AF664220

PLATE NO. I.

तत्सवितुर्वरेण्यं भर्गो देवस्य धीमहि ।
धियो यो नः प्रचोदयान् ॥

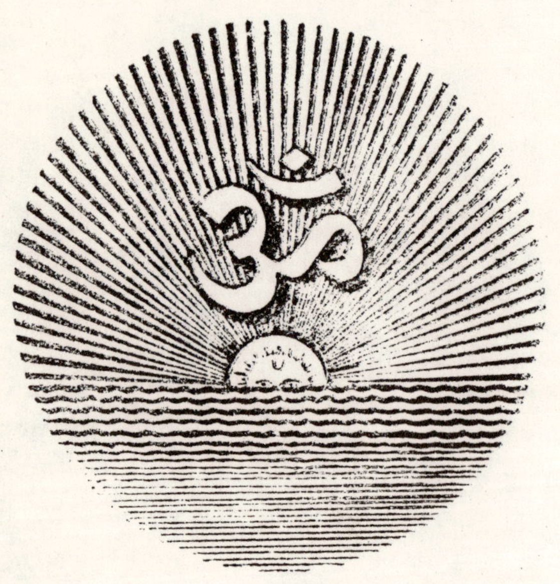

स्तुता मया वरदा वेदमाता प्रचोदयन्तां पावमानी द्विजानाम् ।
आयुः प्राणं प्रजां पशुं कीर्तिं द्रविणं ब्रह्मवर्चसं ।
मह्यं दत्त्वा व्रजत ब्रह्मलोकम् ॥ अथर्ववेदे ॥

In this picture the artist has very intelligently depicted the origin of the so-called sectarian marks from the ancient sacred symbol ॐ. Vide p. clvii. *(Frontispiece.)*

वैदिकी लोकव्यवस्था

Ecclesia Divina

Ecclesia Divina

OR

A Selection of Hymns from the

Four Vedas

Collected, arranged, translated into and commented upon in English by

BHUMANANDA SARASVATI

Compiler of "Anthology of Vedic Hymns"

2002

Kaveri Books

New Delhi - 110 002

First Published in 1936
First Reprint 2002

ISBN 81-7479-059-4

Rs. 890

Published by : Rakesh Goel
Kaveri Books
4697/5-21 A, Ansari Road,
New Delhi - 110 002 (India).
Tel.: 328 8140, 324 5799 Fax: 011 719 9029
e-mail: kaveribooks@vsnl.com

Printed at : Chawla Offset Printers, Delhi - 110 052

PRINTED IN INDIA

List of Contents.

List of Plates.

Introduction.

O wad some Pow'r the giftie gie us
To see oursels as others see us!
It wad frae mony a blunder free us,
And foolish notion:
What airs in dress an' gait wad lea'e us,
And ev'n devotion!

—Robert Burns.

Introduction

CHAPTER I.

WHAT ARE THE VEDAS?

Literature unfolds the forgotten "past" of mankind by throwing a flood of light on a people's life and culture, its attainments and victories, its political and social institutions, its religion and morals, its rise and fall. But for the wonderful monuments of literary wealth handed down by the ancients, man must surely have been entirely in the dark about the life and deeds of his ancestors. The work it does of informing the mind by means of attractive and impressive anecdotes woven into the texture of dry matter-of-fact, details of history and daily routine, cannot be accomplished by any other means. Especially in civilised and progressive society, literature fulfils the office of innumerable learned preceptors. Hence its importance in every time and clime is established both from its excellence as well as necessity.

The object of Literature is to teach

Literature has broadly been divided into two main branches, sacred and profane, according as it dealt with religion or otherwise. But most people, from the nature of their own literary heritage, are apt to consider even Sacred literature as merely historical, though a futile attempt is often-times made to prove it to be divinely inspired and revealed. One branch, and that the most important of the literature humanity has come into possession of, does not deal with history unless

Literature is divided into Profane and Sacred.

it is eternal. The four Vedas of the Aryans of India accomplish all that is claimed of literature above without being human documents of past or current history.

The Vedic Literature is not Historical.

Exigencies of justice in scholarly dealing if not charity, requires that the question of the nature of the Vedas be dispassionately considered in all its aspects. The etymology of the term Veda itself is destined greatly to enlighten the path of the enquirer.

The words Vedas is derived in Several Ways.

The word Veda is formed from the root √vid. There is not only one verb pronounced 'vid' in the dhaatu-paa*tha*' of Paa*n*ini; there are five verbs, of this form, viz, (1) √vida *jn*aane (to know) of the adaadi or second conjugation; (2) √vida sattaayaam (to be) of the divaadi or fourth conjugation; (3) √vidl^a laabhe 'to obtain' of the tudaadi or sixth class; (4) √vida vicaara*n*e 'to consider' of the rudhaadi or seventh conjugation and (5) √vida cetanaakhyaananivaaseshu 'to feel, to tell, to dwell', curaadi or tenth conjugation. To each of these roots the termination gha*n* is added according to P. III, 3, 19 in the sense of instrument (means) or location. The fully formed word would then mean "that by means of which or in which all persons (vidanti) know, (vindanti or vindante) acquire mastery in, (vindate) deliberate over, the various lores or (vidyante or vedayante) live or subsist upon them."*

The word thus formed would bear the acute accent either on the initial or final syllable according to P VI, 1, 160. When the termination is applied in the sense of the instrumental the final syllable would have the acute accent and when it is added in the sense of the locative or mere state or existence (P III, 3, 18), the initial syllable would have it.†

All ancient authorities profusely support this view of the formation of the word 'Veda'. From the way in which most ancient Indian authorities have explained its formation, the meaning of this very important word as well as the nature

---

* विद सत्तायाम्, विद्लृ लाभे, विद विचारणे एतेभ्यो हलश्चेति सूत्रेण करणाधिकरणकारकयोर्घञ्प्रत्यये कृते वेदशब्दः साध्यते ॥ ऋग्वेदादिभाष्य भूमिका २० ॥ सत्तायां विद्यते ज्ञाने वेत्ति विन्ते विचारणे । विन्दते विन्दति प्राप्तौ श्यन्लुक्श्नम्शेषु च क्रमात् ॥ Maadhava p. 389.

† उञ्छादीनां च ॥ पा० ६ । १ । १६० । .... वेगवेदवेष्टबन्धाः करणे ॥ वा० ३ ॥ करणकारक में प्रत्यय किया हो तो घञन्त वेग आदि

of the subject matter of the literature called 'the Vedas' can be unmistakably understood. The Taittireeya Samhitaa I, 4, 20 for example, says; "by means of the Veda did the enlightened obtain from the unrighteous their 'wealth' worth acquiring. Hence the Veda came to be called by that name."* Bhatta Bhaaskara here explains the word as formed from vidl*e* laabhe by adding the termination gha*ú* in the sense of the instrumental.† In the Taittireeya Brāhma*n*a III, 3, 9, 69 a story is told conceiving V e d i as a living being hiding from the enlightened who, it is said, found him out by means of the Veda.‡ Here also Bhatta Bhaaskara says "vividuh means they attained"¶ Aanandateertha in his commentary on the Vish*n*utattvanir*n*aya chapter I, says that the Vedas are so called because, as puts down a text of the Pippalaada School, they alone form a valid means to realise the Supreme Being to know whom neither perception nor inference can be of any use.§

From its derivation the word Veda means scientific knowledge.

The author of the Maanava Dharma*s*aastra voices the same opinion as the above, when in aphorism 6 of the 2nd chapter he says that "the Vedas are so called because each statement therein informs a man of the ideal of human life called the Law of Righteousness to understand which, there is no other valid means of proof."* Kapardisvaamin on Aapas-

---

चार शब्द अन्तोदान्त हों । विजयते येन स वेगः । वेत्ति येन स वेदः । वेष्टते येन स वेष्ट : । बध्नाति येन स बन्धः । और भाव वा अधिकरण में प्रत्यय होगा तो आद्युदात्त ही समझे जावेंगे ॥ Maharshi Dayaananda on Vedic Accent P. 13.

* वेदेन वै देवा असुराणां वित्तं वेद्यमविन्दन्त तद्वेदस्य वेदत्वम् ॥ तै० सं० १ । ४ । २० ॥

† विद्यते लभ्यतेऽनेनेति करणे घञ् । उञ्छादित्वादन्तोदात्तत्वम् ॥ Bhatta Bhaaskara on the above.

‡ वेदिर्देवेभ्योऽनिलायत तां वेदेनान्वविन्दन् ॥ वेदेन वेदिं विविदुः ॥ तै० ३ । ३ । ९ । ६९ ॥

¶ विविदुर्लब्धवन्त इति भट्टभास्करमिश्राः ॥

§ नेन्द्रियाणि नानुमानं वेदा ह्येवैनं वेदयन्ति । तस्मादाहुर्वेदा इति पिप्पलादश्रुतिः ॥ Aanandateertha on Vish*n*utattvanir*n*aya I.

* विदन्त्यनन्यप्रमाणवेद्यं धर्मलक्षणमर्थमस्मादिति वेदः । तच्च वेदनमेकैकस्माद्वाक्याद्भवति ॥ मानव० २ । ६ ॥

tamba sootra I, 33 remarks, that 'the Vedas enable a man to understand (and do) deeds that would lead him to final beatitude.'†

In the more secular treatises on medicine also the same view is expressed. The hoary Sus*r*uta, for example, in Sootrasthaana I, 14 says; "aayurveda means that science in which the principles of hygiene (aayuh) exist (vidyate) or by means of which one can secure (vindati), a healthy living (aayuh),"‡ and the scholiast *D*alha*n*a supports this view.‡ Caraka in Sootrasthaana XXX, 20 and his commentator Cakrapaa*n*i derive, the word veda from the causative or the 10th conjugational base (vedaya) meaning to inform (bodhaya).¶ The revered old Bharata, Father of World's Dramatics in his Naatya*s*aastra I, 1 explains the word veda as meaning 'knowledge' (vedanam), 'existence' (sattaa), 'acquisition' (laabhah), and 'deliberation' (vicaarah).$

From the derivations of the word veda given above, any unbiassed reader will be convinced that ancient Indian authorities understood by that word a scientific treatise or rather science itself. From theology to the principles of the art of histrionics they brought every systematic standardised department of knowledge under what they understood by the term veda as its various and infinite branches. The procedure was well thought out and not arbitrary. The consequences of this have been very far-reaching and important, for the conclusion then follows that the Vedas are the highest in all matters whether religious, social, legal or purely literary, and that all sciences must subserve to them. This is exactly the attititude of all Hindu scholars of India even today. It is a tendency inherited from the remotest past going back farther than the period of which any written history is available. Based upon this tendency is the time-honoured principle that all knowledge must be compared with Vedic principles and what does not tally with them or subserve to them, summarily rejected as

All knowledge must conform to the Vedas.

† निःश्रेयसकराणि कर्माण्यावेदयन्ति वेदा : ॥ कपर्दि॰ १ । ३३ ॥

‡ आयुरस्मिन्विद्यतेऽनेन वा आयुर्विन्दतीत्यायुर्वेदः ॥ सुश्रुते सूत्रस्थाने । १ । १४ ॥ आयुरस्मिन्नायुर्वेदे विद्यतेऽस्तीति डल्हणः ॥

¶ तत्रायुर्वेदयतीत्यायुर्वेदः ॥ चरके । सूत्रस्थाने ।३०। २० ॥ वेदयति बोधयतीति चक्रपाणिः ॥ $नाट्यस्य वेदनं सत्ता लाभो विचारश्च यत्र तन्नाट्यवेदशब्देन ॥ भरत नाट्यशास्त्रे १ । १ ॥

heretical.* The etymologies given above of the word veda, are the basis for this attitude and are themselves the fruit of long patient research—the result of sound inductive reasoning and not mere light-hearted assertions. Hence, it is necessary to see here in brief, how far these etymologies are supported by the subject-matter of the Vedas themselves. As the question relates to the subject-matter of the Vedas itself, a detailed consideration of the topic is reserved for the next chapter of this Introduction.

The venerable Yaaska having explained as to what is meant by devataa (meritorious beings) and Yajnas (righteous works) in the Vedas from the seventh to the thirteenth chapter of his work, thereafter in the fourteenth, describes the procedure of the soul's attaining and helping others to attain salvation through devotion to God and Yogic discipline. This he calls oordhvamaargagati, i. e., proceeding through the upward path.† This chapter treats principally of theology as it is taught in the Vedas.

Theology is considered the most important science in the Vedas.

For example the first verse‡ of the hundred and fiftyfirst hymn of the first book of the Rəgveda draws a vivid picture of the rising sun in the following strains and heartens man to rightful effort and industry for personal advance:—"Lo the wonderful diffuser of rays, the sun has risen! (citram devaanaam udagaadaneekam). He is the enlivener of the vital upward and downward breaths in the human frame and he is also the enlightener of the sacrificial fire (caksurmitrasya varu*n*asyaagneh). He has, by means of his all-pervading rays filled all the three regions, the celestial, the earthly and the intermediate (aapraa dyaavaaprəthivee antariksham). By means of his far-spreading rays he has now entered the whole universe movable and immovable (soorya aatmaa jagatastasthusha*s*ca)."

This is the interpretation of the verse given by Yaaska in the 16th section of the 12th chapter of the Nirukta and it

---

* विरुद्धा च विगीता च दृष्टार्थादिष्टकारणे । स्मृतिर्न श्रुतिमूला स्याद्या चैषाऽसंभवश्रुति: ।। (Given by Medhaatithi as II, 19 Manu).

† व्याख्यातं दैवतं यज्ञाङ्गं च । अथात ऊर्ध्वमार्गगतिं व्याख्यास्यामः ।। नि० १४ । १ ।।

‡ चित्रं देवानामुदगादनीकं चक्षुर्मित्रस्य वरुणस्याग्नेः । आप्रा द्यावापृथिवी अन्तरिक्षं सूर्य आत्मा जगतस्तस्थुषश्च ।। ऋ० १ । १५१ । १ ।।

treats of the physical sun and has nothing to do with what he calls here oordhvamaargagati. "Under this latter aspect," he says,* "the Omnipotent Sun (Imparter of vitality to all) is the seer of the deeds of all human beings since He is the Inner Mover of all creatures to action, for even the huge physical sun gets his lustre from Him. A description of this Great Inner Being of all is available in the four verses R. V. I, 164, 46; III, 26, 7; Taittireeya Aara*n*yaka IX, 10 and R^{ə}gveda I, 164, 31."* All these verses he explains, the first in section 18 chapter 7, and the next three here, in chapter 14.

The first lays down that "the wise call the Adorable God (Agni), 'Indra'—the Omnipotent, 'Mitra'—the friend of all, 'Varu*n*a'—the Holiest, and He also is (according to them) 'Divya'—the Shining One, 'Supar*n*a'—the Protector and Preserver of the universe, and 'Garutmaan'—the Mighty Spirit. Though *He is One Unitary Being* they speak of Him in various ways, sometimes calling Him 'Agni'—the self-effulgent, sometimes 'Yama'—the Controller of the world and sometimes 'Maatari*s*van'—the Life Energy of the universe."†

This verse treats of the highest and most important theological aspect of the Being of God viz, His Unity and Indivisibility.

The remaining verses deal with His Purity, Omnipresence and other aspects and lay down the great principle that man must realise Him and then communicate his soul-elevating experience to other travellers to the 'land of salvation'. This is the only oordhvamaargagati.

"I am the self-effulgent (agnirasmi), the knower of all by my very nature (janmanaa jaatavedaah). All light is, as it were, my eye (ghr^{ə}tam me cakshuh) and Immortality [Final Beatitude] is in my mouth (amr^{ə}tam ma aasan). I am the All-holy Supporter of the three regions, the Maker of the various worlds (arkastridhaatuh rajasah vimaanah), I am ever in righteous works by My nature itself (ajasrah gharmah), and I

* सूर्यं आत्मा इत्युदिस्य हि कर्मद्रष्टा। अथैतदनुप्रवदन्ति। अथैतं महान्तमात्मानमेषर्गणः प्रवदति 'इन्द्रं मित्रं वरुणमग्निमाहुः' इति। अथैष महानात्मात्मजिज्ञासयात्मानं प्रोवाच 'अग्निरस्मि जन्मना जातवेदाः' 'अहमस्मि प्रथमजाः' इत्येताभ्यां ॥ नि॰ १४। १ ॥

† इन्द्रं मित्रं वरुणमग्निमाहुरथो दिव्यः स सुपर्णो गरुत्मान्। एकं सद्विप्रा बहुधा वदन्त्यग्निं यमं मातरिश्वानमाहुः ॥ ऋ॰ १। १६४। ३१ ॥

am surely acceptable to all (havirasmi naama)."* "I am the First Enforcer of the Eternal Law of Righteonsness (aham asmi prathamajaa r$^{\partial}$tasya) and the centre of Immortality [=Final Beatitude] even before all the holy liberated souls (poorvam devebhyo amr$^{\partial}$tasya naabhih). That devotee of Mine who having attained Me imparts through truthful teaching right knowledge about Me to others (yo maa dadaati), verily doth obtain this immortality (sah it evam aavat) but though I am the enlivener of all by food physical and spiritual (annam aham) I eat him away [=deprive him of his salvation] who enjoys his spiritual and physical advantages alone (annam adantam admi)".†

Yaaska then adds that the Supreme Being knowing His devotee to possess these merits manifested Himself to him and commanded him to teach about Him to others, —Whom he had realised in his own self. ‡ This is an illustrative story.

The last verse says, "I have seen the Lord the Saviour of all, Who is not knowable by the senses, Who in various ways comes near to the rightminded devotee or goes far away from him who is otherwise inclined. That Supreme Being pervades all beings that go about in life according to His dictates, nay, even those that act contrariwise." ¶

Yaaska commenting on this says in section 3 chapter 14 that "this Great Being (mahaan aatmaa) is pure Light. He is beyond (para), He is the greatest of all (brahma), He is Eternal (satyam), He is formless like the waters (salilam), He is Unmanifest (avyaktam), He is Intangible (asparsam), He is Colourless (aroopam), He cannot be tasted (arasam), He is Odourless (agandham), He is Deathless (amr$^{\partial}$tam) and He is Pure (Suklam). The human soul enveloped in a subtle body composed of the five elements has her refuge in Him. Some

---

* अग्निरस्मि जन्मना जातवेदा घृतं मे चक्षुरमृतम्म आसन् । अर्कस्त्रिधातू रजसो विमानोऽ जस्रो धर्मो हविरस्मि नाम ॥ ऋ० ३ । २६ । ७ ॥

† अहमस्मि प्रथमजा ऋतस्य पूर्वन्देवेभ्यो अमृतस्य नाभिः । यो मा ददाति स इदेव मावा अहमन्नमन्नमदन्तमद्मि ॥ तैआ० ९ । १० ॥

‡ इति स ह ज्ञात्वा प्रादुर्बभूव, एवं तं व्याजहारायम् तमात्मानमध्यात्मजमन्तिकमन्यस्मा आचचक्ष्वेति ॥ नि० १४ । २ ॥

¶ अपश्यं गोपामनिपद्यमानमा च परा च पथिभिश्चरन्तम् । स सध्रीचीः स विषूचीर्वसान आ वरीवर्ति भुवनेष्वन्तः ॥ ऋ० १ । १६४ ॥ ३१ ॥

Two more, but similar translations of this very important verse are given in the next chapter. One of them refers to the individual soul and the other to the Supreme Being.

call Him (bhootaprakrətih) the Prime Cause of all elements (=beings). He is the refuge or abode of all (Kshetram), the kshetra—field of all, knowing Whom (as such), the human soul attains its pure form and becomes bodiless (niraatmakam).

The other great being (mahaan aatmaa)=the individual soul) is three-fold, viz., light (sattvam), activity (rajas), and dullness (tamas). The light principle (sattvam), stands in purity (vi*s*uddham) in the middle (madhye) and the principles of activity and dullness (rajastamasee) surround it. What is called activity (rajas) is the aptitude to like (kaama) and dullness or darkness (tamas) is the aptitude to dislike. [This latter], when the pure (vi*s*udhyatah) [individual soul] which attains by its own efforts diverse powers (vibhootim kurvatah) does not realise its own nature (avi*jn*aatasya) serves to differentiate the soul from its own nature of the knower of the field [the physical embodiment] (kshetra*jn*a prəthaktvaaya kalpate), for this great being [=the individual soul] (mahaan aatmaa) that is by nature characterised by right understanding (pratibhaati lingah) and enlightened by knowledge (vidyaa-praka*as*alingah) is then blinded by the principle of dullness [=darknes] (tamolingah). In spite of this dullness (tamo'pi) its [=of the individual soul], power of certainty (ni*s*caya-lingah) pervades its whole being like space itself (aaka*as*ah)."*

The theological question is the principal subject of the Vedas as can be ascertained from such texts as I, 164, 39.†

---

* आवरीवर्ति भुवनेष्वन्तरिति । अथैष महानात्मा सत्त्वलक्षणः । तत् परं तद्ब्रह्म, तत्सत्यं, तत्सलिलं, तदगन्धं, तदमृतं, तच्छुक्लं, तन्निष्ठो भूतात्मा, सैषा भूतप्रकृतिरित्येके । तत्क्षेत्रं, तज्ज्ञानात्क्षेत्रज्ञमनुप्राप्य निरात्मकम् ॥

अथैष महानात्मा त्रिविधो भवति सत्वं रजस्तम इतिं । सत्त्वं तु मध्ये विशुद्धं तिष्ठत्यभितो रजस्तमसी । रजः काम इति द्वेषस्तम इति । अविज्ञातस्य विशुध्यतो विभूतिम् कुर्वतः क्षेत्रज्ञपृथकत्वाय कल्पते प्रतिभातिलिङ्गो विद्याप्रकाशलिङ्गः । तमोऽपि निश्चयलिङ्गः ॥ नि० १४, ३ ॥

The text is extremely corrupt and difficult, hence the translation is only approximate.

† ऋचो अक्षरे परमे व्योमन्यस्मिन्देवा अधि विश्वे निषेदुः । यस्तन्न वेद किमृचा करिष्यति य इत्तद्विदुस्त इमे समासते ॥ ऋ० १ । १६४ । ३९ ॥

All Vedic statements (rəcah) have their denotation in the Most High (param) Imperishable (akshare) Omnipresent God (vyoman), in Whom (yasmin) all beneficent beings and objects (visve devaah) have their refuge (adhi nisheduh). What profit (kim) can that man derive

R^əgveda, Atharvaveda X. 7, 38.,* XIII, 4 (2)† etc. The innumerable prayers to God and descriptions of His power, attributes and acts in all the four Vedas also come under this head.

Philosophy also finds a good place in the Vedas.

The Vedas have a very large number of texts of a very unique nature treating of the soul. R. V. I, 58; X, 119,‡ for example, are specimens of this type.

The famous Purushasookta, chapter 31 of the Yajurveda§

(karishyate) from the Vedas (r^əcaa) who (yah) does not realise (na veda) the Supreme Being (tat) [but blindly studies the Sacred Text]? [But on the other hand] all these beneficent agents (ta ime) fully resort (samaasate) only (it) to them who (ye) realise (viduh) that Supreme Being (tat) [in their Vedic Studies]."

* महद्यक्षं भुवनस्य मध्ये तपसि क्रान्तं सलिलस्य पृष्ठे । तस्मिन् छ्रयन्ते य उ के च देवा वृक्षस्य स्कन्धः परित इव शाखाः ॥ अ० १० । ७ । ३८ ॥ यन्महत्सर्वेभ्यो महत्तरं यक्षं सर्वमनुष्यैः पूज्यम् भुवनस्य सर्वसंसारस्य मध्ये परिपूर्णम् तपसि विज्ञाने क्रान्तं वृद्धम सलिलस्यान्तरिक्षस्य कारणरूपेण कार्यस्य प्रलयानन्तरं पृष्ठे पश्चात् स्थितमस्ति तदेव ब्रह्म विज्ञेयम् तस्मिन् ब्रह्मणि ये के चापि देवास्त्रयस्त्रिंशद्वस्वादयस्ते सर्वे श्रयन्ति तदाधारेणैव तिष्ठन्ति। कस्य का इव। वृक्षस्य स्कन्धः स्कन्धे परितः सर्वतो लग्नाः शाखा इव ॥

From the R^əgvedaadi Bhaashyabhoomikaa by Swami Dayaananda Sarasvatee, p. 94 Aj.

† कीर्तिश्च यशश्चांभश्च नभश्च ब्राह्मणवर्चसं चान्नं चान्नाद्यं च ॥ य एतं देवमेकवृतं वेद ॥ अ० १३ । ४ (२), १; २ ॥

Fame, renown, prowess, authority, lustre of the knowledge of God, food and other victuals,—all these—fall to the share of that man who knows this Immutable Being.

न द्वितीयो न तृतीयश्चतुर्थो नाप्युच्यते ॥ न पञ्चमो न षष्ठः सप्तमो नाप्युच्यते ॥ नाष्टमो न नवमो दशमो नाप्युच्यते ॥ ३, ४, ५ ॥

This one Immutable God is called neither the second, nor the third nor yet the fourth. He is called neither the fifth nor the sixth nor yet the seventh. He is called neither the eighth, nor the ninth nor yet the tenth. Vide Anthology of Vedic Hymns Vol. 1 Pp. 39-47.

‡ नहि मे रोदसी उभे अन्यं पक्षं चन प्रति । कुवित्सोमस्यापामिति ॥ ऋ० १० । ११९, । ७ ॥

Both the earth and the heavens together cannot be compared to a part of my powers, which fact I know, having many a time enjoyed the advantages of spiritual discipline. Vide Anthology ot Vedic Hymns Vol. 1 Pp. 166-186.

$ ब्राह्मणोऽस्य मुखमासीद्बाहू राजन्यः कृतः । ऊरू तदस्य यद्वैश्यः पद्भ्यां शूद्रो अजायत ॥ य० ३१ । ११ । ॥

" Oh ye who are desirous to learn ! know that in creation i. e.,,

principally treats of the status of the four classes of men in human society, their functions, attributes etc., and other things related to the order of the universe.

The physical sciences also have their origin in the Vedas.

Subjects with which the physical sciences are concerned are profusely treated of in the Vedas. See for example, the 36* verse of the Hymn on the Motherland where the division of the year into six seasons is clearly mentioned.

Seasons & Motion of the Earth are referred to in the Vedas.

The next verse† of the same hymn clearly refers to the double motion of the Earth which causes these seasons and divisions of time. It cannot be satisfactorily rendered in any other way. It says :— "that Earth, much to be sought after, who *moves along gliding* in whom the different types of heat exist that are found working in the bodies of living beings, that Motherland who casts away the wicked that revile (or persecute) the righteous, and who prefers a virtuous man of great abilities to one who obstructs the good, is established for the powerful, manly and vigorous."

The 12th hymn of the 8th book of the R^{a}gveda treats,

---

of the Viraa*t* Purusha, the body of all the bodies, mentioned in verse five above) the Braahma*n*a (the man knowing God and given to teaching and preaching) occupies the position of the face i. e. being created with the best and the highest qualities of head and heart he is highest in the social scale (according to God's dispensation.) The next in order (you should know) is the Kshatriya (or the governing and warrior class) who can be said to be the arms of this Purusha created as he is with such qualities as strength valour etc. The agricultural and commercial class (endowed with qualities necessary for farming, business etc. occupying the middlemost position in the scale of human society) can be compared to the thighs of this Viraa*t* Purusha. Finally the Soodra occupies the position of his feet (being lowest in the social scale) on account of such qualities as lack of intelligence etc.

* ग्रीष्मस्ते भूमे वर्षाणि शरद्धेमन्तः शिशिरो वसन्तः । ऋतवस्ते विहिता हायनीरहोरात्रे पृथिवि नो दुहाताम् ॥ अ० १२ । १ । ३६ ॥

"The summer, the rains, the autumn, the winter, the frosts and the spring are the seasons due to the (motion of the) earth. On the spacious Land, our Mother, may the years of our life assigned by God be completed by her days and nights."

† याप सर्पं विजमाना विमृग्वरी यस्यामासन्नग्नयो ये अप्स्वन्तः । परा दस्यून्ददती देवपीयूनिन्द्रं वृणाना पृथिवी न वृत्रम् । शक्राय दध्रे वृषभाय वृष्णे ॥ अ० १२ । १ । ३७ ॥

among other topics, of astronomical truths as well. The 30th verse especially is very significant as it states that the whole group of planets is brought into regulation by the presence of the sun. Even Saaya*na*'s rendering of it gives out this theory in clear language.*

Astronomical truths are also treated of.

The sixteenth hymn of the fifth book of the Atharvaveda mentions eleven cardinal numbers in regular succession at the same time giving, in pithy, mnemonic style, good advice for personal development. The previous hymn sets forth the principles of addition, multiplication and perhaps also, division.‡

Mathematical principles are mentioned in the Vedas.

On medicine there are very important theses in the Atharvaveda. The twelfth hymn of the fourth book treats of the Rohi*n*i herb and says that it can join fractured bones. The identity of this herb seems to have been lost to the modern Aayurveda. Its other name seems to be Arundhatee.

There are many hymns on medicine.

The seventeenth, eighteenth and nineteenth hymns¶ of the fourth book of the Atharvaveda give a long account of the wonderful herb Apaamaarga—*Achyrantes Aspera.* It is said to be the greatest of all medicinal herbs and to cure piles and many other diseases. Many Indian physicians today use it profusely for the treatment of piles, asthma and other ailments

---

* यदा सूर्यममुं दिवि शुक्रं ज्योतिरधारयः । आदित्ते विश्वा भुवनानि येमिरे ॥ ऋ० ८ । १२ । ३० ॥ हे इन्द्र अमुं विप्रकृष्टं शुक्रं निर्मलं ज्योतिर्द्योतमानं सूर्यं सर्वस्य प्रेरकं शोभनवीर्यं वा आदित्यं दिवि द्युलोके जगतः प्रकाशनाय यदा यस्मिन्काले अधारयः धारितवानसि आदित् अनन्तरमेव ते त्वया विश्वा विश्वानि सर्वाणि भुवनानि भूतजातानि येमिरे नियम्यन्तेस्म ॥ सायणाचार्याः ॥

† यद्येकवृषोऽसि सृजारसोऽसि ।··············यद्येकादशोऽसि सोपोदकोऽसि ॥ अ० ५ । १६ ॥ See A. V. H. pp. 118-165.

‡ एका च मे दश च मेऽपवक्तार ओषधे । ऋतजात ऋतावरि मधु मे मधुला करः ॥ अ० ५ । १५ ॥

Oh Lord Dispeller of all evil, whether I am pursued by only one detractor or ten of them, Thou Who art Ever-loving, of a righteous disposition and having the Eternal Law of Righteousness in Thy control, bestow on me a sweet disposition." It is quite probable this hymn contains good advice for physicians whose character and practice many people vilify. A true physician must not be disheartened at this but should, on the contrary, be kind and generous even to his detractors and never harbour a grudge against them.

¶ See the 2nd chapter of this introduction.

with great advantage. A physician is defined in R. V. X, 97, 6* as a wise man who knows the use of and possesses a large number of medical herbs.

In several hymns of the Atharvaveda disease 'germs' and organic poisons are said to be the cause of all disease.† The special word for 'disease-germs', is 'rakshas'* and for poison 'visha'. Along with medicine‡ to be given internally the Sun's rays,‡ moonlight, colour § and water ¶ also are mentioned as very

---

*यत्रौषधीः समग्मत राजानः समिताविव । विप्रः स उच्यते भिषग्रक्षोहाऽमीव-चातनः ॥ R. V. X, 97, 6.

† ये क्रिमयः शितिकक्षा ये कृष्णाः शितिबाहवः । ये के च विश्वरूपास्तान् क्रिमीन् जंभयामसि ॥ अ० ५ । २३ । ५ ॥

"We destroy all disease-germs having black sides or completely black-bodied or with black arms or those having all colours."

यास्ते शतं धमनयोऽङ्गान्यनु विष्ठिताः । तासां ते सर्वासां वयं निर्विषाणि ह्वयामसि ॥ अ० ६ । ९० । २ ॥

"We will call out all the organic poisons in the hundreds of arteries (veins and nerves) that are in various ways disposed in the different parts of your body."

‡ यत्ते माता यत्ते पिता जामिर्भ्राता च सर्जतः । प्रत्यक्सेवस्व भेषजं जरदष्टिं कृणोमि त्वा ॥ अ० ५ । ३० । ५ ॥

"The medicine that is being administered to you by your (near and dear ones e.g., your) mother, your father, your sister or your brother, that you should directly take, for by it will I make you live up to a good old age."

अपचितः प्र पतत सुपर्णो वसतेरिव । सूर्यः कृणोतु भेषजं चन्द्रमा वोऽपोच्छतु ॥ अ० ६ । ८३ । १ ॥

"Let indigestion and other ills fly away (from you) just as the vulture takes to flight from human habitations. May the sun afford remedy for thy malady and may the moon dispel it."

§ अनुसूर्यमुदयतां हृद्द्योतो हरिमा च ते । गो रोहितस्य वर्णेन तेन त्वा परि दध्मसि ॥ अ० १ । २२ । १ ॥

"We strengthen thee by means of the red colour of the rising sun (and the milk of a red cow). May thy jaundice and heartburning flee away at the rise of the sun favourable to thee."

¶ आप इद्वा उ भेषजीरापो अमीवचातनीः । आपः सर्वस्य भेषजीस्तास्ते कृण्वन्तु भेषजम् ॥ ऋ० १० । १३७ । ६ ॥

"Water indeed, is medicine; water is the dispeller of the root of all disease and water itself is the remedy for all ills. May that water afford thee a cure for thy ailment."

potent curative agents. The control or regulation of the breath is also highly commended as a very important and unfailing means for the maintenance of good health. The vital breath forms the theme of many hymns*.

While treating his patients a doctor is asked to hearten them by encouraging words.† In Yajurveda 16, 5, God Himself is said to be the First Doctor.‡

Hymn second of the tenth book of the Atharvaveda is a basic text on anatomy.$ Having failed to understand its main

Anatomy also is a Vedic Subject.

tenor Winternitz, in his "History of Indian Literature," in writing about some portions of the Atharvaveda has used language quite unbecoming of a scholar.

---

* प्रविशत प्राणापानावनड्वाहाविव व्रजम् । व्यन्ये यन्तु मृत्यवो यानाहुरितराञ्छतम् ॥ अ० ३ । ११ । ५ ॥

"Let 'on-breath' and 'off-breath' enter (the patient's person) as do bulls enter the stall, and let all the hundreds of deaths go far away."

† मा बिभेर्न मरिष्यसि जरदष्टिं कृणोमि त्वा । निरवोचमहं यक्ष्ममंगेभ्यो अंगज्वरं तव ॥ अ० ५ । ३० । ८ ॥ ‡ अध्यवोचदधिवक्ता प्रथमो दैव्यो भिषक् etc. Vide also Atharvaveda XI, 4, 11; 15; VII, 53; R. V. X, 137; 168; 186; etc.

$ केन पार्ष्णी आभृते पूरुषस्य केन मांसं संभृतं केन गुल्फौ । केनाङ्गुलीः पेशनीः केन खानि केनोच्छ्लङ्खौ मध्यतः कः प्रतिष्ठाम् ॥ अ० १० । २ । १ ॥ अष्टचक्रा नवद्वारा देवानां पूरयोध्या । तस्यां हिरण्ययः कोशः स्वर्गो ज्योतिषावृतः ॥ ३१ ॥ तस्मिन्हिरण्यये कोशे त्र्यरे त्रिप्रतिष्ठिते । तस्मिन्यद्यक्षमात्मन्वत्तद्वै ब्रह्मविदो विदुः ॥ ३२ ॥ प्रभ्राजमानां हरिणीं यशसा संपरीवृताम् । पुरं हिरण्ययीं ब्रह्मा विवेशापराजिताम् ॥ ३३ ॥

"Who is it that has fitted man with two heels, who has padded him with flesh, who has made his two ankles, who has formed his fingers with beautiful joints, who has provided him with his sense organs, who has fitted palms to his feet and put firmness in his waist?"

"There is an impregnable city (in the shape of the human body) with nine portals (=seven apertures in the head and two below) and eight circles in which dwell celestial (=very powerful) beings (the mind, the will, the ego, the five senses etc.) and in which there is a golden (=very powerful) celestial (=advancing towards final beatitude) treasure-chest (=the human soul) surrounded by Light (=God the self-effulgent)." [In Anthology of Vedic Hymns Vol. I p. 147 kosa is rendered by 'heart' which does not fit in quite gracefully with the next two verses].

"Possessors of divine knowledge know that most Holy and Powerful Being to be God Almighty who resides in that treasure-chest with three 'spokes' (=birth, name and place) established in three diverse ways (=works=karma, worship of God=upaasanaa and right knowledge of things=*jn*aana)".

On the basis of human anatomy it teaches great moral and spiritual truths. Similar texts are found in the Yajurveda* also where long lists of animals etc., are given for the instruction of humanity.

Agriculture and cloth-weaving also are treated of in the Vedas. It is impossible to give in this brief introduction a detailed account of the sciences and arts that form the subject matter of Vedic hymns.

From the above it ought to be clear to the reader that the derivation of the word veda from each of the five roots pronounced 'vid' is quite appropriate. According to this etymology the Vedas are revealed texts on all the principal or basic sciences and arts the cultivation of which is essential for the happiness and advancement of human society.

The Word Veda cannot mean a bundle of grass

The word veda bearing the acute accent on the first syllable is interpreted by some to mean a bundle of grass. This interpretation is adopted by Griffith in his translation of A. V. XIX, 72,† but considering the natural interpretation of the verse it seems to be entirely inappropriate. "In that treasury from which (yasmaat ko*s*aat) we bore up the Veda (udabharaama vedam,) we replace it (tasminnantaravadadhma enam). What was desirable (ish*t*am) has been done (kr^o^tam) by the power (veerye*n*a) of the Word of God (brahma*n*ah). May all beneficent objects (devaah) tend to my safety (maa aavat) in this life (iha) by means of this act of righteousness (tena tapasaa)". The very wording of the verse protests against the translation of the word veda by 'a bundle of grass'. The use of a bundle of grass during a particular sacrifice and then replacing it in

---

" Almighty God has entered from all sides that unconquered golden city, lustrous, giving relief from all fatigue, and surrounded by glory from all round."

*ऊर्क् च मे सूनृता च मे पयश्च मे रसश्च मे घृतं च मे मधु च मे सग्धिश्च मे सपीतिश्च मे कृषिश्च मे वृष्टिश्च मे जैत्रञ्च मे औद्भिद्यं च मे यज्ञेन कल्पन्ताम् ॥ य० १८ । ६ ॥ व्रीहयश्च मे यवाश्च मे माषाश्च मे तिलाश्च मे मुद्गाश्च मे खल्वाश्च मे प्रियङ्गवश्च मेऽणवश्च मे श्यामाकाश्च मे नीवाराश्च मे गोधूमाश्च मे मसूराश्च मे यज्ञेन कल्पन्ताम् ॥ ९२ ॥

† यस्मात्कोशादुदभराम वेदं तस्मिन्नन्तरवदध्म एनम् । कृतमिष्टं ब्रह्मणो वीर्येण तेन मा देवास्तपसावतेह ॥ अ० १६ । ७२ ॥

the box from which it was taken does not justify such high-worded eulogium.

There are other names also for the Vedas which deserve to be considered here. The word '*S*ruti' is sometimes used instead of 'Veda.' Derived from the verb √ *S*ru sravan*e* to hear, by the addition of the suffix ktin as explained by Paa*n*ini in 'striyaam ktin' III 3, 94, i.e., 'the termination ktin is affixed to a verb in any sense but that of the agent," and the Vaartika thereon, '*s*ruyajistubhyah' kara*n*e' which adds that "the suffix ktin is added to the roots √ *s*ru, √ yaja devapoojaasangatikara*n*adaaneshu and √ sh*t*uu stutau, in the sense of the instrumental." Hence *s*ruti means that by means of which all the seers beginning with Brahmaa, have heard or learnt and all men will hear or learn, i.e., all true sciences and arts.*

The Vedas have other names also

The word 'brahma' in the neuter gender is another synonym for Veda. It is derived from the verb pronounced (br^{ə}h), viz. √ br^{ə}ha, √ br^{ə}hi vr^{ə}ddhau, √ br^{ə}hi *s*abde br^{ə}hirityeke; by adding the U*n*aadi suffix manin according to the U*n*aadi aphorism sarvadhaatubhyo manin IV, 145; i.e., "the termination manin is added to any root" and the next aphorism, br^{ə}*m*herno'cca which lays down that "after the root √ br^{ə}h √ br^{ə}hi vr^{ə}ddhau the final न is dropped and the preceding अ remains short." According to the former rule the word would bemasculine brahman—'hmaa' nom, singular, having the acute accent on the final syllable, but according to the latter, it would be brahman—hma (having the acute accent on the initial syllable) and neuter gender. The sense would vary in a number of ways in as much as the U*n*aadi terminations are affixed in various ways and in various senses as lays down Paa*n*ini in his rule 'u*n*aadayo bahulam', III, 3, 1.†

The word brahma is derived in many ways

---

* श्रु श्रवण इत्यस्माद्ध ातोः करणकारके क्तिन्प्रत्यये कृते श्रुतिशब्दो व्युत्पद्यते। ....आदिसृष्टिमारभ्याद्यपर्यन्तं ब्रह्मादिभिः सर्वाः सत्या विद्याः श्रूयन्तेऽनया सा श्रुतिः ॥ R. B. B. 20,

†It will not be out of place here to consider the main principles of U*n*aadi formations with Maharshi Daya*n*anda's clear exposition of them :—

उणादयो बहुलम् ॥ पा० ३ । ३ । १ ॥ वर्तमानकालमें धातुओं से उणादि प्रत्यय बहुल करके होते हैं ॥

The U*n*aadi terminations are affixed to verbs in various ways and the resulting form is a noun denoting an agent etc., doing something or being affected by something done in the present time.

U*n*aadi principles are applied in various ways

भूतेऽपि दृश्यन्ते ॥ पा० ३ । ३ । २ ॥ और कहीं कहीं भूतकाल में भी इनका विधान दीख पड़ता है ॥

In some instances they are found used in the sense of the past tense as well.

भविष्यति गम्यादयः ॥ पा० ३ । ३ । ३ ॥ और गमी आदि गणपठित वक्ष्यमाण शब्द भविष्यत्काल ही में होते हैं ॥

But the words gamee etc., which will be mentioned hereafter are used only in the sense of the future tense.

उणादि प्रत्ययों के होने के लिए यह तीनों काल का नियम है ॥

This is the principle according to which the U*n*aadi terminations can be used in the sense of all the three tenses.

गम्यादि शब्द

The following is a list of the words 'gamee' etc:—

गमी = who will go.

आगामी = who will come.

प्रस्थायी = that will start.

प्रतिरोधी = that will obstruct.

प्रतिबोधी = that will awaken.

प्रतियोधी = that will fight against.

प्रतियोगी = that will come counter or come into being over against.

प्रतियायी = that will go back.

भावी = that will come into being.

इनसे अन्य शब्द भूत और वर्तमान अर्थों के बोधक होते हैं ॥

Words other than these are indicative of the present and past tenses.

अब जितनी प्रकृतियों में जितने उणादि प्रत्यय कहे है उतने ही जानना चाहिये वा कुछ विशेष ॥

Here a question arises. Are we to understand by U*n*aadi affixes only so many terminations as are given along with their bases in the U*n*aadi list, or, are there some more ?

इसलिये ।

The answer to this is given in the following:—

बाहुलकं प्रकृतेस्तनुदृष्टेः प्रायसमुच्चयनादपि तेषाम् । कार्यसशेषविधेश्च तदुक्तं नैगमरूढिभवं हि सुसाधु ॥ १ ॥ नाम च धातुजमाह निरुक्ते व्याकरणे शक-

टस्य च तोकम्। यन्न पदार्थविशेषसमुत्थं प्रत्ययतः प्रकृतेश्च तदूह्यम् ॥ २ ॥ संज्ञासु धातुरूपाणि प्रत्ययाश्च ततः परे । कार्याद्विद्यादनूबन्धमेतच्छास्त्रमुणादिषु ॥ ३ ॥ महाभाष्ये ॥

इसी सूत्रकी व्याख्या में महाभाष्यकार पतञ्जलि मुनि उणादिपाठ की व्यवस्था बांधते हैं ॥

In his interpretation of the above aphorism of Paa*n*ini's, the sage Patanjali, the author of the 'Great Commentary,' lays down the following rules for the correct application of the terminations given in the list.

—कि (बाहुलकम्) उणादिपाठमें थोड़े से धातुओं से प्रत्ययविधान किया है सो बहुल [शब्द] के होने से ये प्रत्यय अन्य धातुओं से भी होते हैं ॥

He says that in the ancient list of U*n*aadi formations affixes have been ordained only after a few roots. By the presence of the word bahula—'various' in Paa*n*ini's aphorism cited above, it should be understood that these terminations are to be applied to other verbs also when necessary.

इसीप्रकार प्रत्ययभी थोड़े से संकेतमात्र पढ़े हैं ॥

In the same manner only a few rerminations are mentioned which imply others to be assumed and used when occasion arises.

सत्प्रयोगों में देख के इनसे अन्य भी नवीन प्रत्ययों की कल्पना कर लेनी चाहिये ॥

From good usage (i. e., in the Vedas and works of ancient authoritative writers) other terminations different from these should be assumed.

जैसे (ऋफिडः) इस शब्द में ऋ धातु से फिड प्रत्यय समझा जाता है ॥

For example there is an imaginary word Rᵊphi*d*a (a proper noun coined by some one). In this it is assumed that the Unaadi affix 'phi*d*a' is added to the root √rᵊ gatau.

इसी प्रकार अन्यत्र भी जानना चाहिये ॥

Such assumptions should be made elsewhere also when necessary.

तथा जितने शब्द उणादिगणसे सिद्ध होते हैं उनमें जितने कार्य सूत्रों से प्राप्त हैं वे सब नहीं होते यह भी बहुलग्रहण का ही प्रताप है ॥

It should also be borne in mind that all the processes enjoined by the U*n*aadi aphorisms in the formations of the words given in the Unaadi list, do not take place. This should also be inferred from the word 'bahula' in Paa*n*ini's apborism III, 3, 1.

इसमें यदि कोई ऐसा प्रश्न करे कि उणादि पाठ में जितने धातुओं से जितने प्रत्यय विधान किये और शब्दों के सिद्धि में जितने कार्य सूत्रों से हो सकते हैं उनसे अधिक वा न्यून क्यों होते हैं ॥

Somebody may ask here, why is it that the number of terminations given in the U*n*aadi list and the processes that take place in the formation of the words as stated there, either exceed or fall short of, the actual need.

तो इसका उत्तर यह है कि (नैगम०) वैदिक शब्द और लौकिक संज्ञा शब्द ये सब अच्छे प्रकार सिद्ध नहीं हो सकते ॥

In answer to this it should be stated that not all the words used in the Vedas and the nouns in the living idiom, can be satisfactorily derived by putting together a root and a suffix.

इस लिये पूर्वोक्त तीन प्रकार के कार्य उणादिगण में बहुलवचन से होते हैं इस बहुल [शब्द] के होने से अनेक प्रकार के सहस्रों शब्द सिद्ध होते हैं ॥

The three results mentioned above, it must be noted, are rendered possible by the presence of the expression 'bahula' which helps us to evolve thousands of words of various types.

संज्ञा शब्द वेही कहाते हैं जो किसी निज वाच्य के साथ सम्बन्ध रक्खें फिर उनकी सिद्धि करने से क्यां प्रयोजन है क्योंकि वे संज्ञा शब्द जिस निज अर्थ के बोधक हैं उनका बोध तो प्रकृति प्रत्ययार्थ के सम्बन्ध के विना भी कराते ही हैं वही पश्चात् होगा ॥

Only those words are called nouns which denote realities existing in the world, hence, it is not necessary to explain them as being formed by putting together verbs and suffixes, for even on the strength of such derivation they will bear only that import which they already carry without such aid.

इसलिये (नाम च०) इस विषय में निरुक्तकारों और वैयाकरणों में शाकटायन ऋषि का ऐसा मत है कि सब संज्ञा (रूढि) शब्द प्रकृति प्रत्ययार्थ के सम्बन्ध से यौगिक तथा योग रूढता से अर्थों के बोधक होते हैं ॥

Hence Vedic exigetes and the sage Shaaka*t*aayana among grammarians, hold the opinion that all nouns bear their significations as a result of the combination of a root and suffix or of accepted usage upheld by such derivation.

इन से भिन्न अन्य ऋषियों के मतानुसार सब संज्ञा शब्द रूढि अर्थात् अव्युत्पन्न होते हैं ॥

According to the opinion of other sages noun-words are conventional or underived.

अब जहां शब्दों में प्रकृतिप्रत्यय कुछ भी नहीं जानपड़ता वहां (प्रत्ययतः०) यदि प्रत्यय जान पड़े तो धातु की कल्पना और धातु जान पड़े तो नवीन प्रत्यय की कल्पना कर लेनी चाहिये। इस प्रकार उन शब्दों का अर्थज्ञान कर लेना चाहिये ॥ २ ॥

Now in the case of those words in which either the root or the suffix is not clearly distinguishable, if by some means the termination can be traced then the root should be assumed or vice versa and thus the meaning of the word determined.

संज्ञा शब्दों में धातुओं का रूप पूर्व भाग में और शब्द के पर भाग में धातु से परे प्रत्यय की कल्पना करनी चाहिये ॥

In noun-words the first portion should be considered to be the root and the latter portion after the root to be the suffix.

और जिस शब्द में जिस अनुबन्धका कार्य दीख पड़े वैसे ही सानुबन्धक धातु वा प्रत्ययों की ऊहा करनी चाहिये ॥

From the modifications that may be noticeable in the word thus derived, the indicatory letter of the root or termination, should also be ascertained.

अर्थात् आत्मनेपद दीख पड़े तो अनुदात्तेत् वा ङित् धातु जानना और जो आद्युदात्त स्वर हो तो ञित् वा नित् प्रत्यय की कल्पना करनी चाहिये ॥

If the assumed root is Aatmanepadee it should be understood to have the grave accent or ṅ for its indicatory letter and if the word has the acute accent on the first syllable then the suffix should be understood to have either ñ or n as its indicatory letter.

यह कल्पना सर्वत्र नहीं करनी किन्तु वैदिक वा लौकिक सत्प्रयुक्त शब्दों के अर्थ जानने के लिये शब्दों के पूर्व भाग में धात्वर्थ की और पर भाग में प्रत्ययार्थ की कल्पना करनी चाहिये ॥

It should be borne in mind that these provisions for the assumption of the root in the earlier part of the word concerned and of the termination in the latter, are not made with a view to justify each and every formation, but just to enable the reader to grasp the correct meaning of words used in the Vedas and by authoritative writers.

यह सब सम्बन्ध ऋषि लोगों ने इसलिये बांधा है कि अथाह शब्दों के सागर की थाह व्याकरण से भी नहीं मिल सकती ॥

These principles have been enunciated by the ancient sages because even by means of grammar one cannot have a complete mastery over the unfathomable ocean of Sanskrit vocabulary.

जो कहे कि ऐसा व्याकरण क्यों नहीं बनाया कि जिससे शब्द सागर के पार पहूँच जाते तो यह समझना चाहिये कि कितने ही पोथे बनाते और जन्म जन्मान्तरों भर पढ़ते तो भी पार होना दुर्लभ ही था इसलिये यह पूर्वोक्त व्याकरण से सब प्रबन्ध जताया है ॥ ३ ॥

It was not possible to compile such a grammar as would enable one to steer through the ocean of Sanskrit vocables, for, any number of tomes written on the subject and studied during a long succession of lives, would not have helped one to accomplish the purpose.

उणादिगण में कारकव्यवस्थाका यह नियम है कि—

The following are the principles according to which the case terminations in the sense of which U*n*aadi suffixes are applied are to be determined:—

दाशगोघ्नौ सम्प्रदाने ॥ पा० ३ । ४ । ७३ ॥

यह सूत्र सामान्य कृदन्तका नियामक है कि दाश और गोघ्न शब्द औणादिक हों वा अष्टाध्यायी से सिद्ध हों परन्तु प्रत्यय सम्प्रदान कारक में ही हों । इस नियम से ये दोही शब्द सम्प्रदान में होते हैं अन्य नहीं ॥

This rule regulates the ordinary participial formations. It says that the words 'daasa' and 'goghna' whether they are formed in accordance with U*n*aadi principles or the rules of the Ash*t*aadhyaayee the suffixes utilised in their evolution would be used only in the sense of the dative, the result being that only these two words are formed in the sense of the dative.

भीमादयोऽपादाने ॥ पा० ३ । ४ । ७४ ॥

भीमादि शब्दों में अपादानकारक में ही प्रत्यय होते हैं। भीमादि शब्द औणादिक हैं जैसे—भीमः। भीष्मः। भयानकः। वरुः। चरुः। भूमिः। रजः। संस्कारः। संक्रन्दनः। प्रतपनः। समुद्रः। स्रुवः। स्रुक्। खलतिः। इति भीमादिगणः॥

In the formation of the words of the 'bheemaadi' group the suffixes are applied in the sense of the ablative. The words of the 'bheemaadi' group are U*n*aadi formations. The following is a list of the 'bheemaadi' group :—

Bheema √ञिभी भये+मक् U. I, 145; 148.

Bheeshma √ञिभी भये+षुक्+मक् U. I. 148.

Bhayaanaka √ञिभी भये+आनक U. III, 82.

Varu*h* √वृङ् संभक्तौ, वृञ् वरणे आवरणे च+उ U. I, 7.

Caruh चर भक्षणे, गतौ संशये च+उ U. I, 7.

Bhoomih √भू सत्तायम्+मि U. IV, 45

Rajah √रञ्ज रागे+असुन् U. IV, 189; 217.

Sa*m*skaarah सम्+√डुकृञ् करणे+घञ् P. VI, 1, 135 & III, 3,18.

Sa*m*krandanah सम्+√क्रदि+ल्यु P. III, 1, 134.

Pratapanah प्र+√तप ऐश्वर्यसंतापदाहेषु+ल्युट् P. III, 3, 113.

Samudrah सम्+उत्+√द्रु गतौ+ड Nir II, 11; सम्+√मुद हर्षे संसर्गे च+रक् U. II, 13; सम्+उदक+र P. V, 2, 107 and VI, I, 63 or सम्+√उन्दी क्लेदने+रक् U. II, 13.

Sruvah √स्रु गतौ+क U. II, 61.

Sruk √स्रु गतौ+चिक् U. II, 62.

Khalatih √स्खल संचलने+अतच् U. III, 112.

ताभ्यामन्यत्रोणादयः ॥ पा० ३ । ४ । ७५ ॥

उन सम्प्रदान और अपादान कारकों से भिन्न अन्य कारकों में उणादि प्रत्यय होते हैं ॥

U*n*aadi suffixes are used in the sense of case terminations other than the dative and the ablative.

व्युत्पन्न पक्ष में उणादि प्रत्ययान्त शब्दों के यौगिक होने से प्रत्ययों को कृत्संज्ञक मान के कर्ता में प्राप्त हैं इसलिये यह कारक नियम है ॥

According to the opinion of those that maintain that all noun words are derivative formations U*n*aadi words being derivable, the U*n*aadi suffixes like all 'kr*i*t' suffixes will have to be applied in the

Hence the word 'brahma' can be derived by assuming the termination to be affixed in the sense of any case termination, and according to the sense in which it is affixed, the word would mean either God, the human soul, the Holy Scriptures (Vedas), food, happiness etc. For example nirantaram vardhate-'saaviti=who always grows in His glory brahman=God. Yam sarve nirantaram vardhante=that which all persons try to advance=brahman=the soul or happiness. Yenaadheetena sarve vardhante=brahma=the Vedas by the study, and living up to the teachings of which man advances in every way. Yasmai vardhate=that for which man grows is surely the Supreme Being, soul or salvation (bliss of emancipation). Yasmaat (yat praapya or yasmin sthitvaa P. II, 3, 28 & V., lyablope karma*n*-yupasa*m*khyaanam and adhikara*n*e ca) sarve vardhante tat brahma=the Supreme Being arriving at, or being established in, Whom, by devotion and spiritual discipline all grow, that is, attain divine bliss or salvation. It means, in this sense, the Vedas also, in which case the 'vigraha' would be yasmaat (yat adheetya) sarve manushyaa vardhante i. e., by studying which all men advance in life. The word 'brahma' meaning food also is to be similarly derived. Yasmaat (yat praapya bhuktvaa vaa) sarve praa*n*inah vardhante tat, by obtaining or eating which all creatures grow. It can be derived also in the sense of the instrumental, as yena (praaptena muktena vaa) sarve vardhante. Yasya vardhanam i. e., God, of whom it can always be predicated that He grows in His glory. Yasmin sarvam jagadvardhate, God in Whom all the universe grows or advances from one stage to another. The formation it must be remembered, is Vedic and exceptional, and cannot be taken as a precedent for building up other and similar forms.

---

sense of the nominative, hence this aphorism to further extend their application.

और भाव में भी उणादि प्रत्यय होते हैं ॥

It should be remembered that U*n*aadi suffixes are added in the abstract sense of state or existence also.

सम्प्रदान और अपादान को छोड़ के अन्य कारकों में तो उणादि प्रत्ययों का यथेष्ट विधान है परन्तु बहुल वचन से कहीं सम्प्रदान में भी कोई प्रत्यय कर दिये हों तो चिन्ता नहीं ॥

There is ample provision to derive U*n*aadi formations by applying suffixes in the sense of case terminations other than the dative and ablative, but still, the reader should not stand aghast at the fact, if he finds some author forming an U*n*aadi word by applying an U*n*aadi suffix in the sense of the dative under the force of the word 'bahula' in the aphorism of Paa*n*ini quoted above.

Other names of the Vedas less frequently used are vaac, sookta, mantra, rəc, vaa*n*ee, arka, gir, chandas, stoma, uktham, sarasvatee, *s*abda, aagama, aamnaaya, and nigama. Of these the last four as well as *s*ruti are not used in the Vedas. They are descriptive terms coined by philosophers and jurists.

The word vaac is used in the very first verse of the Atharvaveda to mean the revealed vedas :—Vaacaspatirbalaa teshaam tanvo adya dadaatu me. Also in the Saamaveda II, 21, 7, 2 :—Yunje vaacam *s*atapadeem. In the Yajurveda XXVI, 2 ,we have:—Yathemaam vaacam kalyaa*n*eem aavadaani janebhyah. In R. V., I, 113, 17 we have:—Syoomanaa vaaca udiyarti vahnih.

The word Sookta meaning the Vedas occurs in the following texts :—Upa no na ramasi sooktena vacasaa vayam bhadre*n*a vacasaa vayam. AV. XX, 127, 14. Brahma*n*aspate tvamasya yantaa sooklasya bodhi tanaya*m*ca jinva. Y. XXXIV, 58.

The words mantra, rəc, vaa*n*ee, gir, chandas, stoma, uktham and sarasvatee are illustrated in the following statements culled from the four Vedas:—Pra noonam brahma*n*aspatirmantram vadatyuktham; yasminnindro varu*n*o mitro aryamaa devaa okaa*m*si cakrire. Y.V. XXXIV, 57. Rəco akshare parame vyoman etc. R.V. I, 164, 39. Yo jaagaara tam rəca*h* kaamayante R. V., V, 44, 14. Imaa asmai matayo vaaco asmadaam rəco girah sush*t*utaya*h* samagmata. R.V. X, 91, 12. Yo vidyaadbrahma pratyaksham paroo*m*shi yasya sambhaaraa rəco yasyaanookyam. R.V. IX, 6, 1. Indramidgaathino brəhadindramarkebhirarki*nah*; indram vaa*n*eeranooshata. R.V., I, 7, 1; A.V., XX, 38, 4; 47, 4; and 70,7. Tvaam stomaa aveevrədha*m*stvaamukthaa *s*atakrato; tvaam vardhantu no girah. R.V., I, 5, 8. Etonvindram stavaama *s*uddham *s*uddhena saamnaa; suddhairukthair vaavrəddhvaa*m*sam; *s*uddha aa*s*eervaanmamattu. R.V., VII, 95, 7. Paavakaa nah sarasvatee vaajebhirvaajineevatee; yaj*n*am vash*t*u dhiyaavasu*h*. R. V. I, 3, 10. Asrəgramindra te gira*h* prati tvaamudahaasata; ajoshaa vrəshabham patim. R.V. I, 9, 4. Trikadrukebhi*h* pavate sha*d*urveerekamidbrəhat; trish*t*ubgaayatree chandaa*m*si sarvaa taa yama aarpitaa. A.V., XVIII, 2, 6. Gaayanti tvaa gaayatri*n*or'cantyarkamarki*nah*; brahmaa*n*astvaa *s*atakrata udva*ms*amiva yemire. R.V., I, 10, 1. Yasyaajasram *s*avasaa maanamuktham paribhujadrodasee vi*s*vata*h* seem. R.V. I, 100, 14.

The other expressions viz., *s*abda, aagama, nigama, aamnaaya and *s*ruti are not used in the Vedas. They are descriptive terms coined by philosophers and jurists.

॥ ॐ ॥

CHAPTER II.

THE SUBJECT-MATTER OF THE VEDAS.

Totally wrong and unjustifiable constructions have been put upon very important Vedic hymns by European scholars and their blind Indian followers, owing to their misunderstanding of the term devataa used in the directions given at the top of every hymn in the four Vedas. For a full and clear grasp of the subjects treated in the sacred text it is essential that the term 'devataa' be first, rightly understood. It must also be borne in mind that these directions preceding every hymn in the printed text of the Vedas, do not form parts of the texts themselves, but are entirely external to them and composed by scholars who probably flourished not earlier than some four thousand years before the Christian era. It is very probable they are the compositions of the Sage Saunaka the compiler of the Vedic padapaatha. In these directions the student of the Veda is given, in a very brief compass, very important details intimately concerned with the exigesis of the Vedic text. For example, at the top of the first hymn of the R^{ə}gveda we are told that (1), the Sage of the hymn is Madhucchandas, (2), the Devataa Agni, (3), the Metre Gaayatree and (4), the Tone Shadja. From these details it can be very easily gathered that the Vedic hymns are poetical 'compositions' intended to be sung or chanted according to the principles of music. But out of these details, two items have, unfortunately, been the cause of probably wilful misrepresentation of the Vedic literature on the part of narrow-minded scholars. The words 'R^{ə}shi' and 'Devataa' have either proved very hard nuts to crack for half-learned Sanskritists, or very convenient weapons in the hands of scheming politicians with a smattering of Sanskrit whose one aim in pursuing Sanskrit studies is to represent the oldest and the most cultured Asiatic race viz, the so-called "Hindu", to be a savage and the descendant of savages. It is safe "to give the dog a bad name before killing it". An explanation of the word 'R^{ə}shi' will be found in this Introduction in the chapter on Vedic interpretation.

In a discussion on the word Devataa it is essential first to see what the Vedas themselves have to say on it.

In the twenty second hymn of the first book of the Rəgveda (verse 5) we have the following :- Hira*n*yapaa*n*imootaye savitaaramupahvaye I Sa cettaa devataa padam II In this text the word devataa is used as an appellation of Savitrə, i. e., God the Creator. In the following verse, R. V., I, 100, 15, the words deva and devataa are used for human beings :- Na yasya devaa devataa na martaavapascana *s*avaso antamaapuh I Sa prarikvaa tvakshasaa kshmo diva*s*cā marutvaanno bhavatvindra ootee II Saaya*n*a in his commentary on this verse takes the word Devataa to be genetive singular according to P. VII, 1, 39 and says: devataa daanaadigu*n*ayuktasya indrasya. But on the word devaah he remarks: devaah svaadyaa devaga*n*aah. This means he has very often to take recourse to the derivation of a word in order to explain it. Both the words devaah and devataah here mean righteous, learned or holy men. In the second half of Yajurveda XII, 19 :- Agnish*t*vaabhipaatu mayyaa svastyaa chardishaa *s*antamena tayaa devatayaangirasvaddhruvaa seeda, both the words agni and devataa are used as the appellations of a good husband and the wife is advised to be ever in harmony with her spouse. In the 24th and 25th verses also the word devataa is used similarly.

But the most significant of all Vedic verses on the interpretation of the word devataa is the 20th verse of the 14th chapter of the Yajurveda. In a very simple and easy style it gives almost all the senses of the word:—

ओ३म् ॥ अग्निर्देवता वातो देवता सूर्यो देवता
चन्द्रमा देवता वसवो देवता रुद्रा देवतादित्या देवता
मरुतो देवता विश्वे देवा देवता बृहस्पतिर्देवतेन्द्रो
देवता वरुणो देवता ॥ यजुर्वेदे १४ । २० ॥

Agnir devataa vaato devataa sooryo devataa candramaa devataa vasavo devataa rudraa devataa 'dityaa devataa maruto devataa vi*s*ve devaa devataa brəhaspatir devatendro devataa maruto devataa varu*n*o devataa II Y. XIV, 20.*

According to this verse the following are called "devataa" in Vedic literature:— (1) Agni = heat energy; (2)

* The seer of this stanza is 'Visvedevaah', the devataa' Agni etc., the metre Bhurigbraahmee Trish*t*up and the key Dhaivata.

Vaata = atmosphere; (3) Sooryah = the Sun (i. e., the Constellation Sol); (4) Candramas = the Moon (i.e., the Constellation Luna); (5) Vasavah = the following eight objects called vasu in Vedic language:— (a) Agni = fire; (b) Prəthivee = earth; (c) Vaayu = breeze; (d) Antariksham = the intermediate region; (e) Aadityah = the gravitational and heat-light-imparting energy of the Sun; (f) Dyauh = the celestial region (i. e. the sphere of the Sun and planets which are far above the atmospheric region intervening between them and the earth); (g) Candramas = the cooling and "waxing" force of the moon; (h) Nakshatraa*n*i = the other planets in the celestial region; (6) the following vital "principles" which render life possible:— (a) the soul; (b) the ten vital airs in the body of all living beings:— (i) Praa*n*a; (ii) Apaana; (iii) Samaana; (iv) Udaana; (v) Vyaana; (vi) Naaga; (vii) Koorma; (viii) Krəkala; (ix) Devadatta and (x) Dhananjaya. (7) Aadityaah = the twelve months of the year. (8) Marutah = yogis, preachers of the Word of God and righteous men of fame. (9) Vi*s*ve devaah = all other men of learning and virtuous life, as well as objects possessing beneficent features. (10) Brəhaspati = the Supreme Being, the Revealer of His Eternal Vedic Law. (11) Indra = the lightning (= electricity) and such beneficent qualities in living beings and all natural objects as give them their essential features and (12) Varu*n*ah = water and natural objects of excellence.

This list is very exhaustive and is copied in the Braahma*n*as with some variation. For example, in the *S*atapatha Braahma*n*a we are told that the beings called deva or devataa are thirty three in number and that Prajaapati is the thirty fourth.* The famous grandmother's tale about the thirty three gods by which so much store is laid by European Sanskritists has its foundation in the Braahma*n*as, nay, the Vedas themselves. The other Braahma*n*as also give the same details the difference being only in the wording, the essential features of the account remaining the same.† The number thirty three itself is not

---

* अष्टौ वसवः। एकादश रुद्रा द्वादशादित्या इमे एव द्यावापृथिवी त्रयस्त्रिंश्यौ। त्रयस्त्रिंशद्वै देवाः। प्रजापतिश्चतुस्त्रिंशः ॥ श० ४।५।७।२ ॥ † त्रयस्त्रिंशद्देवताः। प्रजापतिश्चतुस्त्रिंशः ॥ तां० १०।१।१६ ॥ १२।१३।२४ ॥ अष्टौ वसव एकादश रुद्रा द्वादशादित्त्या वाग्द्वात्रिंशी स्वरस्त्रयस्त्रिंशस्त्रयस्त्रिंशद्देवाः ॥ गो० २।२।१३ ॥ त्रयस्त्रिंशद्वै देवाः सोमपास्त्रयस्त्रिंशदसोमपा अष्टौ वसव एकादश रुद्रा द्वादशादित्याः प्रजापतिश्च वषट्कारश्चैते देवाः सोमपा एकादश प्रयाजा एकादशानुयाजा एकादशोपयाजा एते सोमपाः पशुभाजनाः ॥ ऐ० २।१८ ॥ त्रय-

arbitrary but entirely based upon genuine Vedic texts. In R^ə^gveda I, 45, 2; VIII, 30, 2; Yajurveda, XX, 11; 36; XXXIV, 47 and Atharvaveda X, 7, 23; 27; XII, 3, 16; XIX, 27, 10 etc., the number thirty three itself directly, or as a product of three and eleven, is given. In the 19th verse of the 7th chapter of Yajurveda, this is very clearly mentioned:—Ye devaaso divy-ekaadas*a* stha pr^ə^thivyaamadhyekaadas*a* stha | Apsukshitomahi-naikaadas*a* stha te devaaso yaj*n*amimam jushadhvam. This verse divides the thirty three of Y. V. XIV, 20, into three divisions of eleven each, the first being of the nature of light or electricity (divi stha), the second of the earth (pr^ə^thivyaam adhi stha) and the last of the atmosphere (apsukshitah). This verse is a mystic statement of the principle basic ingredients of the external universe (mahaa brahmaan*d*a) as well as of the animal body, especially the human body (pin*d*a brahmaan*d*a). Just as the external universe is divided into three main divisions the Earth, the Celestial or Planetary Region and the Region extending between these two, called in mystic language "Svah" or 'Svarloka', "Bhuvah" or 'Bhuvarloka' and "Bhooh" or 'Bhooloka', so also in the human frame there are three divisions, the abode, of these three groups of objects called "Devataa". These three divisions are in another way divided into seven, named:- (1) Bhooh, (2) Bhuvah, (3) Svah, (4) Mahah, (5) Janah, (6) Tapah, and (7) Satyam. The exact parts of the body which cover the seats of these seven are in order (1), the perinaeum, (2) the root of the genitals, (3), the navel, (4), the heart, (5), the thyroid cartilage (the so-called Adam's apple), (6), the forehead, and (7), the crown. The external universe also is a globe made of seven spheres called by these very names and constituted of matter akin to that of which each of these regions in the human body are constructed. In other words the human body is a miniature structure in the erection of which these thirty three objects are the essential ingredients.

This, in brief, is what the Vedas themselves have to say about the much-disputed word "Devataa." Many more Vedic texts could be quoted to make the position still more clear, but it would require a big independent treatise to deal with the matter in full. A careful and serious study of the texts that deal with the term itself, as well as of the various objects called by some or other name coming under the general heading "Devataa," will enable any one to understand as to

---

स्त्रिशद्वै सोमपाः देवता याः सोमाहुतीरन्वायत्ता अष्टौ वसव एकादश रुद्रा द्वादशा दित्या इन्द्रो द्वात्रिंशः प्रजापतिस्त्रयस्त्रिंशस्त्रयस्त्रिंशः त्पशुभाजनाः ॥ शा० १२ । ६ ॥

what exactly is meant by "Devataa." But in spite of this, European scholars, either owing to their natural inaptitude to understand Vedic literature aright or to an intentional and studied attitude to misinterpret certain Vedic teachings that would, if not garbled, redound to the honour of India and the Vedic Religion, and thus raise them high above Europe and Christianity in the eyes of the world, have found it feasible to represent the objects called "Devataa" in a very pampered manner to the world. A few extracts regarding the subject from the voluminous literature which has done enormous harm to India politically and culturally, are appended.

The late Professor Sir A. A. Macdonell thus writes on the Vedic "gods" :—

The Vedas teach polytheism.

"When the Indo-Aryans entered the north west of India, they brought with them a religion in which the gods were mostly personified powers of nature. A few of these, such as Dyaus, "Heaven," and Usa, "Dawn," come down from Indo-European times; others, such as Mitra, Varuna, and Indra, from the Indo-Iranian age; while yet others were the creation of Aryans on Indian Soil." (From 'Hymns from Rigveda,' by A. A. MACDONELL, in the so-called "Heritage of India Series" published by the Y. M. C. A., Calcutta, Introduction p. 7, ll.15-22.)

The religion of the Rigveda is mainly concerned with the worship of the gods that are largely personifications of the powers of nature. The hymns are predominantly invocations of these gods, being meant to accompany the oblation of Soma juice and the fire sacrifice of melted butter. *The religion of the Veda is thus essentially a polytheistic one but it receives a pantheistic colouring in a few of the latest hymns of the Rigveda. The gods are stated to number thirty three, a figure which, of course, does not include groups like the Maruts or Storm-gods.* The gods are regarded as having had a beginning, but not as having all come into being at the same time, for earlier gods are occasionally referred to and some deities are described as the offspring of others. They are considered to have been mortal first; for they are said to have acquired immortality by drinking Soma or as a gift of Agni and Savitar. *The gods are human in appearance. Their bodily parts are often merely illustrative of the phenomena of nature which they represent. Thus the tongue and the limbs of the fire-god, Agni—merely denote his flames. Some of the gods are warriors especially Indra; others are priests, especially Agni and Brihaspati.* All of them drive through the air in cars, drawn chiefly by horses, but sometimes by other animals. *Their favourite food consists in milk, butter, grain and the flesh of sheep, goats and cattle.* They receive it in the sacrifice, which is either conveyed to them in heaven by Agni, or which they come in their cars to enjoy on the litter of grass prepared for them. Their favourite drink is the intoxicating juice of the Soma plant. Their abode is heaven, the third heaven, or the highest step of *Visnu,* where, cheered by draughts of Soma, they live in a life of bliss.

The most prominent attribute of the gods is power, they regulate the order of nature and overcome the mighty forces of evil they hold sway over all creatures; no one can thwart their laws or live beyond the time they appoint; and the fulfilment of desires depends on them. The gods are also benevolent and bestow welfare on mankind, Rudra being the only one showing injurious traits. They are "true" and "not deceitful"; friends and protectors of the honest and righteous, but punishers of sin and guilt. As in most cases the gods of the Rigveda have not yet become detached from their physical basis, they are indefinite and lacking in individuality. Having many qualities such as power, brilliance, benevolence, and wisdom, in common with others, each god has very few distinctive traits. This vagueness is increased by the practice of invoking deities in couples, when both gods share characteristics that properly belong to one alone. When nearly every quality can thus be ascribed to every god, the identification of one deity with another becomes easy. Several such identifications actually appear in the Rigveda. *The idea even occurs in more than one late hymn, that various deities are but different forms of a single god. The idea, however, never developed into monotheism.* Finally in other late hymns we find the deities, Aditi and Prajapati, identified not only with all the gods, but with nature as well. This brings us to the beginning of that pantheism which became characteristic of later Indian thought in the form of the Vedanta philosophy.

In some Texts there is the idea of a single god also.

The most convenient classification of the Vedic gods is in accordance with the three fold division of the universe, into heaven, air and earth, found by the Rigveda itself. The celestial deities are Dyaus, Varuna, the Adityas, Surya, Savitar, Pusan,

Visnu, Mitra the Asvins, Usas, and Ratri. The deities of the atmosphere are Indra, Rudra, the Maruts, Vayu or Vata, Apam-Napat, Parjanya, Apas. The terrestrial deities are Prithivi, Agni, Brihaspati and Soma. Among these are included certain rivers, the Sindhu (Indus), the Vipas (Bias), the Sutudri (Sutlej) and the Saraswati. All these are personified and invoked. The personification goes farthest in the case of Saraswati, though the connection of the goddess with the river is never lost sight of.

Alongside of the great nature gods there arose during the period of the Rigveda a class of abstract deities of two types. The first and earlier seems to have started from epithets which were applicable to one or move older deities, but which became detached and acquired an independent character as the want of a god exercising the particular activity in question began to be felt. Some of these names denote an agent (formed with the suffiix *tar*). Such is Dhatar, otherwise an epithet of Indra, appearing as an independent deity, the Creator of heaven and earth, sun and moon. The only agent god of this kind at all often mentioned in the Rigveda, though never invoked in an entire hymn, is *Tvastar", the "Artificer" the most skilled of workmen,* who fashioned the hall of Indra and a new drinking cup for the gods. A few other abstract deities, whose names, compound in form, originally epithets of older gods, represent the supreme god that was being invoked at the end of the Rigveda period. These names are rare and late. The most important is Prajapati Lord of creatures. Originally an epithet of a god like Savitar and Soma, this name is employed in a late verse of the tenth book to designate a distinct deity in the character of a creator. Similarly, the epithet Visvakarma, "all-creating", appears as the name of an independent deity to whom two hymns are addressed. The only abstract deity of this type occuring in the oldest as well as the latest hymns of the Rigveda is Brihaspati, the "Lord of Prayer".

"Second class" gods.

The second and smaller class of abstract deities comprises personifications of abstract nouns. There are seven or eight of these all found in the last book. *Thus two hymns are addressed to Manyu, "Wrath" and one to Sraddha, "faith".* The rest occur only in a few isolated passages. *There is besides a purely abstract deity, often incidentally celebrated throughout the Rigveda as Aditi, "Freedom" whose main characteristic is the power of delivering from the bonds of physical suffering and moral guilt. She is the mother of the small group of deities called Adityas. These were according to a common idiom, called the "Sons of freedom", originally only in a figurative sense, which easily led to the personification of Aditi. Goddesses play an insignificant part in the Rigveda. The only one of importance is Usas "Dawn." Next comes Saraswati, the river goddess and Vac, "Speech," each invoked in two hymns. Prithivi, "Earth", Ratri, "Night," and Aranyani, goddess of the forest, are each addressed in one hymn.* Others are mentioned, only in detached verse. The wives of the great gods are still more insignificant, lacking all individuality. They are mere names formed from those of their consorts, as Indrani, "Wife of Indra".

A peculiar feature of the religion of the Rigveda is the invocation of pairs of deities, whose names are combined as compounds, each member being in the dual. About a dozen such pairs are invoked in entire hymns and about a dozen more in detached stanzas. Mitra, Varuna, are addressed in by far the most hymns, though the names of this type oftenest mentioned are Dyava-Prithivi, "Heaven and Earth." The latter pair, having been associated as universal parents from the Indo-European period downwards, probably furnished the analogy for this dual type.

There are a few more or less definite groups of deities generally associated with some particular god. The Maruts, the attendants of Indra, are the most numerous group. The much smaller group of the Adityas is constantly mentioned in Company with their mother, Aditi. The Visvedevas, the "All gods" invoked in about forty hymns, form a comprehensive sacrificial group, intended to include all the gods so that none should be left out; they are, strange to say, sometimes regarded as a narrower group associated with other groups like the Adityas.

Associate gods!

Besides the higher gods, several lesser deities are known to the Rigveda. The most prominent of these are the Ribhus, who are invoked in eleven hymns. Thy are a defthanded trio, who by their marvellous skill acquire the rank of deities. Among their five great feats of dexterity the greatest consisted in transforming the bowl of Tvastar into four shining cups. They further exhibited their skill in renewing the life of their parents, by whom heaven and earth seem to have been meant. A few of the lesser deities are of the tutelary

"Third class" gods.

order. Such is the rarely mentioned Vastospati, "Lord of the dwelling", who is invoked to grant a favourable entry, to remove disease and to bestow protection and prosperity.

Besides the great phenomena of nature, various natural and artificial objects are found deified in the Rigveda. In addition to the rivers and waters already mentioned, mountains are often addressed as divinities, but only along with other natural objects, or in association with gods. One entire hymn is addressed to plants regarded as divine powers, chiefly with reference to their healing properties. Sacrificial implements are also deified, such as the sacrificial post, the sacrificial grass, and the "divine doors," leading to the sacrificial ground, the mortor and pestle used in pounding the Soma plant, and in three whole hymns the pressing stones, which are described as immortal, unaging, mightier then heaven, and driving away demons and destruction. Weapons, finally, are sometimes deified, armour, bow, quiver, arrows, and drum are invoked in one hymn.

Inanimate gods !

Demons often appear in the Rigveda and are of two kinds. The higher and more powerful are the aerial foes of the gods. The conflict is regularly one between a single god and a single demon, as exemplified by Indra and Vritra. The latter is by far the oftenest mentioned. Another powerful demon is Vala, the personified Cave of the cows, which are set free by Indra. Other demon adversaries of Indra are Arbuda, a wily beast whose cows Indra drove out, Visvarupa, a three-headed demon slain by Indra, who seized his cows, and Svarbhanu, who eclipsed the sun. A group of demons are the Panis, primarily foes of Indra, who with the aid of Sarama, tracked the cows concealed by them. *The second or lower class of demons are terrestrial goblins, enemies of man. By far the commonest generic name for them is Raksas.* They are nearly always mentioned in connection with some god who destroys them. The much less frequent term Yatu or Yatudhana (primarily "Sorcerer") alternates with Raksas and perhaps expresses a species". (Ibid., p. 10 l. 36-p. 15 l. 40)

Demons in the Vedas,

Prof. Max Müller, whose avowed object in pursuin Sanskrit studies, was to convert "poor infidel" India to Christianity, thus delivers himself on the subject:—

"The transition from a natural worship to an artificial may take place gradually. It had taken place long before the beginning of the Brahmana period, and the process of corruption continued during this and the succeeding periods, till at last the very corruption became a principle of new life. *But there is throughout the Brahmanas such a complete misunderstanding of the original intention of the Vedic hymns that we can hardly understand how such an estrangement could have taken place, unless there had been at some time or other a sudden and violent break in the chain of tradition. The authors of the Brahmanas evidently imagined that those ancient hymns were written simply for the sake of their sacrifices and whatever interpretation they thought fit to assign to these acts the same they supposed, had to be borne out by the hymns. This idea has vitiated the whole system of Indian exegesis.* It may be justified perhaps, if it had only been applied to the purely sacrificial hymns, particularly to those which are found in the Sanhitas of the Sama veda and Yajur-veda. But the Rig-veda too has experienced the same treatment at the hands of Indian commentators, and the stream of tradition, flowing from the fountain head of the original poets, has, like the waters of Sarasvati, disappeared in the sands of desert. *Not only was the true nature of the gods, as conceived by the early poets, completely lost sight of,* but new gods were actually created out of words which were never intended as names of divine beings. There are several hymns in the Rigveda containing questions as to who is the true or the most powerful god. One is particularly well known, in which each verse ends with the inquiring exclamation of the poet, "Kasmai devaya havisa vidhema ?". "To which god shall we sacrifice with our offering?" This, and similar hymns, in which the interrogative pronoun occured were employed at various sacrifices. A rule had been laid down, that in every sacrificial hymn, there must be a deity addressed by the poet. In order to discover a deity where no deity existed, the most extraordinary objects, such as a present, a drum, stones, plants, were raised to the artificial rank of deities. In accordance with the same system, we find that the authors of the Brahmanas had so completely broken with the past, that, forgetful of the poetical character of the hymns and the *yearning of the poets after the unknown god,* they exalted the interrogative pronoun itself into a deity, and acknowledged a god ka or Who ? In the Taittiriya-sanhita i, 7, 6, 6), in the Kaushitaki-brahmana

Original and later gods

(XXIV. 4.), in the Tandy-brahmana (XV. 10.), and in the 'Satapatha-brahmana, wherever interrogative verses occur, the author states, that Ka is Prajapati, or the Lord of creatures (Prajapatir vai Kah). Nor did they stop here. Some of the hymns in which the interrogative pronoun occured were called Kadvat, i. e., having *kad*, or *quid*. But soon a new adjective was formed, and not only the hymns, but the sacrifice also, offered to the god, were called *Kaya*, or who-ish. This word, which is not to be identified with the Latin, cujus, cuja, cujum, but is merely *the artificial product of an effete mind*, is found in the Taittiriya Sanhita (i,8,3,1), and in the Vajasaneyi-Sanhita (XXV, 15). At the time of Panini this word had acquired such legitimacy as to call for a separate rule explaining its formation (Pan. IV. 2, 25). The commentator here explains Ka by Brahman. After this, we can hardly wonder that in the later Sanskrit literature of the Puranas, Ka appears as a recognised god, as the supreme god, with a genealogy of his own, perhaps even with a wife, and in the laws of Manu, one of the recognised forms of marriage, generally known by the name of the Prajapati marriage, occurs under the monstrous title of Kaya". ("A History of Ancient Sanskrit Literature". by Max Müller, M. A; p. 222 l, 22 p. 223. l. 30.)

Dr. 'Allan Menzies, D. D., in his "History of Religion" thus writes on the subject–"Vedic gods":—

Vedic Sacrifice

"Indian ritual is an immense subject. In the Vedic period there were several orders of sacrifice—the hymns of the Rigveda have to do with the Soma sacrifice alone—and several kinds of priests, and it stands to reason that an elaborate ritual derived from a distant age and cherished by a priestly caste which was growing in power, could not quickly change. In spite of the considerable amount of material accessible in the Brahmanas and Sutras, a history of Indian sarifice as a whole has still to be written.

It is characteristic of early Indian sacrifice that it is not confined to a temple or to any sacred spot, and that it does not require any image of deity. Instructions are always given for choosing and preparing a place for the rite, and for erecting an altar, a place had to be prepared on each occasion. The gods were asked to come, or were thought to be seated in heaven looking on the sacrifice in the open air. While the celebration proceeded according to a certain ritual, it lay with the worshippers to

"Gods" invited to the sacrifice

fix to what god, or gods the sacrifice should be addressed. There was not one ritual for Agni and another for Indra, but the same would serve for either or for both. The sacrifices of which we hear in the Brahmanas are domestic rites; they are offered by the heads of the household who invite ancestors also to be present. A Brahman is present to direct those who sacrifice and the inferior priests, who assist them, and the benefits of the act extended to the dependents of the household. The time was determined by natural seasons or by household events. Some sacrifices were greater than others, the more elaborate ones requiring several days, months, or even years for their celebration. Among the kinds of offering which might be made we find that of man enumerated; *human sacrifice, however, if it had prevailed in earlier times had now grown obsolete.*

Human Sacrifice

The rise of the Brahmans into a caste changed the character of the sacrifice by making its due celebration depend more on special knowledge, and by increasing its elaborate mystery. Once the hymns were recognised as an essential element of such an act, the person who could interpret the hymn and explain its effects acquired great importance. And when the explanation of all the various features of the sacrifice was once begun, a wide door was opened to minute ingenuity. It is astonishing to what trifles these priestly directories descend, what explanations are brought from every part of earth and heaven of the most trivial circumstances, and what sacredness is found in the very blades of grass around the altar. Now the effect of such a treatment of ritual is inevitably this that the rite itself, the outward mechanical performance, comes to be regarded as important, and that the ethical and religious end which was originally aimed at, is lost sight of. The priest and those he acts for are so intent on the minutiae of their celebration that they forget about the god it is intended for. And as they are quite convinced that the sacrifice, if offered with perfect correctness and with nothing left out, must produce its effects, the sacrifice itself comes to appear as the agent of the desired blessings; the god grows less but the sacrifice grows more. This process, which may be observed wherever ritualism exists, was carried in the period of Brahmanism to its utmost length. In this period the old gods lost the strong hold they had before over the people's mind; men ceased to look for their gods to the sky or to the tempest, and began to look instead to the long ceremonies of the priest or to the hymn he chanted at the altar, or to the austerities he practised. Gods of a new type now make their appearance. *As in the vedic period we saw that Brahmanaspati, lord of prayer, had a place besides Indra and Varuna, so now we see that the supreme deity is named Brahma.* The prayer connected with the sacrifice has given its name to the ruler of the universe. Other names for the supreme deity are also found to be making their way to general use, as the old historical and mythological gods fall into the background, and an abstract divine unity is sought after. Prajapati, lord of creatures, who is little heard of in the hymns, is frequently invoked as the head of all the gods, and a triad of gods is heard of, consisting of Agni, Vayu, Surya, fire, the air, the sun and summing up the divine energies. The attributes of the gods are personified, and a set of pale abstractions is thus added to the Pantheon; and spirits and goblins not heard of in the hymns, though not therefore necessarily unknown in the former period, make their appearance. These are, perhaps, the gods of the aborigines, who thus revenge themselves, as the religion of the invaders which at first suppressed them, loses its earlier vigour. The strong gods retire and weak gods, many and shadowy, and bad as well as good, are worshipped. The Asuras were formerly the gods generally, now they are evil beings with whom the good gods have to contend." ("History of Religion," by ALLAN MENZIES D. D. pp. 340-342).

Old and new gods

Historical & Mythological gods,

"Seeking to escape from the confusion, of many gods the Indian mind is looking out even from the Vedic period for some means to conceive of them all as one. In the earliest period each reigned in turn as the supreme; a god is supreme not because he is essentially the greatest of the gods, but because circumstances have brought him to the front. This is Henotheism. Then we have attempts to sum them all up in one expression. Prajapati, lord of creatures, Visvakarma, maker of all things, represent such attempts. Then we have as the supreme, Brahma the power of prayer, a being of different character from all his predecessors. Brahma is an intellectual deity. He is a thinker, a Knower, he is the "Mahan Atma" or great Spirit, which sits in

The "supreme god".

Brahma.

"Mahan Atma".

unbroken calm above the change and distraction of the universe. In rendering Mahan Atma by great spirit, however, we are anticipating. Atma, originally breath or life, comes afterwards, to mean the person, the self when all that is accidental is removed from it, the essential, innermost self. Now Brahma is the great self, inmost essence of all things, which was before them, and is unaffected by their changes. But man also has an atma, a self, it may be very small and lodged in a part of the body where it cannot be detected, but it is there, and the small atma is the same as the great one. By what physiological doctrines this is upheld, cannot here be traced; but the notion of the atma, the great form of which in Brahma is identical with its small form in man, lives at the basis of Brahmanic thought." (Ibid pp. 346-7).

"And we find, in fact, two religions prevailing in India in the period of Brahmanism, that which we have described, for the enlightened who escapes in it from all law, all creed, all ritual, whose whole religion more than any other which ever flourished in the world is within the mind and on the other hand, a religion in which outward gods are worshipped, an outward law enforced which is counted sacred because a god or gods inspired it, and in which superstition gathered from all quarters find shelter. The higher religion by no means killed the lower one, as we see in India to this day. On the contrary, the withdrawal of the higher religion of the country to a region whither the people could not follow, left the religion of the people to sink into degradation, unknown before. One doctrine must be noticed. *The belief in transmigration which Budhism received from the religion it found existing in India, does not belong lo the higher thought of Brahmanism described in this section: the Atma or self, which is identical with the supreme self belongs to quite a different order of thought from the soul which was formerly in some one else, is now in me, and may come to be in many another being.* The doctrine is thought to have been an importation into India about the time we are speaking of. It admits of being made a powerful deterrent from vice and incentive to virtue. If present sufferings are due not to my acts, but to the acts of the person in whom the soul dwelt before, it is possible for me so to act that my soul's future existence may be better and not worse than this

Two religions

Re-incarnation

one, and that it shall not sink but rise in the order of beings and draw near to its final deliverance.

The further development of Indian religion, apart from Buddhism, is in two directions. There is a philosophical movement in which the Brahmanic ideas on God, the world, the soul and its changes, are further worked out, and which leads to the six schools of Hindu philosophy, on the other hand, the gods have their history. Brahma remains the great god, but as his character is so undefined he is little worshipped. Indra, the old national god, yields to Vishnu, the old sun god of the three steps (heaven, the air, the earth) who becomes the favourite deity. The stern and destructive Siva is a new figure, and seems to be partly an adaptation of a god of the savage aborigines: his worship is the most fanatical. These three, the creator, the upholder and the destroyer, form the Trimurti, or divine trinity of India,—a trinity arrived at not by unfolding the riches of the one great god, but by compounding the claims of three gods who are rivals. The doctrine of incarnation is also found here. Vishnu has the ten avatars or incarnations in human form; he comes down to the earth when there is a special reason for his interference. In these avatars, specially in *Krishna, the dark god,* whose exploits as a hero are told in the great epic the Mahabharata, the need is to some extent met, of which both Budhism and christianity lay hold, of a *divine figure who is not too far away from man, and who can be regarded with personal affection.*" (*Ibid. pp 349-51*).

"Old sun god of the three steps."

The divine trinity of India.

The "dark God"

In the above extracts from Macdonell, Max Müller and Menzies the Italics are *ours*. Their main contentions—the gist of what they have to say—singled out by the Italicised passages, can be given as follows :—

1. By the word "Devataa" the writers of the Vedas meant an imaginary god—a fetish.

2. The Vedas teach polytheism—the cult of many imaginary gods, mostly the forces of nature.

3. The Vedic poets themselves conceived of the forces of Nature as gods and extolled them in their poetical writings known as the hymns of the Vedas. But later people invented other and more gods, deified abstract virtues and mere names, as *S*raddha —Faith, etc.

The contention of all European writers on the Vedas.

4. Even inanimate objects such as doors, pestle and mortar etc., are deified in the Vedas.

5. The Vedic poets also believed in the existence of demons of whom they have written in the Vedas.

6. Later and more philosophically-minded people tried to harmonize the polytheistic teachings of the ancient Vedic sages by taking all names such as, Mitra Varuna, Indra etc., to represent one single god but the process did not culminate in monotheism. For this purpose it is that the purely interrogative pronoun 'ka' in the burden "kasmai devaaya havishaa vidhema" of the famous hymn beginning "hiranyagarbhah samavartataagre" has been explained by them as a name of the god Prajaapati—the Lord of creatures.

This in brief is the contention, of all European writers on Vedic literature. This view was held by the earliest of them, is still held by those that are living and will, it seems, be jealously preserved by those that are still to come in the arena of Sanskrit studies. Circumstances have changed, researches have revolutionised methods of Vedic interpretation, but the white man still persists in his old, wrong and damaging views about India's heritage, "the Vedas", for "the Negro may change his skin and the leopard his spots," but the otherwise chameleon-like European, must stick to these ideas as it politically suits him.

Race-prejudice is the one cause of the continuance of such views.

In other words it is race-prejudice pure and simple that has prevailed upon the white man to persist in his view*s* about India. There was a time when these views could be excused as the tentative opinions of inexperienced, callow researchists, but those days are now long past. Yaaska's Nirukta and its commentaries, the Mahaabhaashya of Patanjali, and the many commentaries on the Vedas themselves recently unearthed are accessible to all. Many auxiliary treatises ancient and modern are available in the market. In the face of these to persist in the old, uncouth, and unlearned methods of interpreting literature pertaining to other people's religion does not in the least become a scholar. Those unfortunate days when the great Vedic scholar Aacaarya Saaya*n*a took upon himself the responsibility of explaining the Vedas where astoundingly different from our own times. He had to gather material from all over India with very great difficulty when the whole country was groaning under the oppression of brigandage, devastation and invasion, and, nobody's life and property were safe. The high position that God had bestowed upon him as the Treasurer and Prime Minister of the Kings of

Vijayanagara, Saayana utilised most conscientiously and with the help of his own wealth and the government funds at his disposal, invited scholars from all over the country to set about the most important and difficult task of reviving and preserving the Vedas and Vedic literature that lay buried in the forgotten nooks and corners of the houses of orthodox, superstitious and illiterate people who were most reluctant to part with the sacred handwritten tomes the heirlooms of their families for centuries past. We cannot too highly admire the pertinacity and fidelity of the man who set about such an arduous task not undertaken for centuries by one men all over the world before him, nor now after him. But the task he had undertaken was superhuman and fraught with the most insurmountable difficulties and interminable. With the resources at his disposal, when such things were simply unimaginable, he did what only an intrepid scholar of his acumen and wealth could do. Considering the times it is impossible more could have been done, nay, even so much could be accomplished. The world ought to be thankful to him for his noble endeavour, but it is not wise to stick to his interpretations and exegetical methods better than which it was impossible for him to adopt for lack of trustworthy data. It should be remembered also, that Saayana was not himself the writer of the Vedic and other commentaries but rather the editor who supervised over a conclave of scholars who did the work allotted to them.

The work of Aacaarya Saaya*n*a.

In their writings on the Vedas all European scholars follow Saayana especially where his interpretations seem to be derogatory to Vedic teachings, and flatly refuse to have anything to do with his great predecessors on whom he himself depends, such as Yaaska etc. As for the Ashtaadhyaayee of Paanini and his great commentator, Patanjali's monumental treatise the Mahaabhaashya, European scholars have not the ability to understand them. Nay, these great ancient sages, the white man considers far inferior to his own countrymen who have attained some smattering in Sanskrit. Great harm has been done to Vedic exegesis by the St. Petersburgh Lexicon of Roth and Boehtlingk, in which the authors have abandoned all ancient Indian authorities, even Saayana, in explaining Vedic words, and have set up their own interpretative apparatus for which they had absolutely no justification. The work was highly praised in its own time but nobody now-a-days cares for it. The interpretations of words given in it are so fanciful,

Saaya*n*a the chief source of European Vedic exegesis.

ridiculous and unfounded that it is difficult to understand how two such scholars could pass them on to the world as lexicographical matter. To speak the truth, the major part of the money spent over this voluminous and equally useless work must be considered to have been wasted. Modern European scholars use this dictionary as an authoritative work on Vedic exegesis. with such material to work with, it is no wonder they write such stuff about the Vedas.

Hence the observation on all the too bold afforts of European savants in the Vedic field that one can make, is, that *they have not understood Vedic literature and should therefore, pursue their studies and researches patiently till they are sufficiently enlightened.*

On the first contention of the European researchists viz., "the word devataa means a fetish", enough has already been said in the beginning of this chapter, adducing the authority of the Vedas themselves. Even in common converse the word davataa does not have this restricted sense of an imaginary god or fetish. When it is said that a certain man is "a devataa" it is clearly intended to be conveyed to the hearer that he is endowed with great and good qualities. The attributive idea of the term is uppermost in the mind of the speaker, which also is the principle note of the expression in all writings. The import, viz., a god or something imaginary adored in the place of the Supreme Being is the secondary and external sense superimposed upon the word and not its real signification. A person worships a stone not because he takes it to be a god but rather because he takes it to be a symbol for the deity. If he were to be asked whether he was worshipping the stone, he would flatly deny the charge, and reply that he used it as a means to concentrate his attention on God or to prevent his mind from distraction. Humanity has yet to produce a pure idolater who worships the idol for its own sake without in the least harbouring any idea of the Supreme Being. The so-called idolatry thoughtlessly condemned by the so-called monotheistic religions like Christianity, exists only in the bigotted brain of some "unco guid"* self-righteous people. Hence such foolish tales as the following† about idolatry cannot be too severely condemned:. "There is a great city far away, where people

Derivation and interpretation of the word devataa.

A silly tale about idolatry.

* Robert Burns.

† From "Reading without Tears", Longmans Green and Co., part 2, pp. 184-5.

worship images of wood and stone, and say they are gods. The people in that city are nearly black. *A kind, white lady* tried to teach them about the true God. One day she saw a poor woman lying on the ground with a little boy by her side. The kind lady spoke to them; but the woman was too ill to answer her. The little boy said, "My mother is sick and has nothing to eat, and I fear she will die". The lady sent her servant home with this message, "Let some men come to help a poor sick woman." Some men came and took the woman and the child to the lady's cottage. The mother and child were placed on a nice clean mat with a blanket to cover them. But the mother died that night. Then the lady took care of the little boy *She found that he was proud of his name, because it was the name of an image. His name was Ramchunder. But soon the boy wished for a new name, and he was named John. Soon he loved Jesus and hated images.*"

The foolishness of the above tale is patent on the very face of it. It is false in the first place that "Ramchunder" is the name of an image, for every one knows that it is the name of a very great Aryan king who was an ideal righteous man. Secondly it is false also that "Jesus" and "John" are not the names of images, for the Roman Catholic church is full of Jesuses" and "Johns" made of plaster of Paris, terra cotta and wood. The writer should have thought twice before writing such nonsense, but what "great scholars" like Max Müller have written is not any thing better.

It is easy to prove that "Ramchunder" (correctly spelt Ramchandra) is not the name of an image and nobody uses it because it is such. But it is not difficult to prove also that the word "Devataa" is not used for any fetish or imaginary god in the Vedas but for something quite real and tangible. Ancient Sanskrit scholars of India have written very clearly on the subject leaving no room for doubt, but it is no question of their inability to convince European "scholars," but rather of the unpreparedness of the later to accept what the former have to say even if it be correct.

The words "Deva" and "Devataa" are synonymous. In the Braahmanas the word "Deva" is interpreted as follows:— "Water stands for all the beneficent objects." A. B. II 16. The whole chapter is allegorical explaining through a popular story as to how the Praatanuvaaka (=the morning Vedic lesson of the praises of God and all beneficent objects) is to be recited.

The word "Deva in the Braahmanas.

Prof. Martin Haug's "school-boy's" translation of the first part of the chapter will serve as a good illustration on this point:— "Prajapati being just about to repeat the Prataranuvaka when he was himself Hotar (at his own sacrifice), all the gods were in a state of anxious expectation, as to who of them would be first mentioned. Prajapati looked about (and, seeing the state of anxiety in which the gods were, thought), if I commence by addressing (the mantra) to one deity only, how will the other deities have a share (in such an invocation)? He then saw (with his mental eyes) the verse: *apo revatir*, i. e., the wealthy waters (10, 30, 12). *Apo*, i. e., waters, means all deities, and *revatih*, (rich) means also all deities. He thus commenced the Prataranuvaka by this verse, at which all the goods felt joy: (for each of them thought), he first has mentioned *me*; they all then felt joy when he was repeating the Prataranuvaka"* This is a very "neat" translation, i. e., the translator has not made the least effort to understand what really the passage means. The translation is a mere substitution of plain English words selected from a Sanskrit-English dictionary in the place of Sanskrit words in the original. Speaking plainly, the reader can make something out of the original, e.g., he can think over the many meanings of the various words and pick out such as would suggest something corresponding to the inner idea of the text, but the translator has, by fixing one haphazard signification of each word, debarred the reader from getting any benefit from the passage, for, the English language, if handled in this manner, is not suggestive. It should also be remembered that, in spite of the very recent dates assigned by European writers to the Braahma*n*as, it is quite probable that the Aitareya Braahma*n*a goes back to, say, some four thousand years before the Christian era, and if this is the case then, it is impossible to get out anything from this passage by assigning the words in it those meanings that are prevalent now. It is worse than translating Chaucer's "whan" by the modern English "van"! Good Dr. Martin Luther's famous translation of the Bible is already out of date, for if it were to be read now and translated literally by assigning the vocables their current meaning it will raise a laughter! In spite of Dr. Trench's still expensive dictionary of the biography of

* प्रजापतौ वै स्वयं होतरि प्रातरनुवाकमनुवक्ष्यति सर्वा देवता आशंसंत मामभिप्रतिपत्स्यति मामभीति । स प्रजापतिरैक्षत यद्येकां देवतामादिष्टामभिप्रतिपत्स्यामीतरामेकेन देवता उपाप्ता भविष्यंतीति स एतामृचमपश्यदापोरेवतीरित्यापो वै सर्वा देवता रेवत्यः सर्वा देवताः॥ ऐ० २ । १६ ॥

English words, the European "Sanskritist" has not learnt to assign proper values to the Vedic words.

Current idiom plays a terrible havoc in the use of words by twisting them out of their original forms as far as their sense is concerned, though, it may retain them in the same external as far as utterance is concerned. In the city of Madras there are two localities called "Barbar's Bridge" and "Chintadripet" respectively. The former was originally named after an Englishman and called "Hamilton's Bridge". But the people distorted the pronunciation into "ambattan" meaning in Tamil, "barbar", so that in course of time it became known as "Barbar's Bridge". "Chintadripet" was originally named after St. Andrew and called "St. Andrew's Pet". Here also the Tamil "tongue" accustomed to pronounce 's' as 'ch' (in chair) slowly twisted the whole expression and made it what it is now. He who tries to revive the original names now would be laughed at. But all the same, if documents of those days were to be interpreted, it would be very essential to identify the two names, otherwise, without a flood or an earthquake two localities will have been lost!

In interpreting Vedic words therefore, it would be the wisest plan to depend upon the derivation of the words and not their current usage. The Sanskrit language is known for its partiality towards the *derivative* interpretation of words. Even in modern (Classical) Sanskrit a word is invariably explained as being made up of a root and a suffix which together yield the form as well as the peculiar meaning assigned to a given word. The word "abhyaagata", for example, means, in later Sanskrit a guest, i. e., "one who has casually or by previous arrangement arrived at somebody's house" in which signification the combined sense of the root 'gam', the prefixes 'abhi-aa' and the past participial passive termination 'kta' does persist. This principle will be found to hold good universally in the case of all Sanskrit words, the exceptions being very few. Usage does not deviate from this main principle, but still it is quite probable that it restricts a word to one of its many significations. In that case a particular word used in a passage will have to be translated according to the convention then prevalent so that the particular restricted sense may be clearly expressed.

Derivation of words in Sanskrit

In spite of this it will have to be admitted that certain words, whether nouns, adjectives or verbs can never be thus restricted to connote only particular ideas and nothing else.

Derivation of 'gold'.

There are, in all the living languages current, words, which for centuries have been maintaining the same sense. For example, the word 'gold', in English, keeps on its main sense of something precious in the idioms "a gold ring', 'all that glitters is not gold', and 'a golden opportunity.' Like the Sanskrit word 'su-var*n*a' (*s*obhanah var*n*ah yasya tat), the English word 'gold' also seems to be made up of two elements the first of which can, with certainty be identified with the common adjective 'good'. The second may, very probably be an old word now lost, meaning 'colour.' It is quite probable the part—ld is the same as the modern English 'lead'. Gold also is malleable like 'lead.' This is, however, only a guess. But the Oxford English Dictionary has its own derivation of the word which does not seem to agree either with the external form or with the sense of the word for, there it is said that the word is *perhaps derived from the Old Teutonic root 'ghel' meaning yellow*. An idiom almost coinciding with the English "all that glitters is not gold" is found in the 40th chapter of the Yajurveda (hira*n*mayena paatre*n*a satyasyaapihitam mukham), where the word hira*n*maya means 'shining' or glittering' like gold. The word 'yellow' cannot bring out the full idea of 'gold' as brass, a base metal, also is yellow.

Haug's translation of A. B. II, 16 faulty.

Haug's translation of the passage from the Aitareya Braahma*n*a referred to above, fails in this direction. The word Prajaapati must not have been reproduced "neat," but translated into English. So also the word "devataa" should not have been translated by the English word "gods," but by some other expression capable of clearly bringing out the signification of the original. As it stands, the translation is more unintelligible than the difficult original itself and is therefore, futile. If this is a story it should have been clearly stated in the translation itself by the use of such words within brackets or otherwise, as would make the matter clear to the reader. Even a story must have some purpose, especially in a treatise like the Aitareya Braahma*n*a, the very *raison d'etre* of which is popular demand for an explanation of the Vedic sacrificial system and other details necessary for the clear grasp of Vedic teaching. Haug's translation entirely overlooks this fact. It is quite probable he could not explain it otherwise as he did not possess the exegetical apparatus necessary for the purpose. It is also quite probable that those "learned pandits" who guided him in this work were themselves ill-informed on the subject. But it is also quite probable he must have insisted in using his own faulty reasoning power in explaining things relating to the religion of others. Anyhow, he himself does not seem to have understood the passage. This is the secret of all European scholars who presume they have to say something damaging about the Vedas and Vedic teachings.

The word "devataa" in the above passage does not mean an imaginary fetish, but all good men and all beneficent forces of nature. An illustration from the Gopatha Braahma*n*a will make this point about the word "devataa" clear.

A passage from the Gopatha Braahma*n*a.

In book second, lesson the first and clause 1* of that book, there is a very beautiful interpretation of certain sacrificial details which can be given in English as follows:—"Now when he (the sacrificer) throws the straw from the seat of the Brahmaa, it should be understood that he cleans the whole sacrificial place." The throwing of the straw is here symbolical of the fact that he has already got the whole house and, especially, the place where the sacrifice is to be conducted, swept clean of all rubbish. The straw is a 'sign' for rubbish. "The Brahmaa then sits on his seat reciting the formula :—I am sitting in the seat of him who is in the neighbourhood of the righteous and beneficent men and forces of nature, for such, surely is their Brahmaa (high priest) and he who dwells far from them is the Brahmaa of those that are opposed to all righteous works." The Vedic high priest or Brahmaa is learned in all the Vedas and *S*astras, and a man of good character and righteous living. These attainments are not possible without continuous association with, and following in the footsteps of, good and wise people.

---

* अथ यद्ब्रह्मसदनात्तृणं निरस्यति शोधयत्येवैनं । तदथोपविशतीदमहमर्वाग्वसोः सदनं सीदामीत्यर्वाग्वसुर्ह वै देवानां ब्रह्मा पराग्वसुरसुराणां तमेवैतत् पूर्वे सादयत्यरिष्टं यज्ञं तनुतादिति । अथोपविश्य जपति बृहस्पतिर्ब्रह्मेति । बृहस्पतिर्वा आंगिरसो देवानां ब्रह्मा तस्मिन्नेवैतदनुज्ञातुमिच्छति । प्रणीतासु प्रणीयमानासु वाचं यच्छत्या हविस्कृत उद्वादनादेतद्वै यज्ञस्य द्वारं तदेतदशून्यं करोति । इष्टे च स्विष्टकृतानुयाजानां प्रसवादित्येतद्वै यज्ञस्य द्वितीयं द्वारं तदेवैतदशून्यं करोति । यत्परिधयः परिधीयन्ते यज्ञस्य गोपीथाय परिधीन्परिधत्ते । यज्ञस्य सात्मत्वाय परिधीन्संमार्ष्टि । पुनात्येवैनं त्रिर्मध्यमं । त्रय इमे प्राणाः प्राणानभिजयति । त्रिर्दक्षिणार्धे त्रयो वै लोका लोकानेवाभिजयति । त्रिरुत्तरार्द्धे त्रयो वै देवलोका देवलोकानेवाभिजयति । त्रिरुपवा जयति त्रयो वै देवयानाः पन्थानः । तानेवाभिजयति । ते वै द्वादश भवन्ति । द्वादश ह वै मासाः संवत्सरः । संवत्सरमेव तेन प्रीणाति । अथो संवत्सरमेवात्मोपदधाति स्वर्गस्य लोकस्य समष्ट्यै ।।गो० २ । १ । १ ।।

Here the word 'vasu' does not mean a fanciful being with an invisible body like that of a human being or otherwise, but simply 'one who dwells.' It is derived from the root 'vasa, nivaase,' by adding to it the U*n*aadi termination 'u' according to U*n*aadi aphorism No. I, 10, in the sense of the agent or nominative case as already explained. By 'devaanaam Brahmaa' it is meant that only a man of clean life and known to men of righteous life and high social status, is to be selected for this high and responsible office. It is on the Brahmaa that the successful performance of the whole sacrifice depends. The word 'asura' is explained in the text as having a number of significations out of which, just as in the case of the word 'gold' in the instances given above, only that has to be selected which will fit in under these special circumstances. To translate 'asura' by the English word 'demon,' therefore, is to betray gross ignorance of the rudimentary principles of Vedic exegesis. The Aryans, for millenniums past, have never believed in evil spirits, except such ignorant folk of them as could be easily led away into accepting the wretched theory of 'a satan' or 'power of evil' as opposed to Divinity. Once admitting 'a satan' the door is flung open for the whole host of the satellites of that imaginary being, including 'hobgoblins,' 'will o'the wisps,' 'nightmares' etc. The Vedas have never laid before humanity the abominable doctrine that the human soul falls so low from her noble nature as to become troublesome to the living humanity. The soul is, of her own nature, a very subtle, a highly noble and righteous spiritual being possessing immense capacities of which one cannot even imagine, and as such, there is no power—not even God Almighty—that can bring her down to such detestable levels as to make her the enemy of mankind playing small and great mischiefs to hurt them.* Hence, by 'paraagvasuh' a person shirking the company of the good is meant. The expression 'paraagvasuh asuraa*n*aam Brahmaa' involves a figure of speech which should first be unravelled to arrive at the inner meaning of the words themselves in relation with the context. The many meanings of the word 'brahmaa' are also given elsewhere in the book, of which life, food, etc., are some. Hence 'asuraa*n*aam Brahmaa" may very well be rendered:— "the high priest of those who live only to satisfy their senses."

What sensible objection can one take to the above rendering and why? Any sensible or reasonable objection

---

* Vide 'Anthology of Vedic Hymns,' pp., 166-86.

must have unprejudiced, intelligent and well-weighed arguments in its favour. Max Müller's statement* that "there is throughout the Brahmanas such a complete misunderstanding of the original intention of the Vedic hymns that we can hardly understand how such an estrangement could have taken place, unless there had been at some time or other a sudden violent break in the chain of tradition", does not possess these features. If there had been "a break in the chain of tradition" of the interpretation of the Vedas when the writers of the Braahmanas sat down to write, it is not known how those shattered links could be restored by a foreign scholar from far away Germany sitting comfortably in England in apartments supplied with comforts provided by the East India Company with Indian money, even if such a scholar were to be learned to the very tips of his toes? Is it possible a young man with a smattering of Sanskrit, hardly able to pronounce रामः, रामौ, रामाः correctly, and not having even read a p a r t at least of Paanini's Ashtaadhyaayee, could span that horrible chasm of which this 'scholar' is complaining in the passage quoted above? Given the writer of the Braahmana, a good Sanskrit scholar, well-read in the four Vedas, fully equipped with all the ancillary learning necessary for the task of interpreting the Vedas, and a foreign bungler not able to read even a single sentence from the Vedas correctly and without possessing even a shadow of the preparation necessary for understanding Vedic poetry, is it possible that the "gods or demons" presiding over that chasm would select only the latter to serve as an interpreter of the Vedas ? What qualification does that foreign 'scholar' hold to recommend him to the position of the interpreter of the Vedas? is it his poor training in Sanskrit literature in a far off European country for some four or five or say, even ten years? Did not the writers of the Braahmanas possess much better—million times better—qualifications than this? Then, if in spite of this, they stumbled in their attempts to interpret the Vedas, we may rest assured that a Max Müller can never, be able to interpret a single sentence from those hallowed tomes correctly, and this is exactly what has happened. These European scholars, when they sat down to write, felt themselves to be judges sent down from some region far away from and high above the world of humanity, and the Vedas and the country of the Vedas to be criminals whose case they had to judge. They did not approach the temple of the Vedas in

Are the writers of the Braahmanas mistaken?

* Vide p. xxxii.

an attitude of reverence and awe, but rather with the feelings of a police detective who sees crime everywhere. Hence as they willed, so they saw. "The learned Smellfungus went from London to Paris; from Paris to Boulogne and from Boulogne to Rome, but he carried his jaundice along with him and everything he saw seemed to be distorted and disfigured out of recognition. I will tell it to the world, said he. You had better tell it to your doctor, said I." In some such strains, Lawrence Sterne, in his Sentimental Journey describes, the interested human "view-finder" that had been to Rome. This holds good in the case of all European Vedic scholars, the Bhatta Moksha Moolara, The Mugdhaanalaacarya, and the host of them.

Max Müller further complains:—"The authors of the Brahma*n*as evidently imagined that those ancient hymns were written simply for the sake of their sacrifices and whatever interpretation they thought fit to assign to these acts the same they supposed, had to be borne out by the hymns. This idea has vitiated the whole system of Indian exegesis." This wonderful argument applies the other way also. Without altering it to any considerable extent we get the following:—"The author of the "History of Ancient Sanscrit Literature" and other European scholars evidently imagined that those ancient hymns were written simply to support their views and whatever signification they thought fit to assign to Vedic words like "devataa" the same they supposed had to be borne out by the hymns." Quite true it is, and this is exactly what has happened.

The passage from the Gopatha Braahma*n*a.

The passage from the Gopatha Braahma*n*a runs on thus :—" The sacrificer, therefore, seats first the Brahmaa himself because he thinks he will accomplish the sacrifice without any mishap. He then himself, seated, says, 'the Lord God the Protector of the Vedic Law Himself is Brahmaa (the Master and Revealer of the Vedas).' 'Aangirasa Brəhaspati' (God Almighty the Lord of the Vedas who pervades the whole universe as the very pith of its ('limbs') is the High Priest of all the learned and righteous, and all beneficent objects. In Him (knowing Him to be present) he wants to carry on this work according to the commandment ". On the words 'Aangirasa' and 'Brəhasprti' there is a pun. The word Aangirasa is the name of the Atharvaveda also as it was revealed through the Sage Angiras. A person knowing the Atharvaveda also, is called 'Aangirasa.' 'Brəhaspati' also means protector of speech in the shape of the Vedas or of his own faculty of speech, by truthfulness. In this latter sense the two words will mean the Brahmaa engaged by the present sacrificer. "When the water vessels are brought in, he, (the Brahmaa) keeps silent till the Vedic verse for the offering of the oblation is recited. This is the very door (commencement) so to say, of the sacrifice, which he, by his silence, sees accomplished without any mishap. Then from the offering of the oblation for good intention till it is time for the accompanying oblation to be offered, he again keeps silent. This is the second door of the sacrifice, i.e., its continuation which he thus gets accomplished without any hitch. The drawing of the circumferential lines round the sacrificial ground he gets done for the safety of the sacrificial ground. Then to put life into (i.e., for the completion of) the sacrifice, he gets them cleaned. The middle circumference he gets cleaned thrice as a symbol of his subduing the three principal vital airs (praa*n*a, apaana and udaana). The southern half of the sacrificial ground he gets cleaned thrice to show his subdual of the three accidents of his life (place, name and birth). The northern half also he gets cleaned thrice to express his intention of subduing beneficent objects of the earthly, atmospheric and planetary regions (devaloka). The space nearer to the 'altar' he cleans thrice to show his desire to conquer the three paths of the learned (activity, practice of the presence of God and close observation of all beneficent objects, and right knowledge of God, the soul and the material world). All these acts amount to twelve in number corresponding to the twelve months of the year. By these acts he makes his routine the whole year round lovely, and the soul of man makes the time of the whole year rouud thus favourable for his celestial and 'eternal' happiness (the highest worldly happiness during life and emancipation after death"). *

The above rendering is not a full translation of tho passage but rather a brief paraphrase of it. To explain the text fully and bring out all the inlying ideas in all their grandeur, it would require ten times more space and research. From a close study of such passages, it seems that the writers of the Braahma*n*as were men of great moral and spiritual perfection, which fact is disclosed by every word of the text, provided it isr ead in the right spirit. To pick holes it is not difficult any where. A cynical, rotten-hearted man will smell the rat every where. Not even the highest and best will escape his sceptical

* Vide p. xlv, footnote.

observations. If he looks at a fine building he will begin to calculate how long it will take it to pull it down. The sight of grown up golden, crops will suggest to him the idea of burning the whole field down in a minute. The sight of .a beautiful, well-nourished animal, will put him in mind of his gun to shoot it down or of his sword to cut its throat with.

Fetishes and Totems.

If Prajaapati is the name of a fetish called the 'lord of creatures,' Vish*n*u of a totem supposed to have *stepped thrice*, Vi*s*vakarman of a fabulous artizan of the "gods" who built a hall for Indra another totem or fetish, Mitra the fabulous being with divine potencies come down from the Indo-Iranian age, Varu*n*a an imaginary fetish presiding over justice, so on and so forth, will it not be opportune to ask whom do the following names denote, totems, fetishes, imaginary beings, many or only one ? (1) Jesus. (2) Christ. (3) Jesus Christ. (4) Saviour. (5) Messiah. (6) Son of Man. (7) Son of God. (8) Son of Mary. (9) Son of Joseph etc. Another group is :—(1) God. (2) Jehova. (3) Elohim. (4) Yehva. (5) The Lord. (6) Creator. (7) Providence. (8) God Almighty. (9) Holy God. (10) God of our fathers. (11) God of Israel. (12) God of Abraham. (13) God of Jacob. (14) God of David, etc.

A criticism of the above 9000 years hence

A very large number of such names can be cited and. supposing, after some nine thousand years hence researchful notes were to be written on them by a "Chiropoy" scholar in the following strains they will be higly valued by the then "intelligentsia" as quite up to date and very scholarly:—"The people of 'Collecoonto'* whose motley religion had the one redeeming feature of unity in their holding in reverence a wooden gallows pillar, the symbol and reminder of many of their political leaders having suffered a violent death at the hands of......, were rank polytheists. They offered divine honours to a 'bundle of yarn' ('jes'-bundle and 'us' yarn in the language of the 'Chiropoys' nine thousand years hence) a cock ('kruost'—a cock in the 'Chiropoy' language), and to these two together combined into one pair but looked upon as one unitary being, a razor ('saviour'—shaver in that language)," and so on and so forth. This looks very fantastic now, but nine thousand years hence it will be the sort of literature most appreciated and put into the compulsory courses of study then. Now, however it looks very strange but just wait for nine thousand years and you will see whal it is.

---

*This is the equivalent of 'the cold continent' a descriptive name of Europe in the language of the 'Chiropoys' nine thousand years hence.

But it is not necessary to take a long journey to the land of the "Chiropoys" of nine thousand years hence to test the truthfulness of the above remarks. England's great modern "evolutionary" historian, H. G. Wells (to mention only one of many such 'fast' thinkers), has already done the work for us. Just listen to the following pleasant tale told by him :—

"The Jews who returned after an interval of more than two generations, to Jerusalem from Babylonia in the time of Cyrus were a very different people from the warring Baal-worshippers and Jehovah-worshippers, the sacrificers in the high places and sacrificers at Jerusalem of the Kingdom of Israel and Judah. The plain fact of the Bible narrative is that the Jews went to Babylon barbarians and came back civilised. They went a confused and divided multitude, with no national self-consciousness; they came back with an intense and exclusive spirit. They went with no common literature generally known to them, for it was only about forty years before the captivity that King Josiah is said to have discovered, "a book of the law" in the temple (II Kings XVII) and besides that, there is not a hint in the record of any reading of books; and they returned with most of their material for the old testament. It is manifest that, relieved of their bickering and murderous kings, restrained from politics and in the intellectually stimulating atmosphere of that Babylonian world, the Jewish mind made a great step forward during the captivity.

The evolution of "Jehovah-worshippers".

It was an age of historical inquiry and learning in Babylonia. The Babylonian influences that had made Sardanapalus collect a great library of ancient writings in Nineveh were still at work. We have already told how Nabonidus was so preoccupied with antiquarian research as to neglect the defence of his kingdom against Cyrus. Everything, therefore, contributed to set the exiled Jews inquiring into their own history, and they found an inspiring leader in the prophet Ezekiel. From such hidden and forgotten records as they had with them, genealogies, contemporary histories of David, Solomon and their other kings, legends and traditions, they made out and amplified their own story and told it to Babylon and themselves. The story of creation and the flood, much of the story of Moses, much of Samson were probably incorporated from Babylonian sources. One version of the creation story and one of the Eden story, though originally from Babylon, seem to have been known to the Hebrews before the excile. When the

Jews returned to Jerusalem, only the Pentateuch had been put together into one book, but the grouping of the rest of the historical books was bound to follow.

The rest of the literature remained for some centuries as separate books, to which a very variable amount of respect was paid. Some of the later books are frankly post-captivity compositions. Over all this literature were thrown certain leading ideas. There was an i d e a, which even these books themselves gainsay in detail, that all the people were pure-blooded children of Abraham, there was next an idea of a promise made by Jehovah to Abraham that he would exalt the Jewish race above all other races; and, thirdly, there was the belief first of all that Jehovah was the greatest and most powerful of tribal gods, and then that he was the only true god. The Jews became convinced at last, as a people, that they were the chosen people of the one God of all the earth.

And rising very naturally out of these three ideas, was a fourth, the idea of a coming leader, a saviour, a Messiah, who would realise the long-postponed promise of Jehovah.

This welding together of the Jews into one tradition-cemented people in the course of the "Seventy years," is the first instance in the history of the new power of the written word in human affairs. It was a mental consolidation that did much more than unite the people who returned to Jerusalem. This idea of belonging to a chosen race predestined to pre-eminence was a very attractive one. It possessed also those Jews who remained in Babylonia. Its literature reached the Jews now established in Egypt. It affected the mixed people who had been placed in Samaria, the old capital of the King of Israel when the ten tribes were deported to Media. It inspired a great number of Babylonians and the like to claim Abraham as their father, and thrust their company upon the returning Jews. Ammonites and Moabites became adherents. The book of Nehemiah is full of the distress occasioned by this invasion of the privileges of the chosen. The Jews were already a people dispersed in many lands and cities, wnen their minds and hopes were unified and they became an exclusive people. But at first their exclusiveness is merely to preserve soundness of doctrine and worship, warned, by such lamentable lapses as those of King Solomon. To genuine proselytes of whatever race, Judaism long held out welcoming arms.

To Phoenicians after the fall of Tyre and Carthage, conversion to Judaism must have been particularly easy and attractive. Their language was closely akin to Hebrew. It is possible that the great majority of Africans and Spanish are really of Phoenician origin. There were also great Arabian accessions. In south Russia, as we shall note later there were even Mongolian Jews." *

"But with the broadening of ideas that came with the captivity, the tenor of prophecy broadens and changes. The jealous pettiness that disfigures the earlier tribal ideas of God gives place to a new idea of a god of universal righteousness. It is clear that the increasing influence of prophets was not confined to the Jewish people ; it was something that was going on in those days all over the Semitic world. The breaking down of nations and kingdoms to form the great and changing empires of that age, the smashing up of cult and priesthood, the mutual discrediting of temple by temple in their rivalries and disputes—all these influences were releasing men's minds to a freer and wider religious outlook. The temples had great accumulated stores of golden vessels and lost their hold upon the imaginations of men.

It is difficult to estimate whether amidst these constant wars, life had become more uncertain and unhappy, than it had ever been before, but there can be no doubt that man had become more conscious of its miseries and insecurities. Except for the weak and the women, there remained little comfort or assurance in the sacrifices, ritual and formal devotions of the temples. Such was the world to which the latter prophet of Israel began to talk of the One God, and of a Promise that some day the world should come to peace and unity and happiness. This great God that men were now discovering lived in a temple "not made with hands, eternal in the heavens." There can be little doubt of a great body of such thought and utterance in Babylonia, Egypt and throughout the Semitic east. The prophetic books of the Bible can be but specimens of the prophesying of that time.

We have already drawn attention to the gradual escape of writing and knowledge from their original limitation to the priest-hood and the temple precincts, from the shell in which they were first developed and cherished. We have taken Herodotus as an interesting specimen of what we have called the free inlelligence of mankind. Now here we are dealing with a

*From "A New Outline of History" by H. G. Wells, pp. 266-8.

similar overflow of moral ideas into the general community. The Hebrew prophets and the steady expansion of their ideas towards one God in all the world, is a parallel development of the free conscience of mankind. From this time onwards there runs through human thought, now weakly and obscurely, now gathering power, the ideas of one rule in the world, and of a prômise and possibility of an active and splendid peacc and happiness in human affairs. From being a temple religion of the old type, the Jewish religion becomes, to a large extent, a prophetic and creative religion of a new type. Prophet succeeds Prophet.

Later on as we shall tell, there was born a prophet of unprecedented power, Jesus, whose followers founded the great universal religion of Christianity. Still later Muhammad, another prophet, appears in Arabia and founds Islam. In spite of very distinctive features of their own, these two teachers too, in a manner, arise out of, and in succession to, these Jewish prophets. It is not the place of a historian to discuss the truth and falsity of religion, but it is his business to record the appearance of great constructive ideas. Two thousand four hundred years ago, and six or seven or eight thousand years after the walls of the first Sumerian cities arose, the ideas of the moral unity of mankind and of a world peace had come into the world." *

Just read what Winternitz has to say about two "canonnised" saints of the Roman Catholic Church:—

"On the other hand, it is a fully established fact that one of the favourite books of the whole of Christendom in the Middle Ages, the Story of Barlaam and Josaphat, was composed by a devout Christian on the basis of the Buddha legend, with which he might have become acquainted from the Lalita-Vistara. This story, which is other-wise entirely imbued with the spirit of Christianity has a Buddhist setting—the main features of the Buddha legend, the three excursions, at which the Bodhisattva becomes acquainted with age, disease and death, recur in it, a few of the interpolated parables (e. g. that of the "man in the well") are familiar from Indian literature, and references to India, occur in the story itself. In eastern Iran or in central Asia, where, as we know through the finds of Sir Aurel Stein, Grünwedel and v Le Cog in Khotan and Turfan, Zoroastrians, Buddhists Christians, and Manicheans lived together in closest proximity, a Christian monk could easily become acquainted with the Buddha

Sts. Barlaam and Josaphat.

* Ibid. pp., 269-70,

legend, and be stimulated by it to compose a work which was to import Christian doctrines. This work was presumably written in the 6th or 7th century, first in the Pahlavi language and afterwards translated into Arabic and Syriac. The Georgian and Greek translations might be traced back to the Syriac text. Tne Greek text gave rise to Arabian, Hebrew, Aethiopian, Ecclesiastical Russian and Rumanian versious, which came into being in later times. The numerous European translations and recensious (Lope de Vega has even dramatised the story) can be traced back to the Latin text translated from the Greek. German recensions have been in existence since 1220 A D. In course of centuries the characters in this work had grown so familiar to the Christian peoples, that they were regarded as pious Christian men who had really lived and taught, so that the Catholic Church finally made the two heroes of the story, Barlaam and Josaphat, into saints. Josaphat, however, is none other than the Bodhisattva." *

Dr. A. B. Keith (not a great friend of India and the Vedas) also has to say something on this point:—

"The effort, however, has been made with special emphasis in the case of Buddhist legends, as we find them both in Pali and Sanskrit texts, to prove derivation of events in the gospels, including the apocryphal gospels from India. The argument is also supported by hagiographic legends, beyond all by the tale of Barlaam and Josaphat for it is generally admitted that the Bodhisatva is the figure whence Josaphat is derived. But the parallel of the legends is clearly very small beyond the presence of this figure, and the late date of the story renders it extremely probable that India was only remotely concerned. The figure of the Bodhisattva was most probably taken up by Persian thought in Mahomedan times, made into a typical Sufi, taken thence to Bagdad and Syria, where under christian hands it was converted into a saint. Other cases are far less plausible; the man-eating monster Christophoros cannot fairly be compared with the Bodhisattva—bearing Brahmadatta; the figures in their respective legends have little in common, and it becomes necessary to suppose that the idea was transferred through pictorial delineations misunderstood, while the Christophoros legend can be explained as a variant of the Märchen of the stronger—the effort to find out who is the strongest of all—and conjectural explanations of names. Similarly, the attempt to parallel the legend of Placidas who becomes the

* From a "History of Indian Litereture" by Maurice Winternitz, Vol., II, pp., 416-8

holy Eustachios as the outcome of pursuing a deer, loses and finds again his wife and children, by a combination of a Jataka of a deer which brings about the conversation of a king, of a woman who lost her children, and the sufferings of the hero of the *Vessantara Jataka* is clearly fallacious. The essential parts of the legends belong to the realm of myth or Märchen, and for borrowing there is no real evidence."*

Thus it is not only the credulous Hindu that indulged in the creation of imaginary 'gods'. Today there exists a Church in the city of Madras in the locality called San Thomé, the southern extremity of that ancient place called Mylapore (in the Pa*m*catantra Mihilaaropya) known after St. Lazarus. That St. Lazarus never existed! The Roman Catholic Church has not canonised any Indian saints. There is absolutely no record that any such pious Cristian Indian or non-Indian, ever flourished in Madras and that after his death he was canonised by the Roman Catholic Church in whose name the church in question was built. It may be argued that the poor man of whom the good Jesus speaks in Luke XVI, 19-25 may be the patron saint of the church concerned. This view is wrong, since the account is only a parable related by Jesus to explain "the vanity" of riches. The rich man and Lazarus are only imaginary. Nor is it the other Lazarus, the brother of Mary and Martha whom Jesus 'raised' from the dead as is related in John XI, 1-44. It is quite probable the Roman Catholic Church has, erelong, canonised the brother and sisters spoken of in this account, and if it be so, it would be better to name the Madras church now after this Lazarus!

St. Lazarus' Church, Mylapore.

It is possible these real and unreal saints of the Roman Catholic Church would be represented by the 'Chiropoys' of nine thousand years hence to be so many gods and demi-gods of an idolatrous people. Even if proof were available that these saints were only pious and virtuous human beings it will not be possible for the then critics to take this as anything but the deification of man. In his anxiety to please a choleric god made after his own finite image, man creates a number of agents to intercede for him with that peevish being that all may be well with him in his worldly life full of wilful blunders and sin.

Even granting that the Vedas were written only three thousand years back, it looks simply horrible, unjust, inhuman

*From "History of Sanskrit Literature" by A. B. Keith, pp , 501-2.

and altogether unbelievable that the poor writer of three thousand years back should write:— "Indram mitram varu*n*amagnimaahuratho divyassa supar*n*o garutmaan | Ekam sadvipraa bahudhaa vadantyagnim yaman maatari*s*vaanamaahuh," that is, 'He is one, but out of their immense love for Him they call Him by innumerable beautiful names, Lord of wealth, Loving Friend etc., just as a loving mother would call her baby, my doll my flower, my life,' etc., and that his statement should now, after three thousand years, be twisted and distorted out of all proportion in spite of itself, and a polytheistic garble forcibly put upon it. Nothing can be more unfortunate and unnatural than this. When the ancient writer lays down the rules of interpretation in black and white all of which are available intact and quite intelligible unlike the attitude of the 'Chiropoys' (the race existing in.........nine thousand years hence referred to above), they should not and must not have been, in fairness to scholarship, thus consigned to the waste paper basket and fanciful apparatus constructed after the saying "give the dog a bad name and then kill it."

Dr. Allan Menzies, already quoted, pleads in favour of a Vedic totemism as the basis of evolution into a higher religion in the following words:—

Religion like civilisation, is evolved

"It has been ascribed to a primitive revelation. At the beginning, it is said, God, with the other gifts He gave to man, gave him religion; that is to say, gave him not only a disposition for reverence and piety; but a certain amount of religious knowledge, so that he set out with a stock of religious ideas which were not elaborated by his own efforts, but bestowed on him ready made. It is impossible, however, to conceive how this could be done. If the religion given at first was a lofty and pure one,—and no other need be thought of in such a connection,—then it implies a condition of human life far above the struggles and uncertainties of savage existence, and both the civilisation and the religion must have been lost afterwards. But how could all mankind forget a pure religion ? Mankind in that case cannot have been fit for the possession of it; it was given prematurely. No. The history of early civilisation is the history of a struggle in which man has every thing to conquer, and in which he is not remembering something he had lost, but advancing by new routes to a land he never reached before. And if civilisation was won for the first time, so was religion."*

* "History of Religion" by Allan Menzies D. D. (Page 23. ll., 14-35.)

"It was from the savage state that civilisation was by degrees produced. The theory that man was originally civilised and human, and that it was by a fall, by a degeneration from that earliest condition, that the state of savagery made its appearance, is now generally abandoned. There may be instances of such degeneration having taken place, but on the whole, the conviction now obtains that civilisation is the result of progressive development, and was the result man conquered for himself by his agelong struggle with his environment."*

Religion has gradually evolved

"Now what is true of civilisation generally will be true also of religion, which is one of the principal elements. If every country was once inhabited by savages, then the original religion of every country must have been a religion of savages, and there will be features in the later religion which have been carried on from the earlier one. This indeed, we must in any case expect to find. No new religion can enter on its career as a soil quite unoccupied on which no gods have been worshipped before. That would imply that there had been races in the world without religion, which we do not admit. A faith has always to begin by adjusting itself to that which it found in possession of the soil, and it always adopts what it can of the old system."†

"There is a great family likeness in the religions of savages, and we may even allow ourselves to speak not of religions but of the religion of early races."‡

Dr. Allan Menzie's argument that religion like civilisation is evolved, i. e., just as man from his naked state of the time 'when wild in the woods the noble savage ran" grazed grass, ate fruit fallen from the trees and gobbled up live lice and cockroaches and lived a life lower than that of a tame dog now-a-days,—rose up gradually through centuries and millenniums to the present state of weaving and wearing fine clothes—trousers, coats, collars, neckties, hats, driving in motor cars with a thick cigar in his mouth, nay, flying in aeroplanes, so also religion from the lowest of totemisms rose slowly to the highest pinnacle of the doctrine of 'the father, son and holy ghost, one in three and three in one,' and remember please, that that totemistic stage is described in the Vedas. But if one were to ask Dr. Menzies as to what he has to say about the verse quoted above, "Indram mitram" etc., well he says, sometimes there was a faint idea of a single god but it never developed into worship of a Supreme

* Ibid., p. 10 l, 2. p. 17 l. 6. † Ibid., p. 18 ll. 15 28. ‡ Ibid., p, 19 ll. 21-4

Being. This latter has been reserved only for Christianity. Just see what he has to say on this point:—

"Kathenotheism.—The Vedic poets, as we shall see, speak of the god they are immediately addressing as supreme, and heap upon him all the highest attributes, while not thinking of denying the divinity of other gods.

The language of Henotheism is—"Thou, O Jehovah, art far above all the earth, thou art exalted far above all gods," (Ps. xcvii 9). "There is none like unto thee among the gods, O Lord ?...Thou art great and doest wondrous things. Thou art God alone." (Ps lxxxvi, 8; 10). Here the other gods are recognised as existing, but only one is worshipped. Compare also St. Paul: "There are gods many, and Lords many, but to us there is one God." (I Cor. viii, 5, 6).

The Supreme Being is a Christian monopoly

The language of monotheism is:—"All the gods of people are idols, but Jehovah made the heavens" (Ps xcvi 5), and "Thou shalt have no other god before me."*

"A Supreme Being,—Is it necessary to add another class of deity to these three, and to say besides nature-gods and spirits early man also worshipped a Supreme Being above all these ? In most savage religions there is a principle deity to whom the others are subordinate. But if we together examine one by one the supreme gods of these religions, we find reason to doubt whether they really have a common character so as to form a class by themselves. Many of them are nature-gods who have out-grown the other deities of that class and come to accupy an isolated position. The North American Indians, as we saw, worship the great spirit, the heaven with its breadth, to whom sun and moon and other ordinances of nature fulfil the part of ministers. Many other cases occur in which heaven is the highest god. In others again it is the sun who is supreme. Ukko the great god of the Finns is a heaven and rain-god. Perkunas the god of the Lithuanians is conneeted with thunder. On the other hand there are instances in which the supreme god appears to be a different being from the nature gods. The Samoyedes worship the sun and moon and the spirit of other parts of nature; but they also believe in a good spirit who is above all. *The Supreme Being of the islands of the Pacific bears in New Zealand the name of Tangaroa,*

* "History of Religion" by Allan Menzies D. D. p. 53, ll. 11—29.

and is spoken of in quite metaphysical terms as the uncreated and eternal creator. Here we may suspect Christian influence. With the Zulus Unkulunkulu 'the old-old one' might be supposed to be a kind of first cause. But on looking nearer we find he is distinctly a man, the first man, the common ancestor, beyond which idea speculation does not seem to go. Among many North American tribes an animal is principal deity,—the hare or the musc-rat or the coyate. It is very common to find in savage belief a vague far-off god who is at the back of all the others, takes little part in the management of things, and receives little worship. But it is impossible to judge what that being was at an earlier time, he may have been a nature-god or a spirit who has by degrees grown faint and come to occupy the position. We cannot judge from this that the supreme being was generally diffused in the world in the earliest times and is not to be derived from any of the processes from which the other gods arose. We shall see afterwards how natural the tendency is which, where there are several gods, brings one of them to the front while the others lose importance. For a theory of primitive monotheism the supreme gods of savages certainly do not furnish sufficient evidence, they do not appear to have advanced from very different quarters to the supreme position, in obedience to that native instinct of man's mind which causes him, even when he believes in many gods, to make one of them supreme."*

A Spiritual religion is not evolved

This is simply horrible. The worship of totems—even millions of them—cannot lead to the worship of that One, Unitary, Spiritual Being, Whom humanity from its very 'childhood' has been addressing as God, Father Supreme Being etc. This latter, is impossible to be arrived at by evolution. Evolution is possible only with in very restricted limits. A mongrel dog can, for example, be tamed and trained, its puppies improved till after several generations, say, ten, it is quite possible to have a very fine hunting dog worth hundreds and thousands. But train however much you like, feed the animal on gold if you can and will, even after a million generations a dog will not be able to give you a little leopard, nay, not even a goat. Cross a bitch with a panther if you can, and you will, if possible, get neither a panther nor a dog, but something indescribable. Evolution can explain only this much that from very small beginnings you can have great

The idea of the True God can not be arrived at by evolution

*Ibid, p. 33. l. 28-p. 35 l. 11.

results within certain very definite limits, but not that beginning with something you can produce from it something entirely heterogeneous, It is possible for a man to become an emperor but there are no evolutionary nor revolutionary means by utilising which he can become a huge, fearful, speaking lion! In Scholastic philosophy it is very clearly postulated that lack of good is evil. *Quid est malum? carentia boni.* What is evil? The lack of goodness. According to the Scholastic system it is only a being that can be good etc. *Ens est verum, bonum, utile, pulchrum etc.* So also lack of goodness, *carentia boni, palchri, utilis* etc., can be predicted only of *Ens*—Being and not of *non-Ens*, non-Being. A non-being is some thing unpredictable, something entirely lacking of predictibility. *Veritas metaphysica*—the metaphysical reality of every being is its essential characteristic, called in Sanskrit, "dharma". The metaphysical verity of a horse is its "horseness" and not its being a swift, beautiful or strong horse. This metaphysical verity can never be got by evolution. Evolution can bring in only traits that will remove lack of goodness till the metaphysical verity of a particular thing shines out in all its brilliance.

Spiritual religion is not a result of evolution

Hence an entire absence of spiritual religion cannot, by any means, be so transformed as to become the highest possible spiritual religion. Just as there are animals and animals, but not all are horses, so also there are riligions and religions but not all spiritual religions. A metaphysical system cannot develop into a spiritual religion by any amount of evolution. The religion of a rationalist is his disorderly ordered reasoning with in certain limits. Any amount of his pet ratiocination will not lead him to believe in a spiritual God. For him, it is quite reasonable to say:— *God may exist*, or *God exists if*, or *god exists, but*—etc. If pressed hard sand may yield oil but even an infinite mumber of rationalist processes will not produce belief in spiritual religion. If a rationalist cannot do so how can a savage do it? A savage entirely lacking in ideas of a spiritual religion cannot develop it out of his children's play of totemism. He can acquire it anew from outside, surely, but not develop it out of his own silly *-ism.* This acquisition also will be possible only if he has the necessary qualifications to grasp it and not otherwise.

Polytheism is the worship of many different and independent somethings not always human, wrongly called "gods" and *pantheism is the adoration of every blessed thing as God.* Both are wrong attitudes developed out of a mistaken view of the Supreme Being. He who offers obeisance to many gods or pays divine honors to every imaginable being considered as god, must necessarily know about god as such. He is acquainted with the nature of divinity, but some obstacles have intervened to mar his vision so that he now retains a hazy idea of true divinity, which on account of his mind not efficiently responding* to his soul, seems to him to tally with many objects of a particular type or everything his physical eye meets with. The dimness of his mental vision makes him identify the divinity he had 'seen' or heard of with some other thing or things. Rather it makes him search in many things or all things for what he has lost, forgotten or misplaced. His mind is a palimpsest which still bears the indelible original writing dimly visible through the later scribble rendering its clear outline vague and unrecognisable, all the same it is there. This is one way in which the polytheistic or pantheitee position can be explained.

Another explanation also is possible. A man highly developed in spiritual life will see God in everything. His position is described in Yajurveda XL, 1 thus.

"*Both the mobile and immobile creation in this infinite universe is pervaded by the Supreme Eternal Spirit*, the Repository

---

*This is an extremely difficult and abstruse metaphysical point. Something about this has been stated in the comment on the Naasadeeya as well as the Brahmacarya hymns. The body with all its sense organs being gross matter can have no vision of the highest, spiritual being, God. The mind also being subtle matter, cannot, except with the aid of the soul, visualise God—or rather serve as a means for the composite being called man (described in the Geetaa as "aatmendriyamanoyuktam bhoktetyaahurmaneeshi*n*ah"), to have a vision of the Supreme Being. But this is possible only when the material mind is so 'pliable' as to entirely subserve to the soul in her designs; for, it is only the soul that is naturally so constituted as to have a vision of God continually. But the corporeal veil prevents her from seeing God on account of the predominance of either "rajas" (element producing physical activity) or "tamas" (element which occasions dull material reaction), since, encased as she is in the body, the soul can act only through the mind. If the mind is in order, and quite responsive to the soul, the composite will receive the impression of the Deity from the mind reflected on the latter by the soul. If the mind, on account of the predominance of rajas or tamas in it, receives only very faint, vague and unrecognizable reflection from the soul, the transmission of that impression to the composite also will be vague and uncertain, like groping in the dark. This is what is 'exposed' as polytheism or pantheism.

and the prime source of all wealth and energy, Enjoy, O mortal the righteous pleasures of this world *in a spirit of indifference*, and do not covet the wealth of any fellowbeing."*

It is not physical vision that is meant here. God cannot be visualised physically since there is no physical composition in His Being. A perpetual feeling of His Immanence, His presence, that is what is depicted in the above verse. The following lines from the Canariese poet Sarvajna will explain the point:— "I have the begging bowl in my hand ; the whole expanse of the country lies before me that I may go and freely beg my bread and *God the Bestower of all good, is with me*, who is richer than I am?"†

Such noble souls see God everywhere and in everything. Their nobility is time and again reflected in their words and deeds, for example, they will never utter filthy or angry words. They will not do this even in jest. There will be no travesty of truth or mental restriction in their conversation. In handling things they will be always careful and regardful. While working eating, speaking to others or sleeping, they will feel the presence of the ever present Eternal Father, and hence behave in a manner befitting a well-bred child in the presence of his parents. If such noble souls have seen Him everywhere and in everything and have described Him as such, they have done absolutely no wrong. Granting, for arguments' sake, that the Vedas were written by the sages whose names are prefixed to the hymns in the printed text, it is reasonabl to suppose that they were such noble souls.

Menzies' contention that the idea of the Supreme Being is a Christian 'monopoly' and transmitted thence to other religions is baseless, for the idea of God in the Bible is anthropomorphic. The Christian trinity "father, son and holy ghost, one in three and three in one, three persons and one nature" is no monotheism, nay, it does not seem to be even theism at all. Such a haphazard doctrine cannot produce the beautiful idea about the True God which the following lines from the Yajurveda (XL, 8) lay down:—"He pervades the entire universe. He is of infinite might and the Creator of all. He is

---

* ईशावास्यमिदं सर्वं यत्किञ्च जगत्यां जगत् ।
तेन त्यक्तेन भुञ्जीथा मा गृधः कस्यस्विद्धनम् ॥

† करदि कप्पर उंटु तिरिदुणलु नाडुंटु । हरनैम्ब दैव नमगिरलु ।
नमगिंत सिरिमंतरारु सर्वज्ञ ॥

incorporeal and exempt from birth and death. He is indivisible and impenetrable by the minutest conceivable object. He is free from the bonds of nerves and muscles. He is holy and above every phase of ignorance. He is free from sin and every sinful desire. He is Omniscient and privy to our inmost thoughts. He presides over all, is self-existent and the efficient cause of the universe. He reveals to his eternal subjects the true knowledge of the Vedas."*

The grand idea of the Supreme Being as the One and only God, the Creator, Sustainer and Dissolver of the whole universe that is so clearly expressed in the Vedas,† does not have its counterpart in the sacred books and doctrines of any other religion or country. Other religions have a mere shadow of this marvelous teaching about the oneness of God. To say that god is one and almighty and in the same breath to represent him as a choleric, whimsical, peevish old man crying night and day over the wickedness of mankind, harbouring feelings of utter partiality towards a particular race or community and going about killing and destroying all those that are either opposed to the favoured race or trying to safeguard their interests from the wicked wiles of that race, is no mono-

---

* स पर्यगाच्छुक्रमकायमव्रणमस्नाविरं शुद्धमपापविद्धं । कविर्मनीषी परिभूः स्वयंभूर्याथातथ्यतोऽर्थान्व्यदधाच्छाश्वतीभ्यः समाभ्यः ॥ य० ४० । ८ ॥ †य एकश्चर्षणीनां वसूनामिरज्यति । इन्द्रः पञ्चक्षितीनाम् ॥ ऋ० १ । ७ । ६ ॥ य एक इद्विदयते वसु मर्ताय दाशुषे । ईशानो अप्रतिष्कुत इन्द्रो अङ्ग ॥ ऋ० १ । ८४ । ७ ॥ य इत्तमु ष्टुहि कृष्टीनां विचर्षणिः । पतिर्जज्ञे वृषक्रतुः ॥ ऋ० ६ । ४५ । १६ ॥ य एक इद्धव्यश्चर्षणीनामिन्द्रं तं गीर्भिरभ्यर्च आभिः । यः पत्यते वृषभो वृष्ण्यावान्त्सत्यः सत्वा पुरुमायः ॥ ऋ० ६ । २२ । १ ॥ त्वमग्न इन्द्र वृषभः सतामसि त्वं विष्णुरुरुगायो नमस्यः । त्वं ब्रह्मा रयिविद् ब्रह्मणस्पते त्वं विधर्तः सचसे पुरन्ध्या ॥ ऋ० २ । १ । ३ ॥ त्वमग्ने राजा वरुणो धृतव्रतस्त्वं मित्र भवसि दस्म ईड्यः । त्वमर्यमा सत्पतिर्यस्य सम्भुजं त्वमंशो विदथे देव भाजयुः ॥ ४ ॥ त्वमग्ने रुद्रो असुरो महो दिवस्त्वं शर्धो मारुतं पृक्ष ईशिषे । त्वं वातैररुणैर्यासि शङ्गयस्त्वं पूषा विधतः पासि नु त्मना ॥ ६ ॥ त्वमग्ने द्रविणोदा अरं कृते त्वं देवः सविता रत्नधा असि । त्वं भगो नृपते वस्व ईशिषे त्वं पायुर्दमे यस्तेऽविधत् ॥ ७ ॥ आदित्यानां वसूनां रुद्रियाणां देवो तेवानां न मिनामि धाम । ते मा भद्राय शवसे ततक्षुरपराजितमस्तृतमषाळ्हम् ॥ ऋ० १० । ४८ । ११ ॥ अभीदमेकमेको अस्मि निष्षाळभी द्वा किमु त्रयः करन्त । खले न पर्षान्प्रति हन्मि भूरि किं मा निन्दन्ति शत्रवोऽनिन्द्राः ॥ ऋ० १० । ४८ । ७ ॥

theism, nay, it is no theism at all, it is the meanest of anthropomorphisms. A being having such paltry pettifogging inclinations and steeped overhead in the quagmire of gross partiality is no god at all but at best 'the subliminal self of the modern capitalists'.* To represent Almighty God, the Eternal Father, the Everlasting Source of True Love, Kindness and Perfect Justice as fawning and doting upon a particular race and thirsting after others' throat's blood, is the most heinous blasphemy.

The Vedas, surely, do not teach of such an imbecile god. Even atheism is far preferable to such sham monotheism.

The Vedas describe the forces of nature but do not deify them. Personification, a poetical device can never be equal to deification. European scholars seem to think that figures of speech are the sole monopoly of European languages. In the same manner abstract ideas like 'Manyu' (indignation) and *S*raddhaa (faith) are also personified and not deified.

Inanimate objects like the mortar and pestle, the grindstone, the knife etc., being articles of human use have necessarily to be described. This is exactly what the Vedas have done. European savants have mistaken the forms in which the names of these things have been used, for the vocative. This topic will be dealt with in the chapter on Vedic Interpretation.

The Vedas do not teach about demons or the devil. The words 'raakshasa', 'asura' do not mean devil. See the chapter on interpretation regarding this point.

A disposal of Max Müller's objections to the interpretation of the ancient word 'ka' a name of God Almighty will also be found in the chapter on Vedic interpretation.

The distinctive features of the True Divine Church.

The Vedic subjects treated of in this book clearly point out that it is only the Vedic Society that deserves to be called the True Church of God—the "Ecclesia Divina". All these themes point out the marks of the True Divine Church in a very simple manner:—

(1) A prayerful life of each member is the first mark of the Divine Church. All the members, young and old, male and female, should always pray to God Almighty feelingly and feeling His presence everywhere and at all times. This is taught in the first

---

* Vide 'the Lodgian Heresy, Chapter III.

and last chapters of the book. This subject is dealt with in "Anthology of Vedic Hymns" also.

(2) The second note of the Divine church is a life pure, regulated, peaceful and philanthropic. *A society which practises these virtues cannot thrive unless it spreads its tenets all over the world and converts all humanity—the most sensible at least, to its own views.* A race, community or religion not based upon such teaching will prove the greatest enemy of humanity. The modern age provides innumerable examples of the violations of this principle.

(3) The third note is the establishment of humanity on such sound religions, i. e., spiritual and moral principles as are laid down in the Vedas. Human society must have its kings, leaders, teachers, assemblies and workers but all these must be based upon true spiritual and moral principles.

(4) The fourth note is patriotism and industry coupled with learning. Each member should have a high regard for others feelings, convenience and happiness. This is possible only if the members take care to see that their patriotism does not assume the sinful form of *nation-worship* and *land-hunger* nor their industry that of a *nationalised industrialism.*

(5) If these four notes are present, the fifth viz., universality of teaching and an all-embracing spirit of catholicity will necessarily be prominently visible.

There are the five principal notes which characterise the Holy Vedic Church,—the true Church of God—the Church after His Divine Heart. Any other society, not possessing these notes, even though the majority of mankind may call it "the true and divine church" cannot be regarded to be really such.

The word 'church' has nothing to do with Christianity.

From the use of the word 'Church' in the above paragraphs it may be argued that these remarks are a mere copy of Christian teachings and that the word Church itself is of Christian origin.* But it is not so. All human communities having a religious and moral law and order for their basis are

* The 'Shorter Oxford Dictionary' (perhaps the large one also is no better) renders no help in tracing the true and full origin of this word. There it is said to be derived (?) from Old English *cirice*, circe, Middle English *chereche*, *chiriche* whence

'Churches'. In this sense it has nothing to do with a building, Sunday-meeting, mass, sermons, music and imaginary images of Jesus, his mother Mary and her husband Joseph, of the Christian 'saints' old and new (but all European!), processions, lenten fasts, bishops' dinners, retreats etc., but it has surely to do with organisers and organisation. Without organisers and organisation there can be no church. But it matters little whether such organisers are called, pope, bishop, priest, deacon, dastoor, mulla or by any orther name. The name itself, in this case, does not matter much, but even in this case, it is the Holy Vedas that carry away the laurels! When some organisation calls its head 'pope,'* the Vedas name him 'indra'. 'Indra†' in ordinary classical Sanskrit means sabhaapati

---

churche, *cherche* etc. Apparently common West German.:—Greek kurakon (sc. doma or the like),='house of the Lord'. From this elaborate data very little can be made out about the origin of the word which is still untraced and unknown. It is quite probable it is formed from Gr. 'kurakon' or the Latin 'curia'. It is a translation but not derivative of the Greek ecclesia', Whatever be its derivation, it does not mean a building where Christian worship is conducted or a gathering or body of Christians, but simply a community of human beings regulated by common religious laws.

* From Old English *papa* adopted from eccelesiastical Latin *papa*, adapted from late Greek *papa*=father (S. O. D. 1933). This is the official title of the Bishop of Rome who is also the head of the Roman Catholic Church the world over. Under him there are all the Roman Catholic bishops. The word bishop is said to be derived from Old English *biscop*, *bisceop*. *biscep*:—Latin *episcopus* Greek: *episkopos* (S. O. D. 1933) and means an overseer, superintendent or superviser. Hence the place and people under his jurisdiction is named 'the diocese' (from Greek dioikein=to keep house) or 'the see' i. e., something seen or supervised. The Protestants (not all of them) have only bishops and no pope. The lowest ecclesiastical executive of the Roman Catholics is the priest. His official title is 'reverend father'. The place and people under him are called his 'parish'. The organisation of the Roman Catholic Church of which Macaulay in his review of Ranke's 'History of the Popes' (see his Historical Essays) writes with subdued critical fervour and to which he 'offers qualified praise,' is a copy of Buddhist ecclesiastical organisation. The latter also have their monks (called 'bhikshu' in Sanskrit) in charge of different parishes. The 'heenayaana' Buddhism does not have any showy ecclesiastical paraphernalia for its monk-priests who more or less resemble the 'Hindu' sanyaasi. But the Mahaayaana school of Tibet and elsewhere have more gorgeous, expensive and varied dress etc., for the priests. The Roman Catholic bishop's mitre, the priests' chasuble, surplice etc., are all copied from the Mahayaana Buddhists.

† इन्द्र—इन्दति परमैश्वर्यवान्भवति इति—√ इदि ऐश्वर्ये + रन् U. II, 28 = इन्द्रः = समर्थोऽन्तरात्मादित्यो योगो वा ॥ ‡ √ हु दानादनयोरादाने

=president. The sacrificial priest are hotrə‡ (Rəgveda), adhvaryu§ (Yajurveda), udgaatrə¶ (Saamaveda) and brahmaa$ (the high priest—Atharvaveda). Every brahmaa--sacrificial high priest is selected for the occasion from among those that have studied all the Vedas. The indra or sabhaapati is quite different from these. His position depends upon popular vote. In the Vedic Church ecclesiastical society is not something subordinate or entirely opposed to political and social organisations of the people. All the three form one unit to be called by the cooperative name 'church.' As such the Divine church has her emperor and kings who are members and officers of, but having equal privileges in, the imperial league. This is expressed through a very beautiful simile in R. V. VII, 34, II (Vide p. 299) where the emperor is compared to the ocean and the various kingdoms that unite under his paramountcy to rivers that flow apart from each other between beautiful banks and in the end fall into the same ocean. The sense of the simile connotes the idea of the impartial dealing of the emperor and the willing and hearty cooperation of the member kingdoms.

The emperor and the imperial league.

The entire svaraajya hymn of sixteen stanzas (vide pp. 301-18) has the very significant burden arcannanu svaraajyam. This little sentence of three words than which there does not

---

चेत्येके+तृन् U. II, 95. § अध्वर्युरध्वरयुः। (१) अध्वरं युनक्ति (२) अध्वरस्य नेता। (३) अध्वरं कामयत इति वा (४) अपिवाऽधीयाने युरुपबन्धः। अध्वर इति यज्ञनाम ध्वरति हिंसाकर्मा तत्प्रतिषेधः। या० १॥ ७॥ In this passage Yaaska derives the word in four ways:—(1) अध्वरं युनक्ति इति—अध्वर+√युजिर् योगे+कु U. I, 37, and 33.—अध्वरयुः—अध्वर्युः, the final अ of the base is irregularly dropped. (2) अध्वरं प्रापयति इति अध्वर+√या प्रापणे+कु U. I, 37. (3) अध्वरं कामयते इति अध्वर+क्यच्+उ P. III, I, 8 and 2, 170. (4) अध्वरं अधीते इति अध्वर+यु which is a termination applied after the analogy of P. IV, 2, 59. The word अध्वर itself is a negation of ध्वृ meaning to kill or injure. नञ्+√ध्वृ हिंसायाम्+घञ् P. III. 3, 118 and Nig. II, 19. An adhvara or a yajna is a good work in which no animal is killed and no injury is inflicted on any one. This completely gives the lie to the absurd contention of certain people that animals were killed during the sacrifice. ¶ उद्+√गै शब्दे+तृन् U. II, 95. $ब्रह्मा see p. xv.

seem to be a shorter one in the Vedas, lays bare the whole inner sense of this hymn. It means that if the emperor wants his imperial sway to be a success he himself must first regard it with respect and awe and act in a manner befitting his great position. This idea is impressed upon the mind of the emperor by comparing his position, power, authority, skill at arms, and indignation with the rigour of the Sun, his dazzling brilliance, terrific heat that melts away the cloud etc. He is even commanded in one place (stanza 5) not to be in the least displeased with his subject if they revile him for the reverses he were to suffer at the hands of his foe but muster all his vigour and take full vengeance upon the latter. In this hymn every stanza contains a simile as the word Indra means both the sun and the emperor.

Griffith's translation of this very important hymn is totally unintelligible. He proceeds:—

Griffith's 'tanslation' of the 'Svaraajya hymn,'

1. Thus in the Soma, in wild joy the Brahman hath exalted thee; Thou mightiest thunderarmed hast driven by force the dragon from the earth, lauding thine own imperial sway.

Remarks:—This seems to be an imaginary description of 'Indra' a 'god' of the European Sanskritists intoxicated with pegs of soma liquor. How can a tipsy man fight ? How can he 'laud his own imperial sway' if he drinks so hard as to be in 'wild joy.'

2. The mighty flowing Soma-draught, brought by the hawk hath gladdened thee, That in thy strength, O thunderer, thou hast struck down Vritra from the floods, lauding thine own imperial sway.

Remarks:—Where is the hawk ? Can a hawk bring liquor ? Perhaps it is trained to perform such feats like pigeons to carry letters. What is the use of importing a legend into the text simply because Saaya*n*a has done it when a better interpretation and an easier, a more intelligible one too, can be given from the derivation of the compound श्येनाभृतः ?

3. Go forward, meet the foe, be bold; thy bolt of thunder is not checked. Manliness, Indra, is thy might; slay Vritra, make the waters thine, lauding thy own imperial sway.

Remarks:—Thus the 'god' is sent out to fight the foe after getting himself tipsy with liquor ! How can the poor fellow fight ? But if Indra is a good fighter is it necessary to imagine him to be a god ? can not a brave and skilful king also fight and defeat his foe ? Are the Vedas debarred from instructing a human king how to perform his kingly duties ? Is it impossible to give such instruction in poetical language as it has been done for centuries in India where thousands of treatises on philosophy, astronomy, law and medicine written in poetry still exist ? Where then is the necessity to assume an imaginary 'god' called 'Indra' to explain this hymn ?

4. Thou smotest Vritra from the earth, smotest him, Indra, from the sky. Let these life-fostering waters flow attended by the Marut host, lauding thine own imperial sway.

Remarks:—A cloud lets flow water when it is struck by the sun's terrific heat. It is a historical fact that the great Aryan king Sagara got, ages ago, a canal dug out to help agriculture in Northern India, and that that canal is now known by the name of 'Ganga' and has after thousands of years assumed the wonderful volume of one of the greatest rivers of the world. Those who doubt this fact should please examine the beautifully shaped stones in the bed of the Ganges which must have taken many thousand years to get their ugly misshapen corners and sides rounded off by constant rolling, rubbing and striking against one another. Sagara was a human king well deserving of the title of 'Indra'.

5. The wrathful Indra with his bolt of thunder rushing on the foe, smote fierce on trembling Vritra's back, and loosed the waters free to run, lauding his own imperial sway.

Remarks:—A king can do this very easily. The Sun does it in every rainy season.

6. With hundred-jointed thunder-bolt Indra hath struck him on the back, And while rejoicing in the juice, seeketh prosparity for friends, lauding his own imperial sway.

Remarks:—*Rejoicing in the juice* is very true of Christian Europe on Christmas day ! It is silly to read such abominable ideas in the Vedas,

7. Indra, unconquered might is thine, thunderer, caster of the stone: For thou with thy surpassing power smotest to death the guileful beast, lauding thine own imperial sway.

Remark:—This reads like a school-board's rough exercise.

8. Far over ninety floods thy thunder-bolts were cast

abroad. Great, Indra, is thy hero might, and strength is seated in thine arms, lauding thine own imperial sway.

Remarks:—This is a hasty and thoughtless rendering of Saayan*a*'s commentary on the verse and not of the verse itself.

9. Laud him a thousand all at once, shout twenty forth the hymn of praise. Hundreds have sung aloud to him, to Indra hath the prayer been raised, lauding his own imperial sway.

Remarks:—If thousands laud first and then only twenty shout, Indra must be in a very bad case indeed! What has happened that his party has dwindled so terribly? The later 'hundreds' singing aloud indicate a slight improvement in his position but still there is a horrible discrepency. This, surely, must be the result of his drinking liquor so hard!

10. Indra hath smitten down the power of Vritra,—might with stronger might. This was his manly exploit; he slew Vritra and let loose the floods, lauding his own imperial sway.

Remarks:—Bravo! he has won at last!! This reads like one of Jules Verne'*s* tales !!!

11. Yea, when this great pair of worlds trembled in terror at thy wrath, When, Indra, thunderer, Marut-girt, thou slewest Vritra in thy strength, lauding thine own imperial sway.

Remarks:—It is better for the toper to laud and laud his own 'imperial sway' when nobody else says a good word for it—nobody cares a straw for it. Alas for imperialism!

12. But Vritra scared not Indra with his shaking or his thunder roar. On him that iron thunder-bolt fell fiercely with its thousand points, lauding his own imperial sway.

13. When with the thunder thou didst make thy dart and Vritra meet in war, Thy might, O Indra, fain to slay the dragon, was set firm in heaven, lauding thine own imperial sway.

14. When at thy shout, O thunder-armed, each thing fixed and moving shook, E'en Twashtar trembled at thy wrath and quaked with fear because of thee, lauding thine own imperial sway.

Remarks:—The Twash*t*ar named here is, perhaps, a 'pagod' of whom Francis Xavier had written to the Society of Jesuits' head-quarters, as it is recorded in his biography by Father Faber?

15. There is not, in our knowledge, one who passeth Indra in his strength; In him the deities have stored manliness, insight, power and might, lauding his own imperial sway.

Remarks:—There you are! This 'Indra' is a fetish conceived by the servile imagination of the ancient Indian bard under the influence of strong waters!

16. Still as of old, whatever rite Atharvan, Manus sire of all, Dadhyach performed, their prayer and praise united in that Indra meet, lauding his own imperial sway.

Remarks:—Ergo–because Griffith translates the hymn thus, the ancient Indians must have been fetish worshippers. Q. E. D.

Griffith translation of the hymn reads like a dirge of imperialism. The burden 'lauding thine own imperial sway' coming after an ill-formed, unpleasantly-worded meaningless and purposeless sentence, is simply tiresome and disgusting. One having read the whole of it is apt to complain at the end that one has been cheated into reading a toper's ugly, useless, meaningless and immoral 'rigmarole' and that one's time has been wasted. This is quite true, and any European scholar does not want his readers to draw any other conclusion. Such a conclusion is damaging to the Vedas surely, and not to the silly rendering, for there are still people all over the world whose egregious foolishness makes them the slaves of—hewers of wood and drawers of water for–the wily scheming thinker.

A translation, if at all it deserves to be called by that name, must enlighten the reader about the inner sense of the original passage and not darken it still more and give rise to baseless and uufavourable conclusion about anything or anybody. To achieve so much it is essential that the translator should know the language of the original well and also clearly grasp the theme in the writing he is going to translate. That means, to translate the Vedas, one must know the Ash*t*aadhyaayee of Paa*n*ini, Patanjali's commentary on it, the Nirukta of Yaaska, etc., etc., which cannot at all be expected of a seeker after lime-light and a drawer of a fat salary by currying the favour of those placed above him. To be able to translate the Vedas, it is necessary that one should devote all one's life and all the twentyfour hours of the day to that hallowed task, severing all ones connection with all other concerns. If the study of mathematics, medicine or any other science needs so much, the study and interpretation of the Vedas will not be achieved with less. He who does this during his leisure is a criminal!

The translation of the hundred and seventy third hymn of the tenth book of the Rəgveda given in this book (pp. 315-8) contains certain words which many "scholars" especially European, will take to be a mere echo of modern European ideas. The expressions 'prime minister', 'finance minister' etc., they will say, are not Vedic. But is the English language Vedic? The. idea surely, is in the original and hence it is sought to be expressed in an un-Vedic language but not in an un-Vedic manner. Just listen to what good Sir Oliver Lodge has to say on this point:—"If we can find a way of interpreting ancient literature in a way intelligible to modern conceptions we can surely be thankful for modes of expression simpler and more poetic than our own, with the flavour of antiquity upon them, that come down to us through the mists of archaic languages,—which nevertheless to scholars are as decipherable and intelligible as are the records of the rocks." *

The hymn on the Earth.

Neither these two hymns nor the grand, voluminous, serious essay of sixty three stanzas viz., the hymn on the Earth (Atharvaveda XII, 1: see pp. 243-98) have anything to do with politics in the modern sense of the term. In the last hymn there is an exposition of 'universal patriotism'—that sort of love of the fatherland that makes a man to look to his own country as an off-spring of the greater—the Earth herself, and thus link up his destiny with those of others—all children of the same Mother Earth. Thus both the Mother-country and the Earth are simultaneously treated of and held up to man's regard. The purpose of the hymn is scientific, spiritual and moral, for there are in it verses which impress upon the reader's heart the necessity of loving and revering his Mother-country, as well as the Earth, the Mother of all humanity. For this purpose, says the hymn, man must be truthful, honest, industrious, self-controlled, engaged in the pursuit of ever fresh knowledge and accustomed to the observance of solemn vows to improve his moral and spiritual life. This is laid down in the very first stanza. The Mother-country (bhoomi) and the Earth (prəthivee) are both described in more than one stanza, as the rendezvous of men and other living beings, the source of food and various types of wealth, of

* "The Making of Man" by Sir Oliver Lodge, p. 93. ll. 3-12.

great oceans, seas and rivers. They possess high mountains looking like and reaching to, the clouds. Their expanse is interspersed with huge forests, cultivable soil, and gardens, and their bosom is the store of precious metals and stones. On such land (the Motherland as well as the Earth) the wise in all ages have lived and by their industry enjoyed the just pleasures of life. The source of wealth and happiness, and the home of oneself and one's near and dear ones, the Motherland and the Earth,—land as such, is to be jealously and intelligently protected by one.

The hymn advises all to devote themselves to the pursuit of knowledge, observation of nature, exploration of unknown lands and experimenting with natural products that their Mother-country and the Earth as a whole can afford them. Again and again it is stated that the Earth deserves to be protected with the greatest care and that only the intelligent and industrious can derive happiness from her.

The Earth is also the place for religious works like sacrifices and deeds of great moral virtues and bravery. She is characterised by a peculiar quality—a feature that distinguishes her from all the other elements, namley what is called 'gandha'—'smell' or fragrance,' which appears in beings endowed with earthly bodies as their various differentiating features. In men, in women, in animals, in herbs and vegetables, in short, in all objects and phenomena that are somehow or other connected with the Earth, her special feature does in some way find an expression. In this respect she is the mother of all and hence must be revered and guarded.

The fifth stanza reminds man of his ancestors as having lived on this hallowed Earth, following their various callings in life and doing deeds of valour! She thus brings the past, present and future together in man's life. The eighth stanza is a wonderful scientific statement full of worldly wisdom as well as the most consummate religious piety! One is inclined to read it over and over again and be reciting it night and day, for, the poetry of the stanza is such that it cannot but appeal even to the most cynical mind. In this wonderful verse the Earth, the Mother of all finite composite beings is described as being engrossed in a perpetual adoration of her Lord and Master, Almighty God! The ring of the very wording of this noble verse is so charming, so grand, so incomprehensible and unfathomable that one may read and read it over and over again and try to grasp all that is compressed within the limited scope of its twenty six short words but then after hard exercise will have to admit that one has been able to carry only a drop from this ocean of varied knowledge. The stanza is typical of Vedic teaching---imparting almost all possible instruction within the fewest possible words and in a manner undetected and unsuspected so that no worry and fatigue may be engendered in the mind of the learner.

There are other stanzas also that teach scientific truths, or impart useful knowledge. The ninth and tenth verses mention the division of time into day and night by the influence of the Sun; the eighteenth verse refers to Earth's astounding motion and tremor; the nineteenth, twentieth and twenty first stanzas state that the Earth is held together by heat energy (or electricity) and that she imparts heat to all, she herself receiving it from the Sun. Hence the intelligent and well-inclined are advised to perform the *havana* to diffuse purifying and health-giving matter in the atmosphere for the benefit of all. In the thirty sixth and thirty seventh stanzas, the seasons and time-divisions are said to be due to Earth's double motion. The fifty second stanza also refers to this point. In the forty second stanza rice and barley are mentioned as food grains. In the ninth verse milk also finds a mention. Molten butter is mentioned in the twenty ninth verse. Herbs and vegetables are mentioned in the second stanza. But nowhere, even once, in the sixty three stanzas do we find the mention of flesh as an article of food. There is no mention of hunting though the lion, tiger and other beasts of prey find a mention in the forty ninth stanza. In the fifty first stanza birds are mentioned but it is not said that certain birds are edible and certain others not so. If flesh-eating was in vogue among the Aryans (granting, just for argument's sake that this hymn was written by a poet who existed a couple of centuries before the Christian era) there should have been a mention of it in this hymn.

In the fourteenth stanza the Earth is said to subdue all foes, i e., all who are inimically inclined towards her 'direct' children. The stanza is the key-note to the teaching on love for one's fatherland the hymn has to give. It is the motherland that is meant here and not the Earth itself since in the fortyfifth verse this latter is described as the common abode of all; in the forty eighth she is represented to be the shelter of all whether good or bad; in the next she is extolled as affording protection from all, even wild beasts, and in the fifty-seventh to dispel the wicked. By suppression of the wicked is meant a complete change of their heart and not their annihilation by killing.

This hymn is a very good specimen of Vedic poetry. Even Prof. Winternitz (not a great friend of the Vedas, to be sure,) has, charily of course, to say something favourable about this hymn. His words, however, are to be taken with caution since the translation he gives as well as his own remarks totally fail accurately to delineate the instruction imparted in the hymn. His words are :—

Winternitz's 'chary' praise of the hymn on the Earth.

"Immeasurably higher than this verse-making, which is neither philosophy nor poetry, stands *one* hymn of the Atharva-veda, which, on account of a few verses which relate to the origin of the earth, is usually included among the cosmogonic hymns, but which is free from any and every kind of mysticism and really contains very little philosophy, but so much the more true poetry. It is the magnificent hymn to the Earth, Ath, XII, 1. In sixty three verses the Mother Earth is here extolled as the supporter and preserver of everything earthly, and entreated for happiness and blessing and protection from all evil. Just a few verses in R. T. H. Griffith's translation must suffice to give an idea of one of the most beautiful productions of the poetry of Ancient India.

'Truth, high and potent law, the consecrating rite.
Fervour, Brahma, and Sacrifice uphold the Earth.
May she, the Queen of all that is and is to be, may,
Prithivi make ample space and room for us [1].

She who at first was water in the ocean, whom with their wonderous powers the sages followed.

May she whose heart is in the highest heaven, compassed about with truth, and everlasting,

May she, this Earth, bestow upon us lustre, and grant us power in loftiest dominion. [8]

She whom the Asvins measured out, over whom the foot of Visnu strode,

Whom Indra, Lord of Power and Might, freed from all foemen for himself,

May Earth pour out her milk for us, a mother unto me her son. [10]

O Prithivi, auspicious be thy woodlands, auspicious be thy hills and snow-clad mountains,

Unslain, unwounded, unsubdued, I have set foot upon the Earth, On Earth, brown, black, ruddy and every coloured, on the firm earth that Indra guards from danger. [11]

Produced from thee, on thee move mortal creatures: thou bearest them, both quadruped and biped.

Thine, Prithivi, are these Five human Races, for whom, though mortal, Surya as he rises, spreads with his rays the light that is immortal. [15]

On earth they offer sacrifice and dressed oblation to the gods; men, mortals, live upon the earth by food in their accustomed way.

May that Earth grant us breath and vital power, Prithivi give me life of long duration? [22]

Let what I dig from thee, O Earth, rapidly spring and grow again, O purifier, let me not pierce through thy vitals or thy heart. [35]

May she, the Earth, whereon men sing and dance with varied shout and noise,

Whereon men meet in battle, and the war-cry and the drum resound,

May she drive off our foemen may Prithivi rid me of my foes [41]

Supporting both the foolish and the weighty she bears the death both of good and evil,

In friendly concord with the boar, Earth opens herself for the wild swine that roams the forest. [48]

O Earth, my Mother, set thou me happily in a place secure,

Of one accord with Heaven, O Sage, set me in glory and in wealth.' [63]

This hymn which might just as well be found in the Rigveda-Samhita, proves that in the Samhita of the Atharvvaveda, too, there are scattered manifold fragments of ancient poetry, although the latter Samhita, more than the Rigveda, pursues one definite purpose. In this collection, too, as in that of the Rigveda, *by the side of much thot is of little value or absolutely worthless, there are rare gems of the oldest Indian poetic art.* Only *both works together* give us a real idea of the oldest poetry of the Aryan Indians"*

*"History of Indian Literature" by Winternitz, Vol. I p. 157 l. 3—p. 158 l. 31

Hymns on human society.

The first section of the sixth chapter of the book is a very brief commentary on the hymn from the Atharvaveda on the growth of human society. It is not historical but legal and doctrinal. It does not describe a state that had once prevailed and had to be tackled with by the then leaders of human society located at a particular place in the world, but rather, irrespective of time and clime gives directions as to what to do when, for some or other reason deterioration sets in in the social organisations of mankind. At such a time, it says, the whole formation of society should be overhauled from the very beginning—from the very first unit—the family. Where family life is rotten, state, government, church and society cannot be expected to be safe. The contagion is sure to spread from the lowest unit all over the organisation, for, the whole social organisation itself is nothing but an aggregate of families. The hymn says that when society gets corrupted thus, only a man of upright life directed by Divine Providence, can bring about a reformation and none else. It is such a man that deserves to be elected the president or king of the nation and not one who has ample of money and is full of wile and cunning. Modern human society has completely neglected this principle. Human social, political or religious organisations all the world over are in this mteriliastic age, under the tutelage of Godless people.

The unity of human society, is a very necessary factor in its organisation. God's Law, the Law of Nature, the order of Divine Providence, is essentially a law of unity. In all His works unity is prominent. Inanimate objects and lower animals that have no free will and rational faculty can, instinctively observe some sort of unity—at least a shadow of it. But man, who through his mind and free will often transgresses the limits set by himself or others—even by God and Nature—does very often create disharmony,—unpleasant friction leading to the ultimate corruption of the whole society if such escapades are not checked at the very start. Hence the Holy Vedas lay down that mankind should have social organisations where common deliberations, consultations or debates should always be held in the interest of all. People should make it a point to meet together on all possible occasions to trace the defects in their organisations and to devise means for their eradication. For this end, it is said, mutual understanding and sympathy is necessary. Hole and corner methods, in camera deliberations, compartmental and confidential processes are entiraly foreign to Vedic teachings. Modern society, state or government, entirely lacks this feature. God has created all equal. He has given all one speech, and where there is difference of speech men can easily master the language concerned and become fit for common mutual deliberations. Hence there is no need of the "reserved compartment" system. Such are not the ways of the wise says verse 143 page 375. Such methods are sure to create splits and animosity. Verses 150-6 describe the qualifications of a leader of the masses whose life work (vratam) is to serve humanity. The whole book of the Atharvaveda in which this hymn occurs treats of this single topic, but only a few representative verses have been selected to explain the matter. The steps which "the avowed leader" of mankind (vraatya) adopts to achieve his end of doing good to humanity are mentioned in these hymns.

One characteristic point about the teaching of the Vedas on the organisation of society is the great stress laid upon hearty co-operation between the leader and the led—the ruler and the ruled. This important idea is foremost in all the themes treated of in the sacred Text. Unity is possible only if there is co-operation, and this latter is the result of fellow-feeling, sympathy and frankness in dealing.

The Brəhaddevataa on the subject matter of the Vedas.

Any account of the subiect matter of the Vedas cannot be complete in form without direct reference to the remarks thereon of the sage *S*aunaka in the Brəhaddevataa. The extant text of the book, it must be noted, is not* *S*aunaka's work but rather a separate treatise based upon his borrowing and assimilating much† from the original as well as recasting something from it and adding a good deal from other and even later sources not yet traced. In other words, the hallowed ancient

---

* Vide i, 27 सर्वाण्येतानि नामानि कर्मतस्त्वाह शौनकः; ii, 136, नदीवद्देवतावच्च तत्राचार्यस्तु शौनकः; iv, 18, अग्निं मेनेऽदितिं त्वेव कुत्से चेह च शौनकः; v, 37, उदित्यृचि तृतीयायां सविता शौनकोऽब्रवीत्; etc. These statements imply that somebody other than *S*aunaka is the author of this treatise. It may also mean that *S*aunaka himself gives here his own opinion expressed in some other work of his.

† The tale in vi, 86-89; (about catching fish) iv, 126-7 (cooking dog's entrails) etc., if Macdonell's translation of the verses is to be taken seriously are surely of very late concoction and interpolated into the already corrupt text of the Brəhaddevataa to give abominable customs a colour of magic and reality. "My conclusion, therefore, is that the writer was not *S*aunaka himself, but a teacher of his school, who was not separated from him by any great length of time." (From Macdonell's Brəhaddevataa Vol. I, introduction p. xxiv).

Br^{ə}haddevataa on the R^{ə}gveda (by *S*aunaka) is lost to us, as well as similar treatises on the other Vedas.*

The following observations from the extant Br^{ə}haddevataa will throw ample light on the real significance of the general term 'devataa' as well as such special names of *beings* as come under that category:—

मन्त्रदृग्भ्यो नमस्कृत्य समाम्नायानुपूर्वशः ।
सूक्तर्गर्धर्चपादानामृक्षु वक्ष्यामि दैवतम् ॥बृ० दे० १।१॥

Offering my obeisance (namaskr^{ə}tya†) to the seers of Vedic texts (mantradr^{ə}gbhyah‡), I am going to offer (vakshyaami) in proper order (aanupoorva*s*ah) the traditional (samaamnaaya) account of the subject matter (daivatam) of the hymn, the stanza, the hemistich and the 'foot'.§

---

* It must be noted that the Br^{ə}haddevataa deals only with the R^{ə}gveda and that the Yaajusha and Atharva Sarvaanukramanis and the Daivata Braahma*n*a are not similar works.

† Mecdonell gives 'namaskr^{ə}tvaa' which, if true, is an ancient usage cotresponding to vandanam kr^{ə}tvaa, and is not a mistake. If not, 'namaskr^{ə}tya' as giving in other texts should be adopted.

‡ Mantradr^{ə}gbhyah—√matri guptabhaasha*n*e or √mana j*n*aane, √manu avabodhane yield the form 'mantra'. The Nirukta vii, 12 has मन्त्रा मननात्. The word 'devataa' is just the same as deva. This latter is thus derived:—√दिवु क्रीडाविजिगीषाव्यवहारद्युतिस्तुतिमदमोदस्वप्नकांतिगतिषु + अच् P. iii, 1, 134. Yaaska (Nir. vii, 15) says देवो दानाद्वा दीपनाद्वा द्योतनाद्वा द्युस्थानो भवतीति वा । यो देवः सा देवता ॥ The whole of the दैवतकाण्ड of his work—chapters 7-12 treats of this topic. Vide also S. i, 3, 4 12 ; 5, 1, 15 : 8, 3, 8 ; iv, 3, 5, 1 ; vi, 5, 1, 2 ; vii, 5, 1, 4 ; xi, 6, 3, 10 etc.; Taand. iv, 4, 1; 11; A. i, 1 ; ii, 16; 18 ; Saankh. xi, 4 ; xii, 6; T. i, 2, 2, 5 ; 8, 7, 1 ; ii, 7, 1, 3 ; xii, 2, 4, 3 ; 3, 4, 5 ; 7, 3, 4 ; 9, 7, 5 ; etc.; etc.

Formed from whatever root, the word 'mantra' can only mean *counsel*, *knowledge*, *science* etc., but never a magical or other 'formula.' Macdonell's rendering of it as'formula' is, at best, a shallow interpretation. The use of the word mantra to mean a magical formula belongs to a very late stage in Sanakrit literature.

§ Macdonell's translation is:—"With obeisance to the seers of formulas I will, in the sequence of the traditional text, state for (all) stanzas the divinity of the hymn, the stanza, the hemistich and the verse." This is a careful dictionary rendering of the verse in which, it is not intended to lay bare the idea in the original but simply to give

वेदितव्यं दैवतं हि मन्त्रे मन्त्रे प्रयत्नतः ।
दैवतज्ञो हि मन्त्राणां तदर्थमधिगच्छति ॥ २ ॥

since (hi) one should, with full effort, understand the theme of every Vedic statement, for, it is that person who understands the themes of all Vedic texts that realises their [proper] significance (artham = what is laid down),

तद्विदां तदभिप्रायानृषीणां मन्त्रदृष्टिषु ।
विज्ञापयति विज्ञानं कर्माणि विविधानि च ॥ ३ ॥

and is able to teach others (vi*jn*aapayati) also regarding the systematic knowledge (vi*jn*aanam) and the various (vividhaani) works (karmaa*n*i) prescribed in them,—the real motives (tadabhipraayaan) in the visualising of the Vedic texts (mantradr^əshtishu) by the seers (r^əshee*n*aam) who realised them (tadvidaam). †

न हि कश्चिदविज्ञाय याथातथ्येन दैवतम् ।
लौकिकानां वैदिकानां कर्मणां फलमश्नुते ॥ ४ ॥

One (kah cit) cannot (na), surely (hi), without understanding the subject matter [of Vedic texts] rightly (yaathaatathyena), enjoy the fruit of his actions either temporal (laukikaanaam) or spiritual and deliberative (vaidikaanaam).

प्रथमो भजते त्वासां वर्गोऽग्निमिह दैवतम् ।
द्वितीयो वायुमिन्द्रं वा तृतीयः सूर्यमेव च ॥ ५॥

The first group (vargah)* of these Vedic statements

---

an English representative of each Sanskrit vocable!

† Neither Macdonell's text nor his English rendering of the verse are of any use here. For vijnaapayati he substitutes in English 'he is capable of giving an authoritative opinion' in which perhaps he rolls up also the beautiful word *vjn*aanam. *Vijn*aana deserves to be rendered by 'special' or 'perfect knowledge' and not mere 'opinion'. Viseshe*n*a jaanaati yena tat='that by means of which one knows in a special manner', can never be *opinion*, for by this latter one can have only a hazy idea and not special knowledge. Macdonell's rendering of the word is cunning aud venomous. The first three verses, if taken together, give something very intelligible. It is surprising how such a great Sanskrit scholar like Macdonell could not see this point. He goes on drawling out his rigmarole of a 'wordy representation' in English, and his 'glossarial' deputies most satisfactorily discharge their duty of darkening the sense of the original. For devataa he has 'divinity' and for karmaa*n*i 'ceremonies'. *Satis et non amplius.*

* The word vargah here means only a group and not the particular division of the stanzas of the R^əgveda—ash*t*aka, adhyaaya, anuvaaka, *varga* and r^əe. Macdonell's translation has "group of these (deities)."

(aasaam) [r^{ə}caam]† is concerned with the topic called in Vedic parlance 'agni', the second that called 'vaayu' or 'indra', and the third what is named 'soorya'.

These are the three main themes of all knowledge spiritual or temporal and the objective of all human efiort. They are called by four short names, viz.: agni, vaayu, indra and soorya. That these are not the names of the ordinary physical fire, the wind, an imaginary fetish called Indra or the sun shining in the sky, is explained in the Br^{ə}haddevataa itself. If these three (or four) are the Vedic themes how are we to understand which of these is meant in a particular Vedic text? To this the reply is given in the following:—

अर्थमिच्छन्नृषिर्दैवं यं यमाहायमस्त्विति ।
प्राधान्येन स्तुवन्भक्त्या मन्त्रस्तद्देव एव सः ॥ ६ ॥

When a seer wishing to unfold the purport (artham icchan) of a particular Vedic text) *lays down** something to be the subject thereof, extolling it with devotion (bhaktyaa-application) and giving it prominence, that should be understood to be the theme of that particular text.

If this verse refers to the instructions given at the top of every hymn, chapter or 'lesson' of the Vedas, then it follows that they were composed by *S*aunaka's predecessors, and if it is concerned with the text itself and not the 'rubrics' then every thoughtful and healthy-minded scholar of the Vedas has the authority to interpret Vedic hymns in a consistent manner, without caring for the directions. But a *via media* also is possible. It refers to both and means 'the theme or themes as mentioned in the *rubrics* as well as stated in the text.' In the case of these (two) latter interpretations a difficulty arises. Cannot the expression 'icchan' then convey the idea that these

† The word r^{ə}caam is supplied from the first stanza.

* For example in the printed text of the R^{ə}gveda on the top of the very first hymn we have the following details:—Seer-Madhucchandas: Subject—Adoration of God the Self-effulgent: Metre—Gaayatree: Tone—Sha*d*ja. This means that the "propagator" through whom this hymn has been "published" and by whom it was "interpreted in a complete and detailed manner", whose interpretation of it has in some way, come down to this day, was the sage Madhucchandas. He instructs us that the subject matter of this hymn is God the Self-effulgent. Madhucchandas' name does not find a mention in the hymn, but that of Agni does. Agni is the original r^{ə}shi(=sage, seer) through whom the Vedic Law as set forth in the R^{ə}gveda has been published. See the last Chapter,

Vedic texts are the compositions of such sages? This is a very trivial question. It is possible the Vedic hymn concerned was 'visualised' by more than one sage and the rubrics were drawn up by only one of them. It should also be noted that God, though Almighty, cannot transform a man from something into something else unless the latter wills and endeavours for it. Even then his advance will be confined within possible limits. The essence of Divine Nature consists in this that, It does not overstep spiritual, mental or moral and physical possibilities. Hence in order to appeal to the human mind and be beneficial to it, Divine Providence has to utilise human means and agencies as in this case the sages or seers, and once they are utilised all the conditions pertaining thereto must be observed. Hence the Vedic Law, though eternal, is garbed in 'human speech', revealed through human agencies, in a fashion appealing to weak human nature and 'intelligible' to its imperfect reason. Hence comes the human odour about certain vocables in Vedic statements. More light will be thrown on this point in the last chapter.

प्रत्यक्षं देवतानाम यस्मिन्मन्त्रेऽभिधीयते ।
तामेव देवतां विद्यान्मन्त्रे लक्षणसंपदा ॥११॥

When the name of a particular theme is mentioned in a Vedic text, one should, from the presence of the peculiar notes (laksha*n*asampadaa) understand that to be the subject matter of the text concerned.

तस्मात्तु देवतां नाम्ना मन्त्रे मन्त्रे प्रयोगवित् ।
बहुत्वमभिधानां च प्रयत्नेनोपलक्षयेत् ॥१२॥

Therefore, he, who is conversant with the usage should, with effort, carefully distinguish the subject matter and the plurality of its names in every Vedic text.

This verse clearly lays down that the names of Vedic themes—the so-called devataa are innumerable. The seventeenth verse divides these names into three groups according as they concern the whole hymn, or only a particular text, or are merely mentioned incidentally.* The twentysecond stanza says that one should find out from the name the theme of the hymn from the beginning and end of it where *the sage describing it*† does find an occasion to say something about it. Stanzas 23-33‡ state in clear, simple and unmistakable language—without an if or a but—that no fetish but real

* B. D. i, 17. † B. D. i, 22; R. V. i, 35; 133 etc. ‡ B. D. i, 23-33.

'concrete' beings existing and 'acting' are called in the Vedas devataa and none else: *agere* (—to act) is said to be the *sine qua non* of *esse* (—to be) and the various opinions of different scholars are mentioned thereon.

Many stanzas in this work, marvelous though corrupt, are decisive on the method of interpreting the word 'devataa' and the various beings classified under that head. The Almighty Sun is the source of all Being. He is the 'origin' of gross and subtle matter, the Lord of creatures and the Supreme Being. He pervades this whole universe disposing Himself (=His Providence) in a tripartite manner (=past, present and future; material, mental and spiritual, etc.), engrossing somehow all *beneficent objects* (devaan) in His rays (=tentacles). Fire—even the earthly fire—is one of the threefold aspects of Divine Providence, purifying and sustaining everything, present everywhere. The names of the 'beings called devtaa' are, therefore, very comprehensive and hence their application should be carefully observed, for even incorporate objects are called 'devataa'. Then, in the second chapter follow etymologies of a number of 'devataa-names' both masculine and feminine, identical with the derivations given in the Braahmanas and the Nirukta of Yaaska. The verses referred to here have not been quoted and translated because the only two available editions of the Brᵊhaddevataa are *not at all reliable.* One is rough and in the 'construction' of the text of the other from the many available manuscripts, the editor, Sir A. A. Meacdonell, seems to have given too free a play to his own bias. Had it not been so the book should have been quite different from what it is now. These European scholars, in spite of their inability to understand Vedic literature aright, have the boldness to pose as the 'gurus' of Indians and if the latter take them seriously it is their own fault aud not that of the European Scholars. *Caveat emptor* (=let the purchaser beware).

---

* B. D. i, 61-94 ; ii, 24-85 ; A. i, 7 ; ii, 37 ; iii, 48 ; iv, 10 etc., Saankh. v, 2 ; vii, 6 ; xvi, 3 ; etc.; S. ii, 2, 1, 6 ; 3, 22 ; 3, 4, 12 ; 9, 6 ; 5, 1, 5 ; iii, 4, 2, 15 ; iv, 5, 9, 6 etc.; Taand. vii, 3, 7 ; 4, 1 etc.; Nir. i, 7, 12 ; ii, 5 ; 27; 28 ; iii, 9 ; 11 ; 19; 21 ; iv 19 ; 22 ; vii, 14 ; 19-23 ; viii, 1; 2 ; 4 ; 6 ; x, 1-40 ; xii, 14-29 etc. etc.

CHAPTER III.

VEDIC INTERPRETATION.

R. V. X, 71 treats of Vedic interpretation

With regard to Vedic interpretation it is necessary to see what the Vedas themselves have to say on the point. The seventy first hymn of the tenth book of the R^ə^gveda is very important in this connection as it lays down the principles of Vedic exigesis. The Seer of this hymn is Br^ə^haspati and the subject *jn*aana or Sa*m*j*n*aana, i. e., right understanding of the Vedic Law. Incidentally the word Br^ə^haspati is the name of the historical personage who propagated the principles laid down in this verse but principally it means God or the scholar who exerts himself for the propagation and peservation of the Vedic Law. The eleven stanzas of the hymn with an English translation are given below:—

बृहस्पते प्रथमं वाचो अग्रं यत्प्रैरत नामधेयं दधानाः । यदेषां श्रेष्ठं यदरिप्रमासीत्प्रेणा तदेषां निहितं गुहाविः ॥१॥

If expanded this statement would stand in Sanskrit thus:—

हे बृहस्पते यत् (=यदा) स भगवान् श्रुतिनियामकः बृहस्पतिः ऋषिषु निखिलपदार्थानां तत्तद्धर्मानुसारेण नामधेयं दधानाः वेदरूपिण्यः वाचः प्रथमं (सृष्ट्यारम्भे) प्रैरत तदेव मनुष्येषु परस्परव्यवहारधर्माचरणादिविधायकं (वाचः) अग्रं (=सूत्रपातः) अभवत् । तत् श्रेष्ठं अरिप्रम् वेदविज्ञानम् यत् एषां ऋषीणां गुहा (=हृदयगुफायां=अन्तरात्मनि) निहितं आसीत् तत् एव अखिलजगदुपकारार्थं तस्य सत्यस्वरूपपरमात्मनः प्रेणा (=प्रेरणया) तेषां ऋषीणां हृदयगुफाया आविः (प्रकाशितम्) अभूत् ॥

Oh propagator and protector of the Vedic Speech, when Almighty God the Master and Controller of the Vedic Law (at the beginning of the creation) infused into the hearts of the worthy sages the Vedic Speech that assigns to all things names according to their true and essential features, that Divine act itself became, so to say, the initiative to all the mutual dealings and right conduct of human beings. That excellent and pure revealed knowledge itself, deposited in the innermost recesses of the hearts of the seers, was, for the benefit of the whole world, revealed, by the impulse of that Truthful God.*

सक्तुमिव तितउना पुनन्तो यत्र धीरा मनसा वाचमक्रत । अत्रा सखायः सख्यानि जानते भद्रैषां लक्ष्मीर्निहिताधि वाचि ॥२॥

Great good fortune favours the speech of those wise men who, like sifting flour with a sieve, properly sift their words in interpreting the Revealed Word, rightly realising and valuing the opinions of their colleagues with whom they take counsel in the matter.†

यज्ञेन वाचः पदवीयमायन्तामन्वविन्दन्नृषिषु प्रविष्टाम् । तामाभृत्या व्यदधुः पुरुत्रा तां सप्त रेभा अभि संनवन्ते ॥३॥

The intelligent by associating with the wise have access to the path of the Eternal Vedic Speech, and attain her who inheres to the conclave of sages, wherefrom they carry her, so to say, all over the world. That Speech (it should be borne in mind) is resorted to by all the seven poetical metres as birds resort to a tree.‡

उत त्वः पश्यन्न ददर्श वाचमुत त्वः शृण्वन्न शृणोत्येनाम् । उतो त्वस्मै तन्वं विसस्रे जायेव पत्य उशती सुवासाः ॥४॥

One, seeing her [—the Written Word] (with one's eyes) does not behold [—understand] her true nature. Another, hearing about her from others does not listen to [—rightly understand] her. A third there is whose mind is well disposed and who is sincere in his quest. To such the Eternal Speech reveals herself fully just like an ardent wife dressed and decked in her best, submits herself to her husband.§

उत त्वं सख्ये स्थिरपीतमाहुर्नैनं हिन्वन्त्यपि वाजिनेषु । अधेन्वा चरति माययैष वाचं शुश्रुवां अफलामपुष्पाम् ॥५॥

Expanded in prose and with the necessary links supplied this stanza stands as follows:—

एष अन्यः एतद्विपरीतः यः वेदवाणीं दृष्ट्वापि न पश्यति श्रुत्वापि न गृह्णाति अर्थहीनत्वात् प्रतिकूलार्थत्वात् वा धर्मरूपसाधनाभावात् अपुष्पाम् ततः च अर्थ काममोक्षानुत्पादकत्वात् अफलाम् वाचं शुश्रुवान् अधेन्वा मायया चरति एनं

---

* AA. i, 3,3,4; Aa. S iv, 11,6; S. S. ix, 26,3; Rvidh. iii, 14,1; V. H. Dh. viii, 24.; †Nir. iv, 9; M. B. i, 1,1. ‡ Aa. S iii, 8, 1. §Nir, i, 19; M. B. !, 1, 1.

(=एतादृशम् पुरुषम्) उपरिनिर्दिष्टाः विदितवेदार्थाः सज्जनाः विद्वांसम् न आहुः अपितु मूर्खमेव आहुः । किन्तु ते एतादृशम् अपि जनं सख्ये स्थिरपीतम् कृत्वा वाजिनेषु हिन्वन्ति ॥

This other person who having seen the (Written) Word fails to understand it, or having heard it taught does not grasp its significance, goes through life, growing in the soil of his heart the tree of the Eternal Speech, which because it is either not at all understood or entirely misunderstood, bears no flowers in the shape of a right conduct of life and no fruit in the form of the possession of useful means, fulfilment of all one's just desires and attainment of final beatitude. Such a one, the wise whose hearts are 'enlightened' with the right teaching of the Vedas know to be, and call, ignorant; but yet they befriend him, nourish him with the milk of right guidance till he is firm in the Truth (sthirapeetam), and thus advance him in all great and good undertakings (vaajineshu).*

यस्तित्याज सचिविदं सखायं न तस्य वाच्यपि भागो अस्ति । यदीं शृणोत्यलकं शृणोति नहि प्रवेद सुकृतस्य पन्थाम् ॥६॥

On the contrary he who abandons the Eternal Truth his well wisher and benevolent counsellor, (सचिविदं) will derive no benefit from his learning sacred or profane (वाच्यपि भागो नास्ति), and in as much as he either does not understand the scriptures correctly or totally abstains from them, his mind will not be well disposed to understand aright and follow any good advice given him, the ultimate result being decline and ruin.†

अक्षण्वन्तः कर्णवन्तः सखायो मनोजवेष्वसमा बभूवुः । आदघ्नास उपकक्षास उ त्वे ह्रदा इव स्नात्वा उ त्वे ददृश्रे ॥७॥

Men endowed with eyes and ears are alike but they are unequal so far as the versatility of the mind is concerned; some of them can be compared to ponds the water of which reaches upto the mouth, and some look like those the water of which comes upto the armpits, whereas there are others who are like a large tank which is abundantly filled with water and is fit to bathe in.‡

---

*Nir, i, 20. †A .A iii. 2,4; T.A. i, 3,1; ii, 15,1.

‡Nir, i. 9 and xi, 13 on the word मनोजवेषु has मनसां प्रजवेषु. But Skanda Maheswara's commentary runs;—मनसा ज्ञायन्ते ये ते मनोजवाः and on the letter they say:—मनसो जवेषु—जवतो मनस ऊहापोहाभ्यां ये सम्यगूह्यन्ते न चाचार्योपदेशमात्रेण तेषु परिच्छिन्नेषु शब्देन मनसा वावगन्तव्ये तस्य मानार्थस्त्वान् मनसावच्छिद्येत्यर्थः ।

हृदा तष्टेषु मनसो जवेषु यद्ब्राह्मणा सं यजन्ते सखायः। अत्राह त्वं विजहुर्वेद्याभिरोहब्रह्माणो वि चरन्त्यु त्वे ॥८॥

When the enlightened followers of Vedic teachings join together to deliberate over and decide as to the right significance of some part of the Divine Scriptures, they surely sometimes exclude from their discussions some one who is incapable of understanding the matter rightly on account of his mental proclivities yet undecided; while such of them as depend upon right reasoning as their only guide derive full benefit from the subjects treated of in the Vedas.*

इमे ये नार्वाङ्न परश्चरन्ति न ब्राह्मणासो न सुतेकरासः। त एते वाचमभिपद्य पापया सिरीस्तन्त्रं तन्वते अप्रजज्ञयः ॥९॥

Expanded and rearranged the above stanza would be:—

इमे न सुतेकरासः ये न अर्वाक् चरन्ति। इमे न ब्राह्मणासः ये न परः चरन्ति। ते एते उभयविधाः अपि पापया मत्या वाचं अभिपद्य अप्रजज्ञयः भवन्ति इह वा अन्यस्मिन् जन्मनि वा सिरीः तन्त्रम् तत्वते (=कृष्यादिदुष्करकार्याणि कर्तुम् बाधिताः सन्तः पशुवत् पारतन्त्र्ये जीवन्ति म्रियन्ते च) ॥

These are not true workers of righteousness who do not accomplish their worldly transactions in a satisfactory manner (though they may study the Divine Word). Neither are these (others) the genuine knowers of the Eternal Speech who in their daily life do not rise above the world. These two types of people receive the Divine Word but owing to their sinful iuclinations their mental faculties are rendered blunt (and incapable of grasping it aright) the result being, that (either in this life or the next) they are compelled (by the inexorable Law of Destiny) to sweat for others tilling the soil or doing such other hard work (and to live and die like beasts in slavery).†

सर्वे नन्दन्ति यशसागतेन सभासाहेन सख्या सखायः। किल्बिषस्पृत् पितुषणिर्ह्येषामरं हितो भवति वाजिनाय ॥१०॥

All brethren rejoice with the friend who omes laden with laurels in token of his victory at the assembly, for such a one wipes out stains of sin on his society, helps his friends with wealth and is a great help to them in all their worldly affairs.‡

ऋचां त्वः पोषमास्ते पुपुष्वान्गायत्रं त्वा गायति शक्करीषु। ब्रह्मा त्वो वदति जातविद्यां यज्ञस्य मात्रां विमिमीत उ त्वः ॥११॥

* Nir. xiii, 13, † B. Dh. ii, 6,11,32. ‡ A. B, i, 13,7; Aa. S. iv, 4,4.

(The four sacrificial priests are intended to keep alive the study of the Vedas and to propagate Vedic teachings). The first, the Hotrᵊ by his study of the Rᵊgveda, prompting the sacrificer and helping him to perform the sacrifice by the recitation of verses from the Rᵊgveda, sustains, so to say, that Veda (पोषम् आस्ते) The Udgaatrᵊ on his part, helps in the sacrifice by singing the *S*akvaree hymns from the Saamaveda, and the Adhvaryu attends to the manual part of the ceremonial (यज्ञस्य मात्रां विमिमीते) as laid down in the Yajurveda, while the fourth, the Brahmaa who has studied all the four Vedas, supervises the whole and helps in its consummation by giving directions and rectifying mistakes committed at the sacrifice.

The Vedic language and the later Sanskrit were both spoken languages.

The very first stanza of this hymn says that the Vedic language* is a spoken language. The following stanzas clearly support this view. In the 4th verse there is even a mention of writing. The most important point raised in this great hymn is that the Vedic statements cannot be correctly understood by all and that co-operation of learned men and

* The Sanskrit language is nameless. The word Sa*m*skrᵊta itself as applied to the language does not seem to be much older than the Christian era. It must have come into use long after Paa*n*ini's grammar came to assume authority all over India and many corrupt froms of the language and provincial dialects made it necessary to distinguish between the original idiom and its offshoots. The word Sa*m*skrᵊta itself occurs in all the four Vedas¶ in the sense of refined or purified and it is in this very sense that it is applied to the language in question to distinguish it from its corrupt offshoots. The etymology of the word should not be understood to imply the idea of purification subsequent to corruption but rather to indicate the setting apart of the incorrupt from the corrupt. If the word samskrᵊta were to be construed to signify artificiality, the word French also would mean something imaginary, since french=frank=noble i. e., something contrived out of what was ignoble. The name of a language, a people or a country is invariably a word bearing a very pleasant and beautiful connotation for, in as much as it is assigued by the people concerned, it cannot but have a good and beautiful import,—the expression of their heart's love and yearning. The words 'protestant' 'non-conformist', etc., are living examples of the principle. What they signify are 'things' which already existed, the names subsequently given serving only to distinguish them from others and thus prevent confusion in human intercourse.

¶ R. V. viii, 33,9 "sthiro ra*n*aaya samskrᵊtah"; vi, 28,4 "na sa*m*skrᵊtatram upayanti;" and v, 76, 2 "na sa*m*skrᵊtam pra mimeeto". Y. iv, 34 "tanno samskrᵊtam;" and vii, 14 "saa prathamaa sa*m*skrᵊtih;" S.V . ii, 8 15, 3 "sthiro ra*n*aaya samskrᵊtah" and A. V. xx, 53,3 "sthiro ra*n*aaya sa*m*skrᵊtah;" 57,13 ditto; xi, 1, 35 "tatra nau sa*m*skrᵊtam" and iv, 21,4 "na sa*m*skrᵊtatram upayanti." In all these instance the root krᵊ with the prefix sam connotes the idea of purification, refinement etc.

guidance of virtuous and experienced Vedic scholars is at all times necessary to decide upon their meaning. It also lays down that those, whose actions and utterances are such as to arouse suspicions about their sincerity, should not be admitted into a conclave meeting for this purpose but all the same, they must not be forced to become heretics openly. They must be tolerated, treated kindly and endeavours always made to bring them round. These beautiful ideas are involved in the difficult words of stt. 7-10. Stanzas 5 and 6 call the Vedas 'friends of humanity' to disregard or abandon whom, would result in untold harm to those who might take such a foolish step. Modern India is a living example of the consequences of the viola tion of this principle.

Though European* scholars doubt, in spite of the hymn cited and explained above, that Sanskrit was ever a spoken and written language, yet we have, in the ancient records proof incontrovertible that Sanskrit was both a spoken and written language. As will appear from the extract given below from the Mahaabhaashya, its author Patanjali, who, as Western scholars would have it, lived some three hundred years before the Christian era, is decisive on the point:—

---

*"... ... ... The relation in which Sanskrit stands to the Prakrits and the modern vernaculars is not identical with the relation in which the dead languages of Europe stand to the *living* languages descended from them. The so-called dead languages of Europe were at one time living tongues, spoken nearly as they were written, as, e. g., the speeches of Demosthenes and Cicero testify. When we call these languages dead, we merely mean to describe them as the speech of the dead past, not that of the living present. Sanskrit cannot properly be called a dead language in this sense. *Probably it was never the actual, every-day speech, of any portion of the Aryans of India at any period of their history, however remote. Its name Samskrta, the elaborated or developed speech, illustrates its origin.* It was the language not of any race or district, but of a class—the class of bards and priests, the literary men of the first ages; or rather it was the language of literature; and as literary culture made progress, the language of literature became ever more copious, euphonious and refined. *If life means growth, and if growth means change, Sanskrit must be regarded as having for a long period been, not a dead but a living tongue*; though it must be admitted that it changed slowly, like everythhing else in India —more slowly, doubtless, than the colloquial dialects. *The Sanskrit of the Puranas differed from the Sanskrit of the Vedas; and in the Vedas themselves the style of the later hymns differed from that of the earlier. The earliest Sanskrit extant is evidently the result of a process of refinement, originating in the literary activity of a still earlier period, of which*

Caldwell on the Sanskrit Language.

पृषोदरादीनि यथोपदिष्टम् ॥ P. vi, 3, 109, i.e., words 'belonging to the group (of words) beginning with पृषोदर (=an antelope) are irregularly formed and should be considered as valid as formations which can be fully explained and justified according to the rules of Sanskrit grammar.

The word उपदिष्टम् used in the above aphorism and the inability confessed in it to explain the formation of the words concerned, is a clear expression (not merely an implication) of the fact that the grammarian Paa*n*ini had to accept them as they were found in the popular idiom. It is absurd to say that a language contrived by the "intelligentsia" of the time for their own use should have such irregular expressions as would be beyond the power of Paa*n*ini to explain, for, in that case all words should have been quite regular and formed with the guidance of grammar. Patanjali also, the author of the Mahaabhaashya on the Ash*t*aadhyaayee, who, according to European scholars flourished about the second century before the Christian era, strongly supports the view that Sanskrit was a spoken language at his own time. He says:—पृषोदरादीनीत्युच्यते. Words of the group beginning with prəshodara are mentioned in this aphorism. कानि पृषोदरादीनि. Now which are these words of the prəshodaraadi group? पृषोदरप्रका-

Patanjali's evidence.

---

no records survive. A composition is not necessarily ancient because written in Sanskrit; for all through the ages, down to very recent times, all the *literati* of Northern and Western India, with the exception of the Buddhists, together with a considerable proportion of the *literati* of the South, have been accustomed to regard Sanskrit as the most orthodox vehicle for the expression of every variety of orthodox thought." (From "A Comparative Grammar of the Dravidian Languages" by Rev. R. Caldwell, D. D., LL. D., Second edn., Trübner and Co., London, 1875, Int, p. 81 l. 12 p. 82 l. 2.)

"Now, if we look for any similar traces in the history of Indian literature, our search is completely disappointed. There is no mention of writing-materials, whether paper, bark, or skins, at the time when the Indian Diaskeuasts collected the songs of their Rishis; nor is there any allusion to writing during the whole of the Brahmana period. This upsets the common theories about the origin of prose literature. According to Wolf, prose composition is a safe sign of a written literature. It is not so in India. The whole of the Brahmana literature, however incredible it may seem,

No mention of writing and writing materials

राणि. By the expression pr^əshodaraadi are meant all words of the type of pr^əshodara. कानि पुनः पृषोदरप्रकाराणि. But which are these words of the pr^əshodara type please? येषु लोपागमवर्णविकाराः श्रूयन्ते न चोच्यन्ते. They are those words in which changes in the form of elision and augmentation of letters do take place, but are not taught in grammar. अथ यथेति किमिदम्. Then what is meant by the word yathaa? प्रकारवचने थाल्. The word yathaa used in this aphorism is formed by appending to the word 'yád' the secondary termination 'thaal' in the sense of 'manner,' according to rule v, 3, 23 of the Ash*t*aadhyaayee. अथ किमिदमुपदिष्टानीति. Well, what does the word upadish*t*aani signify? उच्चरितानि. It means 'uttered.' कुत एतत्. Whence is this interpretation got? दिशिरुच्चारणक्रियः. The root √ dis*i* denotes the act of utterance. उच्चार्य हि वर्णानाहोपदिष्टा इमे वर्णा इति. Having uttered the letters one says 'here now, these letters have been pronounced.' कैः पुनरुपदिष्टाः. By whom have they been uttered? शिष्टैः, By people of authority. के पुनः शिष्टाः. Who are these people of authority please? वैयाकरणाः. The grammarians (those who are well-versed in grammar), of course. कुत एतत्. Whence is this interpretation? शास्त्रपूर्विका हि

---

shows not a single vestige of the art of writing. Nay, more than this, even during the Sutra period all the evidence we can get would lead us to supose that even then, thongh the art of writing began to be known, the whole literature of India was preserved by oral tradition only. (From "A History of Ancient Sanskrit Literature by Max Müller, M. A.) Max Müller's contention is unjustifiable. It is not necessary that there should be a mention of writing and writing materials in every possible book. Some mention of the art of writing is found in the Vedas and the old Dhaatupaa*th*a. See page lxxxvi above. The meaning of the root 'likh' has from very ancient times, been given as 'aksharavinyaase' the scratching of letters, and implies the process of writing with a stilus on a leaf or thick paperlike material and then filling up the scratches with pigment. All know very well that the number of Sanskrit works extant is a very small part of the total Sanskrit literature of ancient and mediaeval Indla, a great lot of them having been destroyed by the brutal invaders of the land. In a hellish atmosphere when to profess the Hindu religion was a capital crime a few zealous Braahmans succeeded in preserving only such important writings as the Vedas. It is very probable, some tmportant records may be available if India-wide excavations are carried on. But parchment, paper, cloth, palm leaves and any such perishable material gets carbonised in a few centuries and is entirely lost. Hence it is possible excavations may not yield anything satisfactory of this type, but it is quite probable something tangible can be found to satisfy our curiosity.

शिष्टिर्वैय्याकरणाश्च शास्त्रज्ञाः. Authority comes from well-grounded scientific knowledge and those who are well versed in grammar know the science (of language), to be sure. यदि तर्हि शास्त्रपूर्विका शिष्टिः शिष्टिपूर्वकं च शास्त्रं तदितरेतराश्रयं भवति. If authority must be preceded by science and science by authority then it means the twain are mutually dependent, इतरेतराश्रयाणि च न प्रकल्पयन्ते, and it is impossible (you know), to conceive of things mutually dependent. एवं तर्हि निवासत आचारतश्च. If that be so, understand that the authority spoken of here springs from residence and usage; स चाचार आर्यावर्त एव, that usage exists only in the country of Aaryaavarta. कः पुनरार्यावर्तः. Which is the country called Aaryaavarta? प्रागादर्शात्प्रत्यक्कालकवनाद्दक्षिणेन हिमवन्तमुत्तरेण पारियात्रम्. The country called Aaryaavarta is bounded on the East by the mountain chain called Aadar*s*a, on the West by the forest named Kaalakavana and lies between the Himalayas on the North and Paariyaatra on the South. एतस्मिन्नार्यनिवासे ये ब्राह्मणाः कुम्भीधान्या अलोलुपा अगृह्यमाणकारणाः किंचिदंतरेण कस्याश्चिद्विद्यायाः पारगास्तत्रभवन्तः शिष्टाः. In this country, the home of the Aaryas those honoured Braahma*nas* are considered to have authority in these matters who do not store grain for more than six days' use, are entirely untouched by the craving for lucre, who do not accept gifts on any account and who are perfectly efficient in any department or departments of learning. यदि तर्हि शिष्टाः शब्देषु प्रमाणं किमष्टाध्याय्या क्रियते. If persons of authority be guides in the use of words, then what is the use of the Ash*t*aadhyaayee? शिष्टज्ञानार्थाष्टाध्यायी. The purpose of the Ashtaadhyaayee is to help one recognise people who have authority in the usages of speech. कथं पुनरष्टाध्याय्या शिष्टाः शक्या विज्ञातुम्. How can people of authority be recognised with the help of the Ash*t*aadhyaayee? अष्टाध्यायीमधीयानोऽन्यं पश्यत्यनधीयानं येऽत्र विहिता शब्दास्तान्प्रयुञ्जानम्. A person studying the Ashtaadhyaayee sees another person who does not study it but all the same uses words enjoined in it. स पश्यति. He then thinks: नूनमस्य दैवानुग्रहः स्वभावो वा योऽयं न चाष्टाध्यायीमधीते ये चात्र विहिताः शब्दास्तांश्च प्रयुङ्क्ते. Indeed it must be that either fortune favours this man or he is naturally so constituted that without studying the Ash*t*aadhyaayee he is able to use words laid down in it. अयं नूनमन्यानपि जानाति. Surely he must be acquainted with other words as well. एवमेषा शिष्टज्ञानार्थाष्टाध्यायी thus the Ash*t*aadhyaayee is intended to help one find out persons having authority in the usages of speech.

This passage clearly proves that Sanskrit was, during Patanjali's time a spoken language. The passage एतस्मिन्नार्यनिवासे—एवमेषा शिष्टज्ञानार्थाष्टाध्यायी decisively corroborates this contention.*

The Vedic language is different from Sanskrit.

But it must not be supposed that the Vedic language and the so-called Sanskrit are one and the same. The former has many peculiarities† which distinguish it from the latter, its direct descendant. A person well versed in Sanskrit cannot understand Vedic texts without the aid of a commentary. A student of the Vedas has to face not only linguistic and grammatical difficulties, but something more and far more serious. It is possible with the aid of a good grammar and dictionary to master Greek,

* Vide also P. ii, 4, 66; iii, 1, 90; iv, 1, 17; i, 2,51-61; ii, 4, 63-70; iv, 1, 130; Nir. i, 4 (and the commentaries of Durgaacaaryaa and Skanda-Mahesvara thereon); 6; 14; ii, 2; etc.

† The letters ळ, ळ्ह and ँ are Vedic. The accent also is Vedic. Vide P. i, 2, 29-40. For Vedic euphony see P. viii, 2, 87--89; vi, 1, 94; 132, 133: viii, 3, 49; for declensional peculiarities see P. vii, i, 10; 39; for conjugational peculiarities vide P. iii, 4, 9; i, 4, 81; 82. The following words, are only a few of the innumerable peculiar terms in the Vedic vocabulary:—Atyah R. V. i, 56, 1; Nig. i, 14, a horse. Atharee, R. V. iv, 6, 8; an inviolate woman. Atharyah,—yaah,—yavah, Nig. ii, 5 fingers. Arushah, i, 14 a horse. Asuneetih (see the text). Astremaa iii. greatness. Aavayaah i, 12 water. Aataah i, 6 the cardinal points. Aasaa ii, 16 near. Aake, aare iii, 26 far. Induh i, 12 water. Eem i, 12 water. Utsah iii, 23 a well. Udhaah, oodhah i, 7 night. Oork ii, 7 food. Oormyaa i. 7 night. R^ətasya yonih i, 12 water. R^ə*n*aati i, 14 goes. Etagvah, etagvaa i, 14 a horse. Odana i, 10 a cloud. Ka*n*vah iii, 15 a wise man. Kaaluh ii, 23 a well. Kimeedin iv, 3 an inquisitive interfering sort of fellow who pokes his nose into everything. Keestasah ii, 15 the wise. Kshitayah ii, 3 men. Kshu ii, 7 food. Khaado ar*n*aah i, 13 rivers. Gagnuh, galdah, gaathaa i, 11 speech, Ghr^ə*n*ih i, 9 the day. Citraamaghaa i,8 the dawn. Tugryaa i, 12 water. Parema*n*i (see the text.) This word occurs only in S. V. i, 209 and is thus formed: √pr^{əə}+manin. U. iv, 145=par-e-man. The e is *irregularly* inserted between the root and the termination. The Saaya*n*ic commentator seems to take this word to mean 'paratve' which leaves its formation unexplained. Bharatasvaamin, however, in his commentary on the Saamaveda (which is not as yet published) says 'pr^{əə} paalanapoora*na*yorityasmaat............paremaa tasmin nimitte' in which statement after '—smaat' there seems to be an eillipsis. Perhaps the word 'manin' alone or some phrase containing it is dropped out. But Sir Monier Monier-Williams in his Sanskrit-English dictionary has this

Latin, Hebrew, Arabic or any other language, but to understand Vedic 'Sanskrit' Paa*n*ini's grammar with the Mahaabhashya, and Yaaska's Nirukta are not quite enough. A knowledge of the Braahma*n*as, the sutras on ritual etc., and the ancient philosophical and legal treatises, is also essential. But more than all this, a deep and sincere research into the real nature of Vedic vocables, is very essential, for the Vedic scholar has to deal with a language which was a living idiom thousands of years ago when the values of its words must have been quite different from what they bore at the time of A*s*oka. European scholars have entirely failed to grasp this point. Hence it is, that Mecdonell says:—

"He (Yaaska) gives the names of no fewer than seventeen predecessors, whose explanations of the Vedas are often conflicting."

European scholarship has failed fo grasp the real nature of the Vedic language.

...........The gap between the poets and the early interpreters was indeed so great that one of Yaaska's predecessors, named Kautsa, actually had the audacity to assert that.........

...the Vedic hymns and formulas were obscure, unmeaning or mutually contradictory.............He (Yaaska) largely depends on etymological considerations..... ....often gives two or more alternative or optional senses to the same word.........Saaya*n*a, independently of Yaaska, gives a variety of inconsistent explanations..........he limits his views in most cases to the single verse he has before him.........It would be......unreasonable to take him for our sole guide.........there is litte information to be derived from him...........Roth,† then, rejected the commentators as our

---

note on the word:—"pareman prob. w. r. for pareeman." Here w. r. stands for 'wrong reading'. This formula is a very handy one to explain away difficult expressions besides its affording one a 'bumptious' air to pose as a great scholar! On 'pareman' itself he writes—"pareeman (pr^{aa}?), bounty, plenty; ('ma*n*i') ind. plentifully." The question mark betrays the weakness of this writer who though endowed with a fertile imagination, does not here feel himself on firm ground.

† P. Vi*s*vabandhu S*a*astri, M. A., M. O. L. in his excellent work "A Vedic Concordance" the first volume of which is recently published by the Vi*s*ve*s*varaananda Research Institute, Lahore, points out innumerable blunders, grammatical, lexigraphical and others, in the St. Petersburgh Lexicon, Monier Williams' Dictionary, Macdonell's Vedic grammers and many other European works. Vide his footnotes on pp. 16,22,31,37,45,49,61, etc. The kind critic has overlooked many of the flaws of these 'infallible' writers! The bombastic St. Petersburgh Lexicon, a work costing Rs. 12,00/- bristles with a large number of mistakes of printing and

P, Visvabandhu's eritic. tiom of Western Scholars

chief guides in interpreting the Rigveda............*a qualified European* (*sic!*) is better able to arrive at the *true meaning* of the Rigveda than *a Brahman intetpreter* (*sic!*),......equipped as he (the former) is with all the resources of scientific scholarship.........Roth subjected the Rigveda, to a historical treatment ....utilising the help of the *Avesta*,..................by result of comparative philology, *resources unknown to the traditional* scholar............*the historical sense has succeeded in grasping the spirit of Indian antiquity, long obscured by native* misinterpretation.*

The above passage shows what a wrong attitude the European scholar has assumed towards the Vedas. To discard Yaaska is a great mistake. As for Paa*n*ini these poor people have not the ability to grasp him! The passage has the offensive smell of race-hatred for India, Indian schorship and even Indians as a people. There is no reason why such a foolish reference to the Braahman interpreter be made. After almost a century of so-called research, after having depleted India of hundreds of thousands of precious and rare manuscripts and archaeological finds, and after having mulcted the poor Indian tex-payer to the extent of several crores in the name of Sanskrit research, European scholarship today sheds crocodile tears over her find(?)—India has nothing to teach us, the sooner the Hindu is converted to Christianity† the better, the Vedas are "mad-man's raving and child's prattle!" Macdonell and his ilk pelt stones from inside their glass-houses on the cottages of their neighbours.

---

proof reading in addition to its being printed on a very ordinary sort of antique paper! To err is human, to forgive divine !!

* From "History of Sanskrit Literature" Macdonell pp. 61-64.

†Max Muller's sole object in pursuing Sanskrit studies as he himself often expressed, was to convert India to Christianity. A letter addressed to him by E. B. Pusey runs thus:—"...........Your work will form a new era in the efforts for the conversion of India and Oxford will have reason to be thankful that, by giving you a home, it will have facilitated a work of such primary and lasting importance for the conversion of India, and which by enabling us to compare that early false religion with the true illustrates the more than blessedness of what we enjoy."

In 1866 Max Müller thus wrote to his wife:—

"........I hope I shall finish that work, and I feel convinced though I shall not live to see it, yet this edition of mine and the translation of the Veda will hereafter tell to a great extent on the fate of India and on the growth of millions of souls in that country. It is the root of their religion and to show them what the root, is I feel sure, is the only way of uprooting all that has sprung from it during the last three thousand years."

He intended to convert India to Christianity

To the then Secretary of State for India, the Duke of Argyle, he writes thus in his letter of 16th December 1868:--

"...............The ancient religion of India is doomed and if Christianity does not step in, whose fault will it be?"

To Byramjee Malabari Esq., he wrote thus on 29th January 1882:—"As I told you on a former occasion, my thoughts while writing the lectures (the Hibbert) were with the people of India. I wanted to tell to those few at least whom I might hope to reach in English what the true historical value of this ancient religion is, as looked upon, not from an exclusively European or Christian, but from a historical point of view. I wished to warn against two dangers, that of undervaluing and despising the ancient national religion, as is done so often by your half-Europeanised youths and that of overvaluing it and interpreting it as it was never meant to be interpreted, of which you may see a painful instance in Dayananda Sarasvati's labour on the Veda. Accept the Veda as an ancient historical document, containing thoughts in accordance with the character of an ancient and simple-minded race of men, and you will be able to admire it, and to retain some of it, particularly the teaching of the Upanishads even in these modern days. But discover in it "*steam engines and electricity and European philosophy and morality*", and you deprive it of its true character, you destroy its real value, and you break the historical continuity that ought to bind the present with the past. Accept the past as a reality, study it, and try to understand it, and you will then have less difficulty in finding the right way towards the future.

He splashes mud on Maharshi Dayaananda

The following is from a letter to his son:—

Would you say that anyone sacred book is superior to all others in the world? It may sound prejudiced, but, taking all in all, I say the New Testament. After that, I should place the Koran, which, in its moral teachings, is hardly more than a later edition of the New Testament. Then would follow according to my opinion, the old Testament, the Southern Buddhist Tripitaka, the Taote King of Laotze, the Kings of Confucius, the Veda and the Avesta. But this is a very rough classification, and not likely to be accepted by others. There is no doubt, however, that the ethical teaching is far more prominent in the Old and New Testament than in any other sacred book. Therein lies the distinctiveness of the

His best Sacred book was the New Testament.

Bible. Other sacred books are generally collections of whatever was remembered of ancient times. For instance in the Veda, you get a description of the flood, simply as a *deluge in the Old Testament it takes the ethical meaning, it is a punishment and a reward;* there is the difference between the two; and that distinction runs through the whole of the sacred books. There is, of course, plenty of moral teaching in the other sacred books also, but the distinguishing feature of the Old Testament is that the Jews felt themselves the chosen people of God. That idea runs through the whole book. The Jewish people always referred everything that happened to them, whether happiness or misfortune, to a Divine Government; it was meant for them; there was a meaning in it; they were made to feel that God was angry or pleased."

To N. K. Majumdar, a Brahmo Samajist he wrote as follows in 1899:—

"...............You know for how many years I have watched your efforts to purify the popular religion of India and thereby to bring it nearer to the purity and perfection of other religions, particularly of Christianity......................

He tried to wheedle the Braahmo Samajists into the fold of Christianity.

Now it seems to me the first thing you have to do is to try to remove the differences that still exist among yourselves, and to settle how much of your ancient religion you are willing to give up, if not as utterly false, still as antiquated. You have given up a great deal, polytheism, idolatry, and your elaborate sacrificial worship. You have surrendered also, as far as I can judge, the claim of divine revelation which had been so carefully formulated by your ancient theologians, in support of the truth of the Vedas. These were great sacrifices...................................

Take then the New Testament and read it for yourselves, and judge for yourselves, whether the words of Christ as contained in it satisfy you or not.

I know that yourself as Rammohan Roy and Keshab Chandra Sen, have done that. I know one countryman of yours who wrote a searching criticism on the Old and New Testaments, and joined the Christian Church as established in England, as there was something in its teaching and life of Christ which he could not withstand. I know this is not an argument yet it is something to reflect on.

Christ comes to you as he comes to us in the only trustworthy records preserved of him in the Gospels. *We have not even the right to dictate our interpretation of these Gospels to you, particularly if we consider how differently we interpret them ourselves.* If you accept his teachings as there recorded, you are a Christian... ....

Tell me some of your chief difficulties that prevent you and your countrymen from openly following Christ, and when I write to you I shall do my best to explain how I and many who

The Vedic language as well as its direct descendent the later Sanskrit, both have a tendency to analyse all their words into ultimate vocables, the smallest sounds (= words) possible of making some sense and these are called 'roots' —dhaatu in Sanskrit.* In Sanskrit, this process has attained perfection, for there are in it, very few words which are underived and the roots of which cannot be traced. This process obtains in some other languages also but to a very small extent and from its haphazard nature, cannot be taken to be original. It is a mere copy of the Sanskrit method. Nay, the Sanskrit language has from time immemorial been assigning values even to the letters of its alphabet.† All these are not mere imaginary or fanci-

---

agree with me have met them, and solved them. I do not hesitate to say that some of these points we may have to learn from you more than we can teach you, and I say this honestly, and from personal experience. That too will be a lesson difficult to learn from our bishops and missionaries but in Christian humility they will have to learn it. From my point of view, India, at least the best part of it, is already converted to Christianity. You want no persuasion to become a follower of Christ. Then make up your mind to work for yourselves. Unite your flock..................... ....to hold them together, and to prevent them from straying. The bridge has been built for you by those who came before you. Step boldly forward, it will not break under you, and you will find many friends to welcome you on the other shore, and among them none more delighted then your old friend and fellow labourer, F. Max Müller." (From "Life and Letters of Frederich Max Müller.")

*The following derivations handed down from time immemorial should be noted.—√as to throw + madik U. i, 139 = asmad (I). √yusha to serve + madik = yushmad (you). √tyaj to renounce + adi U. i,132 = tyad (that). √tan to spread + adi = tad (that). √yaj to worship etc. + adi = yad (who or which). √*in* to go + adi = etad (this). √vad to speak + sa U. iii, 62 = vatsa = (a child or a calf). √ram to sport + kthan U. ii, 2 = ratha (a chariot). Baalaka = √bal to breathe, nourish + gha*u* or gha or *na* + ka. See also the etymologies given in the footnotes in the text.

†Note for example:—अ = सर्वम्, पूर्णं, व्यापकं, अव्ययं, एकं, अखंडं, अभावः, शून्यं ॥ इ = स्वस्वामिभावः (मतुप् प्रत्ययवत्), गतिः, समीपं ॥ ए = गत्यभावः, निश्चलः, पूर्णं, अव्ययं ॥ उ = उपरि, दूरम्, तत्, तथा, च इत्यादयः॥ ओ = अनन्यः, तद् एव॥ ऋ = सत्यं, गतिः, बहिः॥ लृ = (ऋकारवत्) । ञ, ण, न, ङ, म, ꣳ = नञ्, अभावः, शून्यं॥ :, ह = निश्चयः, अन्तः, अभावः, संकोचः, निषेधः॥ क = बन्धनं, बलवत्, विशालं, प्रभावशालिन्, सुखं ॥ ख = आकाशं, शून्यं, व्यावृत्तं, छिद्रः॥ ग = गमनं, सरणं स्थानत्यागः, पृथग्भवनं ॥ घ = प्रतिबन्धकः, स्थितिः, एकाग्रता॥ च = समुच्चयः, पुन;, पश्चात्, अन्यः, भिन्नं, अपूर्णं,

ful devices but the results of very serious research and invariably found to be correct* as far as Sanskrit is concerned, and absolutely no harm is done to the argument advanced if they do not hold good in the case of other languages. In the Vedic language† and Sanskrit, of course, they have full force.

These are the features of an ideal language,—the very

अंगहीनं, खण्डः ॥ छ=छाया, आच्छादनं, छत्रं, परिच्छदः, अखण्डं इत्यादयः॥ ज=जननं, जन्म, उत्पत्तिः, नूतनत्वं, गतिः॥ झ=नाशः॥ ट=मध्यमं, साधारणं, निर्बलं, संकोचः इच्छाविरुद्धं ॥ ठ=निश्चयः, प्रगल्भता, पूर्णता ॥ ड=क्रिया, प्रकृतिः, अचेतनं, जडं ॥ ढ=निश्चितं, निश्चलं, धारितं, चेतनं ॥ त=तलं, नीचैः, अत्र, आधारः, अवरं, तीरः, अन्त्यस्थानं॥ थ=स्थितिः, आधेयः, उपरि, तत्र, पारं ॥ द=गतिः, दानं, ह्रासः॥ ध=दानाभावः, धारणं, ग्रहणं ॥ प=रक्षा ॥ फ=व्यादानं उद्घाटनं ॥ ब=प्रवेशः, समावेशः, निलयनं ॥ भ=प्रकटं, प्रकाशं, बहिः, प्रकाशः॥ य=पूर्णा गतिः, यत्, भिन्नं वस्तु ॥ र=दानं, रमणं ॥ ल=ग्रहणं ॥ व=अन्यं, पूर्णं भिन्नं, अथवा, गतिः, गन्धः ॥ श=प्रकाशः ॥ ष=ज्ञानं ॥ स=सार्धं शब्दः, तत् ॥ क्ष=अज्ञानं, निर्जीवं, नाशः, मृत्युः ॥ त्र=पूर्णं दानं, सर्वदानं, सर्वं, समग्रं, निखिलं ॥ ज्ञ=अजन्म, नित्यं, कर्म, ज्ञानं ॥ ळ= वाणी ॥ (Adapted from P. Raghunandan *S*armaa's "Vaidika Sampatti" pp. 317-8). Add आ=समन्तात्, पूर्णं, व्यापकं ॥

*भग्=(भ=प्रकाशः+ग=गतिः=) गतिमान् प्रकाशः ऐश्वर्यः (growing lustre, i. e.), great power or virtue.

मृ=(म्=अभावः+ऋ=सत्यं अथवा गतिः) सत्याभावः, गत्यभावः= मृत्युः (the absence of reality or motion i. e.), death.

णश=(ण=अभावः+श्=प्रकाशः=प्रकाशाभावः=) अदर्शनम् (absence of publicity i. e.), disappearance.

अद=(अ=अभावः+द=दानं=)अदानं, ग्रहणं, भक्षण (not giving, appropriating to oneself=)eating.

Malum=mal= (m=negation+a=complete or one that is partial+l=enjoyment that state or thing in which there can be little or no joy=) something bad.

God=(g=motion+o=other+d=matter, immovable= other than movable or immovable)=Omnipresent Being.

Man=(m = negation+a=ए=perfect+n =negation)= who is neither non-existent nor a perfect rational being. (Ibid p.319).

†Macdonell also uses the appellation 'Vedic language' in contrast with Sanskrit, *Vide* "Vedic Grammar for Beginners" pp. 1, 2 etc.

pattern for, and basis or source of—all human speech.* In fact, no scholar has, till now, been able to advance any satisfactory arguments to prove that Sanskrit has sprung from some other language. The original, primary or primordial speech of mankind is Vedic Sanskrit and no rival has, till now, laid its claims to that title. The existing living and dead languages and even such as are just getting to be known through archaeological excavations here and there, do not have those features which the Vedic language possesses and which are very essential to justify the claim of being the mother of other languages.†

Language also is evloved.

European Sanskrit scholars and their Indian disciples try to demonstrate that the Vedic language cannot be the original or primitive speech of humanity. They cannot conceive and concede that anything can be original or primitive unless, at the same time, it is elementary, crude and shabby like a naughty third form boy's English essay and this again, they think, is a state evolved out of "speechlessness." Their contention is quite

*"What are called families of languages are only dialects of an earlier speech." (China's Place in Philosophy.)

"This does not, however, exclude the possibility that both (Sanskrit and Semitic) are diverging streams of the same source, and the comparisons that have been instituted between the Semitic roots reduced to their simpler forms and the roots of the Aryan languages have made it more than probable that the material elements with which they both started were originally the same." (Lectures on the Science of Language. Vol. i p. 316.)

"Delitzsch goes deeper. He claims to have identified one hundred Semitic roots with Aryan roots." (Tailor's Origin of the Aryans.)

"The aboriginal tribes in Southern and Western Australia use almost the same words for I, thou, he, we, you, etc., as the fishermen on the Madras coast and resemble in many ways the Madras hill tribes, as in the use of their national weapon, the boomerang". (Encyclopaedia Britannica, ninth edition, Vol. III p. 778)

"It has been generally asserted and indeed believed that the Telugu has its origin in the language of the Vedas." (Campbell's Telugu Grammar, Introduction p. xv)".

The above quotations have been copied from P. Raghunandan Sarmaa, op. c.

†In eight articles contributed to the "Illustrated Weekly of India" at different times between 7th July to 3rd November 1935 a writer has made this claim for the dead Sumerian (and Egyptian also?) supporting his views with all sorts of specious, unscholarly arguments. His research is, like that of his European gurus, of the shallowest type and results attained a foregone conclusion. His views will be examined later on.

in contradiction to the old scholastic principle *nemo dat qui non habet* ("none gives what one has not").* *Contraria contrariis curentur* says the allopath; *contraria contrariis evolvuntur* (all things are evolved from things of quite a contrary nature) say our evolutionists. For the law of causality they have little regard. Given a dumb man it is impossible to see our way to 'evolve' a tolerable 'speaker' out of him. We can treat him medically and cure him of the defects of his vocal organs consequently enabling him to use his tongue in producing articulate sounds. But is this evolution? If it is, then every fever patient must be said to have been evolved when he or she gets cured of that malady! We have had with us, our horses, cows, goats and dogs for many centuries, nay, millenniums past, but unfortunately, none of them have started speaking as yet!! A speaking horse, for example, should have been of greater use than merely pulling a tom-tom. He would have cooked his master's food, washed his clothes and run errands for him!!! But then no precautions would have prevented that quadruped—who can count among his ancestors the worthy Bucephalos, Pegasos and Uccaiśravas—from making love to his master's wife or daughter!!!!

Primitive Indo-Germanic concocted by European philologists.

In their anxiety to relegate Sanskrit and the Vedic language to the position of 'third clsss' dialects, the European philologists have invented the wretched primitive Indo-Germanic—a fib of their imagination—with very strange vocabulary having a highly exaggerated pronunciation. For example the Sanskrit root 'budh' there appears as 'bheudh'! That means they have been, will they nill they, constrained to proceed quite against their own pet principle of evolution from crude and simple beginnings and to postulate a dialect—for this is, after all, only a dialect—of the most confounding complexities. Imagination, you know, is a wonderful faculty. Good Sir Oliver Lodge says: "And it seems probable that the information we thus acquire as to actual occurrences within our ken may be speculatively enlarged in imagination to cover a universal system of growth and development, in regions many of them essentially beyond any knowledge that we possess at present."† Facts, and not imagination, can be of any use here.

---

*नासतो विद्यते भावो नाभावो विद्यते सतः। उभयोरपि दृष्टोऽन्तस्त्वनयोस्तत्वदर्शिभिः ॥ गी० २ । १६ ॥

†From "The Making of Man" by Sir Oliver Lodge p. 42 ll. 22-28.

It is not wise to fight shy of the facts as scholars have been doing for almost the past century.

Plain facts, if we handle them in an unsophisticated manner, reveal such features of the Vedic language as cannot but compel us to admit that that language alone can, surely be the mother* of all the human idioms known till now. Its alphabetical system is perfect, its vocabulary is based upon ascertained and recognised roots, and its syntax is free from complexities and artificiality.

How various and entirely divergent languages sprang from the Vedic.

It is not difficult and not at all impossible to explain how such divergent dialects sprang from the one original Vedic Sanskrit. Members of the same family dispersed over a vast country and developed different manners and customs, different traditions, differont laws and religions. The Bible twice develops the whole motley human race and all languages, once from a single man—Adam†—and one primitive language (not Hebrew, surely), and again after the deluge from Noah‡ and his family. There can be no difficulty, therefore, in taking Vedic Sanskrit to be the primitive human speech.

The great divergence in the known languages has sprung from the entire loss of contact between some of

---

*यह देखा जाता है कि जिस भाषा में अधिक और क्लिष्ट उच्चारण होते हैं उससे जब कोई दूसरी भाषा पृथक् होकर नवीन रूप धारण करती है तो उसके दो रूप होते हैं एक मूर्खों का दूसरा पढ़े लिखों का। पढ़े लिखे उसके समस्त उच्चारणों को स्वीकार करते हैं पर मूर्ख और असभ्य उसके क्लिष्ट उच्चारणों को छोड़ देते हैं। उनसे क्लिष्ट उच्चारण करते बनता ही नहीं। इससे उनकी भाषा में आवाजें संकुचित हो जाती हैं और थोड़ी रह जाती हैं अर्थात् मूर्खों की भाषा में ध्वनियां कम और विद्वानों की भाषा में पूरी होती हैं। इन असभ्यों अर्थात् कम उच्चारण वालों में जब विद्या—सभ्यता—उत्पन्न होती है और विद्वानों की सृष्टि होती है तो इनमें समस्त बातों की वृद्धि होती है—धन दौलत, बलबुद्धि, ज्ञानविज्ञान और राजपाट बढ़ता है परन्तु उनकी भाषा में उच्चारणों की वृद्धि नहीं होती। शब्दों की तो वृद्धि होती है, कोश बढ़ जाता है पर आवाजों की—उच्चारणों की—वृद्धि नहीं होती। योरप में ये दोनों नमूने मौजूद हैं। सभी जानते हैं कि योरप की भाषाएं आर्य भाषाओं से ली गई हैं। जिस समय ये भाषाएं ली गयी थीं उस समय भी आर्य भाषाओं में विस्तृत वर्णमाला थी—विस्तृत उच्चारण थे पर योरप वालों के पूर्वज असभ्य थे और क्लिष्ट उच्चारण नहीं कर सकते थे। इसलिए उनकी भाषा संकुचित हो गई और आवाजें कम हो गईं। ४७ आवाजों के स्थान

† Genesis, v and vi. ‡ Genesie, x and xi.

the separated branches and the main family. Such of them as went to far "countries" and failed to keep themselves in communication with the main family could not maintain their manners and customs as well as the idiom intact. Most of them had to live in the vicinities of big forests haunted by all sorts of dangerous beasts. Imminent danger of life and their inability to grow cereals and vegetables forced some of them to kill and eat the carcases of animals and such harmful vegetable products as were available in those uninviting and uncouth surroundings. The climate also must have been very unfavourable. These are the principal causes of their forgetting the true pronunciation of the words of their mother tongue, the Vedic Sanskrit, and ultimately developing an imperfect system of alphabet and idiom like the Semitic. These were the ancestors of the 'Sumerians', the ancient Egyptians the ancient Semites, the Mongolians etc.

Another branch was just able to maintain some slight contact with those branches that were in close touch with the original home. They spoke those languages that can be described as the ancestors of Greek, Latin, Gothic etc. These languages therefore, bear greater resemblance to the

---

में २८ ही आवाज़ें रह गईं । आजकल योरप वालों ने हर विषय में उन्नति की है पर उच्चारणों में उन्नति नहीं हुई। वे 'तुम' के स्थान में अब भी 'टुम' ही कहते हैं। यही हाल यहां के मूर्खों में भी देखा जाता है। मूर्ख सदैव सूक्ष्म को 'सुच्छिम' कहते हैं। उनसे क्ष का उच्चारण चला गया है। जो लोग वर्षा को 'बरखा' कहते हैं उनसे भी 'ष' का उच्चारण लुप्त हो गया है। इसी तरह 'ज्ञान' को 'ग्यान' कहने वालों से भी 'ज्ञ' का उच्चारण जाता रहा है। कहने का मतलब यह है कि मूर्खता—असभ्यता—आवाजों को कम तो कर देती है पर सभ्यता और विद्वत्ता आवाज़ों को बढ़ा नहीं सकती। इससे यह सिद्ध हुआ कि विस्तृत और क्लिष्ट उच्चारण मौलिक हैं और संकुचित तथा सरल उच्चारण अपभ्रंश हैं—परिवर्तन हैं। अर्थात् जिन भाषाओं में अधिक और क्लिष्ट आवाजें हैं वे सभ्यों की हैं, प्राचीन और मौलिक (असल) हैं पर जिन भाषाओं में कम और सरल आवाज़ें हैं वे मूर्खों की हैं नवीन हैं और अपभ्रंश हैं। इस कसौटी से देखते हैं वैदिक भाषा की वर्णमाला संसार की समस्त भाषाओं से विस्तृत, विज्ञान पूर्ण और क्लिष्ट है अतः सिद्ध है कि वही प्राचीन है, मौलिक है, ज्ञानियों की है और असल है। शेष समस्त भाषायें उसकी बिगड़ी हुई शाखा और प्रशाखा हैं॥ (From P. Raghunandan *S*armaa, Op. c. pp. 263-4.)

(M)—E.D.

Vedic. The third, like the ancestors of the Medes, the Persians etc., could be in closer touch with their original home, ard hence could preserve to a greater extent the vestiges of their traditions and language. To this class, belong also many of the dialects of India. The classical Sanskrit is the direct descendant of the Vedic and was spoken by the later generations of the original 'Aryans' themselves who succeeded in keeping their ancient traditions safe from pollution.

The following illustrations will be helpful in grasping the truth about this difficult point:—

(१) हाव्॒नीम्· आ· रतूम्· आ·
हओमो· उपाइत्· ज़॒रथुश़्त्रॅम्·
आत्रॅम्· पइरि· यओज़॒दथॅतॅम्· गाथा॒स्च· स्राव्॒यं॒तॅम्·
आ· दिम्· पृसत्· ज़॒रथुश्त्रो ჻ को· नरॅ· अही·
यिम्· अज़॒म्॒ वीस्पहॅ· अङ्ह॒उश्·
अस्त्व्॒तो· स्रएश़॒तम् दादॅरॅस·
हॅहे· गयॅ॒हे· ह्वन्व्॒तो· अॅमषहॅ ჻
(Avesta).

Sanskrit rendering of the above:—
सावनम् आ ऋतुम् आ, सोमः उपैत् जरथुश्त्रम
अत्रिम परियोर्दधन्तम् गाथाश्च श्रावयन्तम्।
आ तम् पृच्छत् जरथुश्त्रः को नर असि
यम् अहं विश्वस्य असोः अस्थन्वतः श्रेष्ठं ददर्श
स्वस्य गयस्य स्वन्वतो अमृतस्य॥
(२) सिय पिन् सिरिन् सरु
दैनिस् लकुणैन् विसितुरु।
कैलेसुन् कैरैन् दुरु
वन्दिम् मुनि उतुमन् तिलोगुरु॥
(Classical Sinhalese.)

Sanskrit:—शत पुण्या श्रित साराय।
द्वात्रिंशत् लक्षणैः विचित्राय,
क्लेशेभ्यः दूरीभूताय
वन्दे मुनिपुंगवाय त्रिलोकगुरवे॥

The first text quoted above is the first stanza of the 9th Yasna of the Haom Yasta of the Avesta. It can be approximately translated as follows:—'At the proper time of the savana, Soma came to Zarathustra who was consecrating the fire for the sacrifice and was reciting the gaathaas. Him Zarathustra asked, "Oh man who art thou whom I see resplendent with the lustre of immortality, and the best of all embodied beings?'

The second is the first verse of the famous Sinhalese classic the Guttila Kaavyaya, and can be rendered thus:—'I salute that Lord Buddha, the lord of the three worlds, the greatest of the sages, whose essence is resorted to by hundreds of merits, who is beautified with the thirty two virtues and who is beyond all suffering'.

It will be seen that in both these pieces the original Sanskrit words are transformed in such a manner as to demand great care and patience to identify in them the original expressions more difficult and complicated, surely, but yet more pleasant to pronounce and charming to hear. The Hindi, Marathi, Gujerathi, Bengali, and some other dialects of India—in their old and current forms, resemble these two.

These are languages of the second group mentioned. Instances of the 1st group are:—

(1) A Sumerian inscription:—dingir Utu I En an—ki—bi—da I lugal—a—ni—ir I Ha—am—mu-ra—bi I Gu—de—a II 5 II An—na I dingir En—lil da—I ga—ni I se—ga dingir Utu I siba ki—ag II 10 II dingir Marduk—ge I lugal lig—ga I lugal Ka—dingir—ra (ki) I lugal Ki—en—gi I (ki) Urdu II 15 II lugal (an) ub—da I tab—tab—ba—ge I lugal bara—bara I dingir—gal—gal—e—ne I su—gi II 20 II ne—in—ag—a I ud (dingir) Utu I Ki—en—gi (ki) Urdu I nam—en—bi I ag—ne II 25 II mu—na—an—sum — I ma—ta I dur—ka—bi I su—ni—ku I ne—in—si—a II 30 II dingir Utu I en si+um^2 I ti—la—ni—ir I Ararma (ki)—ma I uru nam—en—na— II 35 II ka—na I E—babbar I e-ki-ag-ga-ni I mu—na—ni—in—ru II (From "Inscriptions of Hammurabi," King, Vol. iii, pp. 130—1.)

Translation of the above:—For Samas (Utu), the lord of heaven and earth his king Hammurabi, the minister of Anu, the servant of Bel, the beloved of Samas, the shepherd who delighteth Marduk's heart, the mighty king, the king of Babylon, the king of Sumer and Akkad, the king of the four quarters of the world, the king who hath built anew the shrines

PLATE II

A part of Hammurabi's inscription about the building of the temple of Utu (Samas) in Larsa.

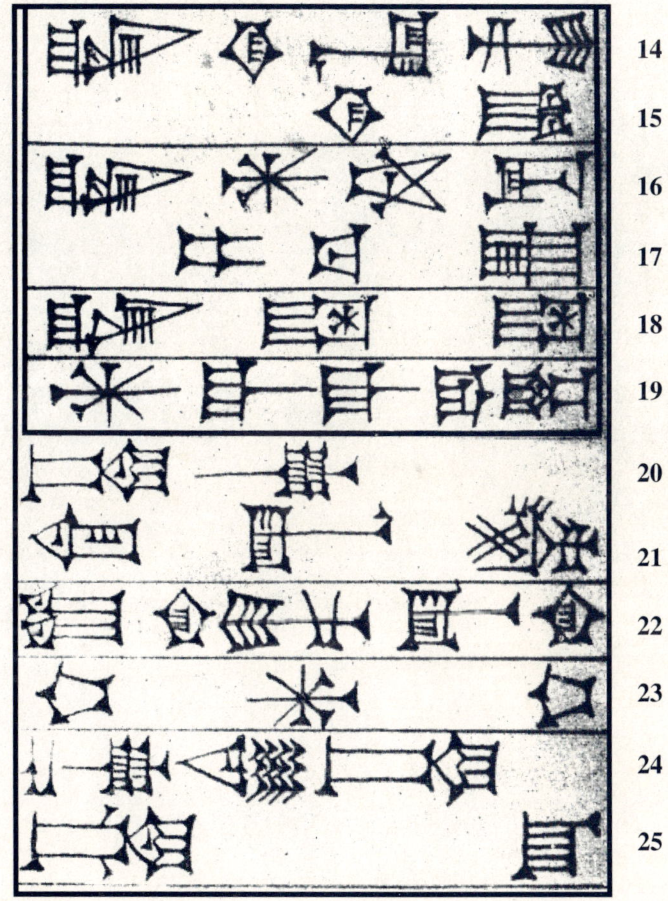

For transliteration see page cvi from lines 14-25 numbered therein, and for translation pages cvi and cvii.
(To face p. cvi.)

of the great gods,--When *S*ama*s* gave unto him Sumer and Akkad to rule, and entrusted their sceptre to his hands, then did (Hammurabi) build for *S*ama*s*, the lord who is the protector of his life, the temple E--babbar, his temple, in Larsa, the city of his rule. (L. W. king, op. cit., p. 182.)

(2) An extract from Hammurabi's Sumerian code:--

The Sumerian words are intentionally transcribed in the Naagaree script to show how beautifully it yields to the sounds:--

If (तुकुन्दि–बि) a son (दुमु) to his father (अद्–द–न–र) 'my father (अद्–द–मु) thou art not' (दु–मै–अ) says (ब–अन्–न–अन्–दुग्), he [the father] shall shave him, (दुब्बिन्–मि–नि–इन्–किद्–अ) to the brand (क़र्–र–अश्) he shall put him (मि–नि–इन्–दु–ऐ) and (उ) for silver (कु–ग–अ–श्) shall sell him (मि–नि–इन्–सि).

तुकुन्दिबि दुमु अम नर अममु नुमैऐन् बअन्न अन्दुग् किशि अनि दुब्बिन्उनै इन् किद् ऐश् उरुकि अ मिनि इब्र निगिन्ऐनै उ ऐत बर ऐनै ॥

If a son to his mother 'my mother thou art not' says, his forehead let them shave, in the city they shall lead him round, and from the house shall expel him.

तुकुन्दिबि अद्द दुमुबिर दुमुमु नुमैऐन् बअन्न अन्दुग् ऐ इन्गर्त बरऐनै ॥

If a father to his son 'my son thou art not' says, from the house and wall thereof they shall expel him.

तुकुन्दिबि अम दुमुनर दुमुमु नुमैऐन् बअन्नअन्दुग् ऐनिग् गुनत बरऐनै ॥

If a mother to her son 'my son thou art not' says, from house and furniture they shall expel her.

तुकुन्दिबि दम्ऐे दम्न हुल्बअन्दगिग्अनि दम्मु नुमैऐन् बअन्नअन्दुग् इद्दशु बअन्शिमु ॥

If a wife to her husband, who is hateful to her, 'my husband thou art not' says, into the river she shall be cast.

तुकुन्दिबि दम्ऐे दम्नर दम्मु नुमैऐन् बअन्न अन्दुग् बर्मनकुत इलल् ऐ ॥

If a husband to his wife 'my wife thou art not' says, one half a mina of silver he shall pay.

तुकुंदिबि लुसग्गऐ लुहुन्गऐदै बउग् बअन्ज़ह् उगुबिअन्दैऐ गन्लबअन्दग् उ तुरबअबअग् अबिउद्इकम् बन्शैतअम् अन्अगग ॥

If a nobleman having hired a labourer, he (the latter)

die, run away, disappear, escape, or fall sick, as his hire per day a *ban* of corn he shall measure out.' (From "Sumerian Reading Book," Budge pp. 167 ff.)

The following lists of words* will clearly show the affinity between Sanskrit and most other languages of the world for the languages selected are quite representative of all the existing (both living and dead) human idioms.

LIST No. I.

In the following list, in the first column are given certain difficult letters which are still current in Sanskrit but lost in the current corrupt 'dialects;' in the second are given illustrations of their uses in Sanskrit and in the last those of their corrupt forms in other languages.

ऋ	ऋत	orthos (Gr.)	प	गोप	gobaa (Ar.)
		right (E.)	"	कौपीन	kafan (Ar.)
घ	मेघ	meha.	भ	गृभ	giraft (P.)
च	चरक	sarak (Ar.)			biraadar (P.)
"	चन्द्रगुप्त	sandracoitos(Gr)	"	भ्रातृ	brother (E.)
"	वनचर	banajar (P.)	"	अभ्र	abra (A.)
छ	छाया	saayaa (P.)	"	भ्रू	brow (E.)
ट	विष्टर	bistar (P.)	"	भ्रष्ट	worst (E.)
थ	स्थान	staan (P.)	ष	पुष्ट	pukht (P.)
द	द्वौ	two (E.)	"	हृष्ट	sakht (P.)
"	धनी	gani (Ar.)	ह	होम	ghoma (Ch.)
"	विधवा	widow (E.)	क्ष	क्षुद्र	khurd (P.)
"	सिन्धु	hindu (P.)	"	क्षत	khat (P,)
"	बुद्ध	but (Ar.)	"	यक्ष्म	zakhm (P.)
ध	दधि	dog (Ar.)	"	उक्षन्	ox (E.)
प	अप्	aab (P.)	"	वक्ष	box (E.)
"	कोटपाल	kotwaal (P.)	ज्ञ	ज्ञा	know (E)

LIST No. II.

In this list the first column gives Sanskrit words.

N. B.—Ar. stands for Arabic, A. S. for Anglo Saxon, Cel. for Celtic, Gr. D. for Doric Greek, O. H. G. for Old High Ger-

*No further examples of passages in different languages have been found necessary to illustrate the fact of 'close connection' between the Vedic and other languages.

man, Go. for Gothic, L. for Latin, O. Pr. for Old Prussian, P. for Persian, Sum. for Sumerian, Dr. for Dravidian and E. for English.

प्रथम	frat'hema (Av.)	protos (Gr.D)	primus (L)	fruma (Go.)
द्वितीय	bitya „	deuteros „	alter „	aut'hara „
तृतीय	thritya „	tritos „	tertius „	thridyo „
ददामि	dadhaami „	didomi „	do „	
तिष्ठामि	histaami „	histemi „	sto „	stand (E.)
असि	ahi „	essi „	es „	is
सर्पिष्	helpos (Gr. D.)	sealf (A. S.)	sälyapä (Tochar?)	
आज्य	unguentum (L.)	imb (Cel.)	anch (O.H.G.)	anctan (O.Pr.)
मृत्यु	mors (L.)	mout (Ar.)		
विंशति	viginti (L.)	twenty (E.)	zwanzig (G.)	
दुहिता	thugater (Gr.)	dukhtar (P.)	daughter (E.)	Tochter (G.)
हंस	chen (Gr.)	anser (L.)	goose (E.)	gans (G)
अम्बा	ama (Sum.)	umma (Ar.)	amma (Dr)	
मातृ	maader (P.)	meter (Gr.)	mater (L.)	mother (E.)	muder (G.)
पितृ	pidar „	pater „	pater „	father „	fader „
सप्त	hafta „	heptos „	septem „	seven „	

LIST No. III.

Avestic words derived from Sanskrit.

असुर	ahura	god.	सोम	homa	the soma creeper.
सेना	henaa	an army.	हस्त	zasta	the hand.
होतृ	zotaa	the hotrə priest.	आहुति	aazuti	an oblation.
बाहु	baazu	an arm.	अहि	azi	a snake.
जानु	zaanu	the knee.	अजा	azaa	a shegoat.
जिह्वा	hizvaa	the tongue.	विश्व	vispa	the world.
अश्व	aspa	a horse.	गृभ	giraft	to sieze.
पशु	pa*s*u	an animal.	उक्षन्	ukshan	an ox.
वायु	vaayu	air.	इषु	ishu	an arrow.

रथ ratha a chariot.

LIST IV.

The second column gives Persian words.

तनु	tan	the body.	शिर	sar	the head.
हस्त	dasta	the hand.	पृष्ठ	pu*s*ta	the back.
पाद	paa	the foot.	दन्त	dandaa*m*	the teeth.

नाभि	naaf	the navel.	कृमि	kiram	a germ.
गल	gulu	the throat.	काक	zaaga	a crow.
ग्रीवा	girebaam	the neck.	कर्पूर	kafoor	camphor.
वदन	badan	the body.	अहिफेन	afyoon	opium.
भ्रू	abroo	the brow.	चन्दन	sandal	sandal.
चर्म	chiram	the skin.	श्वेत	safed	white.
मेष	mesa	a sheep.	द्वार	dar	door.
खर	khar	an ass.	बन्ध	band	bound
उष्ट्र	ustar, sutar	a camal.	तारा	sitaaraa	a star.
गौ	gaava	a cow.	शर्करा	sakar	sugar.
मूषक	moosa	a mouse.	विधवा	bewaa	widow
शृगाल	sagaal	a jackal.	नाम	naam	name.

LIST No. V.

The second column gives Egyptian words.

आदि	aat	begining.	नाश	naasesha	destruction.
अक	ak	to turn.	परि	pari	all round.
अक्ष	akh	to see.	पूर	poor	to bring out.
अन्त	antu	limit.	पुष्प	push	a flower.
अपूप	pupu	bread.	रसना	ras	the tongue.
आप	aap	water.	सेवा	sev	worship.
अर्म	rem	to cry.	श्वेत	hoot	white.
आत्मा	aatmu	of the sevanth heaven.	उषस्	usha	the dawn.
			वास	aas	a house.
दिव्	tep	the sky.	क	ka	the soul.
			नर	nraa	a man.

LIST No. VI.

The second column gives Arabic words.

हर्म्य	haram	a mansion.	गल्भ	balgh	to be proficient.
सुर	hoor	a 'god'			
नरक	naar	the hell.	आजहार	izahaar	to give out.
अन्तकाल	inteqaal	death	लोहित	lahu	blood.
कर्त	qaat	to cut.	मा	maa	negation.
कीर्तन	kirataiyan	to read, recite.	ये	ya	and, which.
			वा	wa	and, or.

षष्ठ	sittaa	six	ख	ḳhalaa	the sky.
सप्त	sabbaa	seven.	औरस	waaris	son, an heir.
सिंह	haisim	a lion.	शरद्	*s*irat	cold
मन्यु	manwu'a	indignation	भ्रम	waham	superstition
दोहन	duhan	butter.	द्यौः	yoh	the sun.
सृ (सर)	harkat	motion.	दिवम्	yom	the day.
नः	naa	we.	धनी	g̣ani	a rich man.

अर्वन् araban a horse.

LIST No VII.

The second column gives Swaahili words.

ध्यान	dhaani	thinking.	सिंह	simbaa	a lion.
कर्त	kaataa	cut.	गौ	gombe	the cow.
मृत्यु	maati	death	गोधूम	gaano	wheat.
द्यौ, ज्योति	juaa	the sun.	षष्ठ	seetaa	six.
जम्बु	zambaraoo	jumblum.	सप्त	savaa	seven.

LIST No VIII.

The second column gives Chinese words.

स्थान	taan	place.	डुकृञ्	do	duty.
श्री	*s*iram	preceptor	जनस्थान	jinataan	the earth
ज्योतिस्थान	jitan	the temple of the sun.	द्युस्थान	tientaan	the heaven
			होम	ghoma	a sacrifice.
जन	jin	a man.	द्यौ	tau	shining, the sun.
अम्बा	maa	mother.			

LIST No. IX.

The second column gives Japanese words.

का, कः (किम्)	kaa	what.	शिष्य	*s*osei	a disciple.
			कनक	kinkaa	gold.
द्यौ	de	sunrise.	अहिफेन	aahen	opium.
उक्षन्	odа*s*i	an ox.	सः	sore	that.
बहुत्व	bhotto	much.	मार्ग	maac	road,
नित्यनित्य	nichi nichi	always, ever & ever.	ध्यान	gen	thinking.
			यम	immaa	angel of death.

LIST No. X.

The 2nd, 3rd and 4th columns give Dravidian words.

Sanskrit.	Tamil.	Telugu	Canarese.	English
मनुष्य	मनिदन्	मनुजुड्ड	...	a man.
अन्य	...	अन्नि	...	another.
तालु	तलै	तला	तले	head etc.
इह	इंगे	ई	इल्ले	here.
मंजु	...	मंछि	...	nice.
अम्बुद	...	मब्बु	मौब्बु	cloud.
नीर	तएणीर्	नीळु	नीरु	whater.
पत्नी	पैरण्जादि	पैंडली	हैंडती	wife.
गौ	...	आवु	आवु	cow.
मेष	...	मे	मेके	goat, sheep.
उष्ट्र	औट्टकम्	औंटे	औंटे	a camel.
राजम्	अरसन्	राजु	अरसनु	a king.
अटवि	...	अड़वि	अड़िवे	a forest.
काक	काका	काकि	कागै	a crow.

LIST No. XI.

This is a tentative but important list of some difficult words the Sanskrit originals of which are not easily ascertainable.

1. Aannipadda (Su.) इन पाद. The word इन in Vedic Sanskrit means lord or master and is an appellation of God. See A. V, xx, 21, 2; 94, 4, Nig. ii, 22 and U. iii, 2.

2. Alexander (Gr.) √रक्ष to protect and √अन to breathe—रक्षकः अनितॄणाम्=the protector of men.

3. Amenhotep (Ancient Egyptian) ओम+√हे to invoke or√हु to sacrifica, accept, impart.

4. Amenophis, ओम्+आविस्.

5. Awan, awal or awar (Su.) √अव to protect, move, be lovely, please, satisfy, know, enter, hear, own, beg, act, desire, shine, obtain, embrace, kill, take, be, and grow.

(N)—E.D.

6. Allah (Ar.) √ अल् to adorn, be competent, able, ward off.

7. Anu (Su.) इन.

8. Apsu „ अप्+√ सू to produce.

9. Banda „ बन्धु.

10. Dingir „ दिनकर (?)

11. En lil „ इन लीला. Almighty God इन for whom the creation of the universe is a mere sport.

12. Inninni „ इन.

13. Ishtar „ √ ईश् to rule+√ तृ to protect. लक्ष्मी, the Omnipotent Providence of God.

14. Kish „ कीच or कीचक (?).

15. Lagash „ लक्ष. The home of a hundred thousand people.

16. Lugal „ लोक. The short form of ओ is उ. Vide P. i, 1, 48 एच इग्घ्रस्वादेशे.

17. Lugal Banda „ लोकबन्धु.

18. Ouranos (Gr.) वरुण. God the Just so often invoked in Vedic hymns.

19. Pharao (Anc. Eg.) √ भृ to support. भूभृत् the supporter of the Earth, a king.

20. Ra „ √ रा to give. God the bestower of all goods. The Sun which imparts vitality to all living beings and trees and plants.

21. Rameses „ रामेश or रमेश.

22. Sag (Su.) √ शक to be able.

23. Shirpur „ श्रीपुर.

24. Shippar „ शिवपार्(वती).

25. Nippur „ नृपुर.

26. Susa „ शूष Power.

27. Tiamat „ तैमात A. V. v, 13, 6; 18, 4. √ तिम to water, damp+√ अत to move. This seems to be the same as वृत्र or अहि meaning the cloud, depicted as a serpent.

28. Tammuz „ तमस्.

29. Tello „ तरु (?)

30. Tutuli „ √ तृ to protect or त्वर् to haste.

31. Ur „ उरु spacious or ऊर्क् food or prosperity; the spacious or prosperous city, the city well-provided with food.

32. Yawe „ यह्व God the great. Vide R. V. i, 36,1 ; iii, 1, 12; 2, 9 etc.

33. Zu „ जटायु (?).

The eleven lists of words* given above are not exhaustive. They are merely representative and can be indefinitely increased. Yet the successful comparison of a number of words taken from different languages with those of Vedic Sanskrit is expected to convince an unprejudiced mind that there is a very substantial contact between this language and the others. On this contact being established, as all sensible European and Indian scholars do admit, a question arises as to which of these have borrowed from the other or others. Remember please, that we have the Vedic on one side and the remaining languages, on the other. Those who think that the former is the oldest, will at once answer that all the others, have, in some way unknown and unintelligible to us, surely borrowed nay, themselves completely sprung from, it. The latter, in the face of the facts adduced, is the only tenable position.

All other languages have sprung from the Vedic.

It would be a very novel position to maintain the contrary, i.e., that the Vedic language went aborrowing from the others.† The vast array of evidence already adduced on

*Ten of these are based upon the "Vaidika Sampatti" of P. Raghunandana Sarmaa.

†This is what the writer in the "Illustrated Weekly of India" already referred to, seems to hold. In his article dated 7th July he takes the Vedic word 'taturim' to be a corruption of Tutuli. The latter (tutuli) sounds like a Praakr^{ə}ta or Apabhra*m*sa formation, but this gentleman being a believer in the theory propounded by his European gurus that the Sanskrit is a refined language—refined from corrupt idioms—cannot but postulate such a topsy turvy theory. He reads 'tuturva*n*i' of R. V. i, 168 1, as Tutur-Bani for it suits his policy to do so. If you were to object to his reading 'b' for 'v' and 'n' for '*n*' he would readily answer that there are very old grammatical principles supporting him, e.g., 'vabayorna bhedah', and the rule of euphony justifying such formations as '*eette*' —(*eed*+te)!! The Vedic 'uru' (vast, spacious etc.,) is a corruption of the Sum. Ur the name of the city, and he is wroth with the 'Indian pandits' who have 'misinterpreted' the word to mean 'heaven.' He perpetrates the 'monstrosity' of breaking up the word 'maghavan' into mah—Awan and interprets it as 'the mighty king of Awan!' For him the Vedic 'Sardha' is a corrupt and later form of 'Chaldea', 'erma' of Elam', 'ruru-bhu' or 'rurukshani' of Lulu-bu' and so on and so forth. In his 2nd article of the 21st July, he gives a 'watersoup' interpretation of R. V. i,

pp. xcix-cxiv, entirely falsifies this view. It will be absurd to think that the ancient Aryans of India have been going aborrowing their vocabulary from the dead Sumerian down to the modern English.

The contention, therefore, that the Vedic language is the original of which the others are copies is the most reasonable.

The Vedic language is the primitive language of humanity.

In other words, it means, that the Vedic is the primordial speech of mankind. This proposition conflicts with the views of European philologists who assert that the Vedas cannot be older than 3000 B. C. Their facile position they prop up with a million assertions the only authority for which can be adduced in no other way than in the form: "Macdonell says",

---

133, 1-7. The heading of the performance is worth quoting: 'Land-grant of Awal—The Lord of Susa, (3500—3150 B. C.)'. Then follows:—'The Rigvedic hymns 1-7 of Mandala 1, and of Sukta 134,...

In this concoction of his that doctor of two European universities wrenches 'Babylonians' out of 'abhivlagya' (which he begins with a capital A to throw dust into the eyes of the reader), equates 'vail-asthaanam' to 'Shir mountain-dweller,' 'yaatumateenaam' to 'Yahows', 'sushmintamah' to 'the noble Lord of Susa' and 'sushmibhih' to 'with brave Suzians'. The word pisaacim he thinks is derived from 'Weshesh'. To support his fanciful interpretation he takes the expressions 'va*t*oori*n*aa padaa' and 'mahaava*t*oori*n*aa padaa', as two unitary compound words and then breaks them up in two different ways, viz., 'Vat-U-Ur-Inaa-padaa' and 'Mahaa-Vatur-Inaa-padaa'. His interpretation of the first is 'the high walled-Ur's High-priest' and of the second 'Mighty Balulu Aanni-padda'. He thus most foolishly adheres to the silly method of squeezing out 1004 interpretations out of a single sentence which he, in his sixth article dated the 22nd September, is audacious enough to criticise. Those who have an axe to grind or a fad to boom, do commit such blunders for they are blinded by their pet theories. This writer's fad is that "the Brahmins and their most sacred book the Rigveda are non-Indian in their origin" (article viii 3rd November 1935). He believes that "the Rigveda is a Sumerian document," sub-heading ofarticle i,) and that the Sanskrit language is derived from the dead Sumerian. With such a fad to boom he could not but cut such curious literary capers, for a straight-forward, serious research would have demanded much labour and time and entirely falsified his foregone conclusions. He does not care a straw for Paa*n*ini's grammar, Yaaska's Nirukta or any such hallowed ancient authority, but 'poses' as his own super Paa*n*ini and super-Yaaska. According to him all ancient Vedic scholars have gone wrong. How can he, then, prove that he is right? by specious arguments? Ebullitions of such vapid scholarship deserve only one place, the waste-paper basket. The hymn this writer is trying to make capital out of, it must be said, is 133rd of the 1st book of the Rᵊgveda and not the 134th. Obviously, he does not much care for accuracy.

"Max Müller maintains," "Roth declares," etc. It should not be supposed that an attempt is being made in these pages to derive from the Vedic all the other languages of the world. Oh no. It will be simply absurd to attempt such a thing at this stage when Vedic research and Archaeology are almost in their infancy. Years of labours in the right direction and with an honest selfless motive, may enable us to trace, to some reasonable extent, the lost links between the Vedic and other languages. As matters stand now, it can be safely stated that the classical Sanskrit is the only language which has directly descended from the Vedic. This truth can be approximately represented by means of a diagram in the form of a genealogical tree as follows:—

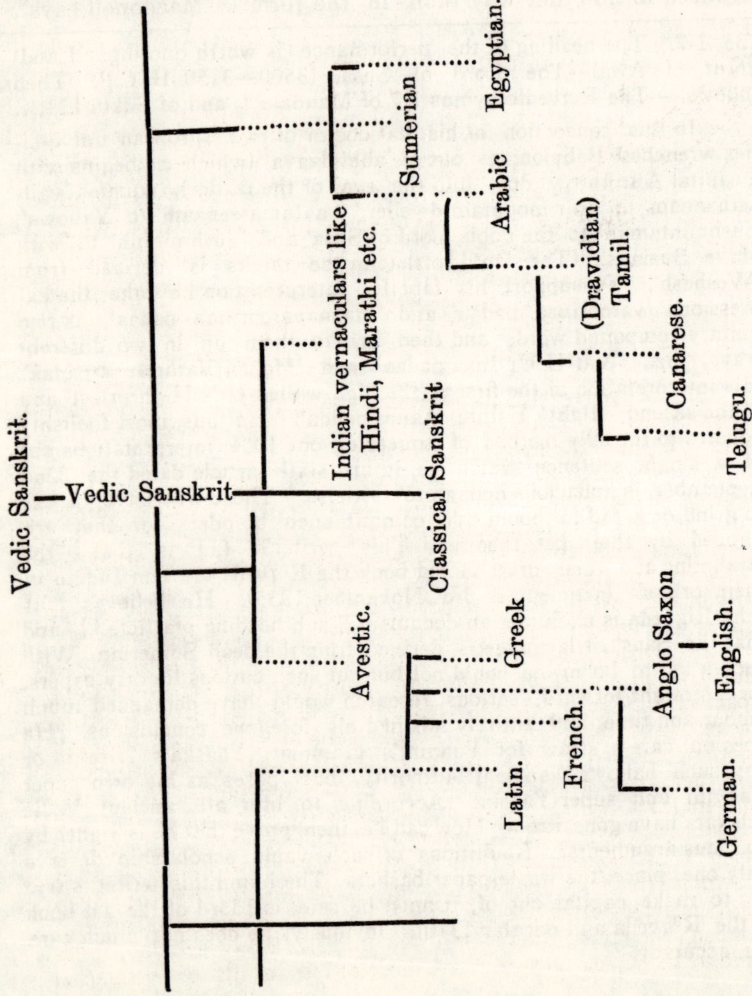

In the above diagram the dots represent those languages that descended from the Vedic Sanskrit but which are now so entirely lost to us that we do not know even their very names. The earliest of them must have substantially resembled their hallowed ancestor. Ages of transformation have brought forth the 'modern' languages which, therefore, have very few clear points of contact with the Vedic. Their unrecognisable vocables are an outcome of the mixture of expressions of the dialects that sprang collaterally from the descendents of the Vedic. A foolish pretention of weakness and intentional negligence on the part of the speakers facilitated these horrible transformations in such a manner that the finished results entirely lost all their semblance to the primitive ancestor. These phenomena are at work even now-a-days. 'Byculla' and 'Muttra' are 'names' of certain places in India. Their orignals were 'Bhaayakha*l*aa' and 'Mathuraa'—**भायखळा** and **मथुरा**—but the slovenly English men who transcribed these words into English depended upon their own silly pronunciation and did not care to consult genuine Indians themselves. The ultimate result of this egregious foolishness has been two obscene* words substituted for quite good Sanskritic names!! Obstinacy in foolishly sticking to their mistakes on the part of lazy people has brought these words into existence and facetious stupidity keeps them still in vogue.

Lost languages

---

*For, Byculla=(in Marathee) baayee kulaa=baayeecaa kulaa = a lady's buttocks. Muttra=(in Marathee or Hindi) = muttraa=one who urinates at the slightest provocation. The transformation of 'Hamilton's Bridge' and 'Saint Andrew's Pettah' has been referred to elsewhere. Note the following also. On the Tanjore-Tirut-turaip-poon*d*i line there is a place called 'A*d*iakka-mangalam', which also has attached to it a very funny story, perhaps concocted. It is said that two sisters went about at the morning time gathering cow-dung in the vicinity of this place. In those days the Railway company had started its survey and commenced naming the stations of their future railway line. An engineer, an English man to be sure, was just then out on his duty of survey. As he wanted to know the name of the place he approached the cow-dung-gathering girl as none else was to be seen and asked her in English:—"What is the name of this place?" The poor girl got frightened at the too near approach of a white man and called out to her elder sister whose name was 'Mangalam'. "A*d*i akkaa Mangalam," the cry she uttered therefore simply meant, "Oh sister Mangalam (please come)." The English man's purpose was, however, completely served. He said, "thank you," and noted down in his diary 'A*d*iakkamangalam'. That is the origin of the name as the story goes. Such hybrid expressions also as 'Islampura', 'Akbarpura', 'Mariabad', 'Lyallpur', and the very funny 'Edwardesabad,' also deserve to be noted. All these are more or less results of obstinacy.

Hence two more causes of the transformation of speech come up for consideration namely obstinacy and desire for secrecy. When the original human family dispersed, some branches of it invented their own secret* languages which in time came to obtain currency, and almost all, except the original stock, obstinately† insisted upon their wrong pronunciation. Changes brought about by these factors can be unravelled with very great difficulty. Allowance has to be made to these two factors also in researches into the origins of the non-Vedic languages.

Obstinacy and desire for secrecy are the causes of divergence of speech.

European philologists have entirely failed to take note of these very important factors in the growth of languages. As Latin and Greek do not exactly coincide with the Vedic, they try to derive, Sanskrit, Greek and Latin together from the 'Primitive-Indo-Germanic' a concoction of their fertile brains.

The Sumerian, the Egyptian and such other languages just getting to be known through Archaeological excavations are, really, such code or secret languages. Their vocabulary is highly artificial and 'unexpressive'. Much of it must have been built up while the speakers of these languages had not, as yet, entirely lost their contact with their original 'Aryan' brethren. The cuneiform, linear, or hieroglyphic method of writing invented by these people tells volumes about their ingeniousness. It is essentially a code script and is intended to reserve the matter inscribed to a strictly limited circle of trusted communicants.

The Sumerian and Egyptian are artificial languages.

It is better to know something about these Sumerians:—

---

* The European 'Esperanto' is a living example. The daughters of an Indian prince (who recently died) have invented their own language which even their relatives cannot understand!

† North of Bombay and Madras cities the true distinction in the pronunciation of *s* (palatal), sh (cerebral) and s (dental) is entirely lost sight of by the speakers of Hindi and cognate dialects. This is a result of shere obstinacy. The Bengali cannot pronounce the Sanskrit 'a'—he changes it into 'o' as in 'pot'. The famous Calcutta Bengali daily is according to him 'Bos + shu moti' and not 'Vasumati'. For 'where will you stop? aap kahaa*m* rahenge'—he says 'aap kohaa*m* royenge?' i. e., 'where will you weep.'' His dental 's' is something resembling that letter and the cerebral 'sh'. A well-known Sanskrit grammatical work of Madras is named 'Dhaaturoopamuktaava*l*ee'. The southerner is very fond of the cerebral *l*. The well-known Sanskrit scholar, Dr. Keith cannot pronounce the cerebrals, hence he obstinately asserts that they are not Aryan !!

"The alternation of settlement, nomadic conquest, refinement, fresh conquest and refinement, which is characteristic of this phase of human history, is particularly to be noted in the region of the Euphrates and Tigris, which lay open in every direction to great areas which are not arid enough to be complete deserts, but which were not fertile enough to support civilised populations. Perhaps the earliest people to form real cities in this part of the world or indeed, in any part of the world, were the people called Sumerians. They were probably brunets of Iberian or Dravidian affinities. They used a kind of writing which they scratched upon clay and their language has been deciphered. It was a language more like the unclassified Caucasic language groups than any others that do now exist. These languages may be connected with Basque, and may represent what was once a wide-spread primitive language group extending from Spain and western Europe to Eastern India, and reaching southwards to central Africa.

Who were the Sumerians?

Excavations conducted at Eridu by Captain R. Campbell Thompson during the recent war have revealed an early Neolithic agricultural stage, before the invention of writing or the use of bronze beneath the earliest Sumerian foundations. The crops of the pre-Sumerians were cut by sickles of earthenware.

The Sumerians shaved their heads and wore simple tunic-like garments of wool. They settled first on the lower courses of the great river and not very far from the Persian Gulf, which in those days ran up for a hundred and thirty miles and more beyond its present head. Sayce in "Babylonian and Assyrian Life," estimates that in 6,500 B. C. Eridu was on the sea coast. The Sumerians fertilized their fields by letting water run through the irrigation trenches, and they gradually became very skilful hydraulic engineers; they had cattle, asses, sheep and goats, but no horses; their collections of mud huts grew into towns, and their religion raised up tower-like temple buildings.

Clay dried in the sun, was a very great fact in the lives of these people. This lower country of the Euphrates-Tigris valley had little or no stone. They built of brick, they made pottery and earthenware images, and they drew and presently wrote upon thin tile-like cakes of clay. They do not seem to have had paper or to have used parchment. Their books and memoranda, even their letters, were potsherds.

At Nippur they built a great tower of brick to their chief god El-li (Enlil) the memory of which is supposed to be preserved in the story of the tower of Babel. They seem to have been divided up into city states, which warred among themselves and maintained for many centuries their military capacity. Their soldiers carried long spears and shields and fought in close formation. Sumerians conquered Sumerians, Sumer remained unconquered by any stranger race for a very long period of time indeed. They developed their civilisation, their writing, and their shipping, through a period that may be twice as long as the whole period from the Christian era to the present time. Then slowly they gave way before the Semitic people.

The first of all known empires was that founded by the high priest of the god of the Sumerian city of Erech. It reached, says an inscription of Nippur, from the Lower (Persian Gulf to the upper (Mediterranean or Red?) Sea. Among the mud heaps of the Euphrates-Tigris valley the record of that vast period of history, that first half of the Age of Cultivation, is buried. There flourished the first temples and the first priest-ruler that we know of among mankind.

Traces of Sumerian trade and perhaps of Sumerian settlement, have been found in North East India, but it is still uncertain whether the Sumerian reached India overland or by the sea. Probably it was by sea. They may have been quite nearly related in race and culture to the people then inhabiting the Ganges valley." (From the "New Outline of History" by H. G. Wells pp. 164-6.)

The same writer thus describes Sumerian culture:—

The Sumerian Civilisation.

"The story of the Tigris and Euphrates civilization, is ......a story of conquest following after conquest, and each conquest replaces old rulers and ruling classes by new; races like the Sumerian and the Elamities are swallowed up, their languages vanish, they interbreed and are lost; the Assyrian melts away into the Chaldean and Syrian, the Hittites lose distinction, the Semites who swallowed up the Sumerians give place to rulers of these new Aryan tribes from the North: Medes and Persians appear in the place of the Elamites, and the (Aryan) Persian language dominates the Empire until the Aryan Greek ousts it from official life.*

---

*What Wells describes above is formulated by an American

Meanwhile the plough does its work year by year, the harvests are gathered, the builders build as they are told, the tradesmen work and invent fresh devices; the knowledge of writing spreads novel things, the horses and wheeled vehicles and iron are introduced and become part of the permanent inheritance of mankind, the volume of trade upon sea and desert increases, man's ideas widen and knowledge grows. There are set-backs, massacres, pestilence, but the story is, on the whole, one of enlargement. For four thousand years this new thing, civilisation, which had set its root into the soil of the two rivers, grew as a tree grows; now losing a limb, not stripped by a storm, but always growing and resuming its growth. It changed its dominant race; it changed its language, but it remained essentially the same development. After four thousand years the warriors and conquerors were still going to and fro over this growing thing they did not understand, but man had by that time (330 B. C.) got iron, horses, writing and computation, money, a far greater variety of foods and textiles, a far wider knowledge of their world than the old Sumerians.

The time that elapsed between the empire of Sargon I and

---

writer, Joseph P. Widney in his "Race Life of the Aryan Peoples", (Funk and Wagnalls Company New York 1907) Vol. II 'The new World': "The strife for survival which came between families as to the Negroid, the Yellow man, and the White man, has come within the family to the Aryan. Had we the history no doubt we should find that it was so likewise within the families of the Negroid and Yellow man in their day of struggle, in each the weaker members dying out through attrition, and the stronger surviving through process of natural selection.

* * *

A race is a family upon a broader scale, subject much to the same laws and limitations. In the family no two children are born equal or alike in vitality, in season of maturity, or in period of decay. And this difference, less strongly marked, it may be, in the first generation, grows more marked, and the divergence more pronounced, with successive generations of removal from the common parent stock. Some come to maturity quickly, and as quickly reach the period of exhaustion. Others mature slowly but are more enduring. It is the working out of the law of variation within the species. Back of the variety it is the law of the variation of species within the genus. And as in the process of generation some species have received the stamp of an ancestry so strong, so marked, so full of vitality, that they live on long after others have died, even through their superior strength crowding aside, and in the end supplanting the others; so within the species itself the stronger variety crowds aside, represses, and in the end extinguishes and survives the weaker."

the conquest of Babylon, by Alexander the Great was as long, be it noted, at the least estimate, as the time from Alexander the Great to the present day. And before the time of Sargon I men had been settled in the Sumerian land, living in towns, worshipping in temples, following an orderly agricultural life in an organised community, for at least as long again. "Eridu, Lagash, Ur, Isin, Larsa, have already an immemorial past when first they appear in history.

One of the most difficult things for both the writer and student of history is to sustain the sense of these time-intervals and prevent these ages becoming shortened by perspective in his imagination. Half the duration of human civilisation and the keys to all its chief institutions are to be found before Sargon I. Moreover, the reader can not too often compare the scale of the dates in these latter fuller pages of man's history with the succession of countless generations.."

Later the Kassite 'Aryans' came and overpowered and mingled with the Sumerians:—

The Kassite Aryans.

"The probability has long been recognised that they (the Kassites) were Aryan by race, and we may with some confidence regard them as akin to the later rulers of Mitanni, who imposed themselves upon the earlier non-Aryan population of Subartu, or Northern Mesopotamia. Like the Mitannian king, the Kassites of Babylonia were a ruling caste or aristocracy, and though they doubtless brought with them numbers of humbler followers, their domination did not affect the linguistic nor the racial character of the country in any marked degree................................In place of the unwieldy system of date-formulae, inherited by the Semites from the Sumerians, under which each year was known by an elaborate title taken from some great event or cult observance, the Kassites introduced the simpler plan of dating by the years of the king's reign........................

But, on the material side, the greatest change they effected in the life of Babylonia was due to their introduction of the horse. There can be little doubt that they were a horse-keeping race, and the success of their invasion may in large part be traced to their greater mobility." (From "History of Babylon" L. W. King p: 214 l. 16—p. 215 l. 17).

The Egyptians also were affected by contact with the 'Aryans'.

"The mounds known as Tell-el-Amarna in Upper Egypt mark the site of a city which had a brief but brilliant existence under Amen-hetep* IV, or Akhenaten, one of the later kings of the Eighteenth Dynasty. He was the famous "heretic" king, who attempted to suppress the established religion of Egypt and to substitute for it a pantheistic monotheism associated with the worship of the solar disc. In pursuance of his religious ideas he deserted Thebes, the ancient capital of the country, and built a new capital further to the north, which he called Akhetaten"† (L. W. King. Op. Cit. 219, ll. 11—21.)

The Sumerian religion was a highly developed system of true theism perhaps with a good mixture of pantheism. It died away but gave rise to the modern Semitic creeds wrongly called 'theistic religions'. European scholars have failed rightly to grasp that ancient religious cult as will be gathered from the following extracts:—

The religion of the Sumerians was not totemistic.

"After long study of the Semtic and Sumerian sources I have become convinced that totemism and demonology have nothing to do with the origins of Sumerian or Semitic religions. The former cannot be proved at all; the latter is a secondary aspect of them. I may fail to carry conviction in concluding that both in Sumerian and Semitic religions, monotheism preceded polytheism and belief in good and evil spirits............It is, I trust, the conclusion of knowledge and not of audacious preconception." (From "Semitic Mythology" by Stephen Herbert Langdon, M. A., Introduction p. xviii ll. 14-25.)

The Sumero-Semitic trinity was composed of the following:—

"The Sun, Venus and Moon were the three principal and perhaps the only deities worshipped by the Semites." (Ibid. p. 3.)

The origin of the Islamic Allah is the Sumero-Aryan 'moon-god':—

"Arabian religion has no mythology at all concerning the gods and goddesses of its pantheon. A few names of Arabic

* European scholars are not uniform in the spelling of many words. Some spell 'Amenhotep'. Dr. Langdon on p. 14 of his "Semitic Mythology" spells "Inninni" in two different ways, i. e., with one 'n' between the first two 'i's and two between the 2nd and 3rd, and vice vera !!

† The glory of the disc.

deities of pre-Islamic times have survived in the Coran (sic) of Mohammed, who founded a thorough monotheism on the deity Allah,* the old Ilah, or title of the Moon-god Wadd, Shahar, Ilmuqah of the earlier pantheon." (Ibid p. 7. ll, 6-11).

The following opinion is due to a misunderstanding of the 'esoteric' nature of the Sumero-Semitic religions:—

"Now these great Canaanite gods, Eshmun, Kemosh, Melqart, and Adon of Gebal, are sometimes regarded as the husbands, sometimes as the sons, sometimes as the brothers of the Earth-goddess Astarte, as we know from Sumerian and Babylonian religion." (Ibid p. 13 ll. 30—4).

The following statements contradict the above:—

"In Accadian, and Babylonian, and Assyrian religion, the virgin Earth-mother goddesses, Innini—Ishtar, Nintud, Aruru, Ninhursag, Ninlil, are all Sumerian, and borrowed by the Semites in prehistoric times." (Ibid. p. 10 ll. 10—4).

"Worship of a dying god, son of the Earth-mother, was the principal cult of this North Arabian people during the period immediately before and after the life of Jesus of Nazareth in Palestine."† (Ibid p. 17 ll. 1-5.)

"As morning star she is goddess of War (in the west 'Anat), and as evening star patroness of love and harlotry."‡ (Ibid. p. 25. ll. 3—5).

"The cult of the "Queen of Heaven"§ was widely spread in Canaan and observed by the Hebrews also." Ibid p. 25. l. 25).

"...........the warlike goddess of the morning star has a rival in "Discord" or "Hostility" even more dreadful than herself." (Ibid p. 27 ll. 26—28).

"She had no consort and really loved only the unfortunate youth Tammuz, who perished annually with the dying corn." (Ibid. p. 28 ll. 2—4.)

"The myth of Ishtar, Astarte, Atargatis, is one of the principal factors in Sumerian and Semitic religion. She is often

---

*The idea of Allah as the True God was very old in Arabia. See Lavi's poem quoted later on.

†It is a historical fact that the good Jesus was crucified. But what brought about his resurrection and deification is this myth. ‡Mary the mother of Jesus has this as one of her appellations according to the Roman Catholic Church. §The Roman Catholic Church calls Mary "Queen of heaven."

represented as a mother with a child at her breasts (the Babylonian Nintud)" * (Ibid. p. 34 ll. 15-20.)

"Bambyce, the ancient Nappigi, is said to have been founded by the legendary Babylonian survivor of Deluge, Sisythus, in Lucian, a corruption of Xisouthros, the Sumerian Ziusudra. Lucian, like all Greek and Roman writers of the period, transforms Semitic mythology into Greek and Roman terms and assigns the legend of the Flood to the Greek Deucalion. This Sumerian legend, based as we now know upon an ancient catastrophe in lower Mesopotamia, looms largely in the mythology of Asia". (Ibid. p.37 l. 32—p. 38 l. 5.)

The Sumerian myth of creation also has striking features which ought to be taken careful note of:—

The Sumero-Semitic Myth of creation

"But there is no evidence in the extensive Sumerian literature that they had any considered theory of the creation of the world. That all things exist and were created by the Word or Logos of the Water-god Enki was a theory developed by them. *But cosmological reflections upon the creation of the universe by the Sun-god, after he had slain the dragon of Chaos*, which resulted in a considered myth and an epical masterpiece, are apparently of Accadian origin. The name of the dragon of Chaos, which appears in the great Epic of Creation, is also Semitic and not Sumerian. Moreover the dragon of the epic is a female, whereas in every Sumerian reference to this primeval battle of Bel and the Dragon the latter is a male monster, and either the storm-bird Zu or the fubulous serpent Mushussu. Both of these dragons are reduced to the role of cohorts in the host of Tiamat, female dragon of the sea, in the Babylonian myth. Moreover every known representation of the battle of Bel and the dragon in Babylonia and Assyria represents the dragon either as a winged lion wtth scaly body and bird talons, or as a serpent monster. None of these representations on seals and monuments is earlier than the tenth century B. C., and even the prolific glyptique of the Hammurabi period, when this epic was probably written, shews no trace of the myth!" (Ibid p. 276 ll. 7-29).

---

* This is the origin of the representation by the Roman Catholic Church of Mary with the infant Jesus as "the Madonna with the Child."

"The combat between light and darkness is the basis of the later myth of Marduk and Tiamat, but the cosmological aud theological speculation is new and based upon the theory that all things sprang from watery chaos, for this reason the female serpent-dragon Tiamat, literally the word for the bitter ocean, became the principal dragon of Chaos and foe of the Sun-god. The dragon Zu of the old Sumerian myth does not survive in the new Babylonian epic of creation. Here the dragons in the train of Tiamat are Basmu, "Viper," Mushussu, "Raging serpent" latterly the constellation Hydra, Lahamu, Ugallu, "Great-lion," probably Leo in Astronomy, Uridimmu, "the Gruesome-lion", the constellation Lupus, Girtabbili, "the Scorpion-man", the constellation Sagittarius, Ulmu dapruti, "the Destructive Spirits", used as a singular (pluralis majestatis), Kulilu, "the Fish-man", the constellation Aquarius, Kusariqqu, "the Fish-man", the constellation Capricorn. Other lists based upon this epic have also Zu and Asakku.

Of all these dragons of Chaos (according to the new philosophy of the epic), only Zu appears with certainty as a foe of the sun in the older system of mythology. In the representations of the battle of Marduk and the dragons the lion is probably Ugallu; the serpent monster with two forefeet of a lion or beast of prey is Mushussu. The winged horse is a form of a Zu, based on an astronomical identification; possibly the eagle-headed lion is also Zu. The Scorpion-man is clear enough and leaves no doubt. The winged sphinx, the winged unicorn, the ostrich, the winged human headed beast with a long beard, are not identifiable with any of these dragons. The bearded beast with legs and body of a lion may perhaps be Kingu, husband of Tiamat and leader of her host. The sphinx has forefeet of a lion and hind legs of a bird of prey." (Ibid, p. 282 l. 4-p. 283.)

The following is the Accadian myth of battle between Ninurta and Labbu.—

"Who *bore* this great serpent?
The sea (Tamtu=Tiamat) it is that bore this great serpent
Enlil designed him in the Heavens.
Fifty miles in his length, one mile long his *head*?
Six cubits (wide) is his mouth, twelve cubits is his....

Twelve cubits are the borders of his ears,
At a distance of sixty cubits he...birds.
In the water he drags his *tail* nine cubits.
He lifts high his tail........."
"Who will go and slay the Labbu,
Deliver the wide land,
And exercise the kingship?
Go, O Tishpak, slay the Labbu,
Deliver the wide land,
And exercise kingship".

Enlil sends Tishpak to destroy Labbu.

"Cause a cloud to go up, a hurricane [*unchain.*]
The seal of thy soul before thy face [hold]
Rush forth, slay the Labbu".

"And so he sent forth a cloud and *unchained* a hurricane; he held his seal of life before him, rushed forth, and slew Labbu. For three years, three months, one day, and ten......the blood of Labbu ran upon the [*sea*]."

This text provides one of the few clear evidences that Sumerian mythology actually contained the basis of all later Babylonian speculations concerning the origin of the universe from water, and furnished the Babylonian schoolmen with material for the myth of Tamtu or Tiamat, dragon of the sea. The old Sumerian word for the salt-sea was *a-ab-ba* or simply *ab* and they had a liturgy know as "a-ab-ba the terrifying." The Sumerian dragon of the primeval bitter sea was a male dragon subdued by Ninurta. In the later Babylonian speculation the Semitic word for the salt-sea, *tamtu, tiamtu, ta-a-wa-tu, tu-amat, ti-amat* as it is variously spelled supplanted the male dragon Ugga, Mushussu of Sumerian mythology, and became a female monster solely because this *word* is feminine in Semitic.

The Babylonian Epic of creation was written in six books or tablets, with a late appendix added as the seventh book, as a commentary on the fifty sacred Sumerian titles of Marduk. No copies of the Babylonian text exist earlier than the age of Nebuchadnezzar.

The epic is known from its first line *enuma elis la nabu samamu*, "When on high the Heavens were not named," involving the theory that nothing existed before the gods had conceived its form and given it a name. And "beneath home(s) bore no name(s)." Then the apsu of underworld freshwater sea, the primevai engenderer of all things, and tiamtu, the salt sea, bearer of all, mingled their principles of the Watery Chaos, and there was Mummu, messenger of Apsu (personified as a divine creature) whose name means "intelligence," the creative word or principle inherent in water. Damascius, a Greek philosopher of the sixth century A. D., reports this theory more accurately then any classical author. He says that the Babylonians pass over the first principle of all things and begin with two, Tauthe and Apason, making Apason the husband of Tauthe; from them proceeded the only begotten Moymis. He interprets Moymis to mean the intelligible world. The Babylonians themselves interpreted Mummu to mean both "utterance," i. e., "word," "Logos," and "life." Berossus, who wrote at Babylon when these doctrines were still well known, describes their theories as having been revealed by Oannes himself. He says that there was a time when all was darkness and water in which came to life monsters of peculiar forms. There were men with two wings and some with four wings, and two faces. They had two heads, one of a male, the other of a female, and were androgynous. Some had legs and horns of goat, some horses' feet; some had the bodies of men and hindquarters of horses like hippocentaurs. There were men with heads of bulls, and dogs with four bodies and tails of fisbes; there were horses with heads of dogs and there were men and animals having heads and bodies of horses, with tails of fishes. All sorts of monstrous beings existed in this Chaos, and Berossus saw designs of them in the temple of Bel in Babylon" (Ibid p. 290)

Ea then slays Apsu but Tiamat still persecutes the gods; the latter approach Anu the father of heaven and beg him to save them from the monster. He sends Bel in compliance with their prayers:—

"Bel spread his net, which Anu had given him, and enmeshed her. He let loose the Imhullu wind in her face. As Tiamat opened her mouth to devour him, the Imhullu wind blew into her, the raging winds filled her belly. His arrow tore her belly, severed her inwards, and rent asunder her heart. He bound her and stood upon her corpse. Her host of dragons scattered and fled in terror. They sought to save their souls alive but were trapped and bound.

He split her into parts, and with half of her he made the Heavens. He drew out her skin and caused watchmen to take charge of it.... ... .The canopy of Heaven was made from the stretched-out skin of Tiamat, and he confined the waters which cause rain above this canopy."(Ibid p. 303.)

The Sumerian religion was a copy of the Vedic.

The evidence adduced above from European authors of renown clearly prove that the Sumerian religion was an imitation of the Vedic with certain Puranic accretions transformed through local influences so as to lose their true original character. But yet there are so many important ideas prominent that we can see through the veil of changes and later additions, the same ancient doctrine of the trinity referred to in the Vedas as 'Soorya, Indra and Vaayu'. Inninni, Ishtar and the other female deities also are echoes of the Glory and Providence of God so often extolled in the Vedas*. The veil that darkens the true features of these is, it should be borne in mind, Pura*n*ic. The eighteen Pura*n*as that have come down to us in a very garbled form and with a good deal of matter recently interpolated, are not their own original selves. They have mostly originated from the 'Braahma*n*as,' the hallowed ancient commentaries on the Vedas. They contain a good deal of genuine ancient historical material which, if carefully sifted, will provide us, along with the Mahaabhaarata, the Raamaaya*n*a, the Braahma*n*as and the inscriptions and archaeological finds (of which alas! we have very few left in India), a complete record of the genuine history of India's past. In their declining age they must have poisoned the traditions of those who were far beyond India but between whom and the latter country there was commercial contact. The matter may be quite the other way as well, e. g., the Pura*n*ic ideas of Paarvatee etc., might have been borrowed from Babylonia. Anyhow, we find in the Sumerian doctrines a garbled form of the original Vedic trinity.

The eighteen Pura*n*as are historical.

The Sumerian myth of creation is also borrowed from the Vedas

The myth of the creation also has clear unmistakable points of contact with the Vedic teaching thereon, as laid down e. g., in the great Naasadeeya Sookta (see elsewhere in this book.) That famous hymn refers to the state before creation by words meaning 'water': in the first verse we have 'ambhah,' and in the third 'salilam'. The third verse says 'tama aaseet tamasaa goo*lh*am' etc., which also is noteworthy.

* See for example Y. V. xxxi; R. V. i, 3, 10—12 etc.

These two Vedic ideas of the state before creation find an echo in the Sumerian legend. Mushussu, Labbu etc., are all copies of Vr^{ə}tra, and Tiamat finds an unmistakable mention in the Atharvaveda as Taimaata—a serpent!!

Surely, the Sumerians must have been a branch of that human family which, at that early time, had begun to call itself 'Aarya'.* Thus it is the Sumerians that separated from the Aryans, it is the Sumerians who borrowed from the latter, it is the Sumerians who got their religion and literature from them and not vice versa.†

---

*The word 'Aarya' occurs in the Vedas a number of times, e.g., R. V. i,183,3 'aaryam saho vardhayaa dyumnamindra'; v,34,6 'yathaavasam nayati daasam aaryah' etc., Y. V. xxxiii, 82 yasyaayam visva aaryo daasah sevadhipaa arih, etc. The word simply meant a good pious, righteous and well-behaved person and has nothing to do with any tribe as far as the Vedas are concerned. The later use of it to denote a particular people was rendered necessary by the evil ways into which their separated brethren had fallen, e.g., disregard of the Vedas, flesh-eating, drinking intoxicating liquors, promiscuous sexual relations, forgetting their mother-tongue Sanskrit, etc., the very essential features of the original family. The term simply means a well-behaved respectable person, and the so-called 'Aaryan race' who came to India from somewhere outside, is a mere figment of the fertile brain of the European scholar. It suits his policy, his political creed, to harangue time and again regarding this particular class of rational bipeds who never existed and hence never came.

† The topsy-turvy thinker whose articles in the "Illustrated Weekly of India" have already been referred to, with his europeanised mind, thinks quite the other way about:—

"...............the people of the Indus Valley worshipped gods and goddesses of whom some were local and others Sumerian or foreign. Gaurisa, Nagesa, Sisna, Hri, Sri, Kli, etc., appear to be the names of deities of the Indus people. Inni, Yini, Ninsianna, Nanna, Gaga, Gi or Ge etc., on the other hand, are well known Sumerian gods and goddesses, which occur frequently in the inscripitions on the Indus seals. Some, such as Iloib, Illu etc. I would class as foreign, but they are so few in number that their occurrence may be due to a few traders of Semitic race residing at Mohenjo daro. The gods and goddesses of the Indus people *continue to figure in the Hindu pantheon at the present day.* The occurrence of the names of Sumerian deities was a puzzle. With a view to solve it I decided to make a thorough search in the Pauranic and Tantric literature for some clue. The discovery of the text is divided into thirteen adhyayas and contains 701 short mantras. The following table may give some idea of the nature of the text:—

ॐ ऐं किं नमः v, 95 Um-En-Kin-Na-Mah. Enkin & Enki probably Sumerian Enki Water-god fish symbol.

That the Vedas were very well known to the Semitic and Sumerian people long long before the Christian era there is ample of documentary evidence incontrovertible. A court poet of Haroun-ar-Rascheed named Asma'iee Malek-us-Sha'araa, had saved from oblivion and destruction a number of ancient documents of ancient Hindu Mecca which had escaped the hands of Islamic invaders. A few of them are still to be seen at the Cairo (?) museum. Malek compiled a selection of these "Searul 'uqool" which is now published by the Berut Publishing Co., Berut, Palestine.* One of these is a short poem by a poet Lavi bine Akhtab bine Turfaa who lived somewhere about 2350—2400 before Mahommed, i. e.. not less than 17 centuries before the Christian era and full 12 centuries before Alexander the Great the ruler of Macedon of which ancient Sumer and Akkad formed parts, and till whose time Sumerian language and script were in use. Lavi is a pure Arab and a great scholar in that language for his style of writing is very simple at the same time the most charming classical Arabic. On p. 118* of the above named book the following beautiful poem from his pen is given:—

ॐ ऎं. सीं. नमः V, 112. Ūm En Sīn na-Mah. Sīn, Sī Sīn. Moon god. Siva in Tantra lit."

The Mohenjo Daro Inscriptions have the symbols of men, fish, and scorpion. 'Purusa' and Adipurusa, according to him is a man or a homo-sign. The Vedic Ka he says occurs among pot marks. (From the "Indian Historical Quarterly," June 1932).

In List no. x p. cxii, in illustration no. 2 p. cv, in the Sumerian text given on p. cvii and in Tamil and Canarese quotations in the text, it must be noted the compiler has been constrained to use ऐ and ओ or ॆ and ो for the short or long sound of the Dravidian languages e and o, as in the English word 'men', 'man', 'pot' and 'all'. This is a modern and corruptm ethod and ought not to be widely and indiscriminately adopted for it gives rise to serious mispronunciation and consequent misunderstanding of text. But to represent the Sanskrit ऐ by the English 'e' is quite a novel procedure. The Sanskrit ऐ has its equivalent in English 'ai' as is well known among Sanskritists but the writer quoted above is so blinded by his fad that he has cast this important point of pronunciation to the winds. ॐ can never be the same as Um. The comparisons instituted in the above article can prove only one thing that the Sumerians have borrowed from the Aryans and not vice versa.

*Available from Haji Hamza Shirazi & Co., Publishers and Booksellers, Bundar Road, Bombay. The compiler is indebted to Soufi Jnaanendraji of the Dayananda Salvation mission for this text.

أيا مُبَارَكَ الأرضِ يُشَيِّنُهَا مِنَ الهِندِ فَأَرَادَكَ اللهُ مَن يُنَزِّلَ ذِكرَةً

وَهَل تَجَلِّيَةٌ عَينَانِ صَحبِى أَربَعَةً هٰذِهِ يُنَزِّلُ رَسُولٌ ذِكرَةً مِنَ الهِندَةِ

يَقُولُونَ اللهَ يَا أَهلَ الأَرضِ عَالِمِينَ كُلَّهُم فَتَبِعُوا ذِكرَةَ الوِيدِ حَقًّا مَا لَم يُنَزِّلَه

وَهُوَ أَعلَمُ السَّامَ وَاليَجرَ مِنَ اللهِ تَنزِيلًا فَأَينَمَا يَا أَخِي مُتَّبِعًا يُبَشِّرِى نَجَاة

وَاثنَينِ هُمَا رِكَ وَأَتَرَ نَاصِحِينَ كَأُخُوَّةٍ وَأَصنَاتَ عَلَى عُودًا وَهُوَ مَشعَرَةٌ

The above can be transcribed thus:—

Ayaa mubaarakal arze yosheyye nuhaa minal Hinde;
Faaraadakal laaho mayyo nazzelaa zikratun. (1)

Wahal tajalleeyatun ʻainaane sahabee arbaʻatun;
Haazahee yunazzelar rasoolo zikratun minal Hindatun. (2)

Yaqoolunallaaha yaa ahalal arze ʻaalameena kullahum;
Fattabeʻoo zikratul Veda haqqan maalam yunazzelatun. (3)

Wahowa ʻaalam us Saama wal Yujra minallahe tanzeelan;
Fa ʻainamaa yaa akheeyo muttabe ʻan yo basshareeyo najaatun. (4)

Wa asnaina humaa Rik wa Atar naasaheena ka akhoowatun;
Wa asnaata alaa ʻoodan wahowa mashaʻaratun. (5)

It can be translated as follows:—

Oh blessed land of Hind (India) thou art worthy of reverence for in thee has God revealed True Knowledge of Him. (1).

What a pure light do these four revealed books afford to our (mind's) eyes like the (charming and cool) lustre of the dawn! These four God revealed unto His prophets (rəshis) in Hind, (2)

and He thus teaches all races of mankind that inhabit His Earth: "observe (in your life) the knowledge I have revealed in the Vedas," for surely God has revealed them. (3)

Those treasuries are the Saama and Yajus (Yujra= Yajur) which God has published. O my brothers! revere these, for they tell us the good news of salvation! (4)

The two next, of these four, Rik and Atharva (Atar) teach us lessons of (universal) brother-hood. These two (Vedas) are the beacons that warn us to turn towards that goal (universal brotherhood). (5)

Lavi's poem proves that the pure cult of the Vedas had spread far and wide all over the world even during the days of the Sumerians. One more authority will now be quoted in this connection.

Vedic Literature is not 'primitive'

Barth says:—"An attempt has been made to estimate length of time that would be necessary for the gradual formation of this literature, and the eleventh century before the Christain era has been suggested as the age in which the poetry that produced these hymns must have flourished. But taking into account all the circumstances, we are of opinion that this term is too recent, and that the great body of the chants of Rigveda must be referred back to a much earlier period. Contrary to an opinion that is often advanced, we consider also a goodly number of the hymns of the Atharvaveda to be of a date not much more recent; and some of the formulae prescribed in the Yajurveda are in all probability quite as ancient." (From Barth's "The Religion of India" p. 7.)

The same writer says elsewhere in the book:—

"Neither in the language nor in the thought of the Rigveda have I been able to discover that quality of primitive natural simplicity which so many* are fain to see in it. The poetry it contain appears to me, on the contrary, to be of a singularly refined character and artificially elaborated, full of allusions and reticenses, of pretensions to mysticism and theosophic insight, and the manner of its expression is such as reminds one more frequently of the phraseology in use among certain small groups of initiated than the poetic language of a large community." (Barth, op. cit. preface p. xiii.)

"The Hymns, as I have already remarked, do not appear to me to show the least trace of popular derivation. I rather imagine that *they emanate from a narrow circle of priests, and that they reflect a somewhat singular view of things. Not only can I not accept the generally received opinion that Vedic and Aryan are synonymous terms, I am even not at all sure to what extent we are right in*

*For example Max Muller, see p. xcvii letter to Byramji Malabari.

speaking of a Vedic people. Not that communities did not then worship the Gods of the Veda, but I doubt very much if they regarded them as they are represented in the Hymns, any more than that they afterwards sacrificed to them in community after the rites prescribed in the Brahmanas. If there is any justice in these views, it is evident that a literature such as this will only embrace what is within the scope of limited horizon, and will have authoritative weight only in regard to things in a more or less special reference, and that the negative conclusions especially which may be deduced from such documents must be received with not a little reservation. A single instance, to which I limit myself, will suffice for illustration. Suppose that certain hymns of the tenth book of Rig-Veda—a book which the majority of critics look upon with distrust—had not come down to us, what would we learn from the rest of the collection respecting the worship of the manes of the departed? We might know that *India paid homage* to certain powers called Pitris, or Fathers, but we could not infer from that any more than from the later worship of the Matris or mothers, this worship of ancestors or spirits of the dead, which, as the comparative study of the beliefs, customs, and institutions of Greece and Rome shows us, was nevertheless from the remotest antiquity one of the principle sources of public and private right, one of the bases of the family and the civic community." (Ibid. p. xv.)

The Vedas which Lavi knew, therefore, according to Barth's contention, must have been in circulation for several thousand years before him. To attain the position which Barth claims for it, Vedic literature must have taken thousands of years, hence, it may safely be concluded that it is the Sumerians who borrowed their culture, literature, religion, nay, their very existence itself from the ancestor of the Aryans.

Hence there can be no obstacles but race-hatred and obstinacy, in the way of European Orientalists in accepting the Vedic language to be the primitive human speech. Yet, casting off all chances of a satisfactory solution of the origin of man based upon his available and most reliable history, the Western scholar goes about searching for imaginary data that never and nowhere existed. If he fails in his foolish attempt, he sits down quietly and concocts his fib of a

Race-hatred and obstinacy are the cause of European Sanskritists' not recognising claims of the Vedic.

primitive 'Indo-Germanic', which then, with all eclat, is forced down the throat of university students all the world over!! These perpetrations of the Western savant, have, as is his ardent desire, made India and Hindu Indians the butt of ridicule all the world over, but he should remember well, that he has, thereby, alienated the sympathies of the direct and only true descendents of his 'Aryan' ancestors, the only one of all the living branches of the human family to preserve faithfully, even in these bad days his fore-fathers' traditions.

European philology is useless in Vedic interpretation

Hence in the department of Vedic exigesis that pseudoscience (European philology) has done absolutely no appreciable good, nay, it has done immense harm and has now almost barred the progress of serious oriental research. It is pre-eminently a communal and racial cobweb of fortuitous and bumptious theories broadcast to keep under and reduce to servility in the sphere of literature, culture and fine arts, the oldest and most cultured of the Asiatic races. In Vedic interpretation therefore, the theories of European philologists ought not to be considered to have any value, especially as they have entirely failed to solve the least possible difficulty in that sphere. The European scholar need not strut out as a Vedic r^ashi to interpret the Vedas to Indians. He has absolutely no qualifications for that 'job'. Philology has existed for milleniums past and the European scholar is not its founder. Comparative philology also is no new thing and the Western savant is not the founder of this either. Nay, he has not understood its principles of unifying and befriending human races, for, he has been insisting upon decentralising and pitching everything and everybody one against the other.

True Vedic exigetes and their works

Hence our Vedic exigetes are the authors of the Braahma*n*as, the grammarian and philologist Paanini, and the etymologist Yaaska. These are not mere names but great and very serious realities for, their monumental works, our principle guides in Vedic interpretation, are extant. These works are so old that their age cannot be accurately computed by any available means. Paa*n*ini and Yaaska are, to speak the truth, mere compilers of the Ashtaadhyaayee and Nirukta and not the authors. The materials they collected from older sources lost to us, had been in existence for millenniums before them. They critically sifted the whole and interspersed it with the necessary connecting links and explanations. They were hard pressed for books on the subjects to be put into the hands of their students for, they were both professors in some ancient educational institutions of renown like Takshasilaa and Naalanda. This is what impelled them to compile the existing treatises.

It is the fidelity and life-long endeavours of these great scholars and scientists and their worthy predecessors that have preserved the Vedic language from getting 'barbarianised', and thus saved the Vedas from corruption and total loss. It must be borne in mind that no other religion, no other community, no other country in the whole world can afford such a wonderful example of preserving intact its ancient traditions and literature. This is principally due to the presence in ancient Indian Aryan society of those righteous people who, on account of their profound Vedic scholarship, belief in God and rectitude of life were called 'Braahma*n*as'. It is they, who made it their life work to study and teach the Vedas safeguarding both their language and interpretation. In this onerous task of their's they were helped by three factors inherent in the Vedic language itself, viz., (1) its very scientific alphabetical system; (2) its grammatical structure and (3) its method of accentuation. These three features are unknown to other languages. Without some sort of alphabet, grammar and accent, perhaps, no language has yet been known to exist, but a pure and scientifically graded and arranged alphabet, a faultless and perfect grammar based on immutable philological principles and able to account for every formation allowing no exception to escape, and lastly a method of accentuation that determines the formation and meaning of vocables, is indeed, very much more.

How is the Vedic language preserved in its purity?

Each of these three items would require a volume in itself to tread it fully, as each forms, according to the ancient traditions of Aryan India, a great scientific subject.* In this introduction it is possible just to touch upon a few salient points bearing upon the special topic of Vedic interpretation with which we are principally concerned.

The great merits of the Vedic alphabetical system will be recognised from the following comparative tables:—

* Those who wish to know more about the Vedic alphabet should consult P. Raghunandana Sarmaa's Hindi work "Vaidika Sampatti" pp. 300—19 or his monograph अक्षरविज्ञान. On grammar and accent of the Vedas only Paa*n*ini's great work can be consulted.

TABLE No. I.
THE VEDIC ALPHABETICAL SYSTEM

Class.	Vowels.					Consonants.											
	Simple.			Diphthongs			Harsh		Soft				Aspirates				Semivowels.
	Short	Long	Prolated	Long	Prolated	Group	Unaspirate	Aspirate	Unaspirate	Aspirate	Nasal	Sibilants	Pure	Vicarious	Pure nasal	Vicarious Cerebral	
Gutturals	अ	आ	अ३	....	....	१	क	ख	ग	घ	ङ	....	ःह	≍*	....	....	....
Palatals	इ	ई	इ३	....	....	२	च	छ	ज	झ	ञ	श	....	....	....	....	य
Labials	उ	ऊ	उ३	....	....	५	प	फ	ब	भ	म	....	....	≍†	....	....	....
Cerebrals	ऋ	ॠ	ऋ३	....	....	३	ट	ठ	ड	ढ	ण	ष	....	....	....	ळ	र
Dentals	ऌ	....	ऌ३	....	....	४	त	थ	द	ध	न	स	....	....	....	....	ल
Gutturo-palatals	....	....	....	ए	ए३	....	....	....	....	....	....	....	....	....	....	....	....
"	....	....	....	ऐ	ऐ३	....	....	....	....	....	....	....	....	....	....	....	....
Gutturo-labials	....	....	....	ओ	ओ३	....	....	....	....	....	....	....	....	....	....	....	....
"	....	....	....	औ	औ३	....	....	....	....	....	....	....	....	....	....	....	....
Dento-labial	....	....	....	....	....	....	....	....	....	....	....	....	....	....	....	....	व
Pure nasals	ॐ	ँ	....	....	....	....	....	....	....	....	....	....	....	....	ँ	....	....

* 'Jihvaamooleeya' like 'ch' in 'loch.' † 'Upadhmaaneeya' like the English 'f.'

TABLE No. II.*

Schemes of transliteration used in this book:—

Vowels:—

(1) a ā i ī u ū ṛ ṝ ḷ ē ai ō au.

(2) a aa i ee u oo rə rəə ḷə e ai o au.

Consonants

Gutturals:—k kh g gh ṃ (2)ɯ.

Palatals:—c ch j jh ñ (2)*ɯ*.

Cerebrals:—ṭ ṭh ḍ ḍh ṇ.

(2) *t th d dh n.*

Dentals:—t th d dh n.

Labials:—p ph b bh m.

Semevowels:—y r l v.

Sibilants:—ś (2)*s* ṣ (2)sh s.

Aspirate:—h

Visarga:—h (2)*h*. Anusvaara ṃ (2)*m*. Vicarious cerebral (2)*l*.

TABLE No III.

Dravidian alphabets.

(Transliterated).

a ā i ī u ū r ṛ ḷ e ē ai o ō au;

Consonants:—gutturals as table 2 but pure Tamil has only the first and last letters e. g., k, ɯ.

Palatals, cerebrals, dentals, labials——do—

A hard cerebral r(r).

" 'dental' nasal n(n)*.

Telugu and Canarese have the full Sanskrit as well as Dravidian schemes combined lacking only*above.

The Si*m*halese alphabet is just the same as the Dravidian and Sanskrit combined. In modern Simhalese the vowels a in man etc., and consonants like f have been improvised.

---

*N. B. The nos. (1) and (2) refer to the two different schemes used. Other particulars are identical in both.

TABLE No. IV

The European alphabetical scheme. The most wayward is the English Scheme.

Vowels.	Consonants.	
	k, c, g, q.	Guttural.
a e i.	j, d, t, y.	Palatal.
	r.*	Cerebral.
	l, n.	Dental.
o u.	p, b, f, v, w, m,	Labial.
	h.	Aspirate.
	s, z.	Sibilants.
	x.	Conjunct.

But the above English scheme is only deceptive for each of these five vowels is only a symbol for innumerable sounds. For example the symbol a occurs in man, far, all, affect, alone, clear, etc., but the sound in each word is different. So also e does duty for a number of sounds as in, bet, we, uses, fete, etc., i and o each for several as in mind, thin, first, suite, not, bottom, stood, flood, ford; and finally u also represents a good many sounds, e. g., put, us, pure, etc.

TABLE No V.

The Avestic alphabetical scheme.

Vowels:—अ आ इ ई उ ऊ अॅ एॅ अ॒ ए ऑ ओ आ॒ आँ

Consonants: Guttural:—क् ख़् ग् ग़्

Palatals:—च् .... ज् ....

Dentals:—त् थ़् द् द़् त़्

Labials:—प् फ़् ब् व़्

Nasals:—ङ् ङ़् न् ∸ म्

Semivowels:—य् (य़्) र् व् (व़्)

Sibilants:—स् श् श़् ष़् ज़् ज़़्

Aspirates:—ह् ह़्

Conjunct:—ह्व़्

*This is a trilled barbarian sound, for, Dr. Keith Calls the Sanskrit cerebrals barbarian!

TABLE No VI.

The Sumerian alphabet.

Vowels:—a, e, i, u.

Consonants::—b, d, g, h, k, ḳ, l, m, n, p,r, s, s[1], s[2], t, ṭ, z.

(From "Sumerian Reading Book", Budge, p. 4.)

TABLE No VII.

Semitic Alphabetical Scheme.

Vowels:—a, u, i.

Consonants, Gutturals:—k. ḳ, kḥ, ḥ, ġ, a.

Palatals:—j, y.

Cerebrals:—ẓ, r.

Dental:s—t d ṭh ṭ l.

Labials:—p b m w f.

Sibilants:—s, sh, ṣ, ẓ z̤ ẕ.

The scheme shown in the fifth table is clearly taken from the Sanskrit Alphabet and added to. About the sixth scheme, viz., the Sumerian, full and trust-worthy records are lacking. The details given by European scholars are few and far between, besides, there seems to be something radically wrong in the method of deciphering the records since the things reported 'read out' are all very fanciful and exaggerated. The last or Semitic scheme given in table VII is based upon the Hebrew and Arabic alphabet. It is replete with gutturals and sibilants.

It will be clearly gathered from all these tables that only the first, the Vedic Sanskrit is the most scientific and must be the original. The haphazard arrangement of the letters in the recognised alphabets of the other languages is a sure indication of their being mere copies of the perfect Vedic arrangement. The hatred of vowels that is so prominent in the Semitic languages could not help the borrowers in hiding away the true nature of the worlds' best alphabetical system, for, after all, they have been compelled to place अ first. The revered Tiruva*ll*uva Naayanaar* has declared at the very commencement of his work that the alphabetical systems of all the languages begin with the hallowed letter अ, the first of the vowels, the symbol of God.

---

* Tirukkura*l* i, 1. Vide "Anthology of Vedic Hymns" p. 90.

The science of grammar of which Paanini was one of the earliest of propagators has achieved all that an advanced science could be expected to achieve. Had it not been for this great treatise the ancient Braahmanas of Aryan India might not have succeeded in preserving the Vedas in their pristine purity.

Ashtaadyayee is Vedic grammar

Paanini's Ash*ta*adhyayee is pre-eminently a Vedic grammar, for though he frequently refers to local usages yet he gives so much instruction on the special features of Vedic Sanskrit that there is no Vedic word which cannot be justified and explained on the basis of the Ash*ta*adhyaayee.

Some are inclined to think that Paa*n*ini's grammar principally deals with popular Sanskrit and only in a secondary manner or as an exception with the Vedic, but this view is not correct. The Vedic language and later Sanskrit being akin in formation though not with regard to the sense of many of their words, can be easily coupled together as far as derivation and formation of words is concerned. Being a direct descendant and heir to all the traditions of the Vedic, the classical Sanskrit retains the largest share of the Vedic formations. If it has deviated at all from its ancestor, it is only admitting very large compounds and strictly adhering to rules of euphony where particular letters collide. Excepting these two particulars, there are no other features of the classical Sanskrit which may not be found in the Vedic. In inflexions and conjugations the Vedic is more copious than later Sanskrit. In syntax also the latter is poorer.

Having in view all these points, Paa*n*ini thought it just and feasible to treat of both the languages in the same treatise. Had the languages differed in the essentials of their formation Paa*n*ini should have completely failed in his task.

The great service Paa*n*ini's grammar has rendered to the student of the Vedas consists in the infallible methods he has laid down to determine the derivation of words. The ancient list of verbs (dhaatupaa*t*ha) gives some 2000 Sanskrit roots from which all the words of the language are derived. In the old Nigha*nt*u commented upon by Yaaska in his Nirukta some peculiar Vedic roots also are given. A few more Vedic roots can be culled from the Vedic texts themselves. All these together form the assured field in which the Vedic student has to carry on his research. The Ash*t*aadhyaayee has also found out infallible principles according to which all nouns and adjectives can be declined.

The accent of Vedic words also comes within the sphere of grammar. Paa*n*ini has spared no pains in giving a full explanation of this very difficult theme in his admirable treatise. His aphorisms on the subject, if collected together, would form a good and complete thesis on the subject. In his treatment of Vedic accent Paanini makes full use of the 'Phi*t*' aphorisms of *S*aantanavaacarya on the accent of 'underived' and 'original' words.

Vedic accent is fully treated of by Paanini.

Vedic accent according to Paa*n*ini* is three-fold: acute, grave and circumflex; and prevails in all Vedic literature if one were to care to see. Its having been marked in the four original Vedic 'codes' and some other Vedic treatises, should not be considered to be an indication that accent is reserved only for the Vedas. No, this type of accent is natural to every 'natural' language and can be traced and determined with some effort.

In Vedic Sanskrit the accent is a 'regulation of the pitch' and concerns itself with the formation and meaning of a word. In ancient Greek also it seems to have been pitch accent. In Latin and modern European languages it is stress accent and has no 'graduation'. With the foolish neglect of the special and advanced study of Greek and Latin, the current languages of Europe have been evincing a tendency to get rid of the 'shackles' of even this last vestige of their contact with their great ancestor the Vedic Sanskrit. It may be noted *in passim* that the Semitic and Dravidian languages have no method of accentuation. They know only emphasis.

An illustration of how the principles laid down by Paa*n*ini regarding Vedic accent work will not be out of place here. In the first verse of the text, for example, we have the word नमस् which, though indeclinable, has the two elements in it clearly exposed to view, viz., root and termination √ नम्. and असुन्. In the ancient dhaatupaa*th*a this particular root is given as grave-accented and the termination असुन् by P. iii,1,2 आद्युदात्तश्च (i. e., 'the first vowel of a termination has the acute accent'), has the acute on its first vowel. Hence we have नम्+असुन्=नम्+अस् At this stage P. VI,1,197 ञ्नित्यादिर्नित्यम् ('when a termination having an indicatory ञ् or न् follows the initial vowel of the base will have the acute') applies and we have नम्+अस्, as P. VI, 1, 158 अनुदात्तं पदमेकवर्जं ('when in a word the acute or circumflex accent is ordained to a

* P. i, 2, 29-31 उच्चैरुदात्तः ॥ नीचैरनुदात्तः ॥ समाहार : स्वरितः ॥

particular vowel, all other vowels should be grave accented'), the अ of the termination becomes grave. Here intervenes P. VIII, 4,66 उदात्तादनुदात्तस्य स्वरितः ('the grave accent of a syllable coming after an acute accented one gives place to the circumflex') and transforms the grave of the termination to a circumflex and so we have नमः. The next word ते is grave accented by P. VIII, 1, 22 तेमयावेकवचनस्य. Here the accent determines the formation and meaning of the word ते. For, had the accent not been marked', it should not have been possible for us to find out easily whether this word is (1) the short form of the dative or genitive singular of the second personal pronoun युष्मद् or (2) the nominative plural masculine gender, or (3) the nominative or (4) accusative dual of the feminine gender or (5 and 6) of the neuter gender, of the third personal pronoune तद्. The latter is acute accented being formed as follows:— √तन्+अदि U. i, 132. Here the root as given in the dhaatupaa*th*a has the acute accent on its initial vowel and so has the termination. But P. vi, 1, 158 allows only one acute accent, and as the final syllable of तन् is dropped before the termination अदि which operates as if it had an indicatory ड्, the acute accent of the latter survives. When the dual or plural nominative or accusative terminations come up for application the accent of the word remains unaltered since these terminations are grave accented by P. iii, 1, 3 अनुदात्तौ सुप्पितौ ('all case terminations and all other terminations that have an indicatory प् are grave accented'). The verb अस्तु is all grave accented by P. viii, 1,28 तिङ्ङतिङः ('a fully formed verbal form coming after a fully formed non-verbal form is grave accented.') In the accentuation of the next word विद्युते the following elements are involved, viz., the prefix वि is acute by Phi*t* rule 81 उपसर्गाश्चाभिवर्जं ('all verbal prefixes [so named by P. 1, 4, 58 प्रादय उपसर्गाः क्रियायोगे i. e., the words प्र and others when they are syntactically connected with verbs are called 'upasarga'] excepting अभि have the accent on their initial syllable') and the root द्युत् also is acute accented in the dhaatupaa*th*a. But the noun-forming termination क्विप् added by P. iii, 2, 177 having an indicatory प् is grave accented by P. iii, 1, 4. Therefore we have वि+द्युत्+क्विप्=वि+द्युत्.* Here Phi*t* 1, फिषोऽन्त उदात्तः ('nominal bases, unless otherwise stated, have the acute accent on the final syllable') deprives the prefix of its natural acute accent in obedience

*This termination is invariably elided by the application of P. i, 3, 3, हलन्त्यम्; 2 उपदेशेऽजनुनासिक इत्: 8 लशक्वतद्धिते: 41 अपृक्त एकाल्-प्रत्ययः and vi, 1, 67 वेरपृक्तस्य.

to the rule अनुदात्तं पदमेकवर्जं P. vi, 1,158. In the next word स्तनयित्नवे the root स्तन् according to the dhaatupaa*t*ha is acute accented and the termination इत्नुच् having an indicatory च् occasions application of the rule चितः P. vi, 1, 163 ('that word which is formed by adding a termination with an indicatory च् will have the acute accent on its final syllable') and hence the word has only one acute accent (P. vi, 1, 158) and that on the last syllable. The accent of this word agrees also with Phi*t* 1. In अश्मने the root अश् is given acute accented in the dhaatupaa*t*ha and the termination मनिन् having an indicatory न् the word अश्मन् has acute on the initial syllable. The word येन follows Phi*t* 1. The word दूडाशे belongs to the पृषोदरादि group and is given with the acute accent on the second syllable. The final word अस्यसि is a verbal form and as such, should have been accented grave by P. viii, 1, 28 but 66 यद्वृत्तान्नित्यम् ('a verbal form directly or indirectly coming into contact with a word connected with the pronoun यत् or its derivative is not wholly grave accented') prevents this in-as-much-as अस्यसि is preceded by येन and दूडाशे. Therefore P. iii, 1, 8 determines that the word should have the acute on the initial syllable.

This elaborate process of accentuation according to formation and meaning does not exist in any other language. But it must be remembered that the accentuation should subserve the sense and not vice versa.

The Source of Vedic accent

The origin of Vedic accent is not traceable. A.v.xi,7,5 says that the Vedic accent has its source in the Most High God * (Ucchista Brahman). This may simply mean that the method of accentuation has been prevailent from the time of the earliest creation and has the same source as the concrete universe itself viz., the Providence of God. No sages or scholars, have, ever come forward to lay claim to this device. From the principles of accentuation laid down by Paanini in his grammar, by Saantanavaacaarya in his Phi*t* aphorisms and by the authors of the Praati*s*aakhyas it may safely be stated that accentuation is an inherent merit of the Vedic language. The very letters of its alphahet, if carefully seen, will be found to be accented.

A necessary implication of this process of accentuation is that the language which adopts it is necessarily an idiom composed of words derived from ultimate elementary roots.

---

* ऋक्साम यजुरुच्छिष्ट उद्गीथः प्रस्तुतं स्तुतं । हिङ्कार उच्छिष्टे स्वरः साम्नो मेडिश्च तन्मयि ॥ अ० ११ । ७ । ५ ॥

This scientific method of marking the accents in all words whether substantives, adjectives or verbs, declinables or indeclinables, simple or compound, can have no place in 'concocted' languages. An artificial speech does not require all such precautions to keep it intact. A language that goes on changing according to times can have nothing to do with such an elaborate process to hamper its growth! Artificial and developing languages lack those elements of stability that conduce to the preservation of the purity of vocables. Vedic Sanskrit, on the contrary, is primarily concerned with the preservation of its words as well as method of interpretation intact, hence, the Original Propagator of the Vedas Himself has provided this most excellent means to safeguard its integrity.

How far is Vedic accent dependable in determining the sense of Vedic Statements

A question now arises whether one is bound to adhere to the accent of Vedic words in explaining Vedic statements. This is a very important question and cannot be answered glibly or flippantly. As it has been pointed out above, the purpose of accentu-ation being to ascertain the meaning of words, it will not do to overlook it while explaining Vedic texts. Vedic scholars are heard remarking that there are statements in the Vedas which, if their accent were to be borne in mind, would either fetch something very obscene or absurd in return for the pains in trying to interpret them or would dwindle down to mere senseless jargon.

There is, no doubt, a way of interpreting other peoples' words which can yield all sorts of horrible 'innuendos', abuse, hatred, infidelity, irreligion, etc., to which partisans have often to take recourse to, to save themselves and their colleagues from harm or to advance their cause. In a world where such methods are the very staple of human dealings, it is but reasonable that we should carefully sift the evidence, before giving our verdict either way when Vedic interpretation is concerned. But it is extremely unjust and uncharitable to expect one to accept an ugly and unpalatable interpretation of a passage as sound, simply because the accent of its words seems to support it. Given that the method of accentuation is intended to clarify the sense of a passage it must help us to arrive at its true signification which, considering propriety, cannot but be good in the case of the Vedas.

Hence Yaaska and other ancient Vedic scholars have differed from *S*aakalya (whose accented word-text of the Vedas has come down to us) in interpreting certain texts where his pada-paa*t*ha hampered their procedure. Besides it must be remembered that though *S*aakalya's marked word text has come down to our own days and is accepted by all scholars, there are other works of the kind viz., the Saamapadapaa*t*ha of Gaargya and the Rәk padapaa*t*ha of Raava*n*a,* which, though less known, are yet a clear indication that scholars from the earliest days of Vedic exigesis have not been coolly allowing themselves to be led away into pitfalls of faulty methods pretending to be sound ones. The science of Vedic exigesis as taught in Yaaska's Nirukta has its *raison d'etre* in the improper† and impertinent interpretations of Vedic texts given by certain half-learned authors and the attacks made upon Vedic style by men like

Nirukti the science of Vedic exigeses

---

* रावणकृत पदपाठ शाकल्य के पदपाठ से कुछ भिन्न है। ऋ० २०। २७। २४ में मास्मैतादृक् का पदपाठ रावण ने मा, अस्मै, तादृक् पढ़ा है। यही पदपाठ उद्गीथने स्वीकार किया है, और यही दुर्गने निरुक्त ५। १६ के व्याख्यान में। ......ऋ० १०। १२६। १ में शाकल्य दो पद पढ़ता है—कुह, कस्य। इसके स्थान में रावण अपने भाष्य में लिखता है—कुहकस्यैन्द्रजालिकस्य—अर्थात्—रावण कुहकस्य एक पद मानता है। (See Bhagavaddatt's वैदिक वाड्मय का इतिहास Vol. i part 2 D. A. V. College, Lahore, p. 66.)

.........................सामवेद के पदपाठकारका नाम गार्ग्य था। सामवेद का पदपाठ दूसरे पदपाठों की अपेक्षा कुछ नूतनता रखता है। यह नूतनता अनेक पदों के कुछ अधिक तोड़ने में है। ....गार्ग्य का उल्लेख यास्क तीन वार करता है।...............ऋग्वेदके पदपाठ में विप्र पद में कोई अवग्रह नहीं। साम में वि, प्रासः ऐसा पदपाठ है। इसी प्रकार ऋग्वेद के पदपाठ में सूनृता पद में कोई अवग्रह नहीं। सामपदपाठ में सू, नृता है।..................गार्ग्य का नाम एक बार बृहद्देवता १। २६ में मिलता है।................एक गार्ग्य अष्टाध्यायी में तीन वार उद्धृत है॥ (Ibid. p. 153, 168-9.)

†Propriety in style forms the subject of a short but very important and difficult treatise by the famous Kashmirian poet Kshemendra named 'Aucityavicaaracarcaa'. At the very commencement of the work he says:—

किं तदौचित्यमित्याह—उचितं प्राहुराचार्याः सदृशं किल यस्य यत्। उचितस्य च यो भावस्तदौचित्यं प्रचक्षते॥ यत्किल यस्यानुरूपं तदुचितमुच्यते तस्य भावमौचित्यं कथयन्ति॥ अधुना सकलकाव्यशरीरजीवितभूतस्यौचित्यस्य प्राधान्येनोपलभ्यां स्थितिं दर्शयितुमाह—पदे वाक्ये प्रबन्धार्थे गुणेऽलंकरणे रसे। क्रियायां कारके लिङ्गे वचने च विशेषणे॥ उपसर्गे निपाते च काले देशे कुले व्रते। तत्वे सत्वे-

Kautsa. Yaaska mentions by name exactly a dozen* authorities on Vedic exigesis from which number it can be said that in ancient Aryan India Vedic scholarship was highly honoured and was considered to be the consummation of learning. Of these 13 Vedic exigetes including Yaaska only the last one is known to us. His work simply called 'Nirukta' is an interpretation of merely 2000 difficult and important words culled from the Vedas and arranged in a list called Nighantu. This work seems to be an ancient one, nay, even Yaaska's Nirukta is a redaction* of very ancient treatises on the subject.

ऽप्यभिप्राये स्वभावे सारसंग्रहे ॥ प्रतिभायामवस्थायां विचारे नाम्न्यथाशिषि । काव्यस्याङ्गेषु च प्राहुरौचित्यं व्यापिजीवितम् ॥ एतेषु पदप्रभृतिषु स्थानेषु मर्मस्विव काव्यस्य सकलशरीरव्यापि जीवितमौचित्यं स्फुटत्वेन स्फुरदवभासते ॥

This propriety of style ought to be recognised in Vedic poetry also and the process of interpretation directed accordingly.

*यास्क अपने निरुक्त में जिन प्राचीन आचार्यों को उद्धृत करता है, उन में से निम्नलिखित बारह निरुक्तकार प्रतीत होते हैं:—(१)औपमन्यव (२) औदुम्बरायण (३) वार्ष्यायणि (४) गार्ग्य (५) आग्रायण (६) शाकपूणि (७) और्णवाभ (८) तैटीकि (९) गालव (१०) स्थौलाष्ठीवि (११) क्रौष्टुकि (१२) कात्थक्य । तेरहवां निरुक्तकार यास्क स्वयं है । चौदहवां कौन था, यह अभी ज्ञात नहीं हो सका । संभव है वह शाकपूणि का पुत्र हो इस का उल्लेख निरुक्त १३ । ११ में मिलता है । इससे भी अधिक संभव है कि वह कौत्सव्य हो इसका निरुक्त निघंटु आथर्वण परिशिष्टों में से एक है ।....................नैरुक्तोंकी श्रेणी में यास्क सब से अन्तिम है । उसने उस सारी सामग्री से काम लिया है जो उस के पूर्वज उसके लिए छोड़ गये थे ॥ (Bhagavaddatt, op. cit. p. 162-3.)

*See for example what Yaaska himself has to say on this point:—

साक्षात्कृतधर्माण ऋषयो बभूवुस्तेऽवरेभ्योऽसाक्षात्कृतधर्मभ्य उपदेशेन मन्त्रान्संप्रादुरुपदेशाय ग्लायन्तोऽवरे बिल्मग्रहणायेमं ग्रन्थं समाम्नासिषुर्वेदं च वेदाङ्गानि च ।

Nir. i, 20, which seems to mean. "there were once enlightened persons who had visualised (fully understood and lived up to) the law of righteousness; they, through their teaching, laid bare the meaning of Vedic texts for such as were unable to understand the Vedas. Later on there came a time when people were unable to understand the Vedas even through these teachings of the ancient seers. For such people, later scholars compiled this Vedic dictionary (the Nighantu and Nirukta) so that they may, with some effort be able to grasp the meaning of Vedic texts," (From "Anthology of Vedic Hymns" p. 14.) It is obvious the passage can be rendered in a different way also. Skanda-Mahesvara's commentary on this is very important:—

एवमुक्तप्रयोजनस्य निरुक्तस्य परेणागमः कथ्यते । साक्षात्कृतधर्माण ऋषयो

From Yaaska's Nirukta it can be gathered that from time immemorial the science of Vedic exigesis has attracted the attention of the greatest of scholars. It is also a fact to be carefully noted that ancient Aryan scholars of India have spared no pains in interpreting the Vedas. Though different treatises on this important subject exposing different points of view in tackling with the question of Vedic interpretation have not come down to us, yet from what Yaaska sometimes cites as some other's opinion, it clearly follows that there were not less than half a dozen different schools of Vedic interpretation. Though we can call all of them 'Vedic exigesis' yet the term 'Nirukta' is reserved for a particular school only though its scope, considering the etymo-

The history and methods of Vedic exigesis.

बभूवुः । धर्मस्यातीन्द्रियत्वात् साक्षात्करणस्यासम्भवात् धर्मशब्देनात्र तदर्थं मन्त्रब्राह्मणमुच्यते, तत्साक्षात्कृतो धर्मो यैस्ते साक्षात्कृतधर्माण ऋषयः । कथं पुनस्तैः साक्षात्कृतम् ? उच्यते, स्मृतिकारैरैतिहासिकैश्चाभ्युपगतत्वाच्छ्रुत्या चाविरोधादन्तरालप्रलयः पुनः सृष्टिश्चास्ति । तत्र सृष्ट्यादौ य ऋषयस्तेऽतीतसृष्टावधीतं सुप्तप्रतिबुद्धन्यायेन मन्त्रब्राह्मणं स्मरन्ति । कश्चित्किञ्चिद्यो यत्स्मरति तत्तेन दृष्टं तेन साक्षात्कृतं तेन प्रोक्तं तस्यार्षमिति चोच्यते । यस्य यावदार्षं तेन तावदेव साक्षात्कृतम्, अन्यत्तु तेनापि यत्साक्षान्न कृतं तदुपदेशेनैवाधिगतम् । न च जन्मान्तरानुभूतं नियमेन न स्मर्यते, दृश्यन्ते ह्यद्यत्वेऽपि जातिस्मराः किञ्चित्स्मरन्तः । ते चर्षयो यद्यपि प्रतिसृष्ट्यन्येऽन्य उत्पद्यन्ते, तथाप्यतीतसृष्टिकृतपुण्यविशेषवशात्तत्कर्माणस्तन्नामानश्चोत्पद्यन्ते । तेनैकस्यां सृष्टौ विश्वामित्रनाम्ना यत्स्मृतं सृष्ट्यन्तरेऽपि विश्वामित्रनामैव तत्स्मरति । अतो नित्यत्वेऽपि वेदस्य नार्षव्यपदेशस्य नापि साक्षात्करणस्य कश्चिद्विरोधः, एतदभिप्रेत्यैतदुच्यते—साक्षात्कृतधर्माण ऋषयो बभूवुः इति । तेऽवरेभ्योऽवरकालीनेभ्यः शक्तिहीनेभ्योऽतीतसृष्टिकृतपुण्यविशेषाभावात्, शक्तिभारैः असाक्षात्कृतधर्मभ्य उपदेशेन शिष्योपाध्यायिकया वृत्या मन्त्रान् ग्रन्थतोऽर्थतश्च संप्रादुः । तेषु हि पूर्वसृष्टावधीतेषु तेषामुपदेशमात्रेणैव स्मृतिर्बभूव, यथेदानीं छन्दो नष्टं गणयतः कस्यचित् । मन्त्रग्रहणं चात्र ब्राह्मणानां प्रदर्शनार्थम्, मन्त्रान् ब्राह्मणानीति संप्रादुः । उपदेशाय ग्लायंतोऽवरे तेष्ववरतमेभ्य उपदेशायोपदेशार्थं ग्लायन्तो 'ग्लै म्लै हर्षक्षये' उपदेशमात्रेण ग्रहीतुमशक्नुवन्तस्तदनुकम्पया क्षीयमाणहर्षास्ताननुकम्पमाना इत्यर्थः । बिल्मग्रहणाय, बिल्म उपायः, तेन ग्रन्थस्य चार्थस्य च ग्रहणार्थम्, ग्रन्थस्य ग्रहणोपायोऽष्टसंधकेन दशसंधकेन वा, ग्रहणमध्ययनमर्थस्योपाध्यायात्पुनः पुनः श्रवणम् । वेदाङ्गज्ञानं च इमं ग्रन्थं समाम्नासिषुः, वेदं च वेदाङ्गानि च । यद्यस्य साक्षात्कृतधर्मण आर्षं तत् तस्मादुपश्रुत्य कृत्स्नं वेदं ग्रन्थग्रहणार्थं समाम्नातवन्तः, अर्थग्रहणार्थं वेदांगानीत्यत एवोपश्रुत्य स्वयं च कल्पयित्वा निरुक्तं च वेदाङ्गम् । तदेवमागमिकस्येदमागमकथनम् । ये तु सृष्टिप्रलयौ नेच्छन्ति, त एतं ग्रन्थमेवं व्याचक्षते—साक्षाद्धर्मवचनोपदेशनिरपेक्षं कृतः प्रतिपन्नो धर्मो यैस्ते साक्षात्कृतधर्माण ऋषयो बभूवुः,

logy of the term (nir + √ vac to explain), can very accurately include all of them. The following methods or schools of Vedic interpretation must have had separate recognition in ancient Aryan India:—

The Nairukta or philological method.

(1) *The nairukta*. This method was pre-eminently philological as in its attempt to interpret Vedic words it invariably insisted upon enquiring into the origins of Vedic speech. This was the most fastidious, thorough-going and perfectly critical method. It has come down to us in Yaaska's Nirukta and is known to consist in a full enquiry into the etymology and history of words and expressions it has to interpret. In Vedic interpretation this is the only faultless and at the same time intelligible method.

The Aitihaasika or historical method.

(2) ***The historical method.*** This is the aitihaasika method as Yaaska calls it. It consisted in elucidating a Vedic passage by referring to particular events in known history. The names of kings and great men in India have, from the earliest ages, conformed to Vedic words. It has never been difficult therefore to find some king, or wise man having a name occurring in one of the four Vedas and their innumerable schools. Hence it was easy for teachers to refer to events in the lives of such men to illustrate and explain Vedic statements. In course of time, however, this method lost its force as, people were thereby, often led astray into attaching greater importance to the historical illustration

---

तेऽवरेभ्योऽसाक्षात्कृतधर्मभ्यो वेदवचनादेवोपदेशनिरपेक्षं धर्मं प्रतिपत्तुमसमर्थेभ्य- इत्यर्थः । उपदेशेन चार्थस्य मन्त्रान् ब्राह्मणानि च संप्रादुः । अस्य मन्त्रस्यायमस्य चायमित्येवमुपदेशेन मन्त्रार्थं ब्राह्मणार्थं च कथितवन्त इत्यर्थः । उपदेशाय ग्लायन्तोऽवरे, ये तु ततोऽप्यवरे वेदवचनात्स्वयमुपदेशमात्रेण वा तदर्थं प्रतिपत्तुमसमर्थास्त आत्मन उपदेशार्थं समाम्नातस्य सत उपाध्याया अर्थमुपदेक्ष्यन्ति, उपदिष्टार्थात्ततो वेदार्थं प्रतिपत्स्यामह इत्येवमर्थमित्यर्थः । इमं ग्रन्थं गवादि देवपत्न्यन्तं समाम्नातवन्तः, वेदं धर्मप्रतिपत्त्यर्थम्, वेदाङ्गानि च अन्यान्यपि वेदार्थप्रतिपत्त्यर्थम् । बिल्मग्रहणाय—बिल्म उपायः ॥

The bit "imam grantham sampraaduh" means that Yaaska counts himself among those who have, from time immemorial helped in the propagation of these principles of Vedic exigesis. It does not at all mean that this particular treatise (in which the passage quoted at the outset occurs) was written by a number of scholars including Yaaska ! !

than to the Vedic truth itself. The Saaya*n*ic commentator has made use of the first as well as this method.

(3) *The mythological.* It was not possible to find historical examples for every possible Vedic statement, hence to make up for the deficiency, scholars were often led to refer to folklore or to invent stories to exemplify Vedic truths. The available "grand-mothers' tales" or "old wive's fables" as they might be called, were collected together and utilised from time to time to explain Vedic statements to the commonalty. Like the historical, this method was very attractive and appealing, but it was more advantageous as it hardly left any Vedic statement unillustrated. Besides it was quite easy to frame a tale just at the nick of time to explain things to the audience. Yaaska calls this also 'itihaasa'. Whenever he criticises these or other methods which seem faulty to him, he uses language that very often savours of assent, but it is not so; he is really criticising the advocates of mythology but his style is so charming and gentle that he often seems to agree with his opponents.

The Mythological method

(4) *The scientific.* After the nairukta method this is the most difficult. It consists in identifying Vedic truths with natural phenomena and explaining them as physical-scientific truths. This method though difficult and abstruse is very frequently resorted to by all scholars as in many cases it is the only process that yields the right meaning. Besides there are certain portions in the Vedas which clearly treat of scientific truths.

The Scientific method

(5) *The esoteric or intuitional.* This is an extremely abstract and abstruse method of interpretation and is possible only for those who are given to Yogic spiritual discipline. It deals with God, the soul, and the human body taking account of the 'outside' world only as an external phenomenon. Yaaska uses this method in the fourteenth chapter of his book. There are some Vedic texts which cannot be explained in any other way but this, e.g., R. V. x, 119. When other methods are employed they yield faulty results.

The Esoteric or Intuitional method

(6) *The ritualistic method.* Perhaps this is the easiest and the most direct way of interpreting Vedic texts. A Vedic passage, for example, embodies a scientific truth or a prayer to God, but at the time of the child's tonsure it is used with reference to the barbar or the razor. Here in interpreting the statement it may be supposed, for the time being, to concern only with the barbar or the razor, and the vocative, if any, rendered accordingly.

The Ritualistic method

Of all these methods, it will be seen at a glance, the 2nd historical, the 3rd mythological and the 6th ritualistic are only shabby time-serving devices and cannot be depended upon. They are, at best, rough processes intended to bring home to the less deliberative, Vedic truths in tentative and attractive, though not enduring and correct forms. The Saaya*n*ic* commentator has committed a great fault in utilising these methods in season and out of season to explain the texts of the Rəgveda.

The Etymological or Derivative method of Vedic interpretion

The first and most important method of Vedic interpretation, viz., the nairukta, includes in itself the so-called etymological or derivative method as opposed to the conventional. It is called in Sanskrit by some, यौगिक† (from √ युज् to join), and the latter in contradistinction with this, रूढ (from √ रुह् to grow). This is no novel process but simply a legitimate application of

---

*It is a mistake to speak of certain books as the work of Saaya*n*a. He was not the author of all the works that go under his *nom de plume*. The following occurs on p. 24 of the introduction to the Mahaabhaashya by Mahaamahopaadhyaaya P. *S*ivadatta *S*aastri Kudaal :—

ततश्च श्रीविष्णुसर्वज्ञ-शङ्करानन्दशिष्यो रामकृष्णस्य गुरुः सायणगोत्रः, मायणपुत्रो माधवः विद्यानगरीय (विजयनगरीय) बुक्कस्य तदुत्तराधिकारिहरिहरस्य चामात्यतायां चकार कारयामास च पण्डितप्रकाण्डैर्ग्रन्थान् ॥ On this the following footnote is given:—बहुभिः पण्डितप्रकाण्डैर्जीविकालोभेन ग्रन्थान् निर्माय माधवीयत्वेन ख्यातिं नीताः । यथा हि :—

तेन मायणपुत्रेण सायणेन मनीषिणा ।
आख्यया माधवीयेयं धातुवृत्तिर्विरच्यते ॥
तत्कटाक्षेण तद्रूपं दधद्बुक्कमहीपतिः ।
आदिशन्माधवाचार्यं वेदार्थस्य प्रकाशने ॥
स प्राह नृपतिं राजन् सायणार्यो ममानुजः ।
सर्वं वेत्त्येष वेदानां व्याख्यातृत्वे नियुज्यताम् ॥
इत्युक्तो माधवार्येण वीरबुक्कमहीपतिः ।
अन्वशात्सायणाचार्यं वेदार्थस्य प्रकाशने ॥

He then mentions the names of 103 works! All these could not have been written by Saayana, especially when we know that the commentary on the Rəgveda itself can be a man's life-work.

† The glib and absurd writer in the "Illustrated Weekly of India" in his article dated 22nd September 1935 makes a very thoughtless and puerile reference to this. His words are: "Among the old Pandit class there is a belief that Vedic Sanskrit contains an

the nairukta method itself. Its justification lies in the nature of the Vedic language itself, which unlike any other living or dead language, insists upon analysing all its vocables to ultimate roots consisting of pure vowels, or a vowel and one or more consonants enclosing, following or preceding

---

enormous number of yaugika words, i. e, words, the meaning of which has nothing to do with the current accepted meanings of those words. *Hitherto the only chance of ascertaining their meaning was to look up to the grammar of Panini and the old Dhaatupaatha, and then make conjectures. This has now proved to be a dangerous weapon. The school of the Arya-Samajists have found out a new method of interpretation by which they show that the Vedas contain all the knowledge of the world."*

With regard to his ridiculing the 'old Pandit class' the following extract from his Hindi edition of 'Kau*t*ilya Arthasaastra' will be enough:—

गुरुकुल कांगड़ी में पन्द्रह वर्ष तक संस्कृत पढ़ने के कारण लेखक इस काम को हाथ में लेने के लिये योग्य हो सका।............अर्थशास्त्र सम्बन्धी महत्वपूर्ण बारह ग्रन्थों के लिखने के बाद लेखक ने जर्मनी इङ्गलैण्ड आदि देशों में जाकर विशेष अध्ययन करने के लिये उद्योग किया। इस उद्योग में श्री पूज्य डाक्टर प्राणजीवन महता तथा घनश्यामदास जी बिरला की उदारता ने बड़ी भारी सहायता पहुंचाई। इधर मोतीलाल बनारसीदास के सत्यपूर्ण व्यवहार ने कौटिल्य अर्थशास्त्र की हिन्दी भाषान्तर रूपी मेरी अभिलाषा को पूर्ण कर दिया। हिन्दी पाठकों की अब तक मैंने जो सेवा की है, वह इतनी अपर्याप्त तथा तुच्छ है कि मैंने योरुप प्रस्थान् के लिये तैय्यारी की और इसीलिये मातृभाषा के अर्थशास्त्र सम्बन्धी साहित्य को किसी तरह पूरा कर सकूं। इसी ग्रन्थ की समाप्ति के साथ ही मैं मातृभूमि तथा हिन्दी पाठकों से पांच साल के लिये विदाई मांगता हूं। (Preface p. 2 dated 1st March 1923).

This product of the 'old Pandits,' and the Arya Samaj, having visited European universities at the expense of some generous millionaires has come back to India with two fat degrees the sign of his having discarded all old ideas! The education he received at an Arya Samajic institution mainly at the expense of the half-starved Indian peasant-proletariat, consummated with his visit to European universities, has equipped him with such infallible knowledge that he can now work miracles! He says "hitherto the only chance..................to look up to the grammar of Panini and the old Dhaatupaatha, and then make conjectures". This is an audacious and insulting statement and extremely silly at the same time. His repetition of the word 'old' is an unpardonable affront. If a reference to Paanini's grammar and the Dhaatupaatha is necessitated to justify a particular formation, there can be no conjecture at all. A conjecture is 'a guess', a piece of 'imperfect knowledge' and as such can have

it. The huge apparatus of primitive and secondary terminations as well as the methods of compounding substantives among themselves or with adjectives and even verbs to yield new vocables, are clear features of the Vedic Sanskrit pointing out unmistakably that it is an analytical language.

It has been proved already that the Vedic language is the primitive speech of humanity. As such it cannot but be analytical. When humanity began its career, there was no convention to settle the sense of vocables according to prevalent usage. The language had roots and terminations which joined together yielded the exact word required to name something or to express some idea according to its nature. All words were, therefore, derivative. This is the 'differentia' of the Vedic language and according to this it can yield its true meaning only to the nairukta or derivative method.

---

nothing to support and justify it. This 'buffoonish' writer perhaps means that the 'old Pandits' first fix upon what construction to put upon a word and then call in the Ash*t*aadhyaayee and Dhaatupaa*t*ha to support it. Is it possible to do so? What really happens is this: The writer or lecturer, whoever he may be, takes a Vedic passage and sets about to study it. His guides in the task are a dictionary (probably the Nirukta of Yaaska) and the Ash*t*aadhyaayee of Paa*n*ini with the help of which books he rectifies his understanding of the passage and thus tries to make out what it means. Is this guessing? To break up vatoori*n*aa padaa once into Vat+U+Ur+Inaa+padaa and then again into Vatur+Inaa+padaa and render that one expression in two different ways in the same sentence; to identify the Taantric 'ai*m*' with Sumerian 'En;' to squeeze 'Babylonians' out of the Vedic 'abhivlagya'; these capers, surely, are super-somersaults of a literary buffoon and no guesses at all!! He further complains that 'this has now proved to be a dangerous weapon', but why should it? Just because it beats the literary juggler with his Europeanised mind hollow exposing his silly tricks to the whole world? Why should it prove dangerous to explain Vedic words with the aid of the Ash*t*aadhyaayee and the Dhaatupaat*t*ha? If this is really dangerous as this doctor of two European universities bumptiously declares, steps ought to be taken to ban all use of grammars and dictionaries in all schools and colleges all the world over. It cannot be that only the 'old' Sanskrit grammar is dangerous. Who knows; 'doctors' know better! Perhaps Macdonell's 'Sodom-apple' of a Vedic grammar may not be dangerous! He then blurts out "The School of Arya Samajists have found out a new method of interpretation by which they show that the Vedas contain *all the knowledge of the world.*" If the basic truths of the key sciences, and an accurate account of the principal natural phenomena can be the foundation of all 'scientific advance,' then surely the Vedic scholars from Yaaska down to Dayaananda Sarasvatee should be thanked for pointing them out in the Vedas. The fortuitous dragging in of the name of the Arya Samajists exposes the hollowness of the critic's European scholarship.

The analytical or derivative method of interpretation has been utilised by all scholars as can be easily found out by a reference to the various commentaries on the Vedas. The late Vedic scholar Maharshi Dayaananda Sarasvatee was not its inventor but discoverer if we may say so. He followed in the footsteps of the great ancient sage Yaaska, who himself adopted the exigetical methods of the Braahma*n*as. But Dayaananda flourished at a time when Vedic scholarship was conspicuous by its absence. When he attempted to bring about a religious and social revival based upon the pure teaching of the Vedas—pre-eminently the heritage of Aryan India there were few who could really understand him. "The proudest among our forefathers bowed their head before two and two alone, namely, the Almighty Father and His word. And, well did the great Swami Dayananda Sarasvati—that giant among men and peerless embodiment of the Vedic life and thought turn our face once more towards the selfsame source of light and strength in order that we may become fit for passing successfully as a nation through the tough trial that is confronting us today".*

Dayananda revived the Nairukta Method.

Quite true, the Vedas have always been the cause of great movements in India. Religious and social reformers of the sincere type, even political leaders have, till very recently, felt drawn towards these hallowed repositories of wisdom to breathe inspiration therefrom to sustain them in their struggle. But when Dayananda proclaimed his message of the Vedas he was not understood aright. His revival of the nairukta or derivative method of interpretation of the Vedas people took for a revolution under cover. They thought that the saadhu was simply trying to impose upon them and drag them into the net of Christianity or piay some such mean trick upon them, and that for this unhallowed purpose of his, he found the Vedas quite handy. The suspicion was so deep-rooted and general that even today even the very admirers of Dayananda are infected with it. The serious-minded scholar whose remarks have been quoted above has found it necessary to make pointed reference to Dayananda's interpretation of certain Vedic words. To clear Dayananda's position is to support the nairukta and Braahma*n*a method of interpreting the Vedas——the only right method.

The scholar referred to above in his work mentioned

* From "A Complete Etymological Dictionary of the Vedic Language", Visvabandhu, Lahore, Introduction p. vii *ll.* 32—38.

already raises a number of queries on Dayaananda's interpretation of certain Vedic words. Serietim they are given below with their answers:—(1) amsa Y. V. x. 5 of which the interpretation by Dayaananda is 'paramaanuroopo bhaagah;' (2) Y, V. xxxiv, 54 'vibhaajakah;' (3) R. V. ii, 27, 1 'samyagghaatakah' and (4) ii, 1, 4 'prerakah'. In this collection the first interpretation 'para maanuroopo bhaagah' i. e., 'a part in the shape of an atom or electron' is quite correct and need not be questioned. 'Amsa'- 'part' may be anything from $\frac{999}{1000}$ to $\frac{1}{100000}$ i. e., a shade less than 'unit' to an infinitesimal particle of it! The explanation may vary between these two limits and to restrict it, it will be unjust. The second interpretation also is quite in keeping with the text. The termination added to the root 'ams' here may be ac, ghau, gha, na, etc., in the sense of the agent etc. The Vedic language being 'primitive' the explanation of such words would depend upon the roots and terminations of which they are composed and the special influence exerted upon them by other words near by in the context. In odinary Sanskrit also such words are met with now and then. For example 'jeeva' means both 'life' and 'that which possesses life'. The third interpetation refers to 'destruction through disintegration' and the fourth to 'division and allotment'. It is by 'dividing' all the 'goods' of the universe by His Providence and 'allotting' them to creatures according to their deserts that He can make all enjoy or suffer. (5) The next word 'amsu' is formed by appending the Unaadi termination 'u' to the root 'ams' according to U. ii, 7 and the Unaadi terminations can be applied in the sense of any case termination (vide pp. xx & xxi above), and in the sense either of the present or past (see p. xvi above). (6) In R. V. iv, 34, 9 the adjectives all agree with the word 'asvinaa' which naturally is in the nominative dual. Hence according to P. vii, 1, 39 'amsatraa', 'rəbhavah' etc., can all be taken to be in the nominative dual. (7) The root 'am' means 'to afflict with pain' or 'to go, sound, eat,' physically or merely metaphorically. To this, the termination 'asun' (U. iv, 189) and the augment 'huk' (U. iv, 220) are added and the form 'amhas' (Vide R. V. i, 42, 1; Y. V. vii, 30) got. (8) So also by appending to it the termination 'u' by U. ii, 7 we have 'amhu' both of which may mean the 'heat' or 'force' of quickness, 'motion,' 'knowledge,' etc. The sense will have to be decided according to the context. (9) The root 'ku' or 'koo' means 'to sound'. When articulate sound is produced by the vocal organs, for example, it will either be praiseworthy or blameworthy. Hence expressions like 'akava' (R. V. vi, 33, 4) akavaari' (Y. V.

P. Visvabandhu's queries.

vii, 36) etc., will have two contrary imports according to the context. (10) In R, V. i, 53, 2 the word 'akaamakarsanah' is explained by Dayaananda to mean "he who reduces or supplants those that have no 'kaama' or righteous ambition". The idea is beautiful and quite in keeping with the spirit of the passage.

In all the above cases we have an example of Svaami Dayaananda's style of Vedic interpretation. A staunch follower of Yaaska's nairukta or derivative method, he first examines the context, then analyses the expression to be explained and proceeds with his task of interpetation supplying such links as are needed to adapt the passage for paraphrasing. In this process he always has an eye on the exigencies of grammar and gives special heed to accent. Lastly he never loses sight of the logical sequence or contact of the several elements of the passage on hand. These are the essential features of Maharshi Dayaananda's style of interpretation and they are simply unassailable. The Vedas are highly poetical and to understand them one has to live and think as they teach, like Dayananda.

"The true poet does, I believe, of necessity, see the infinite in his subject; and he so presents his vision to his readers that they too, if their eyes are open, are enabled in some degree to share in its lessons.

The same gift belongs in a certain degree to the artist. But the range of the poet is unlimited; while the artist's choice of subject is conditioned by the requirement that its treatment shall come within the dominion of the beatiful.

The ground of this difference obviously lies in the different means which the poet and the artist use to express what they see with the eye of the soul. The mode in which words and the melody of words (not now to speak of music) affect us is different in kind from the action of form and colour.

All life, all nature, is therefore the legitimate field of the poet, as prophet. There is an infinite, an eternal meaning in all, and it is his office to make this intelligible to his students.

Our knowlege is inevitably partial in regard of the object and of the subject and of the conditions of its acquisition. In each respect an infinite mystery enwraps a little spot of light.

It requires a serious effort to enter with a living sympathy into the character of another man, or of another class, or of another nation, or of another

PLATE III

The so-called sectarian symbols in use in India and elsewhere.

Numbers 2-6 are some of the so-called caste-marks used by different Hindu 'sects' of India. No. 9 is the Dravidian symbol for ॐ. See p. Clvii.

(To face p. clvii.)

course of thought; to feel, not with a sense of gracious superiority, but of devout thankfulness, that here and here that is supplied which we could not have provided: to acknowledge how peculiar gifts or a peculiar environment, how long discipline or an intense struggle, have conferred upon others the power of seeing that which we can not see."*

Sanskrit Script

It has been proved above that the Aryans of India knew the art of writing from the most ancient times. The earliest mode of writing must have been something like the so-called 'Braahmee' script. The modern Naagaree script is a direct descendent of the ancient script, is very scientific—perfect, we may say, for it is quite adaptable. With a dot below some of its consonants and a stroke above some of its vowels, its symbols can very well represent the sounds of any language on this side of the grave.

There is one very ancient symbol in this script viz., ॐ, which is quite universal and has given rise to the ancient Crescent and Star of Arabia, the Svastikaa, the Cross and all the Caste Marks which the Hindu sects of India draw on their foreheads. These latter, really very significant and edifying symbols, have, by followers of Semitic creeds, been grossly misrepresented. The three lined symbols Nos. 2 & 3 in the plate opposite, are signs of the Vedic Trinity as manifestation of God's Providence. A single line used by some sects and a point by others are signs of the unity and perfection of God. The Crescent or the Crescent and the Point, (see Nos. 11 & 10) the three broad horizontal lines with or without a point in the middle (Nos. 5 & 6) are all modelled after the sacred symbol ॐ, and are simply representations of God, intended to remind the person using them that he or she is always and everywhere seen by his or her Maker. They are very useful as means to prevail upon a person to perform his or her devotional exercises and deal fairly with others. They also serve to point out to what sect a person belongs. If they have dwindled down to sectarian marks it is not their fault, to be sure, but the gross misrepresentation to which they have been subjected by Semitic religions is more than criminal. (See also the frontispiece.)

---

* From "Thoughts on Life and Revelation" by Brooks Foss Westcott p. 291 ll. 1-14.

With regard to Sumerian writing this is what Wells thinks of the cuneiform script:—

"The Sumerian picture-writing, which had to be done upon clay, and with little styles which made curved marks with difficulty and inaccurately, rapidly degenerated by a conventionalised dabbing down of wedge-shaped marks (cuneiform—wedge-shaped) into almost unrecognizable hints of the shapes intended. It helped the Sumerians greatly to learn to write, that they had to draw so badly. They got very soon to the Chinese pictographs ideographs, and phonograms, and beyond them.

Most people know a sort of puzzle called a rebus. It is a way of representing words to pictures, not of the things having a similar sound. For example, two gates and a head is a rebus for Gates-head; a little streamlet (beck), a crowned monarch, and a ham, Beckingham. The Sumerian language was a language well adapted to this sort of representation. It was accurately a language of often quite vast polysyllables, made up of very distinct inalterable syllables; and many of the syllables taken separately were the names of concrete things...

When presently the semites conquered Sumeria, they adopted the syllabic system to their own speech, and so this writing became entirely a sign-for-a-sound writing. It was so used by the Assyrians and by the Chaldeans. But it was not a letter-writing, it was a syllable-writing. This cuneiform script prevailed for long ages over Assyria, Babylonia and the Near East generally; its survival is evident in several of the letters of our alphabet to-day."*

The above is the type of the various fortuitous views of Europeans. The Sumerian writing is a clever contrivance to conserve and hide from the general public certain important matters. It was the invention of people who knew other modes of writing. An inscription of the king Dushratta who was a contemporary of the Sumerians is in a different script.

---

* "The New Outline of History" p. 202. Budge thinks that "——they (the Sumerians) were apparently the first race of mankind to succeed in giving permanent form to their thoughts by the invention of writing,"...the invention of such writing might with some probability be assigned to the period between 3500 and 3000 B. C. (From "Sumerian Reading Book" pp. 7 & 8). The Sumerian language and script were in use till the time of Alexander the Great.

CHAPTER IV.

VEDIC DOCTRINES AND SEERS.

The Naasadeeya hymn, R. V. x, 129 which forms the subject of the fifth chapter of the text treats of the Ultimate Realities, viz; the Supreme Being, the Soul and the Primordial Matter. It is a very difficult and terse text but at the same time clear, direct and definite. The following passage from the pen of one of the leading scientists of Europe will show how differently the European thinks:—

The Ultimate Realities

"Or it may be that no such substantial or material dress will ever be found, and that our knowledge of the universe will for ever remain similar in kind to our present knowledge, a knowledge of our perceptions expressed as a group of mathematical formulae stamped with the stamp of the pure mathematician —the kind of formulae which result from the operation of thought working within its own sphere. In such an event, there may or may not be a non-mental reality behind the form; if there is, it will be beyond our scientific capacity to imagine.

Sir James Jeans no sure of the Ultimate Reality

All these possibitities are in the field, since all refer to the future and the unknown. Our positive knowledge of the road along which science is travelling is confined to that which lies behind it. We can not say how much farther, if at all the road extends in front, or what the far end of it is like; at best we can only guess.

Some may think that the most plausible conjecture is that the end of the road will be like what is at the halfway house, or perhaps more so. We have already described recent progress in physical science as resulting from a continuous emancipation from the purely human point of view. Our last impression of nature, before we began to take our human spectacles off, was of an ocean of mechanism surrounding us on all sides. As we gradually discard our spectacles, we see mechanical concepts continually giving place to mental. If from the nature of things we can never discard them entirely, we may yet conjecture that the effect of doing so would be the total disappearance of matter and mechanism, mind reigning supreme and alone.

Others may think it more likely that the pendulum will swing back in time.

Broadly speaking, the two conjectures are those of the idealist and realist—or, if we prefer, the mentalist and materialist—views of nature. So far the pendulum shews no signs of swinging back, and the law and order which we find in the universe are most easily described—and also, I think, most easily explained—in the language of idealism. Thus, subject to the reservations already mentioned, we may say that present day science is favourable to idealism. In brief, idealism has always maintained that, as the beginning of the road by which we explore nature is mental, the chances are that the end also will be mental. To this, present day science adds that, at the farthest point she has so far reached, much and possibly all, that was not mental has disappeared, and nothing new has come in that is not mental. Yet who shall say what may find awaiting us round the next corner?"*

It is possible by some means to have a vision of subtle matter, e. g., ether. It is possible Western science may succeed in devising some means, an instrument for example, which may aid man's eyesight to catch a glimpse of the waves of ether, but to think that the ultimate atoms of matter, the mind, the soul and the Supreme Being might be 'visualised' by physical means, is absurd.

"'I desire any one', says Berkeley,' to reflect and try whether he can, by any abstraction of thought, conceive the extension and motion of a body, without all other sensible qualities. For my own part, I see evidently that it is not in my power to frame an idea of a body extended and moved, but I must withal give it some colour or other sensible qualities.........In short, extension, figure, and motion, abstracted from all other qualities, are inconceivable'.

*From "The Background of Science" by Sir James Jeans M. A., D. Sc., Sc. D., LL. D., F. R. S., p. 297. l. 19.—p. 298. l. 22. (T)—E. D.

Taking for granted that all other qualities only qualify sense, and therefore can exist in the mind alone, Berkeley cogently infers that the same must be true of extension, figure and motion. For us this reasoning has to be reversed. The primary qualities being physically real, it follows that the secondary must be so as well. It also follows that throughout the physical world the primary qualities are, by their intrinsic nature, so inseparable in existence from the secondary that they can not have the mutual independence which is presupposed in interaction. They are only distinguishable as abstract aspects of one concrete fact. In the course of natural process they may vary concomitantly but do not causally determine each other. The objective value of what perceptually appears as 'red colour' is a secondary quality of the physical object, inseparable from the reflection of light in certain wave-lengths. The physicist has no means of determining with sufficient precision what such qualities are, so as to connect them and their changes with each other in a coherent system. Hence he subsitutes for them their equivalent in terms of the primary qualities, and reserves for these alone the title of 'objective'."*

Some qualities are inferred to be real from the presence of others.

Qualities and properties of matter are real but it is impossible to 'locate' them and inspect their shape, size and colour if any. 'Atomic' matter also is a very great reality but man has not the power to 'visualise' atoms. Every moment of our life we see extended gross matter—a conglomeration of millions of atoms, but to see each of them separately is beyond our power or means.

"The atom cannot be observed; it is too small. Its existence is inferred from the events which take place in its neighbourhood, which events it is said to cause. Now, so long as the atom remains in a constant state, it has no external effects and its existence cannot, therefore be inferred. It is only when an electronic jump occurs, when, that is to say, the atom either absorbs or radiates energy, or when the atom changes in some other way that we know of its existence.

The existence of the Atom is inferred and not directly perceived.

Let us suppose that, as a result of the movement of an electron from an outer to an inner orbit, the atom radiates energy.

*From "Mind and Matter" by G. F. Stout M. A., LL. D., D. Litt p. 278. l. 28—p. 289. l. 21.

A series of events will travel outward from the atom like ripples in a pool, which will sooner or later impinge upon objects in their environment producing effects in these objects. These effects in the environment may be observed, and if they are, we infer that an atom of a certain sort which is giving out energy is responsible for the phenomena observed. Thus we infer the existence of the atom from the effects which it produces, when it changes, in the surrounding neighbourhood. To use a convenient simile of Earl Russell's, let us suppose that a ticket collector is permanently on duty at the exit of the station of a particular town. What will be the nature of his knowledge of the town's population? In the first place, he will only know something about the population when it changes, that is, when somebody enters the town or leaves it. In the second, he will not be aware of these changes where they originally take place, that is in the town itself, but only of the effects of the changes when they manifest themselves at the station. Our knowledge of the atoms is of a similarly indirect kind. All that we are really entitled to say is not that we know atoms, but that events in a certain neighbourhood are such as are compatible with and can be calculated on the assumption that there is an electric charge of a certain magnitude in the middle of the neighbourhood. Energy, in fact, spreads outwards from a particular centre. We may, if we like, conceive that there is an arrangement of electrons and protons there which is the source of the energy of radiation. But the conception is by no means necessitated. 'The idea that there is a hard lump there, which is the electron or proton, is an illegitimate intrusion of common-sense notions derived from touch. For ought we know, the atom may consist entirely of the radiations which come out of it.' Now matter is made of atoms. Matter, therefore, to quote an epigram of Earl Russell's has become 'a convenient formula for describing what happens where it isn't.'

If the atom resolves itself into the effects which the atom, if it existed, would produce when it changed in the surrounding neighbourhood, they will take the form of occurrences or events. These occurrences or events will be physical. Therefore, they will ultimately be susceptible of the same analysis as that which is applicable to the atom, and will be known only in so far as they produce effects elsewhere. To quote Earl Russell again, 'there is a certain air of taking in each other's washing about the whole business. Events in empty space are only known as regards their abstract mathematical characterisation; matter is only an abstract mathematical characteristic of events in empty space.' In other words, we describe what there is at place B in terms of events at places E, F and G, and so on indefinitely."*

The same thinker writes thus on the relationship between mind and body:—

"For at this point the question may well be asked, 'What about mind? *Mind assuredly is not material and, so far from being determined by matter, can in some degree control it. If, for example, I† will to chisel a lump of stone into the shape of a human head, am I‡ not freely altering my† environment to please myself?*† Can it in any sense be maintained that I am merely adopting myself to or reacting to my environment?'

'Mind' says C. E. M. Joad, 'is not matter.'

The answer to this question was provided by nineteenth-century psychology which constituted the second main source of materialist philosophy. In order to realise the significance and plausibility of the answer, let us consider for a moment the astonishing fact of the mind-body relationship. That mind and body are continually interacting is obvious. If I get drunk, I see double; *if I take a late supper of cold pork*¶ *and pickles*, I have a nightmare and dream about blue devils; if I inhale nitrous-oxide gas, I experience an ecstatic vision in which I find myself in Paradise enjoying the converse of God and his angels. These are instances of the influence of the body upon the mind.

---

* From "Guide to Modern Thought" by C. E. M. Joad, pp. 82-84.

†This 'I' makes the whole difference. Without this factor Mind is mere inert matter. ‡Yes, you are, surely, but not your mind.

¶ The reader is requested to tolerate this meat-eater's dirty illustration. "An educated man is educated in various ways and degrees, and he responds in varying ways and degrees to the training which he receives. Huxley and Newman were both highly educated. The general trend of education also varies in accordance with the prevailing interest of the age—according as religion or science or art is the fashion of the hour. The revolt of the younger against the older generation is another source of bias. When a man is no longer young his views are more or less settled, and he resents what tends to disturb them; to the enthusiastic youth on the contrary, the received tradition is likely to appear stale and insipid, so that he is led to grasp at what for him are novelties and to plume himself on being in the van of progress.

Man is made by education and environment

From "Mind and Matter" by G F Stout. M. A., LL. D., D. Litt. p. 8. ll 14-27.

If I see a ghost, my hair stands on end; if I am to address a public meeting, I sweat; if I see a cricket ball coming, I hold out my hands or flinch and duck as the case may be. These are instances of the influence of the mind on the body. Examples could be multiplied indefinitely, the interaction of mind and body being a fact which is testified by every moment of our waking lives. Yet, when we come to reflect upon it, how odd a fact it is.

The body is a piece of matter; as such it possesses the properties of matter, weight, mass, shape, size and so forth, and obeys the laws of physics. How then, if mind and matter are so different that they have not a single quality in common, can they influence one another? How indeed can they 'get at' one another at all? A paving-stone can crush a butterfly because the butterfly, like itself, possesses mass and substance; but how can it effect a wish? The length of the arm can be measured, but who can measure the inspiration which went to the composition of Beethoven's Fifth Symphony? It is no exaggeration to say that this fundamental problem is one which all psychology must attempt to solve and no psychology has yet satisfactorily solved".*

In Indian philosophy, it must be remembered, mind is material. It is so subtle—more subtle than ether—that it can easily come into contact with the spiritual entity—the soul. Being material it cannot of itself act for "matter has no power of changing its own state, whether of rest or motion."† If mind were non-material the connection between body and life (—soul) would be impossible. If it were gross matter it would maintain its contact with the body but never would it unite itself with the soul. It is really a wonderful principle discovered by the Aryan philosophers of India that Mind is subtle 'matter'—the eldest evolute of Primordial Matter.‡

---

*C. E. M. Joad, op cit. pp. 33. ff. †From "The Making of Man" by Sir Oliver Lodge, p. 52 ll. 8 & 9.

‡सत्वरजस्तमसां साम्यावस्था प्रकृतिः प्रकृतेर्महान्महतोऽहङ्कारोऽहङ्कारात्पञ्चतन्मात्राण्युभयमिन्द्रियं तन्मात्रेभ्यः स्थूलभूतानि पुरुष इति पंचविंशतिर्गणः ॥ सांख्य १ । ६१ ॥

"The East has very much to instruct the West. We can instruct them in business habits and practical things. They can instruct us in things relating to the soul and meditation. They enter into the silence and meditate a great deal more than we do." ("Science and Religion by Seven men of Science—Help from the Unseen" by Oliver Lodge, p. 16. l. 33—p. 17 l. 4.) *This is a mere platitude which the author himself does not take seriously*!

Life cannot assume "phenomenal existence" without the aid of matter and a material body cannot be clapped on to it without the 'mediation' of Mind, but it must be borne in mind that Mind has no vehicular capacity. It is the body that is the vehicle. Sir Oliver Lodge says:—

"Hence we can begin to speculate on the probability that herein lies the clue to the association of Life and Mind with Matter, that the connection is not direct but indirect. The instinct of Biologists has always led them to assume that Life and Mind must have some kind of material vehicle; that is to say some close connection with what we otherwise think of at the material Universe. But the material Universe consists not of Matter alone, but of Light, Electricity, and Ether as well. Biologists have been liable to assume, and many do assume to this day, that the material vehicle must be formed of Matter. And some have even supposed that Life and Mind are functions of Matter. But that is only because they were insufficiently acquainted with the other material existences, of which Matter is only a part. It is, I agree, difficult to suppose that Life and Mind can exist without some sort of body or instrument of manifestation or at least of utilisation; nor can we expect it to operate effectively without some control of Energy; but there is no need to conjecture any such deprivation. To think of atomic Matter only, leaves us with all manner of unsolved difficulties. In terms of Matter only, we can not conceive the action of the Sun upon the earth, nor of any other action across space; and it really does not matter whether the space is measured in millions of miles or in millionths of an inch: the puzzle is the same ".*

"Life—whatever Life may be—was able to take hold and utilise the structure provided, utilise it for its own further development. As when a heap of stones or rubbish by the roadside is made use of by floating germs, and clothes itself in verdure: so it may be that Life: always waiting its opportunity, seized hold of the more complex molecules on the planet, and began to enter into its kingdom."†

"That which moves from place to place (is matter)".‡ "Matter is that which moves through space"§ "You push the

*"The Making of Man" p. 25 l. 12- p. 26 l. 17. †Ibid p. 73 ll. 10-19. ‡ Ibid p. 59 ll. 20 & 21. §. P. 59 ll. 23 & 25.

truck; it pushes you. It feels your force; you feel its reaction. It experiences acceleration, that is, it begins to move faster".* "So far from limitation, reaction is an assistance"† "Spirit and Matter interact; the one active, the other passive; the one designing, planning, executing; the other being moulded, obediently responsive, docile yet passively obstructive, with an obstruction which does not oppose but actually assists the object in view, rendering possible what else could not be managed, namely, an active exertion capable of achieving some far-foreseen and desired end‡".

But the problem regarding the existence of the soul is still more difficult. Prof. William James after a long discussion of it gave it up altogether as hopeless, concluding the theme with the following words:—

Prof. William James doubted the existence of the Soul?

"One great use of the Soul has always been to account for, and at the same time to guarantee, the closed individuality of each personal consciousness. The thoughts of one soul must unite into oneself, it was supposed, and must be eternally insulated from those of every other soul. But we have already begun to see that, although unity is the rule of each man's consciousness, yet in some individuals, at least, thoughts may split away from the others and form separate selves. As for insulation, it would be rash, in view of the phenomena of thought-transference, mesmeric influence and spirit-control, which are being alleged now-a-days on better authority than ever before, to be too sure about that point either. The definitively closed nature of our personal consciousness is probably an average statistical resultant of many conditions, but not an elementary force or fact; so that, if one wishes to preserve the Soul, the less he draws his arguments from that quarter the better. So long as our self, on the whole, makes itself good and practically maintains itself as a closed individual, why, as Lotze says, is not that enough? And why is the being an individual in some inaccessible metaphysical way so much prouder an achievement ?

My final conclusion, then, about the substantial Soul is that it explains nothing and guarantees nothing. Its successive thoughts are the only intelligible and verifiable things about it, and definitely to ascertain the correlations of these with brain processes

*Ibid p. 62 ll. 9—12. † P. 66 ll. 22 & 23. ‡ P. 67 ll. 4—13.

is as much as psychology can empyrically do. From the metaphysical point of view, it is true that one may claim that the correlations have a rational ground; and if the word Soul could be taken to mean merely some such vague problematic ground, it would be unobjectionable. But the trouble is that it professes to give the ground in positive terms of a very dubiously credible sort. I therefore feel entirely free to discard the word Soul from the rest of this book. If I ever use it, it will be in the vaguest and most popular way. The reader who finds any comfort in the idea of the Soul, is, however, perfectly free to continue to believe in it; for our reasonings have not established the non-existence of the Soul; they have not proved its superfluity for scientific purposes."*

Professor William James is no more in our midst but we cannot, unfortunately pray for him *requiescat in pace* (may he rest in peace) for this refers to the soul and he did not believe in the existence of such a 'commodity!'

When the poor Soul herself is meted out such shabby treatment by European philosophers† what can we say of things pertaining to her. Just listen to what an author says:—

C.E.M. Joad says, re-incarnation is impossible.

"No less well attested than the so-called wonders of clairvoyance have been the stories current in all ages of those who have apparently possessed the power of going back to the past. This power has usually been regarded as providing evidence for reincarnationist theories. *In certain physical*† *states*, it is said, we remember experiences which we lived through in previous lives. This supposition is, however, by no means necessitated. To any theory of reincarnation serious objections are immediately suggested by a consideration of the facts of

---

* From "Psychology" by Prof. William James, Vol. i, p. 350.

† No, not so please, but 'under certain circumstances'. If you want to criticise represent the position accurately, do not mis-state. The circumstances are these: If the body is favourable, if the mind is free from all impurities of past actions,—the dross of flesh-eating, the dross of tobacco-smoking, the dross of race-hatred, the dross of land-lust and power-lust, the love of wine-woman-and-song *et hoc genus omne*, then it is that a person may remember his or her past deeds and not otherwise. An ordinary person if reminded of his or her past life will have to weep and bewail throughout life, while past memory will incite some to anger, some to malice and yet others to take vengeance upon somebody who may have done them evil then.

Dross vitiates the mind and interferes with the memory of past life.

the relationship between mind* and body to which I drew attention in chapter II. The relationship, as I there pointed out, is obviously very close. An invalid, for example, has a different mentality from a healthy, a hunchback from a straight man: character is bound up with the secretions of the duct-

---

* It is not the gross body alone that makes the person, The soul, till (A) it is emancipated from phenomenal existence. carries along with it a "subtle body, which comprises seventeen principles:—Five *nervauric or vital principles*, five *principles of sensation*, and five *physical principles* such as *Prithivee, Apah Agni*,, etc., in subtle form, and the principles of *volition* and *discernment.* It also accompanies the soul in all births and deaths. It is of two kinds:—*(a) material* which is derived from the fine particles of subtle matter. *(b) Spiritual* or *natural* which comprises the natural powers and attributes of the soul. Both (B) of these remain with the soul in the state of *Emancipation,* and it is through them that the soul enjoys the bliss of emancipation." (From the "Light of Truth" Lahore edn. p. 273).

The subtle or spiritual body is necessary to make the person.

The expressions marked (A) and (B) in the above passage may be taken to be contradictory. The Kathopanishad has the following passage; "Yadaa pancaavatish*t*hante jnaanaani manasaa saha ; buddhisca na vicesh*t*ate taam aahuh paramaam gatim. Ka*t*h, i, 10. "That condition of the soul in which it possesses a pure *manas*—the principle of thought—the five *principles of sensation*, and in which the *deliberations* of *the principle* of *discernment* are true and constant, is called the *supreme state* or Emancipation". ("Light of Truth" p. 265) "The *emancipated* soul leaves off her mortal coil and roams about in space in the All-pervading God by the help of the *Spiritual body.*" (Ibid. p. 266.) From these statements it appears Maharshi Dayaananda thinks that the soul does not become a *spiritus purus* (—pure spirit) in the state of emancipation. The other rendering of the Ka*t*h. passage quoted above is as follows:—"Yadaa yasmin kaale panca jnaanaani srotraadipancajnaanendriyaa*n*i manasaa saha manoyuktaani avatish*t*hante nivr$^{\partial}$ttavyaapaaraa*n*i bhavanti buddhisca vyavasaaya laksha*n*aa yadaa na viceshtate vyaapaaravatee na bhavati taam uktajnaanendriyamanobuddhinaiscalyaroopaam avasthaam paramaam utkr$^{\partial}$sh*t*aam gatim aanandaatmano bhaanasya saadhanabhootaam aahuh uktavanto yogina ityarthah" (Ma*n*iprabhaa.) This interpretation seems to mean that the condition described is one of trance and not of 'final emacipation'.

In the state of 'final' emancipation the soul becomes a *spiritus purus* having her spiritual attributes of volition, like, dislike etc., and it is the first coupled with her *finitude of intelligence* that again compels her to assume corporeal existence after the 'great deluge' (mahaa pralaya). *In limited states of emancipation the Subtle body must accompany.* The difference seems to be more verbal and academical than real and practical.

(U)—E. D.

less glands; an insufficiency of thyroid produces a half-wit and an excess of adrenalin a coward. *Change a man's body* and you change the man.*

If a man's nature is largely determined by his body, it is bound up no less with his memories. My knowledge, such as it is, is largely a memory of things I have learned; my outlook on life the effect of the things I have experienced. If I had not fallen out of the window at the age of five, I should not be afraid of heights now. As one gets older, memories become more important; very aged people live entirely in their memories; in fact *they are* their memories.

Again, a man is very largely the product of his environment. I, for example, am a child of the twentieth century, with the outlook, beliefs and attainments of my generation. Body, memories and environment—these go far to make a man what he is; his personality is, at least in part, their joint out-come.

Now nobody who believes in reincarnation holds, so far as I know, that one inhabits the same body in different lives.† Obviously not, since we know what happens to old bodies; they become worms.‡ People do not normally have any memory of their past lives, so that their memories in each life would be different. Given a different body, different memories and environment, the difficulty is to see in what sense a man *could be said to be the same person* in different lives. If I may commit an Irishism, if it is really I who live through each one of a number of different lives, then I must be a different person§ each time.

---

*When therefore the body is changed the man surely changes but not the soul and not his *fine deliberative apparatus called the spiritual body.*

†Surely they do maintain that the soul in separate phenomenal existences clad in different *gross bodies,* does carry with her the same subtle body vitiated though it may be by various kinds of dross. Why, dross dirties even the soul herself !

‡No, not at all. The 'old body' does not become worms. The worm are as good individuals as a philosopher! The 'old body' gets 'scrapped' or 'broken up into its various elements' for the formation of new bodies. Emotional expressions are unbecoming in serious philosophical discussions.

This old body does not become 'worms',

§Surely the believers in re-incarnation do not say that the 'same person' travels on with the same bodies! They say that the soul along with the spiritual body is the same.

Just listen also to what H. G. Wells has to say on Re-incarnation:—

"Apart from such speculations we may say this much; upon the continuity of any individual consciousness after bodily cessation and disintegration, *The Science of Life* has no word of assurance, and on the other hand it assembles much that points towards its improbability. But so far as our lives go, as matters of fact apart from consciousness, *The Science of Life* has no doubts; it does not speculate, it states. Our lives do not begin afresh at birth, and do not end inconclusively; they take up a physical inheritance, they take over a tradition, they enter into a set drama, they are conditioned from the outset, and each has a rôle to play, different from any role that has ever been played before or will ever be played again. And our lives do not end with death: they stream on, not merely in direct offspring, but more importantly perhaps in the influence they have had on the rest of life. According to the playing of the role the unending consequences are determined. They endure in the fabric of things accomplished for ever. That at least is not theory or speculation; it is as much a statement of fact as that every stream that flows upon this planet earth flows down towards the sea".*

On the re-incarnation of the soul Wells writes verbiage in his "The Science ofLife."

The above passage is floral and ornate but inconclusive. It is Blimberine verbiage ! Listen to the following:—

"Christ announces to us the unbroken continuity of all life which is truly life. There is no likelihood that we shall ever underrate the changes which we can see, the separations which sadden us, the losses which mar our capacity for action; but, on the other hand, we lose much by not dwelling day by day on that which as yet we can grasp of the permanence of our being; we lose much by constructing a future out of some fragments of the present, and transferring it to some remote scene which serves to obscure the solemn beauty of the earth. We lose much by not striving to behold, little by little, it may be in fleeting visions, the eternal which is about us and in us, and which remains unaltered by all vicissitudes".†

The good Jesus said that life continues.

*From "The Science of Life" by H. G. and G. P. Wells and J. Huxley, Cassell and Co., London 1931 p. 853.

† From "Thoughts on Revelation and Life" P. 295 ll. 17—31.

This is what good Sir Oliver Lodge, the great English scientist, has to say on this knotty question:—

"As regards Reincarnation, it is probably a mistake to suppose that the same individual whom we know in bodily form is likely to appear again, at some future date. There may be exceptions, but as a rule that seems unlikely to happen. What may happen, however, is *that some other portion of the larger self becomes incarnate; and if so it would be likely to feel a strong affinity, though often in a vague and puzzled way, with some other portion which had been embodied previously. And, again, if this second incarnate portion happened to include some part of what had gone to make the previous individual, then there might not only be sense of affinity, but some kind of reminiscence, some memory of places and surrounding which had previously been familiar.*

The Lodgean Heresy.

Many people have felt the odd sensation of having been at a place before, and of knowing instinctively what would be found round the corner or through the door. The experience has been called *deja vu*. It is difficult to explain, but the inclusion of some fraction of a former personality, with overlapping fragments of memory from a previous existence, is a working hypothesis towards an explanation of a faculty which, in a few exceptional people, is fairly strong.

This idea seems to help us to contemplate the Platonic doctrine of Reminiscence as a possible reality in some cases,—that the truths of geometry, for instance, were really known by each individual but forgotten; that "our birth was a sleep and a forgetting"; that the developed brain tends to inhibit the reproduction of ancient memories and to isolate us from our previous surroundings and our larger self. Indeed some such doctrine may be necessary to explain the aptitudes and powers and instincts, both of animals and of children, especially when those children show signs of exceptionally early precocity. When they can calculate, for instance, or play a musical instrument, without having learnt. The only alternative to reminiscence in such cases, would appear to be some doctrine of direct Control by another intelligence. This, too, is a hypothesis not to be overlooked, though some form of subliminal explanation seems simpler, if it is sufficient; which is doubtful.

He postulales a subliminal self.

How large a subliminal self may be, one does not know, but one can imagine that in some cases it is very large, so that it contains the potentiality for the incarnation not only of a succession of ordinary individuals, but of really great men. It would be a mistake to suppose that Dante and Tennyson were reincarnations of Virgil, but one might, though presumptuously, imagine that all three were incarnations of one great Subliminal self, which was able to manifest itself in different portions, having a certain family likeness, though without any necessary bodily consanguinity or inheritance in the ordinary sense.

The heredity link appears to be of a quite different order from the subliminal link; and mother and son need have no spiritual or subliminal relationship, in spite of their great similarity. The similarity of the bodily instrument would be sufficient, in that case, to account for the similarity of that portion of the son's larger self which automatically selected this means of manifestation. And the importance of parenthood, in providing a suitable corporeal instrument or vehicle for the manifestation of a really great personality, can hardly be overestimated. But the indwelling spirit need not come from the parents at all. It can be drawn, as it were, from some independent source, by the perfection or other quality of the material vehicle provided.

In some cases it may happen that the portion incarnate is so great that the embodied personality exhibits the phenomenon of transcendent Genius, and is by universal consent accounted a "great man." Though there are cases in which exceptional powers are manifested by one who is not a great man in an ordinary sense, but who has channels of inspiration open occasionally to a non-incarnate portion, apart from the exceptional periods, may be of ordinary magnitude, or, in the ordinary affairs of life, may even be foolish or commonplace. Occasional access to higher source of information or inspiration is not to be denied to personalities of mediocre grade. The normal portion of such individuals is small, the subliminal portion large by comparison, and occasionally accessible."*

"Not only, moreover, can there be different degrees or proportions of incarnation developed from any ordinary subliminal self, but there may be many grades among those selves; so that,

---

* From "The Making of Man" by Sir Oliver Lodge p. 120, l. 27—p. 124 l. 19.

if ever an infinitely large and comprehensive Self allowed any portion to take human form and associate itself with matter, that portion would recognise itself, and be gradually recognised by others, as in close touch with the Infinite and the Eternal. And humanity would perceive that something far above their own grade, something beyond any previous experience, had dwelt among them, and by origin and personality was essentially Divine. It may be that only through such an incarnation as that could we get any knowledge or perception of that higher, but otherwise inaccessible, being.

The incarnation of a fraction of God's being in Christ, says Sir Oliver Lodge, is a fact!

Deity, indeed, is not a thing which we mortals can conceive. We can formulate certain attributes, and try to grasp them, but Infinity is beyond our grasp. All that we can apprehend during our sojourn in matter and probably for long afterwards, is something in human form, something anthropomorphic. And though we may have qualms at suggesting that any spirit inhabiting a material body of human shape can be anything more than man, yet if the doctrine of the Subliminal self be true, and if a Self of Divine magnitude, if in fact Deity, allowed Itself or some portion of Itself to become Incarnate,—humanity would recognise the Kinship and the Identity, and would realise that in this exceptional manifestation there was as much as it was able to grasp of the Infinite Existence, and would be right in speaking of such an Individual as the Son of God." (Ibid pp. 174-177).

The Vedic position is very beautifully summarised in the following three stanzas.

ओ३म् ॥ पतंगमक्तमसुरस्य मायया हृदा पश्यन्ति मनसा विपश्चितः ।
समुद्रे अन्तः कवयो वि चक्षते मरीचीनां पदमिच्छंति वेधसः ॥
ऋग्वेदे १० । १७७ । १ ॥ पतंगो वाचं मनसा बिभर्ति तां गन्धर्वोऽवदद्गर्भे
अन्तः । तां द्योतमानां स्वर्यं मनीषामृतस्य पदे कवयो नि पान्ति ॥ २ ॥
अपश्यं गोपामनिपद्यमानमा च परा च पथिभिश्चरन्तम् । स सध्रीचीः स
विषूचीर्वसान आ वरीवर्ति भुवनेष्वन्तः ॥३॥*

(1) The wise by devotion and cogitation perceive the soul that becomes manifest by assuming a body through the wise providence of God the giver of life. With a poet's vision they carefully observe each object in the world and thus becoming enlightened wish to attain to the source of Light Itself.

* The Nirukta and the Jaiminiyopanishadbraahma*n*a explain these verses as describing reincarnation. Hans Oertell's translation of them in the latter book is absurd in the extreme.

(2) The soul keeps the faculty of speech in (the interior of) the heart and when the time for utterance comes the vital air begins to express it inside, but when it flashes out as the manifestation of sound revealing the contents of the mind the far-sighted wise protect it most assiduously as the very basis of truth. (3) May I see the individual soul, the imperishable lord of the sense organs, ever coming and going by the paths of births and deaths. It travels assuming various conditions of life accompanying it (from birth) and brought about by the residua of its past actions, and thus keeps frequently coming into the various worlds.

This is not the only Vedic text on the reincarnation of the soul. The 58th and 164th hymns of the 1st book of the Rəgveda treat of several aspects of the soul. There are long passages in all the four Vedas that fully treat of this subject. An exposition of the Vedic view-point on this theme is the subject of a separate book.

Does not good Jesus refer to the reincarnation of the soul in Matthew xii, 14? "And if ye will receive *it*, this is Elias, which was for to come." What does this statement mean? How is this coming of Elias again to the world of embodied beings possible except by means of a body? That body may now be 'John the Baptist' for human custom refers to the embodied person and not to the abstract soul. *Satis it non amplius.*

The intention of these "philosophers" is to boom Christianity.

The "philosophers" whose views have been quoted above, betray, like Max Müller, a great tendency to boom Christianity. The scientific education they have received, the high positions they hold or the great regard and confidence they enjoy in the modern world misled by English education, they thus use to lead the whole human race into the folds of Christianity. His great anxiety for somehow reconciling the absurd view of the incarnation of God, has led Sir Oliver Lodge to propound the absurd and heretical theory of the partial incarnation of his imaginary "subliminal self." This heresy can be thus explained by means of a diagram.

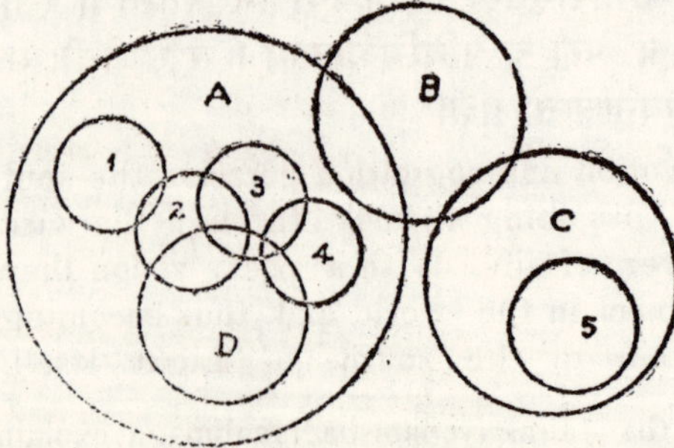

Suppose circles A, B, and C are "subliminal selves" and suppose circles 1—5 and D are incarnated selves. It is clear from the diagram that 1, 2, 3, 4 and D are incarnations of parts of the "subliminal self" A. Suppose part 1 incarnated itself in 1793 and part 2 in 1863; then the latter would remember something ("falling from the window"* in 1802) which is represented in the diagram by the intersection of the circumferences of 1 and 2. Poor No. 3 would be a horrible mess of such memories and cross-memories for 'he' cuts and cross-cuts through four incarnations being himself a part of the "subliminal self" A. Incarnations D and 5 being large would be very successful in the world, enjoy high life, be ever in the limelight, have immense wealth, have a lot of hangers-on and boomers or "hewers of wood and drawers of water" to sweat for them.

Thus it is clear, according to Sir Oliver Lodge there is no such entity as the Individual Soul. There are only "subliminal selves" which can be sliced and served out in various incarnations! Thus this wretched worm of a subliminal self resembles the amoeba. It must be borne in mind that this absurd theory reduces God to a non-entity, for a being having no 'personality' and no individuality can be anything but God. The Semitic creeds have no God, and one need not wonder if the follower of one of these propounds such a heretical and atheistic theory. For real atheism is nothing but to deny the existence of the soul either in an overt or a covert manner, and the latter is more serious and dangerous than the former.†

It is better for a man to think twice before writing anything down, for wrong views broadcast corrode into the hearts of the younger generation and ruin humanity. The political supremacy of Europe does not indicate that her religion and morals are sound. Europe has nothing to teach the world. Especially India has nothing to learn from her. There is a widespread opinion that the modern means of communication have brought the different races nearer that they may mutually learn from and teach, one another, but this is only a silly platitude intended to flout the disputant. Had it not been so, "great European scientists" at least, would not have ventured to write without know-

---

* See page clxix ll. 7 & 8.

† Disbelief in a Supreme Being or Creator is more or less a technical difficulty and can be solved if the person beset with it admits an individual and personal soul. A denial of the latter, however, is the chimax of atheism for the man prone to it can never be brought round to believe in anything beyond the senses.

ing the principal languages and philosophical systems of the world, chief among which is Sanskrit and the philosophy of ancient Aryan India.

The long and short of the cry of these "scientists" can be put briefly thus: "*We have not seen, therefore we refuse to believe*". Along with this there is another maxim: "*We have been told by our padres that Christianity is true hence it must be so*".

The following matter is not doctrinal but it gives the scientific side of Vedic teaching:—

"Achyrantes Aspera, Linn., H. F. B. I., IV, 730; Roxb. 22.

Sans.—Apaamaarga, aghata, apangaka.

The Achyrantes Aspera or Prickly Chaff flower plant is a great medicinal herb.

Vern:—Apanga (Beng. and Ass.). Latjiraa, Chirchiraa Chirchittaa (Hindi); Putkandaa (Punj.) Oonghaa (Rohtak Dist.); Aghaa*d*aa (Bomb. and Mahr.); Uttareni; Antisha; Apaamaargamu (Tel.); Naayurivi (Tamil); Ka*t*alaati (Mal.); Utraa*n*i gi*d*avu; uttaraa*n*e (Kan.); Aghe*d*o (Guj.); Margiaa (Sind).

English:—The Prickly Chaff Flower.

Habitat:—A shrub found all over India, ascending to 3000 ft.

Annual herbs. Stems 1-2 ft., erect, stiff, with long spreading branches thickened above nodes, striate, pubescent. Leaves few, usually thick, leathery, broadly ovate to orbicular, 3·5 by 2-3 in., tapering to base, usually rounded, on short petioles, sometimes acute, or apex entire, but often very undulate, very finely and softly pubescent both sides. Flowers in robust woolly pubescent spikes upto 18 in. long, numerous, stiffly reflexed against rachis, densely crowded. Bracts short, reflexed, ovate, membranous, with a long and very acute point, bractlets very sharply spinescent (very hard in fruit), with a

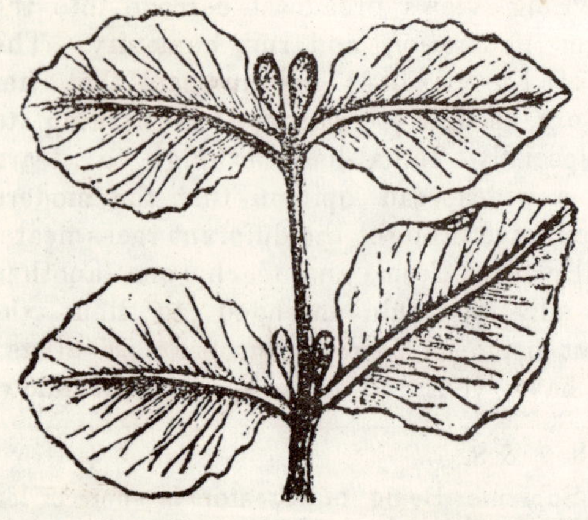

PLATE IV

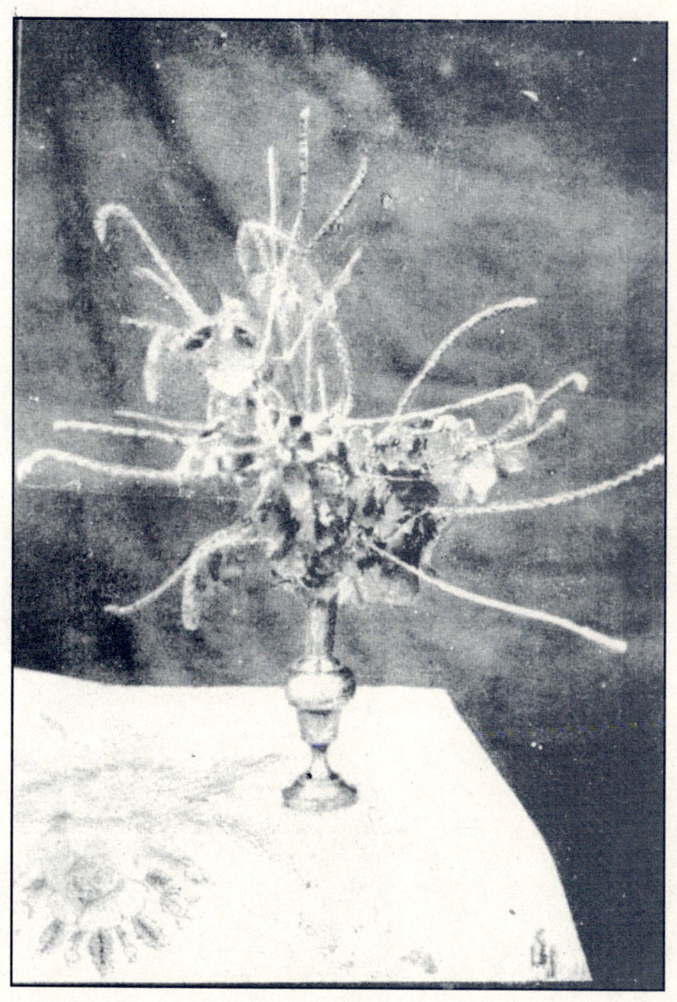

Asclepias Aspera.

(To face p. clxxvi.)

broad membranous wing at base. Perianth leaves about 1/8 in., oblong, oval, acute, glabrous and shining, with a narrow white membranous margin. Stamens 5, staminodes, large, truncate, fimbriate. Fruit very small, oblong, cylindrical, truncate, nearly smooth, brown, enclosed in a hard perianth.

A very common weed throughout the Tropics in India, Ceylon, in waste land and in grass. Trimen observes that the perianth containing the fruit disarticulates from the rachis above the bract carrying away with it the spinescent bractlets by which it becomes attached to other objects and is transported. Flowers greenish white.

Uses:—It possesses valuable medicinal properties as a pungent and laxative, and is considered useful in dropsy, piles, boils, eruptions of the skin, etc. The seeds and leaves are considered emetic, and are useful in hydrophobia and snakebites. (T. N. Mukerji's Amsterdam Catalogue). The dried plant is given to children for colic and also as an astringent in gonorrhoea. (Stewart's Punjab Plants,) Major Madden says that the flowering spikes are regarded as a protective against scorpions, the insects being paralised through the presence of a twig. The ash yields a valuable quantity of potash, rendering it useful in the arts as well as in medicine. Mixed with orpiment this ash is used externally in the treatment of ulcers, and of warts on the penis and other parts of the body. (U. C. Dutt.) Sesamum oil and the ash (*apamarga taila*) are used in the treatment of diseases of the ear, being poured into the meatus. Dr. Bidie says: "Various English practitioners agree as to its marked diuretic properties in the form of a decoction." Dr. Cornish reports favourably, having found it efficacious in the treatment of dropsy. Short reports on its use as an external applicant in the treatment of the bites of insects; and Dr. Turner, calls attention to it as a remedy in snake-bite. (Pharm. Indica). Used in cases of abscess; its ashes are used in cases of asthma and cough. (Ibbetson's Gujrat.) In Sind, it is used by the native foresters as an application to wounds caused by Babool thorns (Murray p. 101). To an infusion of the root is ascribed a mild astringent virtue (Konigberger, Vol. II., 222). The flowering spike made into pills with a little sugar is a popular preventive medicine in Behar for persons bitten by rabid dogs. (Balfour.) As an ash, however, there seems no reason to think it possesses any virtues other than those of the simple alkali of our shops.

"The drug may be useful in all conditions arising from nervousness. Thus it is used as a talisman in hysteria, and I know personally of cases that were benefited by it. How it acts in such a way,

I cannot say; it may be possible that the good effects are obtained by iodisation only, if anything of such nature there is in the drug. But that it is undoubtedly useful in hysteria and such nervous disorders, there is no gainsaying. In hysteria what we find is that there is extreme nervous sensibility attended with muscular contraction, either violent or mild; it is preceded generally by irregular heart or palpitation. (Dr. Lal Mohan Ghoshal, in 'Food and Drugs' for Oct. 1912 pp. 84,85)".*

(१) ईशानां त्वा भेषजानामुज्जेष आ रभामहे । चक्रे सहस्रवीर्यं
सर्वस्मा ओषधे त्वा ॥ अथर्व० ४ । १७ । १ ॥ (२) सत्यजितं शपथयावनीं
सहमानां पुनः सराम् । सर्वाः समह्व्योषधीरितो नः पारयादिति ॥२॥ (३) या
शशाप शपनेन याघं मूरमादधे । या रसस्य हरणाय जातमारेभे तोकमत्तु
सा ॥३॥ (४) दौःष्वप्न्यं । दौर्जीवित्यं रक्षो अभ्वमराय्यः । दुर्णाम्नीः सर्वा दुर्वा-
चस्ता अस्मन्नाशयामसि ॥५॥ (५) क्षुधामारं तृष्णामारमगोतामनपत्यताम् ।
अपामार्ग त्वया वयं सर्वं तदप मृज्महे ॥ ६ ॥ (६) तृष्णामारं क्षुधामारमथो
अक्षपराजयम् । अपामार्ग त्वया वयं सर्वं तदप मृज्महे ॥ ७ ॥ (७) अपामार्ग
ओषधीनां सर्वासामेक इद्वशी । तेन ते मृज्म आस्थितमथ त्वमगदश्चर ॥ ८ ॥
(८) अनयाहमोषध्या सर्वाः कृत्या अदूदुषम् । यां क्षेत्रे चक्रुर्यां गोषु यां वा
ते पुरुषेषु ॥ १८ । ५ ॥ (९) अपामार्गोऽप मार्ष्टु क्षेत्रियं शपथश्च यः ।
अपाह यातुधानीरप सर्वा अराय्यः ॥ ७ ॥ (१०) ब्राह्मणेन पर्युक्तासि कण्वेन
नार्षदेन । सेनेवैषि त्विषीमती न तत्र भयमस्ति यत्र प्राप्नोष्योषधे ॥ १९ । २ ॥
(११) अग्रमेष्योषधीनां ज्योतिषेवाभिदीपयन् । उत त्रातासि पाकस्याथो
हन्तासि रक्षसः ॥ ३ ॥ (१२) प्रत्यङ् हि संबभूविथ प्रतीचीनफलस्त्वम् ।
सर्वान्मच्छपथाँ अधि वरीयो यावया वधम् ॥ ७ ॥ (१३) शतेन मा
परिपाहि सहस्रेणाभि रक्ष मा । इन्द्रस्ते वीरुधां पत उग्र ओज्मानमा
दधत् ॥ ८ ॥

The following is the substance of the above stanzas:—Achyrantes Aspera is the greatest and most potent of all medicinal plants (1,7,11,13). Its 'fruit' grows upside down (12). With certain other herbs it becomes still more potent (1), is an unfailing remedy for irritability and worry giving rise to cursing and use of abusive language (2,4,9); it invigorates (2), dispels anaemia and such weakness in the parents as makes the offspring short-lived (3). Lack of proper thirst, loss of appetite, stammering (agotaam), barrenness, lassitude of the senses (5,6), all kinds of piles (dur*n*aamneeh 4), insomnia and

* From "Indian Medicinal Plants" by Lt. Col. K. K. Kirtikar, Panini Office, Allahabad, India. pp. 1061 ff.

bad dreams (daushshvapnyam 4), melancholia (daurjeevityam 4), emaciation (abhvam 4), pallor (araayyah 4), worms and germs causing disease (rakshah 4), in all these cases also it is very effective. It is a purgative also (punahsaraam 2). In certain acts of 'magic' so-called done by evil-minded people for the destruction of the crops and cattle it serves as a good preventive (8). It cures even hereditary diseases (9). It is a great nutritive agent (11), and one need not fear of being helpless in case of illness where this herb grows (10).

The same properties and uses of the wonderful plant are given in later Sanskrit medical works.

Drive away penury,

The following is the Vedic teaching on the evils of poverty and on the means to remove it:—

ओ३म् ॥ अरायि काणे विकटे गिरिं गच्छ सदान्वे । शिरिम्बिठस्य सत्वभिस्तेभिष्ट्वा चातयामसि ॥ ऋग्वेदे १० । १५५ । १ ॥ चत्तो इतश्चत्तामुत: सर्वा भ्रूणान्यारूषी । अराय्यं ब्रह्मणस्पते तीक्ष्णश्रृङ्गोदृषन्निहि ॥ २ ॥ अदो यद्दारु प्लवते सिन्धोः पारे अपूरुषम् । तदारभस्व दुर्हणो तेन गच्छ परस्तरम् ॥ ३ ॥ यद्ध प्राचीरजगन्तोरो मण्डूरधाणिकीः । हता इन्द्रस्य शत्रवः सर्वे बुद्बुदयाशवः ॥ ४ ॥ परीमे गामनेषत पर्यग्निमहृषत । देवेष्वक्रत श्रवः क इमाँ आदधर्षति ॥ ५ ॥

(1) The ugly, one-eyed, ever groaning Penury should be compelled to take recourse to such uninhabited places as the mountain. All should with the potent yield of the cloud (viz., water) expel her from inhabited places (by adopting good methods of agriculture). (2) The (propagator and) protector of Vedic teachings should (by following them in his own life first), by his incomparable lustre [=vigour] (of industry) chase away Penury—pitch her out from here, there and everywhere, and wipe out the evil effects of all her doings that kill the very seed of life. (3) To escape merciless onslaught of the industrious follower of Vedic teachings, Penury who kills creatures by inflicting untold sufferings on them, will, so to say, take advantage of the earliest opportunity to sieze the first casual sleeper floating along the current of the river without the effort of any human being, and betake herself, as fast as it would carry her, to the opposite bank. (4) Then surely the murderous Penury that (putting enmity between man and man) cuts the bond of fellow-feeling, will go on and on till she is no more seem, for it is a fact that all the foes of an industrious and righteous person living according to God's Law—the Vedas) dispurse like bubbles and vanish! (5) Such

industrious persons as propagate Vedic teachings far and wide carry on, religious sacrifices (and other good works) and enhance the fame of the wise (those are the dispellers of Penury). Who can disparage them?*

The 'pornosophists' or haitairiologists.

The condemnation on pp. 216-37 of the evil and barbarous booming of contraception by the interested gang of pornosophists of Europe who are crossing the seven seas with their nepharious propaganda is not severe enough. The following extract from one of their "doctrinal texts" is enough to show how serious and heinous the affair is :—

> "Technical knowledge of how to utilize science to control conception has become essential to nearly every medical practitioner.
>
> Before entering into the technicalities of the numerous methods now available for use, it may be wise first to define exactly what is meant by the control of conception, popularly called "Birth Control." The public mind has been confused by the innocently vague or the deliberately polemical misuse of terms: So before entering into the scientific and critical considerations attempted in this book, let us be explicit in our definition of what we are discussing.
>
> Defnition: Contraception (Birth Control) is the use by either sex of any means whatsoever whereby coitus (the act of union between man and woman) may be experienced while at the same time the fusion of the ovum with the spermatozoon may be averted, so that conception does not take place.
>
> The careful reader will note that this rules out absolutely the inaccurate arguments sometimes put forward in polemical discussions that celibacy (that is in its accepted sense of life in the unmarried state) is a form of Birth Control: Celibacy may be looked upon as a mode of keeping down the total numbers of the population, but in a strictly accurate and scientific sense it is not a form of contraception or Birth Control. Neither is temporary abstinence from the act of union within marriage a form of Birth Control, though it be adopted by some married persons with a view to avoiding the procreation of offspring and thus to

---

* The whole of Chap. iv of the 'Anthology of Vedic Hymns' and especially pp. 156-61 of that book deserve to be referred to here.

restrict the total number of children. The couple depriving themselves of the completion of their married state are living as unmarried persons do, and are not exercising contraception or Birth Control. The acts of those, however, who for the same reason limit their unions to certain specified dates on which they think that union may safely be experienced without a conception following, come within the definition of contraception given above, for they are exercising the act of union while taking steps for the purpose of avoiding the consequent procreation of children."*

One of the "world-teachers" of this hellish science of 'pornosophy' paid a flying visit to India. She met a 'leader' and in her 'cross-questions' pulled his legs and elicited from him the undesirable reply that he had with difficulty, been able to curb his sexual inclinations and maintain 'brahmacarya'.* 'If you, Mr. So and So, so strong in your moral life, found it difficult to maintain............how can you expect the common masses of India to succeed?' The 'leader' then smiled at this quick repartee. She did not finish here. She went about booming in the papers that Mr. So and So smiled and she asked 'Why did Mr. So and so smile?' She must be replied. "He smiled at the audacious and unfeeling manner you, a woman, have been going about in, holding forth on the dirtiest points of sexual life—exposing so to say the lavatory sink to the view of all. He smiled for he could not clearly grasp what your 'stock-in-trade' was. Finally, oh fair pornosophist, remember that he smiled for he was puzzled as to what you would do if some curious people among your audience were to request you to give a practical demonstration on the public platform of the practical side of your art of pornosophy!"†

The Vedic Seer is a person of righteous life.

The Vedic Seer is a poet and prophet but his poetry is not imaginary and his prophecy is not a mystery unless by that term we mean something beyond our comprehension and not something entirely opposed to the order of Nature. A seer of 'second sight' in the spiritist parlance is not a Vedic Seer or Rəshi. A person who voices out a number of incoherent statements

---

* "Contraception, Birth Control, Its Theory and Practice" by Marie Stopes; Messrs G. P. Putnam's Sons, London, 1932 pp., 1 and 2. † All literature on this subject is picaresque and pornographic. It is highly venomous and deserves to be proscribed and burnt where there will be no aftermath. See pp. 239-40, where the great harm methods of birth control do is mentioned which the pornosophists have intentionally neglected.

void of any clear, rational significance like the "Revelation" of John in the New Testament, is also no R^əshi. A Vedic Seer is the inspired recipient or medium of Divine Revelation—a person who, by his righteous, pure and holy life is able to grasp higher and Divine things which are far above the ken of the generality of mankind. Hence it is necessary first to know what is the idea conveyed by the words "revelation" and "inspiration." The following are Christian views of the matter:—

"Revelation is not so much the disclosure of the truth as the presentment of the facts on which the truth can be discerned.

It is given through life and to living men. It finds us men and it leaves us men. It is the ground of unending, untiring effort towards a larger vital apprehension of that which is laid open. It is not for the satisfaction of the intellectual part of our nature alone, but for the unfolding of our whole nature.

Men were made to seek God: that is the foundation of revelation; *to know Him as mun :* that is the condition of revelation; to grow into His likness: that is the test of revelation".*

"The great men of the race† the inspired men of the race, have felt more at home with the Higher Intelligences than with the things of daily life.‡

And by the process of Inspiration we get help and assistance in understanding things which else would be beyond us. The ordinary material methods are not the only methods. And through all time the great and inspired men have had these visions and intuitions, they have perceived realities, and they have tried to record what they have seen, for the benefit of others. That is the way in which we have to explore some of these things. That at any rate is the method of religion."$

"Revelation is the development of the relation in which God has placed Himself to the world in bringing it into existence. The basis of revelation is laid in the fact that the world was called into existence by the *word* of God, and was animated by His *spirit.* The production of different classes of beings advances teleologically, and reaches its goal only when God has created man

*Westcott, op. cit. p. 13. The italicised bit ruins the quotation. † 'The peaks of the race' as he calls them elsewhere. ‡ "Science and Religion by Seven Men of Science" p. 21 ll. 5-8. $ Ibid, p. 21. ll. 11-20.

in His own image. *In this progression the foundation of revelation is laid.* For *revelation is, in general, God's witness and communication of himself to the world for the ralization of the end of creation,* and for re-establishment of full-communion of man with God. After the tearing asunder through sin of the bond of the original communion of man with God, God testifies. partly *in nature* and the *historical guidance of mankind,* and partly in each one's conscience of His power, goodness, and justice, and thus draws man to seek God."*

"The Pentateuch plainly distinguishes four periods in the history of revelation.--

1. The *primeval age,* with ten patriarchs, closing with the deluge.

2. Beginning with the *world covenant* in Noah's time; the time of the division of the peoples, by which the separation of the race of revelation is prepared; again with ten generations.

3. The time of the three great patriarchs, beginning with Abraham's election, and the *covenant of promise* made with him; and ending with the sojourn of the chosen people in Egypt.

4. The fourth period opens with the redemption of Israel from Egyptian bondage; it includes the giving of the *covenant of the law,* and the establishment of the theory, with its regulations."†

"The notion of a man-god or a human being endowed with divine or supernatural powers, belongs essentially to that earlier period of religious history in which gods and men are still viewed as beings of much the same order, and before they are divided by the impassable gulf which, to later thought, opens out between them. Strange, therefore, as may seem to us the idea of a god incarnate in human form, it has nothing very startling for early man, who sees in a man-god or a god-man only a higher degree of the same supernatural powers which he arrogates in perfect good faith to himself. Such incarnate gods are common in rude society. The incarnation may be temporary or permanent. In the former case, the incarnation—commonly known as inspiration or possession—reveals itself in supernatural knowledge rather than in supernatural power. In other words, its usual manifestations

---

*Oehler's "Old Testament Theology" T. and T. Clarke Edinburgh, p. 17. The last sentence 'After......seek God' is absurd and ugly. †Ibid. p. 49. ll. 8-19.

are divination and prophesy rather than miracles. On the other hand, when the incarnation is not merely temporary, when the divine spirit has permanently taken up its abode in a human body, the god-man is usually expected to vindicate his character by working miracles. Only we have to remember that by men at this stage of thought miracles are not considered as breaches of natural law. Not conceiving the existence of a natural law, primitive man cannot conceive a breach of it. A miracle to him is merely an usually striking manifestation of a common power."*

"Do you believe in the verbal inspiration of the Bible? I do. That is, I believe that the writers of the various books in the Bible were guided by the Holy spirit, not only in the thought to which they gave expression but also in the choice of the words in which they expressed the thought. They spoke from God, being moved by the Holy Ghost", (2 Peter 1: 20 R.V.). It was the Holy Ghost who spake (Hebrews 3: 7; 10:15, 16; Acts 28: 25.) The word uttered was His word (2 Samuel 23: 2. R.V.) The very words used were the words which the Holy Ghost teaches (1 Corinthians 2: 13). Nothing could be plainer than Paul's statement: "In words which the Spirit teacheth."

The Holy spirit Himself anticipated all these modern ingenious but unbiblical and false theories regarding His own work in the apostles. The more carefully and minutely one studies the wording of the statements made in the Bible, the more he will become convinced of the marvellous accuracy of the words used to produce the thought. To a superficial student the doctrine of verbal inspiration may appear questionable or even absurd, but any regenerated and spirit-taught man who ponders the words of Scripture day after day and year after year will become increasingly convinced that the Wisdom of God is in the very words used, as well as in the thought which is expressed in the words.

It is a very suggestive fact that our difficulties with the Bible rapidly disappear when we come to notice the precise language used. The change of a word or a letter, of a tense, case or number, often-times lands a person in contradiction or untruth, but by taking the words just as written, difficulties disappear and the truth shines forth. The more microspically we

---

*Frazer's "Golden Bow," Vol. I. p. 32 l. 19—p. 33 l. 14.

study the Bible, the more clearly does its divine origin shine forth as we see its perfection of form as well as substance."*

The Vedic idea of revelation.

The above is the Christian idea of revelation and is poles apart from the Vedic view of it. The passages are arranged in order, the most reasonable first, from which the succeeding quickly march towards the goal of the Christian padre viz., the dogma that the Bible is revealed and each word of it is divinely inspired. It is really impossible to realize in what sense a historical record of events that occurred in some forgotten corner of the world among tribes of half-cultured and uncultured people could be said to be revealed and inspired. Is it necessary that God should reveal to somebody what happened in Babylon some 4000 years back? and does he go about doing such a thing for the benefit of his near and dear ones? If it be so why not European scientists go about their business in a more reasonable fashion and instead of advancing all sorts of silly and specious arguments to 'prove' (*prove! pshaw!*) that an inaccurate, incomplete and biassed historical record is revealed and inspired, just experiment and devise ways and means to call that 'god' down and take down from him a full account of all races! That will go against these European capitalistic intelligentsia for he will tell them that the Aryans of India are the oldest and most cultured race and that the Vedas are the only revealed law!!. Trial costs nothing, these gentlemen should try, especially as he (the Semitic god) makes gold also the 'chemical' formula of which they can easily get from him and turn every stono in Europe into gold!! As matters stand today, Europe is not self-supporting and has to depend every second of her life even for her food and raiment on the coloured "hewers of wood and drawers of water." From their very nature the Biblical books are interested and inaccurate accounts of historical events compiled from the sources then available by men most of whom were not learned. Hence interested Christian writers cannnot be expected to give a correct definition of Divine Revelation.

What is Divine Revelation?

When a man divulges a secret confided to him he is said to reveal it. With this human revelation we are not concerned. Divine Revelation is quite different from this. *As Drs. Westcott and Oehler quoted above, say, it is concerned with humanity and creation. It is given to the 'peaks of humanity', as Sir Oliver Lodge calls them,*

*From "Practical and Perplexing Questions Answered," R. A. Torrey p. 13 l. 31—p. 14 l. 29.

at the time of creation for the benefit of all beings. For this obviously there must be a reason. The Supreme Being 'hands down' this Revelation because it is absolutely necessary for the safety and growth of mankind. It must be that without such Revelation humanity would have been so much the worse and ever groping in the dark compelled to live like beasts. It can, under no circumstances, be admitted that God created mankind able to find out their own way in creation, and yet, as if to tease them, imposed upon them what may be called a Revelation! If mankind by their very nature were able to find their own way to the problem of Law and Order and a right knowledge of the Providential Disposal of Nature's goods then, surely, to saddle them with a revelation is to penalise them!

Hence the position is this: God Almighty in His Omnipotent Wisdom creates the animate and inanimate universe, the latter first, after this the lower animals and finally man—His most favoured creation! Such a huge universe, it should be understood, must have been 'caused' according to some law, and when kingdoms, nay even very small associations of men require statutes, rules, bye-laws and regulations for their conduct, it would be foolish to think that God creates His universe without law and leaves it destitute of it. *Hence Divine Revelation is nothing but that everlasting Law according to which He creates and sustains the universe and which He hands down to humanity for their guidance.*

This revelation is not done through dictation but by 'inspiring' the eternal principles of that Divine Law into the hearts of such of the 'peaks of humanity' as are able to receive it. It is something like the gramophone record which if the lines over it are blurred cannot receive any impression of the sound 'dealt on' to it. Ordinary human beings are like such blurred records and hence incapable of accepting or responding to truths of the higher sphere.

Those 'peaks of humanity' who being capable of it receive Divine Revelation inspired into their souls, minds and hearts are the Vedic Seers or Rashis, and the Revealed Law itself are the four Vedas. These four Repositories of Divine Law are enough for the 'management' of the universe and human society. They contain the Divine *Magna Carta* of the *Ecclesia Divina* and all other revelations so-called, are merely very distant and faint echoes of it reaching us from over the remote millenniums through vitiated human agencies. They can be found out from their interested, imperfect, incorrect and even false accounts of things, visions and hostile propaganda against some branches of the human family itself, wrong and opprobrious ideas about the Supreme Being and the soul etc. Only the four Vedas are free from all these defects.*

The Vedas are four in as much as a sensible person, in order to rise in material, moral and spiritual life, has to adopt a fourfold method in his daily endeavours for advance, viz., jnaana, (knowledge), karma (activity), upaasanaa (practice of the presence of God), and lastly stuti (praise of God and relation of his experiences before others). The number of the Vedas corresponds to this division of man's duties, the four stages of man's life, tne four social divisions etc., etc. There is no point in the question which some raise on this number, for it could still be raised even if the Vedas were to be five. But such a question cannot arise with regard to the Bible, for if one were to ask as to why there are only four Gospels, the answer is quite ready and can be given without a moment's delay that they are four because four men wrote them severally! But if some mischievous fellow were still to persist in questioning why should not Barnabas' Gospel also be counted along with these, then the padre's ready answer though given with an ill-grace will be; 'oh well, we don't include it because it goes against us.'

The first four Seers of the Vedas,

These four Vedas were, at the beginning of creation, i. e., just when human beings were created, revealed to the four prime Seers Agni, Vaayu, Soorya and Angiras respectively. In the hearts of these four, the Vedic Law was first impressed at one and the same time. How it happened it cannot be known now, but something like the filling of the gramophone record may be

* (1) The Vedas are revealed at the time of the creation, not so the other so-called revealed books. (2) They are revealed in the primitive language of humanity viz, the Vedic Sanskrit. (3) In the Vedas the attributes, nature and work of God are rightly described. He is called 'akaayam,' [Y. V. 40] 'soorya aatmaa jagatastasthushasca' [R.V. 1.115], 'dyaavaabhoomee janayan deva ekah' [Y.V. 17], 'na tasya pratimaa asti' [Y. V. 32]. (4) They teach man to be good [R.V. 7,104,22], [Y.V 40] advance in life [A. V. 5,16] and be at peace with his brothers [R.V. 10, 191]. They do not exaggerate man's age but reckon it as a hundred years [R.V. 10,85,39; 1,158,6: Y.V-25,22 etc.]. Man is not omniscient or almighty and can never become such [Y.V. 20, 24; 1, 5; R.V 10, 129, 6 etc.] These and many more details are given by P. Sivasankar Sarmaa Kaavyateeratha in his little Hindi tract 'Veda hi eesvareeya jnaana hai' published by the Arya Samaj Kaasi.

imagined. These four then propagated the Law through the Brahmaa and other sages whose hearts were afire with Divine inspiration. This hierarchy of inspired teachers of the original Revealed Law of God has never been entirely non-existent in that true Divine formation of human society called the *Ecclesia Divina.* The true Vedic Church has ever been faithfully preserving God's original Revelation whereas others out of pride, ignorance, selfishness and such other passions and base motives have 'invented' their own god and revelation consisting of inaccurate historical accounts and ugly teachings calculated to generate enmity between man and man. The preservation of the Vedas has been possible only because of such disinterested and zealous teachers.

The last of these inspired Seers of the Vedic Word are named in the 'rubrics' at the head of the hymns in the printed text. The mention of such Vedic teachers in this manner is a very old practice and before the five thousand years that have elapsed since the drawing up of the last rubrics, perhaps by *S*aunaka or *S*aakalya, it is quite probable there may have been some difference in the list. It is also quite probable that these lists come down intact from the very first publication of the Vedas, but yet they are of human origin.

The last Seers of the Vedas.

In the 'rubrics' there are several types of inspired seers mentioned. A large number of these are names of men of all social orders* (?), some of these are of ladies and others of animals and inanimate things. The last two are not seers but subjects of minor hymns purposely repeated to lay greater stress upon the signification of these texts. Anyhow the tradition according to which these rubrics were drawn up having been lost it is not now possible easily to ascertain how the names of these 'Seers' were decided upon.

The contention, however, of European Sanskritists that the rubrics contain the names of the writers of the hymns holds no water, for, there are records that a good many hymns existed long before their 'Seers'.† It should also be noted that

* Kavasha Ailusha the Seer of R.V.X, 30 seems to have been formerly a *S*oodra. Vide Aitareya Br. II, 19

† The Seer of the two hymns 61 and 62 of the tenth book of R$^{\partial}$gveda is Naabhaanedish*t*ha according to the 'rubrics.' But history says these two hymns were given to him by his father Manu. Vide Bhagavaddatta's History of Vedic Literature Vol. i, pp. 246-7, The Seer of R.V. iii, 22 is Visvaamitra but the texts existed even at the time of his father Gaadhi. Ibid. p. 248. Also his "Lecture on the R$^{\partial}$gveda pp. 41-7.

one hymn has no less than a hundred seers.* Surely such Seers or Sages cannot be the writers of the hymns.†

Hence in Vedic interpretation a good deal of serious and sincere research is still necessary. To decide what these Seers are, nobody has as yet been able to put forward any substantial data gathered through a disinterested research. The work of a good number of European scholars in this direction till now has been most damnably vitiated by their patent pro-Christian tendencies besides its costing the poor Indian tax-payer crores of rupees. The policy of these people, most of whom have been interested Christian missionary agents and spies, has been to vilify Hinduism and create splits in its fold by various means the most potent of which is a vigorous attempt to engender a distrust in the Vedas by representing them in the worst possible light.

Conclusion.

In how many ways some of the most famous European Sanskritists have endeavoured to poison the mind of the modern Hindu can be understood from the following extract:—

> "A people of this peculiar stamp of mind was never destined to act a prominent part in what is called the history of the world. This exhausting atmosphere of transcendental ideas could not but exercise a detrimental influence on the active and moral character of the Indians. But if we admire in classical history even those heroes in whom the love of country was driven to the highest pitch of fanaticism, we have scarcely a right to despise a nation, in whom the love of a purer and higher life degenerated sometimes into reckless self-sacrifice. No people certainly made a more favourable impression upon the Greeks than the Indians. And when we read the account of their moral and intellectual condition at the time of Alexander, we are obliged to admit that if some of their good qualities are no longer to be met with among the Indians of later times, this is owing, not entirely to an original defect of character, but to that continual system of oppression exercised upon them by foreign conquerors, to

* With regard to R. V. ix, 66 the rubrics say r^{ə}shih satam Vaikhaanasaah i.e., a hundred Vaikhaanasa sages are the 'Seer' (r^{ə}shih) of this hymn. The hymn contains only thirty stanzas. R.V. i, 100 has 19 verses 'seen' by five Seers. † The r^{ə}shi of S.V. i, 435 is vaajinaam stutih i. e, praise of horses; of R.V. ix, 86 (a text of 48 stanzas) aakr^{ə}shtaa maasaah, sikataa nivaavareeh, and pr^{ə}snayo 'jaah, three groups are said to be the Seer.

whose physical power they submitted, while they could not help despising their masters as barbarians. Of the demoralising influence of a foreign occupation we have an instance in the time of Alexander, in the story of Kalanas (Kalyana), who yielded to the flattering offers of the European conqueror, and left his sacred home to follow his royal master as a piece of curiosity. But Megasthenes was afterwards informed that the behaviour of Kalanas was strongly disapproved of by his friends, as ambitious and servile; while Mandanis was praised for his manly answer to Alexander's messengers, not only by his countryman, but by Alexander himself. It was long before Kalanas repented his unworthy ambition, for he burnt himself soon after at Pasargada in the same manner as the only other Brahman who reached Europe in ancient times burned himself at Athens to the astonishment of the Greeks who erected a tomb to him, with the inscription "Here lies the Indian Sarman cheya (Sraman Acharya) from Barygaza, who sought immortality after the old custom of the Indians'."*

The above passage, the unwary Hindu reader will think is a tribute to his ancestors and himself. If it is not the silliest nonsense a writer has ever blackened useful paper with, it must be the worst double dose of slow-poison intentionally administered to the 'heir of a legacy' just to kill him and destroy his heritage!

Listen to what another European "well-wisher of India" "most charitably" remarks for the benefit of the Hindu University student:—"More mystery-mongering than true philosophy is to be found also in the long Rohita hymns, of which Book xiii of the Atharvaveda consists, in which, moreover, all kinds of disconnected matter appears to be thrown together in motley confusion."

This is from Winternitz's so-called 'History of Indian Literature' which from the rabid verbiage quoted above can be said to be the worst possible libel on Vedic literature. This thoughtless writer rates at the Atharvaveda for his own inability to understand the text. There is no 'mystery-mongering' in the Vedas; that 'commodity' is available only in the market of the Semitic religious literature. For example John's 'Revelation' at the end of the New Testament is the most perfect type of 'mystery-mongering'.

---

* Max Müller op. cit. p. 15 l. 15—p. 16 l. 10.

He goes on:—"Thus for instance, Rohita, "the red one," i.e., the sun or a genius of the sun, is extolled as the creative principle—"he created the heaven and the earth,"—at the same time, however, an earthly king is glorified, and the heavenly king Rohita is brought into connection with the earthly king in an intentionally confused manner."

Now 'the cat is out of the bag'. This construction put upon the Atharvan hymn justifies all the rant and cant uttered against it. It is a good instance of 'giving the dog a bad name in order to kill it'. Who told Winternitz that the word Rohita means 'red' only and nothing else? From where did he learn that 'the heavenly king Rohita' is linked up with the earthly king'? This hymn of the Atharvaveda existed long before any earthly king named Rohita. Will he patiently listen to reason and ponder over the hymn guiding himself with the available ancillary literature? His further remarks force us to conclude that he is not open to reason. "Rohita is extolled as the highest being, but a refrain is attached, in which the same Rohita is told to crush, in his anger, him who torments a Brahman...............It would be vain to lighten the mystical semi-darkness which surrounds such and similar verses. I do not think, therefore, that we have to look for great philosophical truths in a hymn like Ath. V. iv, 11 where the Ox is extolled as the creator and preserver of the world:—"The Ox bears the earth and sky. The Ox bears the wide atmosphere. The Ox bears the six wide spheres of heaven. The Ox penetrates the whole universe'. Nor are we much impressed by the fact that this ox is identified with Indra and others of the highest gods, still less by the fact that he yields milk, "his milk is the sacrifice the priestly fee is his milking," and we willingly believe that 'he who knows the seven inexhaustible milkings of the ox, gains offspring and heaven'. This ox is of no more importance than the bull that is extolled extravagantly in Ath.V. ix, 4—he bears all forms in his sides, he was in the beginning an image of the primeval water, and so on, and that is finally discovered to be only an ordinary sacrificial bull which is to be slaughtered. The fact, however, that this pseudo-philosophy and mystery-mongering at bottom pursues a very practical purpose, is proved by such hymns as Ath. x, 10...................Only he who knows this great secret may accept a cow as a gift, and he who gives a cow to the Brahmans, gains all worlds, for in the cow is enclosed all the highest."* Later on he falls foul of Deussen

*"History of Indian Literature" Vol. I pp. 151-7.

for his taking pains to interpret Ath. V. x, 2 and xi, 8 reasonably. Obviously, Winternitz is so dangerously prejudiced against ancient Indian tradition that his remarks cannot be taken more seriously than those of an interested partisan. But his wretched book is published by the Calcutta University and circulated all over India. He interprets Vedic Sanskrit—a language spoken thousands of years ago as if it were modern Sanskrit. He is bent upon misrepresenting Vedic literature, for knowing all the methods of interpretation good and bad, he selects only the bad one for thereby he has a good cause to abuse the Vedas.*

It is high time these tricks were exposed, and this introduction and the text as well as the previous book 'Anthology of Vedic Hymns' is a humble attempt towards this.

It is but natural that there should be some mistakes,† and even serious ones, in such a serious research work; these can be rectified only in a later revision. In most of the extracts quoted from English books there are many slips. In the Arabic poem of Lavi bine Akhtab bine Turfaa also there are mistakes. These are all the copyists' blunders for the originals were not available to tally the final proofs with.

This book is embellished with a Foreword from the pen of the **Rev. Mahatama Hansraj,** but the Compiler himself is responsible for all the views expressed.

Bhūmānanda Sarasvatī.

Delhi; 21st March 1936.

---

*"The Book of the Marvels of India by one Buzurg ibn Shahriyar (in Arabic) and translated into English by L. Marcel Devie, and published by Messrs. George Routledge & sons, Ltd., Broadway House, Carter Lane, E. C., London, contains a large number of 'yarns spun' in the 'opium dens' of far-off Semitic lands to vilify the fair name of India! The curious may look up that worthless book!

†Some may find fault with the derivations given in some parts of this Introduction. They should however remember that none of them are so absurd and puerile as the following snobberies:—Max Müller=मोक्षमूलर, Macdonell=मुग्धानल, Leopold von Schroeder=जनविक्रमिन् श्रोतृ, Vienna=वीणा, Baptist Mission Press=व्यासिष्ठ मिसन यन्त्रम् etc., etc., etc.

ॐ

Ecclesia Divina

Pray to God Always.

ओ३म् ॥ योगेयोगे तवस्तरं वाजेवाजे हवामहे ।
सखाय इन्द्रमूतये ॥ ऋ० १।३०।७॥

Let us all, in unison like true friends, invoke upon God Almighty best known in His Revealed Law, for our protection and help in all our endeavours for the attainment of things even the most difficult to achieve and in all our battles in life.

Ṛgvēda I, 30, 7.

॥ ओ३म् ॥

Ecclesia Divina.

OR

The Constitution & Teaching of

THE DIVINE CHURCH.

CHAPTER I.

Obeisance to God Almighty.

Atharvavēda I, 13.

Subject:—Prayer for protection.

Seer:—The Sage Bhṛgvangiras.

Metre:—Verses 1, and 2 anuṣṭubh, and 3 & 4 jagatī.

(१) ओ३म् ॥ नर्मस्ते अस्तु विद्युते नर्मस्ते
स्तनयित्नवे । नर्मस्ते अस्त्वश्मने येना दूडाशे
अस्यसि ॥ १ ॥

Transliteration:—Namas tē astu vidyutē namas tē stanayitnavē I namas tē astvaśmanē yēnā dūḍāśē asyasi II 1.

पदपाठः— नर्मः । ते । अस्तु । विऽद्युते । नर्मः । ते । स्तनयित्नवे । नर्मः । ते । अस्तु । अश्मने । येन । दुःऽदाशे । अस्यसि ।

अन्वयः—(हे प्रजापते) ते विद्युते नमः अस्तु । ते स्तनयित्नवे नमः अस्तु । ते अश्मने नमः अस्तु येन (विद्युता, स्तनयित्नुना अश्मना च) त्वं दूडाशे अस्यसि ॥

Word-meaning &c. :—नमस्*=Salute, obeisance. **नमस्ते अस्तु**=Let our salute or obeisance be to Thee. **विद्युते**†=in Whose power is the lightning that suddenly flashes with dazzling brilliance and strikes down mighty objects in no time. **स्तनयित्नवे**‡=for the sake of the terrible thunder which at Thy command strikes terror into the hearts of all. **अश्मने**¶=Who hast at Thy command clouds that shut off even the light of the sun. **येन**=by means of which lightning, thunder and cloud. **दूडाशे**§=on the trou-

---

* नमस्—√ णम प्रह्वत्वे शब्दे च+असुन् U. IV,189 सर्वधातुभ्योऽसुन् ="the termination 'asun' is added to all roots." This is an indeclinable.

† विद्युते—वि+√ द्युत दीप्तौ+क्विप P. III, 2, 177 भ्राजभासधुर्विद्युतोर्जिपॄजुग्रावस्तुवः क्विप्=to the roots भ्राज, भास, धु, and 'dyuta' preceded by the preposition 'vi' the termination 'kvip' is added to show someone or something habitually doing the thing indicated by the verb."—विद्युत्—तस्मै.

‡ स्तनयित्नवे—√ ष्टन शब्दे+इत्नुच् U. III, 29 स्तनिहृषिपुषिगदिमदिभ्यो णेरित्नुच्="to the roots 'stana', हृष, पुष, 'gada', and 'mada' in the causal sense the suffix 'itnuc' is added." The final 'c' is indicatory.—स्तनयित्नु—तस्मै.

¶ अश्मने—√ अशुङ् व्याप्तौ or √ अश भोजने+मनिन् U. IV, 147 अशिशकिभ्यां मनिन्="to the roots अश and शक the suffix 'manin' is added in the Unadi sense."—अश्मन्—तस्मै.

§ दूडाशे=दुःदाशे—दुर्+√ दाशृ दाने+घञ् वा खल् P. VI, 3, 109 पृषोदरादीनि यथोपदिष्टम्="the words of the पृषोदरादि group are to be used as they are given," and Vārtika दुरो दाशनाशदभध्येषूत्वमुत्तरपदादेः ष्टुत्वं च="when the prefix 'dus' is prefixed to the roots दाश, नाश दभ and ध्यै, long ऊ is substituted for its penultimate vowel and final consonant; and the initial consonant of the verb is lingualised."—दूडाश—तस्मै.

blesome and oppressive person. अस्यसि=Thou dost hurl; Thou dost put down. Before येन the connecting link should be supplied thus:—यं विद्युतम् स्तनयित्नुम् अश्मानम् त्वम् दूडाशे अशित्वा येन (=तेन) तं दूडाशम् अधः अस्यसि ॥ Or the seventh case of दूडाशे may be explained according to P. VII, I, 39. सुपांसुलुक्पूर्वसवर्णाच्छेयाडाड्यायाजालः i. e., "in Vedic case formations any case termination is found replaced by 'su' the nominative singular termination, or it is dropped the crude form being used instead, or it is replaced by the original final vowel of the base, or 'āt' is substituted for it, or 'śē' 'yā', 'ḍā', 'ḍyā', 'yāc' or'āl' respectively, are used in its place" and the Vārtika on it, सुपां सुपो भवन्तीति वक्तव्यम्="it should be stated that any case termination is substituted for any other case termination". According to this principle the locative singular is used in the place of the accusative and must, therefore, be understood to have the sense of the latter. The substitution is only 'formal' the sense remaining unchanged.

Translation :—With heads bowed in obeisance we approach Thee; Oh Lord Protector of Creatures! (for protection) who hast at Thy disposal the lightning that dazzles the sight of creatures by its sudden flashes of light, the thunder which by its terrific roar strikes terror into their hearts, the cloud that by its vast bulk shuts off and darkens the sun and a host of other phenomena by means of which Thou dost oft hurl the oppressor of Thy true devotees into an abyss of misery.

Purport :—The natural phenomena of lightning and thunder are only symbols or side issues of the grand process of rain-shower which fecundates the earth and brings joy to all beings. But just as the ruler of a realm does, by the very means with which he showers honours and favours on the law-abiding, inflict condign punishment on the disloyal and re-calcitrant, so also God, by these beneficent phenomena, mete out punishment to the sinful and unjust. Hence at the sight of these a man should dispose his heart Godward and try to feel the gravity of the lapses in his life. This attitude will strengthen him to such an extent that he would be peaceful and happy in all calamities even accepting death in a quiet and cheerful mood.

Comment :—It is a well known fact that during the rainy season when the lightning flashes and thunders many men and women try to run and hide themselves. They are seized with terror at the idea of being struck by lightning. They are not all horrible debased sinners but their childish, foolish and ridiculous attitude illustrates the great truth that "cowards die many times before their death", but "the valiant never taste of death but once."* The secret of this fact is laid down in the Bible in the powerful words "the wages of sin is death."† A slavish and selfish attachment to one's own worldly life as if that were all the sum and substance of human existence inspires one with the idea of saving it at all costs. Political slavery, moral turpitude, fall from ideals cherished from ages and ages by one's ancestors and many such evils are the necessary results of such an attitude.

Death is invitable, nay, a necessity. Nobody has ever escaped death. Those religions of the world which maintain that some of their saints and sages have gone up into heaven alive, do in the same breath say that they will have to come down to the world to shed their physical bodies. The greatest of saints, the most righteous of men and women have succumbed to death. The great sages of India, even the four original receivers of the Vedas—the

*Shakespear, New Dictionary of Thoughts, p. 107.

†Paul's Epistle to Romans, VI, 23.

Universal Eternal Revealed Law—succumbed to death. Great heroes, great philanthropists, the benefactors of mankind have all succumbed to death. Men and women known during their lives on earth as paragons of great virtues; great moralists, philosophers, scientists, great learned men have all succumbed to death. Kings and queens, the rich and the poor, have all succumbed to death. The saint as well as the scoundrel, the man of most virtuous life as well as the basest of moral perverts, have all succumbed to death. Death is the leveller and it has taken the toll of all in the same manner and laid them low in the 'vile' earth.

"The wages of sin is death," surely, but it must be borne in mind that the saints died not because they were sinners but simply because they were composite beings and the composite structure of their worldly life had to go to pieces just like childrens' toys. A composite of material atoms can keep together its members only as long as their mutually attracting forces remain in play or till no outside agent intervenes and disintegrates them. The saints' bodies being composite physical structures after all, could not be an exception to this inevitable principle. Their death, in other words, was a disintegration of the particles of their physical frames. They also took their death as such and peacefully left the physical sphere of their life. The thought of death did not terrorise them since they knew that their physical existence was only one of the many phases of the great eternal sun that illumined it—the Soul. They knew the real worth of their life hence they suffered no agony in leaving it. "This outer world is but the pictured scroll of worlds within the soul; a colored chart, a blazoned missal book, wherein who rightly look may spell the splendours with their mortal eyes, and steer to paradise."* They viewed

---

* Alfred Noyce. New Dictionary of Thoughts, p. 341.

life rightly. "Life, if properly viewed in any aspect, is great, but mainly great when viewed in its relation to the world to come."*

Real life is the life of the soul and not that of the body, this latter being only "like a dome of many coloured glass, staining the white radiance of eternity."† "Life is a journey, not a home; a road, not a city of habitation; and the enjoyments and blessings we have are but little inns on the roadside of life, where we may be refreshed for a moment, that we may with new strength press on to the end—to the rest that remaineth for the people of God."‡

The great truth about life is told in the Vedas in the simplest style but most touching language. In the twentyseventh verse of the eighth hymn of the tenth book of the Atharvavēda the embodied soul is thus addressed:—"Thou (त्वं) art now a woman (स्त्री), now a man (पुमान् असि), sometimes a boy (त्वं कुमार:) or sometimes a maid (उत वा कुमारी). Emaciated with age (जीर्णः) thou dost sometimes hobble about (वञ्चसि) with a stick in thy hand, thus being born (जात:) thou assumest existence (भवसि) with innumerable phases (विश्वतोमुखः)".¶ The next verse also is important. It says "sometimes as the father of these (उतैषां पिता), sometimes as their son (उत वा पुत्र एषाम्), sometimes as their elder brother (उतैषां ज्येष्ठः), or sometimes as their younger (उत वा कनिष्ठः). this one refulgent being (एको ह देव:) [the soul] enters the cavity of the heart [in the human form assuming all these relations] (मनसि प्रविष्टः) but he is before all creation

* Albert Barnes. Ibid. 343.

† Shelley. Ibid. 341.

‡ Bonar. Ibid. 345.

¶ त्वं स्त्री त्वं पुमानसि त्वं कुमार उत वा कुमारी । त्वं जीर्णो दण्डेन वञ्चसि त्वं जातो भवसि विश्वतोमुखः ॥ A. V. X, 8, 27.

(प्रथमो जातः) though he [thus often] enters its interior (स उ गर्भे अन्तः)" *

In the Ṛgvēda also (vv. 1 & 2, hymn 24 book 1) the query is raised about the frequent assumption of corporeal existence by the soul and answered. "Who is that amongst all the immortal beings possessed of divine attributes whose charming name we shall contemplate? What is that Being who will give us birth again on earth so that we may see father and mother?" To this question the answer is given in the following words:—"We shall contemplate the charming name of Agni—the Self-effulgent God, Who is the foremost of all the immortal beings possessed of divine attributes; He will give us birth again on earth so that we may see father and mother"†.

To those who know this fact death is not 'the wages of sin'‡ but a necessary phenomenon to which all composite beings have sometime or other to succumb. To those who know this fact the present life is a prepara-

---

* उतैषां पितोत वा पुत्र एषामुतैषां ज्येष्ठ उत वा कनिष्ठः । एको ह देवो मनसि प्रविष्टः प्रथमो जातः स उ गर्भे अन्तः ॥ Ibid. 28. In their explanation of the second line of this verse some scholars take the word 'deva' to mean the Supreme Being. It seems more appropriate to translate it by soul though the former rendering is not incorrect.

† कस्य नूनं कतमस्यामृतानां मनामहे चारु देवस्य नाम । को नो मह्या अदितये पुनर्दात्पितरं च दृशेयं मातरं च ॥ ऋ० १ । २४ । १ ॥ अग्नेर्वयं प्रथमस्यामृतानां मनामहे चारु देवस्य नाम । स नो मह्या अदितये पुनर्दात्पितरं च दृशेयं मातरं च ॥ २ ॥

‡ Christian commentators of the Bible explain this to mean that death came into the world as a result of Adam's sin of disobedience to God (Genesis III, 17-19). It is a pity great European scientists believe this 'orthodox' interpretation to be true. They have 'buried their talents' wilfully.

tion, death the examination and the life after death the promotion. Hence death for them has no sting.

But unfortunately such are very few in this world, for the majority of mankind believe life to be a very rare and precious commodity of enjoyment which they must make much of enjoying all sorts of pleasures of the senses. For such there is only "one life; a little gleam of life between two eternities; no second chance for us for evermore *". Hence there are people in the world who would advise entrants in life like the philosopher who said "if I could get the ear of every young man but for one word, it would be this; *make the most and best of yourself.*—There is no tragedy like a wasted life—a life failing of its true end, and turned to a false end†". Such advice taken wrongly means fall into the abyss of sensuality. There are others again who would advise the credulous in some such strain as the following: "This life's a hollow bubble, don't you know? Just a painted piece of twouble don't you know? We come to earth to cwy, we gwow oldeh and we sigh, oldeh still, and then we die! Don't you know.‡"

Those who are carried away by such pessimistic teaching fall into the quagmire of sensuality never to rise again and wallow therein like swine in a dirty slough. To such and the foolish, illiterate folk who have never once thought upon the nature of their souls and the end of human life, death is the most sorrowful calamity which should never befall one—which must not be even so much as mentioned *en passent* in ordinary conversation. To them this life is all in all and death an

---

* Carlyle. New Dictionary of Thoughts, p. 340.

† T. T. Munger. Ibid P. 342.

‡ Edmund. Ibid. 341.

enormous loss over which tears have to be shed for days, months and years. To them, surely, life is an accidental gain and death "the wages of sin."

What is sin? Sin is poverty. Moral poverty is cowardice. Material poverty is penury or lack of means. The greatest—spiritual, poverty, is a wilful sensual way of living. The least of these is material poverty and it is a sin only in the case of such as feel its pinch. Those who do not feel its pinch will patiently bear it and live up to it. For them it is simply a 'grade of life', a 'status in society' and nothing untoward. There are many grades of life and all of them are good and useful being sanctioned by God. The humblest of them as well as the highest are all good and equal in the eyes of God who ordains them in His Providence. So far so good, but once man begins to feel the pinch of pecuniary poverty it becomes his duty to remove it by all possible legitimate means. The vedas have no good word for penury.* Those who feel the unbearable weight of poverty and allow themselves to be crushed by it without so much as raising a little finger to push it off, are real sinners and to them, life is a burden and death a misfortune. Moral poverty is cowardice which makes a man so mean-minded as to take this life as the first and the last with the result that death is the most unfortunate 'accident' that can befall one. Such shudder at the thought of death and weep and bewail for days and days when a death occurs. Spiritual poverty, a wilful sensual way of living leads a man headlong into annihilation, as he thinks. To such life after death is a mere dream.

It is exactly these three types of mankind that are a great blot on the good name of humanity. It is such that always fear all natural phenomena. The

---

* See the hymn on penury given elsewhere in this book.

rainy season, a great occasion of joy to all creation animate and inanimate, brings them, as they think, an infinite number of dangers to their precious lives. A flash of lightning is an awful warning to them that their precious possession, the like of which can never more be got once it is lost, is going to be snatched away by some unknown adversary. Hence their absurd and abject fears. These truly are the 'cowards that die many times before their death.'

Who are the oppressors of humanity? These three types of sinners oppress humanity in many ways. Those who succumb to penury for sheer lack of industry go about begging—worrying people to give them something. The moral cowards are a great sore on the body of human society for they depend upon others for their safety every minute of their life. The worst atrocities committed on their near and dear ones before their very eyes do not incite them to any valorous action. They allow themselves to be bullied by the wicked just to let them breathe their wretched existence. They wish to be in the world just to enjoy whatever pleasures come handy to them. Beyond this, life has no value for them. Such do oppress humanity—those who are weaker than themselves, in various ways to extort from them as much pleasure as they can. The third type, the sensualists, cannot pass even a moment of their life without bothering others. These have necessarily to oppress their fellow-beings. They consider their duty in life to consist in spoiling the hearth and home of others. It is such oppressors that the verse says, are hurled down into the bottomless abyss of misery and annihilation through the phenomena of lightning &c.

The words 'vidyūtē,' 'stanayitnavē' and 'aśmanē' do not imply that the ancient Aryans worshipped material objects and invoked upon them as gods. The subject of the hymn is 'Prajāpati' the Lord of creatures. A truly pious man is reminded of God by every phenomenon. "In all the vast and the minute, we see the unambiguous footsteps of the God, who gives its luster to the insect's wing, and wheels his throne upon the rolling worlds."* "Nature is too thin a screen; the glory of omnipresent God bursts through everywhere."† "The man who can really, in living union of the mind and heart, converse with God through nature, finds in the material forms around him, a source of power and happiness inexhaustible, and like the life of angels.—The highest life and glory of man is to be alive unto God; and when this grandeur of sensibility to him, and this power of communion with him is carried, as the habit of the soul, into the forms of nature, then the walls of our world are as the gates of heaven."‡ "Nature is the glass reflecting God, as by the sea reflected is the sun, too glorious to be gazed in his sphere."¶

But just see what beautiful directions the Sacred Scriptures have to give to the children of God! "When (यद्) it thunders (स्तनयति) in the atmosphere (वीध्रे), it is as it were the Lord God the Protector of creatures Himself (प्रजापतिरेव) becomes manifest (प्रादुर्भवति) to His creatures (प्रजाभ्यः). [On such occasions,] therefore, (तस्मात्) a man should stand up (तिष्ठे) with his sacred thread under his left arm (प्राचीनोपवीतः) and pray thus:—"Oh Lord God (प्रजापते) be gracious unto me (अनु मा बुध्यस्व इति), To him (एनम्) who knows this [and does so]

* Cowper. New Dictionary of Thoughts, p. 220.

† Emerson. Ibid. 220.

‡ G. B. Cheever. Ibid P. 418.

¶ Young. Ibid P. 419.

(यः एवं वेद) God (प्रजापतिः) as well as all creatures (प्रजाः) will, indeed, show favour (अनु-अनु-बुध्यते),"* (A.V.IX, 1, 24).

(२) नमस्ते प्रवतो नपाद्यतस्तपः समूहसि ।
मृडया नस्तनूभ्यो मयस्तोकेभ्यस्कृधि ॥२॥

Transliteration:—Namas tē pravatō napādyatas-tapah samūhasi । mṛḍayā nastanūbhyō mayastōkēbhyas-kṛdhi ॥ 2.

पदपाठः—नमः । ते । प्रऽवतः । नपात् । यतः । तपः । सम्ऽऊहसि मृडय । नः । तनूभ्यः । मयः । तोकेभ्यः । कृधि ॥

अन्वयः— (हे) प्रवतः नपात् ते नमः यतः त्वं तपः समूहसि । नः तनूभ्यः मृडय तोकेभ्यः (च) मयः कृधि ॥

Wordmeaning &c.:—प्रवतः†=of the devotee, servant,

---

*यद्वीध्रे स्तनयति प्रजापतिरेव तत्प्रजाभ्यः प्रादुर्भवति । तस्मात्प्राचीनोपवीतस्तिष्ठे प्रजापतेऽनु मा बुध्यस्वेति । अन्वेनं प्रजा अनु प्रजापति र्बुध्यते य एवं वेद ॥

The expression 'prācīnōpavītah' is a technical term (See Comment on the Brahmacārī Sūkta A. V. XI, 5 verse 3) and the rendering of it here is quite exact. It may, quite correctly, bear some other import also without contradicting the idea expressed above. The salutary practice of lifting the heart up to God in the manner described in the verse is now obsolete. The reason is not far to seek. The average 'Hindu' Indian misled by his brother spoilt with a non-religious and non-moral (irreligious and immoral?) type of education (English?) thinks that the Vedas consist of ante-deluvian (?) history, and grandmother's tales with a lot of 'madman's raving' and 'child's prattle,' in short 'shibboleth'. Wrong interpretations put upon Vedic statements by foreign (European?) 'scholars' with a smattering of mediaeval Sanskrit are at the bottom of the anti-Vedic tendencies broadcast in India by the faithful Hindu desciples of the European 'guru'.

† प्रवतः—प्र + √ वन संभक्तौ याचने च + क्विप् P. III, 2, 178 अन्ये-

suppliant. **नपात्*** =Who does not let (His devotees) fall; saves from falling. **यतः†** =wherefore. **तपः‡** =trouble, tribulation. **समूहसि**=enjoinest; sendest upon; bringest. **मृडय** =

भ्योऽपि दृश्यते,="the termination 'kvip' is added to other roots also and the resultng iform would mean someone habitually doing something denoted by the verb," VI; 4,40 गमः क्वौ="the final nasal of the root 'gam' is dropped before the terminations beginning with 'kvi'," and the वार्तिक गमादीनामिति वक्तव्यम्="it should be stated that this dropping of the final nasal before terminations beginning with 'kvi' takes place in the case of all roots of the group 'gam' &c." On the removal of the final nasal only 'ga' remains which ends in a short vowel and hence at this stage is to be applied the principle P. VI, 1, 71 ह्रस्वस्य पिति कृति तुक्="the augment 'tuk' is to be added to a root ending in a short vowel before कृत् terminations having an indicatory 'p'."

* नपात्—न पातयति इति नञ्+√पत अधःपतने+णिच्+क्विप् P. III, 1, 26 हेतुमति च="to a verb the sign णिच् is added to signify that someone prevails upon some one else to do something indicated by the verb", and अन्येभ्योऽपि दृश्यते. The णिच् of the causal is dropped before any termination that does not take the इट् of non conjugational forms according to P. III,4,57 णेरनिटि. The negative particle 'na' remains unchanged in a number of forms which are given in P. VI, 3,75, नभ्राण्नपान्नवेदानासत्यानमुचिनकुलनखनपुंसकनक्षत्रनक्रनाकेषु प्रकृत्या. Maharsi Dayananda in his Scholion on the Yajurveda explains this word as न विद्यते पातो धर्मात्पतनं यस्य सः=who does not fall or lapse from righteousness, Vide Y.V. XII, 108,

† यतः—यत्+तसिल् P. V, 3,7 पञ्चम्यास्तसिल्="the termination 'tasil' is added on to 'kim' and other pronouns in the sense of the ablative." The pronouns 'tyad' &c., change their final syllable to 'a' before a case termination as laid down in P. VII, 2, 102, त्यदादीनामः.

‡ तपः—√तप संतापे+असुन् U. IV, 189 सर्वधातुभ्योऽसुन्.

make, render happy. तनूभ्यः* = to the bodies. नः तनूभ्यः मृडय = give us bodily or physical happiness. मयः† = happiness. तोकेभ्य‡ = to our offspring. कृधि = make, bestow upon. तोकेभ्यः मयः कृधि = bestow happiness on our offspring.

Translation :—Oh Lord God, who dost not let Thy devotee fall away from righteousness, wherefore Thou dost send tribulation on him who violates Thy command, we offer obeisance to Thee. Confer on us, we beseech Thee, happiness during our corporeal life and bestow happiness also on our offspring.

Purport:—God through His Natural Laws and Moral Order affords His devotee—the righteous, to rejoice and metes out pain and suffering to the unrighteous. Knowing this man should ever endeavour to live rightly and to diffuse happiness all over the world.

(३) प्रवंतो नपान्नम एवास्तु तुभ्यं नमस्ते हेतये तपुषे च कृण्मः । विद्म ते धाम परमं गुहा यत् समुद्रे अन्तर्निहितासि नाभिः ॥३॥

---

* तनूभ्यः—√तनु विस्तारे+उ U. I, 7 भृमृशीङ्तृचरित्सरितनिधनिमस्जिभ्य उः="to the roots भृ, मृ, शीङ्, तृ, 'car', 'tsar', 'tan', 'dhan' and 'masj' the termination 'u' is added.". The long ऊ is brought about by P. IV, 1, 66 ऊङुतः="the termination ऊङ् is added to nouns endiug in short 'u' and denoting human beings to form the corresponding feminine."

† मयः—मिनोति दुःखम् इति √मिञ् हिंसायाम्+असुन् U. IV, 189 सर्वधातुभ्योऽसुन्. This word is included in the synonyms of happiness in the Nighanṭu III, 6.

‡ तोकेभ्यः—तौति पूरयति गृहम् इति√तु वृद्धौ पूर्तौ वा +क U. III, 40 कृदाधारार्चिकलिभ्यः कः="the suffix 'ka' is added to the roots कृ, दा, धा, रा, 'arc' and 'kal'." —तोकम्—तेभ्यः This word is given among the synonyms of son in the Nighanṭu II, 2.

Transliteration:— Pravatō napānnama ēvāstu tubhyam namas tē hētayē tapuṣē ca krṇmah | vidma tē dhāma paramam guhā yat samudrē antarnihitāsi nābhih || 3.

पदपाठः—प्रवंऽतः। नपात्। नमः। एव। अस्तु। तुभ्यम्। नमः। ते। हेतये। तपुषे। च। कृण्मः। विद्म। ते। धाम। परमम्। गुहा। यत्। समुद्रे। अन्तः। निऽहिता। असि। नाभिः ॥

अन्वयः—(हे) प्रवतः नपात् तुभ्यम् एव नमः अस्तु। ते हेतये च तपुषे नमः कृण्मः यत् ते परमम् धाम गुहा (तत्) विद्म। (त्वं)समुद्रे अन्तः (विश्वस्य) नाभिः निहिता असि ॥

Word-meaning &c.: – **हेतये***=to Him Who is like an adamant in dealing punishment to the wicked **तपुषे**†= to Him Who like a firearm burns the sinful. **नमः कृण्मः**:=we salute, offer obeisance to. **विद्म=विद्मः** =we know. **धाम**‡=place, station, influence, power.

---

* हेतये—√हन वधे गतौ च+क्तिन् P. III, 3,97 ऊतियूतिजूतिसातिहेतिकीर्तयश्च="the forms ऊति, यूति, जूति, साति, हेति and कीर्ति are irregularly formed by adding the termination 'ktin' to the roots 'ava', 'yu', 'ju', सा or 'san', 'han' or 'hi' and कृत् The termination 'ktin' is ordained by P. III, 3, 94 स्त्रियां क्तिन्= "to show mere state or action the suffix 'ktin' is added to a root and the resulting form will be of the feminine gender," Or √हि वर्धने गतौ च+क्तिन्, हन्यन्ते शत्रवः गम्यते जयः वर्धयते वा ऐश्वर्यम् अनया इति हेतिः—तस्मै. This word is included in the names of lethal weapons in the Nighaṇṭu III, 20.

† तपुषे—√तप ऐश्वर्यसंतापदाहेषु+उसि U. II, 117 अर्तिवपियजितनिधनितपिभ्यो नित्—"the Unadi suffix 'usi' is added to the roots ऋ 'vap', 'yaj', 'tan', 'dhan' and 'tap' and in these forms it operates like a termination with an indicatory 'n'." The effect of this latter according to P. VI, 1,197 ञ्नित्यादिर्नित्यम् is to make the initial syllable of the word acute."—तपुस्—तस्मै.

‡ धाम—√डुधाञ् धारणपोषणयोः+मनिन् U. IV, 145 सर्वधातुभ्यो मनिन्="the termination 'manin' is added to any root."

परमम्* =great, very great.= **गुहा**†=in the inaccessible, unapproachable, cavity of the heart. **समुद्रे**‡=in the ocean,

---

* परमम्—पर + √ मा माने + क P. III, 3,3 आतोऽनुपसर्गे कः="the termination 'ka' is added to verbs ending in long आ and not preceded by a prefix when a noun in the accusative case is compounded with it as a subordinate word." परः—तम्.

† गुहा गूहति रक्षति इति—√ गुह संवरणे + क + टाप् P. III, 1,135 इगुपधज्ञाप्रीकिरः कः="to the roots which have for their penultimate a vowel of the इक् pratyāhāra (इ, उ, ऋ and ऌ short or long) the termination 'ka' is added", and IV, 1,4 अजाद्यतष्टाप्—"the feminine of words of the अजादि group and of such as end in short 'a' is formed by adding the suffix टाप्." The initial ट् and final प् are both indicatory only आ being the termination. The word गुहा here is in the locative case according to P. VII, 1, 39 सुपांसुलुक्पूर्वसवर्णाच्छेयाडाड्यायाजालः—गुहा—तस्याम्.

‡ समुद्रे—(1) समुद्द्रवन्ति अस्मात् आपः इति—सम् + उत् + √ द्रु गतौ + ड in the sense of the ablative. The termination is enjoined by P. III, 4, 67 कर्तरि कृत्="the terminations called कृत् are applied to verbs in the sense of the nominative." But the present form though a word of very common use is a Vedic formation. (2) समभिद्रवन्ति एनम् आपः इति—सम् + उत् (in the sense of अभि) + √ द्रु गतौ + ड in the sense of the objective case. (3) सम्मोदन्ते अस्मिन् भूतानि इति सम् + √ मुद हर्षे + रक् U. II,13 स्फायितञ्चिवञ्चिशकिक्षिपिक्षुदिसृपितृपिदृपिवन्द्युन्दिश्वितिवृत्यजिनीपदिमदिमुदिखिदिछिदिभिदिमन्दिचन्दिदहिदसिदम्भिवसिवाशिशीङ्हसिसिधिशुभिभ्यो रक्="to the roots स्फाय् तञ्च् &c, the termination 'rak' is added." (4) समुदको भवति—सम् + उदक + रक् on the analogy of ऊषसुषिमुष्कमधो रः P. V, 2, 107. The word उदक is changed to उदन् by P. VI, 1, 63 पद्दन्नोमास्हृन्निशसन्यूषन्दोषन्यकञ्छकन्नुदन्नासञ्छस्प्रभृतिषु="the words पद्, दत्, नस्, मास् हृद्, निश्, असन्, यूषन्, दोषन्, यकन्, शकन्, उदन्, आसन्, are substituted for the words पाद, दन्त, नासिका, मास, हृदय, निशा, असृज्, यूष, दोष, यकृत्, उदक and आसन before the

sea, intermediate regions. अन्तर* = inside. निहिता = established, placed. नाभिः† =central in the universe like the navel in the human body or like the hub of a wheel.

Translation—Oh Lord Who ever savest Thy devotees from falling away from righteousness, we offer obeisance only to Thee Who art like a terrible adamant or firearm to those who violate Thy law. We know that Thou art even in the most inaccessible place and in the cavity of man's heart. Thou art the centre of all the planetary systems extended in space (holding them together like the navel holding together the whole frame of a living being). [Or Thou art the centre of the whole universe holding it together like a hub holding a wheel together].

Purport:—The whole universe as well as each separate being in it—all depend upon God for their coming into existence as well as continuing in it. He is the centre around which all the planetary systems and all individual beings constituting the visible and invisible

---

termination शस् of the accusative plural and other terminations." The final syllable 'an' is then dropped and we have the form 'samudra'. (5) समुनत्ति जगत् (waters the whole world) इति सम्+√उन्दी क्लेदने+रक् U. II, 13 (vide (2) above).—समुद्रः—तस्मिन्. The Nirukta of 'Yāska on this word runs as follow:—समुद्रः कस्मात् । समुद्द्रवन्त्यस्मादापः समभिद्रवन्त्येनमापः सम्मोदन्तेऽस्मिन्भूतानि, समुदको भवति, समुनत्तीति वा ॥ नि. २ । १० ॥

* अन्तर—अमति गच्छति इति √अम गतौ+सुट्+अरन् U. V, 60 अमेस्तुट् च="in the case of the root 'ama' to go the augment तुट् is inserted between it and the suffix 'aran' (ordained by U. V,59 प्राततेररन् "to the root 'ata' preceded by the preposition 'pra' the suffix 'aran' is added)."

† नाभिः—दुष्टान् नाडीः वा नह्यति बध्नाति इति—णह बन्धने+इञ्= "to the root 'nah' the suffix इञ् is added before which the final ह् of the root is changed to भ्."

universe are severally arranged in their orbits. He is also present directly in every place however inaccessible to finite beings and in the hearts of all. Hence by His Wonderful and Almighty Providence He is able to reward or punish every human being according to his or her good or bad deeds. Therefore, the devotee knowing this, should ever dispose himself in a humble mood to worship Him.

Comment:—The second and third verses of this prayer hymn extol the Omnipotent Providence of God in rewarding or punishing rational beings according as they conformed to His universal Moral Law or not. This idea is expressed in the second verse. The third verse in a very terse and precise manner mentions the essential traits of His Powerful Providence. He is directly present in any place even the most inaccessible to any finite being. The first verse of the fortieth chapter of the Yajurveda describes the Omnipresence of God in the following manner :—"Both the mobile and immobile creation (jagat) in its totality (yat kim) in this (idam) infinite (sarvam) universe (jagatyām) is pervaded (vāsyam) by the Supreme Eternal Spirit, [the repository and the prime source of all wealth and energy] (Iśā). Enjoy (bhuñjīthāh), [O mortal, the righteous pleasures of this world] in a spirit of indifference (tēna tyaktēna) and do not aspire (mā gṛdhah) to the wealth of any fellow being (kasyasvit dhanam)*". In the fourth and fifth verses following the same truth is still forcibly set forth with reasons:—"The Supreme Being is fearless, immutable and uniform (anējat). He is One and One only (ēkam). He surpasses the mind in vigour and energy (manasah

*ईशावास्यमिदं सर्वं यत्किंच जगत्यां जगत् । तेन त्यक्तेन भुञ्जीथा मा गृधः कस्यस्विद्धनम् ॥ य. ४० । १ ॥ The translation given is that of the late Bava Chajju Singh, Editor Arya Patrika, Lahore.

javīyah). The senses (dēvāh) cannot perceive (na āpnuh) Him (ēnat). He pre-exists in every conceivable object or locality (pūrvam arṣat). Though immovable in His own nature, (tiṣṭhat) He (tat) evades the grasp of (ati eti) the subtle mind and the senses over which the mind presides (dhāvatah anyān). Energised by Him (tasmin) the soul (mātariśvā) acts (apah dadhāti)." "The Supreme Being (tat) eludes wholly and entirely the grasp of ignorant minds (ējati) although in His own nature (tat) He is uniform and immovable (na ējati). From those devoid of true knowledge He is far (tat dūrē) though verily (u) He is most adjacent to the wise (tat antikē). He (tat) pervades the inside (antah) of this infinite universe (asya sarvasya) and verily (u) He (tat) engrosses the outside (bāhyatah) of it (asya sarvasya).*" The eighth verse again says:—"The Supreme Being (sah) pervades the entire universe even as space (pari agāt). He is of infinite might and the Creator of all (Śukram). He is incorporeal and exempt from birth and death (akāyam). He is indivisible and impenetrable by the minutest conceivable object (avraṇam). He is free from the bonds of nerves and muscles (asnāviram). He is Holy and above every phase of ignorance (Śuddham). He is free from sin and every sinful desire (apāpaviddham). He is Omniscient (kavih) and privy to our inmost thoughts (manīṣī). He presides over all (paribhūh) is self-existent and the efficient cause of the universe (svayambhūh). He reveals (vyadadhāt) to His eternal (śāśvatībhyah) subjects (samābhyah) the true (yāthātathyatah) knowledge of the Vedas (arthān)†".

---

*अनेजदेकं मनसो जवीयो नैनद्देवा आप्नुवन्पूर्वमर्षत् । तद्धावतोऽन्यानत्येति तिष्ठत्तस्मिन्नपो मातरिश्वा दधाति ॥ ४ ॥ तदेजति तन्नैजति तद्दूरे तद्वन्तिके । तदन्तरस्य सर्वस्य तदु सर्वस्यास्य बाह्यतः ॥ ५ ॥

†स पर्यगाच्छुक्रमकायमव्रणमस्नाविरं शुध्दमपापविद्धम् । कविर्मनीषीः परिभूः स्वयंभूर्याथातथ्यतोऽर्थान्व्यदधाच्छाश्वतीभ्यः समाभ्यः ॥ ८ ॥

A knowledge of this wonderful nature of God's Being ought to dispose the human soul to bear an attitude of the sincerest and most humble reverence towards His Omnipresent Majesty. This is exactly the idea this beautiful hymn purports to teach the devout by the repeated burden 'namas tē'. The present verse by the further expression 'nama ēvāstu tubhyam' purports that only that God who possesses these features is fit to be adored and none else. The verses quoted from the Yajurvēda above also extol His Omnipresent and Omnipotent Providence in various expressions and the result is drawn in the sixteenth verse of the chapter thus—"O self-effulgent Omniscient Lord (agnē vidvān) we bow unto Thee (tē namah uktim vidhēma) with profound humility (bhūyiṣṭhām). Cast out (yuyōdhi) from us (asmat) all debasing and sinful (juhurāṇam)—desires and habits (ēnah) and lead us (naya asmān) by paths of righteousness (supathā) to the acquisition of all true knowledge (viśvāni vayunāni) that we may enjoy true happiness (rāyē)*". This thought is found in our second verse in the expression 'mṛḍayā nastanūbhyō mayastōkēbhyaskṛdhi'. Such a prayer cannot be offered to any god but the Supreme Being.

God is "resident" in the cavity of the heart of the human being. In the thirty second chapter verse eight of the Yajurvēda again we have a clear mention of God's being in the cave—the human heart. It says:—"The enlightened man (vēnah) perceives (paśyat) in his own mind (guhā) that Supreme Being (tat sat nihitam) in Whom (yatra) the whole universe (viśvam) has its one refuge (ēkanīḍam bhavati). The whole universe (idam sarvam)

* अग्ने नय सुपथा राये अस्मान्विश्वानि देव वयुनानि विद्वान्। युयोध्यस्मज्जुहुराणमेनो भूयिष्ठां ते नम उक्तिं विधेम ॥ १६ ॥

[with all the objects in it] comes together at the time of dissolution, in its subtle form (sam ēti) in Him (tasmin) and (ca-ca) becomes separated into gross forms at the time of creation (vi ēti). He (sah) pervades all beings through and through like the warp and-woof of a piece of cloth (ōtah prōtaśca vibhūh prajāsu)*."

In the Puruṣa hymn (Yajurvēda Chapter XXXI, 9) the human heart is called the 'throne of God'. The verse runs as follows:—"Oh men! You should realise that God the Perfect and Adorable (tam yajñam) who manifested† Himself even before the creation (jātam agratah) and Whom the learned (dēvāh), the sages (sādhyāh) and (ca) the seers of the Vedic Law (ṛṣayah) have in all ages worshipped (ayajanta) according to His divine instruction (tēna) and installed exalted high above all (prāukṣan) on the throne of their heart (barhiṣi)".‡

In the Chāndōgyōpaniṣad (VIII, 3, 3) it is said:—"This Supreme Being (ēṣa ātmā) indeed (vāi) is in the heart (hṛdi). He can only be described as residing in the heart (tasyāitadēva niruktam hṛdyayamiti). Therefore He is called the Heart (tasmādhṛdayam). He who knows (ēvamvid) everyday (aharaharvā) enjoys higher and higher bliss (svargam lōkam ētī)¶".

---

*वेनस्तत्पश्यन्निहितं गुहा सद्यत्र विश्वं भवत्येकनीडम् । तस्मिन्निदं सं च वि चैति सर्वं स ओतः प्रोतश्च विभूः प्रजासु: ॥ य. ३२ । ८ ॥

† The past tense here does not mean that there is human history in the Vedas but simply means that the latest creative act on the part of God took place somewhere about 1972949035 years ago or thereabouts which is a fact.

‡तं यज्ञं बर्हिषि प्रौक्षन्पुरुषं जातमग्रतः । तेन देवा अयजन्त साध्या ऋषयश्च ये ॥ य. ३१ । ९ ॥

¶स वा एष आत्मा हृदि । तस्यैतदेव निरुक्तम् हृद्ययमिति । तस्माद्धृदयमिति । अहरहर्वा एवंवित्स्वर्गं लोकमेति ॥ Ch. VIII, 3, 3. This vigorous passage totally gives the lie to the foolish idea prevailing among

In the Antaryāmī Brāhmanam it is stated that though God resides in the interior of the human soul (=heart) the latter does not know Him The human soul is, so to say, His body."* The heart is situated in the body, the soul resides in the heart and God in the soul.

But how can this be since the human soul is finite and the Supreme Being Infinite? Can the finite contain the Infinite? The relation between the human soul and God is not that of the container and the contained for none can contain God Who contains all. The expression 'yasyātmā śarīram' is a figure simply meaning that it is only the human soul that can in any way approach God so as to know Him by direct cognition, for which, she has no need to go far but simply to direct her eyes on her own self which is so near to the Supreme Being as man's body is to his soul. Without soul the body cannot subsist, so also without God the human soul cannot exist. Besides, God's sphere of existence is quite different from that of our physical bodies the sense organs of which are intended only to sense things of the physical sphere. Made of the same matter of which the physical universe is made, they have no power to work in the sphere beyond or other than, the physical. Our inability to see God is due to our not having means appropriate to visualise Him. As He belongs to the

---

the simple-minded and upheld by so many man-made religions that 'svarga'—heaven is a particular place or sphere of existence. If this were true how could one manage to go there daily and come back? 'Svarga' simply means a state in which during earthly life, man secures all the means of happiness and advancement. Such a one 'daily enjoys happiness and advances onward'.

* य आत्मनि तिष्ठन्नात्मनोऽन्तरो यमात्मा न वेद यस्यात्मा शरीरम् ॥ अन्तर्यामी ब्राह्मणम् ॥

subtle spiritual universe and we to the gross material, we cannot perceive Him. We have no means in the physical world by which we could traverse the physical sphere and pass on to the spiritual. As long as such means are not available, and they will never be available in the material world, we must be satisfied with such mental processes as would help us to analyse material things and to pierce through their thick material veil by means of the subtle light of the mind having thereby a peep at the wonderful dazzling radiance of the Supreme Being. In other words, as long as we live in the material world as embodied beings, it is only the mind that will help us to perceive God's Being indirectly, though we cannot see Him directly. This again means that between God and the embodied human soul there is only the mind that can bring about some sort of 'communication' or relation. The mind is material but extremely subtle. On account of its subtleness it can come into contact with the subtle spiritual world and as it is material, it can communicate also with the physical. Partaking thus, of the nature of both the soul as well as matter, it can help us to commune with both the subtle and gross universes of existence.

The soul, a subtle spiritual being, ought to have been able to realise God, but the veil of the gross material body and surroundings has darkened her vision and until this curtain is not lifted by a mental process of eliminative reasoning, coupled with an all round spiritual discipline, it is not possible for her to know about God. Once the veil of gross matter is removed or pierced through, it will be seen that the Supreme Being is very near to the human soul.

God is the centre of the universe. Writing on the Einstein Theory an American writer Samuel Guggenheimer thus expresses himself:—" In the light of the analysis of all substances into one substance, and that one substance a form of energy, we reach by the methods of physical science, something similar to the philosophic deduction that all matter is a manifestation of a force in its nature unknown and unknowable to finite mind; and it must of necessity follow that the age-old controversy between the materialist and the idealist or spiritualist is, in its ancient form at least, a thing of the past. There can be no longer an opposition of a gross, inert matter to active spirit. Matter is reducible to force, or, if you please, spirit. The controversy still persists, however, in a restated form.

"The materialist is the non-sensitive mind * * * * * * who, having carried the analysis thus far, is content to say that the investigation is ended, that the universe rests on or consists of the manifestations of an unknowable, infinite and absolute monistic force which has developed all things up to the consciousness of man, that it is an arrogance of the human mind to conceive itself as of importance in the infinite whole, and that, with the disintegration of the human organism at death, disappears the conscious personality which for a brief instant of infinite time animated it.

"The idealist on the other hand, is lost in admiration at the power of that mind, which hampered in its infinite organism, can, nevertheless, penetrate so deeply into the nature of things, and feel so beautifully the inexpressible things beyond the reach of reason; and reverence it beyond all the tremendous physical forces that threaten it. Perhaps the idealist, in the last analysis, hopes to see demonstrated the fact that, even as underlying the appearances of the physical universe, there exists an unknowable force which may constitute one with the first, so that this one Spirit underlying both consciousness and nature constitutes the universal noumenon sought by the philosopher*."

The above passage is a fine specimen of the horrible struggle the mind of the modern European scientist to state a plain truth the Vedas do so clearly and simply express. Where the Vedic passage being dealt with calls God the centre of the whole universe the modern European scientist starts with a doubt, tries, half assenting, to refute something which he is not sure is wrong and ends in confusion. The passage quoted at length has endeavoured to state in a peculiar style that God 'may' be the centre of the universe. It is said, once an agnostic knelt devoutly to pray but the following words escaped his lips, "Oh God, if Thou dost exist, help me, if Thou canst!" This is exactly the attitude of the modern European scientist. Just compare with this the wonderfully confident and faith-compelling attitude of the Vedic passage being dealt with. "Thou punishest the wicked, Thou dost not allow Thy devotees to fall away from righteousness". Oh the wonderful childlike faith of the worshipper! "Thou art the centre of the whole universe". The faith that gives rise to such noble but involuntary thoughts must be childlike indeed but the thoughts themselves are infinitely more scientific than the straggling, studied, recalcitrant but forced and doubtful conclusions drawn by the European mind. Many phases of European life God is strictly prohibited from encroaching upon. In European politics, for example, God is conspicuous by His absence. Even the severest of religious societies in Christendom that luxuriously indulge in a sumptuous, and pompous ritual in their 'worship' of their God, do not allow that Being even so much as to peep into their politics. Once, it is

*The Einstein Theory by Samuel Guggenheimer, Macmillans New York, Pp. 38—40.

said, a Spanish missionary boasted of his having converted thousands of Moors who are the most impervious to Christian teachings. One of his friends at table admired his noble prowess but asked his reverence where the thousands of his Moorish converts were now practising the 'true religion'. "I took them all under a large military escort", replied his reverence, "and no sooner was each convert baptised in waist-deep sea water than I got him pressed down head and all into the water and held there till he breathed his last. They are all safe now in heaven practising their Christianity. A living Moor, you know, will never be a Christian." This is merely a tale but it tells a good deal more than a mere fictitious story can. When the Pharisees failed to find any just cause to arraign the high-souled Jesus before the Roman Tribunal they tried to trump up some case against him. The Bible tells us:—"Then went the Pharisees, and took counsel how they might entangle him in his talk. And they sent out unto him their disciples with the Herodians saying, Master, we know that thou art true, and teachest the way of God in truth, neither carest thou for any man: for thou regardest not the person of man. Tell us therefore, what thinkest thou? Is it lawful to give tribute unto Caesar, or not? But Jesus perceived their wickedness, and said, Why tempt ye me, ye hypocrites? Shew me the tribute money. And they brought unto him a penny. And he saith unto them, Whose is this image and superscription? They say unto him, Caesar's. Then saith he unto them, *Render therefore unto Caesar the things which are Caesar's; and unto God the things that are God's.*"*

How clear Jesus' teaching is! But he must never for a moment have dreamt that his modern followers, the Europeans, would travesty this grand principle in

* The Gospel of Matthew, XXII, 15–21.

such a manner as to cause a complete rupture between religion and science, religion and philosophy, religion and law, religion and politics etc. The natural conclusion of this heinous attitude has led to confine God to some forgotten corner of some huge legal tomes. European legal codes and treatises scorn and scoff at God, for therein He is remembered in a comical manner only in such ugly and unfortunate occurrences as earthquakes, floods, storms &c. These are called "acts of God"! Could not the European lawyer think of God in some more and better cases?

Be that as it may, the Vedas, surely, consider God to be the Central Power that holds the whole system of universe together. He is the Almighty Sun that keeps all the solar systems in their respective orbits. In law, in politics, in society, in religion, everywhere, He is foremost. Therefore ancient Indian law-givers found it necessary to teach in detail on morality also. They teach that law and ethics are inseparable.

Concerning faith in the providence of God, the Centre of the whole universe, the Guide in life of every human being and the Support that sustains all beings, just listen to what a poet whose heart was "inflamed" with the love of God has to say:—

Revelation

Still, as of old, in Beavor's Vale,
O man of God! our hope and faith
The Elements and Stars assail,
And the awed spirit holds its breath,
Blown over by a wind of death.

Takes Nature thought for such as we,
What place her human atom fills,
The weed-drift of her careless sea,
The mist on her unheeding hills?
What recks she of our helpless wills?

Strange god of Force, with fear, not love,
Its trembling worshipper ! Can prayer
Reach the shut ear of Fate, or move
Unpitying Energy to spare ?
What doth the cosmic Vastness care ?

In vain to this dread Unconcern
For the All-Father's love we look;
In vain, in quest of it, we turn
The storied leaves of Nature's book.
The prints her rocky tablets took.

I pray for faith, I long to trust;
I listen with my heart and hear
A voice without a sound: 'Be just,
Be true, be merciful, revere
The word within thee : God is near !

'A light to sky and earth unknown
Pales all their lights; a mightier force
Than theirs the powers of Nature own,
And, to its goal as at its source,
His spirit moves the Universe.

'Believe and trust. Through stars and suns,
Through life and death, through soul and sense,
His wise, paternal purpose runs;
The darkness of His providence
Is star-lit with benign intents.'

O joy supreme ! I know the Voice,
Like none beside on earth or sea;
Yea, more, O soul of mine, rejoice,
By all that He requires of me,
I know what God Himself must be.

No picture to my aid I call,
I shape no image in my prayer;
I only know in Him is all,

Of life, light, beauty, everywhere,
Eternal Goodness here and there!
I know He is, and what He is,
Whose one great purpose is the good
Of all. I rest my soul on His
Immortal Love and Fatherhood;
And trust Him, as His children should.

I fear no more. The clouded face
Of Nature smiles; through all her things
Of time and space and sense I trace
The moving of the Spirit's wings,
And hear the song of hope she sings*.

(४) यां त्वा देवा असृजन्त विश्व इषुं कृण्वाना असनाय धृष्णुम् । सा नो मृड विदथे गृणाना तस्यै ते नमो अस्तु देवि ॥४॥

Transliteration:—Yām tvā dēvā asṛjanta viśva iṣum kṛṇvānā asanāya dhṛṣṇum I sā nō mṛḍa vidathē gṛṇānā tasyāi tē namō astu dēvi II 4.

पदपाठः—याम् । त्वा । देवाः । असृजन्त । विश्वे । इषुम् । कृण्वानाः । असनाय । धृष्णुम् । सा । नः । मृड । विदथे । गृणाना । तस्यै । ते । नमः । अस्तु । देवि ॥

अन्वयः—विश्वेदेवाः याम् त्वा असनाय धृष्णुम् इषुम् कृण्वानाः असृजन्त सा विदथे गृणाना नः मृड । (हे) देवि तस्यै ते नमः अस्तु ॥

Word-meaning:—**याम्**=to that; to her. **त्वा**=to Thee. **याम् त्वा**=to Thee of such description. The prayer is here addressed to the Divine Majesty of God and hence the feminine gender. **देवाः**=the wise. **असृजन्त**=have

---

* Complete Poetical Works of J. G. Whittier, Oxford University Press, 1898, pp. 506,7.

made; have discharged, fancied, imagined. **विश्वे*** = all; adj. to **देवाः**. **इषुम्**† = spear. **कृण्वानाः** = making. **इषुम् कृण्वानाः असृजन्त** = have made of Thee a spear and discharged Thee; have by their mental faculty, fashioned Thee into a spear. **धृष्णुम्**‡ = very strong, powerful, firm. **असनाय**§ = for throwing, supplanting, destroying all adverse circumstances, beings etc. **सा** = that. **नः** = to us. **मृड** = help, succour.

---

* विश्वे—विशति सर्वत्र इति—√ विश प्रवेशने + कन् U. I, 151 अशूप्रुषिलटिकणिखटिविशिभ्यः क्वन् = "the suffix कन् is added to the root अश, प्रुष, लट, खट and विश." The initial 'k' and final 'n' are indicatory only 'va' being the termination.—विश्वः—ते.

† इषुम—ईषति गच्छति हिनस्ति वा शत्रून् इति √ ईष गतिहिंसादर्शनेषु + उ U. I, 13 ईषेः किच्च = "to the root ईष the termination 'u' ordained by U. I, 7 is added and it operates as if it had an indicatory 'k' and the initial long vowel in the present case is shortened." The effect of the indicatory 'k' is to prevent गुण or वृद्धि as explained in P. I, 1, 5. Or इच्छति वा भक्तजनानाम् इच्छाः पूरयति इति √ इष इच्छायाम् + उ P. III, 3, 1 उणादयो बहुलम् = "the उणादि terminations are variously applied to roots even other than those mentioned in the treatise on the उणादि formations"—इषु—तम्.

‡ धृष्णुम् √ त्रिधृषा प्रागल्भ्ये + क्नु P. III, 2, 140 = त्रसिगृधिधृषिक्षिपेः क्नुः = "to the roots त्रस्, गृध्, धृष् and क्षिप् the termination क्नु is added to show habitual action." The initial 'k' is indicatory only 'nu' being the termination.—धृष्णुः—तम्.

§ असनाय—अस्यति विनाशयति शत्रून् दुरितानि वा इति—√ असु क्षेपणे + ल्युट् P. III, 3, 113 कृत्यल्युटो बहुलम् = "the कृत्य terminations and the termination ल्युट् are added even to other roots than those for which they are expressly ordained." In ल्युट् the initial ल् and the final ट् are indicatory only 'yu' being the *name* of the termination. The termination, is 'ana' as laid down in P. VII, 1, 1 युवोरनाकौ = "for the terminations 'yu' and 'vu' ordained in the अष्टाध्यायी 'ana' and 'aka' should be substituted,"—असनम्—तस्मै.

विदथे*=in philanthropic works; in preaching learning and teaching. . **गृणाना**† = teaching, advising. **तस्यै ते**= to Thee of such description. **देवि**=Oh Divine Majesty! **इषु** also means that by which one desires hence something that can fulfil one's desires. Hence **इषुम् कृण्वानाः असृजन्त** would mean "representing" Thee by means of their rational faculty to be the fulfiller of all desires. **कृण्वानाः** can be construed also with **असनाय** the expression then meaning, "having made up their minds to remove all obstacles—the foe, from the path of their desires. **असनाय कृण्वानाः त्वा इषुम् असृजन्त**=having determined to remove the foe from their path have fashioned Thee into a powerful weapon therefor; having made up their minds to remove all obstacles from the path of their desires, have found Thee, by their rational faculty to be a means to fulfil their wishes.

Translation:—Oh Divine Majesty! all the wise have by their rational faculty, fashioned Thee into a powerful means to fulfil their wishes by destroying all that is adverse to their desires. Thou teachest us to engage ourselves in righteous works and helpest us therefor. Oh Providence! to Thee, Who alone art of this description, do we offer our obeisance.

---

* विदथे—√ विंद ज्ञाने विचारणे सत्तायाम् √ विदलृ लाभे वा+अथ U. III, 115 रुविदिभ्यां ङिच्च=to the roots रु and विद् the termination अथ is added and it operates like one having an indicatory ङ्." According to P. I, 1, 5 क्ङिति च the indicatory ङ् prevents गुण or वृद्धि.—विदथः—तस्मिन्.

† गृणाना —√ गॄ शब्दे+शानच् P. III, 2, 124 लटः शतृशानचावप्रथमासमानाधिकरणे="when agreement of a verb with a noun in the nominative case is not intended either the termination शतृ or शानच् is added on to it to denote something being done in the present time. The initial श and final ऋ and च् are indicatory only अत् and आन being the terminations of the present participle. अत् is parasmaipadi and आन आत्मनेपदि ।

Purport:—That Providence of God which is the means of the creation and sustenance of the universe, is also the means for dealing out justice to both the righteous and the unrighteous. The Divine disposal of things cannot brook any violation of, or interference with it. As soon as somebody transgresses it he is punished then and there. Knowing this the wise man—he, who can properly utilise his rational faculty—should direct his own life Godward, i.e. in accordance with the Laws of Nature—God's Providence, and teach others also accordingly.

Comment:—In this verse God's Providence has been addressed and She has been described as a weapon fashioned by the righteous and wise, to destroy the foe and accomplish all their righteous desires. The Providence of God here, it must be understood, is personified and spoken of in the feminine gender. In the last verse of the Puruṣa hymn "the whole splendour (Śrī) and all the power [and pelf] of the entire universe [visible and invisible] (lakṣmī)" are said to be "entirely submissive to His Divine Majesty like an obedient wife unto her husband".* This is Vedic poetry and not anthropomorphism—a process in which God is attributed human passions, body and limbs. When His attributes, nature and deeds are poetically referred to, it is essential that they should be described with words of some gender. This is a linguistic and grammatical contingency which cannot be avoided. As the Eternal Law is revealed in the primordial human speech, it must submit to the principles of grammar according to which that language is used. It must also be borne in mind that if God ever ordains any language for human convenience it can only be the Vedic Sanskrit as has already been proved in the introduction and none else. There can be only one divinely ordained language and that one must conform

*श्रीश्च ते लक्ष्मीश्च पत्न्यौ ॥ य० ३१ । २२ ॥

to all the conditions arising out of its relation with the world of human exigencies. Even the Creator of the universe must conform to the rules of grammar and idiom if He wishes to communicate His Law to the human mind. Hence there is nothing awkward in the uses of the various figures of speech in the Vedic style, nay, it would have been a great misfortune had not these been used, for in that case, the world's poetry, since it is based on Vedic poetry. should have been void of all beauty and impressiveness of diction. As matters stand, it is Vedic poetry that carries the palm in this connection since it is brimful of all the beauties of speech.

The expression 'dhṛsṇum iṣum asṛjanta' has its equivalent in the English phrase 'created him a knight' etc. Just as in this latter expression it is not hinted at that the whole man, muscle, bone and skin etc., was 'dismantled' and then built limb by limb and with the breath of life breathed into his nostrils, was let off to trudge about with a tailormade uniform on and a sword dangling by his side from the waist, so also here, the sentence, 'they have fashioned Thee into a strong weapon' does not mean that they—the righteous wise men—used the blacksmith's forge etc., heated and melted Him off and then, pouring Him into a mould, hammered and brought Him out in the shape of a fine, large glittering spear! This is a figure and has many parallels in Vedic poetry.

For example in the Sāmavēda a hymn of praise is compared to a chariot. The verse runs: "We send forth this hymn of praise through our minds, like advancing a chariot, to God the Revealer of the Vedas Who deserves our eulogy, for, in His presence our understanding becomes sanctified. Oh Refulgent God! may we not, remaining in Thy favour, injure others or be injured ourselves."*

---

*इमं स्तोममर्हते जातवेदसे रथमिव सम्महेमा मनीषया । भद्रा हि नः प्रमतिरस्य संसद्यग्ने सख्ये मा रिषामा वयं तव ॥ सामवेद १ । ६६ ॥

In another verse it is said that God Himself is fashioned into a chariot and a missile !! "Oh Lord God, always invoked by the pious ! the (righteous) men fashion Thee by (meditation) into a chariot in which they wish to finish quickly the journey to the liberation of their souls, and oh Lustrous One! the enlightened man advanced in spiritual knowledge makes of Thee (by contemplation) a powerful missile with which he desires to kill his foes (in the shape of lust, anger and other passions)*"

European writers also have used such figures. Empedocles wrote :—"God is a circle whose centre is everywhere, and its circumference nowhere†". Another says :—"An old mystic says somewhere, "God is an unutterable sigh in the innermost depths of the soul." With still greater justice, we may reverse the position, and say the soul is a never ending sigh after God.‡"

This is the teaching of the Divine Church on the worship of God. Worship, she says, is to be offered only to that Supreme Being (1) Who has in His Almighty Providence the creation and direction of all natural phenomena; (2) Who is the Rewarder of the righteous and adoration of Whom keeps the devotee in the path of righteousness and truth ; (3) Who is the punisher of the wicked—the wilful miscreants who disobey His Revealed Commandments and oppress others in various ways and (4) Who is the centre of the whole system of the universe on Whom the whole universe always depends for its creation and sustenance, all the planetary systems and all creatures being kept in their respective orbits and order by His Almighty Providence.

---

*अनवस्ते रथमश्वाय तक्षुस्त्वष्टा वज्रं पुरुहूत द्युमन्तम् ॥ सामवेद १ ।४४० ॥

†Empedocles, New Dictionary of Thoughts, p. 226.

‡Christlieb, Ibid, pp. 220—1.

In the second point mentioned above there is a very important principle involved, which Aryan India has followed all through the long ages past even at the sacrifice of her wealth and political liberty. Even today, it may be safely asserted that, it is only the genuine Aryan Indians—the so-called Hindus, out of the whole family of ***home sapiens*** that follow this divine principle. The principle is very important and Truth herself depends upon it for her sustenance. It is this that God Himself supports His true devotee, the man of righteousness, and keeps Him in the path of Truth and righteousness. In other words it means, a true devotee of God will be a man of righteousness never swerving from his righteous life, i.e., he will never in any way persecute others for the sake of his religion or country but even-handed, mete out justice to all. Religion can never interfere with the legitimate liberty, peace and happiness of others not of the same persuasion. Its adherents will never find it necessary to protrude their religion on others by pomp and show. They will never worry others not of their persuasion by legal actions, killing of animals, ravishing their women or any such steps as are entirely opposed to the Divine Law of Righteousness according to which all human beings are equal being children of the same Divine Father. Religion is for man and not man for religion is true in the case of all man-made religions which are no better than tailor-made coats which, if they are tight or unshapely, must be thrown away. But the Divine Religion, the Teaching of the Divine Church which She has received from Her Divine Father from all eternity, is a peculiar soulful training which can make a man a man and without undergoing which, a man will not grow to his full moral and spiritual stature but though a giant corporally, wlll remain much less than man—something between man and beast.

This hymn lays down that true soul-worship of God will keep a man within the limits of Righteousness This trait is found only in Vedic teaching and nowhere else as has been pointed out in the introduction and will be proved conclusively at the end of this book.

A sincere pursuit of true and useful knowledge.

ओ३म् ॥ ब्रह्मचारी चरति वे विषद्विषः स देवानां भवत्येकमङ्गम् । तेन जायामन्वविन्दद्बृहस्पतिः सोमेन नीतां जुह्वं१ न देवाः ॥ अथर्ववेदे । ५ । १७ । ५ ॥

The student of the Eternal Universal Revealed Law ever entering the subject of his pursuit (with an undivided attention and singleness of purpose), becomes (so to say), an indispensable member of the conclave of the wise. Hence it is, that he—the (indefatigable and ever vigilant) guardian of all the branches of the Eternal Lore, attains that Bounteous Divine Science introduced into the world by the August Creator which yields all sorts of happiness (including final emancipation).

Atharvavēda, V, 17, 5.

CHAPTER II.

The Student of the Eternal Universal Revealed Law
OR
Pursuit of True Knowledge.

Atharvaveda XI, 5.

(५) ओ३म् ॥ ब्रह्मचारीष्णंश्चरति रोदसी उभे तस्मिन् देवाः संमनसो भवन्ति । स दाधार पृथिवीं दिवं च स आचार्यं१ तपसा पिपर्ति ॥१॥

Transliteration :—Brahmacārīṣṇaṅścarati rōdasī ubhē tasmin dēvāh sammanasō bhavanti । sa dādhāra pṛthivīm divaṃ ca sa ācāryam tapasā piparti ॥ 1.

पदपाठः—ब्रह्मऽचारी । इष्णन् । चरति । रोदसी इति । उभे इति । तस्मिन् । देवाः । समऽमनसः । भवन्ति । सः । दाधार । पृथिवीम् । दिवम् । च । सः । आऽचार्यम् । तपसा पिपर्ति ॥

अन्वयः—ब्रह्मचारी उभे रोदसी इष्णन् चरति । देवाः तस्मिन् संमनसः भवन्ति । स पृथिवीं दिवं च दाधार । स आचार्यं तपसा पिपर्ति ॥

Word-meaning &c:—ब्रह्मचारी*=the student who pursues the study of the Vedas (the Eternal Revealed Law)

---

* ब्रह्मचारी—√ बृहि वृद्धौ+मनिन्, U. IV, 146, बृहेर्नोऽच्च="to the root बृहि the suffix मनिन् is added (in which—इन् is indicatory the suffix being only मन्) of which the final न् is dropped in the neuter, nominative and accusative cases and changed to 'a' in the first five case forms of the masculine, the ऋ of the root being changed to र् throughout."—ब्रह्मन्, ब्रह्मणे वेदाय चरितुं

observing the vow of perfect chastity. **इष्णन्***=exploring continually; desiring. **चरति**=goes about. **रोदसी**†=the earth and the sun or the heavens. **उभे**=both. **तस्मिन्**=in him. **देवा**‡:=all who crave after glory; all beneficent objects, all forces of nature. **संमनसः**¶=of one mind. **भवन्ति**=become;

शीलमस्य अस्ति इति—ब्रह्मन्+√चर गतौ+णिनि ब्रह्मचारिन् P. III, 3, 170 आवश्यकाधमर्ण्ययोर्णिनिः="the termination णिनि is added to a root to denote the agent who out of necessity does something indicated by the verb or who borrows." This termination shows also habitual action. The initial ण् and final इ are indicatory.

* इष्णन्—√इष आभीक्ष्ण्ये+श्ना+शतृ. P. III, 1, 81 क्र्यादिभ्यः श्ना="to the roots क्री &c. of the ninth conjugation the sign श्ना is added in the conjugational tenses and moods (viz., the present, the imperfect, the imperative and potential)" and 2, 184 लटः शतृशानचावप्रथमासमानाधिकरणे="when no agreement of a verb with a noun in the nominative case is intended the termination शतृ and शानच् are added on to it to denote action being done in the present time." The initial श्, the final ऋ and च् are indicatory letters only ना अत् and आन remaining to be added to the root.

† रोदसी—√रुदिर् अश्रुविमोचने+असुन् U. IV, 189 सर्वधातुभ्योऽसुन् ="the termination असुन् is added to all roots.," and P. IV, 1, 41 षिद्गौरादिभ्यश्च="the feminine suffix ङीष् is added to a word of the group of words beginning with गौर &c." The गौरादि group is not complete and includes words of similar type by implication. In असुन् the final उन् and in ङीष् the initial ङ् and final ष् are indicatory letters only अस् and ई being the terminations.

‡ देवाः—√दिवु क्रीडाविजिगीषाव्यवहारद्युतिस्तुतिमोदमदस्वप्नकान्तिगतिषु+अच् P. III, 1, 124 नन्दिग्रहिपचादिभ्यो ल्युणिन्यचः="the terminations ल्यु, णिनि and अच् are added on to the roots of the group beginning with √नन्द्, √ग्रह्, and √पच् respectively to denote someone doing the thing indicated by the verb."

¶ सम्मनसः—समानानि मनांसि येषां ते P. II, 2, 24 अनेकमन्यपदार्थे= "two or more words in apposition to each other are compound-

are. सः=he, दाधार=supports; makes more useful (to humanity). दिवम्*=The sun. आचार्यः†=the preceptor (one who teaches all the Vedas and the ancillarly lores). ‡तपसा=by austerity. पिपर्ति=perfects.

Translation :—The Vedic student observing the vow of perfect chastity goes about exploring the earth and the heavens. All beneficent objects and forces of nature unite in ministering to him. He makes the earth and the heavens (by his explorations) more and more useful to humanity. With the power of his austere and disciplined life he fulfils the aspirations of his preceptor.

Purport :—To study the Vedas—the Eternal Revealed Law—it is necessary that one should have full control over his senses and passions. The truths taught in the Vedas should then be put to a practical use, their

---

ed together and the resulting compound used as an adjective qualifying some other word not included in the compound itself." This is called बहुव्रीहि. The word समान here is irregularly changed to सम् and the suffix अ added on the analogy of P. V, 4, 78 ब्रह्महस्तिभ्यां वर्चसः="अ is added on to the final syllable of the word वर्चस् preceded by either the word ब्रह्मन् or हस्तिन्.

* दिवम्—दीव्यन्ति सर्वे प्राणिनोऽस्मिन्निति √ दिवु क्रीडाविजिगीषाव्यवहारद्युतिस्तुतिमोदमदस्वप्नकान्तिगतिषु + क्विप्—The termination is added after the manner of U. II, 57 क्विब्वचिप्रच्छिश्रिस्रुद्रुप्रुज्वांदीर्घोऽसंप्रसारणं च="the termination क्विप् is added to the roots वच्, प्रच्छ्, श्रि स्रु, द्रु, प्रु, and ज्रु before which the final vowel of the root is lengthened and there is no सम्प्रसारण."

† आचार्यः—आचारं ग्राहयति इति आ + √ चर गतौ + ण्यत् P. III, 1,124 ऋहलोर्ण्यत्="roots ending in ऋ or consonants take the affix ण्यत् in the sense of 'something that ought to be done', according to the sense of the verb concerned."

‡ तपसा—√ तप ऐश्वर्यसन्तापदाहेषु + असुन् U. IV, 189 सर्वधातुभ्योऽसुन्—तपस्—तेन.

full significance ascertained through careful research and experiment and in the end, they should be propagated by teaching others.

Comment :—The 'exploration' ot the earth and the heavens mentioned in this verse is a thorough investigation into all the intricacies of the subject concerned, accompanied with appropriate research and experiment. The expression 'earth and heavens', rodasī ubhē in Sanskrit, is not an exaggeration. Fiom very ancient times it has been maintained by Indian scholars that to understand the Vedas a knowledge of all the ancillary lores including astronomy and medicine is essential. The disciple—brahmacārī—began with the alphabets, proceeded on through grammar, mathematics, philosophy, law, medicine, astronomy etc., etc., and in the end, grappled with the study of the four Vedas which, considering his preparation, could not be such sealed books to him as they are to us. When completing his Vedic studies a brahmacārī in ancient Aryan India, came out of his preceptor's college as a triumphant graduate—snātaka—he was, indeed, considered a very useful and influential member of society and kings and great statesmen took pride and vied with one another in honouring him. His knowledge and upbringing were such as would enable him to bestow happiness on many by word and deed.

This is exactly what the verse means. This stanza being an introduction to the hymn mentions succinctly the gist of the whole. Details will be given in further stanzas. A reference to the Introduction also will be worth while.

(६) ब्रह्मचारिणं पितरो देवजनाः पृथग्देवा अनु संयन्ति सर्वे । गन्धर्वा एनमन्वायन्त्रयस्त्रिंशत्त्रिशताः षट्सहस्राः सर्वान्त्स देवांस्तपसा पिपर्ति ॥२॥

Transliteration:—Brhmacāriṇam pitarō dēvajanāh pṛthagdēvā anusaṃyanti sarvē । gandharvā ēnam anvāyaṃstrayastriñśattriśatāh ṣaṭsasharāh sarvān sa dēvāṃstapasā piparti ॥ 2.

पदपाठः—ब्रह्मऽचारिणम् । पितरः । देवऽजनाः । पृथक् । देवाः । अनुऽसंयन्ति । सर्वे । गन्धर्वाः । एनम् । अनु । आयन् । त्रयःऽत्रिंशत् । त्रिशताः । षट्ऽसहस्राः । सर्वान् । सः । देवान् । तपसा । पिपर्ति ॥

अन्वयः– पितरः देवजनाः देवाः सर्वे ब्रह्मचारिणं पृथक् अनुसंयन्ति । त्रयस्त्रिंशत्त्रिशताः षट्सहस्राः गन्धर्वाः एनम् अनु आयन् । स सर्वान् देवान् तपसा पिपर्ति ॥

Word-meaning &c.:–**पितरः***=the protectors (of society). **देवजनाः**†=men aspiring after victory, or success in life. **पृथक्**‡=separately; in various ways. **देवाः**=wise men. **अनुसंयन्ति**=follow. **सर्वे**¶=all. **गन्धर्वाः**§=the diligent who support the earth. **एनम्**=him. **अनु आयन्**=have followed.

---

*पितरः—√ पा रक्षणे+तृन् U II, 95 नप्तृनेष्टृत्वष्टृहोतृपोतृभ्रातृजामातृमातृदुहितृ="The words नप्तृ, नेष्टृ, त्वष्टृ, होतृ, पोतृ, भ्रातृ, जामातृ, मातृ, and दुहितृ are formed by adding the Unadi terminations तृन् or तृच् to the root concerned."

†देवजनाः—देवाः च ते जनाः P. II, 1, 57 विशेषणं विशेष्येण बहुलम्= "an adjective may be compounded with the noun it qualifies in most cases." The final acute is justified by P. VI, 1, 223 समासस्य ="all compound words have the acute accent on the final syllable."

‡पृथक्—√ प्रथ प्रख्याने+अजि U I. 137="to the root प्रथ् to publish the suffix अजि is added." The final इ is indicatory only अज् being the termination. The word पृथक् is an adverb.

¶ सर्वे—√ सृ. गतौ+वन् U I, 153 सर्वनिघृष्वरिष्वलष्वशिवपद्वप्रह्वेष्वा, अतन्त्रे="the words सर्व, निघृष्व, रिष्व, लष्व, शिव, पद्व, प्रह्व, and ईश्व are formed by adding the suffix वन् to the roots concerned but not those specially mentioned in the grammatical treatise and which are derivative".

§गन्धर्वाः—गाम् धरतीति गन्धर्वः—ते । गो+धृञ् धारणपोषणयोः+व U I., 155 कॄगॄशॄदॄभ्यो वः="to the roots कॄ, गॄ, शॄ, and दॄ the suffix व

त्रयस्त्रिं*शत्त्रिशताः† षट् सहस्राः‡=Six thousand three hundred and thirty three.

Translation :—Protectors of human society, men wishing for success in life, and those well-versed in the affairs of the world, have always in different ways, followed the man of subdued passions given to the pursuit of Vedic learning. Nay, the diligent, the six thousand three hundred and thirtythree supporters of the earth have also allowed themselves to be led by him, for, he fulfils, by his mortified and regulated life, [the wishes of] all those who aspire after success.

---

is added", and P. VI, 3, 109 पृषोदरादीनि यथोपदिष्टम्="words belonging to the group of पृषोदर etc., are to be taken as they are handed down by ancient authorities."

* त्रयस्त्रिंशत्—त्रयः च त्रिशंत् च P. II, 2, 29 चार्थे द्वन्द्वः="any number of nouns put together by the use of the the copulative conjunction च can be compounded together and the resulting compound is called 'dvandva'—copulative." त्रि—√ तॄ प्लवनसंतरणयोः +ड्रि+सुच् U. V, 66 तरतेड्रिः="to the root तॄ the suffix ड्रि is added" and P. VI, 3, 48 त्रेस्त्रयः="त्रयः is substituted for त्रि when the latter is compounded with another numeral and tho resulting compound is not बहुव्रीहि. त्रिंशत्—त्रयो दशतयः परिमाणम् अस्य संघस्य इति त्रि दशत्= त्रिन्+शतिच् P. V, 1,59 पङ्क्तिविंशतित्रिंशच्चत्वारिंशत्पञ्चाशत्षष्टिसप्तत्यशीतिनवतिशतम्—"the words पङ्क्ति etc., are formed irregularly".

† त्रिशताः—त्रिः आवृत्तं शतं येषु ते P. II, 2, 24 अनेकमन्यपदार्थे.

‡ षट् सहस्राः—षड्धा आवृत्तम् सहस्रं येषु ते P. II, 2, 24 अनेकमन्यपदार्थे. सहस्र—√ षह मर्षणे+असुन् U. IV, 189 सर्वधातुभ्योऽसुन्=सहस् (=बहु निघं० ३ । १ ॥)+र P. II, 2, 94 तदस्यास्त्यस्मिन्निति मतुप="the suffix मतुप् is added to a noun in the nominative case and the resulting form indicates 'someone' or 'something possessing the thing denoted by the noun, or 'in which it exists'," and 107 ऊषसुषिमुष्कमधो रः="to the words ऊष, सुषि, मुष्क and मधु, the suffix र is added to show possession." On the analogy of these instances the terminations are to be applied to other cases also when necessary.

Comment :—For an explanation of the number 6333 we have to refer to Bṛhadāraṇyakōpaniṣad III; 9, 1 and 2,* where it is related, being asked by Vidagdha Śākalya about the number of the 'dēvas,' Yājñyavalkya, in reply, stated it to be 3306 and then explained that the 'dëvas' are only 33 viz., the eight vasus (fire, earth, air, the intermediate region, the sun, the heavens, the moon and the stars), the eleven rudras (the five intellectual senses, the five motor organs, and the mind), the twelve ādityas (the twelve months of the year so called because they arise from the revolution of the earth round the sun—āditya), Indra and Prajāpati; but the rest i. e, 3306—33 were the extensions of the glory of these 33. The word **सहस्र** in Vedic language means 'many,' 'all,'† 'glory'‡ 'very great'¶ 'the worlds,' 'the Veda, and speech'§ 'life,'$ 'the beasts,' ⫲ etc. Hence the number

* अथ हैनं विदग्धः शाकल्यः पप्रच्छ कति देवा याज्ञवल्क्येति । स हैतयैव निविदा प्रतिपेदे यावन्तो वैश्वदेवस्य निविद्युच्यन्ते त्रयश्च त्री च शता त्रयश्च त्री च सहस्रेति । ओमिति होवाच । कत्येव देवा याज्ञवल्क्येति त्रयस्त्रिंशदित्योमिति होवाच । कत्येव देवा याज्ञवल्क्येति । षडित्योमिति होवाच । कत्येव देवा याज्ञवल्क्येति द्वावित्योमिति होवाच । कत्येव देवा याज्ञवल्क्येत्यध्यर्ध इत्योमिति होवाच । कत्येव देवा याज्ञवल्क्येत्येक इत्योमिति होवाच । कतमे ते त्रयश्च त्री च शता त्रयश्च त्री च सहस्रेति ॥१॥ स होवाच महिमान एवैषामेते त्रयस्त्रिंशत्त्वेव देवा इति । कतमे ते त्रयस्त्रिंशदित्यष्टौ वसव एकादश रुद्रा द्वादशादित्यास्त एकत्रिंशदिन्द्रश्चैव प्रजापतिश्च त्रयस्त्रिंशाविति ॥२॥ बृ० ३ । ६ ॥

†सर्वं वै तद्यत्सहस्रम् ॥ शां. ११ । ७ ॥ २५ । १४ ॥ श. ४ । ६ । १ । १५ ॥ ६ । ४ । २। ७ ॥

‡भूमा वै सहस्रम् ॥ श. ३ । ३ । ३ । ८॥

¶परमं सहस्रम् ॥ तां. १६ । ९। २ ॥

§तदाहुः किं तत्सहस्रमितीमे लोका इमे वेदा अथो वागिति ब्रूयात् ॥ ऐ. ६ । १५ ॥

$आयुर्वै सहस्रम् ॥ तै. ३ । ८ । १५ । ३ ॥ १६ । २ ॥

⫲ पशवः सहस्रम् ॥ तां. १६ । १० । १२ ॥

6333 also means the same as explained by the sage Yājñyavalkya. Modern astronomy also affords an explanation of the number 6000. "The number of stars of all magnitudes visible to the naked eye is about 6000, so that the greatest number visible at any time—as we can only see one half of the sky at once—is 3000,"* This verse and the hymn as a whole, is a fine specimen of the Vedic style which in its manner is both intensive and extensive. In its purview it takes cognizance of all the notes of a thing it deals with and also refers to all other things that are somehow concerned with its theme. But in spite of the great difficulty and importance of the subject, very often, the language used is so simple and ordinary that a careless and uninterested reader may find only puerilities or foolishness in the description. In handling such statements great care and patient application is necessary. There was a time in the history of the world, no doubt, as the passage III, 9, 1 and 2 from the Bṛhadāraṇyakōpaniṣad bears witness when a good number of people took part in discussions on such topics. Their life did not end with daily routine but continued far into those vistas of the spiritual side of man's existence which are nowadays relegated to rank esotericism. They devoted the most solemn part of their day to meditating over such things and arrived at a full knowledge of their true values. Modern life has sapped the mind of man and rendered him entirely unfit to utilise his thinking faculty. If we do not understand the true significance of such topics as the present verse deals with, it is simply because we have lost the habit of handling them in a proper manner owing to our worldly-mindedness and gross materialistic tendencies. It is the mentality of the modern man that makes the theme

---

*गन्धर्वाः, सप्तविंशतिः (गन्धर्वाः नक्षत्राणि—इति सायणो महीधरश्च) ॥ श. ५ । १ । ४ । ८ ॥ Lockyer's Elements of Astronomy.

esoteric and not the real nature of the subject itself. It would be wrong, therefore, to take such topics as intended for the initiate few to be received at the hands of some august sage at some secret conclave on an auspicious occasion. The Vedas are intended for the whole humanity and not a select few. Hence, if properly approached in the right spirit and with sufficient preparation they will allow any body to carry away plenty of riches from their storehouse.

In the present verse the terms **पितरः, देवजनाः, देवाः** and **गन्धर्वाः** as well as the number six thousand three hundred and thirty three seem to hamper the average reader's way of grasping the true and full significance of the passage. An effort must, therefore, be made to understand these four terms by pondering over them and then the number six thousand three hundred and thirty three will lose much of its mysteriousness.

The word 'dēva' in ordinary converse is used to denote the highest class in human society. Explaining the verse XI, 4 Yajurvēda, the Śatapatha Brāhmaṇa VI, 3, 1, 16 says that Prajāpati is 'vipra' the wise one and wise men viz., the Brāhmaṇas are the dēvas*. The Ṣaḍviṃśa Brāhmaṇa I, 1 says that the Brāhmaṇas are 'gods among men'.† The learned man that feels the presence of God, studies the Eternal Revealed Law and goes about teaching people, is called a dēva in the Brāhmaṇas.‡ The wise, learned and experienced man

---

* विप्रा विप्रस्य (य० ११ । ४) इति प्रजापतिर्वै विप्रो देवा विप्राः ॥ श० ६ । ३ । १ । १६ ॥

† अथ हैते मनुष्यदेवा ये ब्राह्मणाः ॥ ष० १ । १ ॥

‡ आहुतिभिरेव देवान्प्रीणाति दक्षिणाभिर्मनुष्यदेवान्ब्राह्मणांछुश्रुवुषोऽनूचानान् ॥ श० २ । २ । २ । ६ ॥ द्वया वै देवाः । अहैव देवा अथ ये ब्राह्मणाः शुश्रुवांसोऽनू-चानास्ते मनुष्यदेवाः ॥ श० २ । २ । २ । ६ ॥ ४ । ३ । ४ । ४ ॥

is also called a dēva.* In later Sanskṛit literature also the term is used in a similar sense. The Vāijayanti p. 293, l. 92, e. g., says that the word is used in the sense of 'venerable' or 'respectable'†. The Amarakōśa also explains it as meaning the wise.‡

But the word **देव** in Vedic literature has an infinite variety of meanings. This is made clear in the Brāhmaṇas. The mind, the vital air, the senses, the seasons, speech, the day etc., are all called 'dēva.'¶ Hence a reference to the hoary Brāhmaṇa literature is quite necessary to understand the full significance of the word.

The word 'pitarah' also is used in various senses. The Śatapatha Brāhmaṇa e. g., explains it as the night,

---

* विद्वांसो हि देवाः ॥ ३ । ७ । ३ १० ॥

† भगवान्पूज्यपादश्च देवाश्चार्चार्थिकास्तथा ॥ ४६ ॥ The Vaijayanti of Yadavaprakasa p. 293.

‡ देवः = सुरः = विबुधः ॥ अमरकोष १ । १ ॥ See also Medini Kosa Dhantavarga, v. 36.

¶ ऋतवो वै देवाः ॥ २ । श० ७ । २ । ४ । २६ ॥ प्राणा वै देवाः ॥ श० ७ । ५ । १ । २१ ॥ चक्षुर्देवः ॥ गो० १ । २ १० ॥ मनो देवः ॥ गो० १ । २ । १० ॥ वाक् च वै मनश्च देवानां मिथुनम् ॥ ऐ० ५ । २३ ॥ वागेव देवाः ॥ श० १४ । ४ । ३ । १३ ॥ वाग्देवः ॥ गो० १ । २ । १० ॥ वायुर्वै देवः ॥ जैउ० ३ । ४ । ८ ॥ यशो देवाः ॥ श० २ । १ । ४ । ६ ॥ तस्माद् (देवाः) यशः ॥ श० ३ । ४ । २ । ८ ॥ देवा वै यशस्कामाः सत्रमासत ॥ तां० ७ । ५ । ६ ॥ श्रीर्देवाः ॥ श० २ । १ । ४ । ६ ॥ परोऽक्षंवै देवाः ॥ श० ३ । १ । ३ । २५ ॥ परोऽक्षकामा हि देवाः ॥ श० ६ । १ । १ । २ ॥ ७ । ४ । १ । १० ॥ सत्यमेव देवा अनृतं मनुष्याः ॥ श० १ । १ । १ । ४ ॥ २ । १७ ॥ ३ । ३ । २ । २ ॥ ६ । ४ । १ ॥ सत्यसंहिता वै देवाः ॥ ऐ० १ । ६ ॥ अपहतपाप्मानो वै देवाः ॥ श० २ । १ । ३ । ४ ॥ त्रयस्त्रिंशद्वै देवाः प्रजापतिश्चतुस्त्रिंशः ॥ श० १२ । ६ । १ । ३७ ॥ तां० १० । १ । १६ ॥ १२ । १३ । २४ ॥ अष्टौ वसवः । एकादश रुद्रा द्वादशादित्या इमेऽएव द्यावापृथिवी त्रयस्त्रिंश्यौ त्रयस्त्रिंशद्वै देवाः प्रजापतिश्चतुस्त्रिंशः ॥ श० ४ ५ । ७ । २ ॥ तां० ६ । २ । ५ ॥ ऐ० २ । १८ ॥ ३७ ॥ ३ । २२ ॥ गो० २ । २ १३ ॥ शां० १२ । ६ ॥ The references are not exhaustive.

beings inhabiting spheres beyond the human world, the cardinal points etc.*

The word 'gandharva' is variously interpreted in the Brāhmaṇas. In the Śatapatha the wind is called 'gandharva'. The Jāiminīya Upaniṣad Brāhmaṇa also gives the same interpretation of the word. The mind, 'manas', a righteous act, 'yajña', the fire, 'agni', the moon, 'candramas', the sun, 'sūrya' etc. are all called by the name gandharva.† Some other Brāhmanic passages seem to indicate that uxorious or voluptuous‡ persons, such

---

* रात्रिः पितरः ॥ श० २ । १ । ३ । १ ॥ तिर इव वै पितरो मनुष्येभ्यः ॥ श० २ । ४ । २ । २१ ॥ अवान्तरदिशो वै पितरः ॥ श० १ । ८ । १ । ४० ॥ २ । ६ । १ । १० ११ ॥ पितरो नमस्याः (the respectable) श० १ । ५ । २ । ३ ॥ ये वै यज्वानः (the philanthropic or righteons) ते पितरो बर्हिषदः ॥ तै० १ । ६ । ९ । ६ ॥ मासा वै पितरौ बर्हिषदः ॥ तै० १ । ६ । ८ । ३ ॥ ३ । ३ । ६ । ४॥ सोमप्रयाज्ञा हि पितरः ॥ तै० १ । ६ । ९ । ५ ॥ इन्दव इव हि पितरः । मन इव ॥ तां० ६ । ९ । १९ ॥ २० ॥ ओषधिलोको (vegetable world) वै पितरः ॥ श० १३ । ८ । १ । २० ॥ षड्वाऽऋतवः पितरः ॥ श० ९ । ४ । ३ । ८ ॥ ऋतवः पितरः ॥ शां० ५ । ७ । ॥श० २ । ४ २। २४॥ ६ । १ । ४॥ गो० २ । १ । २४॥ ६ । १५ ॥ ऋतवः खलु वै देवाः पितरः । ऋतूनेव देवान्पितॄन्प्रीणाति । तान्प्रीतान्मनुष्याः पितरोऽनुप्रपिपते ॥ तै० १ । ३ । १० । ५ ॥ क्षत्रं (the ruling class) वै यमो (the controller or governor) विशः (the commercial class) पितरः (protectors) श० ७ । १ । १ । ४ ॥ अपराह्णः पितरः ॥ श० २ । १ । ३ । १ ॥ अन्तभाजो वै पितरः ॥ शां० १६ । ८ ॥ मर्त्याः (the mortal) पितरः ॥ श० २ । १ । ३ । ४ ॥ अनपहतपाप्मानः पितरः ॥ श० २ । १ । ३ । ४ ॥ पितृलोकः पितरः ॥ शां० ५ । ७ ॥ गो० २ । १ । २५ ॥ पितरः प्रजापतिः ॥ गो० २ । ६ । १५ ॥ मनः पितरः ॥ श० १४ । ४ । ३ । १३ ॥ देवा वा एते पितरः ॥ शां० ५ । ६ ॥ गो० २ । १ । २४ ॥ स्विष्टकृतो वै पितरः ॥ गो० २ । १ । २५ ॥ The texts are not exhaustive.

† वातो गन्धर्वः ॥ श० ९ । ४ । १ । १० ॥ मनो गंधर्वः ॥ श० ९ । ४ । १ । १२ । यशो गन्धर्व ॥ श० ९ । ४ । १ । ११ ॥ अग्निर्हु गंधर्वः ॥ श० ९ । ४ । १ । ७ ॥ चन्द्रमा गन्धर्वः ॥ श० ९ । ४ । १ । ९ ॥ सूर्यो गन्धर्वः ॥ श० ९ । ४ । १ । ८ ॥ असौ वा आदित्यो दिव्यो गन्धर्वः ॥ श० ६ । ३ । १ । १९ ॥ प्राणो वै गन्धर्वः ॥ जैउ० ३ । ३६ । ३ ॥

‡ योषित्कामा वै गन्धर्वाः ॥ श० ३ । २ । ४ । ३ ॥ ९ । ३ । २० ॥ स्त्रीकामा वै गन्धर्वाः ॥ ऐ० १ । २७ ॥ ते (गन्धर्वाः) उ ह स्त्रीकामाः ॥ शां० १२ । ३ ॥

as are fond of perfumes* and of beautifying their persons† are in Vedic language called 'gandharva'. The primary derivative sense of the word, however, points towards those who themselves support, cultivate, advance whatever is called 'gō' and help others also to do so. These may be peasants, preachers, tutors, rhetoricians and scholars since all these have to do with 'gō', the earth or 'gō', speech, learning or the Vedas. This is the only right interpretation of the term since it is quite in keeping with Vedic style in which each word of the language is used in its original derivative sense as human convention had not yet come into existence at the time of the first creation at the beginning of the present cycle. This question has been considered in detail in the Introduction and need not be restated here.

From the details given above it follows that the words 'dēvāh', 'pitarah', 'gandharvāh' and 'dēvajanāh' are used in the verse under consideration to mean the four divisions or classes of men in human society viz., 'the teachers or preceptors', the guides of society in matters moral, spiritual and temporal; 'the protectors or guardians' of society, who rule over the land and guard the material interests of the populace, 'the supporters of the land' the agriculturists and traders whose duty it is to make it convenient for all classes to eke out their temporal existence by supplying them all their material needs and hoarding abundant means therefor and finally, 'the men of the public', who have to look to the convenience of all the other classes by serving them corporally in various ways. The subdivisions of these four main divisions for the convenience

---

*गन्धो मे मोदो मे प्रमोदो मे । तन्मे युष्मासु (गन्धर्वेषु) ॥ जैउ० ३ ।२५ ।४॥

† गन्धेन च वै रूपेण च गन्धर्वाप्सरसश्चरन्ति ॥ श० ६ । ४ । १ । ४ ॥ रूपमिति गन्धर्वा उपासते ॥ श० १० । ५ । २ । ३० ॥

of the corporate life of society would amount to millions according to time and clime which means that the number six thousand three hundred thirty three means "innumerable divisions and subdivisions as well as the thirty three celestial (very powerful) objects and their extensions." It would be unreasonable to suppose that the number denotes something definite and must not therefore be taken to mean simply innumerable. Such an unreasonable attitude would force upon us the awkward conclusion that the great ancient scholar the sage Yājñyavalkya did not know this point but he has simply evaded the question put by Vidagdha Śākalya and hoodwinked his adversary by telling a barefaced lie.

The word 'sahasra' has already been explained above. The sense of the word relevant here is 'the universe' or 'all the worlds and beings in them'. The other sense 'innumerable' or 'incalculable' is also required side by side with this since in Vedic style words are used in their fullest significance. The word 'ṣaṭ' prefixed to 'sahasra' means the efficient and material cause of the latter. Ṣaṭ indicates the 'product' of the five (2, & 3) primary beings at the root of all creation—'sahasra'. They are viz., the Supreme Being, the soul, the primordial matter, the mind and the ego. The two and three are not the universe by which term we mean all the worlds,—all the planets and beings upon them, the space in which they are and the time which regulates their existence. The universe is temporal but these two and three are not. They are beyond time. The Supreme Being is the '*raison d'etre*' (=the cause of the being) of all. The soul is the '*raison d'etre*' of the creation. Prakṛti or primordial matter is the material omnipotence (sāmarthya) of the first and the manas —mind and ahaṃkāra—ego, are means by which Prakṛti produces her evolutes for the sake of the soul. If the mind and the ego were not to be, it would be impossible to bring about a connection between her and the soul since the former is material and the latter spiritual. These two subtle material and foremost evolutes of Prakṛti exist in a very distinct state even during the post-deluge period as stated in R. V. X, 129, 4 (see the Nāsadīya Hymn given elsewhere in this book). Primordial matter along with these pre-existing elder evolutes of hers is in a manner unintelligible to us and inexplicable in our human idiom, multiplied as it were, with the other two the Supreme Being and the soul, with the result that we have $3 \times 2 = 6 < 1000$. In this wonderful multiplication there is no merging of the figures, e. g., you multiply 3 by 2 and get 6 after which 3 and 2 do not exist. They merge, so to say, in the result, viz., 6. Here however, none merge in the result, but all co-operate and produce it, keeping, at the same time, their separate 'individuality' or identity intact. The arithmetical multiplication is an extremely imperfect process, a mere shadow of this wonderful Divine multiplication. You give 3 and 2 to the giant Arithmos and ask him to give you their product. He, on his part, takes 3 and 2, puts them together, makes them into one mass and then cuts this latter into 6 parts. You have lost your 3 and 2 of two different values and dimensions, for the giant gives in return 6 of smaller value and dimensions. This is not multiplication but a mere exchange! It is, at best, a process of re-arrangement and not of multiplication. Real multiplication is creative. The original items remain intact but there is a growth – a real growth over and above the originals. Such concrete multiplication is ordained by Divine Providence, and is found in the development of the species of embodied living beings. The pair remain the same yet there is a family. What a wonderful thing it is! You multiply 1 by 1 and sometimes get even a dozen the original 1 and 1 remaining intact. That means in this case $1 \times 1 = 14$, but the giant Arithmos gives you $1 \times 1 =$ only 1! Arithmetical multiplication is merely symbolical. But out of symbols you cannot get the reality. Is the science of Arithmetic wrong in this connection then? No. It means $1 \times 1 = 1$, i. e., one living being united with another living being of appropriate nature according to the principles sanctioned by God would co-operate and both grow and the ultimate result would be one aggregate—a family, fused into one being, so to say, by ties of kinship, affection and interest. This is what the symbolic representation $1 \times 1 = 1$ means. The symbol $3 \times 2 = 6$ means that if two and three co-operate they will have the strength of six.

The Divine multiplication of creation takes place at the beginning of the 'cycle.' How does this come about? The attributes and 'properties' of the soul—her wonderful nature affords an answer to this difficult question. The ancient Aryan sage Gāutama, defines soul as the substratum of "desire, repulsion, feelings of pleasure, feelings of pain, conscious exertion (will), and consciousness"* The Vaiśeṣika system describes it as being characterised by "inhalation, exhalation, winking, i. e., the acts of dropping the eyelids and raising them up, vitality, consciousness, motion, variations brought about in the attitude of the sensoria by the influence of sense-objects, the feeling of happiness, the feeling of pain, will, dislike, and effort."† The sum and substance of these statements comes to this that, the soul possesses 'jñāna'—knowledge, 'icchā'—volition and 'kṛtimattva'—

* इच्छाद्वेषप्रयत्नसुखदुःखज्ञानान्यात्मनो लिङ्गम् ॥ न्या० १ । १ । १० ॥

† प्राणापाननिमेषोन्मेषजीवनमनोगतीन्द्रियान्तर्विकाराः सुखदुःखेच्छाद्वेषप्रयत्नाश्चात्मनो लिङ्गानि ॥ वै० ३ । २ । ४ ॥

PLATE V

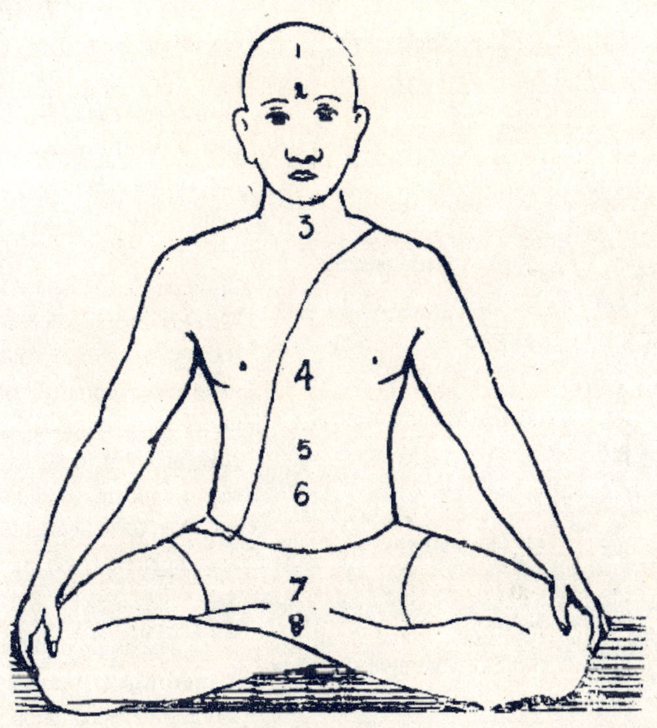

This picture represents the Svaastikaasana and Siddhaasana, two postures of Yogic exercise. The latter is considered to be the best as it is the easiest and the most comfortable. This is the position: The exercitant sits on his haunches placing the ball of his right heel exactly under the perinaeum and below the genitals. The left is then placed upon the genitals exactly in a line with the right below. The trunk, neck and head are kept erect, the arms serving as props to support them. The hands are placed on the knees or a little above them as it suits the exercitant. The eyes should neither be closed nor left open but kept on winking but looking at some particular spot to avoid distraction.

The spots numbered 1-8 are the traditional places in the head and spine of the following:-

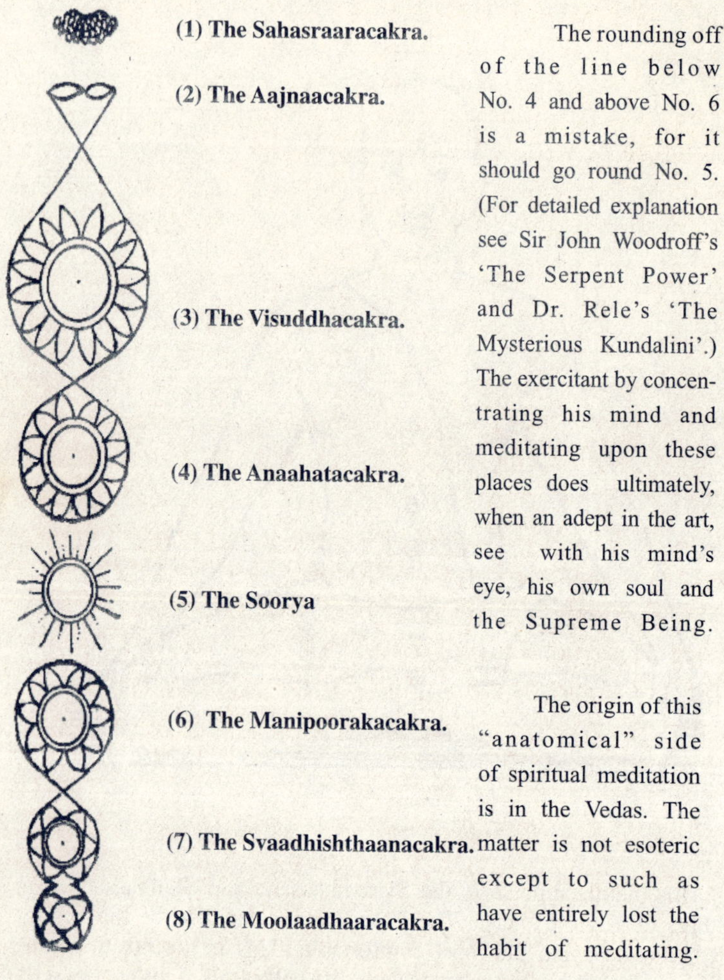

The rounding off of the line below No. 4 and above No. 6 is a mistake, for it should go round No. 5. (For detailed explanation see Sir John Woodroff's 'The Serpent Power' and Dr. Rele's 'The Mysterious Kundalini'.) The exercitant by concentrating his mind and meditating upon these places does ultimately, when an adept in the art, see with his mind's eye, his own soul and the Supreme Being.

The origin of this "anatomical" side of spiritual meditation is in the Vedas. The matter is not esoteric except to such as have entirely lost the habit of meditating.

N.B. In the Svaastikaasana the toes of the right foot are passed through the left calf and thigh from below, and those of the left between the right calf and thigh from above.

(To face p. 57.)

effort in a limited degree whereas the Supreme Being has them in an infinite 'degree'.

These attributes or 'properties' of the soul ever remain with her whether she has a body on or not. In the embodied state continuing for a long time, being tired of the struggle for existence in earthly life, having suffered from various vicissitudes, having gained experience leading on to right knowledge she yearns after her God and calls upon Him saying "Oh Lord! may hymns of praise approach Thy throne of grace lifted up in all the quarters of the universe inhabited by human beings, (resounding through space). Oh bestow on me that, I beseech Thee, which Thou hast not as yet bestowed upon me (i. e., perfect joy), for, Thou, Oh Lord! art my worthy Friend, whom I have won by scaling the seven rungs of the ladder of spiritual discipline, and "Oh Most Excellent Lord! we both are brothers and our nature is akin (i. e., we are both entirely spiritual beings). (To this God replies) I know, oh devotee! that our nature is akin. I now give thee that which I did not give thee before, for thou hast properly won my friendship by scaling the seven rungs of the ladder of spiritual discipline."*

This is the dialogue between the Finite and the Infinite. The two met. The Finite had long awaited the chance. The ups and downs of mortal life prevailed upon the Finite to make a vigorous investigation into her real nature. What did she find? The Finite and the Infinite had a close kinship, both were existence and intelligence, the latter—the Supreme Being—unlimited and independent and the former limited and dependent.

*आ ते स्तोत्राण्युद्यतानि यन्त्वन्तर्विश्वानि मानुषीषु दिक्षु। देहि नु मे यन्मे अदत्तोऽसि युज्यो मे सप्तपदः सखाऽसि ॥ अ० ५। ११। ६ ॥ समा नौ बन्धु वरुण समा जा वेदाहं तद्यन्नावेषा समा जा। ददामि तद्यत्ते अदत्तोऽस्मि युज्यस्ते सप्तपदः सखास्मि ॥ १० ॥

But as long as her knowledge stopped short at this stage the Finite felt elated at the vast gulf of difference that separated her from the vile material universe that had with its tawdry pomp and show and evanescent pleasures, but mostly on account of her own lack of true knowledge of herself, had kept her fettered down to her physical life so long. But, she now thought, the time had come when all material ties would be shattered by heavy blows dealt with the strong club of her realization of her true spiritual nature. How wonderful was her true self as distinct and severed from material attachments! "Face to face with the heavens or this earth," she said to herself in a transport of contemplation of her own self, "my glory is greater, which I have realised while oftentimes enjoying the advantages of spiritual discipline."* She then concluded "well then, here and now, will I sever all my attachments to this earth for, erstwhile have I enjoyed the pleasures of spiritual advance and am now satisfied."†

She did not rest here. A mere resolution was of no consequence. "A good intention clothes itself with power."‡ " If we are but fixed and resolute—bent on high and holy ends, we shall find means to them on every side and at every moment; and even obstacles and opposition will but make us "like the fabled spectre-ships, which sail the fastest in the very teeth of the wind."* "Good resolutions are," therefore, "a pleasant crop to sow.—The seed springs up so readily, and the blossoms open so soon with such a brave show, especially at first. But when the time of flowers has passed,

---

* अभि द्यां महिना भुवमभी३मां पृथिवीं महीम् । कुवित्सोमस्यापामिति ॥ ऋ० १० । ११९ । ८ ॥

† हन्ताहं पृथिवीमिमां निदधानीह वेह वा । कुवित्सोमस्यापामिति ॥ ९ ॥

‡ Emerson, New Dictionary of Thoughts, p. 550.

* Tryon Edwards, Ibid, 550-1.

what as to the fruit?"† But resolutions have their own value and importance. "The block of granite which is an obstacle in the pathway of the weak, becomes a stepping stone in the pathway of the strong."‡ In the case of well-developed souls sincere resolutions bring about altogether 'miraculous' results. It is in connection with such that it can be said that "to think we are able is almost to be so; to determine upon attainment is frequently attainment itself; earnest resolution has often seemed to have about it almost a savour of omnipotence".¶

The resolution of the finite was such, nay, it was much more than this, since it had a very strong and well-disciplined will at its back. She herself felt this. "Just as the mother cow stands near her dear calf (and protects it) so has my reason strengthened by the spiritual training I have erstwhile had, stood me in good stead now."* Such well-balanced will is essential in the world's struggle for existence. "The nerve which never relaxes—the eye which never blanches—the thought which never wanders—the purpose that never wavers—these are the masters of victory"† and these are found only when there is a strong, sincere and practical resolution issuing from a powerful will. Call it reason, call it will, call it what you will, it is the most potent factor in man's life which if well directed makes it or ill directed mars it. The Vedas sing of it in sublime language! "I place before me the auspicious and divine Resolve, the mother of my faculty of reasoning.

† L. Malet, Ibid., 550.

‡ Carlyle, Ibid., 550.

¶ S. Smiles, Ibid., 550.

* उप मां मतिरस्थित वाश्रा पुत्रमिव प्रियम् । कुवित्सोमस्यापामिति ॥ ऋ० १० । ११९ । ४॥

† Anonymous, New Dictionary of Thoughts, p. 550.

May she be ever accessible to me and guide me in the path of achieving my wishes with a singleness of purpose. May I attain to the object of that celestial (=very powerful) resolve which now impregnates my will."* "With powerful good resolve, Oh Lord Guardian of the Eternal Revealed Law, come to us, we beseech Thee, with powerful good resolve. Then give us Thou all great virtues and be ever approachable to us !"† This is what the Vedas teach on good resolves. 'Resolution,' says John Foster, 'is omnipotent.' He that resolves upon any great and good end, has by that very resolution, scaled the chief barrier to it.—He will find such resolution removing difficulties, searching out or making means, giving courage for despondency, and strength for weakness, and like the star to the wise men of old, ever guiding him nearer and nearer to perfection"‡ "But little is vigorously attempted, because difficulties are magnified. A timorously cautious spirit, so far from acting with resolution, will never think itself in possession of the preliminaries for acting at all. Perhaps perseverance has been the radical principle of every truly great character."§

The heroine of our story the Finite was actuated by the most powerful will to put her resolve into force. Hence with the impetus of her firm resolve she went many steps forward on her onward march. "Let me, therefore, here and now indeed, sever all my connection with earthly possessions at once, for I have in many a life enjoyed enough of them "¶ What she saw now was a

---

* आकूतिं देवी सुभगां पुरोदधे चित्तस्य माता सुहवा नो अस्तु । यामाशामेमि केवली सा मे अस्तु विदेयमेनां मनसि प्रविष्टाम् ॥ अ० १६ । ४ । २ ॥

† आकूत्या नो बृहस्पत आकूत्या न उपागहि । अथो भगस्य नो धेह्यथो नः सुहवो भव ॥ ३ ॥

‡ Tryon Edwards, New Dictionary of Thoughts, p. 550.

§ J. Foster, Ibid., p. 550.

¶ ओषमित्पृथिवीमहं जङ्घनानीह वेह वा । कुवित्सोमस्यापामिति ॥ ऋ० १० । ११६ । १० ॥

revelation to her! A defective knowledge of her own spiritual self arrived at through defective investigation had elated her beyond all expectation but what her eyes beheld now was so sublime that she felt powerless to utter her mind's content in any intelligible human speech. How can it be? Experience of things which are not of the physical sphere cannot be expressed in a language of that sphere. She however, somehow burst out, in a faltering manner, says the Divine Vedic Novel, saying :—"One side of my life (my soul—for she was yet in her corporal clothing) I have in the world (=sphere) of light (where there is no hindrance in the shape of matter and ignorance) and only one part have I brought down here in the darkness (of the material world) for in many a life have I enjoyed the pleasures of both."* "Having many a time enjoyed the pleasures of the world and being now released from their fetters I now feel that I am great among the great and that my soul's powers are extended beyond the intermediate regions."†

At this stage, still with the body attached to her, she, through mental abstraction, as if from a great distance through a waving curtain of mist, got a vague glimpse of the holy souls who had, before her, traversed from the world of matter to the bliss of emancipation.‡ The

---

* दिवि मे अन्यः पक्षो३धो अन्यमचीकृषम् । कुवित्सोमस्यापामिति ॥ ११ ॥

† अहमस्मि महामहोऽभिनभ्यमुदीषितः ॥ कुवित्सोमस्यापामिति ॥ १२ ॥

‡ The emancipated soul roams about in the Infinite All-pervading God as it desires, sees all nature through pure knowledge, meets other emancipated souls, sees all the Laws of nature in operation, goes about in all the worlds visible and invisible,, sees all objects that come within its knowledge, the more its knowledge increases the happier it feels. Being altogether pure, the soul acquires perfect knowldge of all hidden things in the state of Emancipation. The Light of truth, Dr. Ch. Bharadwaja's translation, Lahore edn, p. 284.

grand spectacle of millions, billions, trillions, quadrillions, innumerable holy souls passing and repassing the material and non-material regions filled her with an intense longing to be with them. She felt exasperated with joy at the grand possibility and her speech spontaneously burst out into a description of her indescribable feelings at the event. "During many lives have I enjoyed the happiness of worldly possessions and now, adorned with true knowledge through renunciation of the world, and becoming a fitting companion for the liberated souls in their beatific state, I shall go to associate with them on terms of equality."*

Nor is this all. The Finite of our story still in the prison cell of her body continued to develop her powers and many a time during contemplation rose high through trance to the spiritual sphere and had a foretaste of the bliss of emancipation even during her earthly life.† During such spiritual abstraction, she had once, all of a sudden the vision of a very sublime and unique spiritual being the like of whom she had never seen before nor ever dreamt of seeing. Her commune with the holy souls which she held mentally and spiritually was frequent but never before had she seen a spirit of such high order and wonderful beauty. To her soul's eye the beauty and perfection of the extraordinary spirit was so enchanting that she gazed and gazed in wonder at him but could not imagine who he could be. In the end hazy

---

* गृहो याम्यरंकृतो देवेभ्यो हव्यवाहनः । कुवित्सोमस्यापामिति ॥ ऋ० । १० ११९ । १३ ॥

† पृथिव्या अहमुदन्तरिक्षमारुहमन्तरिक्षाद्दिवमारुहम् । दिवो नाकस्य पृष्ठात्स्वर्ज्योतिरगामहम् ॥ य० १० । ६० ॥ The man accomplished in spiritual discipline says:—"From the earth I rose to the intermediate region and thence to the celestial (solar) region. From the solar plane from above the back of the heavens' I went to the sphere of perfect knowledge and happiness."

recollections from very distant past crowded in upon her mental faculty and it struck ner that it could be none but He in search of Whom she had mentally and spiritually travelled all the regions but Whom she had not as yet the good fortune to see face to face. The vision appeared clearly now, her doubts were set at rest and her mind was infused with courage. Offering her obeisance the Finite approached the Infinite and then took place the dialogue quoted above.

This is not the end of the divine drama. Only the first act is over here. What took place at the end of it need not be related in detail for the dialogue itself, if read between the lines, gives all necessary particulars.

* * *

The second act of the holy drama began in the spiritual realm. Belonging to the physical world as we do, we have no means to learn about and report things of the spiritual world. The Holy Vedas written in the earliest, and divinely ordained human speech, set forth only such things as may be intelligible to us. Where they treat of higher things the matter becomes unintelligible or so difficult for us that even after long and laborious research we cannot realise their full and true significance. Hence an account of the life of the Finite after her visit with the Infinite can be summed up in a few words, viz; that she roamed about unhindered in all the spheres physical and spiritual, all the planets, the different worlds, had frequent commune with the Infinite and the holy souls, thus adding to her store of the knowledge of innumerable things. Millions of years of such spirit life made the Finite and all other holy souls all finite like herself, to pause and contemplate over their state and what steps to take next.

Often had some holy soul whose earthly life before emancipation was an exemplar of extraordinary noble deeds assumed, with the sanction and according to the will of the Supreme Being corporeal life on the earth for the amelioration of human ills.†

At this stage, at the end of the 'deluge' period, the Finite of our story and all other holy souls felt a special longing to assume earthly life as embodied 'beings' to gather fresh knowledge by direct personal experience. But to call together the atoms of different types of matter so that by their conglomeration their bodies could be formed, was not within their power. Much less could they create other material forms for the use of their own and others' corporeal existence. Hence all approached the Infinite in a body and after reverent obeisance addressed Him in these words as the Holy Vedic novel relates:—"Oh Lord! We always contemplate (**मनामहे**) on Thy glorious name (**चारु नाम**) for Thou art adorable (**देवस्य**) the Dispenser of happiness (**कस्य**), the most Blissful (**कतमस्य**) of all the immortals (**अमृतानां**). Bliss is Thy nature (**कः**) and Thou sendest us again and again (**नः पुनर्दात**) upon the vast earth (**मह्या अदितये**) that we may see (**दृशेयं**) father (**पितरं**) and mother (**च मातरं**). Oh Lord! Thou art the most Refulgent, (**अग्नेः**). Therefore we meditate (**मनामहे**) on Thy beautiful name (**चारु नाम**) for Thou art All-Holy (**देवस्य**), Oh God it is only Thou of

† * * * * it is possible that Krishna, being very virtuous and being extremely anxious to further the cause of righteousness, might have wished that he would like to be born again and again at different times to protect the good and punish the wicked. If such was the case, there is no harm in it, because whatever the good and the great possess—their wealth, their bodies, aye even their hearts—is at the service of humanity. The Light of Truth, Dr. Ch. Bharadwaja's translation, Lahore edn., p. 206-7,

this nature (सः) that hast the power to send us again and again (पुनर्दात्) upon the vast earth (मह्या अदितये) that we may see (दृशेयं) father (पितरम्) and mother (मातरञ्च)*"

"Oh Lord God Bestower of life! (असुनीते) vouchsafe us, we beseech Thee, (perfect) mental faculties and imparting to us the full span of life (जीवातवे आयुः सु प्रतिरानः) bless us with happiness (रारंधि नः) that we may long see the sun [live vigorously active and industrious lives] (सूर्यस्य संदृशि). Nourish us (त्वं वर्धयस्व) therefore with all bodily (तन्वं) comforts (घृतेन).

"Oh Bestower of life! (असुनीते) give us again (पुनः) we beseech Thee, the sense of sight (चक्षुः) and [all other sensoria], endow us, once more, with the vital airs (पुनः प्राणम्) and bless us with all legitimate physical enjoyments (इह नः धेहि भोगम्) that we may long (ज्योक्) see (पश्येम) the sun (सूर्यम्) rising (उच्चरन्तम्) [live very vigorously active and industrious lives]. Oh Lord! may Thy Holy Will be favourable to us (अनुमते). Succour (मृळया) us (नः) that it may be well with us (स्वस्ति)

*कस्य नूनम् etc. see p. 11. The translation of the two verses here is different from the one given on page eleven. Another rendering slightly different from both these is sub-joined for the information of the reader. Whose name should we hold sacred? Who is that all-glorious, Resplendent Being who is imperishable among all the perishable things; who having made us enjoy the bliss of *Emancipation* again invests us with bodies and thereby gives us the pleasure of seeing our parents? It is the All-glorious, Eternal, Immortal, All-pervading, Supreme Being Whose name we should hold sacred. He it is Who helps us to enjoy the bliss of *Emancipation*, and then brings us back into this world, clothes us with bodies and thereby gives us the pleasure of seeing our parents. The same Divine Spirit it is Who regulates the period of *Emancipation* and lords over all." See the Introduction on the variety of renderings of Vedic texts.

"Vouchsafe Oh Lord! that we (**नः**) may receive (**ददातु**) again (**पुनः**) vitality (**असुम्**) from the earth (**पृथिवी**), the sun and celestial region (**द्यौ देवी**) as well as the intermediate [atmospheric] regions (**अन्तरिक्षम्**) provide us again with vital forces (**पुनः—पुनः—**). May all 'forces' conducive towards the reproduction of the race [or kind] (**सोमः**) unite once more, in the formation of our bodies (**पुनः नः तन्वं ददातु**) and all nutrient things (**पूषा**) provide us with those (**या**) health-giving articles (**पथ्यान्**) that will aid us in our well-being (**स्वस्तिः**)."*

It was a wonderful concurrence. The desire of the holy souls to assume bodily life, the Almighty will of the Infinite to set agoing the giant wheel of creation as well as the termination of the "night of the great deluge"† had

---

* असुनीते मनो अस्मासु धारय जीवातवे सु प्रतिरान आयुः। रारंधि नः सूर्यस्य संदृशि घृतेन त्वं तन्वं वर्धयस्व ॥ ऋग्वेद १०। ५९। ५॥ असुनीते पुनरस्मासु चक्षुः पुनः प्राणमिह नो धेहि भोगम्। ज्योक्पश्येम सूर्यमुच्चरन्तमनुमते मृळया नः स्वस्ति ॥ ६ ॥ पुनर्नो असुं पृथिवी ददातु पुनर्द्यौर्देवी पुनरन्तरिक्षम। पुनर्नः सोमस्तन्वं ददातु पुनः पूषा पथ्यान् या स्वस्तिः ॥ ७ ॥

† Maharsi Dayananda taking for his authority the second line of the following verse from the Mundakopanisad explains this point in his own vigorous style:—

वेदान्तविज्ञानसुनिश्चितार्थाः संन्यासयोगाद्यतयः शुद्धसत्वाः। ते ब्रह्म लोकेषु परान्तकाले परामृताः परिमुच्यन्ति सर्वे ॥ मुं. ३। २। ६ ॥

"The emancipated soul enjoys the bliss of *emancipation* in the Omni-present God till after the end of the *Grand-Dissolution* (*Mahapralaya*), and thereafter parts with that bliss and is again born into this world.' The period covered by *Grand-Dissolution* is calculated thus:—

Time is first divided into four yugas or cycles, viz:—

Satyayuga	...	...	17,28,000 years.
Tretayuga	...	...	12,96,000 "
Dvaparayuga	...	...	8,64,000 "
Kaliyuga	...	...	4,32,000 "
	Total	...	43,20,000

all coincided. During her embodied as well as disembodied life the Finite had invariably carried with her, her will and individuality the basis of her ego.* The unfathomable Providence of the Infinite had so ordained

---

Thus 43,20,000 years make one *Chaturyugi.*

2,000 Chaturyugis (8,640,000,000 years)=an Ahoratra (Day and night).

30 Ahoratras=one Masa (month).

12 Masas=one Varsha (year).

100 Varshas=One Parantakala (*Grand-Dissolution*).

Thus the duration of Emancipation=100×12×30×2,000 ×43,20,000=3,11,040,000,000,000 years.

Light of Truth, (Dr. C. Bharadvaja's translation, Lahore edition, p. 259,

* Maharsi Dayananda says :—"It (the emancipated soul) lives (after emancipation) and keeps its individuality." Ibid., p. 264

Again "it (the innate power of the emancipated soul) is of one kind, but it may be said to consist of the following 24 varieties :—(1) strength ; (2) energy ; (3) attraction ; (4) suggestion ; (5) motion ; (6) intimidation ; (7) analytic power ; (8) skill ; (9) courage ; (10) memory ; (11) discernment ; (12) desire ; (13) love; (14) hatred; (15) association; (16) dissociation; (17) dividing power; (18) combining power; (19) power of sight; (20) hearing; (21) touch ; (22) taste, (23) smell and (24) knowledge.

By the help of these very powers the soul attains and enjoys happiness even in *Emancipation.* If the soul, when emancipated, were to be absorbed into Brahma, who would then enjoy the bliss of *Emancipation.* Those who regard the dissolution of the soul as *Emancipation* are, no doubt, immersed in ignorance because the *Emancipation* of the soul consists in its exemption from all sin and suffering and in the enjoyment of perfect bliss in the All-pervading, All-blissful, Infinite, Omnipotent God." Ibid., p. 264,5.

things that the desire of the Finite and the other holy souls should "ripen" just at the juncture when the period of the long-continued stupor of the disembodied but unliberated souls came to an end. It was a marvellous coincidence. The unliberated souls were in their torpor unable to know or feel anything or put forth any conscious activity, all the same alive, just like a patient prepared for operation lying unconscious on the operation table under the influence of anaesthetics.

Time elapsed. The will of the Infinite had commenced to operate. H i s 'Material Omnipotence'; (sāmarthya) was astir. How and when it was impossible to say, the impact of attraction originating from His Will had siezed the electrons of matter and 'fused' them one with the other into masses of various sizes, shapes and dimensions. Thus objects animate came into being. The various planetary systems were moving in their orbits. The earth was adorned with beautiful vegetation. Vast oceans and seas with rivers falling into them at the end of a long meandering course from the tops of snow-capped mountains, through valleys carpeted with velvety verdure and planes beautified with plants and trees, lakes and ponds and containing all the material that is necessary for sustaining life. Suddenly the Finite and all other holy souls found themselves clothed in bodies of gross matter and placed along with other beings embodied like themselves, amidst material surroundings. A dim recollection of her spiritual past made the Finite of our drama a little sad. But the present life was in no way to be regretted as it opened vistas of multifarious enjoyments and possibilities of the acquisition of immense and varied knowledge.

The divine multiplication had thus been worked out. The two and three had, through union and cooperation, to use our imperfect mundane language, produced the vast universe of composite beings, the creation—sahasra.* This multifold creation extended in all directions (स्रु) along with the cooperation through creation, sustenance and union through Providence on the part of the Supreme Being (**सह**) was the manifestation of the Mighty Divine will. The Finite saw all this but one point struck her most forcibly. It was this that, the Mundus—the Brahmānda—had its miniature representation in her own body. That body also was a product of the Universal Divine Multiplication, no doubt, but in addition to this it was a full representation of both the process and product of that multiplication. Her body a miniature facsimile of the huge universe and hence deservingly called—kṣudra—brahmāṇḍa had innumerable (**सहस्र**) veins, arteries, nerves, glands, sinews, muscles, bones, skin etc., were nourished and kept in working order by six great principles (**षट्**) called† in modern

* सहस्र—ब्रह्मणः मायया (incomrehensible Providence) आत्मनाम् इच्छया समवायेन च प्रकृतिमहदहङ्कारैः सह तान् सततम् अनुसृत्य तैः साकम् मिलित्वा च स्रवति विकृतिरूपेण वर्तते वर्धते च इति—सह + √स्रु गतौ + ड P. III, 4, 67 कर्तरि कृत्, and II, I, 19 उपपदमतिङ् = "a verbal form which is not the conjugated form of a root is invariably compounded with another word and the compound thus formed is a Tatpurusa." This is a Vedic formation.

† Nearly all the different substances we eat are composed of carbon, oxygen, hydrogen, nitrogen, sulphur, and phosphorus. These six kinds of atoms, arranged in various ways and in different numbers, make up an enormous multitude of different kinds of substances. Thus water is composed of two atoms of hydrogen and one atom of oxygen. Starch, albumen, gelatin and other substances occurring in animal and vegetable bodies are far more complicated substances, but all of them made of the above six elements only.

Science and Religion by Seven Men of Science p. 42 l. 29—p. 43 l. 7.

science carbon, oxygen, hydrogen, nitrogen, sulphur and phosphorus. The Infinite and the Finite on the one side, and Primordial Matter with the mind-stuff and ego on the other—the Big Five had thus concurred in the multiplication producing thereby the six (षट्) that nourished the myriad members of the vast universe (सहस्र) that ever moved on in entire consonance with the Almighty and Ever-vigilant Providence of the Infinite.

(७) आचार्यं उपनयमानो ब्रह्मचारिणं कृणुते गर्भमन्तः। तं रात्रीस्तिस्र उदरे बिभर्ति तं जातं द्रष्टुमभि संयन्ति देवाः ॥ ३ ॥

Transliteration:—Acārya upanayamānō brahmacāriṇam kṛṇutē garbham antah ।

Tam ratrīstisra udarē bibharti tam jātam draṣṭum abhi saṃyanti dēvāh ॥ 3.

पदपाठः—आऽचार्यः । उपऽनयमानः । ब्रह्मऽचारिणम् । कृणुते । गर्भम् । अन्तः । तम् । रात्रीः । तिस्रः । उदरे । बिभर्ति । तम् । जातम् । द्रष्टुम् । अभिऽसंयन्ति । देवाः ॥

अन्वयः—आचार्यः उपनयमानः ब्रह्मचारिणम् अन्तः गर्भम् कृणुते तम् तिस्रः रात्रीः उदरे बिभर्ति । तम् (ब्रह्मचारिणम्) जातम् देवाः द्रष्टुम् अभिसंयन्ति ॥

Word-meaning &c.,:– उपनयमानः*=admitting as a

---

* उपनयमानः—उप + √ णीञ् प्रापणे + मुक् + शानच् P. III, 2, 124 शतृशानचावप्रथमासमानाधिकरणे and VII, 2,82 आने मुक् "when the termination आन follows, the augment मुक् is added to the root." The root नी is ubhayapadi, i. e., it takes either the parasmaipadi or atmanepadi terminations as occasion demands. In the present case the atmanepadi present participial termination शानच् (=आन) is used in preference to the parasmaipadi शतृ (=अत्) according to P. I, 3, 36 सम्माननोत्सञ्जनाचार्यकरणज्ञानभृतिविगणनव्ययेषु नियः="the verb नी takes the atmanepadi terminations in prefe-

Vadic student. **गर्भम्***=(as) in the womb. **अन्तः कृणुते**= admits him to his college or hermitage. **तिस्रः**=three. **रात्रीः**† =nights; (**ति॰ रा॰** to remove the triple ignorance arising from one's own self, that arising from natural phenomena and lastly such as originates from creatures). **उदरे**‡=in

---

rence to parasmaipadi when it is used in the sense of 'respecting highly,' 'throwiug up,' 'the action of a preceptor,' 'knowledge,' 'wages,' 'to pay up debts etc.,' or 'to incur expenses in good works." The root नी is read in the ancient Indian list of roots (धातुपाठ) as णीञ् in which the final ञ् being symbolical of the root being ubhayapadi according to P. I, 3, 72 स्वरितञितः कर्त्रभिप्राये क्रियाफले="roots given with the circumflex accent in the धातुपाठ and those having an indicatory ञ् take atmanepadi terminations when the fruit of the action indicated by the verb accrues to the doer himself." The initial ण् of the root gives place to न् as laid down in P. VI, 1, 65 णो नः = "the initial ण् of roots is changed to न्."

* गर्भम् - गिरति गृणाति उपदिशति इति वा √ गॄ शब्दनिगरणविज्ञानेषु +भन् U, III, 152, अर्तिगॄभ्यां भन्="the termination भन् is added to the roots ऋ to go and गॄ to swallow sound or know." The final न् of the termination भन् is indicatory only भ having to be added to the root. गर्भः—तम्.

†रात्रीः—राति सुखं विश्रामं वा ददाति इति—√ रा दाने+त्रिप् U. III, 67 राशदिभ्यां त्रिप् ="the suffix त्रिप् is added to the roots रा to give शद् to perish, decay, kill or cut off". रात्रिः—ताः.

‡ उदरे उद्दृणाति येन अन्नम् इति उद्+√ दृ विदारणे+अच् or अल् U. V, 19 उदि दृणातेरलचौ पूर्वपदलोपश्च="to the root दृ meaning 'to tear' or 'divide' when preceded by the prefix उद् the termination अच् or अल् is added and the final consonant द् of the prefix is dropped." The final च् and ल् are indicatory only अ being the termination. The former, च्, according to P. VI, 1, 163 चितः determines that "the form ending in a termination that had an indicatory च् before application (to the root from which the form is evolved) has the acute accent on its final syllable".

the belly; in his shelter. बिभर्ति=bears, keeps. जातम्*= born; after initiation; after finishing his course of study.

The final ॠ of दृ is changed to अर् and the indicatory न् of the termination dropped in accordance with P. I, 3, 9 तस्य लोपः--उ+दर्+अ=उदरम् When the termination अल् is added P. VI, 1, 193 लिति applies according to which the syllable immediately preceding a termination having an indicatory ल् takes the acute accent. उद्+दृ+अ=उ+दर्+अ=उदरम्. In this form उद् has the acute accent according to the eighty first rule of the fourth book of the rules of accent given in Phit Aphorisms of the Sage शान्तनवाचार्य viz: उपसर्गाश्चाभिवर्जम्, i. e., all prepositions excepting अभि have the acute accent on the first syllable." The root दृ is also acute accented being included in the list of the thirteen roots of the ninth conjugation ending in ॠ in the धातुपाठ. The terminations अच् and अल् are also acute accented according to P. III, 1,2 आद्युदात्तश्च="all terminations ordained to be applied either to nominal or verbal bases have the acute accent on the first syllable". But the rule quoted above, viz., P, III, 1, 193 over-rides these rules and hence in the second formation only the syllable preceding the termination अल्, i. e., the root दृ or दर् is acute accented and all else grave accented, e. g., उ+दर्+अ At this stage P. VIII, 4, 66 उदात्तादनुदात्तस्य स्वरितः intervenes and the final अ bearing the grave accent, being preceded by an acute accented syllable, becomes circumflex. So we have उदरम्—तस्मिन्.

* जातम्—√जनी प्रादुर्भावे+क्त P. III, 4, 72, गत्यर्थाकर्मकश्लिष शीङ्स्थासवसजनरुहजीर्यतिभ्यश्च="the past passive participial termination क्त is added to roots indicating motion, to intransitive verbs and the verbs श्लिष् and others in the sense of the agent." The final ई of the root and the initial क् of the termination are both indicatory. At this stage applies, P. VI, 4, 42 जनसनखनां सञ्झलोः="for the final nasal of the roots जन्, सन् and खन्, आ is substituted before terminations beginning with any consonant except a nasal or a semivowel and directly preceded by the

द्रष्टुम्*=to see, **अभि संयन्ति**=come together. **देवाः**=the learned, the wise. (See v. 2).

Translation : The preceptor admits him to his college and keeps him in his shelter for three days and three nights (*i. e.*, till ignorance of self, natural phenomena and other creatures is removed). When his course of study is completed the learned eagerly assemble to see him.

---

sign of the desiderative suffix सन् or having an indicatory क् or ङ्. The termination क्त is added according to P. III, 1, 102 निष्ठा="the terminations called निष्ठा are applied to roots to denote action done in the past time."

*द्रष्टुम्—√ दृशिर् प्रेक्षणे+तुमुन् P. III, 3, 158 समानकर्तृकेषु तुमुन् ="the termination तुमुन् is added to a root when another verb meaning to desire is adjacent and both are related to the same agent". The final syllable इर् of the root and उन् of the termination are indicatory. Here P. VI, 1, 58 सृजिदृशोर्झल्यमकिति ordains the augment अम् to be added to the roots सृज् and दृश before terminations having no indicatory क् but beginning with any consonant except a nasal or a semivowel. The indicatory म् of the augment points out that as laid down in P. I, 1, 47 मिदचोऽन्त्यात्परः it is to be inserted after the final vowel of the root. दृश् + अम् + तुम् = द + ऋ + अ + श् + तुम्. Here the ऋ of दृश् is changed to र् by P. VI, 1, 77 इको यणचि="When इ, उ, ऋ or लृ short or long is followed by a dissimilar vowel one of the consonants य्, व्, र्, or ल् is substituted for each of them in order." द् +र्+अ+श् +तुम्. Now the palatal श् of द्रश् is changed to the corresponding lingual by P. VIII, 2, 26 व्रश्चभ्रस्ज-सृजमृजयजराजभ्राजच्छशां षः i. e., "the final consonant simple or conjunct of the roots व्रश्च्, भ्रस्ज्, सृज्, मृज्, यज्, राज्, and भ्राज्, and of roots endidg in or छ् श् is chauged to the lingual ष्. Finally intervenes P. VIII, 4, 41 ष्टुना ष्टुः i. e., when स् or a consonant of the dental class comes in contact with ष् or a consonant of the lingual class, a letter of the latter class is substituted for the former." So we have द्रष् + तुम् =द्रष्टुम्.

Comment :—On this verse, Maharṣi Dayānanda in his "Introduction to the Commentary on the Vedas" remarks thus :—"The preceptor, that is, the teacher of learning having invested a Brahmacārin (student), with the sacred thread instructs him to remain firm in his vows and bears him in his womb, as it were, like a foetus, for three days and three nights, *i. e.*, gives him all kinds of directions and points out to him the methods of study. When he becomes learned and fully equipped with knowledge the dēvas (the learned) assemble to see him. They gladly honour him and praise him saying: 'By our great good fortune and the favour of God thou hast become learned amongst us for doing good to all'."* The convocation scenes at any modern university and such other educational institutions all the world over, bear out this statement.

This verse lays down the main principles of the art and science of education as forming a part of the Eternal Revealed Law, the basis of the Church Divine. The principal office of the Church being to teach and lead humanity, the children of God, in the path of righteousness, it is necessary to explain these principles at the very outset in an account of her divine mission.

The Church Divine according to God's law delegates her powers to a number of human agents. Chief of these is the 'rector' or principal as he is often called now-a-days. This verse touches upon the office and qualifications of the rector. The rector or 'ācārya' is the one who initiates the young pupil into the life of a Vedic student, helps him in every way to fit himself for the battle of life by teaching him personally and through other qualified and virtuous teachers as well as by providing him with all that is necessary towards achieving the end of his life as a Vedic student.

The first event in the life of the vedic student is his initiation at the hands of the rector which is expressed by the present participial adjective 'upanayamāṇah.' The real meaning of this expression is 'taking near' or 'admitting.' 'Upanayana', therefore, is the process of admitting a student to a genuine educational institution for training. Now as good and great institutions are expected to have their own symbols, uniform, &c., to distinguish them from others, the Divine Revealed Law lays down certain broad and easy principles for all genuine educational institutions in this connection. The first is the ceremony of "Upanayana" which consists in investing the young student with the sacred thread—'yajñōpavīta.'

What is the 'yajñōpavīta' or the so-called 'sacred thread'? It is a thread* in which three cords are twisted and both the ends of which are joined together in a peculiar manner in a knot, in which the loops of the two ends, before they are fastened, will be in the shape of the sacred symbol 'ॐ'. This is worn around the body being passed over the left shoulder and under the right arm. The first wearing of it by a person after performing certain rites is called the investiture. It is this ceremony of investiture that is referred to in this verse.

The wearing of the sacred thread by the 'dvija'—the twice born is a very old custom in India—as old as the Vedas themselves for its use is enjoined in them. For example, in Rigvēda IX, 86, 32 it is said:—"The student of the Eternal Revealed Law (सः) wearing (तन्वानः) the three-corded (त्रिवृतम्) thread (तन्तुम्) that he may know all that is to be known यथाविदे) and becoming

* The following allows option in the use of the material of which the sacred thread is made; यज्ञोपवीतं कुरुते सूत्रम् वस्त्रम् वाऽपि कुशरज्जुमेव ॥ G. G. S. I, 2, 1. If no cotton thread is available the other material, whatever is available, should he used, but one must not go without one's sacred thread.

'enlightened' (परिव्यत) with lustre like that of the sun's rays (सूर्यस्य रश्मिभिः) guiding himself (नयन्) in the field of ever new (नवीयसीः) applications (प्रशिषम्) of the Sacred Universal Revealed Law (ऋतस्य) becomes a leader (पतिः) of men (जनीनाम्) and freely moves about in the world (उपयाति) discharging his duty (निष्कृतम्)."*

In whatever way the above verse may be rendered the clear reference to the 'sacred thread' cannot be obliterated. The expressions 'ṛtasya praśisō navīyasīh' and 'janīnām patih' unmistakably point towards the accomplished student of the Vedas who puts his 'talents' to practical use in life.

Again in Ṛgvēda III, 8, 4, is found the following beautiful statement:—The young man (युवा) wearing good and clean garments (सुवासाः) [with the sacred thread entwining his person the sign of his] having completed his educational career (परिवीतः), comes to his people (आगात्). He therefore becomes great in the sight of men (स च श्रेयान् भवति) by the successful termination of his educational career (जायमानः). Wise men (धीरासः) able to impart good education to the young (स्वाध्यः कवयः) with hearts disposed to love (मनसा देवयन्तः) [encourage and] advance him [in the path of life] (उन्नयन्ति)."†

The second line of this verse can very well be compared with that of the stanza under consideration. The word 'parivīta' means, as explained by Maharṣi Dayānanda, 'pūrṇavidyah', one that has completed one's education or studied all the lores completely, the secondary and symbolical sense being 'having the sacred thread round his body.' Along with this word parivīta,' there are three others, viz., 'upavīta,' 'prācīnāvīta' and

---

* स सूर्यस्य रश्मिभिः परिव्यत तन्तुं तन्वानस्त्रिवृतं यथा विदे । नयन्नृतस्य प्रशिषो नवीयसीः पतिर्जनीनामुपयाति निष्कृतम् ॥ ऋ० ६ । ८६ । ३२ ॥

† युवा सुवासाः परिवीत आगात् स च श्रेयान्भवति जायमानः । तं धीरासः कवय उन्नयन्ति स्वाध्यो मनसा देवयन्तः ॥ ऋ० १० । ५७ । २ ॥

'nivīta' which directly refer to the sacred thread worn in three different ways.

In the Gōbhila Gṛhya Sūtra I, 2, 2—4* it is laid down that "he is called yajñōpavītī when his sacred thread is taken over the right arm (दक्षिणं बाहुम् उद्धृत्य) let down from over the head (शिरः अव धाय) placed on the left shoulder (सव्ये अंसे प्रतिष्ठापयति) and is worn hanging down under the right arm (दक्षिणं कक्षम् अन्ववलम्बं) when the reverse method is followed he is called prācīnāvītī. It is only in pitṛyajña that a man should follow the prācīnāvītī method. In the beginning† of the treatise it is ordained that the 'sacrificer' during 'dēvayajña should follow the upavītī method. Hence it follows that on all other occasions he should adhere to the nivītī fashion of wearing the thread. The Vāijayantī of Yādavaprakāśa, for example, gives the following information about these technical terms : "The sacred thread is called 'dvijāyanī', 'brahmasūtra,' 'sūtra', 'yajñōpavītaka' and 'pavitra.' When it is worn under the right arm (and on the left shoulder) it is called 'upavīta.' When it is worn under the left arm (and on the right shoulder) it is called 'prācināvīta', while it is named 'nivīta' if worn round the neck."‡

Again in Ṛgvēda X, 57, 2 we are told that "we should all try to attain (नशीमहि) that sacred (आहुतं) thread (तन्तुं) the means for the full accomplishment

* दक्षिणं बाहुमुद्धृत्य शिरोऽवधाय सव्येऽंसे प्रतिष्ठापयति दक्षिणं कक्षमन्ववलम्बं भवत्येवं यज्ञोपवीती भवति ॥ सव्यं बाहुमुद्धृत्य शिरोऽवधाय दक्षिणेंऽसे प्रतिष्ठापयति सव्यं कक्षमन्ववलम्बं भवत्येवं प्राचीनावीती भवति ॥ पितृयज्ञे त्वेव प्राचीनावीती भवति ॥ G. G. S. I, 2, 2—4.

† अथातो गृह्याकर्माणि (=नित्याग्निहोत्रहोमादीनि) उपदेक्ष्यामः ॥ यज्ञोपवीतिनाऽचान्तोदकेन कृत्यम् ॥ Ibid. I, 1, 1 & 2.

‡ द्विजायनी ब्रह्मसूत्रं सूत्रं यज्ञोपवीतकम् । पवित्रञ्चोपवीतन्तु प्रोद्धृते दक्षिणे भुजे ॥ प्राचीनावीतमन्यस्मिन्निवीतं कण्ठलम्बितम् ॥ वैजयन्ती 84, ll. 63–41. Also Manu II, 63:—उद्धृते दक्षिणे पाणावु पवीत्युच्यते द्विजः । सव्ये प्राचीन आवीती निवीती कण्ठसज्जने ॥

(प्रसाधनः) of all works of righteousness (यज्ञस्य) and which is in vogue among the learned (यः देवेषु आततः)."*

In ancient India persons of both sexes young and old wore the sacred thread. That women also were bound to wear it as a duty and not a privilege, can be gathered from the following texts :—

"Then the bridegroom, bringing forward the bride wearing the sacred thread and covered with a mantle, should recite—."*

"Ladies wearing the secred thread as well as those not wearing it."†

In Parāśara-Mādhava and the Harīta smṛti works of the times when India had fallen from her high position, it is stated that women should wear the sacred thread and study the vedas.‡

Bāṇa in his Kādambarī discribes Mahāśvēta the principal female character in the work as wearing the sacred."§

(८) इयं समित्पृथिवी द्यौर्द्वितीयोतान्तरिक्षं समिधा पृणाति। ब्रह्मचारी समिधा मेखलया श्रमेण लोकांस्तपसा पिपर्ति ॥ ४ ॥

---

* यो यज्ञस्य प्रसाधनस्तन्तुर्देवेष्वाततः। तमाहुतं नशीमहि ॥ ऋ० १० । ५७ २ ॥ See also A. V. IX, 1, 24 quoted on p. 15 and 16.

† प्रावृतां यज्ञोपवीतिनीमभ्युदानयञ्जपेत्—॥ G. G. S. II, 1, 19.

‡ स्त्रिय उपनीता अनुपनीताश्च ॥ P. G. S., Siddhavinayaka, Kasi, 1879, p. 84.

¶ द्विविधा : स्त्रियो ब्रह्मवादिन्यः सद्यो वध्वश्च। तत्र ब्रह्मवादिनीनामुपनयनमग्नीन्धनं स्वगृहे भिक्षाचर्येति। वधूनां तूपस्थिते विवाहे कथञ्चिदुपनयनमात्रं कृत्वा विवाहः कार्य इति॥ Parasara Madhava, Asiatic Society of Bengal, Calcutta, 1883.

§चूडामणिचन्द्रमयूखजालेनेव मण्डलीकृतेन ब्रह्मसूत्रेण पवित्रीकृतकायाम् ॥ Kadambari of Bana Nirnaya Sagara Press, Bombay, p. 248 ll. 3 and 4.

Transliteration:—Iyam samit pṛthivī dyāurdvitīyōtāntarikṣam samidhā pṛṇāti ।

Brahmacārī samidhā mēkhalayā śramēṇa lōkāṃstapasā piparti ॥ 4.

पदपाठः— इयम् सम्ऽइत् । पृथिवी । द्यौः । द्वितीया । उत । अन्तरिक्षम् । सम्ऽइधा । पृणाति । ब्रह्मऽचारी । सम्ऽइधा । मेखलया । श्रमेण । लोकान् । तपसा । पिपर्ति ॥

अन्वयः—इयम् पृथिवी (प्रथमा) समित् द्यौः द्वितीया उत अन्तरिक्षं (स तृतीयया) समिधा पृणाति। ब्रह्मचारी लोकान् समिधया मेखलया, श्रमेण, तपसा च पिपर्ति ॥

Word-meaning &c.:—**इयम्**=this. **समित्***=a stick for the sacred fire. **पृथिवी**†=earth. **द्यौः**‡=the heavens. **द्वितीया**¶

---

*समिध :—अग्निरनया समिध्यते सम्यग्दीप्यते इति—सम् + √ञिइन्धी दीप्तौ+क्विप् P. III, 2, 178 अन्येभ्योऽपि दृश्यते.—ताः.

†पृथिवी—प्रथते विस्तीर्णा भवति इति—√प्रथ प्रख्याने+षिवन्+ङीष् U. I, 150 प्रथेः षिवन्षवन्ष्वनः संप्रसारणं च="to the root प्रथ् to become famous, rise or spread out, the termination षिवन्, षवन् or ष्वन् is added and the penultimate र of the root takes सम्प्रसारण." The initial ष् and final न् of the termination are indicatory. प्रथ् + षिवन् or षवन् or ष्वन् =पृथ् +इव or अव or व=पृथिव, पृथव or पृथ्व. Here applies P. IV, 1, 41 षिद्गौरादिभ्यश्च i. e., "the feminine form of words of the masculine gender having an indicatory ष् and of words belonging to the group beginning with गौर etc., is formed by adding the suffix ङीष्." The initial ङ् and final ष् are indicatory only ई being the termination. पृथिवी, पृथवी, पृथ्वी.

‡द्यौः—द्योतन्ते लोकाः अस्यां यया वा इति—√द्युत दीप्तौ+डो U. II, 67="to the root गम् to go the termination डो is added." The initial ड् is indicatory, implying according to P. VI, 4, 143 टेः, that the termination is to be substituted for the टि portion (final syllable containing the last vowel P. I, 1, 63 अचोऽन्त्यादि टिः) of the root द्युत्. द्युत्+डो=द्य्+ओ=द्यो.

¶द्वितीया—द्वयोः पूरणः इति—द्वि+तीय P. V, 2, 54, द्वेस्तीयः="to the word द्वि meaning two, the termination तीय is added to form the

=second. उत=and. अन्तरिक्षम् §=the interior region.

corresponding ordinal." द्वितीयः. Here P. VI, 1, 4 अजाद्यतष्टाप् i. e., "the feminine of words of the masculine gender ending in अ and of words of the group अज etc., is formed by adding the termination टाप् to the masculine." The initial ट् and final प् are indicatory only आ being the termination.–द्वितीया,

§अन्तरिक्षम्—(1) अन्तर्+√ईक्ष दर्शने+घञ् P. III, 3, 19 अकर्तरि च कारके संज्ञायाम् ="nouns are formed from verbs by adding the termination घञ् to them in the sense of any other case but the nominative. The initial घ् and final ञ् are indicatory only अ being the termination. The initial ई of the root is irregularly shortened. (2) अन्तर् मध्ये ऋक्षाणि नक्षत्राणि यस्य, (3) अन्तरा क्षान्तं भवति, (4) अन्तरा इमे द्यावापृथिव्यौ क्षयः (निवासः) यस्य. (5) शरीरेषु अन्तर् (मध्ये) अक्षयम् (अविनाशी) इति वा. The substitution of रि for the final र् of the first word and initial ऋ of the second in (2), the insertion of इ after the first word and dropping of म् at the end of the second in (4), the change of the negative अ to इ and dropping of the final य of the second word in (5), are irregular. Or (3), (4) and (5), may be derived by adding the termination ड irregularly to the roots क्षम् to bear or क्षि to dwell or perish, as follows:--(3) अन्तर्+√क्षमूष सहने+ड; (4) अन्तर्+√क्षि निवासे +ड and (5) अन्तर्+न+क्षि क्षये (विनाशे)+ड P. III, 4,67 कर्तरि कृत् "all कृत् terminations are added to verbs in the sense of the doer." Finally, P. VI, 3, 109 पृषोदरादीनि यथोपदिष्टम् justifies all these formations.

The above interpretation is based upon Yaska's Nirukta Chapter second, section ten which runs as follows:–अन्तरिक्षं कस्मादन्तरा क्षान्तं भवति। अन्तरेमे इति वा शरीरेष्वन्तरक्षयमिति वा ॥ On this the commentator Durgacarya remarks–अन्तरा हीदं द्यावापृथिव्योरवस्थितं क्षान्तं च भवति। पृथिव्यन्तमित्यर्थः। अथवाऽन्तरा द्यावापृथिव्याविमे क्षियति निवसतीत्यन्तरिक्षम्। अथवा शरीरेष्वेतदेवान्तर्मध्येऽवस्थिमक्षयमितराणि पृथिव्यादीनि भूतानि क्षीयन्ते तस्मादक्षयत्वादन्तरिक्षम् ॥ The late Prof. Rajawade points out two

पृणाति=fills. **मेखलया*** = with the girdle, (the sign of chas-

---

inaccuracies in this text. He says:—क्षान्तं=क्षमायुक्तम् । द्यावापृथिव्योर्मध्ये स्थितमेतदतीव क्षमायुक्तम् । क्षमाशीलेनैतेन मेघादि सर्वं धार्यते नाधः पात्यते । दुर्गव्याख्याने 'द्यावापृथिव्योरन्तरा हीदमवस्थितं' पुनरुक्तं भवेत् । 'अन्तरेमे' इत्यस्य तद्व्याख्यानम् । क्षायाः अन्तः = क्षान्त इतिशुध्दं रूपम् । 'अन्त'—शब्दो नैव नपुंसकः । क्षायाः अन्तो यस्मिंस्तद् इति बहुव्रीहौ 'क्षान्तं' कदाचिच्छुध्दं स्यात् ॥ The critic's carelessness in observing rules of euphony is unpardonable especially as he rates at the revered old commentator for copyists' mistakes.

The Scholiast Skandasvamin thus comments upon this passage from the Nirukta :—अन्तरा मध्ये सर्वभूतानां क्षान्तं शान्तं स्थितं निष्क्रियं वा शान्तमव्यूहम्, निष्कम्भस्थानात्मकत्वात् । अन्तरा इमे रोदस्यौ द्यावापृथिव्यौ क्षियतीति वा । अन्तरा इमे क्षोण्याविति वा क्षान्तम् । एवमनेकविकल्पमुत्तरपदम्, अन्तरा शब्दात्पूर्वपदम् शरीरेष्वित्यादि अन्तरा शब्दात्पूर्वपदम् अक्षयशब्दादुत्तरपदमिति विशेषः । विनाशिष्वप्यविनाशीत्यर्थः । The use of commas and lack of euphonic changes is an "improvement(?)" upon the original by the learned editor !!!

As may be gathered from the words of the above quotation Skandasvamin takes अन्तरिक्ष to mean the soul as well as the Supreme Being.

The alternative interpretations of the word अन्तरिक्ष given above are a matter of research and do not imply that the meaning of the verse in question is lost to humanity.

*मेखलया—मीयते प्रक्षिप्यते कायमध्यभागे इति √ डुमिञ् क्षेपे + खलच् P. III, 3, 1, उणादयो बहुलम्="various Unadi terminations even other than those mentioned in the Unadi treatise are applied to roots in various ways and the resulting forms are just as valid as those derived by the application to roots of such suffixes as are enjoined in the Unadi treatise." See Introduction. The initial डु and final ञ् of the root and the final च् of the termination are indicatory. The final vowel of the root takes its guna substitute here. डुमिञ्+खलच्. The final ञ् of the root and च् of the termination are dropped according to P. I, 3, 3 हलन्त्यम् "the final consonant of those forms

tity). **श्रमेण*** = hard work, diligence. **लोकान्**† = the worlds. **तपसा** = with austerity.

Translation:—The earth is the first stick, the heavens the second and he fills the intermediate region

---

of words on the basis of which certain processes are enjoined in such scientific treatises as the Astadhyayi of Panini are indicatory and do not form a part of the word as such." This principle applies to roots also. Such technical forms, it must be borne in mind, are not used in ordinary conversation or writing, e. g., डुकृञ्. Here only the root कृ is conjugated and not the form डुकृञ्. The initial डु is done away with according to P. I, 3 ,5 आदिर्ञिटुडवः "the syllables ञि, टु and डु used in the beginning of such forms are indicatory." These indicatory letters, as laid down in P. I, 3, 9 तस्य लोपः do not form parts of the words concerned and must therefore be dropped when conjugating the latter. मि + खल = मेखल. Now according to P. IV, 1, 4 अजाद्यतष्टाप्, आ is added. मेखल + टाप् = मेखला.— तया.

* श्रमेण—√ श्रमु तपसि खेदे च + घञ् P. III, 3, 18 भावे = "the termination घञ् is added to verbs in the sense of state or condition." The penultimate अ of the root remains unchanged in this case. श्रमु + घञ्. The indicatory उ at the end of the root is dropped according to P. I, 3, 2 उपदेशेऽजनुनासिक इत् = "nasalised vowels used in the 'first utterances' of scientific treatises (see note above) are indicatory." The initial घ् of the termination is also indicatory as laid down in P. I. 3, 8 लशक्वतद्धिते = "ल्, श् and consonants of the guttural class used in the beginning of terminations other than taddhita, are indicatory." Hence both these are dropped by P. I. 3, 9. श्रम् + अ = श्रमः -- तेन.

† लोकान्—लोक ते पश्यन्ति सर्वे एनम् इति—√ लोकृ दर्शने + घञ् P. III, 3, 19 अकर्तरि च कारके संज्ञायाम् i.e., "nouns are formed by adding the termination घञ् to roots in any other sense but the nominative." The final ऋ of the root is indicatory by P. I. 3, 2. लोक् + अ = लोकः — तान्.

with the third. The Vedic student with this fuel for the havana, with his girdle, his hard work and his austerity renders all the worlds perfect.

Purport :—The offering of the three sticks in the 'havana', the wearing of the girdle and other such symbols are indications that the Vedic student solemnly takes the vow of chastity to pursue the study of the sciences relating to the earth, the heavens and the intermediate region for the benefit of the world.

Comment :—Maharṣi Dayānanda's comment on this is.—"With fuel for *homa* the *Brahmacarin* renders the earth, the shining firmament happy, i. e., with his learning and *homa* he confers happiness on the living beings dwelling in those regions. By adopting the smybols of *Brahmacarya*, viz, the *agnihotra*, and the girdle etc., and by his industry as well as by his virtuous conduct, teaching and preaching he makes all beings happy and strong."

(९) पूर्वो जातो ब्रह्मणो ब्रह्मचारी घर्मं वसान-स्तपसोदतिष्ठत् । तस्माज्जातं ब्राह्मणं ब्रह्म ज्येष्ठं देवाश्च सर्वे अमृतेन साकम् ॥ ५ ॥

Transliteration:—Pūrvō jātō brahmaṇō brahmacārī gharmaṃ vasānastapasōdatiṣṭhat ।

Tasmājjātam brāhmaṇam brahma jyēṣṭham dēvāśca sarvē amṛtēna sākam ॥ 5.

पदपाठः—पूर्वः । जातः । ब्रह्मणः । ब्रह्मऽचारी । घर्मम् । वसानः । तपसा । उत् । अतिष्ठत् । तस्मात् । जातम् । ब्राह्मणम् । ब्रह्म । ज्येष्ठम् । देवाः । च । सर्वे । अमृतेन । साकम् ॥

अन्वयः—ब्रह्मचारी ब्रह्मणा पूर्वः जातः घर्मम् वसानः तपसा उत् अतिष्ठत् । तस्मात् ज्येष्ठम् ब्राह्मणम् ब्रह्म जातम् , सर्वे देवाः च अमृतेन साकम् (जाताः) ॥

Wordmeaning &c.—पूर्वः* = first, before. **जातः** = born, known, renowned. **ब्रह्मणः** = owing to his Vedic studies. **घर्मम्†** = lustre, prowess. **वसानः‡** = putting on. **तपसा** = by his austerities. **उत् अतिष्ठत्** = has risen high. **तस्मात्** = from him. **जातम्** = comes to light, is revealed, spreads. **ब्राह्मणम्¶** = the heavenly lore, the knowledge of the Supreme Being.

---

* पूर्वः—√पूर्व निमन्त्रणे निवासे वा + अच् P. III, 1, 134 नन्दिग्रहिपचादिभ्यो ल्युणिन्यचः = "the terminations ल्यु, णिनि and अच् respectively are added to roots belonging to each of the groups beginning with the verbs नन्द्, ग्रह् and पच्." पूर्व + अ = पूर्वः.

† घर्मम्—जिघर्ति क्षरति नश्यति दीप्यते वा जगत् येन इति—√घृ क्षरणदीप्त्योः + मक् U. I, 149 घर्मग्रीष्मौ = "the words घर्म and ग्रीष्म are formed by adding the termination मक् to the roots घृ and ग्रस् respectively." घृ + मक्. Here the final vowel of the root takes guṇa. घर्मः—तम्.

‡ वसानः—√वस आच्छादने + शानच् P. III, 2, 124 लटः शतृशानचावप्रथमासमानाधिकरणे. वस् + आन = वसानः.

¶ ब्राह्मणम्—ब्रह्मणः जातम् इति ब्रह्म + अण् P. IV, 3, 83 प्रभवति—"to a noun in the ablative case any suitable termination from those ordained can be added and the resulting form will convey the idea of something originating from the thing denoted by that noun." The termination अण् can be added to nouns in all the senses in which various terminations are enjoined in the Astadhyayi of Panini from IV, 1, 83 प्राग्दीव्यतोऽण् to IV, 4, 2 तेन दीव्यति खनति जयति जितम्. According to P. VII, 2, 117 तद्धितेष्वचामादेः the first vowel of the base undergoes वृद्धि change when a secondary (तद्धित) termination having an indicatory ण् or ञ् follows.—ब्राह्मणम्.

The word ब्राह्मण is a very important and pretty difficult formation. It is derived in several ways all of which are clearly laid down in the Astadhyayi. A very important point to be noted in connection with the etymology of this word is that it signifies the highest stage in human development to attain which long and even painful preparation is required.

The following etymologies of the word are by no means exhaustive:—

(1) तेन रक्तम् रागात् P. IV, 2, 1="an appropriate secondary termination can be added to a word in the instrumental case signifying colour and the resulting form will mean something dyed in the colour indicated by that word." Metaphorically ब्रह्मन् can be taken to signify "the colour" with which a devotee is "painted." In Indian vernaculars also the expression "to be coloured with" means to be transformed thoroughly ब्रह्मणा रक्तम्—ब्राह्मणम्.

(2) दृष्टं साम P. IV, 2, 7. In the sense of a verse of the "Sama-veda" "seen" (=received and interpreted) by a sage named ब्रह्मन्. ब्रह्मणा दृष्टं साम—ब्राह्मणम्.

(3) साऽस्य देवता P. IV, 2, 24. When ब्रह्मन् (nominative case) is the subject treated of in a Vedic hymn etc., an appropriate termination can be added to the word, *e. g*., ब्रह्मा देवता अस्य इति—ब्राह्मणम्.

(4) तस्य समूहः P. IV, 2, 37, in the sense of a group, crowd or concourse of what are called by the name ब्रह्मन् (the soul—in the genitive case) also we have ब्रह्मणां समूहः—ब्राह्मणम्.

(5) तदधीते तद्वेद P. IV, 2, 58. In the sense of one who studies or knows ब्रह्मन् (accusative case), we get ब्रह्म (वेदं) अधीते जानाति अथवा ब्रह्मन् (परमात्मानम्) जानाति प्राप्नोति वा इति ब्रह्मन्+अण्= ब्राह्मणः. This is the commonest form in use. In ancient times a man who had, by spiritual discipline, realised God, was called ब्राह्मण. A study and understanding of the Eternal Vedic Law also, entitles one to this name. The institution of caste by birth is a later social accretion in India.

(6) तेन निर्वृत्तम् P. IV, 2, 68. In the sense of something 'made' or 'fashioned' by ब्रह्मन् (in the instrumental case), we have ब्रह्मणा (परमात्मना) निर्वृत्तम्—ब्राह्मणम् जगत्.

(7) तस्य निवासः P. IV, 2, 69. According to this principle the word ब्राह्मण is a combination of ब्रह्मन् (soul or the Supreme Being) in the genitive case and a secondary termination, *e. g*., अण्. ब्रह्मणः (परमात्मनः जीवस्य वा) निवासः—ब्राह्मणं शरीरम्.

(8) अदूर भवश्च P. IV, 2, 70. The word ब्राह्मण is got by putting together ब्रह्मन् in the ablative case and a termination in the sense of 'not far from'. ब्रह्मणः अदूरभवम्—ब्राह्मणं जगत्.

In ordinary idiom the above three formations denote place as explained in P. IV, 2, 67 तदस्मिन्नस्तीति देशे तन्नाम्नि="in the sense of 'some one' or 'something dwelling in a place' a noun in the nominative case denoting the name of a place takes an appropriate secondary termination," *e. g.*, उदुम्बरा अस्मिन्सन्ति इति औदुम्बरो देशः a place where there are banian trees. But in Vedic formations this rule cannot be strictly enforced, since God is beyond space. Even space and time depend upon His will.

(9) तत्र जातः P. IV, 3, 25. A noun in the locative case takes a suitable termination and the resulting form would mean someone or something born or r e v e a l e d in what is denoted by that noun. ब्रह्मणि जातः-ब्राह्मणः.

(10) प्रायभवः P. IV, 3, 41. A noun in the locative case combines with a secondary termination in the sense of 'some one' or 'something generally found in.' ब्रह्मणि प्रायेण भवः—ब्राह्मणः.

(11) सम्भूते P. IV, 3, 42. A noun in the locative case takes a secondary termination in the sense of 'found' or 'produced in.' ब्रह्मणि सम्भवति इति—ब्राह्मणः.

(12) तत्र भवः P. IV, 3, 53. A noun in the locative case takes a secondary termination in the sense of someone or something produced in or born of something denoted by that noun. ब्रह्मणि भवः—ब्राह्मणः.

(13) तत आगतः P. IV, 3, 74. A secondary termination is added to a noun in the ablative case to denote 'someone' or 'something coming from.' ब्रह्मण आगतः. In the ordinary form the original word would denote place.

(14) प्रभवति P. IV, 3, 83. The word is formed as above but means 'something arising from'. ब्रह्मणः प्रभवति इति—ब्राह्मणः.

(15). सोऽस्य निवासः P. IV, 3, 89. A secondary termination is appended to a noun in the nominative case and the resulting form would mean the residence of what is denoted by that noun.

(16). तेन प्रोक्तम् P. IV, 3, 101. A secondary termination is affixed to a noun in the instrumental case in the sense of something explained or propagated by someone. ब्रह्मणा प्रोक्तम्—ब्राह्मणम्

(17) तेनैकदिक् P. IV, 3, 112. As above but means "something being in the same 'place' or 'quarter' as—." ब्रह्मणा एकदिक्—ब्राह्मणम्.

(18) कृते ग्रन्थे P. IV, 3, 116. As above but means 'a book made (written—revealed) by—.' ब्रह्मणा कृतः ग्रन्थः—ब्राह्मणः.

(19) संज्ञायाम् P. IV. 3, 117. As above but means 'something made by a group of—.'—ब्रह्मभिः (जीवात्मभिः) कृतम्—ब्राह्मणम्.

(20) तस्येदम् P. IV, 3, 120. A secondary termination is affixed to a noun in the genitive case and the resulting form would signify something belonging to something denoted by that noun. ब्रह्मणः इदम्—ब्राह्मणम्.

(21) तस्य विकारः P. IV, 3, 134. As above but means a modification or effect of.

(22) तस्याऽपत्यम् P. IV, 1, 92. As above but means an offspring of— ब्रह्मणः अपत्यं—ब्राह्मणः. See P. VI, 4, 171 ब्राह्मोऽजातौ.

There are a number of secondary terminations, e. g., अण्, अञ्, ण, क् etc, by the application of which the above forms can be derived but there will be difference of accent only. It should also be borne in mind that the above list of formations is very brief, for many more such interpretations of the word ब्राह्मणम् are possible by applying even those rules of the Astadhyayi where other terminations such as छ, ठक्, फक् etc., are enjoined.

A correct understanding and interpretation of the word is possible only when these niceties of its derivation are borne in mind. Only then will a Vedic passage, where it occurs be rightly understood.

ब्रह्म=ever increasing wealth; food. **ज्येष्ठम्***=excellent; surpassing all. **सर्वे देवाः**=all the wise. **अमृतेन**† **साकम्**‡= with eternal bliss.

---

*ज्येष्ठम्—प्रशस्य+इष्ठन् P. V. 3, 55 अतिशायने तमबिष्ठनौ="to show excess or excellence of some quality, state or action indicated by some adjectival or other word the superlative terminations तमप् and इष्ठन् are added to the latter." Here P. V, 3, 61 ज्य च enjoins the substitution of ज्य for प्रशस्य before the comparative and superlative terminations beginning with vowels, viz., 'ईयसुन्' and इष्ठन्. The final न् is indicatory according to P. I, 3, 3, ज्य+ इष्ठ. Applying P. VI, 1, 87 आद्गुणः="When अ or आ is followed by a dissimilar vowel (any vowel but अ or आ) the corresponding guna vowel is substituted for both." Then according to P. I, 1, 2 अदेङ्गुण : i, e., "the vowels अ, ए and ओ are called guna", we select ए a gutturo-palatal to take the place of अ a guttural and इ a palatal following the principle laid down in P. I, 1, 64 स्थानेऽन्तरतमः ="When the substitution of some letter is ordained in the place of some other letter that substitute should be such as comes nearest to the former in its place of utterance and effort in pronunciation." ज्येष्ठः—तम्.

† अमृतेन—मरणस्य दुःखस्य वा अभावः—नञ्+√मृङ् प्राणत्यागे+क्त P. III, 2, 102 निष्ठा. or the Unadi termination तन् can be added to the root मृ according to U. III, 88 तनिमृङ्भ्यां किच्च="the termination तन् is added to the roots तन् and मृ and it operates as though it had an indicatory क्." The compound with नञ् is laid down in P. II, 2, 6 नञ् "the negative particle न is compounded with a word capable of entering into composition with it and the resulting compound belongs to the Tatpurusa class." The final ञ् is indicatory. The dropping of the initial of the negative particle and retention only of अ when a word beginning with a consonant follows according to P. VI, 3 73 नलोपो नञः. अ+मृत=अमृतम्—तेन.

‡ साकम्—√षो अन्तकर्मणि +कन् U. III, 43 इणभीकापाशल्यतिमर्चिभ्यः कन्="the termination कन् is added to the roots इ to go

Translation :—The Vedic student, by his studies, becomes renowned in good time and putting on lustre attains high esteem among men. From him springs (=is revealed) the most excellent celestial lore (of interpreting the Veda=the Eternal Revealed Law) and ever increasing wealth. All the wise also attain eternal bliss through his help.

Purport : —By his studies, self control and austerities, the Vedic student is honoured by all and he, showing people the way to righteousness and prosperity helps the wise to attain supreme happiness.

Comment :—Maharṣi Dayānanda thus remarks on this verse :—"The Brahmacārin, who has made it his nature (as it were) to move in (*i. e.* study) the Vedas, performs the most difficult austerities, knows the Vedas and God, is the first (*i. e.*) his āśrama being the first in point of order he is the embellisher of all āśramas and remains firm in good behaviour by the practice of virtue (dharma). The learned praise him who is Brahmajyēṣtha *i. e.*, who considers God and learning the greatest (most important) of all, is endowed with the highest happiness on account of his knowledge of God and emancipation and knows God."

भी to fear, कै to make sound, पा to drink, शल्, अत् to go and मर्च् to act. By P. III, 3, 1 उणादयो बहुलम् other roots also take this suffix: Hence षो+कन् . The final न् of the suffix is indicatory. The final ओ of the root is changed to आ as laid down in P. VI, 1, 45, आदेच उपदेशेऽशिति = "the final ए, ऐ, ओ and औ of roots which in the technical rules of grammar are given as ending in any of these vowels, are changed to आ before terminations not having an indicatory श्." The initial ष् of the root is changed to स् as laid down in P. VI, 1, 64 धात्वादेः षः सः. The word साकम् is an indeclinable.

(१०) ब्रह्मचार्यैति समिधा समिद्धः कार्ष्णं वसानो दीक्षितो दीर्घश्मश्रुः । स सद्य एति पूर्वस्मादुत्तरं समुद्रं लोकान्त्संगृभ्य मुहुराचरिक्रत् ॥६॥

Transliteration:—Brahmacāryēti samidhā samiddhah kārsṇam vasānō dīkṣitō dīrghaśmaśruh ।

Sa sadya ēti pūrvasmāduttaram samudram lōkāntsaṃgṛbhhya muhurācarikrat ॥ 6.

पदपाठः—ब्रह्मऽचारी । एति । सम्ऽइधा । सम्ऽइद्धः । कार्ष्णम् । वसानः । दीक्षितः । दीर्घऽश्मश्रुः । सः । सद्य । एति । पूर्वस्मात् । उत्तरम् । समुद्रम् । लोकान् सम्ऽगृभ्य । मुहुः । आऽचरिक्रत् ॥

अन्वयः—ब्रह्मचारी समिधा समिद्धः कार्ष्णं वसानः दीक्षितः दीर्घश्मश्रुः एति । स सद्यः पूर्वस्मात् उत्तरम् समुद्रम् एति लोकान् (च) संगृभ्य मुहुः आचरिक्रत् ।

Word-meaning &c.:—एति = goes. समिधा = by the lustre of learning. समिद्धः* = brilliant, shining. कार्ष्णम्† = dark coloured garment, deerskin. वसानः = putting on.

---

* समिद्धः सम् + √ञिइन्धी दीप्तौ + क्त P. III, 2, 102 निष्ठा and VI, 4, 24 अनिदितां हल उपधायाः क्ङिति = "the penultimate न् of a base not having a short इ for its indicatory letter, is dropped when a termination having an indicatory क् or ङ् follows." सम् + इन्ध + त् = सम् + इध् + त. Here applies P. VIII, 2, 53 झलां जश्झशि = "when a consonant, except a nasal or a semivowel, is followed by a soft unaspirate or aspirate (third or fourth letter of a class) it is changed to the soft unaspirate (third letter) of its class."—सम + इध् + द = समिद्धः.

† कार्ष्णम्—कृष्णेन रागेण रक्तम् P. IV, 2, 1—तेन रक्तं रागात् "a noun in the instrumental case meaning a particular colour takes the termination अण् and the resulting form would indicate something dyed in that colour," or (2) कृष्णस्य (कृष्णमृगस्य चर्मणः) विकारः इति कृष्ण + अण् P. IV, 3, 134. तस्य विकारः = "those secondary terminations which are ordained in this treatise (the Astadhyayi of Panini)

दीक्षितः*=assuming vows. दीर्घश्मश्रुः†=with beard and moustache grown long. सद्यः‡=just. पूर्वस्मात्=from the

---

and for which occasion arises, may be applied to a noun in the sixth case in the sense of a modification (something made) of the thing denoted by the noun." P. IV, 1, 83 प्राग्दीव्यतोऽण् enjoins the termination in all senses in which various terminations are ordained after nouns in Panini's grammar from this aphorism (IV, 1, 83) up to IV, 4, 2 तेन दीव्यति खनति जयति जितं. Hence the termination अण् is added here. This termination having an indicatory ण् according to P. VII, 2, 117 तद्धितेष्वचामादेः occasions vrddhi change in the first of the vowels in the body of the word to which it is applied. Terminations having on indicatory ञ् also have a similar effect. Here P. I, 1, 1 वृद्धिरादैच् points out that the vowels आ, ऐ and औ are vrddhi letters. Hence according to P. I, 1, 51 उरण्परः="any vowel ordained to take the place of ऋ will invariably be followed by र्." We have कृष्ण+अण्—कार्ष्णम्.

* दीक्षितः—दीक्षा अस्य संजाता इति—दीक्षा+इतच् P. V. 2, 36 तदस्य संजातं तारकादिभ्य इतच्="the termination इतच् is added to words of the तारकादि group to show something that has taken place in the thing denoted by the word concerned." Here applies P. VI, 4, 148 यस्येति च="before taddhita terminations and before the termination ई the final अ, आ, इ or ई is elided." दीक्ष्+इत=दीक्षितः .

† दीर्घश्मश्रुः—दीर्घाणि श्मश्रूणि यस्य P. II, 2, 4 अनेकमन्यपदार्थे. According to P. I, 2, 46 कृत्तद्धितसमासाश्च, words ending in कृत् or तद्धित terminations as well as compound words are unitary words—प्रातिपदिक. Hence as laid down in P. II, 4, 71 सुपो धातुप्रातिपदिकयोः—"the terminations at the end of the words which go to form the compound which may be used either as a verb (धातु) or a noun (प्रातिपदिक), are invariably dropped." In the case of the अलुक्समास, however, they are retained. Hence दीर्घश्मश्रुः.

‡ सद्यः—समाने अहनि—समान+अहन् P. V, 3, 22 सद्यःपरुत्परार्यैषमः परेद्यव्यद्यपूर्वेद्युरन्येद्युरन्यतरेद्युरितरेद्युरपरेद्युरधरेद्युरुभयेद्युरुत्तरेद्युः="the words सद्यः

first sea in the form of brahmacarya. उत्तरम्* = the next or latter sea in the form of the housholder's stage. लोकान् = people. संगृभ्य† = leading in masses, guiding, bringing together. मुहुः‡ = often. आचरिक्रत् = challenges, calls upon, calls out, advises.

परुत्, परारि, ऐषम, परेद्यवि, अद्य, पूर्वेद्युः, अन्येद्युः, अन्यतरेद्युः इतरेद्युः, अपरेद्युः, अधरेद्युः, उभयेद्युः, and उत्तरेद्युः are irregularly formed." समान is contracted into स and द्यस् substituted for अहन्.—सद्यः

* उत्तरम्—उद्+तरप् P. V, 3, 57 द्विवचनविभज्योपपदे तरबीयसुनौ = "when out of two things one is to be particularised as possessing some quality in excess over the other, the suffixes तर and ईयस् respectively, are added to the word showing the quality."—उत्तर.

†संगृभ्य—सम्+√ग्रभ् उपादाने+ल्यप् P. VII, 1, 37 समासेऽनञ् पूर्वे क्त्वो ल्यप् = "to a compound formation not having the negative particle नञ् for its first member, the absolute past participial termination ल्यप् is to be added instead of क्त्वा". The compound itself is ordained in P. II, 2, 18 कुगतिप्रादयः = "the particle कु the prepositions प्र etc., and other words which serve as prefixes, enter into composition with words capable of being compounded together and such a compound is compulsory." The penultimate र् of the root is changed to ऋ according to P. VI, 1, 16 ग्रहिज्या वयिव्यधिवष्टि विचतिवृश्चतिपृच्छतिभृज्जतीनां ङिति च = "the semivowel occurring in the roots ग्रह् ज्या, वे, व्यध्, वश्, व्यच्, व्रश्च्, प्रच्छ् and भ्रस्ज् undergoes samprasarana before terminations having an indicatory क् or ङ्. The termination ल्यप् is equal to क्त्वा according to P. I, 1, 55 स्थानिवदादेशोऽनल्विधौ *i. e.* "a letter or letters ordained to take the place of some letter or letters should be considered equal to the original in all respects but not when a rule about some operation in letters themselves is to be applied."

‡ मुहुः—√मुह वैचित्त्ये+उसि—मुहे : किच्च = U. II, 120 "to the root मुह् meaning to faint the termination उसि is added and it operates like one having an indicatory क्." The indicatory क् according to P. I, 1, 5 क्ङिति च prevents guna change of the penultimate short vowel of the root.—मुहुः. This word is an indeclinable.

Translation : Shining with the lustre of true learning, (though) clad in dark-coloured (and coarse) garments, having taken the vows of an initiate (a full fledged graduate), with a flowing beard and moustaches, the student of the Eternal Vedic Lore, now launches at once upon his life's voyage on the vast and deep sea of the householder's stage (being well prepared for it) having, before, successfully come out of the equally unfathomable student's stage. By his virtuous life he brings together, so to say, all the worlds in his own person, and always challenges the attention of all (both by his sane advice and exemplary life).

Purport :—The Vedic student should not care for the polish of his external looks but should enter the householder's stage of life himself living a righteous and austere life, therein guiding people both by precept and example.

Comment :—Maharṣi Dayānanda's remarks here are.—"The Brahmacārin glowing with the aforesaid knowledge wearing deerskin,* etc., with hair and beard which he has worn for a long time, and having been initiated obtains highest happiness and at once passes from the ocean of the practice of *Brahmacarya* to that of the *Grahasthasram*, "the life of a householder" and bringing together all the worlds that are fit for living in (i. e. performing righteous acts and duties the result of which is happy states in future existence) preaches the Law (Dharma) again and again (constantly)".

(११) ब्रह्मचारी जनयन् ब्रह्मापो लोकं प्रजापतिं परमेष्ठिनं विराजम्। गर्भो भूत्वामृतस्य योनाविन्द्रो ह भूत्वासुरांस्ततर्ह ॥७॥

*Regarding the Brahmacari's clothing and such other details see the concluding remarks at the end of this chapter.

Transliteration:—Brahmacārī janayan brahmāpō lōkam prajāpatim paramēṣṭhinam virājam ı
Garbhō bhūtvāmṛtasya yōnāvindrō ha bhūtvāsurāṃstatarha ıı 7.

पदपाठः—ब्रह्मऽचारी। जनयन्। ब्रह्म। अपः। लोकम्। प्रजाऽपतिम्। परमेऽस्थिनम्। विऽराजम्। गर्भः। भूत्वा। अमृतस्य। योनौ। इन्द्रः। ह। भूत्वा। असुरान्। ततर्ह॥

अन्वयः—ब्रह्म अपः लोकम् प्रजापतिम् परमेष्ठिनम् विराजम् जनयन् ब्रह्मचारी अमृतस्य योनौ गर्भः भूत्वा ह इन्द्रः भूत्वा असुरान् ततर्ह॥

Word-meaning &c.:— **जनयन्*** =revealing. **ब्रह्म**=the

---

* जनयन्—√ जनी प्रादुर्भावे+णिच्+शतृ P. III, 1, 26 हेतुमति च="the causal sign णिच् is added to a root to show that another agent prevails upon the doer to do something implied in the verb," and 124 लटः शतृशानचावप्रथमासमानाधिकरणे. The initial ण् and final च् of णिच् are indicatory as laid down in P. I, 3, 7 चुटू *i. e.* "the consonants of the palatal and lingual class used as the initial members of terminations (in the Astadhyayi of Panini) are indicatory", and 3 हलन्त्यम्. √जन् has an indicatory ई at the end, which as laid down in P. VII, 2, 14 श्वीदितो निष्ठायाम् indicates that a root having ई for its indicatory letter does not admit the augment इ before the terminations called निष्ठा. जन्+इ+अत्. Here applies P. VII, 2, 116 अत उपधायाः "before terminations beginning with an indicatory ञ् or ण् the penultimate अ of the base undergoes वृद्धि change." So we should have जानि+अत्, but the Vartika जनीजॄष्क्नसुरञ्जोऽमन्ताश्च (i. e., the roots जनी, जॄष्, क्नसु and all roots ending in the syllable अम् are called मित्) and P. VI, 4, 92 मितां ह्रस्वः (="the penultimate long vowel of the roots called मित् should be shortened before the causal sign णिच्), prevent this. So we have—जनि+अत्. Here P. III, 1, 32 सनाद्यन्ता धातवः="bases terminating with any of the signs सन् of the desiderative (ordained in P III, 1, 7); क्यच्, काम्यच्, क्यङ् and क्यष् of the denominative (ordained in P. III, 1, 8; 9; 11 and 13 respectively); क्विप् showing habit or nature (ordained in P. III, 2, 134; 177 and 178); णिच् of the causal (ordained

Vedic lore. अपः*=(the science of) the vital airs. लोकम्=(the science of) the world. प्रजापतिम्†=the protector of

---

in P. III, 1, 26); यङ् of the frequentative (ordained in P. III, 1, 22); यक् of the passive (ordained in P. III, 1, 67); आय (ordained in P. III, 1, 28); ईयङ् (enjoined by P. III, 1, 29); and णिङ् (laid down in P. III, 1, 30) are called धातु i. e., verbal roots," declares जनि to be a root—धातु. Hence according to P. VII, 2, 84 सार्वधातुकार्धधातुकयोः="before personal terminations and such other terminations as are applied to roots and are characterised by an indicatory श् the final इ, उ, ऋ or लृ short or long of the base undergoes guna change." Therefore following P. I, 1, 2 अदेङ्गुणः We have जने+अत्. Finally applies P. VI, 1, 78 एचोऽयवायावः—"the vowels ए, ऐ, ओ and औ when followed by any vowel are changed to अय्, आय्, अव् and आव् respectively," The question arises which of these four should we substitute for the final ए of जने. The answer is given in P. I, 3. 10 यथासंख्यमनुदेशः समानाम्="when things to be substituted and those for which they are to be subsituted are equal in number the process of substitution should follow the numerical order of both."—जनय्+अत्—जनयन्.

*अपः—आप्यते सुखं येन व्याप्नोति प्रवाहेन सर्वं स्थानं आप्नुवन्ति शरीरम् इति वा √ आप्लृ व्याप्तौ+असुन् U. IV, 189 सर्वधातुभ्योऽसुन् or √ आप्लृ व्याप्तौ +क्विप् U. II, 58 आप्नोतेर्ह्रस्वश्च=to the root आप् to obtain the termination क्विप् is added and its initial long vowel is shortened.—अपः

† प्रजापतिम्—प्रजायाः पतिः P. II, 2, 8 षष्ठी = "a noun in the genitive case can be compounded with another with which it is related and the compound thus formed will be a Tatpurusa." प्रजा—प्रकर्षेण जाता इति—प्र+ √ जनी प्रादुर्भावे+ड P. III, 2, 99 उपसर्गे च संज्ञायाम्="to form a noun the termination ड is added to the root जन् when it is preceded by a preposition." The final syllable अन् of the root is dropped and अ (ड् is indicatory) is added on which gives प्रजा. To this आ (टाप्) is added as laid down in P. IV, 1, 4 अजाद्यतष्टाप्. पतिः—पाति रक्षति इति √ पा रक्षणे +डति U. IV, 57 पातेर्डतिः="to the root पा to protect the suffix डति is

creatures. **परमेष्ठिनम्***=occupying the highest beatific state, **विराजम्**†=the Supreme Being the revealer of the various worlds. **गर्भः**=as a foetus ('germ'-Gr.). **भूत्वा**=becoming. **अमृतस्य योनौ**‡=the source of beatitude, i., e.,

---

added. According to P. VI, 4, 143 टे: the final आ of the root is dropped before डति.

* परमेष्ठिनम्—परमे सर्वोत्तमे पदे तिष्ठति इति—परमे+√ष्ठागतिनिवृत्तौ +इनि P. III, 4, 67 कर्तरि कृत्. The termination in this case operates as one having an indicatory क् and as laid down in P. VI, 4, 64 आतो लोप इटि च the final आ of the root is dropped before it. The locative termination of परमे is retained according to P. VI, 3, 9 हलदन्तात्सप्तम्याः संज्ञायाम्= "when a noun in the locative case, originally ending in a consonant or अ is the first member of a compound, the locative termination is retained." The स् of स्था is in this case changed to ष् according io P. VIII, 3, 97 अम्बाम्बगोभूमिसव्यापद्वित्रिकुशेकुशङ्क्वङ्गमञ्जिपुञ्जिपरमेबर्हिर्दिव्यग्निभ्यः स्थः="the initial स् of the word स्थः is lingualised when it is preceded by the words अम्ब, आम्ब, गो, भूमि, सव्य, अप, द्वि, त्रि, कु, शेकु, शङ्कु, अङ्गु, मञ्जि, पुञ्जि, परमे, बर्हि, दिवि and अग्नि." On this the Vartika स्थास्थिन्स्थृणामिति वक्तव्यम् adds that "along with स्थ, स्था, स्थिन् and स्थृ should also be stated." —परमेष्ठी.—तम्.

† विराजम्—विशेषेण राजते शोभते इति—वि+√राजृ दीप्तौ+क्विप् P. III, 2, 178 अन्येभ्योऽपि दृश्यते—विराट्.—तम्.

‡ योनौ—यौति संयोजयति पृथक्करोति वा इति—√यु मिश्रणामिश्रणयोः +नि U. IV, 51 वह्निश्रिश्रुयुद्रुग्लाहात्वरिभ्यो नित्="tbe termination नि is added to the roots वह्, श्रि, श्रु, यु, द्रु, ग्लै, हा and त्वर् and it operates as one having an indicatory न्." The final vowel of the root undergoes guna change before this termination.—योनिः —तस्मिन्. This word is included in the synonyms of water, house, intermediate region, and place in the Nighantu I, 12; III, 4 and Nir. II, 8 :-मातुर्योनौ माताऽन्तरिक्षम्। निर्मीयन्तेऽस्मिन्भूतानि। योनिरन्तरिक्षम्। महानवयवः। अयमपीतरो योनिरेतस्मादेव. Also Nir. II, 19:—योनिम्... स्थानम्। स्त्रीयोनिरभियुत एनां गर्भः॥

the knowledge of the Supreme Being. इन्द्रः* = most lustrous

---

* इन्द्रः—इन्दति परमैश्वर्यवान्भवति इति—√इदि परमैश्वर्ये+रन् U. II, 28 ऋज्रेन्द्राग्रवज्रविप्रकुब्रचुब्रक्षुरखुरभद्रोग्रभेरभेलशुक्रशुक्लगौरवत्रेरामालाः i. e., "the words ऋज्र, इन्द्र, अग्र, वज्र, विप्र, कुब्र, क्षुर, खुर, भद्र, उग्र, भेर, भेल, शुक्र, शुक्ल, गौर, वत्र, इरा and माला are irregularly formed by the addition of the termination रन् to the roots concerned." The indicatory इ at the end of इदि signifies, as laid down in P. VII, 1, 58 that the augment नुम् is to be added to the root. As नुम् is a मित् augment, P. I, 1, 47 मिदचोऽन्त्यात्परः ordains that it should come after the last vowel of the root. Hence इन्द्+रन्. The final न् of the suffix is indicatory.—इन्द्रः.

The Kasika on P. V, 2, 93 इन्द्रियमिन्द्रलिङ्गमिन्द्रदृष्टमिन्द्रसृष्टमिन्द्रजुष्टमिन्द्रदत्तमिति वा, is worth study. इन्द्रियमित्यन्तोदात्तं शब्दरूपम् निपात्यते। रूढ़िरेषा चक्षुरादीनां करणानाम्। तथा च व्युत्पत्तेरनियमं दर्शयति। इन्द्रशब्दात्षष्ठीसमर्थाल्लिङ्गमित्येतस्मिन्नर्थे घच्प्रत्ययो भवति। इन्द्रस्य लिङ्गमिन्द्रियम्। इन्द्र आत्मा स चक्षुरादिना करणेनानुमीयते। नाकर्तृकं करणमस्ति। इन्द्रेण दृष्टम्। तृतीयासमर्थात्प्रत्ययः। आत्मना दृष्टमित्यर्थः। इन्द्रेण सृष्टम्। आत्मना सृष्टम्। तत्कृतेन शुभाशुभेन कर्मणोत्पन्नमिति कृत्वा। इन्द्रेण जुष्टम् आत्मना जुष्टं सेवितं। तद्द्वारेण विज्ञानोत्पादानात्। इन्द्रदत्तम्। आत्मना विषयेभ्यो दत्तम् यथायथं ग्रहणाय।

The following note from the Nirukta on the word is worth quoting:—"Yaska gives 15 derivations of the word Indra among which one means the soul:—(१) इन्द्र इरां दृणातीति वा। (२) इरां ददातीति वा। (३) इरां दधातीति वा। (४) इरां दारयत इति वा। (५) इरां धारयत इति वा। (६) इन्दवे द्रवतीति वा। (७) इन्दौ रमत इति वा (८) इन्धे भूतानीति वा। (९) तद्यदेनं प्राणैः समैन्धंस्तदिन्द्रस्येंद्रत्वमिति विज्ञायते। (१०) इदं करणादित्याग्रयणः। (११) इदं दर्शनादित्यौपमन्यवः। (१२) इन्दतेर्वैश्वर्यकर्मणः। (१३) इन्दञ्छत्रूणां दारयिता वा (१४) द्रावयिता वा (१५) आदरयिता च यज्वनाम्॥ नि. १०। ८॥

"No. 9 in the above means the soul which is glorified through the senses (and the vital air) by the enlightened. The other derivations mean, lightning, king, etc." Bhumananda Sarasvati, Anthology of Vedic Hymns; The Ram Lall Kapur Tust, Lahore, 1935 p. 113 footnote ll. 5-13.

The following are a few of the interpretations of the word given in the Brahmana literature:—एष वै शुक्रो य एष (सूर्यः) तपत्येष (सूर्य) उ एवेन्द्रः (the sun as the purifier and nourisher of all things by the process of heating through its rays). श. ४।५।५।७॥६।४॥ अथ यः स इन्द्रोऽसौ स आदित्य : ॥ श० ८।५।३।२॥ स यस्स आकाश इन्द्र एव सः (space = ether.) जैउ० १। २८।२॥३१।१॥३२ ।५॥ अथ यत्रैतत्प्रदीप्तो भवति । उच्चैर्धूमः परमया जूत्या बल्बलीति तर्हि हैष (अग्निः) भवतीन्द्रः (a great sacrifice and the sacrificer ?) श० २।३।२।११॥ इन्द्रो वागित्यु वाऽआहुः (the power of speech). श० १।४।५।४॥ See also Ju. B. I, 33, 2; Sankh. B. II, 7; XIII, 5. यो वै वायुः स इन्द्रो य इन्द्र : स वायु : (the atmosphere and the air pervading all space). श० ४।१।३। १६॥ प्राण एवेन्द्रः (the vital air in the body and the air that pervades the world and sustains life). श० १२।६।१।१४॥ हृदयमेवेन्द्रः (the heart). श० १२।६।१।१५॥ यन्मनः स इन्द्रः (the mind or rational faculty). गो० २।४।११॥ See also S. B. XII. 9, 1, 13. रुक्म एवेन्द्रः (glitter, splendour, shining colour, gold, golden hue). श० १०।४।१।६॥ एष वा एत हीन्द्रो यो यजते (the sacrificer, philanthropist) तै० १।३।६।३॥ इन्द्रो यजमानः॥ श० २।१।२।११॥४।५।४।८॥५।१।३।४॥ द्वयेन वाऽएष इन्द्रो भवति यच्च क्षत्रियो यदु च यजमानः॥ श० ५।३।५। २७॥ ऐन्द्रो वै राजन्यः॥ तै० ३।८।२३।२॥ इन्द्रः क्षत्रम्॥ श० १०।४।१। ५॥ See also Sankh. B. XII, 8; T. B. III, 9, 16, 3; S. B. II, 5, 2, 27; 4, 8; III, 9, 1, 16; IV, 3, 3, 6; A, B. IV, 9. यदशनिरिन्द्रस्तेन (lightning) शां० ६।६॥ स्तनयित्नुरेवेन्द्रः (thunder). श० ११।६।३।६॥ तस्मादाहेन्द्रो ब्रह्मेति॥ शां० ६।१४॥ यत्परं भाः प्रजापतिर्वा स इन्द्रो वा॥ श० २।३।१ ।७॥ देवलोको वा इन्द्रः॥ शां० १६।८॥ इन्द्रो बलं बलपतिः॥ श० ११।४।३।१२॥ तै० २।५।७।४॥ वीर्यं वा इन्द्रः (valour, virile power). तां ६।७। ५॥८॥ गो० २।६।७॥ तै० १।७।२।२॥ इन्द्रियं वीर्यमिन्द्रः (the power of the senses). श० २।५।४।८॥३।६।१।१५॥५।४।३।१८॥ शिश्नमिन्द्र : (the power of procreation in the male or female). श. १२।६।१।१६॥ रेत इन्द्रः (semen virile, sperm). श० १२।६।१।१७॥ वृषा वा इन्द्रः (a person of a very powerful or strong physique; a 'breeder'; an athlete; the second type of man according to sanskrit treatises on sexual science). Sankh. B. २०।३॥ एष एवेन्द्रः। यदाहवनीयः ॥ श० २।३।२।२॥ स

like the sun, full of prowess. ह=indeed. **असुरान्***=the wicked, the heretically inclined. **ततर्द**=shatters, destroys.

Translation :—Revealing by his life and teaching the principles of the Vedic Lore, the science of the vital airs, the sciences regarding the world of creatures, the science which treats of the nature of God, the Revealer of all the worlds and the Lord of all creatures in His Highest Beatific state, the Vedic student, lying hidden and growing day by day as a foetus in knowledge of God the source of salvation, becomes most lustrous like the sun and suppresses all that are heretically inclined.

Purport :—It is the life work of a Vedic student who has attained proficiency in all the lores revealed by the Vedas to preach the Vedic Truth and dispel all heresy.

यस्य इन्द्रः सामैव तत् (the Samaveda or hymns or verses from that Veda) जैउ० १ । ३१ । १ ॥ इन्द्र एष यदुद्गाता (the Samavedic priest) जैउ० १ । २२ । २ ॥ इन्द्र आसीत्सीरपतिः शतक्रतुः ॥ तै० २ । ४ । ८ । ७ ॥ सो (इन्द्रः) ऽग्रं देवतानां पर्यैत् । अगच्छत्स्वाराज्यम् ॥ तै० १ । ३ । २ । २ ॥ स (इन्द्रः) वै देवानां वसुर्वीरो ह्येषाम् ॥ श० १ । ६ । ४ । २ ॥ इन्द्रौजसां पते ॥ तै० ३ । ११ । ४ । २ ॥ इन्द्रो मृधां विहन्ता ॥ शां० ४ । १ ॥ इन्द्रायांहोमुचे ॥ तै० १ । ७ । ३ । ७ ॥ ओकःसारी हैषामिन्द्रो भवति यथा गौः प्रज्ञातं गोष्ठम् ॥ गो० ६ । ४ ॥ सेनेन्द्रस्य पत्नी (a very beautiful simile ! the standing army should be as submissive to the king as a good wife to her husband; hence here इन्द्र means king. It is noteworthy that पत्नी etymologically means 'protectress'. The husband and wife together protect the family. So also the king and the standing army ought to protect the subjects.) गो० २ । २ । ६ ॥ ऐन्द्रा वै पशवः ॥ ऐ० ६ । २५ ॥ एतद्वा-इन्द्रस्य रूपम् यदृषभः ॥ श० २ । ५ । ३ । १८ ॥ इन्द्रो वा अश्वः ॥ शां० १५ । ४ ॥

The texts adduced above are not exhaustive but at any rate, they are the result of ancient research in determining the sense of the word इन्द्र in different contexts.

* असुरान्. The following etymologies of this important word are taken from the Anthology of Vedic Hymns (by

Bhumananda Sarasvati, published by the Ram Lall Kapur Trust, Lahore, 1935 pp. 200–205 q. v.):—

(1) अस्यति शत्रून् दुरितं अनर्थान् वा—असेरुरन् U. I, 42="to the root अस् to throw, the termination उरन् is added in the Unadi sense." अस्+उरन्. The final न् of the termination is indicatory used for the exigencies of accent. Vide P. VI, 1, 197.

(2) अस्तः स्थानात् इति U. I, 42 as above, meaning one deposed from his high position as a king dethroned.

(3) असून् राति. Here असु may mean either (*a*) life or vital air, or (*b*) water, or (*c*) intelligence or the reasoning faculty. So also the verb रा means to give or take. Therefore. असुर—असून् प्राणान् प्रज्ञाम् वा राति ददाति अर्थात् सृष्टिकाले जन्मसमये वा जीवात्मानं प्राणबुध्दीन्द्रियाणामधिष्ठानभूतेत शरीरेण संयोजयति, that is, "Who unites the soul at the time of creation or birth with a body the seat of the vital air, intellect and the senses", would mean God. In the same manner असुर meaning असून् राति गृह्णाति मुक्तिसमये प्राणादीन् गृहीत्वा प्रकृतिलीनान् करोति, मरणकाले मनुष्यस्य शरीरात्मवियोगसमये तान् स्वस्मिन् आश्राययति—"Who receives the vital air etc., at the time of the emancipation of a soul and lets them merge in Prakrti or gives them refuge in His Providence at the time of the death i. e., separation of the body and soul, of a person", is also an appellation of God. See Y. V. XXV, 13 and XXIII, 3. When असुर=असून् प्राणान् राति—स्वार्थसिद्धये अन्येषाम् प्राणानपि गृह्णाति हिनस्ति—"who takes destroys—even others' lives for his own selfish motives", it would signify the most wicked oppressor of mankind the worst of tyrants.

On the contrary, derived as अन्येषाम् रक्षणार्थं स्वप्राणानपि अर्पयति—who offers even his own life for the good of others, the word असुर means a very philanthropic and righteous person. Derived as असु जलम् राति ददाति—which gives-showers-water, it means the cloud. On the other hand असून् जलान् राति गृह्णाति बाष्परूपेण अन्तरिक्षे आकर्षति—who receives water, i. e., draws it up in the shape of vapour, it means the sun. See T. B. III, 1, 2 त्वमग्ने रुद्रो असुरो महो दिवः.

The word असु itself is derived according to U. I, 10 शृस्वृस्निहित्रप्यसिवसिहनिक्लिदिबन्धिमनिभ्यश्च, i. e., "to the words शृ, स्वृ, स्निह्, त्रप्, अस्, वस्, हन्, क्लिद्, बन्ध् and मन् the Unadi termination उ is added." अस्यति प्रक्षिपति वायुम् or अस्त: प्राणिनां शरीरे ब्रह्माण्डे वा परमात्मना इति असु: प्राण:. अस्ता: अस्याम् अर्था: (in which the ideals of human life are included), or अस्यति अनर्थान् (which wards off calamities) इति असु: means the intellect or right understanding.

(4) असव: प्राणा: अस्य सन्ति इति—असु+र P. V, 1, 16 तदस्य तदस्मिन् स्यात्="in tbe sense of the genitive or locative case to show something possessed by or inhering in, a suitable termination is appended to a noun in the nominative case denoting the thing possessed or inhering in." असु+र. So also असु: प्रज्ञा अस्य अस्ति इति—the word असुर means a creature having life or intelligence. Derived as असु जलम् अस्य अस्ति, it means a cloud.

(5) असुषु प्राणेषु रमते—असु+रमु क्रीडायाम्+क P. III, 2, 5 कप्रकरणे मूलविभुजादिभ्य उपसंख्यानम्. That which sports in the vital air of creatures, i. e., endows them with life, is the sun. In the neuter gender it is the mind.

(6) वसु उदकं अस्य अस्ति इति—वसु+र as (4) above. व्+असु+र, the initial व् is irregularly dropped.—असुर=the cloud.

(7) अविद्यमाना सुरा यस्य इति—नञ्+सुरा P. II, 2, 24. अनेकमन्यपदार्थे. Vartika नञोऽस्त्यर्थानां वाच्यो वा चोत्तरपदलोपश्च वक्तव्य:="the negative particle नञ् may, sometimes, form Bahuvrihi compounds with substantives but the verbal derivatives used to express their sense are often dropped." P. VI, 3, 73 नलोपो नञ:="the initial न् of the negative particle नञ् is dropped when it is followed by another word" P. VI, 3, 34 स्त्रिया: पुंवद्भाषितपुंस्कादनूङ्समानाधिकरणे स्त्रियामपूरणीप्रियादिषु="in the formation of a Bahuvrihi compound both members of which are in apposition to each other if the first member be a feminine noun derived from the masculine by the addition of any suffix but ऊङ्, the masculine is restored if followed by another feminine noun but not when the second member is a feminine ordinal or one of the words belonging to the group of words commencing with प्रिया" (i. e., प्रिया, मनोज्ञा, कल्याणी, सुभगा

दुर्भगा, भक्तिः, सचिवा, अम्बा कान्ता, श्रान्ता, समा, चपला, दुहिता and वामा). P. I, 2, 48 गोस्त्रियोरुपसर्जनस्य="the final long vowel of a word of the feminine gender which is the final (secondary) member of a compound is shortened." From a successive application of these principles evolves the form असुर meaning not given to drinking liquor.

(8) स्थानेषु न सुष्ठु रताः इति—नञ्+सुष्ठु,+√रमु क्रीडायाम्+ड P. III, 4, 67 कर्तरि कृत्. In compounds the preposition सु (vide P. I, 4, 58 and 94 etc.) is used in the sense of सुष्ठु, (U. I, 25), well, and शोभन (√शुभ or √शुंभ शोभायाम्+ल्युट् P. III, 3, 115), beautiful. E. g., सुष्ठु (adverb) उक्तं+सूक्तम्; शोभना (adjcetive)+उक्तिः =सूक्तिः.—नञ्+सु+रम्+ड=अ+सु+र्+अ (P. VI, 3, 73 नलोपो नञः and 4, 143, टेः. The ञ् of नञ् is done away with *by* P. I, 3, 9). —असुरः. Derived thus, the word means 'restless' or 'not sticking well to a place.'

The above interpretations of the word are based on the following authorities:—

(a.) महच्चास्मै देवानामसुरत्वमेकं प्रज्ञावत्त्वं वानवत्त्वं वा। अपि वासुरिति प्रज्ञानाम अस्यत्यनर्थान। अस्ताश्चास्यामर्थाः। असुरत्वमादिलुप्तम्॥ निरुक्ते १०। ३४॥

असुरिति प्रज्ञानाम। तया तद्वत्त्वम्। तया महत्या प्रज्ञया उदकेन साधनेन सर्वमिदं जनयति पुष्णाति वर्धयति च। अप्रज्ञो हि साधनसंपत्तावपि किं कुर्यात्। अथवा अनवत्त्वम्। असुः प्राणस्तेन तद्वत्त्वम्। एवमपि सति प्राणेनैव शक्यत एतत्सर्वं कर्तुम्। अप्राणो हि किं कुर्यात्। अन्नवत्त्वमिति केचित्। तेषामन्नहेतुनोदकेन तद्वत्त्वम्। तथापि योज्यम्। असुरिति प्रज्ञानाम। तत्कस्मात्। अस्यत्यनर्थान्। प्रज्ञैवहि प्रज्ञावतोऽस्यति क्षिपत्यनर्थान्नाशयति। अस्ताश्चास्यामर्थाः। न हि तदस्ति व्यक्तेर्यत्सर्वं प्रज्ञावतां प्रज्ञायां नास्ति। एतावांस्तु विशेषोऽभिव्यक्तमनभिव्यक्तमिति। अथवा। यदेतदसुरत्वं वसुमतो भावो वसुरत्वमेतत्। रोमत्त्वर्थे। वकारलोपश्च। वसुनोदकेन तद्वान्॥ Thus Durgacarya on the above passage of Yaska's.

(b) Skandasvamin also has the same remarks to make on the passage except the following small differences:. अन्नवत्त्वमित्यपपाठः। असुशब्देनान्नस्य वक्तुमशक्यत्वात्। अथवा वसुरत्वमादिलुप्तं वसुवत्त्वं धनवत्त्वमित्यर्थः। धनमसाधारणं नान्यस्य कस्यचिदीदृशमित्यर्थः। Hence according to Skandsvamin वसु+र=असुर means an extraordinarily wealthy person. This also, as some other etymologies given by him, may very well mean the Supreme Being.

(c) 'अस दीप्त्यादानेषु' भौवादिकः स्वरितेत्पूर्वस्मादेव सूत्रात् [असिमसोरुरन् U. I, 42, 43] उरन्। असति गच्छत्यन्तरिक्षे, दीप्यते स्वयम्, आदत्ते वा जलं वर्षितुं। यद्वा; 'सुर ऐश्वर्ये (तुदा॰ प॰)', इगुपधलक्षणः कः (P. III, 1, 135) सुरतीति सुर ईश्वरः, स्वतन्त्र इत्यर्थः, असुरः अनीश्वरः, इन्द्रादि परतन्त्र इत्यर्थः। "दिवः श्येनासो असुरस्य नीळयः (ऋ॰ सं॰ ८, ४, २४, १)"—"दीर्घाधियो रक्षमाणा असुर्यम् (ऋ॰ सं॰ २, ७, ६, ४)"—इति च निगमौ॥ From Devaraja Yajvan's commentary on the word असुर in the Nighantu, edited by the late P. Satyavrata Samasrami Bhattacharya under the auspices of the Asiatic Society of Bengal, Calcutta 1882. The motley punctuation is the editor's invention of which Devaraja Yajvan had not even dreamt !!

(d) * * * असुरा असुरता स्थानेष्वस्ता स्थानेभ्य इति वापि वासुरिति प्राण (णा Rajwada)नामास्तः शरीरे भवति तेन तद्वन्तः सोर्देवानसृजत तत्सुराणां सुरत्वमसोरसुरानसृजत तदसुराणामसुरत्वमिति विज्ञायते। * * * गन्धर्वाः पितरो देवा असुरा रक्षांसीत्येके चत्वारो वर्णा निषादः पञ्चम इत्यौपमन्यवः॥ Nirukta III. 8. Hence the ancient Vedic exigete--Aupamanyava considers गन्धर्व, पितृ, देव and असुर to be the designations of the four classes in Vedic society. The "non-Vedic" or "general" or "others," to use modern communalistic terminology where to him, the रक्षस् or राक्षस, alias निषाद.

The above passage gives another etymology of the word viz:—

(9) असोरसुरानसृजत तदसुराणामसुरत्वम् in which the particle सु, used here as a noun means good nature--शुभस्वभावः→सुः, and the negative of this, according to P. II, 2, 6 नञ्="the negative particle नञ् is compounded with a word capable of entering in -to composition and the resulting compound is a Tatpurusa" नञ्+सु=असुः (vide P. VI, 3, 73). असुः अस्य अस्ति इति—असुरः (P. V, 1, 16). Here the word means 'evil-natured' or 'wicked' i. e., 'a dangerous person of notoriously bad character wielding immense power and using it to harm others'. When Dr. Samual Johnson said (Vide Journal of a tour to the Hebrides by Boswell) that

Comment:—Maharṣi Dayānaṇda comments on this stanza as follows:—"The *Brahmacarin* learning the Vedic lore, acquiring a knowledge of the vital airs, and of the sensible and visible world, proclaiming God the Lord of creatures, who manifests himsęlf in many ways, entering into the womb of emancipation, *i. e.*, living regularly in knowledge like a foetus, in the womb equipping himself with learning, shining like the sun, and driving away the doers of evil deeds, the ignorant, the hypocrites of malevolent and mischievous disposition, as the sun drives away the clouds and the night, becomes the displayer of all the good qualities and the destroyer of the bad ones."*

(१२) आचार्यस्ततक्ष नभसी उभे इमे उर्वी गम्भीरे पृथिवीं दिवं च । ते रक्षति तपसा ब्रह्मचारी तस्मिन् देवाः संमनसो भवन्ति ॥८॥

---

there was no harm in possessing the power of a giant but that it was wicked to use it like one, he was, in his own peculiar manner, defining a राक्षस. 'The cure for "Materialism,"' says Henry Ford, (New Dictionary of Thoughts, p. 482), 'is to have enough for every body and to spare. When people are sure of having what they need they cease to think about it.' The modern world is infested with 'raksasas' of this type, hence Ford's dream will never come true. A scavenger, a street sweeper, a poor person oppressed by an abnormal social system upholding caste or class division, is not a राक्षस. It is the oppresser and not the oppressed that merits the appellation, but when the whole society is a huge gang of oppressers, the oppressed themselves would be called names. This is the true feature of the modern world.

* These remarks of Maharsi Dayananda's as well as those on some of the previous and subsequent verses are taken from the English translation of his Introduction to the Commentary on the Vedas, pp. 332-5.

Transliteration:—Ācāryastatakṣa nabhasī ubhē imē urvī·gambhīrē pṛthivīm divaṃ ca ।

Tē rakṣati tapasā brahmacārī tasmin dēvāh sammanasō bhavanti ॥ 8.

पदपाठः—आऽचार्यः । ततक्ष । नभसी इति । उभे इति । इमे इति । उर्वी इति । गम्भीरे इति । पृथिवीम् । दिवम् । च । ते इति । रक्षति । तपसा । ब्रह्मऽचारी । तस्मिन् । देवाः । सम्ऽमनसः । भवन्ति ॥

अन्वयः—आचार्यः उभे इमे नभसी उर्वी गम्भीरे पृथिवीं दिवं च ततक्ष । ब्रह्मचारी तपसा ते रक्षति । देवाः तस्मिन् संमनसो भवन्ति ॥

Word-meaning:--**ततक्ष**=made more useful ('fashioned'-Gr.). **नभसी***=inter-related. **उभे**=both. **इमे**=these. **उर्वी**†

---

* नभसी—नह्यति बध्नाति घर्मं परस्परं वा इति—√ णह बन्धने+असुन् U. IV, 211 नहेर्दिवि भश्च="to the root नह् to bind, the termination असुन् is added before which the final ह् of the root is changed to भ् and the resulting form means 'the sky'."—नभस्.—ते.

† उर्वी—आच्छादयति अल्पान् इति—√ ऊर्णुञ् आच्छादने+कु U. I, 31 महति ह्रस्वश्च="to the root ऊर्णु meaning to cover the termination कु is added, the initial long vowel is shortened and the final syllable नु is dropped. The resulting form means vast or great".—उरु. At this stage applies P. IV, 1, 44 वोतो गुणवचनात्="to a base ending in उ and denoting a quality the suffix ङीप् is optionally added in the feminine."— उरु+ङीप्. The final प् is indicatory *by* P. I, 3, 3 but the initial ङ् is not so there being an express enunciation in P. I, 3, 8 to the effect. The letters ल् and श् as well as consonants of the guttural class in the beginning of taddhita (secondary) teminations are not indicatory but either form part of the terminations themselves or have some other force than the indicatory letters. E. g., the termination लच् is enjoined after nouns denoting things pertaining to living beings and ending in आ *by* P. V, 2, 96 प्राणिस्थादातो लजन्यतरस्याम्, as चूडा अस्य अस्ति इति--चूडा+लच्—चूडालः. So also P. V, 2. 100 लोमादिपामादिपिच्छादिभ्यः शनेलचः—लोम+श=लोमशः., पामनः; पिच्छ+इलच्—पिच्छिलः. The ङ् is here used to distinguish

=spacious. **गम्भीरे*** = deep, profound. **पृथिवीं**—the earth. **दिवं†** = the heavens. **ते** = those two. **रक्षति** = he protects. **तपसा** = by an austere way of living.

Translation :—The master renders more useful both these vast and profound regions which are united with each other, namely, the earth and the heavens. The Vedic student by his austerities protects them and all beneficent forces of nature co-operate in him (towards his good).

Purport :—By teaching and learning the Vedic lores through hearing, cogitation and meditation, the master and pupil understand the secrets of the earth and heavens and (propagating knowledge about them), make them more useful to mankind.

---

the three feminine suffixes ङीप्, ङीष् and ङीन् as is done in P. IV, 1, 1 ङ्याप्प्रातिपदिकात्. The ङ् of these terminations is, however, invariably dropped. For *convenience' sake* it has been called indicatory in these notes. The final प्, ष् and न् are, however, indicatory, and are used for the exigencies of accent. The termination ङीप् conforms to P. III, 1, 3 अनुदात्तौ सुप्पितौ = "all case terminations and all terminations that have an indicatory प् are grave accented." Both ङीष् and ङीन् are acute accented according to P. III, 1, 2 आद्युदात्तश्च. The accent of the words to which these terminations are affixed will be regulated by these principles i. e., rules, the observance of which is occasioned by the indicatory letters प्, ष् and न्.—उरु + ङीप् = उरु + ई. The final उ of उरु is changed to व् *by* P. I, 1, 3.—उर्वी.—ते. (Vedic dual).

* गम्भीरे—गम्यते प्राप्यते ज्ञायते वा इति—√ गम्लृ गतौ + ईरन् U. IV, 35 गभीरगम्भीरौ = "the words गभीर and गम्भीर are irregularly formed by adding the Unadi termination ईरन् to the root गम् to go."—गम्भीरः + टाप् (P. IV, 1, 4) गम्भीरा.—ते.

† दिवं—क्रीडन्ति व्यवहरंति सर्वे लोकाः प्राणिनश्च अस्यां इति—√ दिवु क्रीडाविजिगीषा व्यवहारद्युतिस्तुतिमोदमदस्वप्नकान्तिगितषु + क्विप् P. III, 3, 1 उणादयो बहुलम् or 2, 178 अन्येभ्योऽपि दृश्यते.—दिव्.—ताम्.

(१३) इमां भूमिं पृथिवीं ब्रह्मचारी भिक्षामा जभार प्रथमो दिवं च। ते कृत्वा समिधावुपास्ते तयोरार्पिता भुवनानि विश्वा ॥९॥

Transliteration:—Imām bhūmim pṛthivīm brahmacārī bhikṣām ā jabhāra prathamō divaṃ ca ।

Tē kṛtvā samidhāvupāstē tayōrārpitā bhuvanāni viśvā ॥ 9.

पदपाठः—इमाम् । भूमिम् । पृथिवीम् । ब्रह्मऽचारी । भिक्षाम् । आ । जभार । प्रथमः । दिवम् । च । ते इति । कृत्वा । समिधौ । उपऽआस्ते । तयोः । आर्पिता । भुवनानि । विश्वा ॥

अन्वयः—इमाम् पृथिवीम भूमिम् दिवं च प्रथमः ब्रह्मचारी भिक्षाम् आ जभार । ते समिधौ कृत्वा (सः ईश्वरम्) उपास्ते । विश्वा भुवनानि तयोः आर्पिता (सन्ति) ।

Word-meaning &c.:— **इमाम्** = this. **पृथिवीम्** = spacious. **भूमिम्**¶ = earth. **भिक्षाम्**† = alms. **आ जभार**‡ = received; got. **प्रथमः**‡ = first, principal. **दिवम्** = heavens. **कृत्वा** = having made. **समिधौ** = two sticks for the sacrificial fire. **उपास्ते** = he worships God. **तयोः** = in the two.

---

* भूमिम्—भवन्ति पदार्थाः अस्याम् इति—√भू सत्तायाम्+मि U. IV, 45 भुवः कित्="to the root भू to be, the termination मि is added which operates like one having an indicatory क्."—भूमिः—ताम्.

† भिक्षाम्—√भिक्ष् भिक्षायामलाभे लाभे च+अ+टाप्, P. III, 3, 103 गुरोश्च हलः="a root ending in a consonant and having a vowel which is prosodially long takes the suffix अ before the feminine termination."—भिक्ष. Then टाप् is applied by P. IV, 1, 4 अजाद्यतष्टाप्.—भिक्षा.—ताम्.

‡ आजभार—आ+√हृ+अ of the perfect. The भ is substituted according to Vartika हृग्रहोर्भश्छन्दसि.

¶ प्रथमः—प्रथते प्रख्यातः भवति इति—√प्रथ् प्रख्याने+अमच् U. V, 68 प्रथेरमच् ="to the root प्रथ् meaning to spread or rise, the termination अमच् is added." The final च् is indicatory.—प्रथमः,

आर्पिता*=well established. **भुवनानि**†=the worlds. **विश्वा**= all.

Translation:—It is the Brahmacārin (the Vedic student) who is the first to get this spacious earth and the heavens as his alms which he offers as two sticks in the sacrificial fire and worships God. (As) all the worlds are established in these two (they also fall to his share).

Purport:—The wise study the earth and heavens and try to make them more useful to humanity. It is to put

---

* आर्पिता—आ + √ ऋ गतौ + पुक् + णिच् + इट् + क्त P. VII, 3, 36 अर्तिह्रीव्लीरीक्नूयीक्ष्माय्यातां पुग्णौ = "before णिच् the sign of the causal the augment पुक् is added on to the roots ऋ, ह्री, व्ली, री, क्नूयी, क्ष्मायी and to such roots as end in आ," III, 1, 26 हेतुमति च and 102 निष्ठा.—आ + अर्पय् + क्त. The guna change of ऋ to अर् is in accordance with P. VII, 3, 86 पुगन्तलघूपधस्य च = "the final vowel of the verbal base ending in पुक् and the penultimate short of other roots undergoes guna before personal terminations." The augment इट् is added to the root अर्पय् (vide P. III, 1, 32 सनाद्यन्ता धातवः) according to P. VII, 2, 36 आर्धधातुकस्येड्वलादेः. The causal sign is dropped here as explained in P. VI, 4 52 निष्ठायां सेटि = "before the past participial termination when the augment इट् follows, the causal sign at the end of the base is dropped."—आ + अर्पय् + क्त = आ + अर्प् + क्त. The prefix आ and initial अ of the base give place to आ according to P. VI, 1, 101 अकःसवर्णे दीर्घः = "when a vowel of the अक् प्रत्याहार (अइउण् and ऋलृक्) is followed by a similar vowel, the corresponding long vowel is the substitute for both."—आर्प् + क्त = आर्पितः —ते.

† भुवनानि—भवति अथवा भवन्ति भूतानि अस्मिन् इति—√ भू सत्तायाम् + क्युन् U. II, 80 भूसूधूभ्रस्जिभ्यश्छन्दसि = "to the roots भू, सू, धू, and भ्रस्ज् the Unadi termination क्युन् is added." भू + अन (Vide P. VII, 1, 1, युवोरनाकौ). The termination having an indicatory क् guna or vrddhi change of the preceding vowel is forestalled by P. I, 1, 5 क्ङिति च, but उव् is substituted for ऊ according to P. VI, 4, 77 अचिश्नुधातुभ्रुवां य्वोरियङुवङौ = "the final इ and उ of a

us in mind of this principle that the two sticks are offered in the sacrificial fire.

Comment :—A person's life, according to Vedic teachings is divided into four stages, the first of which is brahmacarya, or studentship when as a little boy or girl at about eight years of age when admission to the Guru-kula as described in verse 7 above should take place and study should commence with the Sanskrit language and grammar and other ancillary lores to be consummated with that of the philosophical systems and the Vedas. It is but reasonable to suppose that the student, during the long course of studentship (not less than sixteen years in the case of both boys and girls), was afforded instruction in history and geography as well. A chance to equip himself or herself with practical knowledge of the world was also given. The tuition, it must be noted, was free, nay, the students were fed and clothed by the public* who thought it a great good fortune to feed a Brahmacārin.

Hence of all the four āśramas or stages of human life, the first stage, received a grounding in the knowledge of the earth, the heavens and other planets and regions and also worldly life through the Vedas and the ancillary lores. Therefore, the brahmacārin is appropriately described as receiving earth and heavens as his alms.*

(१४) अर्वागन्यः परो अन्यो दिवस्पृष्ठाद्गुहा निधी निहितौ ब्राह्मणस्य । तौ रक्षति तपसा ब्रह्मचारी तत्केवलं कृणुते ब्रह्म विद्वान् ॥१०॥

---

base ending in the sign श्नु, of roots and of the word भ्रू are changed to इयङ् and उवङ् when a vowel follows."—भुव्+अन= भुवनम्—तानि.

* Regarding these points see concluding remarks.

Transliteration:—Arvāganyah parō anyō divas pṛṣthād guhā nidhī nihitāu brāhmaṇasya ।

Tāu rakṣati tapasā brahmacārī tatkēvalam kṛṇutē brahma vidvān ॥ 10.

पदपाठः—अर्वाक् । अन्यः । परः । अन्यः । दिवः । पृष्ठात् । गुहा । निधी इति निऽधी । निऽहितौ । ब्राह्मणस्य । तौ । रक्षति । तपसा । ब्रह्मऽचारी । तत् । केवलम् । कृणुते । ब्रह्म । विद्वान् ।

अन्वयः—ब्राह्मणस्य निधी गुहा निहितौ, अन्यः अर्वाक्, अन्यः दिवः पृष्ठात् परः । तौ ब्रह्मचारी तपसा रक्षति (च ब्रह्म) विद्वान् तत् ब्रह्म केवलम् कृणुते ॥

Word-meaning &c.—अर्वाक्*=this side. अन्यः†=

---

*अर्वाक्—अवरे काले देशे वा अञ्चति इति—अवर+√ अञ्चु गतौ+क्विन् P. III, 4, 67 कर्तरि कृत्. and III, 2, 59 ऋत्विग्दधृक्स्रग्दिगुष्णिगञ्चुयुजिक्रुञ्चां च="the words ऋत्विग्, दधृष्, स्रज्, दिश्, उष्णिज्, are irregularly formed by adding the termination क्विन् to the roots concerned. This termination is to be added to the roots युज्, क्रुञ्च् and अञ्च् as well to form nouns." For the word अवर अर्व is substituted. The compound is justified by P. II, 3, 109 पृषोदरादीनि यथोपदिष्टम्. The word अर्वाक् is itself indeclinable but अर्वाञ्च् is an adjective and declinable in all the three genders. The elimination of the penultimate nasal is explained in P. VI, 4, 24 अनिदितां हल उपधायाः क्ङिति="the penultimate न् (=nasal) of bases ending in a consonant and not having (short) इ for their indicatory letter is dropped before terminations having an indicatory क् or ङ्." Hence the ञ् of the root is dropped before क्विन्. अर्व+अञ्च्+क्विन्=अर्व+अच्+क्विन्=अर्वाच् (P. VI, 1, 101 अकः सवर्णे दीर्घः). The nominative and accusative singular terminations of the neuter are dropped by P. VII, 1, 23 स्वमोर्नपुंसकात् and the final च् changed to क् *by* P. VIII, 2, 30 चोः कुः="च् at the end of a grammatical form (पद) or when followed by a letter of the झल् प्रत्याहार (i. e., any consonant except a nasel or a semivowel) is changed to क्."—अर्वाक्.

† अन्यः—अनिति जीवति इति—अन प्राणने+य P. III, 3, 1 उणादयो बहुलम् (Vide also U. IV, 101 माछाशसिभ्यो यः)—अन्यः.

one. **परः***=the other. **दिवः**=of the heavens (ether). **पृष्ठात्**† =on the other side. (**दि॰ पृ॰**=in another etheric or spiritual sphere of existence.) **गुहा**‡=concealed. **निधी**¶=

---

* परः—पृणाति पालयति इति—√ पॄ पालने+अप् P. III, 3, 57 ॠदोरप्="the termination अप् is added to verbs ending in long ॠ and उ short or long in the sense of mere state or action or the agent."—पॄ +अप्. The final प् of the termination is indicatory. The ॠ of the root takes guna here according to P. VIII, 3, 84 सार्वधातुकार्धधातुकयोः—पर्+अ=परः. This word will have the acute on the first syllable and hence the final syllable (र) will have circumflex. The form in the verse is got by affixing the termination अच् according to P.III, 1, 134 नन्दिग्रहिपचादिभ्यो ल्युणिन्यचः and VI, 1, 163 चितः.

The two forms are used in the Vedas in different places and surely, in different and distinct senses but owing to the lack of a sincere study of the Vedas such fine points have now become a matter for research.

† पृष्ठात्—पर्षति सिञ्चति यः येन वा इति—√ पृषु सेचने+थक् U. II, 12 तिथपृष्ठगूथयूथप्रोथाः="the Unadi termination थक् is added to the roots तिज्, पृष्, गु, यु and मु and तिथ, पृष्ठ, गूथ, यूथ and प्रोथ are thus irregularly formed."—पृष्ठः.—तस्मात्.

‡ गुहा—गूहति रक्षति इति—√ गुहू संवरणे+क+टाप् P. III, 1, 135 and IV, 1, 4. The form here used is of the locative case singular number *by* P. VII, 1, 39.—गुहा.—तस्याम्.

¶ निधी—नितरां धीयन्ते अस्मिन् इति—नि+√ डुधाञ् धारणपोषणयोः +कि P. III, 3, 92 उपसर्गे घोः किः="when a preposition precedes the termination कि is appended to the roots called घु" (Vide P. I, 1, 19 दाधाघ्वदाप्="the four roots assuming the form दा viz. √ डुदाञ् दाने, √ दाण् दाने, √ दो अवखण्डने and √ देङ् रक्षणे but not √ दाप् लवने and √ दैप् शोधने and such roots as assume the form धा e, g., √ डुधाञ् धारणपोषणयोः and √ धेट् पाने."—नि+धा+कि=नि+ध्+कि. The initial क् of the termination is indicatory suggesting according to P. VI, 4, 64 आतो लोप इटि च that is, the final आ of

two treasures or treasuries. **निहितौ***=are kept. **ब्राह्मणस्य**= of the knowledge of God, **तपसा**=with fervour. **रक्षति**= protects. **केवलम्**†=alone, certain,useful. **कृणुते**=makes. **विद्वान्**‡=knowing.

Translation :—The two treasuries of divine lore are kept concealed, one this side and the other beyond the other side of the heavens (ether). The Vedic student, with his fervour protects the two and knowing the Supreme Being makes Him alone the object to serve.

Purport :—The knowledge of God is available at every place, far and near. The Vedic student and the ascetic realise the Supreme Being by means of their austerities and develop their powers under His aegis.

Comment :—Divine Lore or the knowledge of the Supreme Reality is twofold. The key to both is in the revealed Vedas. In his ordinary mundane existence man has not the qualifications necessary to understand both the aspects of this Divine Lore

---

roots is dropped when an impersonal terminatian with an indicatory क् or the augment इट् follows."—निधिः—तौ.

* निहितौ—नि+√डुधाञ् धारणपोषणयोः+क्त .P. III, 2, 102 निष्ठा and VII, 4, 42 दधातेर्हिः="when a termination itself beginning with त् and having an indicatory क् follows हि is substituted for the root धा."—निहितः.—तौ.

† केवलम्—सेवते सर्वान् सेव्यते वा सर्वैः इति—√केवृ सेवने+कल U. I, 106 वृषादिभ्यश्चित्="the termination कल is added to roots of the group beginning with वृष etc., and it operates as if it had an indicotory च्." The final ऋ of the root and initial क् of the termination are indicatory.—केव्+अल=केवलः.—तम्.

‡ विद्वान—वेत्ति इति—√विद ज्ञाने+शतृ P. VII, 1, 36 विदेः शतुर्वसुः="वसु is substituted for शतृ after the root विद् to know."—विद्वस्→विद्वान् .

as it is revealed in the Vedas. The first or mundane aspect of it we realise by the observation of the world and mundane education. This is a very small fraction of Divine Lore for a man's life is not enough to acquire some tolerable knowledge of it. Just as the visible universe is infinitely small compared with the unseen and what looks to our physical eyes as a vacuum, so also the other aspect of Divine Lore is unfathomable and extremely vast. It belongs to quite another sphere (the etheric, astral as some call it, or rather) the spiritual, and is, hence, to be acquired through the spirit and not the body. This is possible in a state of yogic trance. Such a state, enduring for even a second, will surely enable the soul to grasp the significance of the Vedic statements as they obtain in the spiritual or Divine sphere. This is exactly what is laid down in the Ṛgvēda I, 164, 39*:—

"What good can the *Vedas* do unto him who does not know that Great Being, who is All-pervading and Eternal, the Holiest of all, Who sustains the sun and the earth, and is the support of the wise, Whose realisation is the chief aim of the *Vedas?* But they alone, enjoy eternal bliss who study the *Vedas*, live a righteous life, become perfect yogis and realize God". (The Light of Truth p. 67.)

The realization of God and the higher meaning of the Vedas is not therefore, reserved only for the man who arrives at the fourth stage of life and renounces the world. A person in any stage of life, with subdued passions, continent living accompanied by Vedic study and yogic practice can attain this end. It is not also a matter to be written in books. Anything that a yogi in

---

* ऋचो अक्षरे परमे व्योमन् यस्मिन् देवा अधि विश्वे निषेदुः । यस्तन्न वेद किमृचा करिष्यति य इत्तद्विदुस्त इमे समासते ॥ ऋ० १ । १६४ । ३६ ॥

a state of trance observes on the other (spiritual) sphere cannot be described to beings on the mundane sphere. No human speech can rise to such a high state as to be adequate for the purpose. Only the V e d a s have this power but to understand them fully the limited experience of our mundane life is not a fit training.

(१५) अर्वागन्य इतो अन्यः पृथिव्या अग्नी समेतो नभसी अन्तरेमे । तयोः श्रयन्ते रश्मयोऽधि दृढास्ताना तिष्ठति तपसा ब्रह्मचारी ॥११॥

Transliteration:—Arvāganya itō anya pṛthivyā agnī samētō nabhasī antarēmē ।

Tayōh śrayantē raśmayō'dhi dṛḍhāstān ā tiṣṭhati tapasā brahmacārī.

पदपाठः—अर्वाक् । अन्यः । इतः। अन्यः । पृथिव्याः । अग्नी इति । सम्ऽएतः । नभसी इति । अन्तरा । इमे इति । तयोः । श्रयन्ते । रश्मयः । अधि । दृढाः । तान् । आ । तिष्ठति । तपसा । ब्रह्मऽचारी ॥

अन्वयः- अग्नी इमे नभसी अन्तरा समेतः, अन्यः अर्वाक्, अन्यः इतः पृथिव्याः । तयोः रश्मयः दृढः अधि श्रयन्ते । ब्रह्मचारी तपसा तान् आ तिष्ठति ॥

Word-meaning:—अर्वाक्=here, on the earth. इतः*=away from here. अग्नी=the two fires, viz, the earthly fire and the sun; the heat proceeding from these two fires. समेतः=come together, unite. नभसी=in these two; the

---

*इतः—इदम्+तसिल् P. V, 3, 7 पञ्चम्यास्तसिल्="the termination तसिल् is added to किम् a pronoun and the word बहु." Hence P. V, 3, 3 इदम इश् enjoins the substitution of इश् for इदम्—for the whole of the latter *by* P. I, 1, 55 अनेकाल्शित्सर्वस्य, as implied by its indicatory letter श्. The final syllable इल् of the termination is indicatory according to vartika इर इत्संज्ञा वक्तव्या and P. I, 1, 50 उरण्परः (with its Vartika लपर इति वक्तव्यम्) and therefore dropped *by* I, 3, 9 तस्य लोपः—इदम्+तसिल्=इश्+तस=इतः.

earth and the heavens united together. **अन्तरा**:* = between. **तयोः**=of the two. **अयन्ते**=rest. **रश्मयः**†=rays. **अधि**=in material objects. **दृढाः**‡=firm. **तान्** =on them.

* अन्तरा—अन्तं राति ददाति इति—अन्त+√रा दाने+क P. III, 2, 3 आतोऽनुपसर्गे कः="the termination क is affixed to a root ending in long आ when no preposition precedes the latter." The final आ of the root is dropped before क *by* P. VI, 4, 64 आतो लोप इटि च.—अन्तरम्. In this form the final vowel is irregularly lengthened. The word अन्त itself is formed according to U. III, 86 हसिमृग्रिण्वामिदमिलूपूधुर्विभ्यस्तन् or V, 60 अमेस्तुट् च. In both the cases the word has the acute accent on the final syllable according to P. III, 1, 2 आद्युदात्तश्च and vartika सतिशिष्टस्वरबलीयस्त्वञ्च वक्तव्यम्= "when a subsequent acute accent is ordained when already there is one, the subsequent one is retained in preference to the previous." According to this very principle अन्तरा also has the acute accent on the final syllable. This procedure is to be adopted in all cases except a very few exceptions since in P. VI, 1, 158 अनुदात्तं पदमेकवर्जम्, it is ordained that in every fully formed grammatical form there can be only one syllable bearing the acute accent. The Mahabhasya makes this clear in the following stanza (probably taken from the now lost संग्रह of Katyayana):—

आगमस्य विकारस्य प्रकृतेः प्रत्ययस्य च ।
पृथक्स्वरनिवृत्त्यर्थमेकवर्जे पदस्वरः ॥

On the above Vartika also the Mahabhasya says: सत्येकस्मिन्स्वरे विशिष्टो द्वितीयः स्वरो बलवान्भवति । तच्चानेकप्रत्ययसमासार्थम् ॥

† रश्मयः—अश्नुते व्याप्नोति इति—√अशूङ् व्याप्तौ+मि U. IV, 46 अश्नोते रशच्="for the root अश् meaning to pervade रशच् is substituted before the Unadi termination मि." The final syllable अच् of the substitute रशच् is indicatory, or अ is used to facilitate pronunciation and च् alone is indicatory used to determine the accent of the full form *by* P. VI, 1, 163 चितः.—अश्+मि=रशच्+मि (Vide P. I, 55 अनेकाल्शित्सर्वस्य)=रश्मिः.—ते. Yaska says रश्मिर्यमनात्; Nir. II, 15.√यम उपरमे+इ U. IV, 140 खनिकष्यजि etc., and P. III, 3, 1. रश् is substituted for √यम्.

‡ दृढाः—√दृह or √दृहि वृद्धौ+क्त P. VII, 2, 20 दृढः स्थूलबलयोः

आतिष्ठति=sets, stands, benefits himself by and makes more useful for others. **तपसा**=by his austere living.

Translation :—The *heats* proceeding from these two fires, one here on the earth and the other far away from it, meet between these two inter-related regions, the earth and the heavens. Their rays firmly resort to earthly objects, and the continent Vedic student by his austere life benefits himself by them as well as makes them more useful to others.

Purport :—The sun's heat as well as that of the fire, are essential for the sustenance of all creatures. The brahmacārī and yogi utilise them to their greatest advantage. All people should follow suit.

Comment :—Heat is a purifying agent. It also helps digestion, dispels disease and protects life. Hence the science of yoga recommends the use of fire and the sun's rays. It is a theory of yoga that the adept yogi can reduce his body in bulk and weight to such an extent that he can travel along the rays of the sun.*

(१६) अभिक्रन्दन्स्तनयन्नरुणः शितिङ्गो बृहच्छेपोऽनु भूमौ जभार। ब्रह्मचारी सिञ्चति सानौ रेतः पृथिव्यां तेन जीवन्ति प्रदिशश्चतस्रः ॥१२॥

Transliteration:—Abhikrandan stanayannaruṇah śitingō bṛhacchēpō'nu bhūmāu jabhāra ।
Brahmacārī siñcati sanāu rētah pṛthivyām tēna jīvanti pradiśaścatasrah ॥ 12.

पदपाठः—अभिऽक्रन्दन्। स्तनयन्। अरुणः। शितिङ्गः। बृहत्।

="the word दृढ meaning bulky or strong is irregularly formed by appending the past participial termination क्त to the root दृह or दृहि meaning to grow.—दृढः.—ते.

* See Concluding Remarks at the end of the chapter.

शेपः । अनु । भूमौ । जभार । ब्रह्मऽचारी । सिञ्चति । सानौ । रेतः पृथिव्याम् । तेन । जीवन्ति । प्रऽदिशः । चतस्रः ॥

अन्वयः--अभिक्रन्दन् स्तनयन् अरुणः शितिंगः बृहत् शेपः ब्रह्मचारी भूमौ अनु जभार । (स) सानौ पृथिव्यां (च) रेतः सिञ्चति तेन चतस्रः प्रदिशः जीवन्ति ॥

Word-meaning:—अभिक्रन्दन्* = (cloud) making sound every where because स्तनयन्† = thundering. अभि० स्त० (as applied to the Vedic Student) preaching the Vedic truths at the top of his voice everywhere. अरुणः‡ = (cl.) brown; (br.) like the sun. शितिङ्गः¶ = (cl.) moving between

---

* अभिक्रन्दन्—अभि + √ क्रदि आह्वाने + शतृ P. III, 2, 124 लटः शतृशानचावप्रथमासमानाधिकरणे and VII, 1, 58 इदितो नुम् धातोः.

† स्तनयन् —√ स्तन शब्दे + शतृ P. III, 2, 124 and VI, 1, 64.

‡ अरुणः--√ ऋ गतौ + उनन् U. III, 60 अर्तेश्च = "the Unadi suffix उनन् is appended to the root ऋ and it operates as though it had an indicatory च्." The guna change is in keeping with P. VII, 3, 84 सार्वधातुकार्धधातुकयोः.

¶ शितिङ्गः—शितिः शुक्लः कृष्णश्च तयोर्मध्यतो गच्छति इति--शिति + √ गम्लृ गमने + खच् P. III, 2, 38 Vartika खच्प्रकरणे गमेः सुप्युपसंख्यानम् (= "the termination खच् should be enjoined after the root गम् preceded by a noun") and खच्च डिच्च (= "it should be stated that this खच् operates as if it had an indicatory ड्"). Vide also P. VI, 4, 143. The word शिति itself is formed by appending the termination इन् to the root शत हिंसायाम् according to U. IV, 122 क्रमितमिशतिस्तम्भामत इच्च = "to the roots क्रम्, तम्, शत् and स्तम्भ् the termination इन् (U. IV, 118) is appended before which the penultimate अ of the root is changed to इ the termination itself operating like one having an indicatory क् (U. IV, 120)." शत + इन् + गम् + खच् = शिति + मुम् + गम् + खच्. Here P. VI, 3, 67 अरुर्द्विषदजन्तस्य मुम् = "the augment मुम (= म्) should be added to a word ending in a vowel but not an indeclinable, and to the words अरुष् and द्विषत् when a termination having an indicatory ख् follows". शिति + म् + गम् + खच् = शिति + म् + ग = शितिंगः (Vide P.

darkness and light; (br.) (शितिं गमयति इति—) dispelling the darkness of ignorance. बृहत् =great. शेपः*=(cl.) productive or fertilising force; (br.) power, or influence. भूमौ=on the earth. अनुजभार=has brought; brings; carries. ब्रह्मचारी=the cloud (that which moves about with ब्रह्म=

VIII, 3, 24=नश्चापदान्तस्य झलि="the अनुस्वार is substituted for the nasals न् or म् not at the end of a fully formed grammatical form when any consonant except a nasal or a semivowel follows," and also VII, 4, 57 अनुस्वारस्य ययि परसवर्णः="for the अनुस्वार not at the end of a grammatical form a nasal of the class concerned is substituted when any consonant except a sibilant (श्, ष् or स्) or the aspirate ह् follows."—शितिङ्गः.

* शेपः—शेते येन तत्—√शीङ् स्वप्ने+पुट्+असुन् U. IV, 201 वृङ्शीङ्भ्यां रूपस्वाङ्गयोः पुट् च—"after the roots वृ and शी the termination असुन् takes the augment पुट् and the resulting forms mean 'colour' and 'a limb of the body of a creature' respectively." The final ङ् of the roots, the syllable उट् of the augment and उन् of the termination are indicatory. The first indicates that the roots take the Atmanepadi personal terminations (Vide P. I, 3, 11 अनुदात्तङित आत्मनेपदम्), the second that the augment forms the first part of the 'expression' for which it is ordained (Vide P. I, 1, 46 आद्यन्तौ टकितौ) and the last that the resulting form would have the acute accent on the first syllable (Vide P. VI, 1, 197 ञ्नित्यादिर्नित्यम्).—शेपः. This particular form ends in स्. There is another शेप (Vide Y. V. XXV, 7, शेपेन प्रजां and R. V. X, 85, यस्यामुशन्तः प्रहराम शेपम्) ending in अ formed by affixing the termination प according to U. III, 23 पानीविषिभ्यः पः (="the termination प is added to the roots पा, नी and विष्—पापम्, नीपः, वेष्पः") and P. III, 3, 1, उणादयो बहुलम्. See also the Nighantu III, 29 and Nirukta III, 21; IV, 8; IX, 2 and X, 42. The first of these texts (Nir. III, 21) runs as follows:—शेपो वैतस इति पुंस्प्रजननस्य। शेपः शपतेः स्पृशतिकर्मणः। वैतसो वितस्तं भवयि। Yaska derives it from √शप स्पर्शे by adding the termination घञ् (अ) according to P. III. 3, 19 अकर्तरि च कारके संज्ञायाम्.

water); the Vedic student; **सिञ्चति**=sprinkles. **रेतः***= water. (Br.) **सि० रेतः**=showers down true knowledge. **सानौ**†=on the summit of a hill or mountain. **पृथिव्यां**— on level land; plain. **तेन**—by the act. **जीवन्ति**—live, flourish. **चतस्रः**‡ **प्रदिशः**¶—the creatures living in all the quarters of the earth,

Translation:—Like the brown cloud that roaring noisily moves about between light and darkness and pouring down rain on mountains and plains brings great fertility to the earth, the Vedic student going about on the summits of mountains and low land—wherever there are people—preaching at the top of his voice pours down t r u e knowledge everywhere and like the s u n

---

* रेतः—रीयते स्रवति इति—√रीङ् स्रवणे+तुट्+असुन् U. IV, 202 स्रुरीभ्यां तुट् च—"after the roots स्रु and री the, termination असुन् takes the augment तुट्." The final vowel of the root takes its guna substitute here.—री+त्+अस्+रेतस्.

† सानौ--सनति सम्भजति सनोति ददाति वा इति—√षण सम्भक्तौ√षणु दाने वा+ञुण् U. I, 3 दृसनिजनिचरिचटिरहिभ्यो ञुण्—"the Unadi Suffix ञुण् is added to the roots दृ, सन्, जन्, चर् चट् and रह्". The initial ञ् aud final ण् of the termination are indicatory. The change of अ to आ is in accordance with P. VII, 2. 116 अत उपधायाः.— सानुः—तस्मिन्.

‡ चतस्रः—चतते याचतेऽसौ—√चते याचने+उरन् U. V, 58 चतेरुरन् ="to the root चत् the Unadi termination उरन् is added."—चतुर् चत्वारः In the f e m i n i n e gender this word becomes चतसृ as explained in P. VII. 2, 99 त्रिचतुरो स्त्रियां तिसृचतसृ. Then *by* P. VII, 2 100 we have चतस्रः in the nominative and accusative.

¶ प्रदिशः--दिशति ददाति अवकाशं इति--√दिश् अतिसर्जने+क्विप् P. III, 2, 187 अन्येभ्योऽपि दृश्यते or U. II, 57 क्विब्वचिप्रच्छिश्रिस्रुद्रुप्रुज्वां दीर्घोऽसंप्रसारणं च and P. III, 3, 1 उणादयो बहुलम्. Then *by* Vartika प्रादयो गताद्यर्थे प्रथमया—"the prepositions प्र etc., are compounded with words capable of entering into compositlon but the verbal forms that express their sense are dropped".—प्रकृष्टाः दिशः—प्रदिशः

dispelling the darkness of ignorance imparts great strength to the earth whereby creatures in all the quarters live.

Purport:—It is the duty of every man who understands Vedic teachings to live up to them and preaching them to all, make human life peaceful and fruitful.

(१७) अग्नौ सूर्यै चन्द्रमसि मातरिश्वन् ब्रह्मचार्य१प्सु समिधमादधाति । तासामर्चींषि पृथगभ्रे चरन्ति तासामाज्यं पुरुषो वर्षमापः ॥१३॥

Transliteration:—Agnāu sūryē candramasi mātariśvan brahmacāryapsu samidham ā dadhāti ।

Tāsām arcīmṣi pṛthagabhrē caranti tāsām ājyam puruṣō varṣamāpah ॥ 13.

पदपाठः—अग्नौ । सूर्यै । चन्द्रमसि । मातरिश्वन् । ब्रह्मऽचारी । अप्ऽसु । सम्ऽइधम् । आ । दधाति । तासाम् । अर्चींषि । पृथक् । अभ्रे । चरन्ति । तासाम् । आज्यम् । पुरुषः । वर्षम् । आपः ॥

अन्वयः--ब्रह्मचारी अग्नौ सूर्ये चन्द्रमसि मातरिश्वन् अप्सु समिधम् आदधाति । तासाम् अर्चींषि पृथक् अभ्रे चरन्ति । तासाम् आज्यम् पुरुषः वर्षम् आपः (सन्ति) ॥

Word-meaning &c.:—**अग्नौ**-in the fire. **सूर्ये**= in the sun. **चन्द्रमसि***=in the moon. **मातरिश्वन्**†="in

---

* चन्द्रमसि—चन्द्रं आनन्दं मिमीते इति—चन्द्र+√माङ् माने+असि U. IV, 228 चन्द्रे मो डित्="when the word चन्द्र as a subordinate word, enters into composition with the root मा to measure, the termination असि (U. IV, 223 मिथुनेऽसिः="असि is affixed also to verbs preceded by prepositions") and it operates as if it had an indicatory ड्". That means, the final vowel of मा will be elided (vide P. IV, 4, 143 टेः—)—चन्द्र+मा+अस्, The final इ of असि is indicatory according to P. I, 3, 2 and therefore dropped by 9 तस्य लोपः—चन्द्रमस्.—तस्मिन्. The word चन्द्र is formed *by* U. II, 13 स्फायितञ्चि etc., by putting together the √ चदि आनन्दे+the Unadi suffix रक्.

† मातरिश्वन्—मातरि अन्तरिक्षे श्वयति गच्छति वर्द्धते वा अथवा मातरि

the atmosphere. **ब्रह्मचारी**=the Divine Brahmacārin—God the sustainer of the creation. **अप्सु**=in waters. **समिधम्**= energy. **आदधाति**=puts. **तासाम्**=their; of the waters. **अर्चींषि***=flames. **पृथक्**=in various ways. **अभ्रे**†=in the clouds. **चरन्ति**=move about; spread. **तासाम्**=of those waters. **आज्यं**‡

—मातरि+√ टुओश्वि गतिवृद्धौ: or √ श्वस प्राणने +कनिन् U. I, 159 श्वनुक्षन् etc. This is an irregular formation.—मातरिश्वन्. The form used in the text is of the locative singular, vide P. VII, 1, 39 सुपां सुलुक्पूर्वसवर्णाच्छेयाडाड्यायाजालः. The word मातरि is the locative singular of मातृ which is formed according to U. II, 95 नप्तृनेष्टृत्वष्टृहोतृपोतृभ्रातृजामातृमातृदुहितृ meaning मानयति सत्करोति इति—√ मान् पूजायाम्+तृन् or तृच्—मातृ—माता.

* अर्चींषि—अर्चयति येन तत्—√ अर्च पूजायाम्+इसि U. II, 108 अर्चिशुचिहुसृपिछादिछर्दिभ्य इसिः="to the roots अर्च्, शुच्, हु, सृप्, छाद् and छर्द् the termination इसि is added." The final इ of इसि is indicatory—अर्चिः.—तानि.

† अभ्रे—अपः बिभर्ति इति=अप्+√ भृञ् भरणे+क P. III, 1, 135 इगुपधज्ञाप्रीकिरः कः. The formation is irregular. This word is included among the synonyms of 'cloud' in the Nighantu I, 10. Commenting on अभ्र आं अपः (R. V. V, 48, 1) Yaska in Nirukta V, 5 says अभ्रे आ अपः । अपोऽभ्रेऽधीति. In II, 22 on the word उपर he remarks उपरमन्तेऽस्मिन्नभ्राणि, उपरता आप इति वा.—अभ्रः.—तस्मिन्.

‡ आज्यं—आङ्+√ अञ्जू व्यक्तिम्रक्षणकान्तिगतिषु+क्यप् Vartika आङ्पूर्वादञ्जेः संज्ञायामुपसंख्यानम् ="to the root अञ्ज् preceded by the preposition आ the termination क्यप् is added." The penultimate nasal of the root is dropped according to P. VI, 4, 24 अनिदितां हल उपधायाः क्ङिति.—आ+अज्+य=आज्यम्. The following are a few of the senses in which the word is used in the Brahmana literature:—तेजो वा आज्यम् ॥ तै० ३ । ६ । ४ । ६ ॥ तां० १२ । १० । १८ ॥ देवलोको वा आज्यम् ॥ शां० १६ । ५ ॥ रस आज्यम् ॥ श० ३ । ७ । १ । १३ ॥ पशव आज्यम् ॥ तै० १ । ६ । ३ । ४ ॥ यज्ञो वा आज्यम् ॥ तै० ३ । ३ । ४ । १ ॥ यजमानो वा आज्यम् ॥ तै० ३ । ३ । ४ । ४ ॥ वज्रो ह्याज्यम् ॥ श० १ । ३ । २ । १७ ॥ काम आज्यम् ॥ तै० ३ । १ । ४ । १५ ॥ सत्यमाज्यम् ॥ श० ११ । ३ । १ । १ ॥ प्राणो वा आज्यम् ॥ तै० ३ । ८ । १५ । २ ॥ ३ ॥ रेतो वाऽआज्यम् ॥

essence. **पुरुषः*** = man. **वर्षम्**† = rains. **आपः** = creatures.

श० १ । ६ । २ । ७ ॥ ३ । ६ । ४ । १५ ॥ छन्दांसि वा आज्यम् ॥ तै० ३ । ३ । ५ । ३ ॥ अयातयाम ह्याज्यम् ॥ श० १ । ५ । ३ । २५ ॥ तद्वा इदं षड्विधमाज्यं तूष्णींजपस्तूष्णींशंसः पुरोरुक्सूक्तमुक्थवीर्यं याज्येति ॥ शां० १४ । १ ॥ आत्मा वै यजमानस्याज्यम् ॥ शां० १४ । ४ ॥ वागेवाज्यम् ॥ शां० २८ । ६ ॥ सर्वाणि स्वराण्याज्यानि (स्तोत्राणि) ॥ तां ७ । २ । ५ ॥ Commenting on the word तनूनपात् Yaska in his Nirukta VIII, 5 thus remarks:—तनूनपादाज्यं भवति । नपादित्यनन्तरायाः प्रजाया नामधेयं निर्णततमा भवति । गौरत्र तनूरुच्यते तता अस्यां भोगाः । तस्याः पयो जायते पयस आज्यं जायते ॥

* पुरुषः—(१) पूरति अग्रं गच्छति इति—√ पुर गमने, (२) पूरयति आप्याययति इति—√ पूरी आप्यायने, (३) पृणाति पालयति इति—√ पॄ पालनपूरणयोः +कुषन् U. IV, 74, पुरः कुषन्="to the verb पुर् meaning to go, the Unadi termination कुषन् is added," and P. III, 3, 1 उणादयो बहुलम्. (४) पुरि सीदति इति—पुरि+√ षद्लृ विशरणगत्यवसादनेषु+ड P. III, 4, 67 कर्तरि कृत् and II, 2, 19 उपपदमतिङ्—पुरिषः. पुरुषः. (५) पुरि+√ षद्लृ +घञ् P. III, 67; the rest as before.—पुरिषादः—पुरिषः—पुरुषः. (६) पुरि शेते इति—पुरि+√ शीङ् स्वप्ने+ड as in (४) above—पुरिशः—पुरिषः—पुरुषः. (७) पुरि+√ शीङ्+घ—(पुंसि संज्ञायां घः प्रायेण) the rest as in (४) above—पुरिशयः—पुरिषः—पुरुषः. The formation is irregular. Yaska in Nirukta II, 3 thus comments on this word:—पुरुषः पुरिषादः पुरिशयः पूरयतेर्वा । पूरयत्यन्तरित्यन्तरपुरुषमभिप्रेत्य ।

यस्मात्परं नापरमस्ति किञ्चित् यस्मान्नाणीयो न ज्यायोऽस्ति कश्चित् ।
वृक्ष इव स्तब्धो दिवि तिष्ठत्येकस्तेनेदं पूर्णं पुरुषेण सर्वं ॥

इत्यपि निगमो भवति ॥

A few explanatory remarks on this word culled from Brahmana literature are subjoined:—स वाऽ अयं पुरुषः सर्वासु पूर्षु पुरिशयः ॥ श० १४ । ५ । ५ । १८ ॥ इमे वै लोका पूरयमेव पुरुषो योऽयं (वायुः) पवतेऽस्यां पुरि शेते तस्मात्पुरुषः । श० १३ । ६ । २ । १ ॥ प्राण एष स पुरि शेते स पुरि शेत इति पुरिशयं सन्तं प्राणं पुरुष इत्याचक्षते । गो० १ । १ । ३९ ॥ पुरुषो वाऽ अक्षितिः ॥ श० १४ । ४ । ३ । ७ ॥ पुरुषो वै सहस्रस्य प्रतिमा ॥ श० ७ । ५ २ । १७ ॥ प्राजापत्यो वै पुरुषः ॥ तै० २ । २ । ५ । ३ ॥ पुरुषो वै प्रजापतेर्नेदिष्ठम् ॥ श० ४ । ३ । ४ । ३ ॥ पुरुषः प्रजापतिः ॥ श० ६ । २ । १ । २३ ॥ वैष्णवाः पुरुषाः ॥ श० ५ । २ । ५ । २ ॥ पुरुषं प्रथममालभते । पुरुषो हि प्रथमः पशूनाम् ॥ श० ६ । २ । १ । १८ ॥ पुरुषः पशूनाम् (अधिपतिः) ॥ तां० ६ । २ । ७ ॥ पशवः पुरुषः ॥ तै० ३ । ३ । ८ । २ ॥ पुरुषस्तेन यज्ञो यदेनं पुरुषस्तनुत एष वै तायमानो

Translation:—(God the sustainer of the universe is) the Divine Brahmacārī (Who) puts heat energy everywhere—in fire, in the sun, in the moon, in the atmosphere in the waters. The spreading flames of these waters are seen moving in the clouds in various ways, and their essence appears ultimately in the form of rain, human beings and other creatures.

Purport:—Every man who follows Vedic teaching

यावानेव पुरुषस्तावान् विधीयते तस्मात्पुरुषो यज्ञः ॥ १ । ३ । २ । १ ॥ पुरुषो वै यज्ञः । तस्य यानि चतुर्विंशतिर्वर्षाणि तत्प्रातः सवनम् ।………अथ यानि चतुश्चत्वारिंशद्वर्षाणि तन्माध्यन्दिनं सवनम् . ।………अथ यान्यष्टाचत्वारिंद्वर्षाणि तत्तृतीयसवनम् ।………एतद्ध स्म वै तद्विद्वाना ह महीदास ऐतरेयः स किं म एतदुपतपसि योऽ हमनेन न प्रेष्यामीति । स (महीदासः) ह षोडशं (१६) वर्षशतम् (and 100) जीवति य एवं वेद ॥ छां. ३ । १६ । १–७ ॥ अपाङ्गर्भः पुरुषः स यज्ञः ॥ गो० १ । १ ३९ ॥ पुरुष उद्गीथः ॥ जैउ० १ । ३३ । ६ ॥ पुरुषोऽग्निः ॥ श० १० । ४ । १ । ६ ॥ पुरुषो वै समुद्रः ॥ जैउ० ३ । ३ । ३५ । ५ ॥ पुरुषः सुपर्णः ॥ श० ७ । ४ । २ । ५ ॥ पुरुषो वाव संवत्सरः ॥ गो० १ । ५ । ३ ॥ ५ ॥ पुरुष एव सविता ॥ जैउ० ४ । २७ । १७ ॥ पुरुषो वाव होता ॥ गो० २ । ६ । ६ ॥ पुरुष एव षष्ठमहः ॥ शां० २३ । ४ ॥ अथैष एव पुरुषो योऽयं चक्षुषि ॥ जैउ० १ । २७ । २ ॥ षोडशकलो वै पुरुषः ॥ तै० १ । ७ । ५ । ५ ॥ श० ११ । १ । ६ । ३६ ॥ जैउ० ३ । ३६ । १ ॥ सप्तदशो वै पुरुषो दश प्राणाश्चत्वार्यङ्गान्यात्मा पञ्चदशो ग्रीवाः षोडश्यः शिरः सप्तदशम् ॥ श० ६ । २ । २ । ६ ॥ पुरुषो वै ककुप् ॥ तां० ८ । १० । ६ ॥ १३ । ६ । ४ ॥ १६ । ११ । ७ ॥ १६ । ३ । ४ ॥ २० । ४ । ३ ॥ एतावान्पुरुषो यदात्मा प्रजा जाया ॥ तां० ३ । ४ । ३ ॥ १३ । ३ ॥ शतायुर्वै पुरुषः ॥ शां ० ११ । ७ ॥ शतायुर्वै पुरुषः शतवीर्यः ॥ तै० ३ । ८ । १५ । ३ ॥ १६ । २ ॥ तां० ५ । ६ । १३ ॥

† वर्षम्—वृणोतिस्वीकरोतीति वर्षम्—√वृञ् वरणे+स U. III, 3 वृतृवदिवचिवसिहनिकमिकषिभ्यः सः="the Unadi termination स is appended to the roots वृ, तॄ, वद्, वच्, वस्, हन्, कम् and कष्"—वृ+स. The final ऋ of the root takes its guna before स according to P. VII, 3, 84 सार्वधातुकार्धधातुकयोः. The dental स is lingualised *by* P. VII, 3, 59 आदेशप्रत्यययोः="the initial स् of a termination or a substitute when preceded by any vowel except अ or आ or by the consonants ह्, य्, व्, र् ल् or a letter of the guttural class, is lingualised."—वर्षम्.

should live a continent and mortified life, study the principles working in the disposition of such great natural objects as fire, sun etc., advance in knowledge and help the world to live in a better way.

(१८) आचार्यो मृत्युर्वरुणः सोम ओषधयः पयः ।
जीमूता आसन्त्सत्वानस्तैरिदं स्व१राभृतम् ॥१४॥

Transliteration:—Ācāryō mṛtyurvaruṇah sōma ōṣadhayah payah ।

Jīmūtā āsantsatvāstāiridam svarābhṛtam ॥ 14.

पदपाठः—आऽचार्यः । मृत्युः । वरुणः । सोमः । ओषधयः । पयः । जीमूताः । आसन् । सत्वानः । तैः । इदम् । स्वः । आऽभृतम् ॥

अन्वयः—आचार्यः मृत्युः वरुणः सोमः ओषधयः पयः जीमूताः (अस्ति) । (ते) सत्वानः आसन् तैः इदम् स्वः आ भृतम् ॥

Word-meaning & Translation:—(**आचार्यः**=) The Preceptor (himself a former Brahmacārin), now assuming the role of the director of souls, (**मृत्युः***=) dealing death to the sloth, ignorance and all other draw-backs of those who follow his lead, (**वरुणः**†=) who has the n a c k to

---

* मृत्युः—√ मृङ् प्राणत्यागे+त्युक् U. III, 21 भुजि मृङ्भ्यां युक्त्युकौ ="to the roots भुज् and मृ the Unadi terminations युक् and त्युक् are added." The final क् of the terminations is indicatory.—मृत्युः.

† वरुणः—वृणोति व्रियते वा असौ इति—√ वृञ् वरणे+उनन् U. III, 53 कृवृदारिभ्य उनन्="to the roots कृ, वृ and दृ the Unadi termination is added." The final न् of the termination is indicatory—वरुणः The न् is changed to ण् after ऋ according to the vartika ऋवर्णान्नस्य णत्वं वाच्यम्. Yaska says वरुणो वृणोतीति सतः ॥ Nir. X, 5 See also Nig. V, 4. The following are a few of the interpretations of the word वरुण given in the Brahmanas:—रात्रिर्वरुणः ॥ ऐ० ४। १० ॥ तां० २५ । १० । १० ॥ यः प्राणः स वरुणः ॥ गो० २ । ४ । ११ ॥ यो वै वरुणः सोऽग्निः ॥ श० ५ । २ । ४ । १३ ॥ क्लोमा वरुणः ॥ श० १२ । ६ । १ । १५ ॥ श्रीर्वै वरुणः ॥ शां० १८ । ६ ॥ व्यानो वरुणः ॥ श० १२ । ६ । १ । १६ ॥ पानो वरुणः ॥ श० ८ । ४ । २ । ६ ॥ १२ । ६ । २ । १२ ॥ योनिरेव वरुणः ॥

differentiate between the fit and the unfit, the weak and the strong and accommodate his teaching accordingly, (**सोमः*** =) who by his light and leading imparts joy to his followers like the moon, (**ओषधयः**† =) who strengthens the

शः १२ । ६ । १ । १७ ॥ वरुणो दत्तः ॥ शः ४ । १ । ४ । १ ॥ वरुण एव सविता ॥ जैउ० ४ । २७ । ३ ॥ संवत्सरो वरुणः ॥ शः ४ । ४ । ५ । १८ ॥ क्षत्रं वरुणः ॥ शां० ७ । १० ॥ १२ । ८ ॥ शः ४ । १ । ४ । १ ॥ गो० २ । ६ । ७ ॥ इन्द्र उ वै वरुणः ॥ शां ५ । ४ ॥ सत्यानृते वरुणः ॥ तै० १ । ७ । १० । ४ ॥

* सोमः—सवति ऐश्वर्यहेतुर्भवति इति—√षु प्रसवैश्वर्ययोः+मन् U. I, 140 अर्तिस्तुसुहुसृधृक्षिक्षुभायावापदियक्षिनीभ्यो मन्="to the roots ऋ, स्तु, हु, सृ, धृ, क्षि, क्षु, भा, या, वा, पद् यक्ष्, and नी the termination मन् is added." The final न् of the root is indicatory. The final or penultimate vowel of the root is 'gunated' before the termination according to P. VII, 3, 84. The following are some of the explanations of the word giveu in the Brahmanas:—श्रीर्वै सोमः ॥ शः ४ । १ । ३ । ६ ॥ राजा वे सोमः ॥ शः १४ । १ । ३ । १२ ॥ चन्द्रमा वै सोमः ॥ शां० १६ । ५ ॥ तै० १ । ४ । १० । ७ ॥ शः १२ । १ । १ । २ ॥ पितृलोकः सोमः ॥ शां० १६ । ५ ॥ संवत्सरो वै सोमः ॥ तै० १ । ६ । ८ । २ ॥ ६ । १ ॥ सोमो हि प्रजापतिः ॥ शः । ५ । १ । ५ । २६ ॥ यो वै विष्णुः सोमः सः ॥ शः ३ । ३ । ४ । २१ ॥ ६ । ३ । १६ ॥ सोमः सर्वा देवताः ॥ ऐ० २ । ३ ॥ सोमो रात्रिः ॥ ३ । ४ । ४ । १५ ॥ पशवो हि सोम इति ॥ शः १२ । ७ । २ । २ ॥ सोमो वै दधि ॥ शां० ८ । ६ ॥ वर्चः सोमः ॥ शः ५ । २ । ५ । १० ॥ ११ ॥ क्षत्रं सोमः ॥ ऐ० २ । ३८ ॥ शां० ७ । १० ॥ ६ । ५ ॥ यशो वै सोमः ॥ शः ४ । २ । ४ । ६ ॥ अन्नम् सोमः ॥ शां० ७ । ६ ॥ शः ३ । ३ । ४ । २८ ॥ तां ६ । ६ । १ ॥ प्राणः सोमः ॥ शः ७ । ३ । १ । २ ॥ रेतः सोमः ॥ शां० १३ । ७ ॥ तै० २ । ७ । ४ । १ ॥ शः ३ । ३ । २ । १ ॥ शुक्रः सोमः ॥ तां० ६ । ६ । ६ ॥ रसः सोमः ॥ शः ७ । ३ । १ । ३ ॥ तद्यत्तदमृतं सोमः सः ॥ ६ । ५ । १ । ८ ॥ सर्वं हि सोमः ॥ शः ५ । ५ । ४ । ११ ॥ सोमो वै ब्राह्मणः ॥ तां० २३ । १६ । ५ ॥ सोमः पयः ॥ शः १२ । ७ । ३ । १३ ॥

† ओषधयः—ओषः पाको धीयतेऽस्याम् इति—ओष+√डुधाञ् धारणपोषणयोः+कि P. III, 3, 93 कर्मण्यधिकरणे च= "to the roots called घु (P. I, 1, 20) the termination कि is added in the sense of the locative case when a noun in the accusative case is, as a subordinate word, compounded with the verb" P. II, 2, 19 उपपदमतिङ् and VII, 4, 64 आतो लोप इटि च.—ओषधिः.—ताः. Yaska in his

body, heart, mind and spirit of his followers like nourishing and curative herbs, (**पयः***=) who sustains the social and moral life of the people like milk sustaining the little infant or calf, (**जीमूताः**†=) who showers his bliss-imparting teaching on all without reserve like the clouds raining everywhere alike, (**आसन्**=) is, (**सत्वानः**‡=) powerful; [and full of splendour] for, just as it is (**तैः**=) by these natural phenomena (**इदम्**=) that all this [visible and well known] (**स्वः**¶=) [earthly] happiness

---

Nirukta IX, 27 derives the word as follows:—ओषधय ओषध्द्यन्तीति (√ उष दाहे + शतृ + √ धेट् पाने + कि) वौषत्येना धयन्तीति (√ उष + शतृ + ङि of the locative singular + √धेट् + कि) वा दोषं धयन्तीति (√ दुष वैक्लव्ये + घञ् + √धेट् + कि and elision of the initial consonant द् of the first member) वा ॥ In the शतपथ ब्राह्मणं II, 2, 4, 5 we have the following remark on this word (प्रजापतिः) तां (आहुतिम्) व्यौह्नदोषम् धयेति । तत ओषधयः समभवंस्तस्मादोषधयो नाम ॥

* पयः—पीयते इति—√पीङ् पाने + असुन् U. III, 189 सर्वधातुभ्योऽसुन्. —पयः.

† जीमूताः—जयन्ति अनावृष्टिं ये—√जि जये + मूट् + क्त U. III, 91 जेर्मूट् चोदात्तः ="the augment मूट् acute accented is appended (P. I, 1, 46 आद्यंतौ टकितौ) to the termination क्त affixed to the root जि". The final इ of the root is lengthened. Or जयति नभः, जीयते अनिलेन both formed as above. Or जीवनस्य उदकस्य मूतः ब धः यत्र, जीवनं मूतं बध्दं अनेन इति—√जीव प्राणधारणे + ल्युट् + √मूञ् बन्धने + क्त. Or finally जीवनं मुञ्चति इति—जीवन + √मुच्लृ मोचने + क्त. The composition is irregular and justified by P. VI, 3, 109 पृषोदरादीनि यथोपदिष्टम्:—जीमूतः.—ते.

‡ सत्वानः—√षद्लृ विशरणगत्यवसादनेषु + क्वनिप् P. III, 2, 75 अन्येभ्योऽपि दृश्यन्ते ="the terminations मनिन्, क्वनिप्, वनिप् and विच् are found applied also to other roots than such as end in आ." सद् + वन्; here the द् of the root is chauged to त् —सत्वन्.—ते.

¶ स्वः—(1) सुष्ठु इयर्ति = शोभनं अरणं यस्य इति—सु + √ऋ गतौ + ल्युट्—स्वरणः—स्वर् + अन and then the termination is irregularly dropped. (2) सुष्ठु ईरति = शोभनं ईरणं यस्य—सु + √ईर् गतौ + ल्युट् = स्वीरणः—स्व् + ईर् + अतः the termination is dropped and ई of the

(आभृतम्* =)is brought to the creatures in the world, [so it is by him that all true and lasting happiness including even that of final emancipation is conferred upon all who follow him].

Purport:—God ordains everything for the good of the creatures, rain, moonlight, death etc., according as the universe, in His Omniscience, needs. The Preceptor also should assume a similar role in discharging his duty towards those under him, sometimes putting down evil with the severity of death, sometime imparting peace and dealing lenienty like the cool and charming moon, as circumstances demand.

Comment:—In this verse the term ācārya is the subjective predicate of the 'copula' (as Prof. Bain calls such verbs, vide Higher English Grammar p. 65 ll. 14-26) āsan (=are), the real subjects of which are the words in the verse naming the various objects, varuṇah, payah, jīmūtāh etc. The order has been reversed here to give prominence to the idea of the Brahmacārin, the principal topic of the hymn. More light on this point is thrown in the Introduction.

(१९) अमा घृतं कृणुते केवलमाचार्यों भूत्वा वरुणो यद्यदैच्छत् प्रजापतौ । तद्ब्रह्मचारी प्रायच्छ-स्वान्मित्रो अध्यात्मनः ॥१५॥

---

root changed to श्र—irregularly. (3) सुष्ठु ऋतः रसान् ग्रहीतुम—सु+√ऋ गतौ+क्त—स्वृत—स्वर्+त the termination is dropped and the root gunated. (4) ज्योतिषां चन्द्रादीनां भासं प्रकाशं सुष्ठु ऋतः इति—as (3) above. (5) भासा स्वप्रकाशेन सुष्ठु ऋतः—सु+√ऋ+क्त as (3) above. Yaska says:—स्वरादित्यो भवति । सु अरणः सु ईरणः स्वृतो रसान्स्वृतो भासं ज्योतिषां स्वृतो भासेति वैतेन द्यौर्व्याख्यता ॥ Nir. II, 14.

* आभृतम्—आ+√हृ+क्त P. III, 2, 102 निष्ठा and Vartika हृग्रहोर्भश्छन्दसि.—आभृतम्.

Transliteration:—Amā ghṛtam kṛnutē kēvalamācā-ryō bhūtvā varuṇō yadyadāicchat prajāpatāu ।

Tad brahmacārī prāyacchat svān mitrō adhyātma-nah ॥ 15.

पदपाठः—अमा । घृतम् । कृणुते । केवलम् । आऽचार्यः । भूत्वा । वरुणः । यत्ऽयंत् । ऐच्छंत् । प्रजाऽपंतौ । तत् । ब्रह्मऽचारी । प्र । अयच्छत् । स्वान् । मित्रः । अधि । आत्मनः ।

अन्वयः—**वरुणः आचार्यः भूत्वा अमा घृतं केवलं कृणुते यत् यत् (स) प्रजापतौ ऐच्छत । ब्रह्मचारी मित्रः (भूत्वा) तत् आत्मनः अधि स्वान् प्रायच्छत् ॥**

Word-meaning &c.,:—**अमा***=at home, within his circle of students and friends. **घृतं**†=something enjoy-able. **कृणुते**=makes. **घृ० कृ०**=hands down or imparts for use. **केवलम्**=only. **आचार्यः**=the preceptor. **भूत्वा**‡=be-coming. **वरुणः**=a good man; a man of merits. **व० आ० भू०**= a former Brahmacārin possessing merits, and having an insight into human character assuming the role of the preceptor. **यद्यत्**=whatever. **ऐच्छत्**=he desires. **प्रजापतौ**= in or form God the protector of creatures. **तत्**=that. **प्रायच्छत्**=imparts; hands on. **स्वान्**=to his circle of friends and fellow-students. **मित्रः**¶=becoming their friend.

---

*अमा—an indeclinable formed from the negative particle नञ् and the verb √माङ् माने+क P. III, 2, 3 आतोऽनुपसर्गे कः and the final अ irregularly legthened=measureless. A house is measureless—ample for all living in it. See Nig. III, 4 and Nir. XI, 46 and V, 1. Cf. 'at home', 'go home' etc.

† घृ—√घृ क्षरणदीप्त्योः+क्त P. III, 2, 102 निष्ठा.—घृतम्.

‡ भूत्वा—√भू सत्तायाम्+क्त्वा P. III, 4 21 समानकर्तृकयोः पूर्वकाले.—भूत्वा.

$ मित्रः—√डुमिञ् प्रक्षेपणे+क्त्र U. IV, 164 अमिचिमिशसिभ्यः क्त्रः ="the termination क्त्र is added to the roots अम्, चि, मि, and शस्."—मित्रः=who dispels evil or wards off harm. The sun

आत्मनः* अधि = himself receiving authority from his preceptor.

Translation:—A man of parts himself a former Brahmacārin, having an insight into human nature, assuming the role of the preceptor, should impart to his own circle (of pupils and friends) for use whatever he desires in God the protector of creatures. This, his student of subdued passions, with due authority hands on in a friendly manner to his own friends.

Purport:—The Preceptor should be a man of good character and principles. Teaching should be restricted to a circle of deserving persons. Students who have advanced in their studies and have acquired authority should help their Preceptor by cooperating with him in his work.

---

dispels darkness by his rays. In the neuter the word means a friend. Vide Nig. V, 4. For Dr. Lakshman Sarup this is an 'atmospheric deity'? Index to Nirukta pp. 25 and 225. Yaska gives this as one of the names of the sun in Nir II, 13. Quite against European scholars and their 'aping' Indian followers the hoary Brahmanas interpret the word as follows:—सर्वस्य ह्येव मित्रो मित्रम् ॥ श० ५ । ३। २ । ७ ॥ Look at the gender of the two words equated मित्रः=मित्रम्. Surely the Veteran Sage याज्ञवल्क्य author (?) of the Satapatha Brahmana knew much better than our European friends !! मित्रः (एवैनं) सत्यानां (सुवते) ॥ तै० १।७।४।१॥ मित्र सत्यानामधिपते ॥ तै० ३ । ११ ।४। १ ॥ ब्रह्मैव मित्रः ॥ श० ४ । १ । ४ । १ ॥ मित्रः क्षत्रं क्षत्रपतिः ॥ श० ११ । ४ । ३ । ११ ॥ तै० २ । ५ । ७। ४ ॥ प्राणो वै मित्रः ॥ श० ६ । ५ । १ । ५ ॥ ८ । ४ । २ । ६ ॥ १२ । ६ । २ । १२ ॥ अयं वायुर्मित्रो योऽयं पवते ॥ श० ६ । ५ । ४ । १४ ॥ अहर्मित्रः ॥ तां० २५ । १० । १० ॥ ऐ० ४ । १० ॥ तै० १ । ७ । १० । १ ॥ प्राणो मित्रम् ॥ जैउ० ३ । ३ । ६ ॥ Hence there must be something radically wrong in the method of the 'scholars' who translate मित्र as 'an atmospheric deity'. The late Dr. Rajawade said that it was 'absurd' to translate the Nirukta 'literally'.

*आत्मनः—अतति निरंतरं कर्मफलानि प्राप्नोति व्याप्नोति वा—√ अत

(२०) आचार्यो ब्रह्मचारी ब्रह्मचारी प्रजापतिः ।
प्रजापतिर्वि राजति विराडिन्द्रोऽभवद्वशी ॥१६॥

Transliteration:—Ācāryō brahmacārī brahmacārī prajāpatiḥ ।
Prajāpatirvi rājati virāḍindrō'bhavadvaśī ॥ 16.

पदपाठः—आऽचार्यः । ब्रह्मऽचारी । ब्रह्मऽचारी । प्रजाऽपतिः । प्रजाऽपतिः । वि । राजति । विऽराट् । अभवत् । वशी ॥

अन्वयः—ब्रह्मचारी आचार्यः (अभवत्) । ब्रह्मचारी प्रजापतिः (अभवत्) । प्रजापतिः विराजति । विराट् वशी इन्द्रः अभवत् ॥

Word-meaning &c :- प्रजापतिः=a protector of creatures. विराजति=rules in various ways. विराट्*=an illustrious ruler; an emperor; a great king. इन्द्रः=a great and powerful monarch. वशी†=who can subdue others. अभवत्=has become; becomes.

Translation—A student (finishing his course of studies and properly qualifying himself) becomes a pre-

---

सातत्यगममे+मनिण् U. IV, 153, सातिभ्यां मनिन्मनिणौ="to the roots सो and अत् the terminations मनिन् and मनिण् are added.—अत्+मनिण्. P. VII, 2, 116 अत उपधायाः declares वृद्धि change in the penultimate अ of the root अत्.—आत्+मन्=आत्मन्.

* विराट्—विविधं वा विविधाः प्रजाः वा शास्ति इति—वि+√राज् दीप्तौ+क्विप् P. III, 2, 178 अन्येभ्योऽपि दृश्यते.—वि+राज्.—विराट्.

† वशी—वशः अस्ति अस्य इति—वश+इनि P. V, 1 16 तदस्य तदस्मिन्स्यादिति. The final अ of वश is dropped according to P. I, 4, 18 यचि भम् which lays down that the nominal bases before the स्वादि terminations (ordained from P. IV, 1, 2 स्वौजसमौट्छष्टाभ्यांभिस्ङेभ्यांभ्यस्ङसिभ्यांभ्यस्ङसोसाम्ङ्योस्सुप् to V, 4, 15 उरः प्रभृतिभ्यः कप्) beginning with य् or a vowel are called भ," and VI, 4, 148 यस्येति च="of a nominal base ending in अ or इ short or long and called भ the final vowel is dropped before इ or a secondary termination".—वशिन्.—वशी. वश itself is got by putting together √वश इच्छायाम् and अच् or अप् *by* P. III, 4, 67 कर्तरि कृत्. अच् may also be added *by* P. III, 1, 134 नन्दिग्रहिपचादिभ्योल्युणिन्यचः.

ceptor. It is the student again that becomes a protector of beings and rules over them in various ways. An illustrious ruler of this type becomes a powerful monarch capable of subduing others.

Purport:—Those who wish to rise high in the world should study the Vedic sciences, live a principled and subdued life and thus qualifying themselves put forth effort in the right direction.

(२१) ब्रह्मचर्येण तपसा राजा राष्ट्रं वि रक्षति ।
आचार्यो ब्रह्मचर्येण ब्रह्मचारिणमिच्छते ॥१७॥

Transliteration:—Brahmacaryēṇa tapasā rājā rāṣṭram vi rakṣati ।

Ācāryō brahmacaryēṇa brahmacāriṇam icchatē ॥ 17.

पदपाठः—ब्रह्मऽचर्येण । तपसा । राजा । राष्ट्रं । वि । रक्षति । आऽचार्यः । ब्रह्मऽचर्येण । ब्रह्मऽचारिणम् । इच्छते ॥

अन्वयः—ब्रह्मचर्येण तपसा राजा राष्ट्रं विरक्षति । आचार्यः ब्रह्मचर्येण ब्रह्मचारिणम् इच्छते ॥

Word-meaning &c.:—**ब्रह्मचर्येण** = by Vedic study and control of passions. **तपसा**=by austerity. **राष्ट्रं***= kingdom. **विरक्षति**=protects in various ways. **आचार्यः**= tutor. **इच्छते**=desires for.

Translation.—"By observing brahmacarya (i. e. studying the Vedas and subduing his passions) a king acquires special ability to protect his subjects. By acquiring knowledge through the observance of brahmacarya a teacher is able to take brahmacaris (as his pupils) but not otherwise.

---

* राष्ट्रम्—√ राज़ दीप्तौ (राजति ऐश्वर्यकर्मा इति निघण्टौ २ । २१ ॥)+ ष्ट्रन् U. IV, 157 सर्वधातुभ्यः ष्ट्रन्="the termination ष्ट्रन् is added to all roots," and P. VIII, 2, 36 व्रश्चभ्रस्जसृजमृजयजराजभ्राजच्छशां षः.—राष्ट्रम्. The initial ष् and final न् of the termination are indicatory.

Purport.—Both the king and the Preceptor need study the Vedas, subdue their passions and live principled lives, to be fit for their high and trustworthy positions.

(२२) ब्रह्मचर्येण कन्या३ युवानं विन्दते पतिम् ।
अनड्वान् ब्रह्मचर्येणाश्वो घासं जिगीर्षति ॥१८॥

Transliteration:—Brahmacaryēṇa kanyā yuvānam vindatē patim ।
Anadvān brahmacaryēṇāśvō ghāsam jigīrṣati ॥ 18.

पदपाठः—ब्रह्मऽचर्येण । कन्या । युवानम् । विन्दते । पतिम् ।
अनड्वान् । ब्रह्मऽचर्येण । अश्वः । घासम् । जिगीर्षति ॥

अन्वयः—ब्रह्मचर्येण कन्या युवानम् पतिम् विन्दते । अनड्वान् अश्वः (च) ब्रह्मचर्येण घासं जिगीर्षति ॥

Word-meaning—ब्रह्मचर्येण=after Vedic study and control of the senses. कन्या*=a maiden. युवानं†=a youth. विन्दते=obtains. पतिम्=for husband अनड्वान्‡=bull. ब्रह्मचर्येण=controlling their sexual passion. अश्वः¶=horse.

---

* कन्या—कन्यते दीप्यते कान्यते गच्छति वा असौ—√ कनी दीप्तिकान्तिगतिषु+य+टाप् U. IV, 111 अघ्न्यादयश्च (="the words of the group अघ्न्या etc., are formed by appending the Unadi termination य to the roots concerned,") and P. IV, 1, 4 अजाद्यतष्टाप्.—कन्या.

† युवानम्—यौति मिश्रयत्यामिश्रयति वा सः—√ यु मिश्रणामिश्रणयोः +कनिन् U. I, 156 कनिन् युवृषितक्षिराजिधन्विद्युप्रतिदिवः="to the roots यु, वृष्, तक्ष्, राज्, धन्व्, द्यु and प्रतिदिव्, the Unadi termination कनिन् is added." The final उ of roots is here changed to उव्. The final इन् of the termination is indicatory.

‡ अनड्वान्—अनः शकटं वहति इति—अनस्+√ वह P. III, 2, 178 अन्येभ्योऽपि दृश्यते and II, 2, 19 उपपदमतिङ्. The final स् of the first member is changed to ड्—अनड्वान्.

¶ अश्वः—अश्नुते व्याप्नोति इति—√ अशू व्याप्तौ+क्वन् U. I, 151 अशूप्रुषिलटिकणिखटिविशिभ्यः क्वन्.—अश्वः The initial क् and final न् of the termination are indicatory.

घासम्* = by (eating) grass. (The accusative is here used for the instrumental). जिगीर्षति = bring forth issue; meet the female.

Translation:—A maiden after Vedic study and living in chastity by controlling her senses obtains for her husband a young bachelor of similar qualifications. Even bulls, horses and other beasts nourish themselves with fodder and keep their sexual appetite in control before meeting the female for procreation.

Purport:—The law of checking the sexual appetite is in full force among the dumb animals. Man in addition to this has to qualify himself by a full course of education for life which is an additional reason for keeping the senses under control. Only young men and young women that have undergone such preparation should meet in wedlock.

(२३) ब्रह्मचर्येण तपसा देवा मृत्युमपाघ्नत ।
इन्द्रो ह ब्रह्मचर्येण देवेभ्यः स्व१ राभरत् ॥१९॥

Transliteration:—Brahmacaryēṇa tapasā dēvā mṛtyumapāghnata ।
Indrō ha brahmacaryēṇa dēvēbhyah svarābharat ॥ 19.

पदपाठः—ब्रह्मऽचर्येण । तपसा । देवाः । मृत्युम् । अप । अघ्नत । इन्द्रः । ह । ब्रह्मऽचर्येण । देवेभ्यः । स्वः । आ । अभरत् ॥

अन्वयः—ब्रह्मचर्येण तपसा देवाः मृत्युम् अपाघ्नत । ब्रह्मचर्येण ह इन्द्रः देवेभ्यः स्वः आ अभरत् ॥

Word-meaning:—ब्रह्मचर्येण = by a life of restraint

---

* घासम्—√अद भक्षणे + घञ् P. II, 4, 38 घञपोश्च = "when the termination घञ् or अप् = follows घस्लृ is substituted for अद्" and III, 3, 19 अकर्तरि च कारके संज्ञायाम्.—घस् + अ—घासः. Vide P. VII, 2, 116 अत उपधायाः also.

and Vedic study. **तपसा**=by the observance of the vow. **देवाः**=the wise. **मृत्युम्**=poverty, despondency and such other causes of death. **अपाघ्नत**=destroy. **इन्द्रः**=the sun. **ब्रह्मचर्येण**=according to the law of gravitation and radiation of heat. **देवेभ्यः**=for all beneficent objects that help creatures to live. **स्वः**=heat energy that renders happy. **आ अभरत्**=has fully imparted or dealt.

Translation:—The wise by living a life of restraint and study and practice of the Eternal Revealed Vedic Law dispel all causes of early death (such as despondency, poverty and disease). The sun by observing the law of gravitation and radiation of heat fully imparts to all beneficent objects heat enargy that makes all creatures happy.

Purport:—Restraint over one's mind and senses and especially sexual restraint is quite necessary to guard oneself from, idleness, despair and such other factors that weaken life. It is wise to submit to such restraint and make one's life useful.

Comment:—This and the previous verse lay a great stress on sexual purity and continency. This can be attained only through a self-imposed mental and physical restraint on one's sexual inclinations. This is true not only in the case of the growing youth but also in that of the grown up and married men and women. The sexual organs of the human body, like those of the lower animals, are intended only for reproduction. The lower animals do use them only for this purpose but the depravity of the civilised (?) *homo sapiens* leads him to devise contraceptives to indulge in his lust to the fullest extent without incurring even the least responsibility for his deed. 'Birth control' is a horrible expression, boldly exposing the entire lack of the feeling of shame in modern society. The only method of 'birth control' consists in strong restraint of one's sexual appetite. This point will be treated at some length in the Concluding Remarks.

(२४) ओषधयो भूतभव्यमहोरात्रे वनस्पतिः ।
संवत्सरः सहर्तुभिस्ते जाता ब्रह्मचारिणः ॥२०॥

Transliteration:—Ōṣadhayō bhūtabhavyam ahōrātrē vanaspatiḥ ।
Saṃvatsaraḥ sahartubhistē jātā brahmacāriṇaḥ ॥ 20.

पदपाठः—ओषधयः । भूतऽभव्यम् । अहोरात्रे इति । वनस्पतिः ।
सम्ऽवत्सरः । सह । ऋतुऽभिः । ते । जाताः । ब्रह्मऽचारिणः ॥

अन्वयः—ओषधयः वनस्पतिः भूतभव्यम् अहोरात्रे (च) संवत्सरः सह ऋतुभिः ते ब्रह्मचारिणः जाताः ।

Word-meaning:—ओषधयः=plants and herbs (such as cereals and vegetables). भूतभव्यम्*=the past and the future. अहोरात्रे†=day and night. वनस्पतिः‡=trees. संवत्सरः¶

---

* भूतभव्यम्—भूतं च भव्यं च—P. II, 4, 13 विप्रतिषिद्धं चानधिकरणवाची="words of opposite import not denoting things are optionally compounded into an aggregate copulative compound—समाहारद्वन्द्व."—भूतभव्यम्.

† अहोरात्रे—अहः च रात्रिः च—P. II, 4, 28 हेमन्तशिशिरावहोरात्रे च छन्दसि—"the compounds हेमन्तशिशिरौ and अहोरात्रे used in the Vedas have their gender regulated by that of the first member."

‡ वनस्पतिः—वनस्य पतिः—वन+पति P. VI, 1, 157 पारस्करप्रभृतीनि च संज्ञायाम्="the words पारस्कर etc., all names or nouns, are irregularly formed with the augment सुट् prefixed to the second member."—वनस्पतिः. The word वन itself is formed by adding अच् (P. III, 1, 134 नन्दिग्रहिपचादिभ्यो ल्युणिन्यचः) to the root √ वन सेवनयाचनोपकारेषु.

¶ संवत्सरः—सम्यग्वसन्ति अत्र इति—सम्+√वस निवासे+सरन् U. III, 72 संपूर्वाच्चित्="to the root वस् (71) to dwell, preceded by सम् the termination सरन् (70) is added and it operates as though it had an indicatory च्." P. VII, 4, 49 सः स्यार्धधातुके enjoins the sub-

=the year. सह* =according to. ऋतुभिः† =in the proper seasonal order. जाता=come and go; occur. ब्रह्मचारिणः= are observers of the restraint of the seasonal change and succession.

Translation:—Herbs and plants, the stages of the world that are past and those that are yet to come, day and night, trees, the year, all follow the law of seasonal succession, change and fructification and are therefore observers of the law of restraint.

Purport:—When even such 'inanimate' objects as trees, plants and the year follow the law of seasonal restraint, it is but just that human beings also should observe this law and cohabit with their consorts only at the time of procreation.

(२५) पार्थिवा दिव्याः पशव आरण्या ग्राम्याश्च ये। अपक्षाः पक्षिणश्च ये ते जाता ब्रह्मचारिणः ॥२१॥

Transliteration:—Pārthivā divyāh paśava āranyā grāmyāśca yē ।
Apaksāh paksiṇaśca yē tē jātā brahmacāriṇah ॥ 2 ।.

पदपाठः—पार्थिवाः । दिव्याः । पशवः । आरण्याः । ग्राम्याः । च । ये । अपक्षाः । पक्षिणः । च । ये । ते । जाताः । ब्रह्मऽचारिणः ॥

अन्वयः—पार्थिवाः दिव्याः पशवः ये अपक्षाः च पक्षिणः, ये आरण्याः च ग्राम्याः ते ब्रह्मचारिणः जाताः ॥

---

stitution of त् for the final स् of the base before an impersonal termination." संवत्सरः.

* सह—सहते इति—√षह मर्षणे+अच् P. III, 1, 134.—सह. This word is an indeclinable.

† ऋतुभिः—पुनः पुनः ऋच्छति गच्छति आगच्छति इति—√ऋ गतौ +तु U. I, 72 अर्तेश्च तुः—"to the root ऋ to go, the termination तु is added and it acts as if it had an indicatory क्—ऋतुः.

Word-meaning:—पार्थिवाः* = land. **दिव्याः†** = of the air. **पशवः‡** = animals. **आरण्याः¶** = wild, of the forest. **ग्राम्याः$** = domestic, living near human habitations. **अपक्षाः§** = wing-less. **पक्षिणः£** = winged. **जाताः ब्रह्मचारिणः** = observe the law of restraint.

Translation:—Animals winged and wingless, those that fly in the air and those that live on land, those that betake themselves to the forest and those that live in a domesticated (or semi-domesticated) state in (or near) human habitations, all observe the law of restraint in sexual matters.

Purport:—If dumb animals are such staunch observers of sexual restraint as never to yield to their passions even under change of circumstances, it is much more necessary that man should observe continency

---

* पार्थिवाः—पृथिव्यां भवति इति—पृथिवी+अ or अञ् Vartika पृथिव्या ञा ञौ="to the word पृथिवी the secondary termination अ or अञ् is added in all the senses in which such terminations are enjoined in the Astadhayayi of Panini up to IV, 4, 2 तेन दीव्यति जयति जितम्. —पृथिवी+अ or अञ्. Here P. I, 4, 18 यचि भम् and VI, 4, 148 यस्येति च, come into force and the final ई of the word is elided. P. VII, 2, 117 तद्धितेष्वचामादेः causes वृद्धि change in the ऋ of the word.—पार्थिवः.—ते.

† दिव्याः—दिवि भवः—दिव् + यत् P. V, 1, 67 छन्दसि च="in Vedic style, to any noun the termination यत् is added in the sense of deserving something etc."—दिव्यः.—ते.

‡ ग्राम्याः—ग्रामे भवः—ग्राम+य P. IV, 2, 94 ग्रामाद्यखञौ="to the word ग्राम the secondary termination य or खञ् is added." P. VI, 4, 148.—ग्राम्यः—ते.

§ अपक्षाः—न विद्येते पक्षौ यस्य इति—नञ् +पक्ष P. II, 2, 24 अनेकमन्यपदार्थे, Vartika नञोऽस्त्यर्थानां वाच्यो वा चोत्तरपदलोपश्च वक्तव्यः and P. VI, 3, 73 नलोपो नञः—अपक्षः.—ते.

$ पक्षिणः—पक्षौ अस्य स्तः इति—पक्ष+इनि P. V, 1, 16 तदस्य तदस्मिन् स्यादिति and VI, 4, 148 यस्येति च.—पक्षिन्—ते.

under all circumstances. Every man and every woman must exert himself or herself to fulfil this condition of rational sex life which alone can elevate humanity.

(२६) पृथक्सर्वे प्राजापत्याः प्राणानात्मसु बिभ्रति । तान्सर्वान् ब्रह्म रक्षति ब्रह्मचारिण्याभृतम् ॥२२॥

Transliteration :—Pṛthak sarvē prājāpatyāh prāṇān ātmasu bibhrati ।

Tān sarvān brahma rakṣati brahmacāriṇyābhṛtam ॥ 22.

पदपाठः—पृथक् । सर्वे । प्राजाऽपत्याः । प्राणान । आत्मऽसु । बिभ्रति । तान् । सर्वान् । ब्रह्म । रक्षति । ब्रह्मऽचारिणि । आऽभृतम् ॥

अन्वयः—सर्वे प्राजापात्याः प्राणान् पृथक् बिभ्रति । तान् सर्वान् ब्रह्मचारिणि आभृतम् ब्रह्म रक्षति ॥

Word-meaning:—**पृथक्**=separately. **सर्वे***=all. **प्राजापत्याः**†=creatures created by God the Protector of all creatures. **प्राणान्**‡=vital airs. **आत्मसु**=in their own selves. **बिभ्रति**=keep, have. **ब्रह्म**=Vedic knowledge. **रक्षति**=protects. **ब्रह्मचारिणि**=in the Vedic student of subdued passions. **आभृतम्**¶=stored.

---

* सर्वे—√ सृ सरणे+वन् U. I, 153 सर्वनिघृष्वरिष्वलष्वशिवपद्वप्रह्वेष्वा अतन्त्रे.—सर्वः.—ते.

†प्राजापत्याः—प्रजापति+ण्य P. IV, 1, 85 दित्यदित्यादित्यपत्युत्तरपदाण्ण्यः ="to the words दिति, अदिति, आदित्य and to such compound words as have पति for their second member, the secondary termination ण्य is added". The initial ण् is indicatory of the वृद्धि change of the first vowel in the word *by* P. VII,2, 117 तद्धितेष्वचामादेः. The final इ of the word is dropped *by* P. VI, 4, 148 यस्येति च.—प्राजापत्यः.—ते.

‡ प्राणान्—प्र+√ अन प्राणने+अच् or घञ् P, III, 1, 134. नन्दिग्रहिपचादिभ्यो ल्युणिन्यचः or 3, 19 अकर्तरि च कारके संज्ञायाम्. प्र+अन्+अ =प्राणः.

¶ आभृतम्—आ+√ भृञ् भरणे+क्त P. III, 2, 102 निष्ठा—आभृतम्.

Translation :—All the creatures created by God the Protector of creation, hold in themselves (each according to its capacity) the vital airs separately, and Divine knowledge stored in the man of mortified life given to the learning and teaching of the Vedas, protects them all.

Purport :—It is Divine Law that all creatures should sustain their life by restraining their passions, the reward for the sin of the violation of which is an early death.

(२७) देवानामेतत्परिषूतमनभ्यारूढं चरति रोचमानम्। तस्माज्जातं ब्राह्मणं ब्रह्म ज्येष्ठं देवाश्च सर्वे अमृतेन साकम् ॥२३॥

Transliteration:—Dēvānām ētat parișūtam anabhyā-rūḍham carati rōcamānam।

Tasmājjātaṃ brāhmaṇam brahma jyēṣṭham dēvāśca sarvē amṛtēna sākam ॥ 23.

पदपाठः—देवानाम् । एतत् । परिऽसूतम् । अनभिऽआरूढम् । चरति । रोचमानम् । तस्मात् । जातम् । ब्राह्मणम् । ब्रह्म । ज्येष्ठम् । देवाः । च । सर्वे । अमृतेन । साकम् ॥

अन्वयः—देवानाम् परिषूतम् अनभ्यारूढम् रोचमानम् एतत् (ब्रह्म) चरति । तस्मात् ज्येष्ठम् ब्राह्मणम् (च) ब्रह्म जातम् च सर्वे देवाः अमृतेन साकम् (जाताः) ॥

Word-meaning &c :—**देवानाम्**=of the luminous worlds. **एतत्***=this. (The word **ब्रह्म**=Vedic Lore should be taken

---

* एतत्—एति प्राप्नोति समीपे वर्तते इति—√इण् गतौ+तुट्+अदि U. I, 133 एतेस्तुट् च="to the root इ meaning to go the termination अदि is added but the augment तुट् is prefixed to the latter." इ+तुट्+अदि. The syllable उट् of the augment and the final इ of the termination are indicatory. The final vowel or penultimate short of the root is gunated before अदि. ए+त्+अद्=एतद्—एतत्.

here from the previous stanza). परिषूतम्*=impelling in every way. (The form in क्त here has not the sense of the passive past participle Vide P. III, 3, 134 नपुंसके भावे क्तः). अनभ्यारूढम्†=never over-powered; excellent; surpassing. चरति=moves about; obtains everywhere रोचमानम्‡=resplendent. (Here a connecting link 'एतत् ब्रह्मचारिणि आभृतम्' from the above stanza has to be supplied). तस्मात्=from him (i. e., ब्रह्मचारी). ज्येष्ठम्=superior; great. ब्राह्मणम्=Divine knowlege. ब्रह्म=ever-increasing wealth. देवाः=the wise. सर्वे=all. अमृतेन=immortality. साकम्= are endowed with.

Translation :—The resplendent Vedic Lore obtaining everywhere and never overpowered (by any contrary agent) impels all the luminous worlds. From the man of restraint (given to the study of the Vedas and having his mind stored with it) supreme Divine knowledge and ever increasing wealth spring and all the wise attain immortality.

---

*परिषूतम्—परि+√षू प्रेरणे+क्त P. III, 2, 102 निष्ठा=परि+सू+त. The स is changed to ष according to P. VIII, 3, 57 इणकोः. परिषूतम्.

† अनभ्यारूढम् (अभि+आ+√रुह बीजजन्मनि प्रादुर्भावे च+ क्त P. VI, 1, 77 इको यणचि, and VIII, 2, 31 हो ढः="the final ह् of roots is changed to ढ् when it is followed by any consonant except a nasal or a semivowel or by nothing".)—P. II, 2, 6 नञ्="the negative particle नञ् is compounded with a noun capable of entering into composition with it and the compound thus formed is a Tatpurusa." Vide also P. VI, 3, 73 नलोपो नञः and 74 तस्मान्नुडचि="to the word coming after such नञ् and beginning with a vowel the augment नुट् (न्, उट् indicatory) is added" न+न्+अभ्यारूढम्—अनभ्यारूढम्.

‡ रोचमानम्—√रुच दीप्तावभिप्रीतौ च+मुक्+शानच P. III, 2, 124 लटः शतृशानचावप्रथमासमानाधिकरणे and VII, 2, 82 आने मुक्.

Purport :—The Vedic student of subdued passions reveals the attributes of God and helping the advancement of both wealth and true knowledge renders all fit to attain 'eternal bliss'.

(२८) ब्रह्मचारी ब्रह्म भ्राजद्बिभर्ति तस्मिन्देवा अधि विश्वे समोताः। प्राणापानौ जनयन्नाद्व्यानं वाचं मनो हृदयं ब्रह्म मेधाम् ॥२४॥

Transliteration:—Brahmacārī brahma bhrājad bibharti tasmin dēvā adhi viśvē samōtāh ।

Prāṇāpānāu janayan ādvyānam vācam manō hṛdayam brahma mēdhām ॥ 24.

पदपाठः—ब्रह्मऽचारी। ब्रह्म। भ्राजत्। बिभर्ति। तस्मिन्। देवाः। अधि। विश्वे। सम्ऽओताः। प्राणापानौ। जनयन्। आत्। विऽआनम्। वाचम्। मनः। हृदयम्। ब्रह्म। मेधाम् ॥

अन्वयः—भ्राजत् ब्रह्मचारी ब्रह्म बिभर्ति तस्मिन् विश्वे देवाः अधि समोताः। (स) प्राणापानौ आत व्यानम्, वाचम्, मनः, हृदयम्, ब्रह्म मेधाम् जनयन् (वर्तते) ॥

Word-meaning:—ब्रह्म = Vedic knowledge. भ्राजत्* = shines. बिभर्ति = he possesses. तस्मिन् = in him (Brahmacārin). देवाः = all good qualities. विश्वे = all. अधि = properly, in a fitting manner. समोताः† = are fully intermingled.

---

* भ्राजत्—√ भ्राज् or √ टुभ्राज् दीप्तौ + अदि U. I, 133 शृदृभसोऽदिः = "to the roots शृ, दृ and भस् the termination अदि is added" and P. III, 3, 1 उणादयो बहुलम्.—भ्राजत्.

† समोताः—सम् + आङ + √ वेञ् तन्तु सन्ताने + क्त P. III, 2, 102 निष्ठा and VI, 1, 15 वचिस्वपियजादीनां किति = "the roots वच् and स्वप् and roots of the यजादि group (यजिर्वपिर्वहिश्चैव वसिर्वेञ् व्येञ इत्यपि। ह्वेञ्वदी श्वयतिश्चेति यजाद्याः स्युरिमे नव ॥ Quoted in the तत्त्वबोधिनी on the सिद्धांतकौमुदी on the aphorism) undergo सम्प्रसारण before terminations having an indicatory क्."—सम् + आ + वेञ् + क्त = सम् + आ + उ + ए + त = सम् + आ + उ + त. Vide P. VI, 1, 108 संप्रसारणाच्च =

प्राणापानौ* = inhalation and exhalation. **जनयन्** producing; revealing knowledge of. **आत्**† = and **व्यानं**‡ = vital air, breath. **वाचं**¶ = power of speech. **मनः**§ = a powerful mind. **हृदयं**$ = a pure heart. **ब्रह्म** = knowledge of God. **मेधाम्**£ = wisdom.

Translation :—When the continent Vedic student acquires V e d i c learning, all good qualities fully intermingle in him and he becomes resplendent. He reveals a perfect mastery of his inhalation and exhalation (in particular) and of the vital airs in his person (in general), good eloquence, a powerful mind, pure heart, true knowledge of God and marvelous wisdom (which he goes diffusing about).

Purport :—One who wishes to attain mastery of

"when a vowel follows a सम्प्रसारण letter, the latter is the single substitute in place of both."—समोतः—ते. Vide P. VI, 1, 87 आद्-गुणः also.

* प्राणापानौ—प्राणः च अपानः च—P. II, 2, 22 चार्थे द्वन्द्वः and 4, 26 परवल्लिङ्गं द्वन्द्वतत्पुरुषयोः—प्राणापानौ. The word अपान is formed by putting together the verb √अन् preceded by the prefix अप and the termination अच् or घञ्.

† आत्—√अत सातत्यगमने + क्विप् irregularly applied. This word is an indeclinable and means 'often' or 'and'.

‡ व्यानम्—वि + √अन प्राणने + अच् or घञ् = व्यानम्.

¶ वाचम्—√वच परिभाषणे + क्विप् U. II, 57 क्विब्वचि॰ etc.—वाच् ताम्.

§ मनः—√मन ज्ञाने + असुन् U. IV 189 सर्वधातुभ्योऽसुन्.—मनस्.

$ हृदयम्—हरति विषयान् इति—√हृ हरणे + दुक् + कयन् U. IV, 100 वृहोः षुग्दुकौ च = "to the roots वृ and हृ the augments षुक् and दुक् are prefixed to the Unadi termination कयन् (99)." The final उक् of the augments and the initial क् and final न् of the termination are indicatory.—हृदयम्.

£ मेधाम्—√मिधृ मेधाहिंसयोः + अ P. III, 3, 102 अ प्रत्ययात् + टाप् IV, 1, 4 अजाद्यतष्टाप् or √मेधा आशुग्रहणे + क्विप्—मेधा—ताम्. In the first case the penultimate short of the root is gunated before the termination.

the breath, a good understanding, and other qualities of the heart and soul essential for a good living, should devote himself to a careful study of the Vedic sciences.

Comment :—We are reaching the end of our grand hymn on the Pursuit of True knowledge. Hence these last three stanzas have been devoted to cataloguing the attainments of the full-fledged graduate in the Vedic lores. This stanza states that the Brahmacārin coming out of the college of his Ācārya will be master of his body and mind with all his faculties fully developed. He will have good command over speech, that is, he will be a well-read scholar, a good man of letters and an able speaker. At the end of the verse it is mentioned that he will possess what is called **मेधा**. What is this **मेधा**?

The following occurs in the Vāijayantī of Yādava prakāśa:*—

> **मनीषा शेमुषी बुद्धिर्धीः पूः ख्यातिर्विदा बुधा ॥**
> **ज्ञप्तिः पण्डोपलब्धिस्तु संवित्तिरनुभूश्चितिः ।**
> **अवगत्यनुभूती चिज्ज्ञप्तिर्ज्ञानं च बोधनम् ॥**
> **षोढा धीस्तत्त्वधीः पण्डा मेधा धीर्धारणक्षमा ।**
> **ऊहापोहक्षमा चार्वी गृहीतिर्ग्रहणक्षमा ॥**

धी is therefore a general term for all the 'mental faculties' and is sixfold: (1) **तत्त्वधी**="understanding of the real nature of things", (2) **पण्डा** (**पणायते व्यवहरति स्तौति वा इति**√**पण व्यवहारे स्तुतौ च**+**ड** U, I, 114 **ञमन्ताड्डः**="to roots ending in nasals [**ञ्**, **म्**, **ङ्**, **ण्**, and **न्**] the Unadi termination **ड** is added" and P. IV, 1, 2 **अजाद्यतष्टाप्**)="knowledge acquired by learning or experience", (3) **मेधा** "retentive (?) intelligence", (4) **धी** (√**ध्यै चिन्तायाम्**+**क्विप्** P. III, 2, 178 **अन्येभ्योऽपि दृश्यते**, Vartika **ध्यायतेः संप्रसारणं च** and VI, 1, 108 **संप्रसारणाच्च**) "retentive intelligence" (again), (5) **चार्वी** (**चरति चित्ते इति**√**चर गतौ**+**उ**+**ङीप्** U, I, 3 **दृसनिजनिचरिचटिरहिभ्यो ञ्युण्** and P. IV, 1, 15 **टिड्ढाणञ्द्वयसज्दघ्नञ्मात्रच्तय-**

* Dr. Gustav Oppert's edition, Government Press Madras, 1893, p. 96

ऌक्ऌम्कम्करप:) = "the rational faculty" and (6) गृहीतिः(√ ग्रह उपादाने + क्तिन् P. III, 3, 94 स्त्रियां क्तिन्, VII, 2, 35 आर्ध धातुकस्येड्वलादेः and 37 ग्रहोऽलिटि दीर्घः)

A distinction has to be made between धी and मेधा. The former is a general term meaning any of the mental faculties but the latter means an "intellect that grasps the true nature of things quickly." This is at least the derivative and Vedic significance of the two words though the Vāijayantī equates मेधा to धारणावती धी. In the Nighaṇṭu II, 10 मेधा, III, 15 मेधाविनः, मेधाविनां and मेधाविनामानि the word means 'wisdom' in III, 9 'wisdom' or 'intelligence' and in III, 15 the word धीर, is a synonym of विप्र, वेन, मनीषी, विपश्चित् etc.

It is interesting to note that these two words and their derivatives have been consistently explained in the Nirukta and the commentaries by Durga and Skandasvāmin on it to mean, the first (धी) action or intelligence and the second (मेधा), wisdom. But Dr. Lakshman Sarup in some of these instances, following his European 'masters' gives entirely different significations of the words for which there is absolutely no justification. For example in Nirukta XI, 27 the words धियो विश्वा occuring in R. V. I, 3, 12 are interpreted as सर्वाणि प्रज्ञानानि. Durgācārya repeats the very words of the Nirukta and Skandasvāmin says कर्माणि प्रज्ञा वा. But Dr. Lakshman Sarup has 'devotions'. In the previous section the Nirukta gives for धियावसुः, कर्मवसुः as the synonym and Durga says कर्मधना and Skandasvāmin explains the expression thus:—धीरिति कर्मनाम। वस्विति धननाम। कर्म यागलक्षणं [वसु] धनं यस्याः सा कर्मधना प्रज्ञाधना वा। Dr. Sarup says 'rich in devotion'. For धीतिः in Nir. X, 41 he has 'contemplation', for धियंधाः in VIII, 7 'meditative' and for धियंधियम् in XII, 18 'every thought.' This unauthorised tampering with the 'sanctioned' interpretations of words in the Nirukta reduces the usefulness of

Dr. Lakshman Sarup's Index to the book to the very minimum.

Hence मेधा is the name of that type of intellect which quickly grasps the hidden reality of things and according as this faculty is more or less developed, will one be the better or worse off in the guiding of oneself or others in the affairs of the world. This faculty is the most essential element in the qualifications of one who is going to fight the battle of life and as such, must be the primary thing in the curricula of all training for the young.

(२९) चक्षुः श्रोत्रं यशो अस्मासु धेह्यन्नं रेतो लोहितमुदरम् ॥२५॥

Transliteration:—Cakṣuh śrōtram yaśō asmāsu dhēhyannam rētō lōhitam udaram ॥ 25

पदपाठः—चक्षुः । श्रोत्रम् । यशः । अस्मासु । धेहि । अन्नम् । रेतः । लोहितम् । उदरम् ॥

अन्वयः—(हे ब्रह्मचारिन्) अस्मासु चक्षुः, श्रोत्रं, यशः, अन्नं, रेतः, लोहितम्, उदरम् धेहि ॥

Word-meaning:—चक्षुः* = power of sight. श्रोत्रं† = power of hearing. यशः‡ = fame. अन्नं§ = food. रेतः = seed,

---

* चक्षुः—√ चक्षिङ् दर्शने + उसि U. II, 119 चक्षेः शिच्च = "the termination उसि as added to the root चक्ष् has an indicatory श," —चक्ष् + उस्—चक्षुः. The Unadi terminations are आर्धधातुक terminations, hence *by* P. II, 4, 54 चक्षिङः ख्याञ्, the word ख्याञ् is to be substituted for चक्ष् before उस्. But when it is शित् P. III, 4, 113 तिङ्शित्सार्वधातुकम् applies and the change is forestalled.

† श्रोत्रम्—श्रूयते अनेन इति—√श्रु श्रवणे + त्रन् U. IV, 168 हुयामाश्रुभसिभ्यस्त्रन् = "the Unadi termination त्रन् is added to the roots हु, या, मा, श्रु and भस्." The final vowel and the penultimate short of roots are gunated before this termination.—श्रोत्रम्.

‡ यशः—युट् + √अश देवने + असुन् U. IV, 191 अशेर्देवने युट् च—

semen virile, power of procreation, virility. **लोहितम्***= **blood.** **उदरम्**=good digestion, power of digestion. (This stanza is connected with the previous since the type of accomplished Vedic student is meant here).

Translation:— [To such an accomplished man of restraint learned in the Vedic lores, people (should) approach and request him thus; Oh Sir you are well versed in these matters, Please] help us to attain a good power of sight and of hearing, fame, food, virility, [purity of] blood, and power of digestion.

Purport:—Man should live with restraint and study the Vedas if he wishes to help humanity to live a healthy and prosperous life. People also should approach for guidance only that man who is himself accomplished in these matters.

"the root अश् meaning to sport, takes the augment युट् before the termination असुन् (189),"—यशः,

§ अन्नम्--(१)√अद भक्षणे+क्त P. III, 2, 102 निष्ठा and VIII, 2, 42 रदाभ्यां निष्ठातो नः पूर्वस्य च दः="after र् and द् the initial त् of the past passive participial termination is changed to न् and the final द् of the root also follows suit." अद्+क्त=अन्+न=अन्नम्. (२) अनिति जीवयति इति √अन प्राणने+न U. III, 10 कृवृजृसिद्रुपन्यनिस्वपिभ्यो नित् "the Unadi termination न as added to the roots कृ, वृ, जृ, सि, द्रु, पन्, अन् and स्वप् has an indicatory न्."—अन्+न=अन्नम्. (३) आनतं भूतेभ्यः --आ+√णम प्रह्वत्वे शब्दे च+क्विप् P. III, 2, 178 अन्येभ्योपि दृश्यते. This form is irregular. आ+नम्+क्विप्=अन्नम्. Yaska says:--अन्नं कस्मात्। आनतं भूतेभ्यः। अत्तेर्वा ॥ Nirukta III, 9. The derivation of this word given on p. 44 of Anthology of Vedic Hymns is not accurate. The last attempt on the passage from the Nirukta given here is also only approximate.

*लोहितम्--रोहति प्रादुर्भवति इति—√रुह बीजजन्मनि प्रादुर्भावे च+ इतन् U. III, 94 रुहे रश्च लो वा="the Unadi termination इतन् (93) is added to the root रुह and the initial र् of the root is optionally changed to ल्"--लोहितम्.

Comment:—This extremely terse statement further develops the catalogue of the "graduate's" qualifications. He should be a physician always ready and able to give medical aid to the suffering. He should be so well trained and well disciplined himself as to help others regulate their lives, develop their powers, specialise in matters for which they have vocations and thus lead them on to fame. A 'graduate' who possesses these qualifications will have no need to go from office to office with a petition in his hand for 'service'. There is something awfully wrong in a system of education that saps a young man's vitality, spoils his manners and then sends him out into the world with a vapid title either as a haughty 'rational beast,' or an intriguing schemer or an educated beggar. The ability to read and write in different languages, to reason or discuss on philosophical themes, to solve very difficult problems in higher mathematics is no education but simply acquired habit. "The great end of education is, to discipline rather than to furnish the mind, to train it to the use of its own powers rather than fill it with accumulations of others."* "Education is not learning; it is the exercise and development of the powers of the mind; and the two great methods by which this end may be accomplished are in the halls of learning, or in the conflicts of life."† This is education as it should be, but what is modern education? To speak seriously it is; "Reeling and writhing, of course to begin with," Mock Turtle replied, "and the different branches of arithmetic—ambition, distraction, uglification and derision."‡

(३०) तानि कल्पद्ब्रह्मचारी सलिलस्य पृष्ठे तपोऽतिष्ठत्तप्यमानः समुद्रे । स स्नातो बभ्रुः पिङ्गलः पृथिव्यां बहु रोचते ॥२६॥

---

*Tryon Edwards, New Dictionary of Thoughts, p. 151.
†Princeton Review, Ibid., p. 154.
‡Lewis Carroll, Ibid., p. 153.

Transliteration:—Tāni kalpadbrahmacārī salilasya pṛṣṭhē tapō'tiṣṭhat tapyamānah samudrē ।

Sa snātō babhruh pingalah pṛthivyām bahu rōcatē ॥ 26.

पदपाठः—तानि । कल्पत् । ब्रह्मऽचारी । सलिलस्य । पृष्ठे । तपः । अतिष्ठत् । तप्यमानः । समुद्रे । सः । स्नातः । बभ्रुः । पिङ्गलः । पृथिव्याम् । बहु । रोचते ॥

अन्वयः—ब्रह्मचारी तानि कल्पत् समुद्रे तपः तप्यमानः सलिलस्य पृष्ठे अतिष्ठत् । सः स्नातः बभ्रुः पिंगलः पृथिव्याम् बहु रोचते ॥

Word-meaning:—तानि* = those (duties enjoined upon him viz., of studying the Vedas and the ancillary lores, subduing his passions, and serving his preceptor). **कल्पत्** = doing. **सलिलस्य पृष्ठे**† = on the surface of the water in the shape of learning. **तपः तप्यमानः**‡ = exerting himself to control his senses. **अतिष्ठत्** = has stood. **समुद्रे** = in the first stage (brahmacarya) of man's life which is as unfathomable as the ocean itself. **स्नातः**¶ = having bathed; having finished his studies and training. **बभ्रुः**§ = supporting i. e.,

* तानि—√ तनु विस्तारे + अदि U. I, 132 त्यजि तनियजिभ्यो डित् = "the termination अद् as appended to the roots त्यज्, तन् and यज् has an indicatory ड्"—तन् + अद् = त् + अद् = तद्.—तानि.

† सलिलस्य—√ सल गतौ + इलच् U. I, 54 सलिकल्यनिमहिभडिभण्डिशण्डिपिण्डितुण्डिकुकिभूभ्य इलच् = "to the roots सल्, कल्, अन्, मह्, भड्, भण्ड्, शण्ड्, पिण्ड्, तुण्ड् and कुक् the Unadi termination इलच् is added."–सलिलम्.

‡ तप्यमानः—√ तप सन्तापे + यक् + मुक् + शानच् P. III, 1, 67 सार्वधातुके यक् = "before 'personal' terminations यक् is added on to the root in the passive and 'impersonal' voices," (Vide also P. III, 4, 113 तिङ्शित्सार्वधातुकम्), VII, 2, 82 आने मुक् and III, 2, 124 लटः शतृशानचावप्रथमासमानाधिकरणे.—तप्यमानः.

¶ स्नातः—√ ष्णा शौचे + क्त P. III, 2, 102 निष्ठा—स्नातः

§ बभ्रुः—√ भृञ् भरणे + कु U. I, 22 कुर्भ्रश्च = "before the Unadi termination कु the root भृ to bear or support, is reduplicated." The initial क् of the termination indicates that no गुण or वृद्धि

having stored in himself the learning of the Vedic and ancillary lores. पिङ्गलः*=shining; strong. पृथिव्यां=on the earth; in the world; in society. बहु†= very much. रोचते =he shines.

Translation:—Standing on the surface of the waters of learning in the unfathomable sea of the stage of Brahmacarya, exerting himself to control his senses and performing the duties assigned to him, the Vedic student plunges himself (in the sea of learning), so to say, and bathing therein comes out having stored in himself immense knowledge and shines most brilliantly in the world.

Purport:—The Vedic student by his exercise of mortification of the senses and attainment of high education comes to possess many merits which gain him repute in the world. Parents should aspire to give such an education to their sons and daughters.

CONCLUDING REMARKS.

What the twentysix verses of this grand hymn on the fundamental principles of education teach may now be summed up in brief.

---

change is possible before it.—भ्र+कु=भभ्र+उ=P. VII, 4, 66 उरत्="ऋ at the end of the reduplicated part of a verb is replaced by अ."—भभ्र+उ—P. VIII, 4, 54 अभ्यासे चर्च="in the reduplicated portion of a verb a radical hard or soft aspirate, i. e., the second or fourth letter of a class is replaced by the corresponding hard or soft unaspirate i. e., the first or third letter." बभ्र+उ.—P. VI, 1, 77 इको यणचि.—बभ्रुः.

* पिङ्गलः—√ पिजि वर्णे संपर्चने+कल U. I, 104 कलस्तृपश्च and P. III, 3, 1, उणादयो बहुलम्.—पिञ्+अल, the final ज् of the root is here changed to ग्=पिङ्गलः.

† बहु—√ बहि वृद्धौ+कु U. I, 29 लंघिबंह्योर्नलोपश्च="the termination कु is added to the roots लंघ् and बंह् and the nasal of the roots is dropped."—बहुः.

The Necessity of Educational Institutions for the Young

The hymn lays stress on the necessity of educational institutions for the young. The very first stanza amply suggests this by mentioning the 'Rector'—Ācārya and the 'Student'—Brahmacārin together. In the third verse the ceremony of investiture with the sacred thread as a genuine and serious token of admission to the solemn life of a Vedic student is alluded to. In the fourth the student's regularity in his devotions, in the fifth his solemn vows and austerities are mentioned. In the sixth his clothing and appearance, in the fifteenth his fellow students are briefly described. From all these details we can safely conclude that the hymn lays down the basic principles of a genuine educational institution.

The Rector.

Of such an educational institution, the hymn assures us, the Rector or Ācārya is the very soul. Without him the institution can have no existence. The very first verse says that the Brahmacārin is the fulfilment of the (aspirations of the) Ācārya—sa ācāryam tapasā piparti. The third verse in almost 'symbolic' style describes the relation between the Brahmacārin and the Ācārya. He admits the student not only to the institution but unreservedly to all the stores of knowledge he possesses. He imparts all his varied learning to the pupil till no ignorance is left in the latter. It is a true and complete knowledge of essentials and not of their details or extensions. The process, the verse states, is 'painful', just like the conception and birth of the child. The relation between the Ācārya and Brahmacārin, therefore, is as intimate, cordial and sincere as that between mother and child, nay, the sacred text describes it to be as close as that between the expectant mother and the foetus in her womb!

This cordiality and 'proximity' of the relation between the Rector and his pupils is made possible and continued through the course of studies in which the former is always the leading figure. He himself teaches the students as the eighth and fourteenth verses state. If there are any additional tutors they must be the senior or former Brahmacārins as mentioned in vv. 15—17.

On the part of the Brahmacārins this relation should subsist in their sincere and lively co-operation with the Ācarya through a serious effort in study and work assigned to them by the latter. Verse 12, it must be admitted, is a statement of the various duties of the senior Brahmacārins. There seems to be a hint in it to rural preaching and service. Rural uplift work is not a modern thing; surely, it is as old as the world itself. Now-a-days only the name exists, since machines and factories are reducing all the rural population to what, out of courtesy (?) is not called slavery.

This verse (the 12th) is a description of the rain cloud which rains on all types of land equally, i. e., without making any distinction between place and place. So also the Rector and the Brahmacārins diffuse their learning without stinting among all who are sincere and desire to learn. As for those who do not desire to learn they have to adopt such measures as would arouse their keenness for learning things.

The great Aryan dramatist Bhavabhūti beautifully describes the method in which a good teacher imparts instruction to his pupils in the following words: -

वितरति गुरुः प्राज्ञे विद्यां यथैव तथा जडे
न तु खलु तयोर्ज्ञाने शक्तिं करोत्यपहन्ति वा ।

भवति हि पुनर्भूयान्भेदः फलं प्रति तद्यथा
प्रभवति खलु बिम्बग्राहे मणिर्न मृदादयः ॥

The Uttararamacaritam.

"The tutor imparts tuition to the clever as well as the dull student in the same manner, and does neither make nor mar their power* to grasp things. But yet there is great difference with regard to the result† of the tuition, and that is so because just as a mirror alone is able to take in the reflection of a thing placed before it whereas a clod of earth cannot do so, [clever students grasp what is taught to them and become learned but dull students fail to understand their lessons and remain dunces]".

The sixtyfourth hymn of the nineteenth book of the Atharvaveda seems to be one intended for daily recitation by Brahmacārins at their morning and evening fire-sacrifice (hōma). It consists of only four verses all devoted to the praise of God as the Dispeller of darkness teaching at the same time about the properties of heat or fire. The last verse contains a renewal of the Brahmacārin's pledge of sincere obedience to the Ācarya. It runs:—एतास्ते अग्ने समिधस्त्वमिद्धः समिद्भव । आयुरस्मासु धेह्यमृतत्वमाचार्याय ॥ "We have enkindled the fire and fed it with fuel, may the fire enkindle us now. May we have long life, may we be

---

* This is the मेधा of the 25th verse. It is not acquired, for every human being possesses it from birth, but is sharpened. The Hindi माथा, Marathi माथें and Gujarati माथुं are more probably corruptions of मेधा than of मस्तकम्.

† This is not the modern eye-wash called ***the examination result*** but rather the finished product. In the examination conducted by a genuine Ācarya of genuine Brahmcarins there can be no failures and no bad products.

immortal but let all be for (the fulfilment of the aspirations of) our Ācārya."

This relation of the teacher and the taught continued in another form even after the studies were over and terminated only with death.*

Other Tutors.

The method of tuition in Aryan India seems to have been very simple. The Tutors taught and the Brahmacārins learnt only one subject at a time, over a sufficiently long period till the subject itself was over. A clear hint of this is found in all ancient Aryan text books which have come down to us. For example, the first aphorism commencing the preface to the Aṣṭādhyāyī of Pāṇini is **अथ शब्दानुशासनं** as can be gathered from the Mahābhāṣya of Patanjali. The word **अथ** here as elsewhere, (in the philosophical and other treatises) means 'after', i. e., after the study of other subjects preparing the ground for this. Patanjali himself comments on the word thus:—**अथेत्ययं शब्दोऽधिकारार्थः प्रयुज्यते । शब्दानुशासनं नाम शास्त्रमधिकृतं वेदितव्यं ॥** 'Atha', he says, has the sense of 'adhikāra' fitness—fitness of the students to learn and of the subject to be taught. This fitness can be possible only after the study of some other subjects preparatory to what is being now undertaken. In the case of Pāṇini's Aṣṭādhyāyī a knowledge of reading and writing in the 'current vernacular' and of Sanskrit declensions and conjugations has always been found necessary. To study the Mahābhāṣya itself a

* In the Taittiriyopanisad I, 11 it is said वेदमनूच्याचार्योऽन्तेवासिनमनुशास्ति । सत्यं वद । धर्मं चर । स्वाध्यायान्मा प्रमदः । आचार्याय प्रियं धनमाहृत्य प्रजातन्तुं मा व्यवच्छेत्सीः । सत्यान्न प्रमदितव्यम् । धर्मान्न प्रमदितव्यम् । कुशलान्न प्रमदितव्यम् । भूत्यै न प्रमदितव्यम् । स्वाध्यायप्रवचनाभ्यां न प्रमदितव्यम् ॥ In 2 again we have:—आचार्यदेवो भव ॥ Further in 3 it is said:...... अथ यदि ते कर्मविचिकित्सा वा वृत्तविचिकित्सा वा स्यात्ये तत्र ब्राह्मणाः संमर्शिनः... तत्र वर्तेरन् तथा तत्र वर्तेथाः, one of these, of course, is the Acarya himself.

previous general knowledge of the Aṣṭādhyāyī is essential though it is not impossible to study the two together. But a study of the Yoga philosophy surely pre-supposes knowledge of the Sāṃkhya system, Vāiśēṣika of Nyāya and Mīmāṃsā and Vēdānta of all of these. The following seems to have been the course of studies in ancient Aryan institutions in India:—

A. Knowledge of one's mother-tongue and of Sanskrit declensions and conjugations qualified a boy or girl for admission to the Ācāryakula for the study of the Aṣṭādhyāyī.

B. A knowledge of the Aṣṭādhyāyī was essential to proceed on to higher studies in grammar.

C. A sound knowledge of grammar acquired after a course of study extending over some years qualified the student to proceed on to mathematics and astronomy.

D. Then came the time for philosophy.

E. After philosophy was taken up medicine.

F. At this stage, it seems, the Brahmacārins now sufficiently grown up, took to the Vedas along with the Nirukta and the Brāhmaṇas or these two in their turn preceded the Vedas.

G. 'Military science', the art of war and the use of weapons, perhaps reserved only for the kingly class, preceded Vedic study and so did music, vocal and instrumental.

Only those who came out of the Ācāryakula successful in all these subjects (and their number was always small), were considered to be the full-fledged 'graduates' or snātākas.

In the first section of the seventh book of the Chāndōgyōpaniṣad a beautiful story is told about the interview of the sage Nārada with the sage Sanatkumāra regarding the former's 'post-graduate' studies. This is not a grandmother's tale or myth but a true historical account told in the attractive story (?) style. The account* runs:—"Nārada approached Sanaṭkumāra and said—'Sir, please teach me'. Sanatkumāra replied 'Let me have a full account of all you have studied; I shall then be able to tell you what I can do for you'. Nārada's answer to this question was:—'Sir, I have studied the Ṛgvēda, Yajurvēda, Sāmavēda and the fourth Atharvavēda, the fifth 'ancient history' (in the form of the Brāhmaṇa), (the sixth) the science of Vedic interpretation, (the seventh) the 'science' of the service (?) of the elders, (the eighth) arithmetic, (the ninth) the science of the motions etc., of the celestial bodies, (the tenth) minerology, (the eleventh) logic, (the twelfth) ethics, (the thirteenth) physiology, (the fourteenth) theology, (the fifteenth) zoology, (the sixteenth) the military science, (the seventeenth) astronomy and (the eighteenth) the science of poisonous reptiles. All this, Sir, I have studied'. The modest Nārada further said; 'I may tell you, Sir, I know only the verses of the Vedas—the words alone—and have not realised the essence—the very soul—of all this learning. I have learnt that he who comes to know the soul through the guidance of personages like you, surmounts all suffering. Sir, I am miserable, please lead me out of my misery". Sanatkumāra replied:—'What -ever things you have studied, Oh Nārada ! are nothing

---

*अधीहि भगव इति होपससाद सनत्कुमारं नारदस्तं होवाच यद्वेत्थ तेन मोपसीद ततस्त ऊर्ध्वं वक्ष्यामीति ॥ छां० ७ । १ । १ ॥ स होवाचर्ग्वेदं भगवोऽध्येमि यजुर्वेदं सामवेदमाथर्वणं चतुर्थमितिहासपुराणं पञ्चमं वेदानां वेदं पित्र्यं राशिं दैवं निधिं वाकोवाक्यमेकायनं देवविद्यां ब्रह्मविद्यां भूतविद्यां क्षत्रविद्यां नक्षत्रविद्यां सर्पदेवजनविद्यामेतद्भगवोऽध्येमि ॥ २ ॥ सोऽहं भगवो मन्त्रविदेवास्मि नाऽत्मविच्छ्रुतं ह्येव भगवद्दृशेभ्यस्तरति शोकमात्मविदिति । सोऽहं भगवः शोचामि तं मा भगवाञ्छोकस्य पारं तारयत्विति । तं होवाच यद्वै किञ्चैतदध्यगीष्ठा नामैवैतत् ॥ ३ ॥........
.........स यो नाम ब्रह्मेत्युपास्ते यावन्नाम्नो गतं तत्रास्य यथाकामचारो भवति......
..................॥ ५॥

but extensions of the Most Majestic Name of God......... Therefore as far does the glory of that Name extend so far does the force of the will of him prevail who adheres to the Sacred Name of God taking it to be the true representation of Him............................"

From this long passage it is clear that many subjects were taught in ancient Aryan I n d i a. Who taught all these ? Did the Rector or Ācārya have a staff of qualified Tutors to assist him in tutorial work ? From the use of the word अथ explained at the outset of this section it seems only one Tutor, the Ācārya, taught all the subjects progressively to a group of students. It is quite possible also that different subjects were specialised and 'monopolised' by different scholars and students flocked to them according to their own need and choice. Very often a batch of students continued under the same Ācārya till they had studied all the eighteen (?) subjects. If the Rector had any assistants they must have been his own senior Brahmacārins and past students. The hymn seems to favour this view.

The Brahmacarins.

In ancient India the life of a student was a very serious affair full of responsibilities and discipline. No doubt, the basic principles regarding the status and duties of a Vedic student were derived from our hymn.

The first stanza of the hymn begins with austerities performed for the Ācārya. It is quite probable the little candidates, when the system prevailed, were expected to undergo some mild self-mortification such as a fast for a few hours, special ablutions and some sort of sacrifice. As a general rule they all knew their 'twilight prayers' by heart being taught by their parents to pray at home.

The ceremony of investiture with the sacred thread

at the hands of the Ācārya is the first step in the young condidate's life as a Vedic student. The ceremony is symbolic of the fact that his 'old Adam' is no more and that now begins his new regenerate life. This is his second and real birth and there will never be a repetition of it—no third birth. Hereafter there will be only growth mental, moral and spiritual. Even his physical development will be controlled and properly directed. Hence his self-mortification or tapas.

That the Brahmacārin's life was a life of thorough discipline and mortification is mentioned in the hymn over and over again. The very first verse says:—Sa ācāryam tapasā piparti, the second verse has:—sarvān sa dēvāṃstapasā piparti. The fourth verse is still more explicit. There the words are:—Brahmacārī samidhā mēkhalayā śramēṇa lōkāṃstapasā piparti. The eighth says that the Brahmacārī protects the earth and the heavens by his austerities—tē rakṣati tapasā Brahmacārī. The same statement almost, is repeated in the tenth stanza. The next states that by his austere life he benefits himself by the sun's rays. The nineteenth verse Brahmacaryēṇa tapasā etc., is a very beautiful maxim true for all time for the whole universe and the seventeenth is a special enunciation of it. *He can not be a student who is not mortified. Much less can that wretched man be fit for the Rectorship or the hallowed place of the Acarya of a college of students whose senses are not mortified. Limelight, women, pleasure, 'bossing' it over others and shirking from tutorial work are some of the greatest crimes a man in the place of the Rector can commit.* The principals of modern educational institutions all the world over do not deserve the appellation of Ācārya. That is a sacred word implying mental, moral and spiritual development in the man to whom it is applied. An austere and mortified life, teaching the students *in person* and being in constant communication with them are the very essentials of Ācāryahood. He who is void of these may, because the cabal to which he belongs has the upper hand in affairs, succeed in attaining to and maintaining that position but in truth, he will be the darkest foe of the Brahmacārins and not their friend. Hence for both the teacher and the taught tapas and brahmacarya are essential. In other words brahmacarya and tapas and ācāryahood also where necessary, are always coexistent.

Self-discipline and self-mortification under directions from the Ācārya are the essential features of the life of the Brahmacārin and the hymn lays very great stress upon them. Brahmacārins who possess these great qualities will always find it easy to discharge their duties towards their institution and its head. The hymn mentions various duties of the Brahmacārin of which something has already been said. These can be now described serially as follows:—

I. Observation of the physical world around and a regulated and desciplined use of all the beneficent forces of nature, so that all the physical elements in his person be properly developed and strengthened. Vide verses 1 and 2.

II. At the time of the 'fire-sacrifice' he should, while he throws sticks into the fire, think of his state as a Brahmacārin aglow with his industry and rigours of discipline, to be a great sacrifice at which the earth, the intermediate region and the heavens themselves are offered. Vide verse 4.

III. He should, by his daily life, i. e., in his daily routine, his behaviour and his relations with others, reveal the excellence of Vedic teachings and should always be on the alert to put down any heresy. Vide verse 7.

IV. He should regularly perform the 'fire-sacrifice'

(hōma) twice daily for the purification of the air and to maintain his contact with Vedic studies. He should, while casting the sticks into the fire, try to realise that the whole universe is a sacrifice performed by God in which all the worlds are offered as fuel and that his own life of discipline and mortification is a symbol of that great Universal sacrifice. Vide verse 9.

V. He should look upon himself as the zealous keeper of the treasure of Vedic Lore obtaining in both the mundane and the supramundane (or etheric) spheres and while he is studying the former, should have faith also in the latter. Verse 10.

VI. He should utilise the sun's rays to keep his body fit. He should not therefore hide himself from the sun and rain, cold and air but take advantage of all such natural phenomena to control and strengthen his body that he may successfully cope with his work. Verse 11.

VII According to the fitness of all those that come into contact with him, he should diffuse the learning he has acquired from his preceptors. Except for this condition he should not reserve anything but go on teaching and preaching, helping and serving all who need it wherever they may be on mountains or plains, or cities or the countryside. Verses 12 and 15.

VIII. He should curb and subdue his sexual appetite never allowing it to have the better of him. He should look at the dumb animals which practise 'sex control' and also observe trees and plants that keep strictly within the limits of their species. All these exhibit a wonderful practice of self-restraint which the Brahmacārin should always bear in mind. He should, as a Brahmacārin abstain from all contact with the fair sex and the Brahmacāriṇī also should have nothing to do with men. It is only then that their bodies will develop and be able to stand the strain of the struggle which awaits them in the world. Verses 18—21.

Along with these manifold duties the rigorous discipline he under-went made the Brahmacārin an able man of affairs with a body and mind strong enough to cope with all difficulties. Ancient Aryan Indian Scholars, the leaders of the schools of philosophy etc., had all undergone such rigorous training, and had themselves afterwards become the leaders of India-wide educational schools.

In the sixth verse the words kārṣṇam vasānah are a clear reference to the clothing of the Brahmacārin. Many take the word kārṣṇam to mean 'deerskin'. But this interpretation is not true since nowhere is it clearly stated that in ancient India it was customary for a Brahmacārin to wear deerskin and that he was strictly prohibited from wearing anything else. The derivation of the word kārṣṇa has been given on pp. 90 and 91 from which it will be seen that the word means dark-coloured garments as well. The dark colour required is either yellow, saffron or the dull red colour of ocre usually used by sanyāsins now-a-days. The provision of coloured garments for students is intended to reduce the labour and expenses of washing as white garments get dirty soon. The other sense of the word, viz, 'deerskin', is also derivative and not superior to the former (dark-coloured garment) in any way.

The fourth verse of the eighth hymn of the third book of the Ṛgvēda (quoted on p. 76) calls the Brahmacārin 'yuvā suvāsāh' which means 'a young man dressed in good and clean clothes'. The expression 'vāsas' is invariably used for clothing and not for skins used for putting on if such be anywhere in the world. In the

Āśvalāyana Gṛhya Sūtra, aphorism 9,* section 19 of chapter I it is said: "if the Brahmacārins wear garments those must be coloured. He who is a Brahman by his 'nature and inclinations' should have ochre-coloured, the Kṣatriya should wear madder-coloured and the Vāiśya turmeric-coloured."

From verse 178† of the 2nd chapter of the Bhārgavī Manusmṛti it seems a Brahmacārī is prohibited even from wearing leather shoes. It is therefore difficult to understand how one could, in consistency with truth, be allowed to wear deerskins in the place of cloth while one is being prohibited from using leather shoes even. This license to wear deerskins becomes still more unintelligible when it is known that the Brahmacārin is not allowed to eat flesh or to hurt animals.‡ Would it not then on his part, be tantamount to cooperating with those who did both (eat flesh and hurt animals) by hunting deer, if he were to use the skins of the poor beasts they had wantonly killed? To clothe thousands of Brahmacārins the skins of deer casually killed for the safety of agricultural produce would never be enough and intentional killing for this very purpose would therefore be necessitated. Such killing is entirely opposed to Vedic teachings. In the very first verse of the Yajurvēda God is besought and men are advised to protect§ the cattle of the 'sacrificer'—Yajamāna¶, i. e., one who keeps cattle for such profitable use as farming,

* यदि वासांसि वसीरन्रक्तानि वसीरन्काषायं ब्राह्मणो मांजिष्ठं क्षत्रियो हारिद्रं वैश्य: ॥ A. G. S. I, 19, 9.

† अभ्यङ्गमञ्जनं चाक्ष्णोरुपानच्छत्रधारणम् । कामं क्रोधं च लोभं च नर्तनं गीतवादनं ॥ M. S. II, 178.

‡ वर्जयेन्मधु मांसञ्च गंधं माल्यं रसान्स्त्रियः । शुक्तानि यानि सर्वाणि प्राणिनां चैव हिंसनम् ॥ M. S, II, 177,

§ यजमानस्य पशून्पाहि ॥ य० १ । १ ॥

¶ √यज देवपूजा (for offering in token of respect to a

riding etc. In the same Veda again, there are express injunctions prohibiting the killing of cows and bulls*, of sheep† and of single-hoofed animals.‡ It is true the words gām, avim, ēkaśapham paśum are used metaphorically in these instances but the literal sense also is equally valid.

There have been people in India who adduce evidence from ancient works in support of flesh-eating. They employ a lot of special pleading and equivocation to support their dirty view. The twentysecond aphorism of the eighth section of the sixth book of the Mīmāmsā Sūtra of the sage Jāimini is one of the authorities submitted to this ugly travesty. The aphorism runs:—(Avakīrṇipaśuśca) and the performance of the rite connected with the beast of the Brahmacārin who has violated his vow of celibacy (tadvat) is like a rite to be performed in the ordinary fire, for (aprāptakālatvāt) the time has not as yet arrived for the performer to establish the sacred household fire (ādhānasya)§ The rite itself is described in the Kātyāyana Śrāuta Sūtra Chapter I aphorisms 13-17 thus: "A Vedic student who has broken his vow of sexual restraint should *obtain* an ass at the south-western quarter."¶ What does this mean ?

All the world over the ass is considered to be a mean animal. It is a great injustice to the good beast no doubt, for, in truth, it is more useful than the silly horse or the foolish but gentle bull or the haughty buffalo

---

great personage) संगतिकरण (for conveying things or persons from place to place) दानेषु (to give milk or a cow etc., in charity to the needy)+मुक्+आन P. VII, 2, 82 and III, 2, 124.

* गां मा हिंसीः ॥ य० १३ । ४३ ॥

† अविं मा हिंसीः ॥ य० १३ । ४४ ॥

‡ मा हिंसीरेकशफम् ॥ य० १ । ४८ ॥

§ अवकीर्णिपशुश्च तद्वदाधानस्याप्राप्तकालत्वात् ॥ मी० ६ । ८ । २२ ॥

¶ ब्रह्मचार्यवकीर्णी नैर्ऋतं गर्दभमालभेत ॥ का० श्रौ० सू० १ ॥

or the lordly and extremely expensive elephant. A wayward world going on wrong and utterly selfish principles, cannot but look down upon the humble and submissive. Bred of this wrong spirit the custom prevailed and is still occasionally h e a r d of as prevailing in some parts of India of taking a wrong-doer round on the back of an ass in procession through public thoroughfares. In ancient India also this was the fate of a Brahmacārin who had fallen in evil ways and defiled himself. He was himself compelled to get (ā labh) an ass and ride on it towards the southwestern direction of his Ācāryakula, leave the animal there, bathe and return. This was his penance. After this public penance he was fit for association and he was accepted again by his Ācārya as a prodigal son. But before this rite he had to perform a 'fire-sacrifice' as laid down in the eighteenth section of the second chapter of the Tāittirīya Āraṇyaka thus:*-- "The expounders of the Vedas say that the person of the Brahmacārin who ***(somehow i. e., even accidentally)*** spoils the precious seminal fluid in his body, gets ***decomposed*** and the elements thereof enter the various beneficent agents ***(that have contributed towards its formation)***, for example, his vital airs enter the winds (marutāh), his vigour the sun (indram), the power he has acquired through Vedic studies to God

---

* कतिधावकीर्णी प्रविशति चतुर्धेत्याहुर्ब्रह्मवादिनो । मरुतः प्राणैः । इन्द्रं बलेन । बृहस्पतिम् ब्रह्मवर्चसेन । अग्निमेवेतरेण सर्वेण । तस्यैतां प्रायश्चित्तिं विदाञ्चकार सुदेवः काश्यपः । यो ब्रह्मचार्यवकिरेदमावास्यायां रात्र्यामग्निं प्रणीयोपसमाधाय द्विराज्यस्योपघातं जुहोति कामावकीर्णोऽस्मि काम कामाय स्वाहा कामाभिद्रुग्धोऽस्म्य भिद्रुग्धोऽस्मि काम कामाय स्वाहेति । अमृतं वा आज्यममृतमेवात्मन्धत्ते । हुत्वा प्रयताञ्जलिः कवातिर्यङ्ङग्निमभिमन्त्रयेत । सं मा सिञ्चन्तु मरुतस्समिन्द्रः सं बृहस्पतिः । सं मायमग्निः सिञ्चत्वायुषा च बलेन चायुष्मन्तं करोतु मेति । प्रति हास्मै मरुतः प्राणान्दधाति प्रतीन्द्रो बलं प्रति बृहस्पतिर्ब्रह्मवर्चसं प्रत्यग्निरितरः सर्वं । सर्वतनूर्भूत्वा सर्वमायुरेति । त्रिरभिमन्त्रयेत त्रिषत्या हि देवाः । यो पूत इव मन्येत स इत्थं जुहुयादित्थमभिमन्त्रयेत पुनीत एवात्मानमायुरेवात्मन्धत्ते । * * * तैआ० २ । १८ ॥

the Protector of Revelation (bṛhaspatim) and all the other elements of his physical being go to the universal principle diffusing heat-energy (agnim). The sage Sudēva a dcscendant of the sage Kaśyap lays down the following penance for such offending Brahmacārin. On the last night of the dark half of the month he should light a fire, feed it with fuel and taking molten butter in his hands twice pour it in the fire and pray thus:—'Oh Lord of my desires (Kāma)! I have gone astray [in my desires] (avakirṇō'smi) and broken my vow (avakīrnō'smi). Oh Lord God of my desires (Kāma)! I submit entirely (svāhā) to Thy Holy Will (Kāmāya). Oh Lord God of my desires! I have erred (abhidrugdhō'smi) and revolted against Thy Omnipotent Providence (abhidrugdhō'smi). Oh Lord of my desires! I bow before Thy Holy Will [forgive me]'. Molten butter is nectar, so to say. By performing the rite thus the Brahmacārin calls together the immortal vital principles in his physical being again. He should after this, join the palms of his hands together in reverence and slightly bending his body towards the fire thus pray to God: 'May the winds shower upon me the vital airs, may the sun pour on me his vigour, may the Lord God the Protector of the Revealed Vedas give me true knowledge and may the universal principle of heat advance my life, my strength and make me long-lived.' The winds then bestow on him again the vital airs, the sun vigour, God the Protector of the Vedas the power of true knowledge and the universal principle of heat all the rest. He then becomes whole in body and enjoys the full span of life. He should recite the last prayer thrice for the beneficent principles (mentioned above) are true for all the three divisions of time. One should have faith in this purificatory rite and offer it. He will, then, in truth be purified and receive the promise of long life.*..............."

This was the ancient fire oblation. Then followed

the rite about the ass. Self-inflicted public penance for the least flaw as well as for the greatest crime committed in the darkest nook of the world was considered sufficient atonement in ancient India during the Vedic ages. The then Government also attached great importance to such acts of penance and acknowledged them to be full satisfaction for the requirements of the law. But it must be remembered that during those hallowed times when there were thousands of institutions all over India training Brahmacārins in the various Vedic lores, human nature being what it is, a good number of cases of such minor flaws as referred to in the Taittiriya Āraṇyaka passage quoted above occurred and penances performed so that the poor ass was-nick named 'avakīrṇi paśu'. It is quite probable the ass-rite was performed by that Brahmacārin who had committed the serious 'indiscretion' of becoming a victim to 'woman's wiles'.

But the travesty of the Mīmāṃsā aphorism is horrible in the extreme. The following translation is an instance of it:—"And the animal to be offered as a penance for a breach of the vow by a religious student is to be done like it, because the time for the establishment of fire has not arrived."* The wording of the statement is quite clear. The phrase 'the animal to be offered as penance' simply means killing an ass and burning it as a 'holocaust'. Is it imaginable that such an absurd sacrifice would ever be enjoined by the votaries of any religion on this side of the grave? Well, what will be the effect of such an ugly rite? The young man has committed an indiscretion of a very grave nature and

* The Mimamsa Sutras of Jaimini, translated by Pandit Mohan Lal Sandal, M. A., LL. B., published by the Panini Office, Allahabad, 1923 p. 409.

whether he kills one ass or a thousand of them or roasts them all alive, he can never get his past innocence back, but will surely further incur the sin of ḳilling. It is impossible therefore to understand how great thinkers like Kātyāyana and Jāimini tolerated—much less preached —such a thing? The language of the original texts is old and terse no doubt, but the idea in the translation does not emerge from the original, it is imported by the translator into the text from his own prejudiced mind.*

It is reasonable, therefore, to suppose that the clothing of the Brahmacārins in ancient Indian Ācāryakulas was not deerskin but cotton cloth and in the cold season perhaps even woollen. Their principal clothing seems to have been two pieces of cloth one to be tied below the waist and the other to be thrown over the back, shoulders and chest. Those who could afford to have a deerskin had to sit upon it during devotional exercises and not use it for covering the body with.

In the second section of the second chapter of the first book of the Gōpatha Brāhmaṇa this verse is commented upon. There it is said that the Brahmacārin's lustre derived from Vedic study goes to beasts (मृग=lion

* "The sutra refers to the गर्दभेज्या; in this connection see sutras 13–17 of the chap. I of कात्यायन श्रौत सूत्र. The present sutra embodies the सिद्धान्त. When a religious student who is bound to observe the vow of celibacy, goes astray, he is to perform गर्दभेज्या as a penance. *Now the question is in which fire the animal is to be offered?* The reply according to our author is, that it should be done in the unconsecrated fire because the time for consecration of fire is after the completion of the (ब्रह्मचर्याश्रम) student's life. The subject is fully discussed by कात्यायन in the श्रौत सूत्र. ब्रह्मचार्यवकीर्णी नैर्ऋतं गर्दभमालभेत "A religious student who goes astray, shall offer an ass consecrated to नैर्ऋत." Ibid., p. 409, 10.

or deer) hence when he uses (**वस्ते**=puts on?) deerskins he obstructs his lustre of Vedic study from departing from him*. The cogency of the argument given here is not

---

* जायमानो ह वै ब्राह्मणः सप्तेन्द्रियाण्यभिजायन्ते ब्रह्मवर्चसञ्च यशश्च स्वप्नञ्च क्रोधञ्च श्लाघाञ्च रूपञ्च पुण्यमेव गन्धं सप्तमम्। तानि ह वा अस्यैतानि ब्रह्मचर्यमुपेतोऽपक्रामन्ति मृगानस्य ब्रह्मवर्चसं गच्छत्याचार्यं यशोऽजगरं स्वप्नो वराहं क्रोधोऽपः श्लाघां कुमारीं रूपमोषधिवनस्पतीन्पुण्यो गन्धः। स यन्मृगाजिनानि वस्ते तेन तद्ब्रह्मवर्चसमवरुन्धे यदस्य मृगेषु भवति स ह स्नातो ब्रह्मवर्चसी भवति। * * * * * गो० १।२।२॥ The language of the passage quoted above is elliptical and enigmatic and hence only an approximate translation is subjoined. A literal translation of such a text would lead one nowhere:–"No sooner the candidate undergoes the ceremony of rebirth in the form of investiture with the sacred thread than there starts in his being the proper formation of seven properties, viz., the power (=quickness of intellect) of the Vedic learning he has commenced, fame (of good scholarship and a useful life awaiting him), (a carefree life refreshed with) sound and peaceful sleep, indignation (towards wickedness), praise (of his own self based upon recognition of his merits), beauty (of body, mind and soul) and fragrance of his person. If he is careless or indiscrete during his brahmacarya these properties depart from him and betake themselves, so to say, to other beings. For example the quickness of intellect acquired through study goes as it were, to the deer (or wild beasts which are quick in their senses and movement), his fame goes to his Acarya, his sleep to the python, his anger to the boar, his self-praise to the waters, his good looks to maidens and the fragrance of his person to trees and plants. Hence when he uses deerskins (regularly i. e., sits upon them and meditates or puts them on as a part of penance for any indiscretion he may have committed), he prevents from departing from him the power of his understanding sharpened by Vedic study and resembling the swiftness of deer. When he finishes his studies and comes out as a graduate he possesses this power to the full. * * * * * * * " G. Br. I, 2,2.

intelligible. Besides the passage itself may not be genuine. But in section 21* of the third chapter wearing of deerskin is prescribed as a penance for the initiated who commits an indiscretion. It is quite probable therefore, that someone, as a token of penance, gave up, for the time being, all his clothing, wore only the Kāupīna —privy cloth—and covered his trunk with the deerskin on which he sat during his devotional exercises.

The above details have brought one issue to the fore, namely

What is Krsnajina or deer-skin?

Is the expression Kṛṣṇājina, employed in Vedic lirerature (the four Vedas, the Brahmanas, the Upaniṣads and the Kalpa sūtras), to be taken literally to mean the skin of the black antelope or goat or is it figuratively

---

The above method in translating an ancient Sanskrit text is used not to support a fad but to avoid an absurdity. It is simply revolting to think that a person whose mind was so highly developed as would be necessary to write the Gopatha Brahmana could clothe himself in deerskins. The passage explains why it is that deerskins are used to sit on during spiritual exercises.

* स होवाच द्वादश ह वै वसूनि दीक्षितादुत्क्रामन्ति। न ह वै दीक्षितोऽग्निहोत्रं जुहुयात् न पौर्णमासेन यज्ञेन यजेत नामावास्येनास्मिन्वसीत न पितृयज्ञेन यजेत न तत्र गच्छेद्यत्र मनसा जिगमिषेन्नेष्ट्या यजेत न वाचा यथाकथाचिदभिभाषेत न मिथुनं चरेन्नान्यस्य यथाकाममु युञ्जीत न पशुवन्धेन यज्ञेन यजेत न तत्र गच्छेद्यत्र चक्षुषा परापश्येत् कृष्णाजिनं वसीत कुरीरन्धारयेन्मुष्टीकुर्यादङ्गुष्ठप्रभृतयस्तिस्र उच्छ्रयेन्मृगशृङ्गं गृह्णीयात्तेन कषेताथ यस्य दीक्षितस्य वाग्वायता स्यान्मुष्टी वा विसृष्टौ स एतानि जपेत् ॥ गो० १।३।२१॥

It is irrelevant to attempt at translating this very archaic and enigmatic passage. Suffice it to say that the use of the deerskin here is for devotional and penitential purposes.

PLATE VI

This is the Padmaasana in which the right foot is placed upon the left thigh and the left foot across the right on the right thigh. If the arms were to be crossed at the back and the left hand brought forward to catch the right great toe, and the right hand similarly employed to catch the left great toe, this would be the Baddhapadmaasana.

The merit of these postures consists in the great help they render the devotee in his exercise. They spare the spine from the strain brought about by the weight of the trunk, since that is borne by the thighs and the arms in an equal measure, at the same time, giving full play to the muscles of these, which would not be possible in any other posture of quietude.

(To face p. 169.)

used meaning something else? The following quotations seem to support the latter view :—

"This (earth) itself is the kṛṣṇājina when a reverent guest is entertained thereon." Atharvaveda IX,6,17.*

Commenting on Yajurvēda IX, 35 and 36 respectively the Śatapatha Brāhmaṇa says kṛṣṇājina is the source of good deeds, (Ś. Br. VI,4,2,6) and Kṛṣṇājina is the seat (abode?) of the priest." (VI,4,2,7).†

‡"Brahma is Kṛṣṇājina". Śānkh Br. IV, 11. "The kṛṣṇājina is a ship which can easily sail across'! A. Br. I,13. "This earth, surely, is the Kṛṣṇājina," Ś. Br. VI, 4,1,9. "The sacrifice itself is 'the Kṛṣṇājina" Ś. Br. VI, 4,1,6; ,III. 2,1,8; 28.

There are many more texts of this type in which the expression 'kṛṣṇājina' is used metaphorically. The word 'ajina' itself is formed from the root 'aj' meaning to go or move (also to set in motion) by adding the Uṇādi§ suffix 'inac' and hence something that moves or sets in motion. In this sense the word 'ajina' seems to be related to the more recent English word 'engine' to connect which latter with the Latin *ingenium*¶, does not seem

---

* इयमेव (पृथिवी) कृष्णाजिनम् ॥ अ॰ ६ । ६ । १७ ॥

† सीद होतः स्व उ लोके चिकित्वान्सादया यज्ञम् सुकृतस्य योनौ ॥ य॰ ११ । ३५ ॥ नि होता होतृषदने विदानस्त्वेषो दीदिवां असदत्सुदक्षः ॥ य॰ ११ । ३६ ॥ तस्य (अग्नेः) एष स्वो लोको यत्कृष्णाजिनम् ॥ श॰ ६ । ४ । २ । ६ ॥ कृष्णाजिनम् वै सुकृतस्य योनिः ॥ Ibid. कृष्णाजिनम् हौतृषदनम् ॥ Ibid., 7.

‡ ब्रह्म वै कृष्णाजिनम् ॥ शां॰ ४ । ११ ॥ कृष्णाजिनम् वै सुतर्मा नौः ॥ ऐ॰ १ । १३ ॥ इयं (पृथिवी) वै कृष्णाजिनम् ॥ श॰ ६ । ४ । १ । ९ ॥ यज्ञो वै कृष्णाजिनम् ॥ श॰ ६ । ४ । १ । ६ ॥ ३ । २ । १ । ८ ॥ २८ ॥

§ अजेरज च U. II, 48="to the root अज् to go, the termination इनच् (46) is added."

¶ "Engine (e'ndzin), *sb.* ME. [a. OF. *engin*—L. *ingenium* (whence INGENIOUS), f. *in*+*gen* root of *gignere* to beget.]"

to be quite accurate. The word 'ajina' originally signifying motion implies skin because it is only when the outer covering or skin is safe that all things and animals can go in life. 'Ajina' in this sense seems to have also meant cloth sometime in its history. There is a word in Hindustani 'Zīn'* which means a kind of thick cloth like drill or duck. This word 'Zīn' is connected with the Avestan word pronounced in the same way and meaning 'saddle' which is its common signification now-a-days. A piece of cloth tied to the saddle also was called Zīn-posh. This must have been a particular kind of thick strong cloth, hence thick drill-like cloth is still being called by that name in those parts of India where Hindustani is spoken. The term must have been introduced by the Moghul invaders of India or even their predecessors. It goes back in that case, almost to the tenth century of the Christian era. The ancient Iranian language, Avestan or Zend-Pehlevi whatever it may be called, a direct offshoot of a very late but direct descendant of the Vedic Sanskrit must have borrowed the word 'Zīn' or its predecessor from its hallowed ancestor and the

---

The shorter Oxford English Dictionary, the Clarendon Press Oxford, 1933 p., 611 col., 1. Even when meaning motherwit, genius or ingenuity the word need not be 'derived' from the Latin *in+gignere*, but the more ancient Sanskrit अज+इनच् will answer the purpose quite well. Besides all English words are not directly derived from Latin roots but a good number of them go far back to the older and genuine Aryan source, viz., Vedic Sanskrit. The English language did exist in some form or other alongside of Latin when the latter was a living spoken language.

*زین Zin [Pehl. Zin; Zend, Zaini], S. M. Saddle....Zin-posh, S. M. A cloth fastened over the saddle. A Dictionary of Urdu classical Hindi and English by John T. Platts, M. A., Sampson Low, Marston and Company, London, 1884, p., 620 col., 2.

borrowal must have been our 'ajina'. The process through which the initial (a) was done away with and the (j) changed to (z) is not inexplicable. The words 'Zan' (woman) and (Arabic) 'Zāt' (nature) based on the ancient Sanskrit root—'janī, prādurbhāvē are enough evidences of one part of the change. Hence kṛṣṇājina may mean a black or dark-coloured thick cloth.

In the twenty third stanza of the second chapter of the Bhārgavī Manusmṛti it is said that that part of India is the best suited for yajña—'religious sacrifice' (?) which is the natural abode of the Kṛṣṇasāra—black antelope and the country beyond it is savage land "* This description of the particular province exactly tallies with the derivation of the expression Kṛṣṇājina—where the kṛṣṇa (mṛga) —black antelope—ajina—goes i. e., lives in a natural and free state. (Regarding the application of the termination 'inac' in the sense of the locative case see the Introduction). The word kṛṣṇa also etymologically means something that attracts or repels. Hence, it is quite probable, the Vedic expressions Kārṣṇam and kṛṣṇājina may mean something quite different from 'deerskin' their metaphorical or later developed conventional sense.

Food of the Brahmacarins.

The eighth, ninth and tenth stanzas of the Food hymn, R. V. I, 187 describe the food of human beings in the following words:—

"Oh Lord God! Who pervadest like the air all space [and all things] (**वातापे**), be Thou (**भव**) our Great

---

* कृष्णसारस्तु चरति मृगो यत्र स्वभावतः । स ज्ञेयो यज्ञियो देशो म्लेच्छदेश-स्त्वतः परः ॥ म० २ । २३ ॥

† कृषेर्वर्णे U. III, 4 = "the termination नक् is added to the verb कृष् to draw, and the word thus formed means a kind of colour." Vide also P, III, 3, 1 उणादयो बहुलम्.

Nourisher (**पीवः इत्**) by the gift of such food (**यत्**) as consists of water (**अपाम्**) and herbs like the sōma and other vegetables (**ओषधीनाम्**), the ingredients of which are available every where (**परिंशम्**) and which we can obtain easily (**आरिशामहे**)."*

"Oh Lord God Omnipresent like the air (**वातापे**)! Whose sustaining Providence is manifest in the make up of all trees and plants (**यत् ते सोम**), be Thou our Great Nourisher (**पीवः इत् भव**) by the ingredients of the food which we resort to (**यत् भजामहे**), which is made up of cow's milk and other products of it (**गवाशिरः**) and which is accompanied by preparations from cereal like barley and other grain (**यवाशिरः**)."†

"Oh Lord Who pervadest all like air (**वातापे**)! Thou art (**भव**) the Maker of all (**करम्भः**). Thy Providence is manifest in trees and plants (**ओषधे**). Thou removest disease (**वृक्क**) and helpest in the advance of our health (**उदारथिः**). Be Thou (**भव**) our Great Nourisher (**पीवः इत**)."‡

These three verses give details about the diet of human beings. They lay down, in a descriptive manner, the main principles of human dietary on ethical and not hedonistic grounds. On epicurean, hedonistic or utilitarian principles even cannibalism can be supported, but on an ethical basis, however, only very simple and frugal feeding i. e., eating only so much food and of such a type as is strictly necessary to keep the body and soul together and efficiently going on in the world, is allowed. The first and the most essential item in one's dietary is air. Without fresh and pure air and that in a sufficient quantity no animal, no trees and plants, can thrive. This idea is suggested in the appellation of God used in the sacred

* यदपामोषधीनां परिंशमारिशामहे । वातापे पीव इद्भव ॥ ऋ० १ । १८७ । ८ ॥ † यत्ते सोम गवाशिरो यवाशिरो भजामहे । वातापे पीव इद्भव ॥ ९ ॥ ‡ करंभ ओषधे भव पीवो वृक्क उदारथिः । वातापे पीव इद्भव ॥१०॥

text viz., Vātāpi, Who is considered to be pervading through His Providence even our food. This idea is further enhanced and completed by the burden of the three stanzas quoted here 'pīva id bhava'—be Thou our Great Nourisher. The imperative mood here is simply a substitute for the simple present tense. Thou art our Great Nourisher. This means that food is endowed with ingredients that sustain animal life only as long as His special Providence is visibly working in it, viz., when (food) material is fresh and 'living'. This is possible only when the vital principle, air, persists in its unalloyed form. This test of the presence of vitality in the form of air of a particular assimilable t y p e, excludes all kinds of 'animal food' so called, since this latter is ready for consumption only when the vital principle present in the body of the animal in the form of life is expelled. No sooner this expulsion takes place than decomposition sets in rendering the carcass entirely unfit for any ordinary use but burial or cremation. Vegetables and cereals however, maintain their vitality for an unlimited length fo time.

The second and equally essential item in animal dietary is water. This is clearly mentioned in the eighth stanza by name directly, viz., apām. Without air an animal cannot live for even a minute or two. Hence a living being cannot abstain from fresh air for any perceptible length of time, because life or vitality—in Vedic language prāṇa—is nothing but a kind of air, an essential vehicle for the soul. But without water, it is possible, for a living being to pull on for a considerable time. nutritive or dietetic importance of water is here referred to. Its curative or medical aspect is treated of in the Vedas in many texts but this is not concerned with the topic here.

Next then, the third and last in the dietary of man

come vegetables and cereals, milk and its products the first including even herbs having medicinal properties such as the famous Sōma creeper, now falsely considered to be extinct or unknown. Grain, vegetables and milk make up all the ingredients of man's food. Fruit is a type of vegetable and can easily be left out if vegetables are available, though it is quite true that along with the three main ingredients of diet it serves as a great corrector of the digestive process supplying at the same time a good amount of blood-forming material. Thus the diet prescribed for man in the Vedas is purely vegetarian. Wherever an admission of meat-eating is pointed out in the Vedas it must be understood that it is either a misunderstanding on the part of the critic, or that it is a case of wilful travesty or studied misrepresentation. It is unimaginable that the Revealed Vedas which have such beautiful and complete instruction on agriculture to give us (Vide A. V. III, 17 given elsewhere and R. V. X, 34, 13 etc.) should support the abominable practice of eating meat which is entirely opposed to agriculture.

It must also be borne in mind that the best minds have condemned flesh-eating. The following extracts from modern European books are enough to expose the weakness of the theory that flesh is necessary for the human constitution.

The Bible does not uphold Meat-eating.

"For nigh two thousand years frightful tortures have been inflicted by man on his fellows; poor humanity has been persecuted, hunted, imprisoned, and slain with relentless cruelty and cold-blooded ferocity, and since the Redeemer walked the earth, man has succeeded in deluging the centuries with oceans of innocent blood poured out in His Holy Name. In comparatively modern times the terrible Inquisition swallowed up its countless thousands and even in our own country, the prison, the faggot and the block have claimed their unoffending and helpless Victims." (Is meat-eating Sanctioned by Divine Authority? by Sir W. E. Cooper C. I. E., The Order of the Golden Age, Paignton, Devon, p. 4 l. 28—p. 5 l. 9).

"Many of the religious teachers mentioned in the Bible who "stood up for the Lord" were essentially human and endowed with human tastes and weaknesses. They found the practice of eating animal flesh common among all peoples when they were born into the world, and they simply accepted it just as it stood. They were but *men*, and were liable to finite man's errors when he comes to interpret God's laws and commands." (Ibid., p. 6 lines 8—16.

"Believing then as we do in the immutability of God's word, is it not incredible to suppose that this Omniscient Being, when planning out his marvellous scheme of creation, should have created man a frugivorous creature and have commanded him accordingly to eat of the fruits of the earth, and a few years later have changed His mind?" (Ibid., p. 7 lines 21—28).

"It seems that an explanation of the seeming inconsistency is offered in the fact that Jewish historians have always regarded Jehovah as a Personal God; and once we clothe the Creator with personal attributes, we make Him subject to human weakness. Such a conception of God may well lead the mind into all sorts of errors, and it certainly appears that, as the whole of the old Jewish writers regarded Jehovah as a Personal Being, and moreover as a God possessed of the same passions and attributes as man, they found it easy enough to think that, as He was given to anger, jealousy, repentance and such like weaknesses, He might conceivably change His mind occasionally.

Throughout the Bible we come across passages such as these:—

"And it repented the Lord that He had made man on the earth and it grieved him at His heart"—Gen VI, 6.

"And Lord repented of the evil which He thought to do to His people."—Ex. XXXII, 14.

"For the Lord thy God is a consuming fire, even a jealous God."—Deut. IV, 15.

"That the Lord may turn from the fierceness of His anger and show thee mercy and have compassion on thee."—Deut. XIII, 17.

"Saith the Lord, shall not my soul be avenged on such a nation as this ?=Jerem. IX, 9.

Here is depicted a Being with all the worst attributes of mortals, anger, jealousy fury, fierceness, destructiveness, revenge evil; and then He is given a human heart and made to feel human emotions such as grief, repentance, mercy, compassion.

In other words, God was measured by human standards, and man utterly failed to appreciate Him; failed to arrive at a just estimate of His immeasurable greatness, of the awful magnitude of His might, majesty, and power; and of the profundity of His unchangeableness.

To measure immortality by mortality, the infinite by the finite, is impossible, and the writers of much of the Bible failed to grasp this, and so they formed erroneous conception of the Holy one and invested Him with attributes which essentially belong to man, but which are impossible to God.

The history of Christianity has shown us what terrible errors "zeal for the Lord" has led man into—persecutions, strife, intolerance and worse; and even to-day it is clear that much is put forward and done in the name of the Lord that may be regarded at least as un-Christlike". (Ibid, Pages 8 l. 9—p. 9 l. 31.)

"The men of old who figured so grandly in the history of the jews; the prophets, seers and sages who were filled with a consuming fire to turn the hearts of their beloved people to the Lord again, saw visions and dreamed dreams; they were persistent in their pleading, and passionate in their burning eloquence; they declaimed so much and for so long against the follies, vices, and crimes, the sins and iniquities of their fellow-countrymen, that they might well have been carried away by their fiery zeal into saying more than they had divine authority for at the time. They were unquestionably inspired men, but inspired men were not peculiar to the Jewish people; they have been found in many nations at many times. Even in our own time there are holy men and women who work by Divine Authority as did the men of old; yet because, they are human, because the divine current in man ebbs and flows as a tidal wave; because, in short, he is not and cannot from his nature be constant, we are unable to accept all his utterances as divine as the Vox Dei." (Ibid., p., 10, ll. 1--23.)

"It was their habit, as it is ours today, to honour their friends at their feasts by giving them of their best, and the fattlings of flocks and herds were often killed in proof of their hospitality. This is essentially the custom of a nomadic people, of every people who carry their flocks and herds with them, and it is as common today among the wandering tribes of all Eastern Countries as it was among the Jewish tribes at and before the time of Christ.

The Great Teacher, in putting before His audience this beautiful parable, (Luke XV, 11-32) was merely referring to their own customs, and not to His. In the parable of the Lost Sheep, in verse 4 of the same chapter, this is made clearer. He says :—

'*What man of you, having a hundred sheep.*' He does not say 'What man among us' nor does He all through the Gosples even personally associate Himself with His hearers in such human habits or customs, but invariably uses them as examples, in order to l e a d us along a path that we are accustomed to tread in.

His parables are all grafted on human standards, and the lessons thereof are the fruits of human life and experience, and if in teaching these lessons the Master refers to *our* mode of life, and makes His parables clear by reference to *our* ways, we must admit that He referred in this wise to human habits and customs, not because He Himself was by nature personally identified with them, but because it was the surest and most direct means of appealing to the understanding of His hearers, and we should, therefore, be careful in not committing Him to responsibility in the matter." (Ibid., p. 16 l. 9–p. 17 l. 13).

"It is distinctly recorded by the early Fathers of the Church that several of the Apostles were total abstainers from flesh-food, and it is more than probable that they were following the exalted example of their master.

Clemens of Alexandria tells us that 'Matthew the Apostle lived upon seeds and hard shelled fruits and other vegetables, without touching flesh'. (Pedag. ii, 1).

Hegesippus, the historian of the Church, as Eusebius quoted him (Eccles. His, ii, 2, 3), asserts of St. James, the first head of the Christian Church that 'he never ate animal food'—an assertion repeated by St. Augustine (Ad Faustum xxii, 3), who states that James, the brother of the Lord, lived upon seeds and vegetables, never tasting flesh or wine—'Jacobus frater Domini, seminibus et aleribus usus est, non carno nec vino'.

And abundant evidence will be found in the pages of the Ethics of Diet (by Howard Williams, M. A.) that the most learned and influential of the Christian Fathers – Clemens, Origen, Chrysostom, Tertullian and many others—practised abstinence from flesh-food and declaimed against the carnivorous habit with energy and burning zeal." (Ibid., p. 17 l. 19–p. 19. l. 14.)

"Let us draw a parallel between this case and that of many of the great families of our own country, or, for that matter of any country in Europe. The landed possessions of many of these great ones of the earth are vast and yield great revenues. They are firmly established in them, and the law of the country recognises their proprietorship. Nobody today bothers himself about the equity of their titles, the land is theirs, it has descended for generations from heir to heir, and that is enough.

But trace back the history of some of these lords of the earth; go back generation by generation; back to those days when strife was rife, and breastplate and morion, sword and spear, were important factors in the formation of family estates and the upbuilding of family names.

Go back to those 'good old days' when 'barons held their sway' and serfdom was the portion of the people, to those fine old times when the strong hand took what it wanted and held what it took; when kings confiscated the estates of those who opposed them, and distributed them with lavish hand among courtiers and flatterers, gave away with unstinted generosity that which was not theirs to give and enriched those who had no right to receive, save the right which *might* gives." (Ibid, p. 24 l. 16--p. 25 l. 13).

This is the teaching of the Bible on flesh-eating. Let us now see what science has to say on this ugly topic.

Meat-eating is condemned by science also.

"The habit of eating the bodies of slaughtered animals, which has prevailed amongst the people of the western nations for so long, has flourished unchecked throughout the past centuries in consequence of a popular belief that such diet is both *natural* for mankind and *necessary*."

"As soon, therefore, as Christendom can be made to realise that the practice of flesh-eating is not only *unnecessary* but also *unnatural*, and a violation of both physical and moral law, such an awakening of right sentiment concerning this matter is likely to take place that the wanton butchery and bloodshed, which now so disgrace our civilisation and Christianity, will be brought to an end." ("The Testimony of Science in Favour of Natural and Humane Diet" by Sidney H. Beard, Order of the Golden Age, Paignton, Devon, p. 1. l. 1-6 and 20-27.)

"Imagine a procession of 10,000 cattle marching two by two, in a line fifteen miles long, let 20,000 sheep follow them, bleating along twelve miles of road; after them drive sixteen miles of hogs, 27,000 strong; then let 30,000 fowls bring up the rear, over a space of six miles; aud in this whole caravan, stretching for nearly fifty miles and requiring two days to pass a given point, you will see the animals devoted to death in the packing house of Swift & Co., in a single day.

It is only necessary to think of the numberless processions of victims daily entering similar infernos, such as Armour's, Lipton's and others, and the abattoirs and private slaughter dens which deface every so-called Christian land (London has 400, and even cities like Bristol have 120) in order to realise how urgent is the necessity that this needless system of slaughter which is estimated to cause the cruel death of at least 300 millions of cattle every year (exclusive of smaller animals and birds) should be seriously challenged.

Christendom must be reminded of the words of the Great teacher, 'Go ye and learn what this meaneth, I desire *mercy* and not *Sacrifice*.' I invite the attention, therefore, of all who desire to live in harmony with the Divine Will, and to lessen the sum total of pain, suffering and sorrow in this world, to consider the following statements made by some of our most eminent scientific men." (Ibid., p. 2 ll. 8 – 33.)

"Comparative Anatomy teaches us that man resembles the frugivorous animals in *everything*, the carnivorous in nothing... It is only by softening and disguising dead flesh by culinary preparations that it is rendered susceptible of mastication or digestion, and that the sight of its bloody juices and raw horror does not excite loathing and disgust......

Man resembles no carnivorous animal. There is no exception, unless man be one, to the rule of herbivorous animals having cellulated colons. The orang-outang perfectly resembles man both in the order and in the number of his teeth.

The orang-outang is the most anthropomorphic (man-like) of the ape tribes, all of whom are strictly frugivorous. There is no other species of animals which live on different foods in which this analogy exists." (Prof. Baron. Cuvier. "Leçon d'Anatomie Comparative". Ibid., p. 4. ll. 1–18).

"'The body of man and that of the anthropoids are not only peculiarly similar,' says Haeckel 'but they are practically one and the same in every important respect. The same 200 bones in the same order and structure, make up our inner skeleton; the same 300 muscles affect our movement; the same hair clothes our skins; the same four-chambered heart is the central pulsometer in our circulation; the same 32 teeth are set in the same order in our jaws; the same salivary, hepatic and gastric glands compass our digestion; the same reproductive organs ensure the maintenance of our race.'" (Professor, J. Howard Moore, Chicago University, "The Universal Kinship"., Ibid., p. 5 ll. 24–36.)

"Today, there is the scientific fact assured that man belongs not to the flesh-eaters, but to the fruit-eaters. To-day there is the chemical fact in the hands of all, which none can gainsay, that the products of the vegetable kingdom contain all that is necessary for the fullest sustenance of human life.

Flesh is an unnatural food, and, therefore, tends to create functional disturbance. As it is taken in modern civilisation it is affected with such terrible diseases (readily communicable to man) as Cancer, Consumption, Fever, intestinal worms, etc., to an enormous extent. There is little need for wonder that flesh eating is one of the most serious causes of the disease that carry off ninety-nine out of every hundred people that are born." (Josiah Oldfield, D. C. L., M. A., M. R. C. S, L. R. C. P. Senior Physician, Lady Margaret Hospital, Bombay, "Herald of the Golden Age." Ibid. p. 6. ll. 1—17).

"I was contending that from the conformation of our teeth we do not appear to be adapted by Nature to the use of a flesh diet, since all animals whom nature has formed to feed on flesh have their teeth long, conical, sharp, uneven, and with intervals between them—of which kind are lions, tigers, wolves, dogs, cats and others. But those who are made to subsist only on herbs and fruits have their teeth short, blunt, close to one another, and distributed in even rows." (Professor Pierre Gassendi, Letter to Van Helmont, Ibid p., 6. ll. 24--34).

"The natural food of man, judging from his structure, appears to consist principally of the fruits, roots, and other succulent parts of vegetables. His hands afford every facility for gathering them; his short but moderately strong jaws on the one hand, and his canines being equal only in length to the other teeth, together with his tuberculated molars, on the other, would scarcely permit him either to masticate herbage, or to devour flesh were these condiments not previously prepared by cooking." (Professor Baron Cuvier., "The Animal Kingdom," Ed. 1858. Ibid., p. 6 and 7).

"It is a vulgar error to regard meat in any form as necessary to life. All that is necessary to the human body can be supplied by the vegetable kingdom. The vegetarian can extract from his food all the principles necessary for the growth and support of the body as well as for the production of heat and force. It must be admitted as a fact beyond all question that some persons are stronger and more healthy who live on that food. I know how much of the prevailing meat diet is not merely a wasteful extravagance but a source of serious evil to the consumer." (Sir Henry Thompson M. D., F. R. C. S. "Diet in Relation to Age and Activity", (1886 Ed.) Ibid., pp. 9 and 10).

"I have been a *Vegetarian* for about 13 years, and during that time have found that my faculties were better than before and my health has been excellent. I have found no disadvantage but every advantage in being a vegetarian. Scientists are coming to the conclusion that there are in meat certain things which are absolutely poisonous. My idea is that meat is very much of the nature of a stimulant, it simply bucks people up, and they can not be 'bucked up' without using themselves more than they should. The distinguishing character of vegetarians is their power of endurance. Now that I am a vegetarian it does not make any difference if I do not have a meal at the usual time.

I do not think that you would have any better example of the error people have made in thinking that meat and beer made good fighting men, than in the present war which Japan is carrying on. The peformances of England's allies, both physically and morally, are excellent testimony to the value of the non-meat diet." (G. F. Rogers, M. D., Meeting of Cambridge, May 12th 1905, p. 11 l. I–21).

"I sincerely hope that before the close of the (nineteenth) century, not only will slaughter-houses be abolished, but that the use of animal flesh as food will be absolutely abandoned.

We have also to learn, as a first truth, the truth that the oftener we go to the vegetable world for our food, the oftener we go to the first, and therefore to the cheapest source of supply". (Sir Benjamin W. Richardson, M. D., F. R. C. S. From an Address before the Congress on Public Health., Ibid., p. 11 ll. 22—31).

"The man who suffers from Gout, or Rheumatism is sick because he daily swallows these maladies at the dinner table, possibly at every meal he eats. As long as a man keeps on *eating Gout*, in the shape of juicy beef-steaks and mutton chops etc., he must expect to have painful twinges in his toes.

Eminent French and English physicians have, in recent years, shown that a large share of the maladies from which human beings suffer are due to uric acid.

Dr. Haig, the eminent English physician, has shown that most uric acid diseases are due not only to the failure of the body to destroy or eliminate its uric acid, but to the introduction of uric acid with food. The following are a few of the startling facts which these investigators have brought to light:—

A pound of beefsteak contains fourteen grains of uric Acid.

A pound of liver contains nineteen grains of uric acid.

A pound of sweetbread contains seventy grains of uric acid.

The following list of maladies due to uric acid is copied from Dr. Haig's great work entitled 'Uric Acid and Causation of Disease':—gout, rheumatism, headache, epilepsy, convulsions, chorea, hysteria, neurasthenia, nervousness, mental depression, lethargy, vertigo, syncope, insomnia, paralysis, asthma, dyspepsia, congestion of the liver, glycosuria, diabetes, Bright's disease, albuminuria, dropsy, gravel and calculus, neuritis, retinitis, cerebral and spinal degeneration, local inflammation of all kinds, appendicitis.

The above maladies are due to eating uric acid and it is evident they cannot be cured while a person continues to eat the uric acid by which they are produced.

A person's liver and kidneys may be able to destroy and eliminate the uric acid produced in his own body, while not at all prepared to deal with five, ten or twenty times the quantity." (J. H. Kellogg, M. D., Medical Superintendent of the Battle Creek Sanatorium, Michigan. "The Battle Creek Journal.' Ibid., pp., 13 and 14).

"The effete salts contained in animal tissues act as slow but sure poisons upon the bodies of those who consume them, producing gradually, first, serious functional disturbance, and finally organic changes in the blood vessels which are the structures by which the blood is distributed to the various organs, and which regulate such supply as is necessary in the respective cases.

This supply being interfered with, results in *degeneration* and *disease* of the various organs, and structures. The ultimate effects of this, and the disposition of the poisonous salts in various organs, is manifest as premature senility or localised disease leading to much impairment of usefulness and activity, and to a high total of mortality.

When death ends this sequence of events, the cause commonly given is the most prominent local manifestation–such as 'apoplexy', 'kidney disease', 'heart failure' etc., when in fact, the real and primary cause is *slow poisoning from effete flesh salts.* (Robert Perks, M. D., F. R. C. S., "Herald of the Golden Age," Sep. 1903. Ibid., p. 14. ll. 8—28).

"The influence of flesh-eating in the production of Appendicitis has been studied for the first time by an eminent surgeon of the Hotel Dieu, Dr. Lucas Championniere. The attention of practitioners of various centuries has thus been wakened to enquire into the dietetic causes of Appendicitis, and statistics have been received proving that the frequency of this lesion is proportional to the importance given to flesh foods in the dietaries of different peoples. Appendicitis is common among the North Americans, and also among the people of England, Switzerland and Germany, all very carnivorous. It is rare in the Italian who lives on cereals.

The observations of army physicians has enabled us to ascertain that Appendicitis is frequent in the Arabian who lives after the manner of Europeans and eats meat while *it is never found in those who follow the traditions of their ancestors and do not consume the flesh of animals.*

Members of those religious orders who are vegetarians never have Appendicitis. I have observed or operated upon several hundred cases of Appendicitis. My attention has, therefore, been drawn to this subject, and I think that my observations may be interesting.

But the most characteristic observation is that made upon children, and I invite your whole attention to this fact. We know that Appendicitis is very frequent in children. Very well,

I have never yet seen a case of Appendicitis in a child who had never eaten meat.

We can affirm almost with certainty that a vegetarian never contracts this malady. *The cause of Appendicitis is therefore flesh-eating.*" (Dr. Victor Pauchet, "La Reforme Allmentaire," Ibid., pp. 14 and 15).

"The alimentary canal in the *carnivora* is short—about three times the length of the body—and the colon smooth, so that the excretions, which very rapidly undergo decomposition remain but a very short time in the canal. Now, in Man the canal is long—twelve times the length of the body (trunk)—and the colon sacculated, thus the food remains for a longer period in the system before the residue is voided. It is apparent, therefore, that a flesh diet, which rapidly undergoes decomposition, is not *in any way* suitable to man. Nay, more, it is not only unsuitable, but it is *dangerous*, and is, to a large extent, accountable for the more serious diseases to which the human race is subject". Ibid., p. 18. ll. 24–36.

"A gentleman who lives in this town had a Cancer on his neck for four years. When he discovered it, he left off eating meat and continued to adhere closely to a pure food dietary. He soon began to recover; after a time the Cancer was reduced to a small growth, and finally disappeared and healed up. There is now only a small white scar on the neck where the Cancer was, and during the two years that have elapsed since that time the man has been perfectly well. I sent a specimen of this Cancer to an eminent Professor of Pathology in the Cornell University, and after an examination he pronounced it a case of Cancer in its most deadly form." (J. H. Kellogg, M. D., Founder and Medical Superintendent of the Battle Creek Sanitarium, Michigan. "Herald of the Golden Age," April 1930, Ibid., pp. 19 and 20.)

"Of 19,522 deaths among natives in Cairo during 1891, only 19 were returned as due to Cancer (females 20, males 9), or

1 in 1,023. In England during the same year I have ascertained that proportion of Cancer deaths was 11 in 29.

From these data it appears that the reputation of Egypt for comparative immunity from Cancer is well founded.

In Tunis, Algeria, and Morocco, Cancer almost is as rare among the natives as in Egypt.

It is a curious fact that the lowest European Cancer death rates are to be found in just those parts of the Continent that are contiguous to the North African littoral. Thus the Sardinian Cancer mortality for 1889 was only 1.7 per 10,000 living, that of Calabria 2.4, and Sicily 2.8. The Corsican Cancer mortality is almost equally low, and along the Spanish Mediterranean littoral Cancer is very rare.

In these parts of the world, as in Northern Africa, the conditions of existence are unfavourable to the development of Cancer. If I am asked to define these conditions, it may be answered that they comprise extreme frugality in living, open-air existence, and last but not least an alimentation which includes but *little animal food*." (W. Roger Williams, F. R. C. S., "British Medical Journal," Sep. 20th, 1902., Ibid., p. 21. ll. 14—38.)

"I advocate the simple and single natural food of Original Man even for modern Man, in spite of all the long centuries of mixed and cooked dietary of mankind. I feel strongly, very strongly on this subject. And why? Firstly; because the natural uncooked food has saved my life, has rejuvenated my body and made out of an over-fed, old man, courting apoplexy and rushing blindly into a premature grave, a comparatively young, vigorous and healthy person. And secondly: because it has, through my mediumship, saved many a valuable life threatened by disease, which would have succumbed under the unnatural modern diet, and orthodox treatment." (O. L. Abramawski, M. D. Ch. D., Late medical superintendent to the Mildura District Hospital, "Herald of the Golden Age", July 1910., Ibid., p. 26 ll. 11—25.

"It must be honestly admitted that weight by weight vegetable substances, when they are carefully selected, possess the most striking advantages over animal food in nutritive value. I should like to see the vegetarian and fruit-living plan brought into general use, and I believe it will be." (Sir Benjamin W. Richardson. M. D., F. R. C. S., "Foods for Man–Animal and Vegetable–A Comparison. Ibid., p. 26. ll. 26–33.)

"For the last seven or eight months, I have lived on purely vegetable food, and I am a hundred per cent., the better man for it. The fact that I am alive myself, and that I enjoy my life, and that I am in respectable health and strength, and a great deal stronger than I remember ever having been before, and a great deal lighter and more vigorous, and more full of mental energy than I was, convinces me that if one man can live so, other people can live so." (Revd. Charles Spurgeon, "Temperance Record," Oct. 1st 1885. Ibid., p. 29. ll. 21—31.

"Dr. Adam Ferguson of Edinburgh, the historian, after strokes of paralysis, became a vegetarian at sixty. He got rid of every paralytic symptom, became robust and muscular and lived to ninety-three. Sir Walter Scott thus described him: 'He is, long after his eightieth year, one of the most striking old men it was possible to look at. The mixture of original thinking with high moral feeling and extensive learning, his love of country, contempt of luxury, and especially the strong subjection of his passions and feelings to the dominion of his reason, made him perhaps the most striking example of Stoic philosopher that could be seen in modern days." (Watson's lecture on the "Principle and Practice of Physic," (5th Edition)., Ibid., pp., 29 and 30.

A most noteworthy and valuable personal testimony concerning the benefits which followed the intelligent adoption of fruitarian diet has been recorded by Mr. Eustace H. Miles,

M. A. (Tennis champion, 1899 to 1903, and 1905, 1906, 1909, 1910), in his book entitled 'Muscle, Brain and Diet' 1901). It is as follows:—

"When I began to use these (fruitarian) foods, I had to face 'well meaning' opposition, not only from those who had no education on the subject, but also from most of the medical men with whom I discussed the subjcct. Nay, more, I daresay that many of my friends considered that I was going off my head. It was not an easy life.

But when it was certain that, for two and a half years, my body and mental vigour *steadily increased* when I was abel to keep in constant training of body and mind, when I was ready to play hard Tennis match and do eight or nine hours hard mental work in a single day without feeling any real fatigue, and when my success at games, and the range and amount and quality and success of my work improved instead of the reverse, *then*, by degrees, even my dearest friends and relations, were forced to admit that there *might* be something in it in *my* case.

I found that much of my superfluous fat had disappeared, that my skin was getting a healthier colour, that in exercise and at games my clearness of eye, my skill, my endurance, and a strange thing, surely, between the ages of 27 and 32 my activity and flexibility, were gradually increasing, that my brain work was far better in respect of range of subjects, of sheer quantity, of quickness and of quality, then it had even been before.

All this will sound very like self-illusion 'you imagine all this'; the sceptic will say, 'but it needs *proof*.' In reply I appeal to statistics. That during the last year I have coached nearer to 150 than to 100 Honours' pupils, that since last January I have had the schemes of over ten books accepted by various well-known publishers, and—in the intervals of my coaching—have already written nearly all of them, as well as a good many articles. All this I can prove.

It is less easy to prove that I have never felt so happy as I do now, that I have never taken so much interest in things as I do now, that I feel altogether better in every way than I used to—that my motives in life are higher than they used to be—all this, I say, I can not prove. I can only ask the reader to believe that it is true". Ibid., pp., 37 and 38.

"The following testimony given by Mr. Samuel Saunders, of Market Livington, Devizes, who was personally known to the author of the booklet, was printed in the Herald of the Golden Age, July 1904:—

"I have abstained from fish, flesh and fowl for 62 years, and have been observant of the rules of health. I have never had a headache, never been in bed a whole day from illness, or suffered pain except from trivial accidents. I have had a very happy, and I hope somewhat useful life and now in my 88th year I am as light and lissom and as capable of receiving a new idea as I was twenty years ago." (Ibid., p. 38. ll. 21–32).

"Tuberculosis exists among cattle and other animals to an extent scarcely realized. Evidence from the public slaughter-houses in the large towns of England, as well as from those on the Continent speak with no uncertain sound on this matter.

I may remind you of the facts made public quite recently of the examination of the Queen's herd of cattle, where out of 40 animals, 36 were found to have been affected. If this be the case in the Royal herd, it is probable that Tuberculosis is scarcely likely to be less prevalent in herds less constantly under supervision". (Dr. Jackson, President of the British Medical Association, 1899. Speech at Congress at Barnstaple. Ibid., p. 23. ll. 16–29.)

The following horrid details about the meat trade will convince sensible people about the responsibility of meat-eaters for the untold suffering caused to sensitive living beings. The Sage Kaṇāda, the founder (?) of the famous Vāiśeṣika school of Āryan philosophy clearly points this out in his treatise. He says:—"Duties prescribed by the Vedas cannot produce their fruit, if the man performing them subsists on evil diet. Diet becomes evil when it involves injury (to others). The taint of such diet affects them also who come in contact with the eater thereof."*

Disgusting details of the meat trade.

"In a letter to the 'Standard' I showed that: 'There are three common modes of slaughtering animals, and the less usual methods are generally modifications of one of the chief ones. Animals are killed by either (1) cutting their throats and allowing them to bleed to death; (2) destroying sensibility by stunning with a mallet; or pole-axe or mask-bolt, and then damaging the brain so as to cause death; (3) stabbing the animal in the neck by driving a dagger into the space between the base of the skull and the first cervical vertebra, and so injuring the upper part of the spinal column or possibly the lower part of the medulla (depending on the direction of the stroke), and thus causing immediate paralysis to be followed by throat-cutting, or hammering to hasten death.

In none of these cases can it be said, as your, 'Butcher' correspondent states, that death is 'instantaneous' but none the less, it is probable that he is quite right in fixing two minutes as a period quite long enough for an animal to lose all consciousness in, when the first method of throat-cutting is adopted. For this, however, it is necessary to have both a careful and skilled man, while in a very large number of cases the want of skill of the slaughter man is shown by conscious movements (not the reflex epileptoid movements), which demonstrate that acute pain is still felt when the incisions are made for stripping off the skin.

When, as in the case of cattle, the second method is adopted, the total sum of agony which is inflicted in the public

* तद्दुष्टभोजने न विद्यते ॥ दुष्टं हिंसायाम् ॥ तस्य समभिव्याहारतो दोषः॥ वै॰ ६ । १ । ६-८ ॥

and private slaughter houses of the land is too terrible to contemplate calmly. I have seen a fine young sensitive cow dragged up by the windlass to the ring, and then, as the slaughterman brought down the pointed pole-axe with all his force, he missed the spot, and the weapon struck into the eye and burst it, and tore its way into places where the presence of many sensory nerves would cause the most atrocious agony. With bellowings of anguish, the poor creature dashed her head madly again and again against the wall, and it was some time (which seemed like centuries) before a blow was brought home and she stiffened out and fell.

The third method of slaughter, which is not in vogue in St. Petersburg, Naples, Venice, Mayence and a few other places, probably entails still more suffering, for, though the animal at once falls into a heap, it is through muscle paralysis, and not through loss of consciousness, while the injury to the posterior sensory nerve roots of the spinal cord would necessarily cause the acutest agony. In butcher language, an animal is said to be 'killed' when it is down in such a way that it will die of itself without causing the butcher any further trouble. This, however, is not the language of humanity, and there is no way of ensuring market deaths without the enduring of bitterest suffering by thousands and thousands of sentient creatures". ("The cruelties of the Meat Trade" by Josiah Oldfield, Order of the Golden Age, Paignton, Devon, pp., 10 & 11.)

"The usual method in vogue in England is to drive the animal to the door of the slaughter-house, and then throw a rope or chain over its horns, and then throw the other end of the rope over a beam, or attach it to a windlass, and so pull the animal in till its head is wedged firmly in a corner, or against a barrier while the creature is held in this position the slaughterman takes a pole-axe (which is a very long handled hammer with a heavy head ending in a hollow steel spike), and standing in front of the animal, brings it down with all his force upon the centre of the creature's head. The spike may penetrate the bone and stick fast in, and the man may break away a piece of the skull in getting it loose again, or the bony frontal bone may be so hard that it does not break its way in. In either case the beast may fall at once as if shot while the peculiar stiffening process runs all down the spine to the very end of the tail—a ghastly stiffening out in death, which, once seen, will never be forgotten. In some cases, however, the animal will not fall, but will only bellow and roar, and dash its body from side to side in its agony. If the rope or chain holds taut, so that the head cannot move, the man simply lifts up his axe again, and brings it down again as before with just the same result. If the man is strong and skilled, and the gearing is good, he nearly always succeeds in bringing the animal down in one or at most two or three blows, but if he is not very strong, or not skilled enough to hit exactly in the right spot, or if the animal can get its head at all loose in its agonising struggles, he may hit away for several times, and may even—in rare cases —have to stop and rest awhile, while the poor thing stands in all the terror of death and suffering before him.

Where ropes are used, and these have to be tied in a primitive way, or held by another man, the poor creature is generally able to get its head so far loose that much difficulty is experienced in getting it close up again and in hitting in the right spot; and what agonies are endured when an excited man is bringing down a spiked steel axe, blow after blow, with all his might upon the head, can be conjectured rather than realised. A blow above the orbit would break through and burst the eyeball, above the nose would force its way into the delicately nervous chamber where the olfactory nerves are all spread out and would cause intensest agony, while the front of the head generally below the margin of the frontal bone is highly sensitive, and a life-time of suffering could be crowded into those terrible minutes which prelude unconsciousness and death.

'I can't bear to eat a beefsteak now', said a well known actress, 'because I was passing a shed in a little town where I was staying a few months ago. I heard a great noise and shouting and bellowing inside, and so I peeped in......It was dreadful......Such a beautiful cow straining in agony at the chain round her neck......her lovely great eyes all one blaze of terror ......a great lout behind twisting her tail......a big fellow in front with his pole-axe trying to kill her......I was fascinated, I was hypnotised. I tried to tear myself away, but I could not. ......Every time the axe came down the great creature groaned and bellowed, and shook her head, and strained away in deadly fear and trembling......and every time the axe came down I felt it in my own flesh, and I, too shuddered,......The fellow was clumsy, and the minutes seemed like long centuries to me...... At last she fell—oh! such a thud......such a horrible, stiff, stark, glaring thing......and I, too, felt the pangs of death within me... I rushed home, and buried my head in my pillow and sobbed for the cow I had seen die so terribly........If *this* has to be gone through for my plate of beef I will never touch it again, I vowed; and now I am a fruitarian.'" ("The Cruelties of the Meat Trade" by Josiah Oldfield, pp., 11 and 12.)

"The Jewish method consists in throwing the animal down and then cutting its throat. Of this it is enough to say that the Berlin Society for the protection of animals has circulated millions of leaflets against this Jewish method owing to the cruelty involved in it. Legislators have been moved to forbid it by law, owing to the sufferings it entailed, and yet, horrible though it admittedly is, there is good reason to believe that it is not the worst method in use by far! If that which is upheld by hundreds of thousands of intelligent Jews as being one of the best methods known, be so bad, wherewith shall we classify the worst?" (Ibid., p. 14 ll. 28-39).

"Tolstoi once visited an abattoir near his home, and thus describes what he saw.—'It was the Friday before Trinity. It was a warm June day......The 'work' was in full swing. All the dusty yard was full, and cattle had been driven into all the little yards besides the 'chambers'.

At the gate stood carts with oxen, cows, and calves tied to them. Other carts drawn by fine horses, holding live calves with their heads hanging, dangling down, were unloaded, and other carts containing the carcasses of oxen, with shaking legs and heads protruding, and bright-red lungs and crimson livers, were driving away from the slaughter-house.

Through the door opposite to that where I stood a big red well-fed ox was being led in. Two men were pulling him. He had hardly been led in when I saw a butcher raise a knife upon his neck, and stab. The ox, as if all its four legs had suddenly been broken, fell heavily upon its belly, then turned over and began to struggle with its legs and hind part.

Immediately another butcher threw himself upon the front part of the ox, on the side opposite from the struggling legs caught its horns and twisted its head down upon the ground, while another butcher cut its throat with a knife, and from under the head poured forth a stream of dark-red blood, under which a blood-besmeared boy placed a tin basin.

While all this was being done the ox twitched its head incessantly, as if endeavouring to get up, and fought with its legs in the air. The basin was soon full, but the ox was still alive, heaving with heavy gasps and kicking out all four legs, so that the butchers held aloof. When one basin was full the boy carried it away on his head to the albumin factory aud another boy placed another basin and this one was also filled. But the ox still heaved his body and struggled with his hind legs.

When the blood ceased to flow the butcher raised the ox's head and began to skin it. *The ox still writhed.* The head skinned, showed red with white veins, and stayed in positions as the butcher moved it; from both sides of it the skin hung down, the ox did not cease writhing.

Then another butcher caught the animal by the leg and

broke it, and cut it off. In the stomach and other legs *the convulsions still went on.* The other legs were cut off and thrown where the legs of the oxen of one proprietor were thrown. Then the carcass was dragged a w a y and hung up; and *then* the convulsions ceased. The convulsions were over at last.

Thus from the door I watched the second, third, fourth ox. It was the same with all. The head cut off with the tongue bitten, the same convulsions. The only difference was that the butcher did not always hit his blow so as to fell the ox. Sometimes the butcher missed his aim, then the ox leaped up, roared, and, covered with blood, tried to escape. But then he was pulled under the bar, hit a second time and felled.

I afterwards went round to the door through which the oxen entered. Here I saw the same, only nearer and more clearly; and, moreover, I here saw what I had missed seeing from the other door—how the oxen were forced to enter. Each time that an ox was taken in the yard and pulled forward by a rope tied to his horns, the ox, smelling blood, refused to enter, sometimes roared and retreated backwards. Two men could not drag it by force, and therefore each time one of the butchers went round behind, grasped the ox's t a i l, and twitched it, breaking the stump so that the gristle crackled, and the ox advanced.

When they had finished the oxen of one owner, they led in another's cattle. Of this next lot the first animal was not an ox, but a bull. A well-bred, fine, muscular, energetic young animal, black with white spots and legs. He was pulled, he lowered his head, and sternly resisted. But the butcher, following behind, caught at his tail, just like an engineman grasping the handle of the whistle, twisted, and the gristles crackled. The bull rushed forward, knocking down the men who were pulling the ropes, then again stopped, squinting with its black eyes, the whites of which were suffused with blood.

Again the tail crackled, and the bull jumped forward, and was in the spot where they desired him to be. The striking man approached, took aim, and hit. The hit missed the mark. The bull leaped, shook its head, roared, and, covered with blood, got free and rushed out. All the men in the doorway jumped aside. But the ready butchers, with the pluck bred by perpetual risks, quickly caught the rope, the tail operation was repeated, and again the bull was in the chamber, where he was dragged under the bar, from which he could not escape. The striking man quickly took aim at the spot where the hair separates like a star, and which he found, despite the blood, and then the fine animal, full of life, fell down and writhed its limbs while it was being bled, and its head was cut off.

'There, the cursed devil has even fallen on the wrong side', grumbled the butcher, cutting the vein upon its head.

In five minutes they stuck up a head, red instead of black, without skin, with fixed and glassy eyes—which had shown with such glorious colours only five minutes before". (Ibid., p. 16 l. 22—p. 18 l. 33).

"In the first year of this new century we may calculate that *in England alone* over a million cattle are being done to death, over seven million sheep are offering their throats to the knife, and over two millions of pigs are sending up their piercing cries as they find themselves in the presence of a violent death.

This means that for the purpose of providing a *luxury*—not a *necessary*—of life, not a day passes but that nearly two thousand eight hundred cattle, nearly twenty thousand sheep, and over five thousand pigs are put to death. Divide this still further, and we find that every hour, the whole day long and the whole night through, there are over a hundred cattle knocked down, over seven hundred sheep, and over two hundred pigs' throats cut. Still further we may drive the thought home and impress upon ourselves that every minute of the day, and every minute of the night as well, two cattle fall, and fourteen sheep and four pigs gasp in violent death.

In *England alone* as I sit and write, this tremendous sacrifice is going on all day and all night, and for every single breath I draw in life, an animal ceases to draw its breath in a painful and convulsive death and all unnecessarily—*to satisfy a fashion in diet.*

This calculation of twenty violent deaths a minute day and night refers only to the higher and very sentient creatures and omits all thought of the thousands upon thousands of rabbits, hares, fowls, ducks, geese, turkeys, birds (game and otherwise), deer, etc., etc., which are doomed each day to die to swell "the food supply" of the nation. It also omits the vast number of animals who are slaughtered *in other lands* for shipment to England in connection with the 'dead meat' traffic". (Ibid., p. 20 l. 27—p. 21 l. 18).

The above arguments condemning flesh-diet have been taken from the publications of the good society called "The Order of the Golden Age". The beautiful little booklets written in a fine literary style attractively printed and got up are worth more than their weight in gold. The noble publishers have done a signal service to humanity all the world over in exposing the bare truth about the brutal fashion of eating flesh. It is a score of years since these lovely booklets were first published but the truthful and cogent arguments advanced in them in favour of vegetarian and fruitarian diet do not seem to have much impressed the masses as well as the ***intelligentsia*** of Christendom who in the same heartless, woe-begone fashion as before, have been going on killing and eating living beings. Nay, the consumption of flesh since, must have been on the increase.* A strenuous, worldwide propaganda seems to be more necessary now than ever

---

* But just read the following message of hope from the Leader, Allahabad, 8th November 1935, p., 9 Cols. 3 and 4:—

Not long ago vegetarians were regarded in western countries as 'funny' people and vegetarianism as a fad. But in recent times the progress of medical

before to prevail upon sensible people to leave no stone unturned in putting an end to this wretched evil. The following extremely rational and trenchant criticism of flesh-eating by Maharṣi Dayānanda Sarasvatī ought to be useful in this connection:—

The Economical side of Flesh-eating

"If of two cows one were to yield two seers* of milk and the other twenty it is clear the average yield of each will be eleven seers. According to this calculation a cow gives in a month eight maunds† and a quarter of milk. The shortest period of time after which a cow ceases giving milk is six months and the longest eighteen, between any two successive calving seasons; hence on the average a single milking season of the cow comes to twelve months. Thus each cow yields in one milking season of twelve months, ninety-nine maunds of milk. If

science and the researches in dietetics have led to the discovery of the fact that a vegetable and fruit diet supplemented by such animal products as milk and eggs is the most suitable for healthy existence and that meat diet produces toxins which are responsible for a variety of diseases and distempers. The report of the Vegetarian Society held at Manchester in mail week presented at its eighty-eighth annual meeting stated that today there was no authoritative dietitian who would publicly declare that a fleshless diet was unscientific or incapable of meeting all man's physical needs and that vegetarianism had enormously grown in public favour. If the vegetarian societies were to make satisfactory progress, it is pointed out in the report, there must be an acceptance of vegetarianism not only on health but on ethical and moral grounds also, 'an acceptance that it is not possible for man to attain to the highest moral development while he continues to cause needless suffering and death that he may eat; that vegetarianism is a basic reform on which it would be less difficult to build a healthier and more peaceful world.' This is an aspect of diet reform which the warring west will do well to think over. Peaceful progress of society can best be ensured by bringing about moral development which will be helped by eschewing meat diet. The Hindus are perhaps the most peaceful and tolerant people in the world because they are predominantly vegetarian either through religious conviction or economic causes. Not only in Europe but in the United States also vegetarianism has been making rapid progress. During the last two or three decades the trend in food consumption in America has been towards fruits, vegetables and dairy products, with less emphasis on cereals and meats,

* A seer is about 2 lbs.

† A maund = 40 seers = 80 lbs.

this milk were to be boiled with a sufficient quantity of rice* and sugar, say, two and three ounces of each per two pounds of milk—the average quantity necessary for a man to quench his hunger at a time—1980 men can be fed once with the milk given by a cow during one milking season. The least number of times a cow calves is eight and the greatest eighteen the average of which comes to thirteen. This means that 25,740 persons can be once fed to their satisfaction on the total quantity of m i l k a cow can give during her life-time. Now supposing that out of the thirteen calves a cow gives birth to, six are female and seven male, one cow can be the cause of the sustenance with milk of 1,54,440 persons in the manner described above. The usefulness of the male calves can be understood from the following details:— A farmer can produce, in a year, with the aid of a pair of bulls, 200 maunds of corn, and with three pairs, therefore, will grow 600 maunds. On an average a bull works for about 8 years which means that three pairs of bulls will help to grow 4800 maunds of corn during their life-time. Now supposing a man requires a pound and a half of corn for one meal, the corn grown with the help of three pairs of bulls during their life-time will be enough to feed 2,56,000 persons at a time. If the milk given by the mother cow during this period were to be added to this, 4,10,440 persons can be fed once. In this manner a single cow and her calves support innumerable persons with food. But if a cow were to be killed only 80 (eighty) persons can feed on her flesh once. Hence, to kill such a useful animal for the selfish satisfaction of a few and thereby deprive innumerable people of the benefit derived from it, is a great crime and a horrible sin.

The she-buffalo yields more milk than the cow but

* Wheat, barley, oats etc., can be substituted for rice.

her milk is not so wholesome as that of the latter. Cow's milk is congenial to an intellectual life whereas the she-buffalo's is not so. The he-buffalo also is less useful than the bull.

The she-camel gives more milk than either the cow or the she-buffalo but her milk also is inferior to the cow's.

Now let us consider the case of the goat. The she-goat yields at least one seer and at the most five seers of milk the average of which comes to three seers per she-goat in the day. The she-goat gives milk at a stretch for three to five months, i. e., on an average for four months during one milking season. Her yield in one month, therefore, amounts to 2 maunds and 10 seers, i. e., 9 maunds in 4 months, which latter, calculating as before, is enough to feed 180 persons at a time, and as the she-goat brings forth young ones twice a year, her annual yield of milk is enough for 360 persons. A she-goat brings forth young ones from 4 to 8 years, i. e., on an average duriug six years of her life-time. Hence the total quantity of milk got from a she-goat through her life is enough to feed 2160 persons at a time. If we take her kids also into account, say, 24 on an average two of which number may be supposed to die young, and supposing also that 10 of them are male and 12 female, the total yield of milk of the mother goat and her daughters will be sufficient to feed 25,920 persons once. If all the generations of 'progeny' of a she-goat were to be taken into account it is simply impossible to count the number of persons thus sustained on goat's milk. The he-goats are useful for carrying burden and such other work. Besides, with the wool of goats and sheep cloth can be woven for human wear. The ewe yields less milk than the she-goat but her milk is richer in butter and hence more nourishing. Just in this manner, all animals that yield milk are conducive to man's welfare in various ways. Just like the camel, the horse and the elephant also are useful. The pig, the dog, the fowl, the peacock are all useful each in its own way. He who desires and tries to benefit himself by the deer, the lion, the peacock and such other beasts and birds can very well do so [without killing them.] Two things are absolutely necessary for the protection and advancement of the vitality, life, happiness and strength of all beings and the knowledge and ideals also of mankind, namely food and drink, and clothing. Without the first, man and other living beings will be exterminated and in the absence of the second, man has to suffer untold hardships.

Nothing can be more heinous than the infidelity, ingratitude and tyranny of those people who kill and eat the flesh of those animals which possess innumerable good qualities, i. e., which feed on such worthless things as grass, leaves and fruits and flowers [fallen from trees] and give in return such a valuable commodity as milk, which when yoked to conveyances and the plough help man to grow various kinds of food-grains and thereby give him good health, strength mental and physical as well as courage, which love and are attached to man like his children and friends, which suffer him to tie them down wherever he likes, go wherever he takes them, move away from where he removes them, go to him whenever they see him or he calls them, run to him for protection whenever a tiger or some such cruel beast of prey is about to attack them, even after whose [animals'] death their skins save man's feet from thorns or serve some other useful purpose of his, which grazing in the pastures return at appointed times to appointed places to give suck to the young and milk to their owners, which with all the strength of their being are ever prepared to serve man and whose whole life is dedicated to the welfare of the ruler and the ruled!

Hence it is that by the expression 'aghnyāh........ yajamānasya paśūnpāhi' in the first verse of the Yajurvēda, God commands man not to kill animals but, on the other hand, enjoins on him the duty of protecting the cattle of the good man (yajamāna) who [by his good work of keeping cattle and agriculture] diffuses happiness among mankind, so that it may be well with him also. This is also the reason why from the very ancient age of the great sage Brahmā down to the modern days the Ārya has been considering the killing of animals to be a great sin and crime. If cattle are protected there can never be scarcity of food-grains, since the consumption of these latter will be much reduced by reason of even the poorest of men getting enough of milk for their use. The reduction in the consumption of cereals will lead to reduction in the quantity of refuse voided by the human system which in turn will cause reduction in ill smells. The reduction in ill smells will, turn, in bring about the purification of thc atmosphere and rain water, finally leading to the annihilation of the miasmata of disease which means health and happiness for all.

Hence it will be no exaggeration to say that the destruction of cattle leads to the destruction of the ruler as well as the ruled, for, fall in the number of cattle makes m i l k scarce and farming impossible. It is, now-a-days, difficult to get cattle, milk and its derivatives, even at ten times the prices at which they were available 700 years ago, for, during the last 700 years many flesh-eating races have come to and inhabited India, and they have been indiscriminately killing and eating away cattle, flesh, bone and all! When the root itself is destroyed, leaves and flowers will also be destroyed.* The cause itself being

---

* नष्टे मूले नैव पत्रं न पुष्पम् ॥

annihilated, the effect cannot continue in existence.

Oh flesh-eaters ! when you have killed and eaten the flesh of all animals and they become scarce you will find it difficult to desist from eating the flesh of man himself. Oh merciful God ! will not Thou take pity on the poor dumb animals that are being killed for no offence of their's ? Hast Thou no love for them ? Are the doors of Thy Court of Justice closed to them ? Wilt not Thou listen to their cries for mercy and save them from man's tyranny ? Why dost Thou not shed the lustre of Thy mercy in the hearts of the flesh-eaters and expel thence, cruelty, hardness, selfishness and foolishness that they may turn away from the sin of killing animals ?"

Maharṣi Dayānanda then gives the following imaginary dialogue between a flesh-eater and an advocate of the protection of animals to prove that meat-eating is not unavoidable as those addicted to the dirty habit of eating flesh try to maintain.

Is flesh-eating unavoidable ?

"Flesh-eater—The whole universe including animals and all, has been created by God for man's use and man himself to serve Him. Therefore there is no harm in eating flesh.

Protectionist—The same God has created your bodies Who has created those of the animals. If you maintain that animals are created to be food for you then it can be asserted with equal force that you are intended to be food for other beasts and birds of prey, for, just as you long to eat their flesh, lions, vultures and other beasts and birds long to eat yours. Hence it can very well be argued that you are intended to be food for these latter.

Flesh-eater—Man has sharp, pointed teeth like flesh-eating beasts; hence like them, he also is destined to eat flesh.

Protectionist—Your argument to support flesh-eating by instituting a comparison between the teeth of such savage beasts as the tiger and those of man, is doomed to failure, for, you as a man, in no way resemble them. You are a man they are beasts. You are a biped and they are quadrupeds. You can educate yourself and distinguish right from wrong but they cannot do so. The comparison also is not correct, for why should you not rather compare man's teeth with those of the monkey instead of with those of carnivorous animals? The monkey has teeth like the lion and cat but he does not eat flesh. The monkey resembles man in shape also, for his feet hands and nails [as well as his other limbs] are like those of man. Hence through the semblance of the monkey to the man, God advises the latter to desist from flesh and subsist on fruit and vegetables like the former. The semblance of man to no other beast is so perfect as to the monkey, hence it is right that man should abstain from meat.

Flesh-eater—Carnivorous animals are strong [and bold] whereas those abstaining from meat are weak [and timid], hence it is advantageous to eat meat.

Protectionist—It is thoughtless and foolish to say so. The lion is a carnivorous animal unlike the wild boar or wild buffalo which are pure vegetarians, but when the lion falls in with a number of men he may kill one or two of them and be himself killed with one or two gunshots or sword-thrusts. The wild boar or buffalo on the contrary will charge a number of hunters on horseback or foot and will not die even when wounded with a number of bullets, pierced with spears and cut with swords. The lion slinks away from the boar or buffalo but they are not afraid of him. Practical instances of the superiority of vegetarianism to meat diet are not wanting. Take, for example, a wrestling Chāubē from Mathurā [who is a Brahmin subsisting on vegetables, cereals, milk and butter] and match him with a meat-eating athlete. The former will surely throw down the latter and sit upon his chest and then it will be clearly proved whether flesh-eating is more nourishing or vegetarian diet. Is it possible to get nourishment and vigour from peelings as contrasted with the inner pithy matter? Flesh is like the outer husk whereas milk and its products like butter, are like the inner pith. He who uses these intelligently will get [infinitely] more nourishment than from meat. Therefore it is quite true that flesh-eating is useless, harmful, unjust, wrong and wicked [in the extreme].

Flesh-eater—But there can be nothing wrong in eating flesh in a place where nothing else is available or in an emergency or to ward off sickness.

Protectionist—This argument also holds no water. There must be soil where there are men and soil can be cultivated and cereals and vegetables grown. Where this is impossible man cannot thrive; it is also difficult for man to live in a country where fresh water, fruit and vegetables are not available. In emergencies also one can abstain from flesh-eating just as vegetarians do. Sickness also can be easily averted without touching meat. Hence meat eating is not good.

Flesh-eater.—If meat were not to be eaten, animals would multiply to an enormous extent and the earth would not contain all of them. Hence it is advisable to eat meat, for which reason God also has made them very prolific.

Protectionist—This is a specious argument emanating from a mind perverted with meat-eating. Nobody eats man's flesh yet man-kind do not grow with any great rapidity. Animals grow at a greater pace because a number of them are required to support the life of one man. Hence God has made them prolific.

Flesh-eater—My arguments so far have been

based upon the every-day dealings of man's life. 'Religiously, there is nothing wrong in eating meat. If it is wrong 'religiously' at all, as you seem to maintain, it may be so for you, since your religion prohibits meat-eating. Therefore you should not eat, but we may, since our religion does condemn flesh-eating.

Protectionist—The ideas of right and wrong are inseparably associated with the ordinary dealings of human life and it will be impossible to prove otherwise. All human acts which involve harm to others are wrong, and the contrary, right. Hence you will have to admit that killing animals which are beneficial to thousands is sinful, and protecting them, just. Stealing, adultery and such other deeds are considered sinful because they involve harm to others. Otherwise a thief does all those things by his light-fingered practices which a rich man does with the help of his wealth. Hence those acts are wrong which are harmful and those are right which are not so. When harming one person by stealing his or her property is a sin, it must be a greater sin to harm a large number of human beings by killing cattle. A flesh-eater does not possess those finer feelings which characterise humanity, such as pity. He is ever prepared to accomplish his selfish design by injuring others. When he looks at a robust and fat animal his 'mouth waters' and he says to himself:—'Oh how nice would it be to kill this beast and eat its flesh ?' When a vegetarian, on the contrary, looks at it, he feels happy at its healthy and happy life. In his dealings a flesh-eater quite resembles the lion and other beasts of prey which never do good to anyone but feel happy in interminably going on killing life and eating carcasses of animals thus killed. Hence it is absolutely wicked to eat meat.

Flesh-eater—Well, if that be so, we may not eat the flesh of animals that are serviceable. But when they grow old, useless and die, then of course we may eat their flesh.

Protectionist—The same amount of blame attaches to the killing and eating of the flesh of animals that have grown old and infirm in man's service as to the killing and eating of his old and infirm parents. A man who eats the flesh of animals that have died a natural death will surely get addicted to the meat-eating habit and will never be able to desist from the sin of killing. Hence, it is better never to eat meat.

Flesh-eater—I think one may eat the flesh of animals that live in the forest and are not useful to any body but on the contrary, positively harmful.

Protectionist—Even the flesh of such animals one must not eat, for they also can be turned to good account if man likes to do so. One pig or cock does more of scavenging than a hundred human scavengers can. Peacocks and other birds kill snakes and render human habitations safe. Man would be in a very bad case if other animals were to consume his victuals. These wild animals and birds are intended to be food for other wild beasts and birds, hence man should let them alone. If man were to explore the methods of putting such wild beasts as lion etc., to good use, he can do so. Hence meat-eating should be absolutely prohibited. Animals which give one milk and such other nourishing products deserve to be regarded with as great a care and affection as one's parents. From God's disposal of the creation also it is borne out that the number of animals must be greater than that of man, for He has created their food---grass, fruits, flowers etc.,—in greater quantities than man's food. Besides, these things [the food of dumb animals], is produced without any effort on their part such as cultivating the soil and sowing the seed; and where it is produced, He showers abundance of rain also. All these facts lead us on to the conclusion that He intends to save them and not to kill.

Flesh-eater—It is sinful, surely to kill an animal and eat its flesh, but when meat is sold in the bazaars one can buy and eat it without incurring any guilt. One can also, with impunity, eat meat offered to the deities Bhāirava, Cāmuṇḍā, Durgā, Jakhāiyā or that consecrated in the rites of the Vāmamārgins, for this would be tantamount to observing a religious rule.

Protectionist—If none were to eat meat or advise others to do so or consent in others' eating it, no animals would be killed, for profiteering through selling meat and misleading others therefor to eat it having come to an end, the slaughter of cattle [and other animals and birds] would totally stop. The following statement—verse 51* chapter 5—from the Manusmṛti is noteworthy:—"He who advises another to eat meat, he who chops it, he who kills the animals, he who sells or buys them for such a purpose, he who cooks the flesh, and he who serves it at table, all these eight, incur the sin of killing." It is a grivevous sin to kill or get an animal killed, and offer its flesh, to Bhāirava etc. Hence God the Merciful has laid down no injunction in the Vedas as to the killing of animals and eating their flesh."*

Dr. Peebles the renowned American Spiritualist, Bernard Macfadden the great American Physical Culturist and many other scholars and specialists have condemned meat eating in unqualified terms. For lack of space they have not been quoted.

---

*अनुमन्ता विशसिता निहन्ता क्रयविक्रयी । संस्कर्ता चोपहर्ता च खादकश्चेति घातकाः ॥ म० ५ । ५१ ॥

† From the Gokarunaanidhi of Maharshi Dayaananda Sarasvatee printed in the Dayaananda Birth Centenary edition of his shorter works; the Paropakaarinee Sabhaa, Ajmer 1925, vol. II, pp. 921—30.

The Brahmacārin's diet must therefore be purely vegetarian and fruitarian, his clothing plain and his life simple and innocent.

The following Vedic verses also are worth referring to in this connection:—

ओ३म् । उत्तिष्ठतावपश्यतेन्द्रस्य भागमृत्वियम् ।
Aum । uttiṣṭhatāvapaśyatēndrasya bhāgam ṛtviyam ।
यदि श्रातो जुहोतन यद्यश्रांतो ममत्तन ॥ ऋ० १० १७९ । १ ॥
yadi śrātō juhōtana yadyaśrātō mamattana ॥ R. V. x, 179, 1.

"Arise and look around you. See [the trees, plants fields and cattle] the share allotted to the man of power and genius according to the season. Among these things if any are ripe and ready for use accept them [and offer also to others], but if not ripe and ready, be cheerful [and wait till they become fit for use].'

श्रातं हविरोष्विन्द्र प्रयाहि जगाम सूरो अध्वनो
Śrātam havirōṣvindra prayāhi jagāma sūrō adhvanō
विमध्यम् । परि त्वासते निधिभिः सखायः कुलपा
vimadhyam । pari tvāsatē nidhibhih sakhāyah kulapā
न व्राजपतिं चरन्तम् ॥ २ ॥
na vrājapatim carantam ॥ 2.

"Oh thou who wieldest power, things are done and fit for use; thou shouldst therefore go and accept of them for the sun is already well in the middle of his daily path. All thy friends with their treasures have been waiting for thee just as those [self-respecting persons] who guard the honour of their families gather round the leader of the community who is endeavouring for betterment."

श्रातं मन्य ऊधनि श्रातमग्नौ सुश्रातं मन्ये
Śrātam manya ūdhani śrātam agnāu suśrātam manye

तद्दृतं नवीयः । माध्यन्दिनस्य सवनस्य दध्नः
tadṛtam navīyah । mādhyandinasya savanasya dadhnah
पिबेन्द्र वज्रिन्पुरुकृज्जुषाणः ॥ ३ ॥
pibēndra vajrin purukṛjjuṣāṇah ॥ 3.

"Cow's milk is known to get fit for use in the udder itself. Food is believed to become fit for use when cooked on fire. That is very good and fit for use which is got very fresh [whether cooked or naturally ripened]. Oh man who wieldest power, handlest weapons and art ever busy in thy occupations, accept of thy midday meal and take curds along with it."

The above hymn lays down that man's food consists of:—(1) cooked cereals and vegetables, (2) ripe fruit and (3) milk and curds and other products of milk. It points out also that the principal meal is the midday meal.

The following is a translation of the second verse of the hundred and fortieth hymn of the sixth book of the Atharvavēda:—"The two rows of thy teeth [oh child!] are intended to eat rice, barley, black grams, sesamum and other cereals and vegetables. This is the portion allotted to thee [and all human beings]—a portion calculated to fetch man immense wealth. Let not thy teeth do harm to thy father and mother."*

The following three verses also are of a piece with the above:—

"Whatever thou eatest and whatever thou drinkest, [oh man!] such as cereals or other agricultural produce and milk, old and new, all this food of thine I make free from all poisonous elements." A. V. VIII, 2,19.†

---

* व्रीहिमत्तं यवमत्तमथो माषमथो तिलम् । वां मागो निहितो रत्नधेयाय दन्तौ मा हिंसिष्टं पितरं मातरं च ॥ अ॰ ६ । १४० । २ ॥

† यदश्नासि यत्पिबसि धान्यं कृष्याः पयः । यदाद्यं यदनाद्यं सर्वं ते अन्नमविषं कृणोमिः ॥ अ॰ ८ । १ । १६ ॥

"Oh man! thou shouldst always think thus: 'I provide all those that depend upon me with enough of cow's milk. I give them in sufficient quantities molten butter which helps in the system the healthy flow of juices that keep human constitution in robust health. Thus well provided with healthy diet, may my men be brave and industrious, may this abode of m i n e be the resort of intelligent matrons." A. V. II, 26, 5.*

"The increase of two-legged and four-legged beings in my household is always acceptable to me and of whatever of cereals I possess. May the Creator, the Lord of Revelation bless me with cattle for milk and cereals and vegetables full of health-giving juices." A. V. XIX, 31, 5.†

There is not even the slightest mention of meat in these statements all of which refer only to cereals, milk and vegetables as the food of man.

The following statements also may be looked up here:—

"Those articles of food which are got by churning (**मन्थम्**) [such as butter and whey], cooked rice and the pulp and kernels of fruits that strengthen the brain (**मांसं**) all which I heartily offer to you, may all these be conducive to your vitality and may these palatable things let flow health-giving juices in your system." A. V. XVIII, 4, 42.‡

The word **मांस** is formed according to U. III, 64, **मनेर्दीर्घश्च** (i.e., "to the root **मन्** to meditate, the termination **स** is added before which the penultimate **अ** of the root is lengthened") and hence means something that helps to develop the rational faculty, i. e., a brain tonic.

---

* आ हरामि गवां क्षीरमाहार्षं धान्यं रसम् । आहृता अस्माकं वीरा आ पत्नीरिदमस्तकम् ॥ अ० २ । २६ । ५ ॥ † पुष्टिं पशूनां परि जग्रभाहं चतुष्पदां द्विपदां यच्च धान्यम् । पयः पशूनां रसमोषधीनां बृहस्पतिः सविता मे नि यच्छात्॥ अ० १९ । ३१ । ५ ॥ ‡ यं ते मन्थं यमोदनं यन्मांसं निपृणामि ते । ते ते सन्तु स्वधावन्तो मधुमन्तो घृतश्चुतः ॥ अ० १८ । ४ । ४२ ॥

The following interesting passages occur in the Brāhmaṇas in which the word **मांसम्** does not admit the interpretation 'the flesh of an animal' unless the interpreter means to commit an unpardonable absurdity:—"What is 'māṃsam,' is surely the most ancient of diets (paramānnādyam)" Ś. XI, 7, 1, 3.* "Food indeed is the 'māṃsam' of an animal." Ibid., VII, 5, 2, 42†. "He must not eat 'māṃsam'. Nor should he cohabit with his wife. If he eats māṃsam' or cohabits with his wife he will lose his vigour." T. I, 1, 9, 7; 8.‡ There are a few more passages of the type in all of which the words 'annam', paramānnādyam' and 'māṃsam' are enigmatic. They cannot be rendered in the haphazard manner in which Eggeling and others (even Sāyaṇa) have light-heartedly done. A long passage Ś. VIII, 5, 2, 42 and 43 stands in the w a y and obstructs the translator's progress. This passage 'calls the skin', and even 'the hair' of an animal 'annam.'¶ It is absurd to say that the ancient Āryans of India ate the flesh, the skin and even the hair of an animal. In Ś. VIII, 6, 2, 14; 7, 3, 1 and 4, 19 'māṃsam'

---

* एतदु ह वै परममन्नाद्यं यन्मांसम् ॥ श० ११ । ७ । १ । ३ ॥

† अन्नमु पशोर्मांसम् ॥ श० ७ । ५ । २ । ४२ ॥

‡ न मांसमश्नीयात् । न स्त्रियमुपेयात् । यन्मांसमश्नीयात् । यत्स्त्रियमुपेयात् । निर्वीर्यः स्यात् ॥ तै० १ । १ । ६ । ७ ॥ ८ ॥

¶ अथ या पञ्चोत्तराः । ताश्छन्दस्याः पशवो वै छन्दांस्यन्नं पशवोऽन्नमु पशोर्मांसमथ वाऽएतेभ्यः पशुभ्यो मांसान्युत्क्रान्तानि भवन्ति तद्यच्छन्दस्या उपदधात्येष्वेवैतत्पशुषु मांसानि दधात्यनन्तर्हिताः पशुभ्यः उपदधात्यनन्तर्हितानि तत्पशुभ्यो मांसानि दधात्यन्तरा अपस्या भवन्ति बाह्याश्छन्दस्या अन्तरा ह्यापो बाह्यानि मांसानि ॥ श० ७ । ५ । २ । ४२ ॥ तदाहुः । यदिमा आप एतानि मांसान्यथ क्व त्वक्क्व लोमेत्यन्नं वाव पशोस्त्वगन्नं लोम तद्यच्छन्दस्या उपदधाति सैव पशोस्त्वक्तल्लोमाथो यान्यमून्युखायामजलोमानि तानि लोमानि बाह्योखा भवत्यन्तराणि पशुशीर्षाणि बाह्यानि हि लोमान्यन्तर आत्मा यदीतरेण यदीतरेणेति ह स्माह शाण्डिल्यः सर्वानेव वयं कृत्स्नान्पशून्त्संकुर्म इति ॥ ४३ ॥

is called 'purīṣam'—dung !† In Ś. VIII, 1, 4, 5 'māṃsam' is said to be 'sādanam'—something that repels !!‡

The following verse from the Atharvavēda (II, 24,1) curses meat-eaters in the following strain:—"Oh ye who take delight in killing, who spoil others' happiness, ye pests, ye mean ones, may your weapons of killing revert and attack you! Eat them whose ye are! Eat him who has sent you! Eat your own flesh !"*

There is no mention of meat-eating in the Vedas. Flesh is not in the least conducive to Brahmacarya.

What is Brahmacarya ?

A rational sex-life consisting in the control of one's passions and perfect sexual purity in thought, word and deed is called Brahmacarya. For a sensible man Brahmacarya is a solemn life-long vow, whether he be single or married.

That Brahmacarya consists in the 'mortification' and regulation of the senses has already been discussed. Here the sexual aspect of Brahmacarya has to be considered.

Brahmacarya is sexual purity in thought, word and deed and hence in a narrower and more definite sense, means preservation intact of semen virile in man and the female counterpart of it in woman, by a direct exercise over the body of his or her mind-force and soul-force. Every person is a triple composite consisting of a gross physical body, a spiritual entity—the soul and the hinge between the two—the mind, a very subtle material means

---

† मांसं वै पुरीषम् ॥ श० ८ । ६ । २ । १४ ॥ ७ । ३ । १ ॥ मांसं पुरीषम् ॥ श० ८ । ७ । ४ । १९ ॥

‡ मांसं सादनम् ॥ श० ८ । १ । ४ । ५ ॥

* शेरभक शेरभ पुनर्वो यन्तु यातवः पुनर्हेतिः किमीदिनः । यस्य स्थ तमत्त यो वः प्राहैत्तमत्त स्वा मांसान्यत्त ॥ अ० २ । २४ । १ ॥

which alone renders possible the combination of the former two. The body and its organs being gross matter are attracted by gross material phenomena among which sexual passion is one. The attraction becomes possible and urgent only to what extent the mind relaxes its hold on them, and the mind in turn, loses its grip on the body and senses when the soul becomes so weak as to be unable to exert its spiritual influence over it. Of all the passions that rule a man's life sexual passion is the strongest and therefore needs the strongest control to regulate it. This intensity of the sexual passion is quite necessary, for, without it there would be no sex urge and no propagation of the species.

It is Dame Nature's dispensation that in spite of barriers of thought, convention and breeding men and women should, at a very casual glance sometimes, feel mutually attracted. Of all living beings man is the most conventional. Non-rational animals, depending merely upon their natural instinct go through life with the regularity of a machine without committing any breaches or excesses. Can it be that they also are ruled by a dumb, inexorable convention compelling them to stick closely to the law both in spirit and letter?

Man is rational as well as conventional, but his reason is very often wayward and his convention, with the selfish and self-centred accretions of centuries over it, absurd. Hence with an untrained and ill-directed reason he very often tries to break through it. It is exactly here that excesses are committed, for in the process, man oversteps the limits of his capacities. It is here exactly that Vedic teaching intervenes and advises man to become a Brahmacārin—a man of thoughtfully, rationally, regulated life. For regulation soul-force has to be exerted over the rational faculty or mind, and mind-force thus coupled with soul-force, brought to bear upon the body and senses. The result of this will be a happy, smooth sailing through life.

The Vedas, therefore, teach a man or woman to exercise rational sex-control and not haphazard and silly birth-control. Birth-control is simply another name for 'curtained' prostitution or promiscuous, selfish intentional sexual excesses. The ugly and immoral methods of birth-control teach men and women to give free play to their sexual appetite without incurring the slightest public responsibility and shame for their misdeeds. In other words the modern European methods of birth control such as pessaries, French letters and Onanism (as advocated by the late Dr. Annie Besant) purport to throw every woman open to every man's wiles and make her, so to say, a type of public property—a kind of live stock used for man's basest motives. Modern methods of European birth-control are pre-eminently man's contrivances to take the full glut of his lust grown rampant by means of everyday growing wealth—wealth acquired through preferential trade forced upon non-European races at the point of the bayonet or under the shade of bombing planes and with political legerdemain. The European man practises artificial birth control and to keep up his vigour for the purpose, ingratiates himself with monkey glands or takes recourse to one of the many remedies to keep up sexual strength devised by the good Christian scientists of Europe.*

The Divine Vedic Church, whose foundation are the Divinely Revealed Vedas, teaches that there is only one method of the regulation of the family—birth-

* Just now the Indian bazaars are flooded with many European and indigenous remedies, and Indian papers flared up with glowing advertisements about them.

control—and that through a strict mental and spiritual self-control over the physical aspect of one's life. For this purpose she places before every man and woman the monogamous ideal of marital relation sanctioned and supported by the Divinely ordained Holy Sacrament of Marriage. Sacramental marriage as it prevails in the *Ecclesia Divina* is not a step coming after the termination of Vedic Brahmacarya, but rather a consummation of it—a further grade of it continuing adherence to the same principles of self-control and life of study and service extended to two individuals united in the bonds of life-long comradeship. Their marital relation is not intended for unbridled enjoyment of sexual appetite but a very sparing, careful and intentionally well ordered use of the sexual contacts simply and primarily for the production of good, sound-bodied offspring.

Dr. Marie Stopes, almost at the commencement of her work 'Radiant Motherhood' says:—

"In ancient sanskrit, there is a work dealing minutely with love and with the different forms its expression takes in different t y p e s of people. This has been modified, added to and re-written by many later authors, and under various names works based on this are to be found in Sanskrit and translated into various Indian dialects.*

In these volumes much that is curious, and to Western notions, *absurd*,* is to be found, but also *several** profound observations which *appear** to be based on truths generally ignored by us. One of the interesting themes of these very early writers is a recognition and a description of the characteristics of the best and most perfect type of woman, the "Padmini." In addition to describing fully her physical appearance and characteristics, it is observed that she being a child of light and not of darkness, prefers *the supreme act of love* to take place in the daylight rather than the dark.

* It is a pity she does not name the work.

* Italics *ours*. These expressions denote the platitudes the authoress has imbibed with her breeding.

In this country, owing to our ***artificial, overburdened*** and *overstrained* lives, the physical union of lovers is almost always confined to the night time. Crowded as we are in cities and suburban districts, solitude in Nature is almost impossible; for most, seclusion is only known in a closed room after dark. The Sanskrit writer* of the sixth century, however, takes love more seriously† than we do, and he describes how for the sacred union serious preparation of beauty should be made—a room or natural arbour decked with flowers; and for the supreme expression of love (that is the love between a pair each of the highest and most perfect type), this should take place in the light of day and not the darkness of the night. *Even in our present degraded civilisation*‡ there are some who do realise the sacredness and the value of the bodily embrace in the fresh beauty of nature and sunlight. There must be many beautiful children who were concieved from unions which took place under natural conditions of light and open air radiance. The most spontaneous time for conception is the summer when our air is mild and sweet enough for true love in Nature's way.

In an empire where woodland or seaside solitude is not obtainable by lovers for this their most sacred function the distribution of the population is gravely wrong. It will, however, probably for some time to come be difficult for those who desire such a profound return to natural rectitude, to obtain the necessary security of seclusion amid beautiful surroundings. Therefore, alas, it will in all probability long remain only possible to most lovers to ramble together in nature, and then later to follow the usual course of uniting within their room.

We do not know enough about ourselves or the results of our actions, under our present conditions, to realize to what extent the hour of conception modifies the quality of the offspring. We only know that the child of lovers beautiful in mind and body, the child ardently desired by them, whose coming is prepared with every beauty which it is in their power to obtain, is often well

---

* Has he no name? †Just because it is a serious lifelong marital affair and not seaside flirtation !

‡ *Et tu Brute !* (Shakespear's 'Julius Caesar'.)

worth all the outlay of love and thought. Certainly among those personally known to me who have followed the rather exceptional course I indicate, the children are remarkable for both physical beauty and exquisite vitailty balanced with sweetness and strength of mental and spiritual qualities."*

What the authoress quoted above expresses comes to this:—(1) The marital union is sacred and intended for the propagation of the race and not for the indulgence of the sexual appetite. (2) The process of the conception of the child is a sacred act and hence requires special preparation, time and place for its consummation. (3) There must be mutual love between the parties that undertake this onerous duty upon them and they must be fit for it.

If this is the position where is the room for artificial birth-control? But the authoress in another book of hers proceeds thus:—

"Marriage is too often the grave of romance, and undoubtedly the disabilities of recurrent pregnancies, and the consequent necessity which married people have so long felt of using some means of prevention, have done much to deaden the beauty and undermine the security of the marriage relation. Alas! that it should be so, but without question many of the less worthy people have known better how to retain the adventitious charms of union than have those united in holy wedlock.

Ideally all knowledge of methods of controlling conception should be confined to the married and *those immediately about to marry*. Something approaching a sacred initiation into the rites of marriage should be available, under dignified and impressive circumstances for every wedded pair, but alas! this is a remote ideal, and today far too often the married are in ignorance of what should most vitally concern them.

* * * *

Some people, generally those who have been *brought up in the hazy ignorance of either an idealistic*

---

* "Radiant Motherhood" by Marie Stopes; G. Putnam's Sons, Ltd., London, 1923 pp., 9—12.

or a shamefaced attitude towards sex, refuse to use any preventive method. Not infrequently a woman who has had several children and acquired a fear of pregnancy so refuses and cuts off her husband from all normal intercourse with, possibly, serious effects on the health of both. Such people should try to realise that *because there may be a few inartistic moments in a course of procedure, that cannot rationally be held to prohibit the procedure.* It would be as reasonable to decide that as some of the processes of cooking and the after-affects (?) of digestion are inartistic solid food should not be taken. In this physical world we are to a considerable extent dependent on the physical facts of our bodies, which we cannot override without making grievous trouble either for ourselves or those around us."‡

In the above passage the authoress in plain language advises those who are married and also *those immediately about to marry* to use contraceptive methods and not to go acrying over spilt milk. 'If some inartistic handling of *check pessaries* and *French letters* have caused some little inconvenience, don't fear and don't worry, go on and go ahead, you will be all right, 'try, try again, boys, and you will succeed at last', she seems to say.

A few more gems need be quoted from this authoress' works to make her point of view clear:—

"Among baby's rights, I should perhaps also make it clear that there is his right that he should not be used as a *bulwark* between his mother and another baby in a way which is sometimes recommended so that a mother may go on nursing her infant for a very long time, sometimes even into its second year, in the hope that this nursing may prevent her conceiving again. *Such a course of action is very harmful both to the child and to her and should never be followed.* Such a practice is, of course, much less common in this country (*except among aliens*) than it is abroad where I have seen healthy children of even three or four years of age nursing upon their mother's knees."$

---

‡ "Wise Parenthood" by Marie Stopes; Messrs. G. P. Putnam's Sons., Ltd., London, 1923, pp. 26 and 27.

$ "Radiant Motherhood", p., 180.

What she says here seems to be that the observance of Brahmacarya—sex-control—by the mother who nurses a baby for a pretty long time is bad, she should push away the baby or hand it over to a nurse, indulge in her sexual appetite and bring forth another child, if not, take recourse to artificial methods of birth-control, that is good.

See how she falls foul of poor Count Tolstoy in the following passage:—

"Tolstoy's condemnation of any sex contact while the wife was pregnant or nursing may have influenced some serious men, but, as in many other respects, Tolstoy's teaching is so widely contradictory, and depends so much upon his own age and state at the time, one *cannot but regret the unbalanced influence his literary power has given him.*"*

Tolstoy preaches Brahmacarya, that is bad. Sex control ‡ or rational sex life according to this writer is harmful, birth control is the best.

The following passage, the last to be quoted from her, is very significant:—

"As Dean Inge reminded us (*Outspoken Essays, 1919*), there was a stage in the high civilisation of Greece when slaves were only allowed to rear a child as a reward for their good behaviour. I find a curious parallel to this in the treatment of a section of our society by our present community.

Crushed by the burden of taxation which they have not the resources to meet and to provide for children also: crushed by the national cost of the too numerous children of those who do not contribute to the public funds by taxation, yet *who recklessly bring forth from an inferior stock individuals who are not self-supporting*, the middle and superior artisan classes have, without perceiving it, come almost to take the position of that ancient slave population. It is only as a reward for their thrift

* "Radiant Motherhood" pp. 110-11.

and foresight, for their care and self-denial that they find themselves able (that is allowed by financial circumstances) to have one or perhaps two children. Hence by a strange parallel working of divers forces, the best, the thriftiest, the most serious-minded, the desiring of parenthood are today those who are forced by circumstances into the position of the ancient slave and allowed to rear but one or two children as a result perhaps of a life-time of valuable service and of loving union with a wife well fitted to bear more offspring. While on the other hand, society allows the diseased, the racially negligent, the thriftless, the careless, the feeble-minded, the very lowest and worst members of the community, to produce innumerable tens of thousands of stunted, warped, and *inferior infants.* If they live, a large proportion of these are doomed from their very physical inheritance to be at the best but partly self-supporting, and thus to drain the resources of the classes above them which have a sense of responsibility. The better classes, freed from the cost of the institutions, hospitals, prisons and so on, principally filled by the inferior stock, would be able to afford to enlarge their own families, and at the same time not only to save misery but to multiply a hundredfold the contribution in human life-value to the riches of the State,"*

What standard does this advocate of the capitalistic 'intelligentsia' and petty bourgeois of England has to distinguish between superior and *inferior infants* it is not clear. She complains that there are in England people '*who bring forth recklessly from an inferior stock individuals who ure not self-supporting* !' Has she forgotten from what stock Sir Henry Stanely came ? Aristotle was a man of a stunted and weak frame. Socrates was an ugly-faced, snub-nosed fellow. Of what stock did the good Jesus come ? Guy de Maupassant in one of his short stories says that Swinburne was a large-headed, small-bodied, sickly man and ate monkey's flesh. A cripple, a dwarf or even a sickly man may very often be a great saint, a good scholar or a sound politician.

* "Radiant Motherhood," pp., 210 & 211.

An apparently sound body and good looks are not all that make a man a man. 'All that glitters is not gold'. A person with an apparently sound and handsome body may be all hollow inside. *Mens sana in corpore sano* is perfectly true, but even a cripple can have a sound, i. e., healthy body, for, the lack or defect of a limb or two does not interfere with health. But *mens pulchra in corpore pulchro*, 'a beautiful mind in a beautiful body,' is rarely true. Rotten views are rotten views after all, whether they be expressed by a 'Paris Belle' or a 'Kashmirian Padmini' and are a sign of a rotten mind and so far, along with their authoress, deserve unqualified condemnation.

Such a condemnation in an extremely rational and sensible form from the pen of a great European Authority on the subject of Eugenics is subjoined:—

"The artificial prevention of conception has long been practised in secret, but only recently has it been openly recommended as being indispensable to a higher sexual ethic and to a thorough-going racial hygiene.

It is asserted, in the first place, that the adoption of this practice will protect married women from the injury to health consequent upon too frequent motherhood; in the second place, it will render it possible for weak or otherwise undesirable persons to marry without burdening the community with degenerate offspring. It is therefore maintained that Neo-Malthusian practices should play an important part in the realisation of a far-seeing sense of social responsibility. At the same time it is alleged that our natural instinct of revulsion against their unnatural and calculating character is no more than a foolish prejudice. In every direction we see man subordinating nature to his own intellect and will, so why should he not make use of technical science in the sphere of sex relationships, where so many important interests are at stake?

These arguments are sufficiently plausible to be in the highest degree dangerous. Yet it is easy to reply to them, In the first place, we readily admit that the sphere of sex should be subjected to the human spirit; nay, we might go further and even define sexual ethics as the complete subordination of our sexual conduct to our life as a whole, with all its fundamental interests and responsibilities. But nothing could be more radically false than to imagine that the methods of Neo-Malthusianism mark an advance in the subordination of nature to the spirit. It must be obvious to every thinking person that precisely the opposite is the case. The perfection and popularisation of these practices will not assist men to master their instincts and passions, but will on the contrary make it easier than has ever before been the case for man's sexual and animal self to dominate the will and spirit. For the artificial prevention of conception does not in the least control or discipline the sexual feeling itself. *It merely frees it from producing its normal results: and it is these very results which have, in the past, so powerfully contributed towards self-discipline and self-control.* Remove the proper and natural consequences of sexual intercourse, and a controlling factor of the first importance has been eliminated. We may therefore assume with the utmost confidence that the subjection of men and women to their sensual passions will rapidly increase with the increase of Neo-Malthusian practices. It will increase, moreover, for this further reason that the prevention of conception causes the sex instinct to concentrate itself, in a most unwholesome and dangerous manner, upon mere barren pleasure; here we have naked sensuality, stripped of all the nobility, sanctity, and responsibility which attach to the normally directed sex impulse, associated as it is with *creation.* Those who are today recommending the practices to which we refer, have not the remotest idea of the slippery downward slope upon which they have set their feet. Once let people begin with deliberate scientific purpose to pick out the element of pleasure from sexual activity as a whole, while neglecting its true meaning and purpose in our lives, then their remains no reason why the pleasure itself should not be enhanced by scientific means. It is no accident that this enhancement is most extensively practised in the identical country in which the artificial restriction of the family has been most generally adopted.

But it will be asked : Is not the liberation of women from the burden of excessive motherhood a great success on the part of Neo-Malthusianism ? It is only an apparent success. In reality it is women, in particular, who will be the sufferers through anything which increases sexual irresponsibility in men. Even the most excessive production of children could not endanger women so greatly or so deeply undermine the true necessities of their existence, as will the artificial restriction of the family. The male sex passion, when relieved from all sense of responsibility and from the necessity for periods of self-control, when artificially liberated from the natural consequences which lend it meaning and dignity and link it to the purpose of life as a whole, will necessarily become more pleasure-seeking and more recklessly selfish than it could be under normal conditions. The result will be an increase in every sort of disloyalty and irresponsibility. This will not fail to make itself felt at those times when the wife is least able to respond to the claims of a desire for pleasure, and in cases of illness when she doubly needs her husband's undivided affection. The situations which will necesarily arise from the man's sexuality being exclusively directed towards sensuous gratification and being unaccustomed to control, will far surpass, in tragedy, sordidness, and poisonous consequences, anything which could possibly arise from the most unlimited child-bearing Moreover immoderation in this last respect can be met only by an increasing spiritualisation and control of merely sensual passion, and never by methods which degrade and brutalise the sex impulse itself. It is true that these artificial methods may *momentarily* relieve much suffering. In the long run, however, according to their own inner nature, they must increase the sum total of human suffering in every sphere of life—for their effect is immeasurably to increase the subjection of man to passion and artificial sensuousness. This effect will be felt not only in the sexual sphere. It will spread to all the other departments of life.

We may therefore feel absolutely certain that along these lines there can come nothing but injury to the human race—even if it were assured (which is far from being the case) that these methods would result in the birth of none but the most desirable children. Moreover this result presupposes a superhuman degree of responsibility and selflessness, the very qualities, it will be observed, which will most suffer under the Epicurean philosophy which stands behind the artificial restriction of the family! While speaking of the question of racial health we may remark that it should never be forgotten that not only in the case of the individual but in that of the race, too, the strengthening of character, and the establishment of the spirit as ruler over the body, is the foundation of all health. For this reason, a married life in which all motives for the overcoming of self have been artificially eliminated must necessarily lead in the direction of racial degeneration.

"My teaching is health for all flesh," said CHRIST. Since, however, health is to such a large extent a product of spiritual and moral factors, and physical degeneration is frequently a direct product of weakness of character and spiritual bankruptcy, it is a false general principle to lay too much weight upon the physical conditions of the propagation of the race. Parents with weak physical health are quite capable of producing children whose spiritual and moral qualities are such as not only to convey an increment of innermost life-energy to the race, but to preserve the efficiency of a weak body, nay gradually to regenerate it. On the other hand, robust physical energy is only too readily converted into weak health if it enters upon life without preservative spiritual forces. This point of view applies even to the sphere of psycho-pathology; morbid mental tendencies are often counteracted and disciplined to an extraordinary extent through ethical factors and in general by the inexhaustible regenerative power of the spirit. On the other hand, a lack of moral energy, even in the healthiest men, carries with it the germ of mental morbidity and nervous disturbance. With regard to the whole problem of heredity, it should always be borne in mind that dangerous tendencies on the part of one parent may be balanced by healthy influences derived from the other. *These considerations must not of course be understood in the sense that I deprecate responsibility with regard to really serious and indubitable hereditary dangers.* My desire is to protest against the brutal and superficial "heredity-terrorism" with which certain modern eugenic enthusiasts advocate a regulation of human breeding borrowed from the stables and totally foreign to the human race, where the problem of the right or duty of propagation is so infinitely more difficult and complicated. In the case of humanity, spiritual and ethical factors have to be taken into account. Moreover it is only in the rarest cases that we find two parents who are both of them, physically and psychically, so equally and so heavily tainted or defective, that anything could be safely predicted with regard to their children!

It is indeed no accident that the oldest wisdom directed man's attention rather towards *regeneration* than towards generation, towards *re-birth* rather than towards birth, and forbade him to play at arrangement in a sphere of life where the combinations of the formative life forces are forever concealed from him. For us mortals it is impossible to recognise the real life-tendencies which are handed on from two human beings to a third; we shall never be able really to dominate our existence from this standpoint, but will merely pass from one hypothesis to another. We should therefore direct our whole effort towards the work of healing, reformation and regeneration, towards right care and right education. And all the methods which are thereby tested and practised towards the weakest and most endangered members of the community will come to the good of those who are apparently the most healthy, preserving them and their descendants from degeneration. This is the one and only true "racial hygiene"—all artificial prevention, all imitation of that principle of the survival of the fit, or elimination of the unfit, which reigns upon the subhuman level, rests upon an act of self-deception; we believe ourselves to possess a knowledge which in reality we do not possess. It is an ironical fact that those who are the loudest in calling, in the name of the race, for a death sentence upon the existence of others *are perhaps themselves the true pioneers and precursors of racial extinction*. These remarks are naturally not directed against that influencing of heredity which is demanded under the name of "pre-natal" ethics: physical and mental hygiene on the part of the parents, abstention from alcohol etc. This is rather a species of regeneration: it is not concerned with the prevention or selection of a particular potential child, but with the proper influencing of a particular child, the development of which one cultivates, but the coming or not coming of which has been left in GOD'S hands. This is the only right attitude for men and women to take up. They must hold fast to what is certain, and from that standpoint, in firmness and clearness, direct their outward activities. But in what is uncertain they must refrain from premature interference —it may be that some day, upon a higher level of spiritual experience, the knowledge that is now denied may be granted.

So much with regard to the Eugenic arguments in favour of the preventive methods. There are many other very weighty arguments which might be brought up against these interferences with nature. there is today, unfortunately, an increasing number of men and women who are quite insensitive to the profound *uncleanness* of these methods, either because they are not so constituted as to feel it, or because their feelings have been blunted by so much professional occupation with the sexual side of life. It is in the highest degree desirable, however, that the conduct of the race in this respect should be determined (as was once indeed the case) by those who have retained simple and pure feelings and not by those in whom they have been blunted! Life is coarse and mechanical enough. It must become completely coarsened and uninspired if no higher considerations whatever enter into the base search for pleasure and the dull utilitarianism of modern conditions. The present age is sadly in need of a revival of the feeling that there is a kind of shame and chastity which springs from man's simplest and unspoiled self, and is, in such matters as these, a much safer guide than cold abstract reason and calculating expediency. This inner chastity protests against the most intimate and devoted relationship of two people to one another being torn out of the darkness of elementary feeling into the artificial light of scientific technique and cold-blooded anticipation. The disappear -ance of shame in these matters is far from being a sign of health and strength—as is sometimes supposed. It is an indication of decay and degeneracy. What we call shame is the product of a deep and healthy life-instinct for the preservation of the unconscious and uncalculating element in the sexual sphere. This same shame it is which asserts itself against an "arranged" marriage; because the true position of the sexual should be behind that veil of self-forgetfulness which a great and passionate feeling throws over men:—

Wen Ihr's nicht fühlt—Ihr werdet's nict erjagen!

The suffering caused by excessive childbirth among women is certainly to be taken very seriously. The remedy is to be found, however, in an increasing liberation of the woman from every species of sexual slavery. The full establishment of the woman in her dignity as a human personality will work against abuse of this sort; it will develop a type of domestic custom which, even in the hitherto backward countries, will strongly counterbalance the merely dominating instinct of the man—a result which will be at least as valuable to the man as to the woman. Such an increasing outward resistance to his sensual nature will be of great assistance in man's own moral liberation; and this education of the man to higher spiritual freedom against the sex instinct is the second way to an amelioration of this suffering on the part of woman. Today, unfortunately, the majority of men find themselves in this respect still in an almost purely natural condition—they *must*, however, be raised above this level, just as they have been raised above the blind instinct of revenge which swayed men in the days of the family feud. It seems to me indubitable that the mastering and subjection of natural impulse, as shown in the sex instinct, is superior in cultural value to any other form of dominion over nature. Unfortunately our own age, in particular, instead of applying the great principle of mastery over nature to the sphere of sex, too, has largely sunk back into a sad and deadening naturalism. It appears as if, in this sphere, there was a desire for a complete rest from every king of spiritual effort, and a resolve to allow nature entire sway over the human spirit.

For example, there could not be anything more objectionable than the way in which today, throughout a great part of our sexual literature, the terms "sexual intercourse" and "sexual satisfaction" are used, as if it was a question of mechanical functions which must be performed with the same regularity and imperative necessity as the operations of digestion. From all this jargon the suggestion continually goes out that in this sphere man is born to absolute surrender and slavery. It is perhaps the very worst type of tyranny that public opinion with regard to such matters should be governed, not by the great masters of the will and the great teachers of love (who know that great joys are never won and kept without great denials), but by the great mass of uninspired men of the world, who have not the faintest idea of what is meant by the awakening of the flesh through the spirit, men who have no spiritual sense of honour with which to oppose the blind pressure of the sex-instinct. Here indeed it will be necessary to arouse life to strong and high ideals, and not to allow the true doctrine to be lowered through human weakness. There has never been an age in which there has been so much talk of freedom as in the present, and never one in which the most important struggle for freedom, the struggle against the world of mere impulse, has been so thrust into the background. But, as we have said, this struggle can be carried on only by the highest demands: here, if anywhere, are the words true. "Thou canst; then thou must!" It is precisely the great strong standards and limitations in this sphere which act as a true support and cure by suggestion for large numbers of those in a pathological condition, or of an over-strung type, while the weak following of impulse makes even strong people pathological. The ever-increasing use of excuses based upon "pathological disposition" is the best way to make unsound natures wholly the victims of their abnormal dispositions. Educators, in particular, should be very careful never to lose sight of this fact.

The great majority of human beings will never succeed in more than a partial solution of the sex problem. This is not, in the first place, any concern of the ethical thinker. It is not our business to form theory according to practice, but rather to inspire practice from the point of view of the highest theory. We must answer the question: What is true hygiene, *consistent* responsibility, and *real* enhancement of life in this sphere? Those who will still l i v e in short-sighted hygiene, half responsibility, and apparent enhancement of life, let them remain in their weak condition and endure the consequences. What is above all necessary is the heroic example of pioneers, true men who will bear witness in their own lives to the triumph of the spirit, men who will invade the lower levels with a definite example and testimony—and equally necessary is the example of true women who will demand *men* and not puppets, and will refuse to encourage man in his weakness and mere slavery to instinct, but will demand great tests of will-power, as once upon a time the women of the *Minnezeit* demanded noble deeds of those who sought their favour. In such a fashion, through the strengthening of the soul, will men become fit for true love. In the modern way, however, they will be fit only for the nerve doctor.

Perhaps it is because there is so much talk about freedom of personality in our age that so little of it is practised. If at one time, in the early centuries of Christianity, husbands and wives w e r e able to live together as brothers and sisters, for the glory of CHRIST, as a glad witness of the newly discovered power of the spiritual man, then it should not be altogether too high a goal for the "free" man of today to obtain a sufficient amount of control over his sense-nature not to use or abuse the companion of his life solely in the work of propagation. Or must we accept the sexual impulse as the sole and all-powerful genius of the human race, and is there no omnipotent GOD in life to give us freedom when we earnestly seek it? Through the spiritual domination and education of the sex instinct, that which nature gives to man is neither reduced nor despised. Sex is then linked to the highest spiritual sources of joy, and thereby experienced with a *thousand times greater intensity*. There is an intimate connection between *Seligkeit* (felicity) and *Seele* (the soul). The most elementary condition of all true spiritual culture is *the training of the will*,—not that weak surrender to instinct and illusion through which man ultimately becomes the slave of the outer world and of his own physical and nervous condition!"

* * * * *

"A considerable number of writings in defence of Neo-Malthusian principles have appeared since the foregoing section was completed. The influence of these works is peculiarly insidious, because the suggestions they contain are put forward, not in the interests of individual self-indulgence, but in the interests of *eugenics or racial hygiene*, and in the name of *the emancipation of women* from the burden of excessive childbirth—more especially among the poor.

When, in spite of such considerations, I persist in retaining my convictions, it is perfectly clear to me that I shall be separating myself from the prevailing tendencies of the age. Along with the disappearance of belief in a spiritual world arises the danger that even earnest and noble men and women will be influenced in their consideration of the deeper things of life by the newest and most tangible facts alone, and will be inaccessible to all arguments going beyond the scope of mere practical sense and expediency. It would appear as if the preponderance of an intellect directed towards external things destroyed not only belief in the invisible world in a religious sense, but also undermined the power of grasping the full value and reality of certain *imponderabilia* in earthly life, and of understanding the deep-growing spiritual injuries which may proceed from apparently harmless and even outwardly beneficial things. Closely connected with this is the method of the typical modern reformer (which might be illustrated by a number of examples taken from this book)—a method according to which he bases his suggestions upon some particular evil which is fully described and emphasized, the attention of the public being thereby totally distracted from the consideration of the possibly much greater evils which may lie behind the immediate and obvious advantages which the reformer himself offers!

It is a main argument of the Neo-Malthusians that the prevention of conception is no more than a continuation of the great process of civilisation—the subjection of nature to reason. This is a piece of pure sophistry. In the foregoing remarks we have already pointed out that the artificial restriction of the family is anything but a triumph of the spirit over natural forces. It is merely a mechanical prevention of certain natural consequences of these forces, and it must contribute towards subjecting man still further to the dominion of these forces, since it removes those important restrictions which nature herself has set in the way of natural sexual impulses. We do not go so far as to assert that married people should not come together unless they have the intention and the possibility of producing a child; genuine love is an equally justifiable motive for the consummation, of t h e i r passion. But the conscious, deliberate prevention of conception brings an entirely new factor into the whole sex-relationship. It introduces an element of technical routine into that which should be as far removed as possible from all routine; it represents a concentration upon the mere mechanism of sexual love—a side of life which should be veiled over with a spiritual garment and not be dragged forward into the forefront of our consciousness and made the object of a special technique. Practices of this kind cannot be carried on without a gradual coarsening and disintegration of feeling, in consequence of which (especially in the man) sensibilities will be dulled which can hardly be described in words, but which are of decisive importance for the whole spiritual and moral nature, particularly on the sexual side. In the sexual organisation of the man there is always a danger that the mere impulse towards sexual gratification will break loose from all other physiological and spiritual aspects of sexual life. All deeper masculine education—not least man's education through womanly feeling—has tended to restrain the merely sensual element and to unite the brute instinct with a whole world of higher sensibilities which veil it over and place it more or less in the mental background. But what is the part played by the artificial prevention of conception? It drags this brute element, this thirst for mere sensual gratification, away from its spiritual and moral associations, its great redeeming and sanctifying influences, thereby producing a spiritual injury of incalculable seriousness—an injury the very essence of which is the liberation of the natural from the controlling spiritual. Pure-minded women are often the least able to understand this point of view, because they are either lacking in sensual feeling or their sensuality is of a much more refined type than that of the man. Practices of this kind will therefore be much less injurious to them than to their husbands. Their influence upon the man's whole erotic nature is profoundly corrupting. Our arm-chair "sexual reformers" do not go out of their way to consider this; they have not the faintest notion of the spiritual foundation of racial health, and cannot realise that the psycho-therapeutical standpoint is here of great importance. Even supposing that the adoption of Neo-Malthusian principles would really lead to the suppression of unsound children, and to the breeding of a large number of healthy children, there would still remain the decisive question: Would not this practice operate, physiologically and psychologically, in such a fashion as to corrupt the whole sphere of sex, and produce such a degeneration of natural instinct, such a disturbance of higher erotic feelings, that in the course of a few generations even the best human material would become physically, psychically and nervously degenerate, as a consequence of this disintegrating tendency? These possibilities do not occur to the advocates of Neo-Malthusianism. Like so many other modern reformers, they are Utopians and shallow optimists, who refuse to perceive the darker side of human nature, and have no concrete perception of all the lower tendencies in man which such practices would liberate and morbidly stimulate."

* * * * *

"It will perhaps be said in reply that my own position also involves a great optimism. Will men, for such intangible reasons, really abandon the exceedingly immediate and practical advantages and pleasures, which the artificial restriction of the family places within their grasp? Believe me, I am under no such illusion. My remarks are addressed to a small circle who will understand my meaning without further explanation. I do not for a moment doubt that the modern devices for the prevention of conception will spread like wildfire. But we shall not have long to wait for the results. Then the time will come when large masses of men and women will again enrol themselves under the protection of those great principles which are today scorned and rejected!" "MARRIAGE AND THE SEX PROBLEM." by Dr. F. W. Foerster, Special Lecturer in Ethics and Psychology at the University of Zürich, translated by Dr. Meyrick Booth. B. Sc., Ph. D.; Messrs Wells Gardner, Darton & Co. Ltd., London, 1912 pp., 92—109).

'Birth-control' is only a symptom, so to say, of the growing immorality among sensually-minded people all over the world. To nip the evil in the bud (but it has grown and is growing apace) a sincere change of heart to bring better times is absolutely necessary. Sensual inclinations have much to do with breeding and habits.

The evil effects of breeding can be rectified by good company but a change of habits is very essential. The worst of these habits that has undermined the moral hygiene of the west and westernised people wherever they may be, as also of a very great majority of mankind all over the world during these days, is flesh or meat diet, i. e., the eating of flesh, fish and eggs. Flesh-diet is essentially immoral and sensual as it unnecessarily excites the sexual appetite on account of the presence of certain salts (not always effete) and acids in large quantities which produce unnecessary heat in the human system, and bringing about certain transformations in the blood and nerve cells, ultimately cause sexual pre-occupation and worry in the mind. The use of intoxicants and tobacco also are undesirable in this connection.

A wilful persistence in these unnatural and evil habits and trying to grapple with imaginary causes of the growing immoral practices will not help us solve the difficulty that has beset the whole world and threatens to ruin the human race in the near future. Racial and national immorality backed by a thoughtless life of ease is the last symptom before the downfall of a nation. History bears witness to this fact. The Medes, the ancient Persians, the Phoenicians, the Greeks, the Romans and many other races that rose to political power in the world were all sunk in gross immorality before their fall.

The generous and able writer quoted above has hinted at the evil consequences that will overtake those of the European races that are wilfully encouraging sexual levity under some or other deceptive name. But he has refrained from mentioning any of these clearly. It is better to state the unpleasant truth and awaken the conscience of such fortunate men and women as God intends to send forth as His worthy messengers preaching to the future 'fallen-humanity' a sincere change of heart and return to their Eternal Father.

A good many of the ugly effects of this growing immorality are already apparent among western people, Political falsehoods, breaking of the plighted word, discarding of a religion demanding a high moral standard of life and going after easier, man-made systems of thought and the keeping up of a false and artificial procedure of etiquette in social life, all these are eating into the vitals of European society.

The evil itself is very old, only the symptoms have become very obvious now. Oscar Wilde* was a result of it. It will not be long before many like him will rank among the very pique of society and their ugly deeds will be overlooked even by the opportunist, factious governments of the world. Well-fed, lusty capitalists will give full play to their sensual inclinations without shame and pass for good men. The sin of Sodom,† even sadism will be widely practised. Those women who, playing into the hands of immoral men take recourse to contraceptive methods will find themselves replaced by eunuchs and summarily dismissed from a pseudo-conjugal life. God forbid it should be so, but the world forcibly led by wealthy, war-minded Europe is heading for a moral disaster of the first magnitude.

To quote Dr. Foerster again:—

"The author knows only too well that he will not

---

* In a dirty poem of his, *Charmides*. Wilde describes a man rising from his bed in the morning loosening his embrace of *some dear body*, i. e., a body either male or female! What a heinous, diabolical idea!! What disedification! What scandal!!

‡ See the Old Testament, Genesis XIX. See also Livy's History of the Punic Wars, Book XXII, Sections 3 and 4.

convert the upholders of the "new morality". He therefore appeals, in the first place, to the young men and women of today. It is his sincere hope that they will not be so misled by the plausible phrases of modern writers, and by the term "new morality," as to believe that any fresh vital force lies behind the new gospel of moral license. On the contrary, this whole tendency is a symptom of *weakness and exhaustion.* It is an old and tired phase of thought, which *resigns the will to the dominion of instincts and desires.* Even at its best, it stands for a weak and short-sighted sympathy, lacking in the manly knowledge that the most merciful social system is one founded upon definite order. The conquering spiritual power of the old way of life best corresponds to the temper of youth. Here youthful strength finds its highest aims. Here it meets with its greatest test of will power at the very threshold of life." ("Marriage and the Sex Problem", Foerster, p. 225.)

Oh what a terrible fall! The modern European woman, a dupe of the lusty modern European capitalist man, acts the part of the victim to his pleasure to perfection. She exhibits her charms on the cinema screen for his pleasure; she sings in the gramaphone record to lull him out of his day's money-making business worries and last but not least, she takes recourse to contraceptives to appease his growing sensual appetite.

The ancient Āryan Sages of India very powerfully grappled with this question. For example, the sage Bhṛgu in his edition of the Manusmṛti lays down the following rules for the guidance of the right-minded husband and wife:—(1) A married man or woman must never approach another's spouse. (2) The couple may meet on all *nights* out of the sixteen since the beginning of the wife's monthly 'illness' except the four *nights* of the illness itself, the eleventh, the thirteenth, the fourteenth and the fifteenth of the dark or bright half of the month and any other days when either of the pair is indisposed. (3) They should necessarily meet on these occasions for the production of children, but it should not be understood from this that their occasional union (on other nights not prohibited) for the gratification of one or the other of them is totally forbidden.

Nocturnal meeting is ordained in preference to diurnal since the latter is apt to produce intense heat in the system thus leading to indisposition and even to serious mishaps. The setting apart of the sixteen days is justified by the fact that the right period of fecundation of the ovum with the sperm covers so many days more or less from the day of 'illness.' The exempted days are considered unsuitable on account of certain lunar (and solar) influences on the human system. The removal of the four days of 'illness' and any other days of the spouse's indisposition from the list is easy to understand. But the other 'provisions' also of the Bhārgavī Manusmṛti in this connection are based on very profound and important scientific truths which modern scientists refuse to understand.

Following these rules, says Bhṛgu, the householder will indeed be a Brahmacārin.*

Thus man's life is essentially a life of Brahmacarya and cannot be anything else since his body is a Kṣudrabrahmāṇḍa (=a miniature universe) and his soul—brahma is the abode of God—Brahma. The fulfilment of this

---

* ऋतुकालाभिगामी स्यात्स्वदारनिरतः सदा ।
पर्ववर्जं व्रजेच्चैनां तद्व्रतो रतिकाम्यया ॥ म० ३ । ४५ ॥

ऋतुः स्वाभाविकः स्त्रीणां रात्रयः षोडश स्मृताः ।
चतुर्भिरितरैः सार्धमहोभिः सद्विगर्हितैः ॥ ४६ ॥

तासामाद्याश्चतस्रस्तु निन्दितैकादशी च या ।
त्रयोदशी च शेषास्तु प्रशस्ता दश रात्रयः ॥ ४७ ॥

निन्द्यास्वष्टासु चान्यासु स्त्रियो रात्रिषु वर्जयन् ।
ब्रह्मचार्येव भवति यत्र तत्राश्रमे वसन् ॥ ५० ॥

three-fold existence is what is called Brahmacarya. The maintenance of the

6333

in his kṣudra-brahmāṇḍa and the surrounding universe is possible only through a life of thorough Brahmacarya. The six-fold constitution of a body has already been explained. There is a seven-fold composition also of the living frame known to science of which the ingredients are:—(1) rasa (chyle); (2) rakta (blood); (3) māṃsa (flesh); (4) mēdā (fat); (5) asthi (bone); (6) majjā (marrow) and (7) vīrya (semen, both male and female). A healthy body —*corpus sanum*—is possible only when all these ingredients of the *animal* frame are intact. They form therefore, an aggregate of the natural phenomena that necessarily unite in the formation of a living body.

Each successive item in this list is more important and precious than the preceding, the last being the greatest and rarest of all since it forms the nucleus of the very making of a living being. It forms the very basis, the foundation, nay, the essence itself of all the muscles, bones, sinews, nerves, veins, arteries, capillaries, etc., etc., the great 6333 in the animal system. Those who advocate the use of contraceptives have, unjustly and mischievously belittled the significance of this very important element, *semen*, the loss of which in most cases means the ruin of the life of the loser.

Hence the pertinent question arises

How can Brahmarya be maintained ?

Simple living and high thinking is the best means to attain this end. Light and only sufficient clothing, an entirely vegetarian diet (completely excluding flesh, fish and eggs), total abstinence from all intoxicants, luxuries and 'unnecessaries,' and a life of study, meditation and prayer and hard physical labour—all this forms the only and the surest course to keep Brahmacarya. Fresh air and residence in a healthy and clean locality as well as anatomical exercise is necessary but this is not the subject of this book.

Did the Brahmacarin beg his living?

A reference to the 'Hymn on Penury R̄. V. X, 155 given elsewhere in this book. will make it clear to the reader that the idea of begging on the part of any but the Sannyāsin is repugnant to the Vedas. It seems however probable, that the poor student was asked to beg his bread and study that he may, under no circumstances, remain ignorant. It is reasonable to suppose that if a Brahmacārin were to go abegging, say every three hours a day, his studies would be interfered with. Hence it is not clearly intelligible how certain scholars came to represent the ancient Brahmacārin as a beggar. It is not right to think that the ancient Āryan kings and rich men of India compelled their children to beg, for, ancient authorities do not at all support this view.

The Earth is for the Wise and Righteous. Benefactors of Their People.

ओ३म् ॥ प्रैष स्तोमः पृथिवीमन्तरिक्षं वनस्पतीं-
रोषधी राये अश्याः । देवोदेवः सुहवो भूतु मह्यं मा
नो माता पृथिवी दुर्मतौ धात् ॥ ऋ० ५।४२।१६॥

Every wise person having a good insight into things (and diffusing his knowledge among others) should realise (the properties and uses of) this praiseworthy phenomenon (of heat energy) that vitalizes the earth, the atmosphere, the trees, the plants (and all other things in the universe) in such a manner as to render them capable of producing wealth (and happiness for all beings). May such wise men bestow happiness on me (and others) and may not this Earth support us if we are wicked at heart. R. V., V. 42, 16.

अगऴ्वारै तांगु निलम्पोल तम्मै । इगऴ्वार्पोरुत्तरलै ॥

The highest righteousness consists in one's putting up with those that ill use one just as the Earth supports even those that dig her up. (Saint Tiruvalluva Naaynaar in his Tiruk Kural.)

The waters deluge man with rain, oppress him with hail and drown him with inundations; the air rushes in storms, prepares the tempest, or lights up the volcano; but the earth, gentle and indulgent ever subservient to the wants of man, spreads his walks with flowers, and his table with plenty; returns, with interest, every good committed to her care; and though she produces the poison, she still supplies the antidote; though constantly teased more to furnish the luxuries of man than his necessities, yet even to the last she continues her kind indulgence, and, when life is over, she piously covers his remains in her bosom. (Pliny; the New Dictionary of Thoughts, p. 149.)

The Earth is for the Wise and Righteous, Benefactors of Other People

[illegible]

Every wise person having a good insight into things (and diffusing his knowledge among others) should utilize (the properties and uses of) this praiseworthy [illegible] (of heat energy) that vitalizes the earth, the atmosphere, [illegible] and all other things in the universe) in such a manner as to render them capable of producing wealth (and happiness for all beings). May such wise men bestow happiness on the [illegible] (and others) and may not the Earth support [illegible] wicked at heart. R. V. 1.190.16

[illegible]

The highest [illegible] the Earth [illegible] (Sant Tiruvalluvar [illegible] Tirukkural)

The waters deluge man with rain, oppress him with hail, and drown him with inundations; the air rushes in storms, prepares the tempest, or lights up the volcano; but the earth, gentle and indulgent, ever subservient to the wants of man, spreads his walks with flowers and his table with plenty, returns, with interest, every good committed to her care; and though she produces the poison, she still supplies the antidote; and though constantly teased more to furnish the luxuries of man than his necessities, yet even to the last she continues her kind indulgence, and, when life is over, she piously covers his remains in her bosom. (Pliny: the New Dictionary of Thoughts, p. 149)

CHAPTER III.

Universal Patriotism.

Atharvavēda, XII, 1.

(३१) ओ३म् । सत्यं बृहदृतमुग्रं दीक्षा तपो ब्रह्म यज्ञः पृथिवीं धारयन्ति । सा नो भूतस्य भव्यस्य पत्न्युरुं लोकं पृथिवी नः कृणोतु ॥१॥

(31) Satyam bṛhadṛtam ugram dīkṣā tapō brahma yajnah pṛthivīm dhārayanti | Sā nō bhūtasya patnyurum lōkam pṛthivī nah kṛṇōtu || 1.

पदपाठः—सत्यम् । बृहत् । ऋतम् । उग्रम् । दीक्षा । तपः । ब्रह्म । यज्ञः । पृथिवीम् । धारयन्ति । सा । नः । भूतस्य । भव्यस्य । पत्नी । उरुम् । लोकम् । पृथिवी । नः । कृणोतु ॥

अन्वयः—बृहत् सत्यम् उग्रम् ऋतम् दीक्षा तपः ब्रह्म यज्ञः (च) पृथिवीं धारयन्ति । सा नः भूतस्य (च) पत्नी (अस्ति) । (सा) पृथिवी नः लोकम् कृणोतु ॥

Word-meaning:—बृहत् सत्यम्=Conduct day by day growing in truth. उग्रम् ऋतम्=vigorous pursuit of right knowledge. दीक्षा=self-control. तपः=observance of solemn vows. **ब्रह्म**=pursuit of Vedic study along with the purity of one's morals. **यज्ञः**=sacrifice or good works—honouring the wise, associating with the virtuous and charity. **पृथिवीम्**=Motherland, kingdom, the Earth. **धारयन्ति**= support, uphold. **सा**=that. **नः**=our. **भूतस्य**=of the past. **भव्यस्य**=of the future. **पत्नी** = protector. **उरुम्** =broad **लोकम्**=space. **कृणोतु**=may she make.

Translation :—A people's conduct day by day progressing in truthfulness, their vigorous pursuit of right knowledge, their self-control, their observance of solemn vows, their prosecution of Vedic study accompanied by the purity of morals, their good works (such as honouring the wise, associating with the virtuous and charity), these are the qualities that enable the Motherland to hold her head erect among other nations. May our Mother country who has protected us in the past (is protecting us now) and will protect us in the future, afford us ample room (that we may develop in these virtues.)

Purport :—Truthfulness in one's mental and moral life, control of the senses and meekly commingling with the wise, are essential for one's advance in earthly life. This rule holds good for all times and all climes.

(३२) असंबाधं वध्यतो मानवानां यस्यां उद्वतः प्रवतः समं बहु ।
नानावीर्या ओषधीर्या बिभर्ति पृथिवी नः प्रथतां राध्यतां नः ॥ २ ॥

(32) Asambādham vadhyatō mānavānām yasyā udvatah pravatah samam bahu । Nānāvīryā ōsadhīryā bibharti prthivī nah prathatām rādhyatām nah ॥ 2.

पदपाठः—असम्ऽबाधम् । वध्यतः । मानवानाम् । यस्याः । उत्ऽवतः । प्रऽवतः । समम् । बहु । नानाऽवीर्याः । ओषधीः । या । बिभर्ति । पृथिवी । नः । प्रथताम् । राध्यताम् । नः ॥

अन्वयः—मानवानाम् असंबाधम् वध्यतः यस्याः उद्वतः प्रवतः बहु

समम् (च बभूव), या पृथिवी नानावीर्याः ओषधीः बिभर्ति (सा) नः प्रथताम् (सा) नः राध्यताम् ॥

Word-meaning:—**असंबाधम्** = a phenomenon or factor that impedes progress. **वध्यतः** = removing. **मानवानाम्** = of thoughtful man. **यस्याः** = whose. **उद्वतः** = high (places). **प्रवतः** = low (places). **समम्** = even (places). **बहु** = many. **नानावीर्याः** = of many potencies. **ओषधीः** = herbs. **या** = who. **बिभर्ति** = keeps, bears, produces. **पृथिवी** = Motherland. **नः** = for us. **प्रथताम्** = allow room. **राध्यताम्** = accomplish (happiness.)

Translation :—This Motherland though herself chequered by high, and low places and many plains does remove all causes that impede the progress of the thoughtful. She stores (within her bosom) herbs of multifarious potentialities. May she afford us ample room for progress and accomplish our happiness.

Purport :—Thoughtful people have no regard for even and approachable places or fear for inaccessible high and low lands, for their diligence removes all obstacles enabling them to work for their own and others' happiness.

(३३) यस्यां समुद्र उत सिन्धुरापो यस्यामन्नं कृष्टयः संबभूवुः ।
यस्यामिदं जिन्वति प्राणदेजत् सा नो भूमिः पूर्वपेये दधातु ॥ ३ ॥

(33) Yasyām samudra uta sindhurāpō yasyām-annam kṛṣṭayaḥ sambabhūvuh। Yasyāmidam jinvati prāṇadējat sā nō bhūmih pūrvapēyē dadhātu ॥ 3.

पदपाठः—यस्याम् । समुद्रः । उत । सिन्धुः । आपः । यस्याम् । अन्नम् । कृष्टयः । सम्ऽबभूवुः । यस्याम् । इदम् । जिन्वति । प्राणत् । एजत् । सा । नः । भूमिः । पूर्वऽपेये । दधातु ॥

अन्वयः—यस्यां समुद्रः उत सिन्धुः आपः यस्यां अन्नं कृष्टयः (च) संबभूवुः, यस्यां इदं प्राणत् एजत् जिन्वति, सा भूमिः नः पूर्वपेये दधातु ॥

Word-meaning:—**यस्यां** = on which. **समुद्रः** = the sea.

उत=and. सिन्धुः=big rivers. आपः=streams, lakes, etc. अन्नं = food. कृष्टयः=fields, farms. संबभूवुः=exist. इदम् प्राणत् एजत्=this living and moving world. जिन्वति=goes about. पूर्वपेये=a position deserving to be protected by the great.

Translation:—In whom exist seas, great rivers and other receptacles of water (such as streams, lakes, and wells), food and farms, and in whom this whole world endowed with breath and motion goes about its business, may she advance us to a position that deserves to be protected by the great.

Purport:—men who utilise the sea, rivers, and rain-water, do farming, ply boats and set up machinery to advance the happiness of mankind, deserve to be respected by all.

(३४) यस्याश्चतस्रः प्रदिशः पृथिव्या यस्यामन्नं कृष्टयः संबभूवुः ।
या बिभर्ति । बहुधा प्राणदेजत् सा नो भूमिर्गोष्वप्यन्ने दधातु ॥ ४ ॥

(34) Yasyāścatasrah pradiśah pṛthivyā yasyām annam kṛṣṭayah sambabhūvuh । Yā bibharti bahudhā prāṇadējat sā nō bhūmirgōṣvapyannē dadhātu ॥ 4

पदपाठः—यस्याः । चतस्रः । प्रऽदिशः । पृथिव्याः । यस्यां । अन्नं । कृष्टयः । सम्ऽबभूवुः । या । बिभर्ति । बहुधा । प्राणत् । एजत् । सा । नः । भूमिः । गोषु । अपि । अन्ने । दधातु ॥

अन्वयः—यस्याः पृथिव्याः चतस्रः प्रदिशः (सन्ति), यस्याम् (एकैकस्याम् प्रदिशि) अन्नम् कृष्टयः च संबभूवुः, या भूमिः (इदं) प्राणत् एजत् बहुधा बिभर्ति सा नः गोषु अपि (च) अन्ने दधातु ॥

Word-meaning:—चतस्रः = four. प्रदिशः= the main quarters. यस्याम्=in each of which. भूमिः=Motherland. बिभर्ति=bears, supports. बहुधा=in many ways. गोषु= in (plenty of milch) cows. अन्ने=food, provisions दधातु = establish, place.

Translation:—That Motherland of ours has her four main (and four subordinate) quarters, in each of which food and farms abound, and she, by various means supports this whole *world* endowed with life and motion. May that Motherland establish us in a plenty of (milch) cows and also of food.

Purport:—A man who casts a supervising glance all around and procuring provisions and other necessaries protects all creatures is himself blessed with abundance in domestic animals and food.

(३५) यस्यां पूर्वे पूर्वजना विचक्रिरे यस्यां देवा असुरानभ्यवर्तयन्।
गवामश्वानां वयसश्च विष्ठा भगं वर्चः पृथिवी नो दधातु ॥ ५ ॥

(35) Yasyām pūrvē pūrvajanā vicakrirē yasyām dēvā asurān abhyavartayan। Gavāmaśvānām vayasaśca viṣṭhā bhagam varcah pṛthivī nō dadhātu ॥ 5.

पदपाठः—यस्याम्। पूर्वे। पूर्वऽजनाः। विऽचक्रिरे। यस्याम्। देवाः। असुरान। अभिऽअवर्तयन्। गवाम्। अश्वानाम्। वयसः। च। विऽस्था। भगम्। वर्चः। पृथिवी। नः। दधातु ॥

अन्वयः—यस्यां (पृथिव्यां) पूर्वे पूर्वजनाः विचक्रिरे, यस्यां देवाः असुरान् अभ्यवर्तयन्, (या) गवां अश्वानांम वयसः च विष्ठा, (सा) पृथिवी नः भगं वर्चः (च) दधातु ॥

Word-meaning:—**पूर्वे**=in past creations, ages or times. **पूर्वजनाः**=predecessors or ancestors. **विचक्रिरे**= performed deeds of prowess. **देवाः**=righteous men. **असुरान्** =the wicked. **अभ्यवर्तयन्**=vanquished. **गवां**=of cows. **अश्वानां**=of horses. **वयसः**=of food. **विष्ठा (विऽस्था)**=a special place, shelter, refuge. **भगम्**=prosperity. **वर्चः**=power.

Translation:—May that Motherland (of ours) in whom in past ages (or creations) our predecessors did deeds of prowess, the righteous vanquished the wicked, and who in a special manner shelters cows, horses (and such other domestic animals) and food, bestow on us prosperity and power.

Purport:—Our ancestors by diligent efforts removed all obstacles from their way and attained to prosperity and power. We also should do likewise.

(३६) विश्वंभरा वसुधानी प्रतिष्ठा हिरण्यवक्षा जगतो निवेशनी ।
वैश्वानरं बिभ्रती भूमिरग्निमिन्द्रऋषभा द्रविणे नो दधातु ॥ ६ ॥

(36) Viśvambharā vasudhānī pratiṣṭhā hiraṇya vakṣā jagatō nivēśanī । Vāiśvānaram bibhratī bhūmiragnimindrarṣabhā draviṇē nō dadhātu ॥ 6.

पदपाठः—विश्वंऽभरा । वसुऽधानी । प्रतिऽस्था हिरण्यऽवक्षाः । जगतः । निऽवेशनी वैश्वानरं । बिभ्रती । भूमिः । अग्निं । इन्द्रऽऋषभा । द्रविणे । नः । दधातु ॥

अन्वयः— विश्वंभरा, वसुधानी, प्रतिष्ठा, हिरण्यावक्षाः, जगतः निवेशनी, वैश्वानरं अग्निं बिभ्रती, इन्द्रऋषभा भूमिः नो द्रविणे दधातु ॥

Word-meaning:—विश्वंभरा = sheltering all on her bosom. वसुधानी = the receptacle of wealth. प्रतिष्ठा = firm refuge. हिरण्यवक्षाः = who stores gold and other precious metals in her bosom. जगतः = of the active. निवेशनी = imparter of happiness. वैश्वानरं = doing good to all men. अग्निम् = a man of prowess like fire. बिभ्रती = bearing, supporting. इन्द्रऋषभा = Having God for her control-ler. द्रविणे = in power and wealth.

Translation:—May that Motherland (of ours) who shelters all on her bosom, who is the receptacle of wealth, who affords firm standing to all, who keeps gold and other precious metals in her bosom, who imparts happiness to all that are active, who supports men of fire-like vigorous prowess in doing good to their fellow-men and who has God for her Controller, establish us in power and wealth.

Purport:—The industrious, become leaders of men, secure wealth in the shape of the precious metals etc., and attain happiness.

(३७) यां रक्षन्त्यस्वप्ना विश्वदानीं देवा भूमिं पृथिवीमप्रमादं ।
सा नो मधु प्रियं दुहामथो उक्षतु वर्चसा ॥ ७ ॥

(37) Yām rakṣantyasvapnā viśvadānīm dēvā bhūmim pṛthivīm apramādam । Sā nō madhu priyam duhām athō ukṣatu varcasā ॥ 7.

पदपाठः—यां । रक्षन्ति । अस्वप्नाः । विश्वऽदानीं । देवाः । भूमिम् पृथिवीं । अप्रऽमादं । सा । नः । मधु । प्रियं । दुहां । अथो इति । उक्षतु । वर्चसा ॥

अन्वयः—यां विश्वदानीम् भूमिम् पृथिवीं अस्वप्नाः देवाः अप्रमादम् रक्षन्ति, सा नः प्रियम् मधु दुहां अथो (नः) वर्चसा उक्षतु ॥

Word-meaning:—**विश्वदानीं**=who gives all. **रक्षन्ति**=protect. **अस्वप्नाः**=without sleeping. **देवाः**=the righteous. **पृथिवीं भूमिं**=the spacious Motherland. **अप्रमादं**=without any flaw (in their vigilence). **मधु**=the fruit of past actions, all pleasurable objects, the essence of all worldly things. **प्रियं**=desirable. **दुहां**=bestow on. **अथो** (**अथ+उ**) =and also. **उक्षतु** (√**उक्ष्**)=may shower on, advance. **वर्चसा**=with power, energy, prowess.

Translation:—May that Motherland, the giver of all, the firm and spacious, whom the wise ones sleepless keep a watch over without any flaw in their vigil, give us the means to enjoy the fruit of our past actions, and so help us to develop our powers.

Purport:—Men who protect the land by a vigilant and flawless watch enjoy the best of all things and become wise and powerful.

(३८) यार्ऽणवेऽधि सलिलमग्र आसीद्यां मायाभिरन्वचरन् मनी-

षिणः । यस्या हृदयं परमे व्योमन्त्सत्येनावृतममृतं पृथिव्याः । सा नो भूमिस्त्विषिं बलं राष्ट्रे दधातूत्तमे ॥ ८ ॥

(38) Yā'rṇave'dhi salilam agra āsīdyām māyābhiranvacaran manīṣiṇah । Yasyā hṛdayam paramē vyōmantsatyēnāvṛtam amṛtam pṛthivyāh । Sā nō bhūmistviṣim balam rāṣṭrē dadhātūttamē ॥ 8.

पदपाठः—या । अर्णवे । अधि । सलिलं । अग्रे । आसीत् यां । मायाभिः । अनुऽअचरन् । मनीषिणः । यस्याः । हृदयं । परमे । विऽओमन् । सत्येन । आऽवृतम् । अमृतम् । पृथिव्याः । सा । नः । भूमिः । त्विषिम् । बलम् । राष्ट्रे । दधातु । उत्ऽतमे ॥

अन्वयः—या भूमिः अग्रे अर्णवे अधि सलिलम् आसीत् यां, (अग्रे) मनीषिणः मायाभिः अन्वचरन्, यस्याः पृथिव्याः अमृतं हृदयम् (अग्रे) परमे व्योमन् सत्येन आवृतं (बभूव) सा भूमिः नः उत्तमे राष्ट्रे त्विषिं बलं (च) दधातु ॥

Word-meaning:—**अर्णवे**=in the sea, atmosphere. **अधि**=in, on. **सलिलम्**=water in the form of vapour or mist. **आसीत्**=was. **अग्रे**=in the beginning, before creation. **मायाभिः**=with the intellectual faculties. **अनु अचरन्**=have followed, have served. **मनीषिणः**=the thoughtful. **हृदयम्**=heart, pith, essence. **परमे व्योमन्**=in the Almighty, Omnipresent God. **सत्येन**=by the eternal primordial matter. **आवृतं**=is covered. **अमृतं**=not dead, immortal. **त्विषिं**=light. **बलम्**=power, (armies). **उत्तमे**=in an excelient. **राष्ट्रे**=kingdom. **दधातु**=bestow on.

Translation:—May that Mother Earth, which, before the creation, was in the form of vapour in the ocean of atmosphere, whom, in past ages (or creations) the thoughtful served with their rational faculties, whose immortal heart is established in the Most High God and is enveloped in truth (or whose indestructible essence before the creation covered with Primordial Matter existed in the Most High God), make us an excellent nation endowed with the light of wisdom and power.

Purport:—This Earth has always existed, before the creation as subtle matter, and after the creation as the meeting place of innumerable souls and the receptacle of precious metals and important agricultural products. Those who, knowing this, serve her with diligence and wisdom, will become a great nation endowed with light and power.

(३९) यस्यामापः परिचराः समानीरहोरात्रे अप्रमादं क्षरन्ति । सा नो भूमिर्भूरिधारा पयो दुहामथो उक्षतु वर्चसा ॥९॥

(39) Yasyāmāpah paricarāh samānīrahōrātrē apramādam kṣaranti । Sā nō bhūmih bhūridhārā payō duhāmathō ukṣatu varcasā ॥ 9.

पदपाठः—यस्याम् । आपः । परिऽचराः । समानीः । अहोरात्रे इति । अप्रऽमादम् । क्षरन्ति । सा । नः । भूमिः । भूरिऽधारा । पयः । दुहाम् । अथो इति । उक्षतु । वर्चसा ॥

अन्वयः—यस्यां परिचराः समानीः आपः अहोरात्रे अप्रमादं क्षरन्ति, सा भूरिधारा भूमिः नः पयो दुहां अथो वर्चसा उक्षतु ॥

Word-meaning:—यस्यां = in whom. **आपः** = trustworthy, of good will. **समानीः** = of equal or quiet nature. **परिचराः** = serving others. **अहोरात्रे** = day and night. **अप्रमादं** = without anything untoward. **क्षरन्ति** = flow, pass. **भूरिधारा** = possessing immense power to support creatures. **पयः** = milk, food. **दुहां** = yield.

Translation:—May that Motherland in whom many well-wishers of humanity of quiet nature and serving mankind pass their days and nights without anything untoward happening, and who possesses immense power to support beings, amply provide us with food, and also help us to develop our power.

Purport:—Like noble souls of impartial and philanthropic dispositions, all men, casting off all differences, should work for each other's welfare, and by means of food and other helps rendered by the earth advance in power and valour.

(४०) यामुश्विनावमिमातां विष्णुर्यस्यां विचक्रमे । इन्द्रो यां चक्र आत्मनेऽनमित्रां शचीपतिः । सा नो भूमिर्विसृजतां माता पुत्राय मे पयः ॥ १० ॥

(40) Yāmaśvināvamimātām viṣṇuryasyām vicakramē Indrō yām cakra ātmanē'namitrām śacīpatih। Sā nō bhūmirvisṛjatām mātā putrāya mē payah ॥ 10.

पदपाठः—याम् । अश्विनौ । अमिमाताम् । विष्णुः । यस्याम् । विऽचक्रमे । इन्द्रः । याम् । चक्रे । आत्मने । अनमित्राम् । शचीऽपतिः । सा । नः । भूमिः । वि । सृजताम् । माता । पुत्राय । मे । पयः ॥

अन्वयः—यां अश्विनौ अमिमातां, यस्यां विष्णुः विचक्रमे, यां शचीपतिः इन्द्रः आत्मने अनमित्रां चक्रे, सा माता भूमिः मे पुत्राय पयः विसृजताम् ॥

Word-meaning:—**अश्विनौ**=day and night. **अमिमातां**=have measured. **विष्णुः**=the pervading sun. **विचक्रमे**=placed his foot upon. **इन्द्रः**=the soul. **आत्मने**=for herself. **अनमित्रां**=free from foes. **शचीपतिः**=the protector of speech, actions, or wisdom. **विसृजतां**=bestow on us in various ways. **पयः**=food, milk.

Translation:—May that Motherland whom the day and the night have measured, on whom the pervading sun has placed his feet in the shape of rays, whom for his own sake, the soul the lord of speech (deeds or intellect), has rendered free from foes, provide me with 'milk.'

Purport:—That land which the day and night have rendered fruitful, which the sun keeps fit by his gravitational force, light, rain etc., and on which truth-speaking, righteous and wise men prosper, every man should try to make more useful and thus do the good of mankind.

(४१) गिरयस्ते पर्वता हिमवन्तोऽरण्यं ते पृथिवि स्योनमस्तु। बभ्रुं कृष्णां रोहिणीं विश्वरूपां ध्रुवां भूमिं पृथिवीमिन्द्रगुप्तां। अजीतोऽहतो अक्षतोऽध्यष्ठां पृथिवीमहम् ॥११॥

(41) Girayastē parvatā himavantō'raṇyam tē pṛthivī syōnam astu । Babhrum kṛṣṇām rōhinīm viśvarūpām dhruvām bhūmim pṛthivīmindraguptām । Ajītō'hatō akṣatō'dhyaṣthām prthivīmaham ॥ 11.

पदपाठः—गिरयः। ते। पर्वताः। हिमऽवन्तः। अरण्यं। ते। पृथिवि स्योनं। अस्तु। बभ्रुम्। कृष्णां। रोहिणीं। विश्वऽरूपां। ध्रुवां। भूमिं। पृथिवीं। इन्द्रऽगुप्तां। अजीतः। अहतः। अक्षतः। अधि। अस्थां। पृथिवीं। अहम् ॥

अन्वयः—(हे) पृथिवि ते गिरयः पर्वताः हिमवन्तः अरण्यं (च नः) स्योनं अस्तु। पृथिवीम् बभ्रुम कृष्णां रोहिणीं विश्वरूपां ध्रुवां भूमिं इन्द्रगुप्तां अहं पृथिवीं अजीतः अहतः अक्षतः अध्यष्ठाम् ॥

Word-meaning:—गिरयः ते=her hills. हिमवन्तः पर्वताः =snowclad mountains. अरण्यं=woodland. पृथिवि=Oh Motherland. स्योनम्=pleasant. अस्तु=may be. बभ्रुं=who supports. कृष्णां=fit for agriculture. रोहिणीम्=yielding agricultural products. विश्वरूपां=of various forms, golden, silver etc. ध्रुवां भूमिम्=firm land. पृथिवीं=vast. इन्द्रगुप्तां=protected by great and powerful men. अजीतः= unconquered. अहतः=unslain. अक्षतः=unwounded. अध्यष्ठां =may I possess, rule over, reside in.

Translation:—May the hills, the snowclad mountains and the woodlands of our Motherland be pleasant to us! She, the spacious Motherland, who supports all creatures, fit for agriculture, yielding various kinds of agricultural products, and having innumerable forms (such as golden silver etc., on account of the different precious metals she keeps), who affords firm ground for our residence, and is protected by great and powerful men ! May I reside in (rule over, and possess) her, unconquered, unslain, unwounded.

Purport:—By means of arts, machinery and conveyances man should, without let or hindrance, explore even the most inaccessible parts of the earth and make them fertile and habitable.

(४२) यत् ते मध्यं पृथिवि यच्च नभ्यं यास्त ऊर्जस्तन्वः सम्बभूवुः । तासु नो धेह्यभि नः पवस्व माता भूमिः पुत्रो अहं पृथिव्याः । पर्जन्यः पिता स उ नः पिपर्तु ॥ १२ ॥

(42) Yat tē madhyam pṛthivi yacca nabhyam yāsta ūrjastanvah sambabhūvuh । Tāsu nō dhēhyabhi nah pavasva mātā bhūmih putrō aham pṛthivyāh । Parjanyah pitā sa u nah pipartu ॥ 12.

पदपाठः—यत् । ते । मध्यं । पृथिवि । यत् । च । नभ्यं । याः । ते । ऊर्जः । तन्वः । सम्ऽबभूवुः । तासु । नः । धेहि । अभि । नः । पवस्व । माता । भूमिः । पुत्रः । अहम् । पृथिव्याः । पर्जन्यः । पिता । सः । ऊं इति । नः । पिपर्तु ।

अन्वयः—(हे) पृथिवि यत् ते मध्यम् यत् च नभ्यं याः ते ऊर्जः तन्वः सम्बभूवुः तासु नः धेहि, नः अभि पवस्व, भूमिः माता अहं पृथिव्याः पुत्रः पर्जन्यः पिता, सः उ नः पिपर्तु ।

Word-meaning:—**यत्**=what. **ते**=her. **मध्यं** (**मन्**+**यत्**)= acts of justice. **नभ्यम**= the warrior's beneficent deeds. **ऊर्जः**=bestowing power or strength. **तन्वः**=from the body. **सम्बभूवुः**=have come into being. **तासु**=in all those acts. **धेहि**=may shelter. **अभि पवस्व**=purify from all directions, or completely. **पर्जन्यः**=the rain cloud. **पिता**=protector, father. **पिपर्तु**=may he fill us with plenty.

Translation:—To the Motherland, do all the acts of

justice, and the warriors' beneficent deeds pertain and from her body proceed all the things that nourish and strengthen us. With these she shelters us and purifies us completely. The Earth is a mother unto me and I, like a son, ward off all her calamities. The rain clouds protect us like a father, may they fill us with plenty.

Purport:—Men should attain practical proficiency in politics, geology, agriculture, 'hydrology' and such other key sciences and arts and render the earth more beneficent to humanity,

(४३) यस्यां वेदिं परिगृह्णन्ति भूम्यां यस्यां यज्ञं तन्वते विश्वकर्माणः । यस्यां मीयन्ते स्वरवः पृथिव्यामूर्ध्वाः शुक्रा आहुत्याः पुरस्तात् । सा नो भूमिर्वर्धयद्वर्धमाना ॥१३॥

(43) Yasyām vēdim parigṛhṇanti bhūmyām yasyām yajñam tanvatē viśvakarmāṇah । Yasyām mīyantē svaravah pṛithivyām ūrdhvāh śukrā āhutyāh purastāt । Sā nō bhūmirvardhayadvardhamānā ॥ 13.

पदपाठः—यस्याम् । वेदिं । परिऽगृह्णन्ति । भूम्यां । यस्यां । यज्ञं । तन्वते । विश्वकर्माणः । यस्यां । मीयन्ते । स्वरवः । पृथिव्यां । ऊर्ध्वाः । शुक्राः । आऽहुत्याः । पुरस्तात् । सा । नः । भूमिः । वर्धयत् । वर्धमाना ॥

अन्वयः—यस्यां भूम्यां विश्वकर्माणः वेदिं परिगृह्णन्ति, यस्यां यज्ञम् तन्वते, यस्यां पृथिव्यां आहुत्याः पुरस्तात् ऊर्ध्वाः शुक्राः स्वरवः मीयन्ते, सा भूमिः वर्धमाना नः वर्धयत् ॥

Word-meaning:—**वेदिं**=the sacrificial place. **परिगृह्णन्ति**,=surround. **यज्ञं**=sacrifice in the form of good works viz:—honouring the wise, associating with the righteous and charity. **विश्वकर्माणः**=men proficient in all works. **मीयन्ते**=are constructed. **स्वरवः**=triumphal columns. **ऊर्ध्वाः**=high. **शुक्राः**=white. **आहुत्याः पुरस्तात्**=before the completion of sacrificial good works. **वर्धयत्**=advance, help to advance or develop, make to prosper. **वर्धमाना**=growing, advancing, prospering.

Translation:—On which Earth, men proficient in all works surround the place prepared and purified for sacrificial ceremonies, on which sacrifices in the form of honouring the wise, associating with the righteous and succouring the needy are performed, on which Earth before the consummation of great sacrificial good works, high, white triumphal pillars are built, may that Motherland thus prospering advance our prosperity.

Purport:—It is but meet that becoming experts in all good works, men should advance the fame of their Mother Country and establish their own repute.

(४४) यो नो द्वेषत्पृथिवि यः पृतन्याद्योऽभिदासान्मनसा यो वधेन। तं नो भूमे रन्धय पूर्वकृत्वरि। ॥१४॥

(44) Yō nō dvēṣat pṛthivi yaḥ pṛtanyādyō'bhi dāsānmanasā yō vadhēna। Tam nō bhūmē randhaya pūrvakṛtvari ॥ 14.

पदपाठः—यः। नः। द्वेषत्। पृथिवि। यः। पृतन्यात्। यः। अभिऽदासात्। मनसा। यः। वधेन। तम्। नः। भूमे। रन्धय। पूर्वऽकृत्वरि॥

अन्वयः—(हे) पृथिवि, यः नः द्वेषत्, यः पृतन्यात्, यः मनसा (वा) वधेन (वा) नः अभिदासात् (हे) भूमे, पूर्वकृत्वरि तं नः रन्धय॥

Word-meaning:—**द्वेषत्**=is hostile towards. **पृतन्यात्**=invade with a body of troops. **अभिदासात्**=harass. **मनसा**=in thought, **वधेन**=in action by the use of lethal weapons. **नः**=for us. **रन्धय**=destroy. **पूर्वकृत्वरि**=thou who workest for the good of the great.

Translation:—Him who has hostile inclinations towards us, him who may invade us with a body of troops, him, who may harass us with hostile plans in his mind, or actively with arms, may the Mother Earth, —the Motherland who is firm and does work for the righteous, destroy all such for us.

Purport:—Those who, with a pious regard protect the Earth (motherland) can destroy all foes.

(४५) त्वज्जातास्त्वयिं चरन्ति मर्त्यास्त्वं बिभर्षि द्विपदस्त्वं चतुष्पदः। तवेमे पृथिवि पञ्चं मानवा येभ्यो ज्योतिरमृतं मर्त्येभ्य उद्यन्त्सूर्यो रश्मिभिरातनोति ॥१५॥

(45) Tvajjātāstvayi caranti martyāstvam bibharṣi dvipadastvam catuṣpadah। Tavēmē pṛthivi pañca mānavā yēbhyō jyōtiramṛtam martyēbhya udyantsūryō raśmibhirātanōti ॥ 15.

पदपाठः—त्वत् । जाताः । त्वयिं । चरन्ति । मर्त्याः । त्वम् । बिभर्षि । द्विऽपदः । त्वम् । चतुःऽपदः । तवं । इमे । पृथिवि । पञ्चं । मानवाः । येभ्यः । ज्योतिः । अमृतम् । मर्त्येभ्यः । उत्ऽयन् । सूर्यः । रश्मिऽभिः । आऽतनोति ॥१५॥

अन्वयः—मर्त्याः त्वत् जाताः त्वयि चरन्ति, त्वम् द्विपदः त्वम् चतुष्पदः (च) बिभर्षि। (हे) पृथिवि, इमे पञ्च मानवाः येभ्यः मर्त्येभ्यः उद्यन् सूर्यः रश्मिभिः अमृतम् ज्योतिः आतनोति, तव (एव) ॥

Word-meaning:—त्वत् जाताः=born from thee. त्वयि चरन्ति=live and move in thee. मर्त्याः=the mortal beings. विभर्षि=thou dost support. द्विपदः=bipeds. चतुष्पदः=quadrupeds. इमे पञ्च मानवाः=these human beings related to the five great elements, earth, water, fire, air, and other. येभ्यः =for whom. मर्त्येभ्यः=for mortals. अमृतम् ज्योतिः=immortal light. उद्यत् सूर्यः=the rising sun. रश्मिभिः=with his rays. आतनोति=spreads all around.

Translation:—All these mortal creatures are born of the Motherland and live and move in her. She supports bipeds (on her bosom) and she supports the quadrupeds. Man having an intimate connection with the five great elements earth, water, light, air and ether, for whom, mortal by nature as he is, the sun by means of his rays spreads immortal light all around, is also the subject of the Earth.

Purport:—Men should recognise their indebtedness to their Motherland and endeavour diligently to make her more beneficent to humanity. The sun's light, rain and such other phenomena will surely co-operate with such.

(४६) ता नः प्रजाः सम् दुंहूताम् समुग्रा वाचो मधुं पृथिवि धेहि मह्यंम् ॥ १६ ॥

(46) Tā nah prajāh sam duhratām samagrā vācō madhu pṛthivi dhēhi mahyam ॥ 16.

पदपाठः—ताः । नः । प्रऽजाः । सं । दुहूतां । सम्ऽअग्राः । वाचः । मधुं । पृथिवि । धेहि । मह्यंम् ॥

अन्वयः—समग्राः ताः प्रजाः नः सन्दुह्रतां, हे पृथिवि मह्यम् वाचः मधु धेहि ॥

Word-meaning:—**समग्राः ताः प्रजाः**=all those creatures (mentioned in the above stanza). **नः सन्दुह्रतां**=unite with us and complete our soceity. **वाचः**=of speech. **मधु**= sweetness. **धेहि**=give. **मह्यम्**=to me.

Translation:—May all these creatures unite with us, complete our society and make it perfect. May the Motherland give us sweetness of speech (which is so essential to bring us together).

Purport:—Sweetness of speech that is truth-speaking coupled with gentleness of expression and humility in tone enables a man to derive happiness from all creatures.

(४७) विश्वस्वं मातरमोषधीनां ध्रुवां भूमिं पृथिवीं धर्मणा धृताम् । शिवां स्योनामनु चरेम विश्वहा ॥१७॥

(47) Viśvasvam mātaram ōṣādhīnām dhruvām bhūmim pṛthivīm dharmaṇā dhṛtām । Śivām syōnām anu carēma viśvahā ॥ 17.

पदपाठः—विश्वऽस्वंम् । मातरंम् । ओषंधीनाम् । ध्रुवां । भूमिंम् । पृथिवीम् । धर्मणा । धृताम् । शिवां । स्योनाम् । अनुं । चरम । विश्वहां ॥

अन्वयः—विश्वस्वम् ओषधीनां मातरम् ध्रुवां भूमिं धर्मणा धृतां शिवां स्योनां पृथिवीं विश्वहा अनु चरेम ॥

Word-meaning:—**विश्वस्वं**=who produces and possesses every thing earthly. **मातरं**=mother. **ओषधीनां**=of the herbs. **ध्रुवां**=the firm. **भूमिं**=ground. **पृथिवीं**=spacious. **धर्मणा**=righteousness. **धृतां**=supported. **शिवां**=auspicious. **स्योनां**=pleasant. **अनु चरेम**=let us follow. **विश्वहा**=in various ways.

Translation:—May we, in all ways, follow (live in accordance wtth the 'wishes' of) that Motherland who produces and possesses all terrestrial objects, is the mother (producer) of all herbs, who affords firm stand to all creatures, who is upheld by righteousness, and who is auspicious, charming and spacious.

Purport:—Righteousness should be the norm in accordance with which, the ruler as well as the ruled enjoy the earth. It will then yield them happiness.

(४८) महत् सधस्थं महती बभूविथ महान् वेग एजथुर्वेपथुष्टे । महांस्त्वेन्द्रो रक्षत्यप्रमादम् । सा नो भूमे प्र रोचय हिरण्यस्येव संदृशि मा नो द्विक्षत कश्चन ॥ १८ ॥

(48) Mahat sadhastham mahatī babhūvitha mahān vēga ējathurvepathuṣṭē । Mahāṃstvēndrō rakṣatyapramādam । Sā nō bhūmē prarōcaya hiraṇyasyēva sandṛśi mā nō dvikṣata kaścana ॥ 18.

पदपाठः—मुहत् । सुधऽस्थंम् । मुहती । बुभूविथ । मुहान । वेगंः । एजथुंः । वेपथुंः । ते । मुहान् । त्वा । इन्द्रंः । रक्षति । अप्रंऽमादम् । सा । नः । भूमे । प्र । रोचय । हिरंण्यस्यऽइव । संऽदृशि । मा । नः । द्विक्षत । कः । चन ॥

अन्वयः—(हे पृथिवि) महती (त्वम्) महत् सधस्थम् बभूविथ । ते वेगः, एजथुः, वेपथुः, (च) महान् । महान् इन्द्रः अप्रमादम् त्वा रक्षति । सा भूमे नः हिरण्यस्य इव सन्दृशि प्ररोचय, कश्चन नः मा द्विक्षत् ॥

Word-meaning:—**महत्**=great. **सधस्थं**=place to stay together. **महती**=great. **बभूविथ**=thou art. **महान्**=great **वेगः**=velocity. **एजथुः**=going, moving. **वेपथुः**=trembling, shaking. **महान् इन्द्रः**=the Great God. **रक्षति**=protects. **अप्रमादं**=without any flaw. **प्ररोचय**=make us to shine forth **हिरण्यस्य इव**=like that of gold. **संदृशि**=in form, to look at. **मा नः कश्चन द्विक्षत**=may nobody bear us any ill will.

Translation:—Our Mother is great, and a great place of shelter dost afford for all. Her velocity, her motion and her tremor are all immense. The Great and All-powerful God protects her without any flaw. May the Earth, who is of this description, make us shine with lustre as of gold and may nobody bear us any malice.

Purport:—The diligent by endeavours and co-operation with others procure through their knowledge wealth in the form of gold etc., and become powerful.

(४९) अग्निर्भूम्यामोषधीष्वग्निमापो बिभ्रत्यग्निरश्मसु । अग्निरन्तः पुरुषेषु गोष्वश्वेष्वग्नयः ॥ १९ ॥

(49) Agnirbhūmyām ōṣadhīṣvagnimāpo bibhratyagniraśmasu । Agnirantaḥ puruśēṣu gōṣvaśvēṣvagnayah ॥ 19

पदपाठः—अग्निः । भूम्यांम् । ओषंधीषु । अग्निम् । आपंः । बिभ्रति । अग्निः । अश्मंऽसु । अग्निः । अन्तः । पुरुषेषु । गोषुं । अश्वेषु । अग्नयंः ॥

अन्वयः—भूम्याम् ओषधीषु (च) अग्निः (अस्ति), आपः अग्निं बिभ्रति, अश्मसु (अपि) अग्निः (अस्ति)। पुरुषेषु अन्तः अग्निः, गोषु अश्वेषु (च) अग्नयः सन्ति ॥

Word-meaning:—**अग्निः**=fire, heat, electricity. **भूम्यां**= in the earth. **ओषधीषु**=in herbs, **आपः**=waters. **बिभ्रति**= support, bear, hold. **अश्मसु**=in stones or clouds. **अन्तः**= inside. **पुरुषेषु**=in men. **गोषु**=in cows. **अश्वेषु**=in horses. **अग्नयः**=heat or electricity in differerent forms or grades.

Translation:—Fire (heat-energy and electricity) is present in the Earth. It thence enters the herbs (that grow upon the Earth). The waters bear fire, and fire is an ingredient .in the formation of the cloud (or stone). It is present in the human body, and in different forms it is found in the bodies of animals like the cow and the horse.

Purport:—The heat that is in the Earth enters cereals and vegetables and endows them with nutrient potency. Bodies of animals and all gross forms of matter are held together by the power of this heat or electricity.

(५०) अ॒ग्निर्दि॒व आ त॑पत्य॒ग्नेर्दे॒वस्यो॒र्व१॒॑न्तरि॑क्षम् । अ॒ग्निं मर्ता॑स इन्धते हव्य॒वाहं॑ घृत॒प्रिय॑म् ॥ २० ॥

(50) Agnirdiva ā tapatyagnērdēvasyōrvantarikṣam I Agnim martāsa indhatē havyavāham ghṛtapriyam ‖ 20.

पदपाठः—अ॒ग्निः । दि॒वः । आ । त॒प॒ति॒ । अ॒ग्नेः । दे॒वस्य॑ । उ॒रु । अ॒न्तरि॑क्षं । अ॒ग्निम् । मर्ता॑सः । इ॒न्ध॒ते॒ । ह॒व्य॒ऽवाह॑म् । घृ॒त॒ऽप्रिय॑म् ॥

अन्वयः—अग्निः दिवः आ तपति, देवस्य अग्नेः उरु अन्तरिक्षं । मर्तासः हव्यवाहम् घृतप्रियम् अग्निं इन्धते ॥

Word-meaning:—**दिवः**=from the sun (Nir. VI, 20). **आ तपति**=comes down and shines or heats. **देवस्य**=of the desirable or cherished one. **उरु**=spacious. **अन्तरिक्षम**=the intermediate region. मर्तासः=the mortals. इन्धते (indhatē)= light. हव्यवाहम (havyavāham)=that which carries the fragrance of the articles burnt all around; that which carries the juice of food in the arteries. घृतप्रियम्=which is kept up by greasy and combustible substances.

Translation:—Heat (or electricity) proceeds (originally) from the sun and then finds a shelter on earth. It occupies the spacious intermediate region (sky) as well. Men (the mortals) light it in the form of the sacrificial fire which is kept up by greasy aud combustible substances and which carries the fragrance of articles burnt in it all around (or which carries the juices of food in the form of blood etc., into the arteries and veins).

Purport:—It is heat that through the articles of food eaten nourishes the body. It is heat, again, that cleanses the atmosphere and food materials by carrying in the air the essence of nourishing cleansing and fragrant articles burnt in the sacrificial fire. Hence all should perform the 'havana'—*holocaust.*

(५१) अ॒ग्निवा॑साः पृथि॒व्यसि॑तज्ञूस्त्वि॒षीम॑न्तं॒ संशि॑तं मा कृणोतु ॥२१॥

(51) Agnivāsāh pṛthivyasitajñūstviṣīmantam saṃśitam mā kṛṇōtu ‖ 21.

पदपाठः—अ॒ग्निऽवा॑साः । पृ॒थि॒वी । अ॒सि॒तऽज्ञूः । त्वि॒षिऽम॑न्तम् । सम्ऽशि॑तम् । मा॒ । कृ॒णो॒तु ॥

अन्वयः—अग्निवासाः असितज्ञूः पृथिवी मा त्विषिमन्तम् संशितं कृणोतु ॥

Word-meanig:—**अग्निवासाः**=whose abode is in fire, who wears fire like clothing. **असितज्ञूः**=who actuates creatures to put forth voluntary and unfettered effort.

त्विषिमन्तम्=full of brilliance or power. **संशितं**=vigorous, agile. **कृणोतु**=may make.

Translation:—May this Mother Earth clothed in heat, and aiding (enjoining) unfettered voluntary effort in living creatures make me powerful (or brilliant) and agile.

Purport:—Just as the Earth with force derived from the sun progresses in her motion unhindered, men also should develop their powers and advance in the path of righteousness.

(५२) भूम्यां देवेभ्यो ददति यज्ञं हव्यमरंकृतं । भूम्यां मनुष्या जीवन्ति स्वधयान्नेन मर्त्याः । सा नो भूमिः प्राणमायुर्दधातु जरदष्टिं मा पृथिवी कृणोतु ॥ २२ ॥

(52) Bhūmyām dēvēbhyō dadati yajñam havyam araṃkṛtam। Bhūmyām manuṣyā jīvanti svadhayānnēna martyāh। Sā nō bhūmih prāṇamāyurdadhātū jaradaṣṭim mā pṛthivī kṛṇōtu ॥ 22.

पदपाठः—भूम्यां । देवेभ्यः । ददति । यज्ञं । हव्यं । अरंऽकृतं । भूम्यां । मनुष्याः । जीवन्ति । स्वधया । अन्नेन । मर्त्याः । सा । नः । भूमिः । प्राणम् । आयुः । दधातु । जरत्ऽअष्टिम् । मा । पृथिवी । कृणोतु ॥

अन्वयः—भूम्यां (मनुष्याः) देवेभ्यः हव्यं अरंकृतम् यज्ञम् ददति । भूम्यां मर्त्याः मनुष्याः स्वधया अन्नेन जीवन्ति । सा भूमिः नः प्राणम् आयुः च ददातु, पृथिवी मा जरदष्टिं कृणोतु ॥

Word-meaning:—**भूम्यां**=on the earth **देवेभ्यः**=(for the acquisition of good qualities), to objects of beneficent nature such as fire etc., **ददति**=offer. **यज्ञम्**=(civil intercourse) in a sacrificial rite. **हव्यं**=(possible of exchange) objects of sacrifice. **अरंकृतं**=refined and well prepared. **जीवन्ति**=live. **स्वधया**=by their power of endur-ance. **अन्नेन**=through food. **प्राणं**=vital power. **आयुः**=long life. **जरदष्टिं**=praising God in all actions; till growing old. **कृणोतु**=may make.

Translation:—In the Motherland men keep on a mutual refined civil intercourse for their betterment by the acquisition of good qualities. By means of their power of endurance and through food mortal men live on the earth. May that Motherland, (by these acts) give us vitality and long life and may she help me to live to a good old age.

Purport:—The means of improving oneself is keeping company with good men and trying to imitate their qualities.

(५३) यस्ते गन्धः पृथिवि संबभूव यं बिभ्रत्योषधयो यमापः । यं गन्धर्वा अप्सरसश्च भेजिरे तेन मा सुरभिं कृणु मा नो द्विक्षत कश्चन ॥२३॥

(53) Yastē gandhah pṛthivi sambabhūva yam bibhartyōṣadhayo yamāpah । Yam gandharvā apsarasaśca bhējirē tēna mā surabhim kṛṇu mā nō dvikṣata kaścana ॥ 23.

पदपाठः—यः । ते । गन्धः । पृथिवि । सम्ऽबभूव । यं । बिभ्रति ओषधयः । यं । आपः । यं । गन्धर्वाः । अप्सरसः । च । भेजिरे । तेन । मा । सुरभिम् । कृणु । मा । नः । द्विक्षत । कः । चन ॥

अन्वयः—(हे) पृथिवि यः ते गन्धः संबभूव यम् ओषधयः यम् आपः बिभ्रति, यम् गन्धर्वाः अप्सरसः च भेजिरे तेन मा सुरभिं कृणु। मा नो द्विक्षत कश्चन ॥

Word-meaning:—**गन्धः**=smell. **संबभूव**=is produced, exists. **ओषधयः**=herbs, plants. **गन्धर्वाः**=creatures constituted of particles of earth. **अप्सरसः**=creatures moving in water or space. **भेजिरे**=particles. **सुरभिं**=powerful. **द्विक्षत**=bear ill will. **कः चन**=nobody.

Translation:—May the E a r t h through that characteristic of hers which appears as smell, borne by herbs and waters, which is shared in by creatures constituted of earthly particles and by creatures moving in water (or space), make me powerful. May nobody bear us ill will.

Purport:—Earth is endowed with smell and the bodies of all embodied creatures also are endowed with smell and therefore depend upon the former. Men should investigate the constituents of earth and develop their powers.

(५४) यस्ते गन्धः पुष्करमाविवेश यं संजभ्रुः सूर्याया विवाहे। अमर्त्याः पृथिवि गन्धमग्रे तेनं मा सुरभिं कृणु मा नो द्विक्षत कश्चन ॥२४॥

(54) Yāstē gandhah puṣkaram āvivēśa yam sañjabhruh sūryāyā vivāhē I Amartyāh pṛthivi gandham agrē tēna mā surabhim kṛṇu mā nō dvikṣata kaścana II 24.

पदपाठः—यः। ते। गन्धः। पुष्करम्। आऽविवेश। यम्। सम्ऽजभ्रुः। सूर्यायाः। विऽवाहे। अमर्त्याः। पृथिवि। गन्धम्। अग्रे। तेन। मा। सुरभिम्। कृणु। मा। नः। द्विक्षत। कः। चन ॥

अन्वयः—पृथिवि यः ते गन्धः पुष्करमाविवेश यम् गन्धम् अग्रे अमर्त्याः सूर्यायाः विवाहे संजभ्रुः तेन मा सुरभिं कृणु। मा नो द्विक्षत कश्चन ॥

Word-meaning:—**पुष्करं** = nutrient objects. **आविवेश** = entered. **संजभ्रुः**=gathered, collected. **सूर्यायाः** = of the sun -light. **विवाहे** = in conveying, or carrying. **अमर्त्याः** = the immortals, the industrious.

Translation:—May the Earth by that frgrance of hers which has entered into nutrient objects, which the enterprising noble-minded men have gathered from the diffused light of the sun, make me powerful. May nobody bear us any ill will.

Purport:—The fragrance, that is, the special ingredients of the earth enter different objects and nourish them. Through the sun's heat this fragrance spreads far and wide. Those who know this secret about the earth benefit themselves by it and attain to happiness.

(५५) यस्ते॑ ग॒न्धः पुरु॑षेषु स्त्री॒षु पुं॒सु भगो॒ रुचि॑ः । यो अश्वे॑षु वी॒रेषु॒ यो मृगेषू॒त ह॒स्तिषु॑ । क॒न्यायां॑ वर्चो॒ यद्भू॑मे॒ तेना॒स्माँ अपि॒ सं सृ॑ज मा नो॑ द्विक्षत॒ कश्च॒न ॥ २५ ॥

(55) Yastē gandhah puruṣēṣu strīṣu puṃsu bhagō rucih I Yō aśvēṣu vīrēṣu yō mṛgēṣūta hastiṣu I Kanyāyām varcō yadbhūmē tenāsmāṃ api saṃ sṛja mā nō dvikṣata kaścana II 25.

पदपाठः—यः । ते । ग॒न्धः । पुरु॑षेषु । स्त्री॒षु । पुम्ऽसु । भगः । रुचिः । यः । अश्वे॑षु । वी॒रेषु॑ । यः । मृगेषु॑ । उ॒त । ह॒स्तिषु॑ । क॒न्यांयाम् । वर्चः । यत् । भू॒मे॒ । तेन॑ । अ॒स्मान । अपि॑ । सम् । सृ॒ज । मा । नः॒ । द्वि॒क्षत॒ । कः । च॒न ॥

अन्वयः—पृथिवि यः ते गन्धः पुरुषेषु यः स्त्रीषु पुंसु भगः रुचिः (च) यः वीरेषु अश्वेषु यः मृगेषु उत हस्तिषु, यत् वर्चः कन्यायां, भूमे तेन अस्मान् अपि सं सृज । मा नः कश्चन द्विक्षत ॥

Word-meaning:—**पुरुषेषु**=leaders of men. **भगः**= enjoyable potency. **रुचिः**=lustre. **वीरेषु अश्वेषु**=swift horses. **कन्यायां**=in the constellation virgo, in the maiden. **भूमे**= (in) the shelter or abode of all **वर्चः**=lustre, vigour. **संसृज** =unite.

Translation:—May the Earth, the abode of all, by her special characteristic distinguished by fragrance which appears in leaders of men (as their powerful activity), in male and female creatures as their enjoyable qualities and lustre, in fast running horses, the deer and the elephant as agility and greatness, in the constellation virgo as its lustre (in the maiden as her charming modesty), bestow on us also that virtue of hers. May nobody bear us any ill will.

Purport:—Human beings and other embodied creatures, as well as the stars and planets of the intermediate region exist under the aegis of the earth. Man should, therefore, develop his beneficent powers and remove all obstacles in his and others' way of life.

(५६) शिला भूमिरश्मा पांसुः सा भूमिः सन्धृता धृता । तस्यै हिरण्यवक्षसे पृथिव्या अकरं नमः ॥ २६ ॥

(56) Śilā bhūmiraśmā pāṃsuh sā bhūmih sandhṛta dhṛtā । Tasyāi hiraṇyavakṣasē pṛthivyā akaram namah ॥ 26.

पदपाठः—शिला । भूमिः । अश्मा । पांसुः । सा । भूमिः । सम्ऽधृता । धृता । तस्यै । हिरण्यऽवक्षसे । पृथिव्यै । अकरम् । नमः ॥

अन्वयः—भूमिः शिला, अश्मा, पांसुः; सा भूमिः संधृता धृता । (अहम्) तस्यै हिरण्यवक्षसे पृथिव्यै नमः अकरम् ॥

Word-meaning:—शिला=slabs, small stones. अश्मा =boulders, rocks, stones. पांसुः=dust, gravel. सन्धृता= properly supported according to her qualities mentioned above. धृताः=stands; exists. हिरण्यवक्षसे=having gold or light in her bosom. नमः अकरम्=I salute (that is regard with admiration), I eat food for.

Translation:—The earth appears in the shape of small and big stones and dust. She is standing firmly held together only because of the qualities mentioned above. I nourish my body with food provided by this Motherland to render her service who keeps gold (or light) in her bosom.

Purport:—The land where we are born or which is our present abode and source of livelihood, demands our service in return for what it yields us. If each person were to observe this important rule in his or her life, the whole Earth will be a place of unalloyed happiness, but lack of patriotism on the part of a large number of mankind and an overstrained, self-aggrandising emotion for one's country degenerated into the ugly fetish of 'nation-worship,' renders the Earth uninhabitable.

(५७) यस्यां वृक्षा वानस्पत्या ध्रुवास्तिष्ठन्ति विश्वहा । पृथिवीं विश्वधायसं धृतामच्छावदामसि ॥ २७ ॥

(57) Yasyām vṛkṣā vānaspatyā dhruvāstiṣṭhanti viśvahā । Pṛthivīm viśvadhāyasam dhṛtāmacchāvadāmasi ॥ 27.

पदपाठः—यस्याम् । वृक्षाः । वानस्पत्याः । ध्रुवाः । तिष्ठन्ति । विश्वहा । पृथिवीम् । विश्वऽधायसम् । धृताम् । अच्छऽआवदामसि ॥

अन्वयः—यस्यां वृक्षाः वानस्पत्याः विश्वहा ध्रुवाः तिष्ठन्ति, (ताम्) विश्वधायसम् धृतां पृथिवीम् अच्छावदामसि ॥

Word-meaning:—**वानस्पत्याः**=(lords of the wood) grown from the seeds of huge trees. **ध्रुवाः**=firm. **विश्वहा**=evermore in various ways. **विश्वधायसम**=supporting all these. **धृतां**=supported by brave men. **अच्छ आवदामसि**=we invoke upon and welcome.

Translation:—On whom big trees the lords of the wood evermore stand firm, that Motherland, the supporter of all and herself supported by brave men, we invoke upon and welcome.

Purport:—The Motherland produces trees which yield fruit, flowers, leaves etc., for our use. We should bear this in mind and guard her.

(५८) उदीरा॑णा उतासी॑ना॒स्तिष्ठ॑न्तः प्र॒क्राम॑न्तः । प॒द्भ्यां द॑क्षिण-स॒व्याभ्यां॑ मा व्य॑थिष्महि॒ भूम्या॑म् ॥ २८ ॥

(58) Udīrāṇā utāsīnāstiṣṭhantah prakrāmantah I Padbhyām dakṣiṇasavyābhyām mā vyathiṣmahi bhūmyām II 28.

पदपाठः—उ॒त्ऽईरा॑णाः । उ॒त । आसी॑नाः । तिष्ठ॑न्तः । प्र॒ऽक्राम॑न्तः । प॒त्ऽभ्यां॑म् । द॒क्षि॒ण॒ऽस॒व्याभ्यां॑म् । मा । व्य॒थि॒ष्म॒हि॒ । भूम्यां॑म् ॥

अन्वयः—(वयम्) उदीराणाः उत आसीनाः तिष्ठन्तः प्रक्रामन्तः दक्षिणसव्याभ्यां पद्भ्यां भूम्यां मा व्यथिष्महि ॥

Word-meaning:—उदीराणाः = rising up. प्रक्रामन्तः = going. पद्भ्यां = on either leg or foot. दक्षिणसव्याभ्यां = right or left. व्यथिष्महि = reel, stagger.

Translation:—Whether rising up, or seated, or standing or going, may we not stagger on this Motherland of ours either on the right foot or the left.

Purport:—Men should serve their Mothercountry maintaining always their presence of mind and health, and thereby make all happy.

(५९) वि॒मृग्व॑रीम् पृ॒थि॒वीमा व॑दामि क्ष॒मां भूमि॑म् ब्रह्म॑णा वावृधा॒नां । ऊर्जं॑ पु॒ष्टं बिभ्र॑तीमन्नभा॒गं घृ॒तं त्वा॒भि नि षी॑देम भूमे ॥ २९ ॥

(59) Vimṛgvarīm pṛthivīmā vadāmi kṣamām bhūmim brahmaṇā vāvṛdhānām I Ūrjam puṣṭam bibhratīmannabhāgam ghṛtam tvābhi ni ṣīdēma bhūmē II 29.

पदपाठः—वि॒ऽमृग्व॑रीम् । पृ॒थि॒वीम् । आ । व॒दा॒मि॒ । क्ष॒माम् । भूमि॑म् । ब्रह्म॑णा । वा॒वृ॒धा॒नाम् । ऊर्ज॑म् । पु॒ष्टम् । बिभ्र॑ती॒म् । अ॒न्न॒ऽभा॒गं । घृ॒तम् । त्वा॒ । अ॒भि । नि । सी॒दे॒म॒ । भू॒मे॒ ॥

अन्वयः—विमृग्वरीम्, क्षमां, भूमिं, ब्रह्मणा वावृधानां, ऊर्जम् पुष्टम् अन्नभागम् घृतम् बिभ्रतीम् पृथिवीम् आवदामि । भूमे त्वा अभि निषीदेम ॥

Word-meaning:—**विमृग्वरीं**=fit to be sought after in various ways. **आवदामि**=I invoke upon. **क्षमां**=able to support. **भूमिं**=firm. **ब्रह्मणा**=through Vedic lore or food. **वावृधानां**=grown. **ऊर्जं**=nutritive thing. **पुष्टं**=strengthening. **बिभ्रतीं**=bearing. **अन्नभागं**=portion of food, **घृतं**=molten butter. **त्वा अभि**=on her, **निषीदेम**=may we sit, or rest,

Translation:—I invoke upon that Motherland who is sought after in various ways, who is able to support (all), who is firm, who grows (day by day) by means of the Vedic Lore, who bears strengthening, nourishing and fatty thing's fit for food. May we establish ourselves at peace on that Motherland.

Purport:—Scientists through the knowledge of Geology and other sciences should explore the earth and securing beneficent things advance in health and strength and advise others to do likewise.

(६०) शुद्धा न आपस्तन्वे क्षरन्तु यो नः सेदुरप्रिये तं नि दध्मः। पवित्रेण पृथिवि मोत् पुनामि ॥ ३० ॥

(60) Śuddhā na āpastanvē kṣarantu yō nah sēdurapriyē taṃ ni dadhmah। Pavitrēna pṛthivi mōt punāmi ॥ 30.

पदपाठः—शुद्धाः। नः। आपः। तन्वे। क्षरन्तु। यः। नः। सेदुः। अप्रिये। तम्। नि। दध्मः। पवित्रेण। पृथिवि। मा। उत्। पुनामि ॥

अन्वयः—नः तन्वे शुद्धाः आपः क्षरन्तु, यः नः सेदुः तम् अप्रिये निदध्मः। पृथिवि मा पवित्रेण उत्पुनामि ॥

Word-meaning:—**तन्वे**=for body. **क्षरन्तु**=may flow **सेदुः**=destructive, harmful practices. **अप्रिये**=on the enemy. **निदध्मः**=shift, put on. **पवित्रेण**=good, righteous practices **उत् पुनामि**=I purify, cleanse.

Translation:—May the Motherland, let flow pure waters for the cleansing of our bodies. All evil and ruinous practices we shift on to the foe, and I sanctify myself by good and virtuous dealing.

Purport:—Just as we wash off the dirt sticking to our bodies with water, we should purge our heart and mind also of all impurities and sanctify our soul by righteous living, Evil company also should be given up but this should involve no injury to others, otherwise there would be no purification.

(६१) यास्ते प्राचीः प्रदिशो या उदीचीर्यास्ते भूमे अधराद्याश्च पश्चात् । स्योनास्ता मह्यं चरते भवन्तु मा नि पप्तं भुवने शिश्रियाणः ॥ ३१ ॥

(61) Yāstē prācīh pradiśō yā udīcīryāstē bhūmē adharādyāśca paṣcāt I Syōnāstā mahyam caratē bhavantu mā ni paptam bhuvanē siśriyāṇah II 31.

पदपाठः—याः । ते । प्राचीः । प्रऽदिशः । याः । उदीचीः । याः । ते । भूमे । अधरात् । याः । च । पश्चात् । स्योनाः । ताः । मह्यम् । चरते । भवन्तु । मा । नि । पप्तम् । भुवने । शिश्रियाणः ॥

अन्वयः—(हे) भूमे याः ते प्राचीः प्रदिशः याः उदीचीः याः ते अधरात् याः च पश्चात् ताः मह्यम् चरते स्योनाः भवन्तु । (अहम्) भुवने शिश्रियाणः मा नि पप्तम् ॥

Word-meanig:—प्राचीः =facing, front, eastern, **उदीचीः**=upper, northern, **अधरात्**=lower, nether, southern, **पश्चात्**=behind, back, western. **स्योनाः**=pleasant, tending to happiness. **चरते**=living and moving. **नि पप्तं**=fall down, stumble. **शिश्रियाणः**=resting on.

Translation:—May the eastern and the northern regions of the Motherland, those lying southward and those westward be propitious unto me who am living and moving in her. As long as I tread upon her ground may I not stumble.

Purport:—Men should be diligent and moving about, if they have to enjoy happiness in every direction.

(६२) मा नः पश्चान्मा पुरस्तान्नुदिष्ठा मोत्तरादधरादुत । स्वस्ति भूमे नो भव मा विदन् परिपन्थिनो वरीयो यावया वधम् ॥ ३२ ॥

(62) Mā nah paṣcānmā purastānnudiṣṭhā mōttarād-adharāduta । Svasti bhūmē nō bhava mā vidan paripan-thinō varīyō yāvayā vadham ॥ 32.

पदपाठः—मा । नः । पश्चात् । मा । पुरस्तात् । नुदिष्ठाः । मा । उत्तरात् । अधरात् । उत । स्वस्ति । भूमे । नः । भव । मा । विदन् । परिऽपन्थिनः । वरीयः । यावय । वधम् ॥

अन्वयः—(हे) भूमे नः मा पश्चात् मा पुरस्तात् मा उत्तरात् मा उत अधरात् नुदिष्ठाः । (हे) भूमे नः स्वस्ति भव, परिपन्थिनः (नः) मा विदन्, वधं वरीयः यावय ॥

Word-meaning:—**पुरस्तात्**=from before, **नुदिष्ठाः**= drive, push. **स्वस्ति**=auspicious, **मा विदन्**=may not they overtake, overpower. **परिपन्थिनः**=highwaymen, antagonists, **वरीयः**=very far, **यावय**=remove, **वधं**=lethal or deadly arms.

Translation:—May not the Motherland drive us from before or behind, from above or below, but be gracious unto us. May not she let the robbers find us, but keep the deadly weapons (of war) far away from us.

Purprot:—Man should be on his guard and save himself from the snares of the wicked from every quarter.

(६३) यावत् तेऽभि विपश्यामि भूमे सूर्येण मेदिना । तावन्मे चक्षुर्मा मेष्टोत्तरामुत्तरां समाम् ॥ ३३ ॥

(63) Yāvat tē'bhi vipaśyāmi bhūmē sūryēṇa mēdinā । Tāvanmē caksurmā mēṣṭōttarāmuttarām samām ॥ 33.

Word-meaning:—यावत्—तावत्=as long as. **अभि विपश्यामि**=I look around. **मेदिना**=for a friend. **मेष्ट**=fail in, lose, destroy. **उत्तरामुत्तरां**=(successive) good, excellent. **समां**=favourable or beneficent effort or undertaking.

Translation:—May the Motherland help me so that as long as I look around with the sun for my friend, my eyesight may not fail in successive excellent and beneficent undertakings.

Purport:—Man should always utilise nature and his own faculties in endeavours to do good to himself and others.

(६४) यच्छयानः पर्यावर्ते दक्षिणं सव्यमभि भूमे पार्श्वम् । उत्तानास्त्वा प्रतीचीं यत्पृष्टीभिरधिशेमहे । मा हिंसीस्तत्र नो भूमे सर्वस्य प्रतिशीवरि ॥३४॥

(64) Yacchayānah paryāvartē dakṣiṇam savyamabhi bhūmē pārśvam । Uttānāstvā pratīcīm yatpṛṣṭībhiradhiśēmahē । Mā himsīstatra nō bhūmē sarvasya pratiśīvari ॥ 34.

पदपाठः—यत् । शयानः । परिऽआवर्ते । दक्षिणम् । सव्यम् । अभि । भूमे । पार्श्वम् । उत्तानाः । त्वा । प्रतीचीम् । यत् । पृष्टीभिः । अधिऽशेमहे । मा । हिंसीः । तत्र । नः । भूमे । सर्वस्य । प्रतिऽशीवरि ॥

अन्वयः—भूमे, यत् शयानः दक्षिणम् सव्यम् (वा) पार्श्वम् अभि पर्यावर्ते यत् उत्तानाः प्रतीचीम् त्वा पृष्टीभिः अधिशेमहे, सर्वस्य प्रतीशीवरि भूमे, तत्र नो मा हिंसीः ॥

Word-meaning:—यत्=while. **शयानः**=lying down, sleeping. **पर्यावर्ते**=I turn upon, change sides. **सव्यम्**=left **उत्तानाः**=stretched at full length, with face upwards. **प्रतीचीं**=meeting, touching. **पृष्टीभिः**=with the ribs. **अधिशेमहे**=we sleep upon. **मा**=do not. **हिंसीः**=hurt. **तत्र**=then. **प्रतिशीवरि**=who furnishes a bed or place for sleeping.

Trnaslation:—When, as I lie down, I turn upon my right or left side, or when stretched at full length, we sleep upon the Earth touching our ribs, may not she, then, who furnishes a bed for all, hurt us.

Purport:—Land becomes a source of happiness to those diligent people who level ups and downs and make it even.

(६५) यत् तें भूमे विखनामि क्षिप्रं तदपि रोहतु । मा ते मर्म विमृग्वरि मा ते हृदयमर्पिपम् ॥३५॥

(65) Yat tē bhūmē vikhanāmi kṣipram tadapi rōhatu I Mā tē marma vimṛgvari mā tē hṛdayamarpipam II 35.

पदपाठः—यत् । ते । भूमे । विऽखनामि । क्षिप्रम् । तत् । अपिं । रोहतु । मा । ते । मर्म । विऽमृग्वरि । मा । ते । हृदयम् । अर्पिपम् ॥

अन्वयः—भूमे, यत् ते विखनामि तत् अपि शीघ्रम् रोहतु । विमृग्वरि मा ते मर्म मा ते हृदयम् (अहम्) अर्पिपम् ॥

Word-meaning:—**विखनामि**=I dig out. **शीघ्रम्**=quickly. **रोहतु**=grow, fill up. **विमृग्वरि**=who is fit to be sought after. **मर्म**=vitals, such parts as are essential for vegetation. **अर्पिपं**=injure, damage.

Translation—May the Motherland soon fill up whatever I dig out of her. Of her who is fit to be sought after, may I not damage those parts which are vital to vegetation, or the interior regions where she stores rare and precious things.

Purport—Men proficient in Geology and knowledge of the earth's crust should carefully dig out precious metals and stones from the earth and keep it fit also for farming purposes.

(६६) ग्रीष्मस्तें भूमे वर्षाणिं शरद्धेमन्तः शिशिरो वसन्तः । ऋतवस्ते विहिता हायनीरहोरात्रे पृथिवि नो दुहाताम् ॥३६॥

(66) Grīṣmastē bhūmē varṣāṇi śaraddhēmantah śiśirō vasantah । Ṛtavastē vihitā hāyanīrahōrātrē pṛthivi nō duhātām ॥ 36.

पदपाठः—ग्रीष्मः । ते । भूमे । वर्षाणि । शरत् । हेमन्तः । शिशिरः । वसन्तः । ऋतवः । ते । विऽहिताः । हायनीः । अहोरात्रे इति । पृथिवि । नः । दुहाताम् ॥

अन्वयः—भूमे, ग्रीष्मः, वर्षाणि, शरत्, हेमन्तः, शिशिरः, वसन्तः, ते ऋतवः । पृथिवि, विहिताः हायनीः ते अहोरात्रे नः दुहातां ॥

Word-meaning:—ग्रीष्मः = summer, the hot season. वर्षाणि = the rains. शरत् = the autumn. हेमन्तः = winter. शिशिरः = frost, cold season. वसन्तः = spring. विहिताः = assigned, allotted. हायनीः = years. दुहाताम् = may fulfil.

Translation:—The summer, the rains, the autumn, the winter, the frosts and the spring are the seasons due to the (motions of the) Earth. On the spacious Land, our Mother, may the years of our life assigned by God be completed by her days and nights.

Purport:—Man can and should live a long life on Earth doing proper work and adopting a way of living fit for each season of the year.

(६७) यार्प सर्पं विजमाना विमृग्वरी यस्यामासंन्नग्नयो ये अप्स्व१न्तः । परा दस्यून् ददती देवपीयूनिन्द्रं वृणाना पृथिवी न वृत्रम् । शक्राय दध्रे वृषभाय वृष्णे ॥३७॥

(67) Yāpa sarpam vijamānā vimṛgvarī yasyāmā-sannagnayō yē apsvantah । Parā dasyūn dadatī dēvapīyūnindram vṛṇānā pṛthivī na vṛtram । Śakrāya dadhrē vṛṣabhāya vṛṣnē ॥ 37.

पदपाठः—या । अप । सर्पम् । विजमाना । विऽमृग्वरी । यस्याम् । आसन । अग्नयः । ये । अप्ऽसु । अन्तः । परा । दस्यून । ददती ।

देवऽपीयून् । इन्द्रम् । वृणाना । पृथिवी । न । वृत्रम् । शक्राय । दध्रे ।
वृषभाय । वृष्णे ॥

अन्वयः—या विमृग्वरी (पृथिवी) अप सर्पं विजमाना, यस्यां (ते) अग्नयः आसन् ये अप्सु अन्तः (सन्ति) (सा) पृथिवी देवपीयून् दस्यून परा ददती, इन्द्रं वृणाना न (तु) वृत्रम् , वृषभाय वृष्णे शक्राय दध्रे ॥

Word-meaning:—**अपसर्प** = gliding. **विजमाना** = moving. **विमृग्वरी**=fit to be sought after. **आसन्**=there are. **अग्नयः**=fires, different types of heat. **अप्सु**=in creatures, in living beings. **परा ददती**=leaving far away. **दस्यून्**=the wicked. **देवपीयून्**=revilers or persecutors of the good. **इन्द्रं**=a righteous man of abilities. **वृणाना**=selecting. **वृत्रं**=the foe, the obstructor of the righteous. **शक्राय**=for the vigorous. **वृषभाय**=for the powerful. **वृष्णे**=for the manly. **दध्रे**=is established.

Translation:—That Earth, much to be sought after, who moves along gliding, in whom the different types of heat exist that are found working in the bodies of living beings, that Motherland who casts away the wicked that revile (or persecute) the righteous, and who prefers a virtuous man of great abilities to one who obstructs the good, is established for the powerful, manly and vigorous.

Purport:—The righteous who understand the secrets of the Earth and taking a lesson from her ever forward movement are afire with the spirit of undaunted diligence that baffles all obstacles, will derive happiness from her, whereas the wicked will ever be miserable.

(६८) यस्यां सदोहविर्धाने यूपो यस्यां निमीयते । ब्रह्माणो यस्यामर्चन्त्यृग्भिः साम्ना यजुर्विदः । युज्यन्ते यस्यामृत्विजः सोममिन्द्राय पातवे ॥३८॥

(68) Yasyām sadō havirdhānē yūpō yasyām nimīyatē । Brahmāṇō yasyāmarcantyṛgbhih sāmnā yajurvēdah । Yujyantē yasyāmṛtvijah sōmamindrāya pātavē ॥ 38.

पदपाठः—यस्याम् । सदःऽहविर्धाने । यूपः । यस्याम् । निऽमीयते । ब्रह्माणः । यस्याम् । अर्चन्ति । ऋक्ऽभिः । साम्ना । यजुःऽविदः । युज्यन्ते । यस्याम् । ऋत्विजः । सोमम् । इन्द्राय । पातवे ॥

अन्वयः—यस्यां सदोहविर्धाने यस्यां यूपः निमीयते, यस्यां ब्रह्माणः ऋग्भिः, यजुर्विदः साम्ना अर्चन्ति, यस्यां ऋत्विजः इन्द्राय पातवे सोमम् युज्यन्ते ॥

Word-meanig:—**सदोहविर्धाने**=places for assemblies and granaries. **यूपः**=triumphal posts. **निमीयते**=is erected. **ब्रह्माणः**=learned in Vedic Lore. **अर्चन्ति**=adore. **ऋग्भिः**= with hymns from the Vedas. **साम्ना**=with knowledge leading to final beatitude. **यजुर्विदः**=those who know how to worship God. **युज्यन्ते**=go in trance.

Translation—That Motherland who abounds in places for assemblies for religious works and granaries, on whom triumphal posts are erected at sacrifice, on whom men versed in Vedic Lore praise God with Vedic hymns, on whom those proficient in worshipping Him adore Him by means of knowledge leading to final beatitude, and on whom, the devout accustomed to worship the Lord in all seasons go into trance to give the soul a foretaste of the state of salvation;

Purport:—Let us endeavour to accomplish our legitimate wishes in the Motherland who enables the knowers of Veda and great yogis through right knowledge of God to attain salvation.

(६९) यस्यां पूर्वे भूतकृत ऋषयो गा उदानृचुः । सप्त सत्रेण वेधसो यज्ञेन तपसा सह ॥३९॥

(69) Yasyām pūrvē bhūtakṛta ṛṣayō gā udānṛcuh । Sapta satrēṇa vēdhasō yajñēna tapasā saha ॥

पदपाठः—यस्याम् । पूर्वे । भूतऽकृतः । ऋषयः । गाः । उत् । आनृचुः । सप्त । सत्रेण । वेधसः । यज्ञेन । तपसा । सह ॥

अन्वयः—यस्यां (भूम्यां) पूर्वे भूतकृतः वेधसः सप्त ऋषयः सत्रेण यज्ञेन तपसा सह गाः उदानृचुः ॥

Word-meaning:—पूर्वे = in their abodes in the shape of the human body. भूतकृतः = veracious workers, benefactors of creatures. ऋषयः = the seers that procure sense objects. गाः = the Vedic lore. उदानृचुः = served in an excellent manner. सप्त = seven (viz:—the five sense organs, the mind and the intellect). सत्रेण = by the protector of the virtuous or righteous. वेधसः = possessing knowledge; intellectual. यज्ञेन = by good works, viz: honouring the wise, associating with the good and charity.

Translation:—that Motherland, on whom resident in their abodes (in the shape of human bodies), the seven seers (*of sense objects viz., the five sense organs, the mind and the intellect*), truthful workers possessing knowledge have served the Vedic Lore in the most excellent manner performing good works (*viz: honouring the wise, associating with the righteous and practising charity*) that shield the virtuous accompanied by the observance of austere vows (*such as continence &c.*);

Purport:—Sheltered by the Motherland, man, through the agency of the organs of his person attains Vedic Knowledge and advances spiritually, Hence, if we are diligent for the Motherland, happiness is ours.

(७०) सा नो भूमिरा दिशतु यद्धनं कामयामहे । भगो अनुप्रयुङ्क्तामिन्द्र एतु पुरोगवः ॥४०॥

(70) Sā nō bhūmirā diśatu yaddhanam kāmayāmahe I Bhagō anuprayunktāmindra ētu purōgavaḥ ॥ 40.

पदपाठः—सा । नः । भूमिः । आ । दिशतु । यत । धनम् । कामयामहे । भगः । अनुऽप्रयुङ्क्ताम् । इन्द्रः । एतु । पुरःऽगवः ॥

अन्वयः—सा भूमिः नः धनम् आ दिशतु यत् (वयम्) कामयामहे। भगः (नः) अनुप्रयुङ्क्तां, इन्द्रः पुरोगवः एतु ॥

Word-meaning:—आदिशतु=bestow on us. कामयामहे =we crave after. भगः=fortun . अनुप्रयुङ्क्तां=may ever favour. पुरोगवः=leader, one who heads or goes before.

Translation:—may that Motherland bestow on us that munificence which we crave after, let fortune be ever favourable to us, and may righteous men of worth be our leaders.

Purport:—men should follow great and God-fearing persons, attain Vedic knowledge, develop their powers and become leaders of men.

(७१) यस्यां गायन्ति नृत्यन्ति भूम्यां मर्त्या व्यैलबाः। युध्यन्ते यस्यामाक्रन्दो यस्यां वदति दुन्दुभिः। सा नो भूमिः प्रणुदतां सपत्नानसपत्नं मा पृथिवी कृणोतु ॥४१॥

(71) Yasyām gāyanti nṛtyanti bhūmyām martyā vyāilabāh। Yudhyantē yasyāmākrandō yasyām vadati dundubhih। Sā nō bhūmih praṇudatām sapatnān asa-patnam mā pṛthivī kṛṇōtu ॥ 41.

पदपाठः—यस्याम्। गायन्ति। नृत्यन्ति। भूम्याम्। मर्त्याः। विऽऐलबाः। युध्यन्ते। यस्याम्। आऽक्रन्दः। यस्याम्। वदति। दुन्दुभिः। सा। नः। भूमिः। प्र। नुदताम्। सऽपत्नान्। असपत्नम्। मा। पृथिवी। कृणोतु ॥

अन्वयः—यस्यां भूम्यां व्यैलबाः मर्त्याः गायन्ति नृत्यन्ति (च), यस्यां भूम्यां आक्रन्दः युध्यन्ते, यस्यां दुन्दुभिः वदति, सा भूमिः नः सपत्नान् प्रणुदतां, पृथिवी मा असपत्नम् कृणोतु ॥

Word-meaning:—गायन्ति=they sing. नृत्यन्ति=they dance. व्यैलबाः (वि+इला+अण्+बण्+ड)=speaking different kinds of languages. युध्यन्ते=they fight. आक्रन्दः=shouting (warriors), war-cry, lamentation. वदति=sounds, resounds.

दुन्दुभिः=drum, war drum. प्रणुदतां=may remove. सपत्नान्=enemies, antagonists. असपत्नम्=bereft of enemies.

Translation:—May that Motherland of ours on whom men speaking various tongues sing and dance, on whom they meet in battle and the war-cry and the war drum resound, remove our foes and may the spacious Earth rid us of them.

Purport:—The righteous diligently removing all obstacles from their way attain peace and happiness sheltered by the Motherland, whereon, ordinary people sing, dance, cry, shout and fight.

(७२) यस्यामन्नं व्रीहियवौ यस्यां इमाः पञ्च कृष्टयः । भूम्यै पर्जन्यपत्न्यै नमोऽस्तु वर्षमेदसे ॥४२॥

(72) Yasyāmannaṁ vrīhiyavāu yasyā imāh pañca kṛṣṭayah I Bhūmyāi parjanyapatnyāi namo'stu varṣamēdasē II 42.

पदपाठः—यस्याम् । अन्नम् । व्रीहिऽयवौ । यस्याः । इमाः । पञ्च । कृष्टयः । भूम्यै । पर्जन्यऽपत्न्यै । नमः । अस्तु । वर्षऽमेदसे ॥

अन्वयः—यस्यां (भूमौ) अन्नम् व्रीहियवौ यस्याः इमाः पञ्च कृष्टयः (तस्यै) भूम्यै वर्षमेदसे पर्जन्यपत्न्यै नमः अस्तु ॥

Word-meaning:—पञ्च=five (i. e. related to the five great elements earth, water, light, air and ether). पर्जन्यपत्न्यै=protected by the clouds. वर्षमेदसे=loving rains. नमः=food that we eat, salute.

Translation:—May the food we eat be for the protection of that Motherland of ours on whom rice, barley and such other cereals fit for food abound, to whom belong these human beings related to the five great elements, to whom the rains are dear and who is protected by rain-clouds.

Purport:—With the aid of the five great elements man should procure his food but only for the service of the Motherland who shelters and nourishes him.

(७३) यस्याः पुरो देवकृताः क्षेत्रे यस्या विकुर्वते । प्रजापतिः पृथिवीं विश्वगर्भामाशामाशां रण्यां नः कृणोतु ॥४३॥

(73) Yasyāh purō dēvakṛtāh kṣētrē yasyā vikurvatē Prajāpatih pṛthivīm viśvagarbhām āśāmāśām raṇyām nah kṛnōtu ॥ 43.

पदपाठः—यस्याः । पुरः । देवऽकृताः । क्षेत्रे । यस्याः । विऽकुर्वते । प्रजाऽपतिः । पृथिवीम् । विश्वऽगर्भाम् । आशाम्ऽआशाम् । रण्याम् । नः । कृणोतु ।

अन्वयः—यस्याः पुरः देवकृताः, यस्याः क्षेत्रे(षु) (जनाः) विकुर्वते । प्रजापतिः (तां) पृथिवीम् विश्वगर्भाम् पृथिवीं नः आशामाशां रण्यां कृणोतु ॥

Word-meaning:—**पुरः**=cities (palaces, forts, ramparts &c. included). **देवकृताः**=built by the wise, or learned. **क्षेत्रे (क्षेत्रेषु)**=in fields, on land. **विकुर्वते**=men do various types of work. **प्रजापतिः**=God the Lord of progenies. **विश्वगर्भां**=who bears everything in her interior. **आशामाशां**=in every quarter. **रण्यां**=pleasant, charming.

Translation:—Whose cities are the work of learned men, on whose land men do various types of work, may God the Lord of progenies make that Motherland pleasant for us in every quarter.

Purport:—God bestows happiness on those wise men who build cities, erect forts, establish institutions offices etc., and thus advance their own as well as other people's happiness.

(७४) निधिं बिभ्रती बहुधा गुहा वसु मणिं हिरण्यं पृथिवी ददातु मे । वसूनि नो वसुदा रासमाना देवी दधातु सुमनस्यमाना ॥४४॥

(74) Nidhim bibhratī bahudhā guhā vasu maṇim hiraṇyam pṛthivī dadātu mē । Vasūni nō vasudā rāsamānā dēvī dadhātu sumanasyamānā ॥ 44.

पदपाठः—निऽधिम् । बिभ्रती । बहुऽधा । गुहा । वसु । मणिम् । हिरण्यम् पृथिवी । ददातु । मे । वसूनि । नः । वसुऽदाः । रासमाना । देवी । दधातु । सुऽमनस्यमाना ॥

अन्वयः—गुहा निधिम् बहुधा बिभ्रती पृथिवी, वसु, मणिम्, हिरण्यम् मे ददातु । (सा) वसुदाः वसूनि रासमाना देवी सुमनस्यमाना नः दधातु ॥

Word-meaning:—गुहा=in the interior. निधिम्=treasure. वसुदाः=giver of munificence. रासमाना=giving. देवी=possessing good qualities. सुमनस्यमाना=with a favourable disposition, or a loving heart.

Translation:—May our spacious Motherland who stores in her interior treasure in various ways, bestow on me riches, jewels and gold. Giver of munificence, may she who possesses noble qualities, distributing various kinds of wealth support us with a kind heart.

Purport:—Wise men who investigate the interior of the earth rejoice at the find of wealth, precious stones and metals.

(७५) जनं बिभ्रती बहुधा विवाचसं नानाधर्माणं पृथिवी यथौकसम् । सहस्रं धारा द्रविणस्य मे दुहां ध्रुवेव धेनुरनपस्फुरन्ती ॥४५॥

(75) Janam bibhratī bahudhā vivācasam nānādharmāṇam pṛthivī yathāukasam | Sahasram dhārā draviṇasya mē duhām dhruvēva dhēnuranapasphurantī || 45.

पदपाठः—जनम् । बिभ्रती । बहुऽधा । विऽवाचसम् । नानाऽधर्माणम् पृथिवी । यथाऽओकसम् । सहस्रम् । धाराः । द्रविणस्य । मे । दुहाम् । ध्रुवाऽइव । धेनुः । अनपऽस्फुरन्ती ।

अन्वयः—विवाचसम् नानाधर्माणम् जनम् यथौकसं बहुधा बिभ्रती पृथिवी, अनपस्फुरन्ती ध्रुवेव धेनुः द्रविणस्य सहस्रम धाराः मे दुहां ॥

Word-meanig:—विवाचसं=possessing the power of speech in a special manner. **नानाधर्माणं**=of various qualities. **यथौकसं**=according to their place or desert. **धाराः**=streams. **ध्रुवाऽइव**=firm like. (This is a constant compound but the **इव** has to be construed with **धेनुः**). **अनपस्फुरन्ती**=never-failing.

Translation:—Just as she, according to their deserts in various ways supports the concourse of men of various qualities and specially endowed with the power of speech, may the spacious Motherland, like a constant cow that never fails pour on me a thousand streams of wealth.

Purport:—The cow subsists on fodder which costs little but the cowherd, if he is a clever man, can procure a large quantity of milk which is much more precious than her feed. Just in the same way, by education and diligence, men can develop their abilities and so profit by their Motherland.

(७६) यस्तें सर्पो वृश्चिंकस्तृष्टदंश्मा हेमन्तजंब्धो भृमलो गुहाशयें । क्रिमिर्जिन्वंत् पृथिवि यद्यदेजंति प्रावृषि तन्नः सर्पन्मोप सृपद्यच्छिवं तेनं नो मृड ॥४६॥

(76) Yastē sarpō vṛścikastṛṣṭadaṃśmā hēmanta-jabdhō bhṛmalō guhāśayē I Krimirjinvat pṛthivi yadya-dējati prāvṛṣi tannah sarpanmōpa sṛpadyacchivam tēna nō mṛḍa II 46.

पदपाठः—यः । ते । सर्पः । वृश्चिंकः । तृष्टऽदंश्मा । हेमन्तऽजंब्धः । भृमलः । गुहां । शयें । क्रिमिंः । जिन्वंत् । पृथिवि । यत्ऽयंत् । एजंति । प्रावृषिं । तत् । नः । सर्पंत् । मा । उपं । सृपत् । यत् । शिवम् । तेनं । नः । मृड ॥

अन्वयः—पृथिवि यः ते सर्पः तृष्टदंश्मा हेमन्तजब्धः भृमलः गुहाशये वृश्चिकः, (यः) क्रिमिः यत् यत् प्रावृषि जिन्वत् एजति तत् सर्पत् नः मा अपसृपत् । यत् शिवम् नः तेन मृड ॥

Word-meaning:—वृश्चिकः—scorpion. **तृष्टदंश्मा** = that by the sting of which thirst is caused, sharply-stinging (Gr.) **तृष्ट**=harsh, pungent, rugged, hoarse. **हेमन्तजब्धः**=child with winter cold. **भ्रमलः**=bewildered. **शये**=lies concealed. **जिन्वत्**=being pleased. **प्रावृषि**=in the rains. **सर्पन्**=creeping. **उप सृपत**=come near us. **मृड**=make us happy.

Translation:—The snake, the scorpion, chilled with winter-cold and bewildered lies hidden in the holes, of theEarth, the worm and whatever in the rains pleased moves about, may not these, creeping, come near us. May she bless us with all that is good,

Purport:—Men must always be on their guard lest harmful creatures should injure them,

(७७) ये ते पन्थानो बहवो जनायना रथस्य वर्त्मानसश्च यातवे । यैः संचरन्त्युभये भद्रपापास्तं पन्थानं जयेमानमित्रमतस्करं यच्छिवं तेन नो मृड ॥४७॥

(77) Yē tē panthānō bahavō janāyanā rathasya vartmānasaśca yātavē I Yāih sañcarantyubhayē bhadra-pāpāstam panthānam jayēmānamitram ataskaram yacchivam tēna nō mṛḍa II 47.

पदपाठः—ये । ते । पन्थानः । बहवः । जनऽअयनाः । रथस्य । वर्त्म । अनसः । च । यातवे । यैः । सम्ऽचरन्ति । उभये । भद्रऽपापाः । तम् । पन्थानम् । जयेम । अनमित्रम् । अतस्करम् । यत् । शिवम् । तेन । नः । मृड ।

अन्वयः—ये ते बहवः पन्थानः जनायनाः रथस्य च अनसः यातवे वर्त्म यैः उभये भद्रपापाः संचरन्ति तम् अनमित्रम् अतस्करं पन्थानं जयेम । यत् शिवम् तेन नः मृड ॥

Word-meaning:—जनायनाः=fit for people to travel upon, **वर्त्मा**=road, **अनसः**=of the waggon, **यातवे**=to go over. संचरन्ति=go together. भद्रपापा:=good and sinful. अनमित्रं=without the foe. अतस्करं=without the robber.

Trnaslation—The many ways of the Motherland fit for people to travel upon, the road for car and waggon to journey over, by which both the good and the bad pass together, may we conquer that path rid of the foe and the robber. May she bless us with all that is good.

Purport—Persons who endeavour to distinguish between the high way and the low, the good path and the bad and take to the road to righteousness will be secure from the wicked and thus attain happiness.

(७८) मुल्वं विभ्रंती गुरुभृद्भद्रपापस्यं निधनं तितिक्षुः । वराहेणं पृथिवी संविदाना सूकराय वि जिहीते मृगायं ॥४८॥

(78) Malvam bibhratī gurubhṛdbhadrapāpasya nidhanam titikṣuh I Varāhēṇa pṛthivī saṃvidānā sūkarāya vijihītē mṛgāya II 48.

पदपाठः—मुल्वम् । बिभ्रंती । गुरुभृत् । भद्रऽपापस्यं । निऽधनंम् । तितिक्षुः । वराहेणं । पृथिवी । समऽविदाना । सूकरायं । वि । जिहीते । मृगायं ।

अन्वयः—मल्वं गुरुभृत् च बिभ्रती, भद्रपापस्य निधनं तितिक्षुः, वराहेण संविदाना, पृथिवि मृगाय सूकराय विजिहीते ॥

Word-meaning::—मल्वम् (√मल्+व)=power to support. गुरुभृत्=the power to hold weight, gravitational force. निधनम्=concourse. तितिक्षुः=supporting. वराहेण=with the rain-cloud. संविदाना=in unison, in agrument with. सूकराय =of pleasant rays (the sun). विजिहीते=goes, disposes. मृगाय=the moving.

Translation:—Having the power to support things as well as the force of gravitation, she supports the concourse of the virtuous as well as of the wicked and in unison with rain-cloud, the spacious Earth dispose herself in various ways to the pleasant-rayed sun himself in motion.

Purport::—By her forces of support and attraction the Earth holds all creatures and objects on herself, and owing to her motion with the surface towards the sun water evaporates and falls down on the Earth again as rain. Man should endeavour to use the Earth in a fitting manner.

(७९) ये त आ॒र॒ण्याः प॒शवो॑ मृ॒गा वने॑ हि॒ताः सिं॒हा व्या॒घ्राः पु॑रु॒षाद॒श्चर॑न्ति । उ॒लं वृकं॑ पृथिवि दु॒च्छुना॑मि॒त ऋ॒क्षीकां॒ रक्षो॒ अप॑ बाधया॒स्मत् ॥४९॥

(79) Yē ta āraṇyāḥ paśavō mṛgā vanē hitāḥ vyāghrāḥ puruṣādaścaranti । Ulam vṛkam pṛthivi ducchunāmita ṛkṣīkām rakṣō apa bādhayāsmat ॥ 49.

पदपाठः—ये । ते॒ । आ॒र॒ण्याः । प॒शवः॑ । मृ॒गाः । वने॑ । हि॒ताः । सिं॒हाः । व्या॒घ्राः । पु॒रु॒षऽअदः॑ । चर॑न्ति । उ॒लम् । वृक॑म् । पृ॒थि॒वि॒ । दु॒च्छुना॑म् । इ॒तः । ऋ॒क्षीका॑म् । रक्षः॑ । अप॑ । बा॒ध॒य॒ । अ॒स्मत् ।

अन्वयः—ये ते आरण्याः पशवः, हिताः मृगाः सिंहाः, व्याघ्राः पुरुषादः वने चरन्ति, पृथिवि उलं वृकं, दुच्छुनां ऋक्षीकां इतः अस्मत् अप बाधय ॥

Word-meaning:—**हिताः**=beneficent. **पुरुषादः** = man-eating. **उलम्**=ferocious hyena (Gr.). **वृकम्** =the wolf. **दुच्छुनां**=of ugly gait. **ऋक्षीकां**=the she-bear. **रक्षः**=injurious creatures. **अपबाधय**=chase away.

Translation:—Her beasts of the forest such as the beneficial deer, the man-eating lion and tiger, roam about in the forest. May the Motherland chase away from us here, (these, as well as) the ferocious wolf and the she-bear of the nasty gait.

Purport:—Man should protect and forbear from killing beneficial animals, but destroy those that are harmful.

(८०) ये गन्धर्वा अप्सरसो ये चारायाः किमीदिनः । पिशाचान्त्सर्वा रक्षांसि तानस्मद् भूमे यावय ॥५०॥

(80) Yē gandharvā apsarasō yē cārāyāh kimīdinah I
Piśācāntsarvā rakṣāmsi tānasmadbhūmē yāvaya II 50.

पदपाठः—ये । गन्धर्वाः । अप्सरसः । ये । च । अरायाः । किमीदिनः । पिशाचान । सर्वा । रक्षांसि । तान् । अस्मत् । भूमे । यवय ॥

अन्वयः—ये गन्धर्वाः, अप्सरसः, ये च अरायाः, किमी दिनः, भूमे, तान् पिशाचान् सर्वा रक्षांसि अस्मत् यावय ॥

Word-meaning:—**गन्धर्वाः** (from root √ **गन्ध्**=to injure +**अच्**+**अर्व**)=harmful beings. **अप्सरसः** (**अप**+√**सृ**+**असि**) =those that go against. **अरायाः**=the stingy. **किमीदिनः**= mean persons, the ignoble. (Nir. VI, 12). **पिशाचान्**=flesh-eaters, those who injure others. **रक्षांसि**=wicked beings. **यावय**=remove from us.

Translation:—Those whose nature is to hurt others, those who work against others' welfare, the stingy and the ignoble, may the Motherland remove from our midst (these) as well as the flesh eaters and all other injurious beings.

Purport:—Men should not associate with the harmfully-inclined but only with the righteous and the former should be suppressed and the latter protected.

(८१) यां द्विपादः पक्षिणः सं पतन्ति हंसाः सुपर्णाः शकुना वयांसि । यस्यां वातो मातरिश्वेयते रजांसि कृण्वंश्च्यावयंश्च वृक्षान् । वातस्य प्रवामुपवामनु वात्यर्चिः ॥५१॥

(81) Yām dvipādah pakṣiṇah sam patanti haṃsāh suparṇāh śakunā vayāṃsi । Yasyām vātō mātariśvēyate rajāṃsi kṛṇvañścyāvayañśca vṛkṣān । Vātasya pravām upavām anu vātyarcih ॥ 51.

पदपाठः—याम् । द्विऽपादः । पक्षिणः । सम्ऽपतन्ति । हंसाः । सुऽपर्णाः । शकुनाः । वयांसि । यस्याम् । वातः मातरिश्वा । ईयते । रजांसि । कृण्वन् । च्यावयन् । च । वृक्षान् । वातस्य । प्रऽवाम् । उपऽवाम् । अनु । वाति । अर्चिः ॥

अन्वयः—यां (भूमिं) द्विपादः पक्षिणः हंसाः, सुपर्णाः, शकुनाः वयांसि, संपतन्ति । यस्यां मातरिश्वा वातः रजांसि कृण्वन् वृक्षान् च च्यावयन् ईयते, अर्चिः वातस्य प्रवां उपवां अनु वाति ॥

Word-meaning:—संपतन्ति=fly, fly together. हंसाः= swans. सुपर्णाः=eagle etc. which fly very high. शकुनाः= powerful. वयांसि=birds (like the vulture and). मातरिश्वा= blowing in the intermediate region. ईयते=blows, flows, moves. रजांसि=cloud waded with water, (dust, gr.) च्यावयन्=causing to shake or tremble. प्रवां=moving forward or before. उपवां=moving backward, behind or near. अनु=along with. (For प्रवामुपवामनुवाति=Gr. has 'pursues the blast hither and thither'). वाति=blows. अर्चिः =light, (flame, Gr.).

Translation:—To which fly together the winged bipeds such as the swan, the high flying eagle and strong birds (the vulture, kite etc.,), on whom the wind moving in the intermediate region raises dust, shakes trees and the flame of fire moves backward and forward along with the movement of the wind;

Purport:—Man should learn about birds, wind, fire etc., and profit himself by all these.

(८२) यस्यां कृष्णमरुणम् च संहिते अहोरात्रे विहिते भूम्यामधि ।

वृर्षेण भूमिः पृथिवी वृतावृता सा नो दधातु भद्रया प्रिये धामनि-धामनि ॥५२॥

(82) Yasyām kṛṣṇamaruṇam ca saṃhitē ahōrtārē vihitē bhūmyām adhi । Varṣēṇa bhūmih pṛthivī vṛtāvṛtā sā nō dadhātu bhadrayā priyē dhāmanidhāmani ॥ 52.

पदपाठः—यस्याम् । कृष्णम् । अरुणम् । च । समऽहिते । अहोरात्रे इति । विऽहिते । भूम्याम् । अधि । वर्षेण । भूमिः । पृथिवी । वृता । आऽवृता । सा । नः । दधातु । भद्रया । प्रिये । धामनिऽधामनि ॥

अन्वयः—यस्यां भूम्यां अधि अरुणम् कृष्णं च संहिते अहोरात्रे विहिते । वर्षेण वृतावृता सा पृथिवी भूमिः नः भद्रया प्रिये धामनि-धामनि दधातु ॥

Word-meaning:—कृष्णं=black, dusky. अरुणं=ruddy pertaining to the sun. संहिते=united. विहिते=settled, established. वर्षेण=by the rain. भूमिः पृथिवी=the spacious Earth or Motherland. वृता=surrounded by. आवृता=covered over, encompassed. दधातु=may establish us. भद्रया=with an understanding tending to happiness. प्रिये=delightful. धामनिधामनि=in each place.

Translation:—that Earth, upon whom are settled joined together day and night, the ruddy and the dark, who is surrounded and encompassed by rain, may that spacious Motherland establish us with an understanding tending to happiness in each delightful place.

Purport:—Men, who live with their rational faculty well-disposed, derive happiness in all the places of their Motherland blessed with a well-ordered succession of day and night and timely showers of rain.

(८३) द्यौश्च म इदं पृथिवी चान्तरिक्षं च मे व्यचः । अग्निः सूर्य आपो मेधां विश्वे देवाश्च सं ददुः ॥५३॥

(83) Dyāuśca ma idam pṛthivī cāntarikṣam ca mē vyacah । Agnih sūrya āpō mēdhām viśvē dēvāśca sam daduh ॥ 53.

पदपाठः—द्यौः । च । मे । इदम् । पृथिवी । च । अन्तरिक्षम् । च । मे । व्यचः । अग्निः । सूर्यः । आपः । मेधाम् । विश्वे । देवाः । च । सम् । ददुः ॥

अन्वयः—द्यौः च पृथिवी च अन्तरिक्षं च मे इदम् व्यचः (सं ददुः) अग्निः सूर्यः आपः विश्वे देवाश्च (मे) मेधाम् संददुः

Word-meaning:—व्यचः = expanse.

Translation:—The Heavens, the Earth and the Intermediate Region afford me ample room, and Fire, Sun, Water and all other objects endowed with good qualities have joined together to give me decisive understanding.

Purport:—Those wise men who, by a scientific and rational use of the physical objects of the world advance forward, help others also to advance in knowledge and attain happiness.

(८४) अहमस्मि सहमान उत्तरो नाम भूम्याम् । अभीषाडस्मि विश्वाषाडाशामाशां विषासहिः ॥ ५४ ॥

(84) Ahamasmi sahamāna uttarō nāma bhūmyām । Abhīṣāḍasmi viśvāṣādāśām āśām viṣāsahih ॥ 54

पदपाठः—अहम् । अस्मि । सहमानः । उत्तरः । नाम । भूम्याम् । अभीऽषाट् । अस्मि । विश्वाषाट् । आशाम्ऽआशाम् । विऽससहिः ॥

अन्वयः—अहम् भूम्यां सहमानः उत्तरः नाम । (अहम्) अभीषाट् विश्वाषाट् आशामाशां विषासहिः अस्मि ॥

Word-meaning:—सहमानः = victorious. **उत्तरः** = the superior, the supreme or great. **नाम** = called. **अभीषाट्** = triumphant. **विश्वषाट्** = all-over-powering. **आशामाशां** = in every direction. **विषासहिः** = conqueror.

Translation:—I am victorious and am called on earth the supreme. I am triumphant, all-over-powering and conqueror in every direction.

Purport:—Development of his capacities will help man to progress onwards and he will then attain to fame and a high position.

(८५) अदो यद्देवि प्रथमाना पुरस्ताद्देवैरुक्ता व्यसर्पो महित्वम् ।
आ त्वा सुभूतमविशत् तदानीमकल्पयथाः प्रदिशश्चतस्रः ॥ ५५ ॥

(85) Adō yaddēvi prathamānā purastāddēvāiruktā vyasarpō mahitvam । Ā tvā subhūtamaviśat tadānīmakalpayathāḥ pradiśaścatasrah ॥ 55.

पदपाठः—अदः । यत् । देवि । प्रथमाना । पुरस्तात् । देवैः । उक्ता । विऽअसर्पः । महिऽत्वम् । आ । त्वा । सुऽभूतम् । अविशत् । तदानीम् । अकल्पयथाः । प्रऽदिशः । चतस्रः ॥

अन्वयः—देवि (पृथिवि) देवैः उक्ता (त्वम्) यत् पुरस्तात् प्रथमाना अदः महित्वम् व्यसर्पः तदानीं त्वा सुभूतम् आविशत्, चतस्रः प्रदिशः (च त्वम्) अकल्पयथाः ॥

Word-meaning:—**अदः**=that, well-known. **यद्**=while **देवि**=possessing beneficent qualities. **प्रथमाना**=spreading, expanding. **व्यसर्पः**=advances. **महित्वम्**=glory, magnificence. **आविशत्**=takes recourse to, enters, resorts to. **सुभूतं**=great splendour, grandeur. **अकल्पयथाः**=makes to flourish.

Translation:—While the Motherland, possessed of beneficent qualities, advances forward, as told by the wise, expanding her magnificence still further, great prosperity resorts to her and she makes the four great (and the four subordinate) quarters flourish.

Purport:—Riches and power hasten from all directions to that man who proceeds on and on in his researches into the glories of his Mothercountry.

(८६) ये ग्रामा यदरण्यं याः सभा अधि भूम्याम् । ये संग्रामाः समितयस्तेषु चारु वदेम ते ॥ ५६ ॥

(86) Yē grāmā yadaraṇyam yāh sabhā adhi bhūmyām। Yē sangrāmāh samitayastēṣu cāru vadēma tē ॥ 56.

पदपाठः—ये । ग्रामाः । यत् । अरण्यम् । याः । सभाः । अधि । भूम्याम् । ये । सम्ऽग्रामाः । सम्ऽइतयः । तेषु । चारु । वदेम । ते ॥

अन्वयः—ये ग्रामाः, यत् अरण्यम्, याः सभाः, ये संग्रामाः, (याः) समितयः, भूम्याम् अधि (भवन्ति) तेषु (वयम्) ते चारु वदेम ॥

Word-meaning:—संग्रामाः=battles (gatherings, Gr.) **समितयः**=assemblies. **चारु**=beautiful glory.

Translation:—In villages, in woodland, in all assemblages, in wars (gatherings) and meetings of the peoples on the earth, we will recount the glories of the Motherland.

Purport:—It is right that a man should know and talk of the greatness of his Motherland at all places and on all occasions, regardless whether the assemblies are religious, political or legal.

(८७) अश्वं इव रजो दुधुवे वि तान् जनान् य आक्षियन् पृथिवीम् यादजायत । मन्द्राग्रेत्वरी भुवनस्य गोपा वनस्पतीनाम् गृभिरोषधीनाम् ॥ ५७ ॥

(87) Aśva iva rajō dudhuvē vi tān janān ya ākṣiyan pṛthivīm yādajāyata । Mandrāgrētvarī bhuwanasya gōpā vanaspatīnām gṛbhirōṣadhīnām ॥ 57.

पदपाठः—अश्वःऽइव । रजः । दुधुवे । वि । तान् । जनान् । ये । आऽअक्षियन् । पृथिवीम् । यात् । अजायत । मन्द्रा । अग्रऽइत्वरी । भुवनस्य । गोपाः । वनस्पतीनाम् । गृभिः । ओषधीनाम् ॥

अन्वयः—यात् अजायत अश्वः इव रजः मन्द्रा अग्रेत्वरी भुवनस्य

गोपाः वनस्पतीनां श्रोषधीनां (च) गृभिः (सा पृथिवी) तान् जनान् विदुधुवे ये पृथिवीं श्राक्षियन् ॥

Word-meaning:—विदुधुवे=has shaken off. श्राक्षियन् =worried, oppressed. यात्=since when. मन्द्रा=cheering. श्रग्रेत्वरी=going in advance. गोपाः=protectress. गृभिः= holder, keeper.

Translation:—Since her birth, this cheering, advance-marching Motherland of ours, the protectress of the whole populace, the keeper of trees and plants, has shaken off all those people that oppressed her as a horse shakes off dust.

Purport:—The fatigued horse lies down on the earth to rest and rising up, shakes off the dirty dust sticking to its body. So also the Motherland shakes off those wicked people that try to prosper by oppressing her.

(८८) यद्वदा॑मि मधु॑मत् तद्वदा॑मि यदीक्षे॒ तद्व॑नन्ति मा। त्विषी॑मानस्मि जूति॒मानवा॒न्यान् ह॑न्मि॒ दोध॑तः ॥ ५८ ॥

(88) Yadvadāmi madhumat tadvadāmi yadīkṣē tadvananti mā I Tviṣīmān asmi jūtimān avānyān hanmi dōdhataḥ II 58.

पदपाठः—यत्। वदा॑मि। मधु॑ऽमत्। तत्। व॒दा॒मि॒। यत्। ईक्षे॑। तत्। व॒न॒न्ति॒। मा॒। त्विषि॑ऽमान्। अ॒स्मि॒। जू॒ति॒ऽमान्। अव॑। अ॒न्यान्। ह॒न्मि॒। दोध॑तः ॥

अन्वयः—यत् वदामि तत् मधुमत् वदामि। यद् ईक्षे तत् मा (विदाः) वनन्ति। अहम् त्विषिमान् जूतिमान् अस्मि। दोधतः अन्यान् अवहन्मि ॥

Word-meaning:—यत्-तत्=whatever, (विदाः) वनन्ति= (Divine Laws) serve. त्विषिमान् =brilliant. जूतिमान्=quick. अव हन्मि=I strike down. दोधतः=inimical, angry.

Translation:—Whatever I speak, I speak honey-sweet. Whatever I see, Divine laws serve it out to me. I am brilliant, and quick and I strike down those enemies who are fiercely disposed towards me.

Purport:—Man should speak with deliberation and use his eyes and hands with discretion. If so, the Divine laws will endow him with strength and agility that baffle all obstacles.

(८९) शन्तिवा सुरभिः स्योना कीलालोध्नी पयस्वती । भूमिरधि ब्रवीतु मे पृथिवी पयसा सह ॥ ५९ ॥

(89) Śantivā surabhih syōnā kīlālōdhnī payasvatī I Bhūmiradhi bravītū mē pṛthivī payasā saha II 59.

पदपाठः—शन्तिऽवा । सुरभिः । स्योना । कीलालऽऊध्नी । पयस्वती । भूमिः । अधि । ब्रवीतु । मे । पृथिवी । पयसा । सह ॥

अन्वयः—शन्तिवा सुरभिः स्योना कीलालोध्नी पयस्वती भूमिः पृथिवी पयसा सह मे अधिब्रवीतु ॥

Word-meaning:—**शन्तिवा** = mild, peaceful. **सुरभिः**= powerful, munificent. **स्योना**=giving happiness. **कीलालोध्नी**= having the milk of nectar in her breasts. **पयस्वती**= possessing or yielding much milk or food. **अधि ब्रवीतु**= command, bless.

Translation—May this spacious Motherland of ours, peaceful, powerful, bliss-giving, having nectar in her breasts and yielding much milk, bestow, with food, her benison on me.

Purport:—The diligent 'conspire' together and procure innumerable means of happiness from their Motherland.

(९०) यामन्वैच्छद्धविषा विश्वकर्मान्तरर्णवे रजसि प्रविष्टाम् । भुजिष्यं पात्रं निहितं गुहा यदाविर्भोगे अभवन्मातृमद्भ्यः ॥६०॥

(90) Yāmanvāicchaddhavisa viśvakramāntararṇavē rajasi praviṣṭām I Bhujiṣyam pātram nihitam guhā yadāvirbhōgē abhavanmātṛmadbhyah II 60.

पदपाठः—याम् । अनुऽऐच्छंत् । हविषा । विश्वऽकंर्मा । अन्तः । अर्णवे । रजंसि । प्रऽविंष्टाम् । भुजिष्यंम् । पात्रंम् । निऽहिंतम् । गुहां । यत् । आविः । भोगे । अभवत् । मातृमत्ऽभ्यंः ॥

अन्वयः—यां (पृथिवीम्) रजसि अन्तः अर्णवे प्रविष्टां विश्वकर्मा हविषा अन्वैच्छत् (तस्याः) गुहा यत् भुजिष्यम् पात्रम् (तत्) मातृमद्भ्यः भोगे आविः अभवत् ॥

Word-meaning:—अन्वैच्छत् = searched for. हविषा = oblation (Gr.), mutual dealings. विश्वकर्मा = a man well-versed in all works. रजसि अन्तः = in the middle region. अर्णवे = in the sea (of vapour). प्रविष्टां = entered. भुजिष्यं = fit for enjoyment. पात्रं = object that tends to one's protection or something that tends to protect him that protects it. मातृमद्भ्यः = for those who have their mothers.

Translation:—Those enjoyable objects leading to the protection of beings, which have manifested themselves in the form of food that is enjoyed by young creatures tended by their mothers, are placed in the cavity of that Earth who has entered the ocean (of vapour) in the middle region and for whom men well-versed in all works have searched by means of mutual dealings.

Purport:—Exploration of the Earth with an eye to her surroundings holds out immense possibilities of happiness to the industrious just as a mother yields nourishment to her child.

(९१) त्वमंस्यावपंनी जनांनामदिंतिः कामदुघां पप्रथाना । यत्तं ऊनं तत्त आ पूरयाति प्रजापंतिः प्रथमजा ऋतस्यं ॥६१॥

(91) Tvamasyāvapanī janānām aditih Kāmadughā paprathānā । Yatta ūnam tatta ā pūrayāti prajāpatih prathamajā ṛtasya ॥ 61.

पदपाठः—त्वम् । असि । आऽवपनी । जनांनाम् । अदिंतिः ।

कामऽदुघा । पप्रथाना । यत् । ते । ऊनम् । तत । ते । आ । पूरयाति । प्रजाऽपतिः । प्रथमऽजाः । ऋतस्य ॥

अन्वयः—त्वं आवपनी जनानां अदितिः कामदुघा पप्रथाना असि यत् ते ऊनं तत् ऋतस्य प्रथमजाः प्रजापतिः आपूरयाति ॥

Word-meaning:—**आवपनी**=becoming very fertile. **अदितिः**=perfect. **कामदुघा**=fulfiller of wishes. **पप्रथाना**= famous, well known. **आपूरयाति**=may complete in every way.

Translation:—The Motherland, becoming very fertile is well known as the perfect observer of the vow of fulfilling the wishes of mankind. Whatever is lacking in her may the Lord of Creation, the First Propagator of the universal order, supply in every way.

Purport:—The Earth affords all that is necessary for the sustenance of creatures, and whatever these latter consume is replenished by God through rain and other physical phenomena.

(९२) उपस्थास्ते अनमीवा अयक्ष्मा अस्मभ्यं सन्तु पृथिवि प्रसूताः । दीर्घं न आयुः प्रतिबुध्यमाना वयं तुभ्यं बलिहृतः स्याम ॥६२॥

(92) Upasthāstē anamīvā ayakṣmā asmabhyam santu pṛthivi prasūtāḥ I Dīrgham nah āyuh pratibudhyamānā vayam tubhyam balihṛtah syām II 62.

पदपाठः—उपऽस्थाः । ते । अनमीवाः । अयक्ष्माः । अस्मभ्यम् । सन्तु । पृथिवि । प्रऽसूताः । दीर्घम् । नः । आयुः । प्रतिऽबुध्यमानाः । वयम् । तुभ्यम् । बलिऽहृतः । स्याम ॥

अन्वयः—पृथिवि ते उपस्थाः अस्मभ्यम् अनमीवाः अयक्ष्माः प्रसूताः सन्तु । दीर्घम् आयुः प्रतिबुध्यमानाः वयं तुभ्यं बलिहृतः स्याम ॥

Word-meaning:—उपस्थाः=sides; bosom; laps. अनमीवाः=free from sickness. अयक्ष्माः=free from consumption. प्रसूताः=produced. प्रतिबुध्यमानाः=keeping awake and watching. बलिहृतः=offering tribute in the shape of service.

Translation:—May the shelter the Motherland affords us on her bosom, be free from consumption and all other diseases. May we live our long life keeping ourselves wakeful and watching and paying her the tribute of our service.

Purport:—Men should endeavour by a careful regulation of living, avoid all sickness and render all mutual legitemate service.

(९३) भूमे मातर्नि धेहि मा भद्रया सुप्रतिष्ठितम् । संविदाना
दिवा कवे श्रियां मां धेहि भूत्यांम् ॥ ६३ ॥

(93) Bhūmē mātar ni dhēhi mā bhadrayā supratiṣṭhitam । Saṃvidānā divā kavē śriyām mā dhēhi bhūtyām ॥ 63.

पदपाठः—भूमे । मातः । नि । धेहि । मा । भद्रया । सुऽप्रतिस्थितम् । सम्ऽविदाना । दिवा । कवे । श्रियाम् । मा । धेहि । भूत्यांम् ॥

अन्वयः—मातः भूमे मा भद्रया सुप्रतिष्ठितम् नि धेहि । कवे दिवा संविदाना मा श्रियाम् भूत्याम् धेहि ॥

Word-meaning:—निधेहि=may she keep. भद्रया=with an understanding tending to welfare. सुप्रतिष्ठितं=well -established. संविदाना=in unison with. दिवा=sun; the intermediate region; light; the heavens. कवे=who always moves, on whom all creatures live and move. श्रयां=in prosperity; wealth. भूत्यां=in wealth or prosperity; well being; progress; advancement. धेहि=may establish us.

Translation:—May the Motherland, keep me safe with an understanding leading to happiness. May she who ever moves in unison with the sun establish us in wealth and prosperity.

Purport:—Those who direct their rational faculties towards the proper performance of their duties in life will attain to prosperity and fame.

The righteous shall never be removed; but the wicked shall not inhabit the earth. Proverbs (O. T.); X, 30.

One generation passeth away, and another generation cometh: but the earth abideth for ever. If thou seest the oppression of the poor, and violent perverting of judgment and justice in a province, marvel not at the matter: for he that is higher than the highest regardeth; and there be higher than they. Moreover the profit of the earth is for all: the king himself is served by the field. Ecclesiastes (O. T.); I, 4; V, 8 and 9.

Blessed are the meek: for they shall inherit the earth. Swear not at all: neither by heaven: for it is God's throne: nor by the earth: for it is His footstool: Matthew (N. T.); V, 5; 34 and 35.

Earth, thou great footstool of our God who reigns on high; thou fruitful source of all our raiment, life and food; our house, our parent, and our nurse. Watts, the New Dictionary of Thoughts, p., 149.

The Ruler and the Ruled.

ओ३म् ॥ स्वादोरित्था विषूवतो मध्वः पिबन्ति गौर्यः । या इन्द्रेण सयावरीर्वृष्णा मदन्ति शोभसे वस्वीरनु स्वराज्यम् ॥ ऋग्वेदे । १ । ८४ । १० ॥

The white rays moving along with the sun that showers pleasant light all over, and enabling creatures to live in happiness, do become a cause of rejoicing by the charming light they afford and thus suck up the savoury essences diffused all over in space. So also, subjects acting in agreement with a powerful monarch and living in peace and contentment, rejoice in the act of rendering their sovereign kingdom beautiful by their industry and thus enjoy of all the good things of the world. R. V., I, 84, 10.

राजा राष्ट्रानाम् पेशो नदीनामनुत्तमस्मै क्षत्रं विश्वायु ॥ ऋग्वेदे ७ । ३४ । ११ ॥

The king who keeps united in him his subjects divided by different interests, like the ocean receiving in the end the waters of various rivers the courses of which are different from one another, enjoys his power undisturbed by foes and lives to a good old age. R. V., VII, 34, 11.

CHAPTER IV.

SECTION I.

The Vedic Idea of an Empire.

Ṛgvēda I, 80.

Seer:—The Sage Rāhūgaṇa Gōtama.

Subject:—The Idea of an Empire.

Metre:—Stanzas 1 and 11 nicṛdāstārapanktih, 5, 6, 9, 10, 13 and 14 virāṭpanktih. 2, 4, 7, 12 and 15 bhurigbṛhatī and 8 and 16 bṛhatī.

Key:—Stanzas 1, 5, 6, 9, 10, 11, 13 and 14 pañcama, and 2—4, 7, 8, 12, 15 and 16 madhyama.

(९४) ओ३म् ॥ इत्था हि सोम इन्मदे ब्रह्मा चकार वर्धनम् । शविष्ठ वज्रिन्नोजसा पृथिव्या निः शशा अहिमर्चन्ननु स्वराज्यम् ॥१॥

(94) Itthaa hi soma inmade brahmaa cakaara vardhanam I *S*avish*tha* vajrinnojasaa prəthivyaa nih *sa*saa ahimarcannanu svaraajyam II 1.

(हे) शविष्ठ वज्रिन् (यथा) ब्रह्मा ओजसा पृथिव्याः मदे सोमे

इत्था वर्धनम् चकार (तथा) हि (त्वम्) स्वऽराज्यम् अनु अर्चन् (सर्वान् अन्यायाचारान्) निः शशाः (यथा सूर्यः) अहिम् (निः शशति) ॥

इत्था=thus; in this manner; in such a way. **सोमे** (√सु+मन्, U. I, 140)=that which yields power and prosperity. **मदे** (√मद्)=giving joy. **ब्रह्मा**=a man learned in the Vedic lores. **चकार**=may make. **वर्धनम्**=advancement; progress. **शविष्ठ**=Oh most powerful. **वज्रिन्**=thou who art proficient in wielding weapons of war. **ओजसा**= by prowess. **निः शशाः**=uproot entirely; expel completely. **अहिम्**=the cloud; wickedness; oppression; repression. **अनु अर्चन्**=with the view to make acceptable or worthy of regard, **स्वराज्यं**=a sovereign and independent kingdom; an empire.

Oh powerful emperor skilled in the weapons of war, just as the sun by his rays dispels the clouds, so do thou expel all wickedness and oppression from thy kingdom and make it acceptable to and respected among the people so that the enlightened (learned in the Vedic lores) may live therein in peace and by their prowess derive advantage from the enjoyable objects of the earth and help others also to do likewise and thus progress in life.

(९५) स त्वामदद्वृषा मदः सोमः श्येनाभृतः सुतः । येना वृत्रं निरद्भ्यो जघन्थ वज्रिन्नोजसार्चन्ननु स्वराज्यम् ॥२॥

(95) Sa tvaamadadvr^əshaa madah somah Syenaabhr^ətah sutah । Yenaa vr^ətram niradbhyo jaghantha vajrinnojasaarcannaanu svaraajyam ॥ 2.

(हे) वज्रिन् (येन वृष्णा मदेन श्येनाभृतेन सुतेन सोमेन त्वम्) ओजसा स्वऽराज्यम् अनु अर्चन् (यथा सूर्यः) अत्ऽभ्यः (पृथक् कृत्य जलम् स्वीकुर्वन्तम्) वृत्रम् (निर्जघान तथा प्रजाभ्यः पृथक् कृत्य प्रजा-

सुखम् स्वीकुर्वन्तम् शत्रुम्) निः जघन्थं सः वृषा मदः श्येनऽआंभृतः सुतः सोमः त्वा अमदत् ॥

त्वा=thee. अमदत्=give joy. वृषा=showering justice or happiness. सोमः=the objects produced by nature which give man power and prosperity. श्येनाभृतः=carried about like a hawk. (There is no implication here of hunting animals for food, but the idea involved here simply means expulsion of harmful agencies. The hawk, if utilised properly will destroy birds and vermin harmful to the crops and thus help man). सुतः=being developed; being disturbed. निर्जघन्थ=split into pieces; compelled; put down or dispelled.

Oh powerful wielder of the war weapons just as the sun shatters the cloud that keeps waters bound, so do thou, utilising those objects of the earth like a hawk which, developed, shower blessings on mankind, dispel the foe that robs thy subjects of their peace and happiness thus making thy kingdom acceptable and respected, and so may these objects be to thy rejoicing.

(९६) प्रेह्यभीहि धृष्णुहि न ते वज्रो नि यंसते । इन्द्र नृम्णं हि ते शवो हनो वृत्रं जया अपोऽर्चन्ननु स्वराज्यम् ॥३॥

(96) Prehyabheehi dhrəshnuhi na te vajro ni yamsate I Indra nrəmnam hi te savo hano vrətram jayaa apo'rcannanu svaraajyam ॥ 3.

(हे) इन्द्र (यथा सूर्यस्य) वज्रः वृत्रम् हनः अपः नि यंसते (तथा ये) ते (शत्रवः तान् हत्वा) स्वऽराज्यम् अनु अर्चन् हि नृम्णम् प्र इहि शवः अभि इहि (शरीरात्मबलेन) धृष्णहि जयाः (एवम् कुर्वतः) ते (पराजयः) न (भविष्यति) ॥

प्रेहि=obtain in abundance. अभीहि=develop in all

ways. धृष्णुहि=be bold and valiant. वज्रः=flood of rays. नियंसते=keeps in control. नृम्णम्=wealth. हि=surely. शवः= power. हनः=kills; shatters; thou dost dispel, etc. जयाः= (√ जि)=be victorious. अपः=waters.

Oh king, llke the sun that shatters the cloud by his rays and controls the waters, do thou put down thy antagonists and making thy rule acceptable and respected advance in wealth, acquire full power and becoming bold and valiant in body and spirit, be always victorious. After this there will be no defeat for thee.

(९७) निरिन्द्र भूम्या अधि वृत्रं जघन्थ निर्दिवः। सृजा मरुत्वंतीरव जीवधंन्या इमा अपोऽर्चन्ननु स्वराज्यम् ॥४॥

(97) Nirindra bhoomyaa adhi vr$^{\theta}$tram jaghantha nir-divah I Sr$^{\theta}$jaa marutvateerava jeevadhanyaa imaa apo'rcannanu svaraajyam II 4.

(हे) इन्द्र (यथा सूर्यः) वृत्रम् (हत्वा) भूम्याः अधि (इमाः) जीवऽधंन्याः मरुत्वंतीः अपः निः जघन्थ दिवः (निरवसृजति तथा त्वम् दुष्टाचारान् हत्वा धर्माचारं प्रचार्य) स्वऽराज्यम् अनु अर्चन (राज्यम् शाधि प्रजासुखम् च) निः अव सृजा ॥

इन्द्रः=Oh powerful king, भूम्याः अधि=on the earth. निर्जघन्थ=always shatters or dispels. दिवः=rays; light. निरवसृजा= always accomplish. मरुत्वतीः=beneficial to man and other creatures. जीवधन्याः=helping human beings to earn wealth and other means of life.

Oh powerful king, even as the sun shatters the clouds, diffuses his light-giving rays and lets flow waters that help human beings and other creatures to live in peace, so do thou destroy the wicked, give wide encouragement to righteous conduct and thus making thy empire acceptable and respected rule over it, so that thou and thy subjects may ever enjoy all happiness.

(९८) इन्द्रो वृत्रस्य दोधतः सानुं वज्रेण हीळितः
अभि क्रम्यावजिघ्नतेऽपः समीय चोदयन्नर्चन्ननु स्वराज्यम् ॥५॥

(98) Indro vr^ə^trasya dodhatah saanum vajre*n*a hee*l*itah ।
Abhi kramyaavajighnate'pah sarmaaya codayannarcannanu svaraajyam ॥ 5.

(हे विद्वन् यथा) इन्द्रः वज्रेण वृत्रस्य अपः अभिऽक्रम्य सानुं (छिनत्ति तथा त्वम्) स्वऽराज्यम् अनु अर्चन् अव जिघ्नते समीय (स्वबलम्) चोदयन् दोधतः (शत्रोः बलम् अभिक्रम्य सेनां छित्वा हीळितः (सन् क्रोधम्) अव (सृज) ॥

इन्द्रः=the sun. दोधतः (√दोध Nig. II, 12)=angry. सानुम्=peaks, different parts, the extended portions. वज्रेण =by his fierce heat or light rays. हीळितः (√हीळ्)=being insulted; disregarded. अभिक्रम्य=having attacked. अव जिघ्नते=him who kills and destroys. समीय=him who goes about. चोदयन्=sending. स्वराज्यम् अन्वर्चन्=asserting the sovereignty. छिनत्ति=shatters. स्वबलम्=thy own troups. विजयम् =victory. आप्नुहि=obtain.

Oh learned king! just as the sun attacks all over with his fierce heat and cuts off the different portions of, the cloud, so do thou assert thy sovereignty and send thy troops to attack the army of thy foe that might be going about killing and destroying in thy kingdom. If thy foe happens to disperse thy troops and if, therefore, thy subjects disparage thee, let thy wrath vent itself upon thy foe.

(९९) अधि सानौ जिघ्नते वज्रेण शतपर्वणा ।

 (98)

मन्दान इन्द्रो अन्धसः सखिभ्यो गातुमिच्छत्यर्चन्ननु स्वराज्यम् ॥६॥

(99) Adhi saanau jighnate vajre*n*a sataparva*n*aa | Mandaana indro andhasah sakhibhyo gaatumicchatyarcannanu svaraajyam || 6.

(हे राजन् यथा) इन्द्रः शतऽपर्वणा वज्रेण (वृत्रस्य) सानौ अधि (प्रहरति इव प्रकाशं) नि जिघ्नते (तस्मै सदैव प्रतिकूलो वर्तते तथा एव) गातुम् इच्छति (स भवान्) सखिऽभ्यः मन्दान स्वराज्यं अनु अर्चन् अन्धसः (दाता भव) ॥

अधि सानौ=on the peaks or different extended parts. जिघ्नते=that obstructs (the rays). वज्रेण=by its streaks. शतपर्वणा=of hundreds of branches. मन्दानः=giving greater joy to. इन्द्रः=lightning. अन्धसः=of food. (Nig II, 7). सखिभ्यः=to thy friends and subjects. गातुम् (√ गै+तुन् U. I, 73).=eloquent praise, words of noble teaching. इच्छति =wishes for, likes. प्रहरति=strikes. प्रतिकूलः=hostile. वर्तते= behaves. भवान्=you. दाता=giver, provider.

Oh king ! even as lightning with hundreds of its streaks seems to strike on the different parts of, and to be hostile to, the cloud, which obstructs its light, so shouldst thou, who likest words of noble teaching, regarding thy own sovereign rule first, be the bestower of bread and joy on thy firiends and subjects.

(१००) इन्द्र तुभ्यमिदद्रिवोऽनुत्तं वज्रिन्वीर्यम् । यद्ध त्यं मायिनं मृगं तमु त्वं माययावधी रर्चन्ननु स्वराज्यम् ॥७॥

(100) Indra tubhyam idadrivo'nuttam vajrin veeryam | Yaddha tyam maayinam mr^e^gam tamu tvam maayayaavadheerarcannanu svaraajyam || 7.

(हे) अद्रिऽवः वज्रिन् इन्द्र (त्वं) यत् त्यं मायिनम् मृगं मायया ह अवधीः (दिवः इव) अनुत्तं वीर्यं (गृहीत्वा) स्वऽराज्यम् अनु अर्चन तम उ (दण्डयसि तस्मै) तुभ्यम् इत् (वयम् करान् ददाम) ॥

इन्द्र=oh king who impartest happiness to thy subjects. **तुभ्यम्**=to thee. **इत्**=alone. **अद्रिवः**=ruling over a kingdom adorned with mountains like clouds. **अनुत्तम्**= natural, not acquired. **वज्रिन्**=maintaining perfect war equipment. **वीर्यम्**=power, prowess. **यत्**=that **ह**=surely. **त्यम्**=that. **मायिनम्**=deceitful. **मृगम्**=beast, taking enjoyment like a brute. **उ**=an expletive or interjection of inference. **मायया**=(√मा+य U. IV, 109). by cunning and cleverness. **अवधीः**=dost put down. **दिवः**=of the sun. **गृहीत्वा**=having accepted, possessing. **दण्डयसि**=dost punish. **करान्**=taxes, tributes. **ददाम**=we (shall) give.

(The learned representatives of the people say to the king:—) Oh king who impartest happiness to thy subjects ruling over a kingdom possessing cloud-like mountains! as thou possessing natural prowess as the sun possesses lustre and regarding thy sovereign authority with respect, dost, using proper cunning, severely punish and put down with a strong hand the foe, who, by fraud deprives thy subjects of the good things of the world and enjoys them himself like a brute, we offer tribute to thee alone.

(१०१) वि ते वज्रासोऽअस्थिरन् नवतिं नाव्या३ अनु महत्तं इन्द्र वीर्यम् बाह्वोस्ते बलं हितमर्चन्ननु स्वराज्यम् ॥८॥

(101) Vi te vajraaso asthiran navatim naavyaa anu । Mahat ta indra veeryam baahvoste balam hitamarcannanu svaraajyam ॥ 8,

(हे) इन्द्र! ते वज्रासः नवतिम् नाव्याः अनु वि अस्थिरन् (यत ते)

बाह्वोःमहत वीर्यम् बलम् हितं (अस्ति तेन) स्वऽराज्यम् अनु अर्चन् (राज्यश्रियं त्वं प्राप्नुहि) ॥

वब्रासः=armies well-equipped with arms and ammunition. नवतिम्=ninety. नाव्याः=fleets of ships. अनु वि अस्थिरन्=keep arrayed for immediate use. महत्= great. ते=thy. बाह्वोः=in the arms बलम्=power. हितम्= is, exists (is placed).

Oh supreme king ! ninety armies of well-equipped soldiers with fleets of ships are standing ready to march at thy command. Great prowess is in thy arms and thou possessest mighty power. Honour thy sovereign authority and enjoy the happiness of an independent kingdom.

(१०२) सहस्त्रं साकमर्चत परिष्टोभत विंशतिः ।
शतैनमन्वनोनवुरिन्द्राय ब्रह्मोद्यतमर्चन्ननु स्वराज्यम् ॥९॥

(102) Sahasram saakamarcata parish*t*obhata vi*ms*atih ।
*S*atainamanvanonavurindraaya brahmodyatamarcannanu svaraa-
jyam ॥ 9.

(हे मनुष्याः यूयं यः) स्वऽराज्यं अर्चन् (वर्तते तं आश्रित्य स्वकीय-राष्ट्रं अधर्माचरणात्) परि स्तोभत, साकं सहस्त्रम् अर्चत (यं) विंशतिः शता अनु अनोनवुः (यः) उत्ऽयंतं ब्रह्म (अर्चन् वर्तते तस्मै इन्द्राय अनुस्तुवत) ॥

सहस्रम्=a thousand, innumerable. साकं=together, conjointly. अर्चत=welcome, be snbmissive to. परिष्टोभत= prevent from, save, purge of. विंशतिः शता=twenty hundred, two thousand, scores of hundreds. एनं=him. अन्वनोनवुः= (अनु+ √ नु)=extoll in favourable manner. इन्द्राय=for the king or president. ब्रह्म=the Vedic law or teaching. उद्यतं= famous, ever true, ever useful. आश्रित्य=taking shelter in. स्वकीयराष्ट्रं=one's own country, kingdom or nation. अधर्माचरणात्=from wicked conduct, from those who live evil lives. अनुस्तुवत (अनु + √स्तु) = praise, speak well of, extol.

Oh men ! taking shelter under that king who has a high regard for his sovereign authority, purge your kingdom of all evil. Unite in your thousands to welcome such a ruler and bands of scores of hundreds of you should extol him favourably and submit and offer allegience to him, who accepts with reverence (as his rule of life) the ever useful Vedic teachings.

(१०३) इन्द्रो वृत्रस्य तविषीं निरहन्त्सहसा सहः ।
महत्तदस्य पौंस्यं वृत्रं जघन्वाँ असृजदर्चन्ननु स्व-
राज्यम् ॥१०॥

(103) Indro vr^{ə}trasya tavisheem nirahantsahasaa sahah I
Mahattadasya pau*m*syam vr^{ə}tram jaghauvaan asr^{ə}jadarcannanu
svaraajyam II 10.

(यः) इन्द्रः वृत्रं (सूर्यः इव शत्रुं) जघन्वान् यः सहसा वृत्रस्य (सूर्यः इव शत्रोः) तविषीं निःअहन् (यः च सूर्यः स्वप्रकाशम् इव) स्वऽराज्यम् अनु अर्चन् (सुखम्) असृजत् तत् अस्य महत् पौंस्यम् सहः (च अस्ति) ॥

तविषीं = power. निरहन् = continuously shatters or destroys. सहसा = by his strength or force. सहः = power, endurance, power of endurance. महत् = great. पौंस्यं = virility, vigour, valour. जघन्वान् = strikes down and destroys continually.

That this mighty monarch strikes down and shatters the power of his foe as the sun does the cloud, and that even as the sun diffuses his pleasant light welcoming his sovereign authority imparts happiness to his friends and subjects, is the result of his great prowess and endurance.

(१०४) इमे चित्तव मन्यवे वेपेते भियसा मही ।

यदिन्द्र वज्रिन्नोजसा वृत्रं मरुत्वाँ अवधीरर्चन्ननु स्वराज्यम् ॥११॥

(104) Ime cittava manyave vepete bhiyasaa mahee ।
Yadindra vajrinnojasaa vr^ətran marutvaan avadheerarcannanu svaraajvam ॥ 11.

(हे) वज्रिन् इन्द्र (यथा सूर्यस्य आकर्षणेन ताड़नेन च) इमे मही वेपेते (तत्तुल्यस्य) यत् तव ओजसा भियसा (च) मन्यवे (शत्रवः वेपन्ते यथा च) मरुत्वान् (सूर्यः मेघम् हन्ति तथा सः त्वम्) स्वऽराज्यम् अनु-अर्चन् (अरीन्) चित् अवधीः ॥

इमे=these two. चित्=surely. तव=thine. मन्यवे (मन्यु) =for (the pacification of) thy wrath. वेपेते=both shake or tremble (by the sun's heat and force of gravitation). भियसा=through awe or fear. मही=the two spacious worlds, viz., the earth and the heavens. यत् (=यस्य)= whose. इन्द्र=oh king, the sun. ओजसा=by power. मरुत्वाँ= helped by wind. अवधीः=thou killest, shatterest, destroyest, dost put down.

Oh great king, well-versed in the handling of arms, of whose power and awe the enemy remain in fear and try to pacify thy wrath just as these two vast worlds, the earth and the heavens are kept in motion by the heat and force of gravitation of the sun, so do thou, like the sun shattering the cloud, accept thy sovereign authority and of a certainty put down thy-foe.

(१०५) न वेपसा न तन्यतेन्द्रं वृत्रो वि बींभयत् ।
अभ्येनं वज्र आयसः सहस्रभृष्टिरायतार्चन्ननु स्वराज्यम् ॥१२॥

(105) Na vepasaa na tanyatendram vr^ətro vi beebhayat ।
Abhyenam vajra aayasah sahasrabhr^əsh*t*iraayataarcannanu svaraajyam ॥ 12.

(हे राजन्) स्वऽराज्यम् अनु अर्चन् (त्वम् यथा) वृत्रः इन्द्रं वेपसा न वि बीभयत् तन्यता न (विबीभयत् एनम् मेघम् प्रति सूर्यप्रेरितः) सहस्रंऽभृष्टिः आयसः वज्रः अभि आयत (तथा शत्रून् प्रति भव) ॥

वेपसा = by quickness. तन्यता (= तन्यतुना from √ तन + यतुच् U. IV, 2) = by wind, night, thunderbolt, roaring, thundering. इन्द्रम् = the sun. विबीभयत् = frighten. एनम् = him (the cloud). आयसः = like a steel or fiery missile. सहस्रभृष्टिः (सहस्र + √ भ्रस्ज + क्तिन्) = burning or roasting in a thousand ways. अभ्यायत = falls on or attacks from all round. सूर्यप्रेरितः (सूर्येण प्रेरितः) = sent or discharged by the sun. प्रति = towards.

Oh king! welcoming thy royal authority, thou shouldst behave towards thy enemies just like the sun whom the cloud cannot frighten either by its quick movement or by its roaring thunder, but who attacks the latter from all sides with his hot rays like steel missiles emitting fire and burning in a thousand ways.

(१०६) यद्वृत्रं तव चाशनिं वज्रेण समयोधयः ।
आहिमिन्द्र जिघांसतो दिवि ते बद्बधे शवोऽर्चन्ननु स्वराज्यम् ॥१३॥

(106) Yadvr̥tram tava caaśanim vajreṇa samayodhayah ।
Ahim indra jighaamsato divi te badbadhe śavo'rcannanu svaraajyam ॥ 13.

(हे) इन्द्र स्वऽराज्यम् अनु अर्चन् (त्वम्) यत् दिवि (सूर्यः) अशनिम् (प्रहृत्य) वृत्रम् अहिम् बद्बधे (तथा) वज्रेण (उपेताः स्वसेनाः शत्रुभिः सह) समऽअयोधयः (शत्रून्) जिघांसतः तव शवः ते (यशः) च (वर्धिष्येते) ॥

यत् (= यथा) = as. वृत्रम् √ वृत् + रक् (U. II, 13) = crooked cunning; tricky. अशनिम् = thunderbolt. वज्रेण = with an army equipped fully with arms and ammunition. **समयोधयः**=make them join in full fight with. **अहिम्**=cloud, enemy. **जिघांसतः**=he who kills or puts down. **दिवि**=in the heavens. **बद्बधे** (√ **बाधृ**+**सन्** according to Maharṣi Dayānanda and **यङ्लुक्** according to Macdonell)=repressing, putting down, destroying. **शवः**=power. **प्रहत्य**=striking. **उपेताः**=endowed or equipped with. **स्वसेनाः**=thy forces. **शत्रुभिः**=with the enemy. **वर्धिष्येते**=will both increase.

Oh monarch! welcoming thy sovereign authority; even as the sun strikes the crooked clouds with his thunderbolt and shatters them, so do thou make thy well equipped forces join in full battle with thy foes and destroy the latter. Thy power and fame will thereby advance.

(१०७) अभिष्टने तें अद्रिवो यत्स्था जगच्च रेजते । त्वष्टा चित्तव मन्यव इन्द्र वेविज्यतें भियार्चन्ननुं स्वराज्यम् ॥१४॥

(107) Abhishtane te adrivo yat sthaa jagacca rejate । tvashtaa cit tava manyava indra vevijyate bhiya'rcannanu svaraajyam ॥ 14.

(हे) अद्रिऽवः इन्द्र यत् ते अभिऽस्तने स्थाः जगत् च रेजते त्वष्टा चित् ते भिया तवं मन्यवे वेविज्यतें (तत् भवान) स्वऽराज्यम् अनुं अर्चन् (सुखी भवेत्) ॥

अभिष्टने=thundering fearfully hence striking awe by his justice and power. **यत् (यदा)**=when. **स्थाः** (√ **स्था**+**क्विप**) =immovable objects. **जगत्**=movable objects or creatures. **रेजते**=trembles. **त्वष्टा**=a commander who invariably cuts down the enemy. **चित्**=even. **मन्यवे**=for indignation, righteous anger. **वेविज्यते**=becomes agitated. **तत (=तदा)**=then. **भवान्**=you. **सुखी**=happy.

Oh great king, whose realm is adorned with innumerable cloudlike mountains, when at thy awfully just dealing all objects,—both movable and immovable, tremble, and even thy own mighty commander of troops who never fails to pare down thine enemies in battle becomes agitated with fear at thy indignation, do thou, then, honour thy sovereign authority and feel happy.

(१०८) नहि नु यादधीमसीन्द्रं को वीर्यां परः । तस्मिन्नृम्णमुत क्रतुं देवा ओजांसि सन्दधुरर्चन्ननु स्वराज्यम् ॥१५॥

(108) Nahi nu yaadadheemaseendram ko veeryaa parah I Tasmin nrəm*n*amuta kratum devaa ojaamsi sandadhurarcannanu svaraajyam || 15.

(यः) परः (इन्द्रः) स्वऽराज्यम् अनु अर्चन् (वर्तते यस्मिन्) देवाः नृम्णम् क्रतुम् उत ओजांसि सम् दधुः, (तथा यम् इन्द्रम् प्राप्य वयम्) वीर्यां अधिऽइमसि (तम्) इन्द्रम् (प्राप्य) कः नु (नृम्णम्) नहि यात् कः नु (नृम्णम् क्रतुम, उत ओजांसि नहि सन्दध्यात्) ॥

नहि=not. **नु**=at once, quickly. **यात्**=to obtain, to acquire. **अधीमसि**=we secure by education. **कः**=who. **वीर्यां** (=**वीर्याणि**)=various powers (=qualifications, educational etc.) **परः**=possessed of excellences. **तस्मिन्**=in that kingdom. **नृम्णम्**=wealth. **क्रतुम**=intellectual attainments, industriousness, insight. **देवाः**=the learned, the wise, the enlightened. **ओजांसि**=prowess of body, mind and soul. **सन्दधुः** (**सम √ धा**)=fully attains to. **प्राप्य**=approaching, coming under the patronage of. **सन्दध्यात्**=may fully attain to, acquire.

Who will not acquire those multifarious boons, viz:—wealth, industry perseverance and various powers (of body, mind and soul) under the patronage of that noble king of innumerable excellences, who deals honourably with his sovereign authority, under whose patronage the learned attain all these things and we all secure by education various powers ?

(१०९) यामथर्वा मनुष्पिता दध्यङ् धियमत्नत । तस्मिन्ब्रह्माणि पूर्वथेन्द्रे उक्था समग्मतार्चन्ननु स्वराज्यम् ॥१६॥

(109) Yaamatharvaa manushpitaa dadhyaṃ dhiyamatnata tasmin brahmaani poorvathendra ukthaa samagmataarcannanu svaraajyam ॥ 16.

(हे मनुष्याः यथा) स्वऽराज्यम् अनुं अर्चन् दध्यङ्, अथर्वा, पिता, मनुः, याम् धियम् (प्राप्य यस्मिन् सुखानि तनुते तथा एतां प्राप्य यूयम् सुखानि अत्नत, यस्मिन्) इन्द्रे पूर्वऽथा ब्रह्माणि उक्था (प्राप्नोति तस्मिन् सेविते सति एतानि) सम् अग्मत ॥

यां=which, **अथर्वा**=a righteous man abstaining from injuring others and such other sins. **मनुः**=a wise man, a great thinker. **पिता**=a teacher of the Vedic lore. **दध्यङ्**= a man endowed with great merits. **धियं**=an intellect refined with learning and devoted to good deeds. **अत्नत**= (√**तन्**)=stretch, diffuse, propagate. **तस्मिन्**=in that way of life, adopting those measures. **ब्रह्माणि**=wealth and good food. **पूर्वथा**=like the ancients. **इन्द्रे**=in the God Almighty. **उक्था** (=**उक्थानि**)=wise and good speech, or sayings. **समग्मत**=do attain. **यस्मिन्**=in which way of life, by adopting which measures. (The second **यस्मिन्** is related to **इन्द्रे**). **प्राप्नोति**=obtains. (**तस्मिन्** qualifies **इन्द्रे**—**सेविते सति** locative absolute=if that Almighty God is resorted to or approached, if you resort to or approach Him). **एतानि**= these i. e., **ब्रह्माणि** and **उक्था.**

Oh men ! even as the righteous abstaining from all sorts of injury to creatures, great thinkers and teachers of the Vedic lores—men endowed with great qualities—extending a friendly welcome to all by first developing their own kingdom, attaining an intellectual capacity refined with learning and devoted to good deeds, adopt such measures as would advance the happiness of mankind. You also attaining such an intellectual capacity should do likewise. By serving God Almighty the ancients before you in all ages obtained riches by honourable means, and the faculty to speak well and wisely, which you too, by taking recourse to that Almighty God, can acquire.

SECTION II.

The King and His Ministers

Ṛgvēda X, 173.

Seer:—The Sage Dhruva.
Subject:—The king and his ministers.
Metre:—(Stanzas 1, 3 and 5), anuṣṭup, stanza 2 bhuriganuṣṭup, and 6, nicṛdanuṣṭup.
Key:—Gāndhāra.

(११०) ओ३म् ॥ आ त्वाहार्षमन्तरेधि ध्रुवस्तिष्ठाविचाचलिः । विशस्त्वा सर्वा वाञ्छन्तु मा त्वद्राष्ट्रमधिभ्रशत् ॥१॥

(110) Aa tvaahaarsham antaredhi dhruvastishthaavicaacalih । Visastvaa sarvaa vaanchantu maa tvadraashtramadhibhrasat ॥ 1.

त्वा आ अहार्षम्, अन्तः एधि। ध्रुवः अविऽचाचलिः तिष्ठ । त्वा सर्वाः विशः वाञ्छन्तु । त्वत् राष्ट्रम् मा अधिभ्रशत् ॥

आहार्षम् (**आ**+√**हृ**)=I have elected (thee). I have chosen (thee). **अन्तर्**=inside, amongst, in the midst of. **एधि** (√**अस्**)=be thou. **ध्रुवः** (√**ध्रुव्**+**क** U. II, 61).=firm. **तिष्ठ**=remain. **अविचाचलिः** (**वि**√**चल**)=not staggering, firm, unmoved. **वाञ्छन्तु**=may like thee, may be favourable to thee. **त्वत्**=on account of thee. **राष्ट्रम्**=nation, kingdom. **अधि भ्रशत्**=may not fall, may not be degraded.

Oh king! I have installed thee ruler of this kingdom; be thou therefore firm and unmoved on thy throne. May all the people be well disposed towards thee and may not the kingdom fall on account of thee.

(१११) इहैवैधि मापं च्योष्ठाः पर्वत इवाविचाचलिः । इन्द्र इवेह ध्रुवस्तिष्ठेह राष्ट्रमु धारय ॥२॥

(111) Ihaivaidhi maapa cyosh*th*aah parvata ivaavicaacalih । Indra iveha dhruvastish*th*eha raash*t*ram u dhaaraya ॥ 2.

(हे राजन् !) इह एव एधि, मा अपं च्योष्ठाः । पर्वतःऽइव अविऽचाचलिः इन्द्रःऽइव ध्रुवः इह तिष्ठ उ इह राष्ट्रम् धारय ॥

अपच्योष्ठाः (**अप**+√**च्यु**)=may thou not fall (i. e. may thou not fail to endeavour for the advancement of thine kingdom.) **पर्वतः इव**=like a mountain. **इन्द्रः इव**=like the sun. **इह**=in this kingdom. The third **इह** means 'in thy station as king'. **उ** = and. **धारय** = support, sustain take care of.

Oh king! be thou firm in this kingdom like a rock and do not fail to endeavour for its advancement. Be thou 'firm' in this kingdom like the sun, and remaining in thy station as king, support the nation.

(११२) इममिन्द्रो अदीधरद्ध्रुवं ध्रुवेण हविषा । तस्मै सोमो अधि ब्रवत्तस्मा उ ब्रह्मणस्पतिः ॥३॥

(111) Imamindro adeedharaddhruvam dhruve*n*a havishaa । Tasmai somo adhi bravat tasmaa u brahma*n*aspatih ॥ 3.

इमम् ध्रुवम् (राजानम्) ध्रुवेण हविषा अदीधरत् । तस्मै सोमः अधि ब्रवत् उ तस्मै ब्रह्मणः पतिः (अधिब्रवत्) ॥

इमम् ध्रुवम्=this king thus firmly installed. **इन्द्रः**=finance minister. **अदीधरत्**=should support. **ध्रुवेण**=by a permanent. **हविषा** (√**हु** 3rd conj., to give or receive × **इसि** U. II, 108)=tax, tribute. **सोमः**=the minister of justice, the chief judge. **अधिब्रवत्** (**अधि**+√**ब्रू**)=advise him in matters relating to the administration of justice. ब्रह्मणस्पतिः =the prime minister well versed in the Vedic lores.

Let the finance minister support by means of permanent taxation this king thus firmly installed; let the ministers of justice advise him on matters relating to the administration of justice and, the prime minister well versed in the Vedic lores guide him in his royal duties.

(११३) ध्रुवा द्यौर्ध्रुवा पृथिवी ध्रुवासः पर्वता इमे।
ध्रुवं विश्वमिदं जगद्ध्रुवो राजा विशामयम् ॥४॥

(113) Dhruvaa dyaurdhruvaa prəthivee dhruvaasah parvataa ime । Dhruvam visvamidam jagaddhruvo raajaa visaam ayam ॥ 4.

(यथा) द्यौः ध्रुवा (वर्तते यथा) पृथिवी (च स्वकक्षायाम् ध्रुवा वर्तते यथा) इमे पर्वताः ध्रुवासः (वर्तन्ते, यथा) इदं विश्वं जगत् (स्वस्वनियम-पालने) ध्रुवं (वर्तते तथा एव) अयम् विशाम् राजा (स्वधर्मपालने) ध्रुवः (वर्तताम्) ॥

द्यौः=the sun, the celestial region. पृथिवी=the earth. विश्वम्=the whole. जगत्=the world of living and moving beings as well as of immovables. वर्तते=is, behaves, acts. स्वकक्षायां=in its own orbit. स्वस्वनियमपालने=in the observance of the law regulating its motion etc. स्वधर्मपालने=in the discharge of his duties.

Just as the heavenly region is firm, just as the earth is firm in its own orbit, just as these mountains are firm on the earth, and just as this whole universe of animate and inanimate beings is firm in its observance of the laws governing its motion etc., so also, may this king be firm in the discharge of his onerous duties as ruler of this nation.

(११४) ध्रुवं ते राजा वरुणो ध्रुवं देवो बृहस्पतिः।
ध्रुवं त इन्द्रश्चाग्निश्च राष्ट्रं धारयतां ध्रुवम् ॥५॥

(114) Dhruvam te raajaa varu*n*o dhruvam devo br^ə^haspatih।
Dhruvam ta indra*s*caagni*s*ca raash*t*ram dhaarayataam dhruvam ॥5.

(हे राजन) ते राजा वरुणः (इदम् राष्ट्रम्) ध्रुवम् धारयताम् । देवः बृहस्पतिः (इदम्) ध्रुवम् (धारयताम् तथा एव) ते इन्द्रः च अग्निः च (इदम्) राष्ट्रम् ध्रुवम् (धारयेताम्) ॥

राजा=of a brilliant and cultured mind. **वरुणः**=the minister of education. **देवः**= enlightened, reverent. **बृहस्पतिः**=the prime minister well-versed in the Vedic lores. **अग्निः**=the forward war minister. **ध्रुवम्**=firmly, steadily. **धारयतां**=support and guide in accordance with the rules regulating the duties of their offices.

Oh king! let thy brilliant and cultured educational minister, the reverent prime minister learned in the Vedas, thy finance minister and thy forward (and brave) war minister, each according to the rules regulating the duties of his office steadily support this kingdom.

(११५) ध्रुवं ध्रुवेण हविषाभि सोमं मृशामसि ।
अथो त इन्द्रः केवलीर्विशो बलिहृतस्करत् ॥६॥

(115) Dhruvam dhruve*n*a havishaabhi somam mr^ə^shaamasi । Atho ta indrah kevaleerviso balihr^ə^taskarat ॥ 6.

ध्रुवेणं हविषा ध्रुवं सोमम् अभि मृशामसि । अथो (हे राजन) ते इन्द्रः केवलीः विशः बलिऽहृतः करत् ॥

ध्रुवेण हविषा=by payment of an ascertained amount. **अभिमृशामसि**=get justice administered. **अथो**=and. **केवलीः विशः**=only thy subjects. **बलिहृतः**=payers of taxes. **करत्**= should make. **बलिहृतः करत्**=should levy taxes only from thy subjects.

The minister of justice shall administer the law in return for the payment of a stipulated amount of money to him, and oh king! thy finance minister should levy taxes only from the subjects.

Know Him rather than speak of Him.

ओ३म् ॥ न तं विदाथ य इमा जजानान्यद्युष्मा-
कमन्तरम्बभूव । नीहारेण प्रावृता जल्प्या चासुतृप
उक्थशासश्चरन्ति ॥ य० १७ । ३१ ॥

You do not know Him Who has produced all this visible (and invisible) universe. He is quite different from the one you are searching for and He is in your inner selves. There are people living only to satisfy their senses who go about arguing much and talking tall (to prove the existence of God and exerting their influence upon the common, ignorant people) but are themselves enveloped with a thick mist of ignorance. (You are such).

Submit to Him entirely.

अन्रे ऐन्नन् आवियुमुडलुमुडमै ऐल्लामुङ्,
कुन्रे यनैयाय् यन्नैयाट्कौराडपोदे कौराडलैयो ।
विन्रोरिडैयूरैनक्कुराडो वैराडोरामुक्करणौम्माने,
नन्रे चैय्याय् पिझैच्चैवाय् नानोविदर्कुक्कारणमे ॥

Didst not Thou take my soul, my body, my apparel (my victuals) and all into Thy (Divine) control, oh Lord! Thou Who art like a (huge) mountain (to me who am less than a tiny ant before Thee), when Thou didst accept my submission to *t*hy Sway. Have I anything left for me now to depend upon (but Thy Providence) oh Thou Who hast eight hands (in the form of the eight cardinal points) and three eyes (in the form of the past, present and future)? Whether Th y disposal of my life turns out well or ill for me (from the worldly point of view), may not my self be the cause either of its initiation or fulfilment but let Thy Holy Will be the be-all and end-all of it). (The Saivite devotee Maa*n*ikka Vaacakar in his Tiruvaacakam).

Wait patiently and you will be saved.

देवाचिये द्वारीं । उभा क्षणभरी । तेणें मुक्ति चारी । साधियेल्या ॥

He who waits (patiently) at the Lord's "door" even for a moment, will attain "four-fold" salvation. (From Jnaanesvar the Vaish*n*ava devotee of Mahaaraash*t*ra).

E. D.—40.

PLATE VII
6333

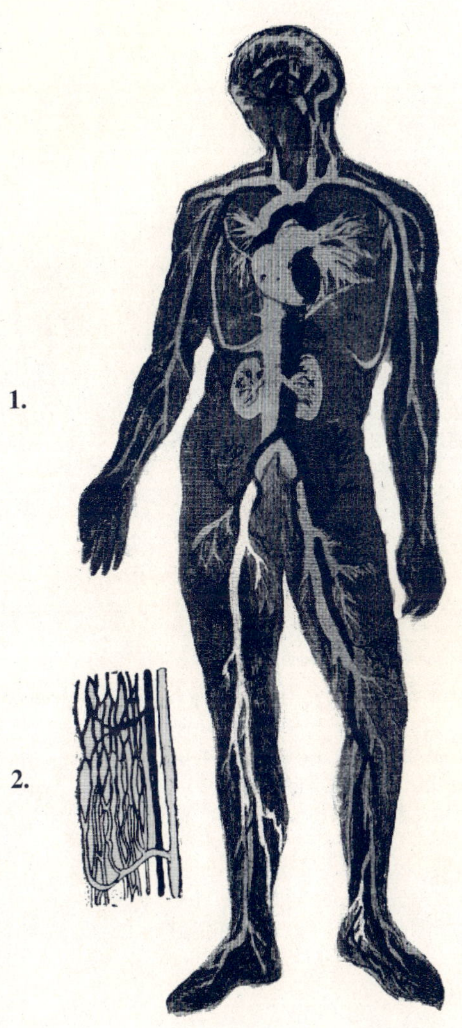

(1) The arteries (white) and veins (black). (2) A section showing the capillaries.

(To face p. 320.)

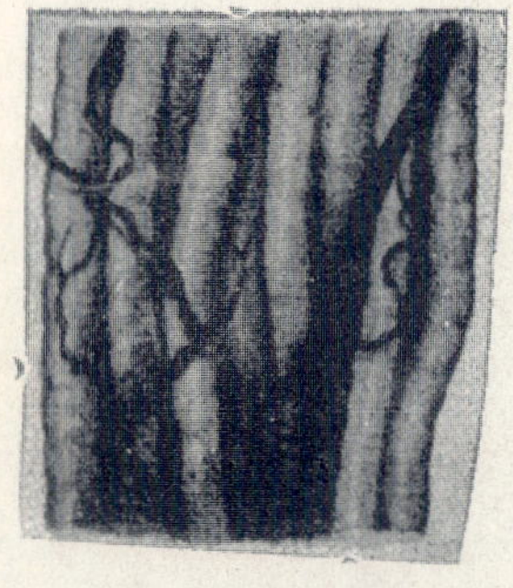

1.

2.

No. 1 is a bit of a muscle in which a bundle of muscle fibres can be seen. No. 2 shows two of these fibres highly magnified. It is all these 'details' of the human body that are called six thousand three hundred and thirty three. (See p. 239). The veins, arteries and nerves are also referred to as rivers. See R. V. x, 75.

CHAPTER V.

The Great Realities at the Root of Creation,

Ṛgvēda X, 129.

Seer:—The Sage Prajāpati Paramēṣthin.*

Subject:—An account of the state before creation and of the three Great Eternal Realities.

Metre:—Verses 1—3 nicṛt triṣṭup; 4—6 triṣṭup and verse 7 pādanicṛttriṣṭup.

Key:—Dhāivata.

(११६) ओ३म् ॥ नासदासीन्नो सदासीत्तदानीं नासीद्रजो नो व्योमापरो यत् । किमावरीवः कुहकस्य शर्मन्नम्भः किमासीद्गहनं गभीरम् ॥१॥

(116) Nāsadasīnnō sadāsīt tadānīm nāsīdrajō nō vyōmāparō yat । Kim āvarīvah kuhakasya śarmannambhah kim āsīdgahanam gabhīram ॥ 1.

पदपाठः—न । असंत् । आसीत् । नो । सत् । आसीत् । तदा-

---

*Prajaapati Paramesh*th*in need not here be taken to mean the Supreme Being. The Asiatics have never been so 'prudish' as to refrain from using the names of God as the *proper names* of ordinary mortals. Hence 'Paramesvara,' 'Prajaapati,' 'Omkaara,' etc., are proper names of common occurrence among the 'Hindus' even today.

नीम् । न । आसीत् । रजः । नो । विऽओम । परः । यत् । किम् । आ । अवरीवर् । कुहं† । कस्य† । शर्मन् । अम्भः । किम् । आसीत् । गह॑नम् । गभीरम् ॥

अन्वयः—तदानीम् असत् न आसीत् । सत् नो आसीत् । रजः न आसीत् । यत् अपरः व्योम (तत् अपि) नो (आसीत्) । किम् कुहकस्य अम्भः गहनम् गभीरम् आसीत् ? किम् (तत्) शर्मन् आ अवरीवः ।

Word-meaning etc:—असत (नञ्+अस्+शतृ P. III, 2, 124 and II, 2, 26)=void, space. न आसीत्=there was not, there were no finite composite beings and hence there was no vogue of the 'realisation' of space by action and speech. सत्=the unmanifest Primordial Matter called by some, 'nature', (प्रकृति), of which the phenomenal world is a remote evolute. तदानीम् (तद्+दानीं P. V, 3, 19; VII, 2, 102)=then, i. e., before creation when the 'great deluge' (महाप्रलय) period had not as yet terminated. रजः (√रञ्ज्+असुन् U. IV, 217)=atoms, atomic matter, an early evolutionary stage of the Primordial Matter. व्योम (√व्ये+मनिन् U. IV, 151 and P. VI, 3, 109)=ether, the etheric evolute of the Primordial Matter, nebulous matter, etheric nebula. अपरः=other, next. आ अवरीवः (आ+√वृ+यङ्लुक+लृ of the past imperfect)=does or did envelop. कुहकस्य (√कुह+वुन् U. II, 37)=of the cloud of mist appearing at morning time in the rainy season. (The double acute accent of this word in the text is irregular). शर्मन् (√शृ+मनिन् U. IV, 145)=house, refuge, hence here, Brahman the Supreme Being, Who is the Refuge of all finite beings. अम्भः (√आप+infix नुम्+भू U. IV, 210)= water. गहनम् (√गाह+क्युन् U. II, 79)=deep, difficult. गभीरम् (√गम्+ईरन् U. IV, 35)=great, vast.

Translation:—There was no void or space then

---

†This is supposed to be the padapaa*th*a of the sage *S*aunaka. The padapaa*th*a, it must be remembered, is not a mere breaking up of Vedic words into their component parts, but a regular, though peculiar, commentary on Vedic verses. Hence Yaaska and other Vedic scholars often differ from it. See the Introduction.

(before creation), nor was their manifest the Primordial Matter, nor atoms, nor even ether ['virāt', the luminous nebular mass of matter] (as there was no vogue of the realisation of these in action owing to the absence of finite composite beings). There was some fine indescribable matter which extended like haze, but like the vanishing cloud of mist seen at morning time in the rainy season; its expanse and depth could not cover Him, the Refuge of all finite beings.

Comment:—Maharṣi Dayānanda's "Introduction to the Vedic Commentary" p. 169-70 has the following explanation of this stanza:—"Before the creation, i. e., when this effect the world had not been made, even the void (*Akasha—space*) was not; because, there were no actions which could take place in it, nor was at that time the causal matter of the world named *sat*, consisting of *prakriti*—unmanifested matter, nor were there the atoms; nor was there the second *akasha*—ether, which fills the universe (*virat*). There was at that time only the subtlest, and the ultimate (material cause of all this world) called God's Sāmarthya i. e., 'material to work with'. As the slight moisture that appears as fog on a morning in the rainy season is neither sufficient to throw a veil over the earth nor to make the rivers flow, nor is it deep because it is so insignificant, even so the entire universe which has been made by God with His *Samarthya* can not be said to be deep in comparison to *Parabrahma*—the Holy and Immaculate. The universe is finite while God is Infinite. Nothing can, therefore, cover Him."

Severed from its context this verse would seem to postulate that before the first creation only the Supreme Being existed and naught else, The hymn as a whole, it must be borne in mind, carries us back to a condition previous to all the states of existence and hence unimaginable. The terminology of the hymn has a solemn incomprehensible rhythm about it, the mark of its unintelligibility to ordinary minds. Not all Vedic statements can be understood by the average man or woman. If even an ordinary school or college text requires preparation to understand, much more study and application is necessary to grasp the great and subtle truths described in the Vedas in a language which does not belong to human concourse. To understand such things a proper disposition of the mind engendered through Yogic exercises is very desirable. Bare human knowledge based upon our ordinary everyday life being only relative, cannot be sufficient to understand great subtle or spiritual truths belonging to other spheres of existence where the usages of space, time and motion of the gross material world are inappropriate.

Imagine a disembodied soul left alone in the midst of this condition of affairs prior to creation. What will she observe ? There will be nothing fit for her observation. Where will she take her stand and where will she move ? There will be no means to mark space and direct her motion or stay in it. How can she distinguish between prior and posterior there being no events and no motion to make calculation of time possible ? These usages presuppose a 'gross material' existence. Hence it is that Maharṣi Dayānanda very aptly observes: "because, there were no actions which could take place in it."

Griffith translates this stanza as follows:—"There was not nonexistent nor existent: there was no realm of air, no sky beyond it. What covered in and when ? Was water their unfathomed depth of water ?" Here an English word or phrase for each Vedic term has been inserted but no attempt made to bring out the inlying idea of the original. The idea conveyed by the translation of the denial of everything is not in the original and is untrue scientifically. The fact of existence as such can never be denied for it is at the base of all and when all ceases, itself persists for ever. A modern scientist says "the mere fact of existence is the fact of eternity."* A more solemn book, the Old Testament, says "And God said unto Moses, *I am that I am*: and he said, Thus shalt thou say unto the children of Israel, *I am* hath sent me unto you."† Griffith did not know the Einstein Theory, and perhaps he did not much care for the Bible also.

Wilson's‡ translation and Macdonell's¶ versified rendering of the verse also follow suit having nothing to recommand them to the serious reader. As interpreters these gentlemen have one and all miserably failed. Their translations of the stanza are at best misinterpretations if not also misrepresentations.

The words 'na asat' and 'no sat' do not deny existence, but, on the other hand, as are interpreted by the great Vedic Scholar Dayānanda, assert it most forcibly. The denial of sat and asat brings out clearly the idea that God, the pure existent, is beyond these two categories and what effect the deluge has on them, it cannot have on the Supreme Being.

In the Tāittirīyōpaniṣad we have:—"From whom

---

* Samuel Guggenheimer, in his 'The Einstein Theory Explained' Macmillan's New York 1925 p. 10. †Exodus (O.T.) III, 15.

‡"The non-existent was not, the existent was not, then the world was not nor the firmament, nor that which is above (the firmament). How could there be any investing envelop, and where? Of what (could there be) felicity? How (could there be) the deep unfathomable water?" H. H. Wilson's Translation of the Rəgveda.

¶"Nor aught existed then, nor naught existed,
There was no air, no heaven beyond,
What covered all? Wherein? In whose shelter was it?
Was it the water, deep and fathomless?" Macdonell's History of Sanskrit Literature.

all the creatures are born, and by whom, being born, are maintained, and to whom they resort and in whom they are finally (at the time of pralaya) 'merged', that is Brahma (the Supreme Being). Try to know Him"*

The phenomenal world is not annihilated but resolved itself into its elementary ingredients by the Will of God and remains in Him. There is no time when material existents completely cease to exist; they are simply transmuted from gross to their subtle forms. As for the souls "they lie idle in the time of chaos (pralaya) as they do in dreamless or profound sleep", as says Maharṣi Dayānanda in his Light of Truth Chapter VIII. Thus all existents undergo a complete change leaving only the ultimate essentials intact, but the Supreme Being is beyond change. In Him there is no change. The period of pralaya is a period of cessation of creative activity for Him but not of change, since His Being consists of nothing but what is essential. His nature is unalloyed and simple, hence the pralaya does not transform Him. By the expression अभिसंविशन्ति in the quotation above, it is hinted that the ultimate, irreducible essentials of all existents, at pralaya, remain in the Supreme Being.

The Chāndōgyōpaniṣad testifies to the persistence of this irreducible minimum of all material existents:—"(Oh Śvētakētu) distinguish water as the original cause from the enjoyable earth, its effect: water as effect from heat as cause, and heat as effect from Sat: Sat (the real), as cause, which is the eternal or noumenal Prakṛti or Primordial Matter, the root and mainstay of all the world."† On this Maharṣi Dayānada thus comments in

---

*यतो वा इमानि भूतानि जायन्ते येन जातानि जीवन्ति यत्प्रयन्त्यभिसंविशन्ति तद्विजिज्ञासस्व तद्ब्रह्म ॥ तै० ३ । १ ॥

†एवमेव खलु सोम्यान्नेन शुङ्गेनापो मूलमन्विच्छाद्भिः सोम्य शुङ्गेन तेजो

his Light of Truth Ch. VIII:—"This whole visible world was like something unreal before the creation, and existed in an invisible form together with the souls in the Brahman and Prakṛti. It was not non-existent."

The following appears in the Yajurveda:—"The wise one beholds with his mind's eye That Supreme Being Who lies hidden in a sphere of existence difficult of access and in Whom the whole universe resumes one aggregate form. In Him all this evolved world 'merges' at the time of dissolution and from Him is it evolved in different forms at creation. He is it that, in various ways, fills all created beings through and through like the warp and woof in the cloth."*

The idea in the above verse refers to the Supreme Being as the efficient cause and not the material.

In Atharvaveda II, 1, 1 it is said:—"The wise one beholds, with his mind's eye, That Supreme Being Who remains hidden in a sphere of existence difficult of access. From Him does Primordial Matter derive various potencies and evolve the beings that are born at creation and to Him, Knowing His Blissful aspect, do the pious offer praise."†

In this, **पृश्नि**, the Primordial Matter is clearly stated to be the material cause of the producible universe. Hence, we may say, the verse **नासदासीन्नो सदासीत्** does not deny the existence of matter but simply hints that all

मूलमन्विच्छ तेजसा सोम्य शुङ्गेन सन्मूलमन्विच्छ । सन्मूलाः सोम्येमाः सर्वाः प्रजा सदायतनाः सत्प्रतिष्ठाः ॥ छां० ६ । ८ । ४ ॥

* वेनस्तत्पश्यन्निहितं गुहा सद्यत्र विश्वं भवत्येकनीडम् । तस्मिन्निदं सञ्च विचैति सर्वं स ओतः प्रोतश्च विभूः प्रजासु ॥ य. ३२ । ८ ॥

† वेनस्तत्पश्यत्परमं गुहा यद्यत्र विश्वं भवत्येकरूपम् । इदं पृश्निरदुहज्जायमानाः स्वर्विदो अभ्यनूषत व्राः ॥ अ. २ । १ । १ ॥

*The difference between this translation and that given on p. 104 'Anthology of Vedic Hymns' is only verbal.

beings other than Brahma, are at that time of chaos in an incomprehensible and indescribable condtion.

(११७) न मृत्युरासीदमृतं न तर्हि न रात्र्या अह्न आसीत्प्रकेतः। आनीदवातं स्वधया तदेकं तस्माद्धान्यन्न परः किंचनास ॥२॥

(117) Na mṛtyurāsīdamṛtaṁ na tarhi na rātryā ahna āsīt prakētah I Ānīdavātam svadhayā tadēkam tasmāddhānyanna parah kiṃcan āsa ‖ 2.

पदपाठः— न। मृत्युः। आसीत्। अमृतम्। न। तर्हि। न। रात्र्याः। अह्नः। आसीत्। प्रऽकेतः। आनीत्। अवातम्। स्वधया। तत्। एकम्। तस्मात्। ह। अन्यत्। न। परः। किम्। चन। आस ॥

अन्वयः—तर्हि मृत्युः न आसीत् अमृतम् अपि न (आसीत्), रात्र्या अह्नः प्रकेतः न आसीत्। तदेकम् स्वधया अवातम् आनीत्, ह तस्मात् परः अन्यत् किंचन न आस ॥

Word-meaning:—तर्हि = then. मृत्युः = dying, death. अमृतम् = life, living. रात्र्याः = from the night. अह्नः = of the day. प्रकेतः = (प्रकृष्टश्चासौ केतश्च—प्र + √ कि ज्ञाने + तन् U. III, 86 and P. III, 3, 1,) = sign, mark. अवातम् (वातं विना यथा स्यात्तथा) = windless, breathless. आनीत् = breathed. स्वधया (स्वस्मिन्धीयते इति स्व + डुधाञ् धारणपोषणयोः + क P. III, 2, 3) = with His own Creative 'Power' i. e. the Primordial Matter. तत् एकम् = that One God. तस्मात् = from Him. ह = surely. अन्यत् = something else. परः = distinct, beyond, greater. न किंचन = nothing at all. आस = existed, was manifest.

Translation:—There was no death then, nor was there life. There was also no sign to distinguish day from night. That (Supreme) One then, with His (great subtle) 'Material Energy' of creation lived breathless and nothing else distinct (or apart) from Him, was manifest.

Comment:—The idea set forth in this verse should

be construed along with that in the previous one. The first verse has mentioned God as existing before creation, and now this verse mentions another thing, viz: 'svadhā' called by Maharṣi Dayānanda, 'Sāmarthya'. This is a name of Prakṛti or Primordial Matter, in its subtlest form, at this stage existing inchoate in the Supreme Being without losing its individual existence. As it exists before the creation it is essentially eternal.

The word 'amṛta' does not deny anything immortal, for such a denial would be a contradiction of the idea in the first verse. Rather it denies life in an embodied form as is associated with the individual souls. Hence we can say, that this verse mentions by implication another eternal entity, the human soul, thus making up the trio of the Vedic creed.

In the second half of the first line of this stanza, time division is denied as being relative to gross existence. Sāyaṇa* in his commentary on this verse has noted the use of **तदानीं**, **(तर्हि)** as being due to **उपचार**—an extended application of the terminolgy of our daily concourse to a condition to which it is not strictly applicable.

The expression 'avātam' denies the existence of air ('prāṇa'—vital air) as a separate entity before creation. In spite of this, He did 'breathe', which means that all the great elements do absolutely depend upon God and exist in Him ever after dissolution. This word 'parah' means, distinct or apart from or greater than, and implies that if some disembodied being, having the power to visualise spiritual existents were to come on the scene it would have seen God and God alone everywhere. This is the glorious state the accomplished yogi finds himself in during samādhi.

---

* कथं तर्हि नो सदासीत्तदानीमिति कालवाची प्रत्ययः उपचारादिति ब्रूमः॥ सायणाचार्याः ॥

Griffith's translation of the last quarter of this stanza is "apart from it was nothing whatever," while Wilson renders it—"other than that there was nothing else whatever", and Macdonell says:—"than that, forsooth, no other thing existed". The two latter convey a flat, categorical denial of everything else but God, in spite of the words 'svadhā' and 'amṛtam' whereas the first approximates to it. Such a rendering is entirely opposed to the spirit of the Veda and cannot be accepted as authentic. It is true, the verse is difficult, but to misconstrue it, would not improve the situation. Griffith's rendering can be excused but the two others are entirely out of court,

The Vedic doctrine of trinity is necessitated by the great disparity between the material and spiritual spheres of existence. The gross material world in which we live cannot be explained as the effect of any non-material, subtle, spiritual entity according to the law of causality which requires that the essential features of the cause must be present in the effect. The theory of creation out of nothing also is equally absurd and repulsive to science. *Ex nihilo nihil fit*—out of nothing only nothing can come.

> The 'no' has nowhere room to be;
> No void is, where the 'yes' is not:—
> This final end of both is seen
> By them that see things as they are."*

This teaching of the trinity is set forth in Ṛgveda I, 164,20† commenting on which Maharṣi Dayānanda in his Satyārthaprakāśa. Ch. VIII says:— "The Brahma (Supreme Being) and the ego (human soul) are both

---

* नासतो विद्यते भावो नाभावो विद्यते सतः । उभयोरपि दृष्टोऽन्तस्त्वनयोस्तत्त्वदर्शिभिः ॥ भ० २ । १६ ॥ † द्वा सुपर्णा सयुजा सखाया समानं वृक्षं परिषस्वजाते । तयोरन्यः पिप्पलं स्वाद्वत्त्यनश्नन्नन्यो अभिचाकशीति ॥ ऋ. १ । १६४ । २० ॥

(dvā) alike in virtue of their consciousness and protective and other qualities (suparṇā). They are related to each other as the pervader and the pervaded (sayujā). Bearing friendship to each other (sakhāyā), they are eternal and unbeginning. So (samānam) is also the tree (vṛkṣa), which is the fundamental cause, whose branches are the phenomena of the material world, and which is developed on till it is resolved into its elementary ingredients at the time of dissolution. It is the third unbeginning substance. The qualities, characters and natures of these three substances are also unbeginning. Of the two, the Supreme Being and the human soul, the latter tastes with satisfaction the fruit of virtue and vice, borne by the tree of the world (svādvatti) ; and the former, is not affected (anaśnan) by the consequences of works, shining everywhere in the interior and exterior through and through. God is distinct from the soul, and nature (Prakṛti) is distinct from both God and the soul. But all the three are eternal and unbeginning,"

The Tāittirīyōpaniṣad* says :— "If a person thinks that Brahma is non-existence, he himself becomes non-existent. But if he thinks that Brahma is existent, he is regarded a saint." "There was chaos in the beginning, i. e., this very world was chaos in the beginning. The visible world (sat) came out of it. It (the Brahma) made itself, hence it is called "well made".†

In the previous passage, II, 6 it is said :—God Who is spirit and Whose Will is absolute, willed, and the 'heaven and earth' came into being. He said, as it were, I am one, I become many, so that I may create. He cogitated and brooded over His cosmic plan, and

---

*असन्नेव स भवति । असद्ब्रह्मेति वेद चेत् । अस्ति ब्रह्मेति चेद्वेद । सन्तमेनं ततो विदुः ॥ II, 6. †असद्वा इदमग्र आसीत् । ततो वै सदजायत । तदात्मानं स्वयमकुरुत । तस्मात्तत्सुकृतमुच्यते ॥ II ,7.

created all this world as it is. Having thus created it He entered it. After His entering it, it became the reality in its atomic and phenomenal forms, i. e., in visible and invisible, mental and material forms, in transient and permanent states. Whatever exists is real. It is called truth or reality.*

The Sāmkhya Sūtra I, 61† mentions these three existents as eternal and on this Maharṣi Dayānanda in his Satyārthaprakāśa Ch. VIII comments thus :—"*Prakriti* or nature is tripartite or the union of three qualities namely, pure (sattva), middling (rajas) and inert (tamas)—subtle, volatile and base states of matter. It produces the brain substances (buddhi) which generates consciousness (ahamkāra). This in its turn creates the five quintessences (pañca tanmātra) correlated or sensitive to five kinds of elements, ten senses, and the *will or conative power*. The five quintessences produce five elements. They all make up the number of 24 essences. The twenty fifth† is the person or mind (puruṣa) human and divine. Of these essences, the *prakriti* or matter in its original state is undecaying, and the brain substance or sublime matter, consciousness or life, and five quintessences or elementals are the products of *prakriti*, modifications of matter and the cause of the senses, the will (manas) and gross elements. The person or mind is neither the nature, material cause or substance, nor the product of any other being."

Another learned commentator (Svāmi Darsanā-

*सोऽकामयत बहुस्यां प्रजायेयेति। स तपोऽप्यत। स तपस्तप्त्वा इदं सर्वमसृजत यदिदं किञ्च। तत्सृष्ट्वा तदेवानुप्रविशत्। तदनुप्रविश्य सच्च त्यच्चाभवत्। निरुक्तं चानिरुक्तं च निलयनञ्चानिलयनञ्च विज्ञानञ्चाविज्ञानञ्च सत्यञ्चानृतं च सत्यमभवत् यदिदं किञ्च। तत्सत्यमित्याचक्षते। तै० २। ६॥ The paraphrase is by the late Durgaa Prasaada of Lahore. †सत्वरजस्तमसां साम्यावस्था प्रकृतिः। प्रकृतेर्महान्महतोऽहंकारोऽहंकारात्पञ्चतन्मात्राण्युभयमिन्द्रियं पञ्चतन्मात्रेभ्यः स्थूलभूतानि पुरुष इति पञ्चविंशतिर्गणः॥ सांख्य० १। ६१.

nanda*) does not count the 24th manas but takes 'puruṣa' as standing for both the human soul and the Supreme Being, thus making up the total of twentyfive categories. Hence, it can safely be averred that from very ancient times Indian philosophical thought has been accustomed to count three essential eternal beings namely matter, souls and God. Of this more will be said at the end.

(११८) तम॑आसीत्तम॑सा गूळ्हमग्रे॑ऽप्रकेतं स॑लिलं सर्वं॑मा इदं । तुच्छ्येनाभ्वपि॑हितं यदासीत्तप॑सस्तन्म॑हिना जा॑यतैकं॑ ॥३॥

(118) Tama āsīttamasā gū*l*ham agrē'prakētam salilam sarvamā 'idam I Tucchyēnābhvapihitam yadāsīt-tapasastanmahinā jāyatāikam || 3.

पदपाठः—तम॑ः । आसीत् । तम॑सा । गूळ्हम् । अग्रे॑ । अप्रऽकेतम् । सलिलम् । सर्वं॑ । आः । इदं । तुच्छ्येन॑ । आभु । अपि॑ऽहितम् । यत् । आसी॑त् । तप॑सः । तत् । महिना । अजायत । एकं॑ ॥

अन्वयः—इदं सर्वं अग्रे तम आसीत् (च) तमसा गूळ्हम् अप्रकेतं सलिलं आः । यत् तुच्छ्येन (तमसा) अपिहितं आसीत तत् आभु (ब्रह्मणः) तपसः महिना एकं अजायत ॥

Word-meaning etc:—इदं सर्वं=all this visible (and invisible) universe. **तमः**(√ **तनु विस्तारे** or √ **तमिर् खेदे** or √ **तमु कांक्षायां+असुन्** U. IV, 189)=chaos, darkness, something not discernible or distinguishable. **तमसा**=by darkness, i. e., absence of light. That state in which the sense organs cannot work, **गूळ्हम्** (√ **गुह्+क्त**)=hidden. **अप्रकेतम्** (**अविद्यमानः प्रकेतः यस्य तत्**)=having no features of distinction, unintelligible. **सलिलम्** (√ **सल गतौ+इलच्** U. I, 54)=like water, diffuse, ethereal, entirely absorbed in. **आः** (√ **अस भुवि** P. VII, 3, 97)=was. **तुच्छ्येन**=by

* See his commentary on the Saamkhyapravacana sootra.

insignificant. तुच्छ्य is Vedic for तुच्छ). आभु (=आभुना P VII, I, 39. आभु= आ+√भू+इ P. III, 2, 180)=by something overpowering, enveloping, all-pervading. तपसः=of omnipotence. महिना=by virtue, power. अजायत=was produced, born. एकम् अजायत=became one, uniform.

Translation :—In the Beginning (=before the creation) there was 'darkness' and concealed in it, all this universe lay (in its rudimentary form) undiscriminated and chaotic. Whatever there was, was 'shapeless', diffuse and enveloped in a pervasive darkness in itself insignificant (as compared with the Supreme Being). By the might of His Omnipotence it assumed uniformity.

Comment :—Maharṣi Dayānanda in chapter VII of his Satyārthaprakāśa thus remarks on this stanza laying bare its inner meaning:—"All this world was enveloped in darkness before creation: It was unknowable and of ethereal form. Insignificant before His Greatness it lay undeveloped at 'a place' in the presence of the Infinite God. By virtue of His Ommipotence it came out of the noumenal into the phenomenal form".

The previous stanza told us that before creation there was nothing to distinguish day from night. Now we are told that it was entirely dark then. Besides this the whole material of which the universe is composed *lay huddled together in a chaotic form* in which one part could not be distinguished from another. This is an elementary scientific truth, for the distinctions of time, place, state, action, quality etc., are relative to a thinking and acting mind. In the absence of such a mind it would be madness to talk of such distinctions.

Griffith's translation of this stanza is as follows :— Darkness then was: at first concealed in darkness this All was indiscriminated chaos. All that existed then was void and formless by the great power of warmth was born that Unit." It is not clear why the first 'All' begins with a capital letter. Perhaps the translator intends to convey the idea of God by it as he surely seems to mean by the funny word 'Unit' at the end. It is also not known whose 'great power of warmth' the translator speaks of. If the original is difficult, the rendering, to say the least, is uncouth and inexact. The idea conveyed by Griffith is tantamount to the theory of creation out of nothing which is said to be a fundamental tenet of the Bible and Christianity, but it has no place in the Vedas. Wilson's verbose translation also is no good. He speaks of "undistinguishable water" an " empty united world which was covered by a mere nothing" and " produced through the power of austerity," which expressions do not in the least lay bare the beautiful idea in the original, Macdonell's versified translation also is of a piece with these two. It is a pity these European scholars have entirely failed to grasp the true meaning of the original but yet they wish to teach the world of something they themselves have not understood.

Sāyana interprets तुच्छ्येन as तुच्छकल्पनेन सदसद्विलक्षणेन भावरूपाज्ञानेन. He means the famous fib of the modern Vedāntins माया (=illusion) for which there is no room in genuine Vedic literature. The word, in the Vedas, has a very good meaning which the reader may look up in the introduction to this book. तुच्छ्येन and आभु both refer to तमसा in the first line and the absence of the instrumental termination need not confuse us since in Vedic poetry terminations are sometimes dropped or used purely for the exigencies of metre.

The Ancient Indian Lawgiver Manu also supports the view expressed in this text. He says:—"This universe, at the time of the great deluge (mahāpralaya) was covered with darkness, indistinct, unthinkable, unknowable, and as if in a state of deep sleep everywhere." "Then the Self-existent, Almighty God, of whom the senses cannot 'take cognizance' and Whose power is unimpeded made manifest this universe consisting of the five great elements (and other evolutes of Prakṛti) and thus the Dispeller of darkness revealed Himself."*

Manu has, in these two verses, thrown sufficient light on the idea expressed in the Vedic text. Further description of the creation by this great sage will be given at the end of the comment on this hymn.

The Bible also upholds a view of creation similar to that expresed in our text, for, in fact the Bible has borrowed this view from the Vedas though not directly. Being a very late compilation, it has taken its tenets from the Zoroastrian Scriptures† much older than the Bible and nearest to the Vedas. Hence, it should not be understood that quotations from the Bible and other later religious books are given here to support Vedic teachings, but simply to illustrate universal the nature of the latter. "In the beginning God created the heaven and the earth. And the earth was without form, and void, and darkness was upon the face of the deep. And the spirit of God moved upon the face of the water."‡

It will be noticed from this quotation that the Biblical theory of creation is restricted only to "the heaven and the earth." Modern science has detected innumerable solar systems and that consisting of our sun and earth, is only one out of the huge number.

---

*आसीदिदं तमोभूतमप्रज्ञातमलक्षणम् । अप्रतर्क्यमविज्ञेयं प्रसुप्तमिव सर्वतः ॥

†ततः स्वयंभूर्भगवानव्यक्तो व्यञ्जयन्निदम् । महाभूतादिवृत्तौजाः प्रादुरासी त्तमोनुदः ॥ म० १ । ५ ॥ ६ ॥

† See 'The Fountainhead of Religion' by Gangaa Prasaada.

‡ Genesis (O. T.) I, 1; 2.

Science is true, of course, since the conclusions drawn from observation and supported directly by the senses, cannot be gainsaid. Hence, there can be only one conclusion possible viz., (1) that in the other solar systems the Bible cannot be in force, or (2) that the Biblical account deals with a later creation and not the first of the cycle, or (3) that it is an inaccurate copy made by an untrained mind of the Vedic description. The quotation says "darkness was upon the face of the deep." This is a very faint echo of "तम असीत्तमसा गूळ्हम्" etc., which propounds a theory entirely in harmony with the assured principles of modern science. What is meant by "the deep" and where was this ? There is a clear hint in this that the earth is flat and immovable. The sentence in the quotation represents God as moving from place to place and hence limited by space. This topic will be dealt with at length, at the end of this hymn.

(११९) कामस्तदग्रे समवर्तताधि मनसो रेतः प्रथमं यदासीत् । सतो बंधुमसति निरविन्दन्हृदि प्रतीष्या कवयो मनीषा ॥४॥

(119) Kāmastadagrē samavartatādhi manasō rētah prathamam yadāsīt । Satō bandhumasati niravindan hrdi pratīṣyā kavayō manīṣā ॥ 4.

पदपाठः—कामः । तत् । अग्रे । सम् । अवर्तत । अधि । मनसः । रेतः । प्रथमम् । यत् । आसीत् । सतः । बंधुम् । असति । निः । अविन्दन् । हृदि । प्रतिऽइष्य । कवयः । मनीषा ॥

अन्वयः—अग्रे यत् मनसः प्रथमं रेतः आसीत् तत् कामः समधि अवर्तत । कवयः हृदि मनीषा प्रतीष्य असति सतः बन्धुम निरविन्दन् ॥

Word-meaning &c:—कामः (√ कमु इच्छायाम्+घञ्=P. III, 3, 18 or घ P. VI, 1, 203 or अच् P. III, 1, 134)=desire of creation etc. समधि अवर्तत = arose or came into being upon. मनसः (√मन ज्ञाने + असुन् U. IV, 189) = of the mind. The universal and not the individual mind is here intended. रेतः (√री गतिरेषणयोः + तुट् + असुन् U. VI, 189) = seed. प्रथमम् आसीत् = already existed. सतः = of the real, permanent. The human soul is meant here. बंधुम् (√बन्ध बन्धने + उ U. I, 10) = friend, relation. असति = in the non-real, that is, matter as opposed to the soul. The world is implied in this expression. निरविन्दन् = found out. हृदि = in the heart. प्रतीष्य (प्रति + √इष गतिहिंसादर्शनेषु + ल्यप् P. VII, 1, 37) = having searched. कवयः (√कु शब्दे + इ U. IV, 139) = the wise. मनीषा (√मन ज्ञाने + इषन् + टाप् U. VI, 26 and P. IV, 2, 4 or मनस् + ईष गतौ + क + टाप् P. III, 2, 5, Vārtika कप्रकरणे मूलविभुजादिभ्य उपसंख्यानम्. IV, 2, 4; I, 1, 16 and Vārtika शकन्ध्वादिषु पररूपं वाच्यं तच्च टेः) = by the intellect.

Translation :—In the beginning then, there arose Desire (for the creation of the universe) which subsisted in the primeval seed of mind. Hence sages, on a careful search by means of the intellect find out in the impermanent material universe a 'kin' of the Eternal Spirit.

Comment :—The Kāma in this verse is an apotheosis of this noble passion described in Atharvavēda XIX, 52* and is hence called the forerunner of all creation. Winternitz calls this in his "History of Indian Literature" p. 99, "sexual desire" which interpretation, considering the use of the term in other hymns, is entirely wrong. Sexual passion which is only one of the many phases of desire cannot explain creation.

Griffith translates मनसो रेतः by "germ of spirit." Manas is not spirit. The Sāmkhyapravacana Sūtra I 61 elsewhere quoted gives manas or mahat as the eldest evolute of Prakṛti. Immediately after the rising of desire this material evolute is evolved. Hence it is

* See the Introduction to this book.

not clear how Griffith could call Manas 'Spirit'. Besides, spirits can have no seed or germ since they are neither produced by, nor produce, anything at all.

The second line of this stanza lays down a very great truth. The soul is a spiritual entity and Prakṛti is material. There can be no union possible between the two. To bring about such a union, a medium partaking of the nature of both is required. This is found in the manas which, though material, is so subtle that it can easily connect itself with the soul and receive the latter's reflection, whereas, being material it can be in agreement with Prakṛti too. Thus it is that the animal body and all the creation is rendered possible.

Prakṛti does not entangle herself with a liberated soul. Nor does she let off an unliberated soul until the latter becomes fit to attain liberation. Hence the whole act of Divine Will in creating the universe is to allow the human soul to extend her knowledge and attain liberation. In the external universe this is not clearly visible. But a direction of the vision inwards towards the mind will clearly show one how one's position is in relation to liberation and what one has to do in order to attain that state. The Yogi therefore, directs his sight inwards by practice to realise this truth. Some Sanskrit poet has very aptly stated this point thus: "It is the mind that extends the good and evil phases of the life of all beings, hence one should dissuade it from evil and direct it towards good."* What is good and what is evil can be seen only in the mirror of the mind. The wise who use this mirror properly will realise what is laid down in Atharvavēda, VIII, 1, 6: "Mayst thou, oh man, always progress onwards and never go downwards, (wherefore) I endow thee with various potencies to enable

*मनो हि सर्वभूतानां संतनोति शुभाशुभम् । अशुभेभ्यस्तदाक्षिप्य शुभेऽर्थे चावधारय ॥ S. U.

thee to live. Ride in this car (in the shape of thy body) leading to immortality and imparting bliss and when thou art grayhaired with age, recount thy experiences to the young traveller on the path of life".*

From this text we learn the following things about the human body:—(1) It is a means that enables the man always to progress upwards. (2) If rightly utilised it will never take him on the downward path of degradation moral and spiritual. (3) It is endowed with innumerable potencies that should make man's life smooth if he knows and tries to take advantage of them. (4) It is a conveyance to perform the journey on the path of life to salvation. (5) It is intended to impart happiness to man and not to make him miserable if he handles it properly. (6) If man uses his body properly, that is, as a means to the end and does not 'dote' over it, he must live up to a good old age. (7) Life in the body is intended to gather salutary experience which is to be laid before others also for their guidance.

The Kaṭhōpaniṣad also describes the body as a chariot:="The spirit is the master of the chariot, the body is the chariot, the intellect the driver, and the will the reins of horses. The senses are the horses, and the objects of the senses are their path. Philosophers call the spirit associated with the senses and the will, the enjoyer (or the human being)."†

If these are the advantages of the body, then surely it is a friend and wellwisher—if we can use these expressions—of the soul.

---

* उद्यानं ते पुरुष नावयानं जीवातुं ते दक्षतातिं कृणोमि । आ हि रोहेममृतं सुखं रथमथ जिर्विर्विदथमावदासि ॥

† आत्मानं रथिनं विद्धि शरीरं रथमेव तु । बुद्धिं तु सारथिं विद्धि मनः प्रग्रहमेव च ॥ इन्द्रियाणि हयानाहुर्विषयांस्तेषु गोचरान् । आत्मेन्द्रियमनोयुक्तं भोक्तेत्याहुर्मनीषिणः ॥ क० ३ । ३ । ४ ॥

This is exactly what the second line of the stanza says.

Griffith's translation of the second line of this stanza is "sages who searched with their heart's thought discovered the existent's kinship in the non-existent." This way of rendering gives the passage a historical setting and contradicts the very previous line which purports that in the 'Universal Mind' there arose in the very beginning desire. If only desire was born where were the sages? 'Nothing' cannot be equated to sages. To understand Vedic poetry a knowledge of Sanskrit rhetorics is quite essential though this latter science is based upon the Vedas and general Sanskrit literature. To explain difficult passages in Vedic poetry this science is very helpful. A special treatise dealing with Vedic rhetorics is yet to be written and hence such manuals as **काव्यादर्श, साहित्यदर्पण** etc., can be used with advantage.

The present stanza is an instance of either arthāntaranyāsa or kāvyalingam, (figures of speech recognised by Sanskrit rhetoricians). If the latter part of it is taken as a general statement supported by a particular statement in the first part, then it is the figure of speech called arthāntaranyāsa. If the latter is taken as an effect or cause of the former then it is kāvyalingam. Either way the stanza can be very well explained without erring on any side.

Griffiith and his followers have, however, found it feasible to carry on the mistake into their translation of the next stanza as well. There the word **एषाम्** they explain as a demonstrative pronoun referring to **कवयः** in this stanza. Griffith is not very clear on this, for he translates: "transversely was their severing line extended," but an Indian follower of his clearly puts it thus:—"Whatever was below, whatever was above, was traversed by the light of these (sages)." This means that the creative action originated from these imaginary sages and not from the Supreme Being! This interpretation is very seriously contradicted, nay, nullified by the second line of the 6th stanza "अर्वाग्देवा अस्य विसर्जनेन etc., i. e., "the wise ones came into being after the creation of the universe etc."

(१२०) तिरश्चीनो विततो रश्मिरेषामधः स्विदासी३दुपरिस्विदासी३त् । रेतोधा आसन्महिमान आसन्स्वधा अवस्तात्प्रयतिः परस्तात् ॥५॥

(120) Tiraścīnō vitatō raśmirēṣām adhah svidasīdupari svidāsīt । Rētōdhā āsan mahimāna āsan svadhā avastāt prayatih parastāt ॥ 5.

पदपाठः—तिरश्चीनः । विऽततः । रश्मिः । एषाम् । अधः । स्वित् आसी३त् । उपरि । स्वित । आसी३त् । रेतःऽधाः । आसन् । महिमानः । आसन् । स्वधा । अवस्तात् । प्रऽयतिः । परस्तात् ॥

अन्वयः—एषां तिरश्चीनः विततः रश्मिः अधः स्वित् आसीत् उपरि स्वित् आसीत् । (तदानीम्) रेतोधाः आसन्, महिमानः आसन्, अवस्तात् स्वधा (आसीत्) परस्तात् प्रयतिः (आसीत्) ॥

Word-meaning etc:—तिरश्चीनः (तिरस + √ अञ्चु गतिपूजनयोः + क्विन् + ख P. III, 2, 59; VI, 4, 138 and V, 4, 7) = slanting. विततः (वि + √ तनु विस्तारे + क्त P. III, 2, 102 and VI, 4, 37) = spread. रश्मिः (√ अशूङ् व्याप्तौ + मि U. IV, 46) = ray, cord. एषाम् = of these (note the plural which means more than two). अधः स्वित् उपरि स्वित् = below and above in a wonderful manner. आसीत् = was. रेतोधाः = souls awaiting to be born to enjoy the fruit of past actions. महिमानः = liberated souls who were waiting to be reborn as their state of liberation had terminated. स्वधा = creative power of God. अवस्तात = this side. प्रयतिः = effort, influence of the past actions of souls. परस्तात् = the other side.

Translation:—The slanting ray of light of these

(viz:—(1) tad ekam [vs. 2]; (2) svadhā [vs. 2] or apraketam salilam [vs. 3] and (3) rētōdhāh and mahimānah) had spread wonderfully both below and above. There were unliberated souls waiting to be reborn to enjoy the residua of their past actions and liberated souls who had enjoyed their state of bliss. This side worked the Divine creative Force and that side the influence of the past actions of individual souls.

Comment:—The simile of the ray of light is here used to connote the idea of the sudden spread of the result of the creative act of the Divine Will. Light travels at the rate of 1,86,000 miles per second. The production of the several objects of the universe also was as quick. Dissolution of the universe into its elements also will be as speedy. An earthquake or a deluge destroys huge thickly peopled regions within a wink of the eye. Sāyaṇa says **सूर्यरश्मिरुदयानंतरं निमेषमात्रेण युगप-त्सर्वजगद्व्याप्नोति** i. e. "after sunrise the ray (=light) of the sun within a wink of the eye instantaneously spreads all over the world." From this we understand that scientific truths about the motion of light etc., are not unknown to the Vedas.

रेतोधाः is explained by Sāyaṇa as **रेतसो बीजभूतस्य कर्मणां विधातारः कर्तारो भोक्तारश्च जीवाः** i. e., "those souls who are the doers and enjoyers of the fruits of deeds that are seed (=origin or source) of other actions to be done or enjoyed in other (=subsequent) births. Here those souls are meant who had not attained their liberation before the 'deluge'. They have now to be reborn to enjoy the residua of the deeds good and bad of their past lives, These residua are the seed or source of their births hereafter. Hence the expression **रेतोधा** is quite appropriate.

Sāyaṇa has failed to interpret the expression **महिमानः** rightly. He tries to profit by his mistake since a deeper research into the etymology of the word would falsify his pet theory of interminable liberation of the human soul.

With regard to the state of the soul after death, it is alleged that there is difference of opinion among the different schools of Indian philosophy. The materialists maintain that after death nothing remains of man. All other schools believe in transmigration. But with regard to salvation there is difference. There are schools of the Buddhist and the Jain sects who maintain that complete annihilation is salvation. This seems to be the general idea signified by the well-known expression निर्वाण (blowing out or extinction). The Vedantins and others maintain that liberation is endless. A liberated soul is for ever exempted from assuming birth. The third and most reasonable school maintains that liberation cannot be endless since being the result of limited efforts such as right knowledge through yogic exercises it cannot itself be indefinite. Sāyaṇa belongs to the second school. This school interprets the term महिमानः as meaning महान्तो वियदादयो भोग्याः i. e., "the huge enjoyable objects such as space etc."

The Puruṣasūkta, (Ch. XXXI of the Yajurveda) stanza 16* uses this word for the liberated souls.

An English translation of a free and very accurate rendering of this verse by Maharṣi Dayānanda in his 'Introduction to the Commentary on the Vedas' is as follows:—"The learned (देवाः) have paid, do and will always pay homage (अयजन्त) to God the Worshipful (यज्ञम्) with praise, prayer and worship (यज्ञेन). All men ought to begin (प्रथमानि) all actions with these (धर्माणि) and no one

* यज्ञेन यज्ञमयजन्त देवास्तानि धर्माणि प्रथमान्यासन् । ते ह नाकं महिमानः सचन्त यत्र पूर्वे साध्याः सन्ति देवाः ॥ य० ३१ ॥ १६ ॥

ought to do anything which is not preceded by them. Verily, do the worshippers of God, exalted in glory (महिमानः), attain to Him and emancipation in which there is no pain or suffering (नाकं). The learned men who qualified themselves in the past (पूर्वे साध्याः देवाः) and those who are qualifying themselves now and those who will qualify themselves in future, obtained and will obtain this highest state of bliss to be enjoyed for a hundred years of Brahma during which period there is no return to the cycle of births and deaths."

From this it will be gathered that महिमानः means the liberated souls. Uvata also commenting on this says,* " those ascetics who are glorified, that is, having shaken off the three attributes are become pure, enter the Supreme Being called Nārāyaṇa, or, in other words, attain emancipation." Hence the word महिमानः ought to be rendered here also in like manner. The association of रेतोधाः a term denoting human souls raises in our minds the expectation that the other term also would stand for human souls. Besides महिमानः is too high a word to be used for such inanimate objects as ether, air etc.

In the Brāhmaṇa literature the word महिमन् does not seem to be used to signify the five great elements alone. In Śatapatha X, 2, 2, 2, we have देवा महिमानः i. e., "the wise (or learned) are the glorified." In VI,3,1,18 it is written यज्ञो वै महिमा "sacrifice indeed is glorification." In XIII,2,11,2 and Taittirīya Brāhmaṇa III,9,10,1 we are told that "the king is the glorified one" राजा महिमा. The word महिमा in the first authority quoted here, if stretched, would mean the five great elements or anything connoted with the root दिव्. In the second quotation

---

* ये तु योगिनो महिमानो जन्मान्तरैर्निर्धूतगुणाः शुध्दास्ते नारायणाख्य-पुरुषमाविशन्ति मुक्तिं गच्छन्तीत्यर्थः" इति उवटभाष्ये ॥

it would mean God the Adorable as यज्ञ means यजनीय as well. In the last text it would mean Soma also, since राजा means the Soma plant as well. But in spite of all these probabilities the only appropriate and intelligent interpretation, on account of association as well as the import of the word in the passage from the Puruṣa Sūkta quoted above is, "liberated souls."

Sāyaṇa has committed another irregularity at least, if not inaccuracy. The word स्वधा has already occured in Stanza 2 above, आनीदवातं स्वधया तदेकं—where his interpretation is quite correct. He says there स्वस्मिन्धीयते ध्रियत आश्रित्य वर्तत इति स्वधा माया, that is, "that which exists depending upon God's own self viz., Māyā, the incomprehensible awful Might of God." Sāyaṇa tries to convey here the neo-Vedantic idea of 'illusion,' but this is a very late, superfluous growth of the idiom, and cannot be traced to the Vedas. Where in Vedic texts it savours of this idea, the sense of something incomprehensible to the human mind is intended and not something false or bogus. The word माया itself is derived from the root मा meaning to measure, with the suffix य and seems to connote the idea of the measure of reality which the Scholastic philosophers describe as "intellectus Dei est norma rerum," which literally means: Divine Intellect is the norm of things (i. e. the mind of God is the standard according to which reality is to be tested). God creates the universe according to His own idea but the ideas of human beings are formed after the things of the universe and have to be tallied with them and not vice versa. The idea is really awful and difficult to grasp.

The terms प्रकृति, माया, स्वधा, शक्ति, ईश्वरी etc., are all synonymous and indicate something awful and incomprehensible, (material though, according to the most reasonable of ancient Indian philosophers) in the power of God, which He manipulates at the time of creation. What is meant by स्वधा in this verse as well as the second is simply the extremely subtle, diffuse form of Primordial Matter in which the universe had 'merged' through the Omnipotence of God. Sāyaṇa's interpretation of this term, therefore, as अन्नम् or भोग्यप्रपञ्चः cannot be accepted.

The next word प्रयतिः derived from the root √यम्, prefix प्र and suffix क्तिन्, means effort or endeavour of the souls arising from the residua of their past deeds. This simple Vedic word need not be stretched as Sāyaṇa does to yield a meaning agreeable to his pet theory of 'māyā'.

It will now have become clear that this hymn really refers to three eternal principles viz., (1) God in the first stanza, (2) Svadhā in the second and (3) Svadhā and 'migrating' and liberated souls in the fifth. To these three, it is, that the demonstrative pronoun एषाम् refers. But in the Comment on the previous stanza it has been shown how Griffith and his school misconstrue it. Sāyaṇa also, to support his fad of the neo-Vedantic doctrine of māyā, says, "अविद्याकामकर्माणि सृष्टिहेतुत्वेनोक्तानि" i. e., "false knowledge, desire and actions are here spoken of as the cause of creation." This trio of causes is nowhere, even so much as hinted at, in the whole hymn. Besides from eulogia from the Atharvaveda and Yajurveda on 'Desire' (see Introduction, Chapter II) the only conclusion drawn can be that desire is a noble passion and the universe is a benefactor of the soul and not her enemy.

(१२१) को अद्धा वेद क इह प्रवोचत्कुत आजाता कुत इयं विसृष्टिः । अर्वाग्देवा अस्य विसर्जनेनाथा को वेद यत आबभूव ॥६॥

(121) Kō addhā vēda ka iha pravōcat kuta ājātā kuta iyam visṛṣṭih । Arvāgdēvā asya visarjanēnāthā kō vēda yata ā babhūva ॥

पदपाठः—कः । अद्धा । वेद । कः । इह । प्र । वोचत् । कुतः । आऽजाता । कुतः । इयम् । विऽसृष्टिः । अर्वाक् । देवाः । अस्य । विऽसर्जनेन । अथ । कः । वेद । यतः । आऽबभूव ॥

अन्वयः—अद्धा कः वेद ? इह कः प्रवोचत् ? कुतः आजाता ? इयम् विसृष्टिः कुतः ? अथ अस्य विसर्जनेन अर्वाक् देवाः (अजायन्त) कः वेद यतः (इयम् विसृष्टिः) आबभूव ? ॥

Word-meaning &c:—कः = who. अद्धा = surely. वेद = knows, can know. इह = here, in this case, about it. प्रवोचत् = declares, can declare it. कुतः = whence, from where. आजाता = has come into being. इयम् = this. विसृष्टिः = creation full of variety, the 'hydra-headed' motley creation. अर्वाक् = later. देवाः = wise men. अस्य = of this. विसर्जनेन = than the creation or formation. अथ = hence कः = who among the finite beings. यतः = whence. आबभूव = came into being.

Translation:—Who verily can know (by personal contact) whence it was born and whence this multifarious creation came into being and who can declare about it? The wise ones who are expected to know (this great secret) are themselves later born than the creation of this universe. Hence how is it possible for any being (other than God) to know how and whence it (the creation first) came into being?

Comment:—This stanza asks a number of questions and if the implied links are supplied, gives only one answer with one reason for it. (1) कः अद्धा वेद (a) कुतः आजाता (b) कुतः इयम् विसृष्टिः ? (2) क इह प्रवोचत् (a) कुतः आजाता (b) कुतः इयम् विसृष्टिः ?

The implied link is:—(3) न कोऽपि वेद (a) कुतः आजाता (b) कुतः इयम् विसृष्टिः । The objector says (4) देवा वेदितुम् अर्हन्ति । The reply is: (5) न देवाः अपि वेदितुम् अर्हन्ति । कुतः ? ।

Then comes the conclusion (6) **अर्वाग्देवाः अस्य विसर्जनेन अथा को वेद यतः इयं विसृष्टिः आ बभूव ? न कोऽपि ॥**

By '**वेद**' here, knowledge (a) complete and (b), through personal contact is meant and not knowledge acquired somehow. Knowledge of the root causes of the various items of the universe and the way in which they have been formed, is not within the scope of human faculties. It is not possible for man to know everything about the rose. With great efforts and patient research he can know only something about it and nothing more. Human nature is so constituted that in order to acquire knowledge man has to depend upon several factors most of which are external to his own self both in time and place. Different types of knowledge is acquired from different sources through different media, by means of different organs and with the help of different means, not all of which can a man command at a time. Even if all these factors are available, man's knowledge assumes only the form of information acquired through external agencies with the help of his senses. All definite or limited beings suffer from these defects. It is not destined that such should know the awful way in which the diffused atoms of Primordial Matter combine, and from a subtle, invisible chaos, all of a sudden, witn greater speed than that at which light travels, an immense, limitless universe of the most formidable gross material objects, comes into being.

To know the secret of creation, our stanza says, is possible only for the eye witness,—for him who existed before it and whose consciousness took note of the whole process. The (ordinary) human souls (saṃsārī jīva) did exist before creation as the previous stanza taught us, but their existence was not a conscious life. They were in an unconscious state (mugdhāvasthā), entirely unfit to receive any knowledge. Even the liberated souls, otherwise capable of gathering knowledge and putting forth effort at will, were then in a condition entirely unfit to 'act physically' except knowing God and communicating with Him and 'visualising' the subtle chaotic matter. Physical activity limited by time and place could not then be possible as there was no gross matter to react. This is explained in the second stanza. The only really conscious existent at this stage, as the fourth stanza has pointed out, being the Divine Self in Whose Mind the Desire for creation arises, the secret of creation is a sealed book to all finite beings.

Hence it should be noted that the denial of knowledge in this stanza is not a total denial. There is one exception, viz., the Supreme Being, Whose conscious existence preceded the creation of the universe, nay, according to Whose Omnipotent Will, the universe took form. He surely knows everything, as the next stanza says.

(१२२) इयं विसृष्टिर्यत आबभूव यदि वा दधे यदि वा न। यो अस्याध्यक्षः परमे व्योमन्त्सो अङ्ग वेद यदि वा न वेद ॥ ७ ॥

(122) Iyam visṛṣtiryata ābabhūva yadi vā dedhē yadi vā na 1 Yō'syādhyakṣah paramē vyōmantsō anga vēda yadi vā na vēda ॥ 7.

पदपाठः—इयम् । विऽसृष्टिः यतः । आऽबभूव । यदि । वा । दधे । यदि । वा । न । यः । अस्य । अधिऽअक्षः । परमे । विऽओमन् । सः । अङ्ग । वेद । यदि । वा । न । वेद ॥

अन्वयः—इयं विसृष्टिः यतः आबभूव यदि वा दधे यदि वा न (दधे)। योऽस्याध्यक्षः स परमे व्योमन् अङ्ग (तम् यः) वेद यदि वा (तम्) न वेद ॥

Word-meaning etc:—विसृष्टिः (वि + √ सृज विसर्गे + क्तिन् P. III, 3, 94 and VIII, 2, 36) = multiform or motley creation यतः (यद्+तसिल् P. V, 3, 7 and VII, 2, 102)=from whom, whence. आबभूव=has come into being. यदि=if. दधे= supports. अध्यक्षः (अक्षे अधिकृतः इति अधि+अक्ष P. II, 2 8, अक्ष=√ अशूङ् व्याप्तौ +स U. III, 65)=controller. परमे= highest, most exalted. व्योमन् (व्योम्नि P. VII,1,39)=in His most blissful state. अङ्ग=oh friend. वेद=knows, attains. यदि वा दधे=He supports it, as long as He continues the support of His Almighty Providence. The *created universe* remains in its motley composite form as long as God, its Controller, thinks it fit to continue it in that state. यदि वा न दधे= if He does not support it. The universe ceases to exist in its created form when he witholds His support, i. e., when He dissolves it. (यः) अङ्ग वेद= Oh friend! he *truly knows* who knows Him. The knowledge of that thoughtful person alone deserves to be called right knowledge who sees the Providence of God behind the screen of the created universe, for he alone is qualified to attain salvation. यदि वा न वेद= his knowledge is futile who rests satisfied with an acquaintance of the material universe and does not like to proceed further in his search.

Translation:—He, from Whom this motley creation has come into being is its Controller, and He ever exists in His most sublime beatific state. This creation remains in existence as long as He supports it and it ceases to exist when He witholds His support. Oh friend! he who knows Him attains happiness and final beatitude but he who does not know Him, does not reach that goal.

Comment:—The above translation of the last and the most difficult stanza of this hymn is based upon the interpretation of it given by Maharṣi Dayānanda in his "Introduction to the Commentary on the Vedas" p. 170 and Satyārthaprakāśa chapter VIII.

Here also the difficulty is rhetorical rather than linguistic or philosophical. All that need be said on the subject has already been said, only the conclusion being left over for this stanza. This awful conclusion has been forced upon the enquirer by the following statements:—(1) God is the Controller of this multifold universe and He is ever in His most exalted and blissful state. (2) It is from Him that the whole universe has come into existence, and it remains as long as He supports it and ceases to exist when He dissolves it into its elementary causal form.

When so much has been said the thoughtful enquirer becomes more ardent to know about the universe but now his attention is focussed on the Supreme Being as the ultimate reality knowing Whom all else can be known. Hence the conclusion inevitably follows that one should spare no pains in attaining true knowledge of Him which is equivalent to accomplishing the emancipation of one's soul, the end of all creation. The knowledge of the universe also is to serve the same end but indirectly. The direct source of salvation being true knowledge of God, the Veda Says that (3), one should not allow himself to be carried away by the awful 'mystery' of creation, but should rather direct his attention to the only object worthy of all human endeavours namely salvation through the right knowledge of God. If one knows Him, one would attain liberation and not otherwise. Hence know God and adore Him alone and none else.

This conclusion has been couched in phraseology that demands on the part of the reader a knowledge of Sanskrit rhetorics. The figure involved here is श्लेष—alliteration—but the pun upon the words दवे and वेद is impossible in English. Each is used in two different senses namely, the first (**दधे**) means (1), to support and (2), to be kept intact, and the latter (**वेद**) (1), to know, and (2), to attain. This is the only sensible way to handle the stanza in and has been adopted by the great modern Vedic exegete, Maharṣi Dayānanda. A deviation from this plan and the adoption of a simpler method is sure to land the interpreter into a horrible contradiction to extricate oneself from which it is impossible. Sāyaṇa, and after him Griffith and other European scholars and their Indian followers, insist upon interpreting the stanza otherwise, as a consequence of which the hymn becomes a bundle of contradictions. It is not true that the translation given above is far-fetched, for those who say so have not, through negligence or incapacity taken notice of the figure involved in the stanza. The style of Vedic poetry is not debarred from the use of figures of speech nor have our scholars the sole monopoly to interpret the Vedas.

Concluding remarks:—In the Taīttirīyōpaniṣad it is said :— "When the Supreme Spirit began to evolve the cosmos, He first produced ether ; from ether came out (was evolved) the gaseous condition ; from the gaseous the igneous condition ; from the igneous the aqueous, (i. e. the liquid or molten) condition ; from the aqueous or molten came out the solid state. From the solid earth were produced the herbs ; from herbs food (or other vegetables), from food was produced the seed of animal life and thence man." II, 2.*

The above passage lays down a great scientific principle. The following passage from a scholar's

---

* तस्माद्वा एतस्मादात्मनः आकाशः संभूतः । आकाशाद्वायुः । वायोरग्निः । अग्नेरापः । अद्भ्यः पृथिवी । पृथिव्या ओषधयः । ओषधिभ्योऽन्नम् । अन्नाद्रेतः । रेतसः पुरुषः ॥ तैउ० २ । २ ॥

writing on the subject is worth quoting :—"How this universe came into being is a riddle of which every religion must attempt the solution. Scientists tell us that there was a time when the earth was on account of extreme heat in a molten state; and they point out that the outer crust of our globe has cooled and become solid. There is still great heat in its interior, as is evidenced by the fact that the substances emitted from the bowels of the earth during volcanic eruptions are generally in a state of fusion. We are also told that prior to this molten condition, the earth was a globe of fire like the sun, and still earlier it was in a gaseous (or nebulous) state. Of course, no animals could live, nor any vegetables grow on the earth when it was so hot. The various stages through which earth has passed in its evolution, and which the Western Science has discovered only recently, are mentioned in the oldest books of the Vedic literature. Modern science stops at the gaseous or nebulous state, but the Aryan Śāstras go back one step further and describe a fifth stage called the ethereal or Ākāśa, which is subtler than the aerial or gaseous state, and is thus the first stage of planetary evolution".*

"The objection which is sometimes raised against this doctrine that it amounts to a belief in three, or a plurality of gods, is too absurd to demand a serious refutation. Though all three substances possess this common attribute of being 'eternal', there is no other attribute which is common to all of them. Matter is, of course, dead and inert, while God and souls are intelligent beings. Of God and souls too, the former is infinite, the latter finite; the former fills all space and pervades all things, the latter is circumscribed in a small body; the former is free from the pleasures and pains to which the latter is subject; the former is omniscient, the latter has only a limited knowledge and so on. Can it

* The Fountainehad of Religion, Madras Edition 133-5.

be reasonably urged that this amounts to a belief in the divinity of matter and soul? Is divinity equivalent to eternity? Is eternity the only attribute connoted by 'God'?

God is the efficient cause of the universe; matter is its material cause. They are both eternal, as are also the souls. But this particular cosmos in which we are living is not eternal (as Buddhists would have it). It has had a beginning and it will have an end. The period during which a particular cosmos lasts is called in Sanskrit 'Kalpa' (literally cosmos), or figuratively a Brāhma dina', i. e., a divine day, and it consists of 4,32,00,00,000 ordinary (human) years. It is preceded and succeeded by an equal period during which matter lies in a state of chaos, and that is called a Brahmarātri, i. e., a "divine night". The evolution of cosmos from chaos may be called a creation (sṛṣti सृष्टि) and its involution a dissolution (pralaya प्रलय). Creation *ex nihilo* and complete annihilation are impossibilities. Before the evolution of this particular cosmos commenced, matter lay in a chaotic state; before that chaos there was a cosmos; before that cosmos another chaos; before that chaos another cosmos; and so on without beginning. Similarly the present universe will be succeeded by a chaos after which there will be another cosmos, and so forth without end. As days and nights succeed each other, so do cosmos and chaos in this eternal cycle of evolutions and involutions.

The reader need hardly be told that this doctrine of co-eternity of matter and souls with God, and of an eternal cycle of creations and dissolutions (better termed evolutions and involutions) is peculiar to Aryan philosophy. The semitic religions teach a totally different hypothesis. According to them this universe is the first and the last of its kind. It was created out of nothing at a particular time, and it will again, go into nothing, when the time comes for it. But the souls will survive the general destruction, some of them being sent to heaven and others consigned to hell for all eternity according to their deserts.

Apart from the unscientific character of the hypothesis that something can come out of nothing and be again reduced to nothing, the supporters of this theory have to be confronted with many a knotty question:— Why did god create this universe out of nothing at a particular time, and why will he again annihilate it at another fixed time? What impelled Him to make this change in His otherwise quiet existence? Why did He not desire to create it before the particular time when it was created? All that our friends who support the above hypothesis can say in answer to these and other similar questions is that they are "mysteries", a word which helps to cover so many weaknesses in a system of religion? From the standpoint of Vedic philosophy these questions do not and cannot arise. For there was never a time when God for the first time created this world. Again it is also worth while to remark that according to the semitic theory it will be difficult to predicate of God before He created this universe or after He will have destroyed it, these attributes which we commonly affirm of Him. How could He be called a creator for He had created nothing before this universe, and how could He be said to be omniscient for there existed nothing which He could possibly know? How could He be said to be just for there were no beings between whom He could adjudge and be just? How could He be merciful for there were none on whom He could show mercy? And yet it cannot be ignored that the period for which this world has lasted or shall last, is insignificant, we may say, is almost nothing, by the side of eternity. A drop bears some proportion to the ocean of which it is a part, but a terminable period however long it may be, can bear no proportion whatever to eternity. God's nature cannot be said to be uniform according to this theory. Further is it not unphilosophical to believe that souls which have had a beginning will yet have no end?"*

The later Zoroastrian scriptures contain the same doctrine about creation as explained above. In Sasan I, we read:— "souls are immaterial, indivisible, without beginning and without end." In his commentary on this text, Sasan V, the last inspired writer of the Parsi religion, first proves that souls are immaterial and indivisible, and then proceeds :—"After this I say that souls are *eternal* because for every created substance there must be a material before it. Thus if the souls are not eternal they must be material which has already been disproved." The same argument has been employed to prove the eternity of matter.

"The doctrine of successive creations and dissolutions is also explicitly enunciated. Each cosmos (with its succeeding chaos) is called in the Parsi scriptures a 'mih charkha' which corresponds to the Sanskrit 'mahā cakra' and means a 'great round' or 'cycle.' We find in Sasan I:— 'In the beginning of a *mih carkha* the work of evolution of the universe commences anew. The forms, actions and knowledge manifested in that *mih carkha* are similar to the previous *mih carkha.* Every *mih carkha* that comes is similar to the previous one from beginning to the end.' On this Sasan V comments:— 'In the beginning of a *mih carkha* the elements begin to combine, and there are manifested forms which in speech and action are similar to those of the previous *mih carkha;* but they are not the very same forms.' ....

The doctrine of cosmogony is not treated of in the Parsi scriptures as elaborately as in the books of Vedic literature. Still the above quotations prove that the

*Ibid 137-9.

Parsi doctrine was derived from the Vedic one................ The order of the creation of various things (viz., heaven, earth, vegetables, animals and man) as described in Zend Avesta, is substantially the same as given in the XXXI chapter of the Yajurveda, and that the Mosaic account of cosmogony as given in Genesis Chapter I, is only a copy of the Zoroastrian account. But the Bible writers borrowed only that much, and do not appear to have extended their thoughts beyond this particular cosmos, or to have ever troubled themselves with the problem as to whether there was any universe before the creation of this particular one, or there will be any after this one is destroyed. Nor do they appear to have ever asked themselves as to whether this universe was created from nothing or out of a previously existing material. For there is, in the Bible, no clear enunciation of the popularly received Semitic doctrine that the world was created out of nothing and for the first time. In fact, it is noteworthy that the Hebrew word 'bara' in the opening verse of the Genesis, which has been translated into 'created' means, accurately speaking, 'cut', 'cut out', 'planned'—which would go to show that the author of the Genesis, perhaps believed in the pre-existence of matter. Later on, as the original Vedic teaching was more forgotten, it became an article of faith with all the three Semitic religions that this universe is the first and the last of its kind, and that it was produced out of nothing, and will pass again into nothing. We have already indicated how unphilosophical this hypothesis is."*

Another point to be noted about this hymn is the note of mysticism about the way in which it delineates the state of things before creation. For example, in the first verse there is a denial of the phenomenal as well as noumenal world before creation but in the second

* Ibid. 140-2.

line of the verse, it is very clearly hinted that the Supreme Being, even then existed in His full Omnipotence 'merging' all within Himself. There is a distant ring of incomprehensibility about the phraseology of the hymn. The whole question is treated with great solemnity filling the intelligent and thinking reader's mind with awe. Explain however much we can, something yet remains to be explained in the unfathomable poesy of this hymn,

In concluding, a remark on a very abstruse point in ancient Indian philosophy would be quite opportune. In the first stanza we have the word **तदानीम्** 'then,' a vocable denoting an artificial and relative division of time. In the successive verses there is a hint at space also. In an air of mysticism the hymn has tackled with a number of difficult philosophical questions. But the description being of a state prior to phenomenal creation how could time and space be postulated then? European philosophers are accustomed to think in a manner quite different from the ancient Indian philosphers. European philosophers consider time and space relative and dependent on material objects. It is true that ideas of time and space are relative, but this does not mean that in the absence of material creation they cease to exist. They only become manifest when phenomenal creation comes into being. In other words, Indian philosophy postulates absolute time and absolute space existing eternally. For example in the Vāiśēṣika philosophy we are told:—**पृथिव्यापस्तेजो वायुराकाशं कालो दिगात्मा मन इति द्रव्याणि** ॥ I, 1, 5, Earth, water, fire, air, ether (space) time, the cardinal points, soul and mind are the nine *substances*. **स्पर्शवान् वायुः** ॥ II, 1, 4. Air is that which can be felt by the touch and its touch is neither hot nor cold. **अद्रव्यत्वेन नित्यत्वमुक्तम्** ॥ II, 1, 13. Air is eternal since no material cause is found to produce it. Aphorism II, 1, 20 describes ether or space. **द्रव्यत्वनित्यत्वे**

वायुना व्याख्याते ॥ II, 1, 28. That space is material and eternal can be proved in the same way as air. Aphorism II, 2, 6 describes time. Aphorism II, 2, 7 reiterates the argument in II, 1, 28 in connection with time. Aphorism II, 2, 10 describes the cardinal points or space and the next proves it to be material and eternal.

We need not proceed further cataloguing the things reckoned eternal in Indian philosophy. What we are concerned with here is whether there are only three eternal existents, namely, the Supreme Being, the soul and Primordial Matter or whether there are many. It must be noted here that the difference between the Vāiśeṣikas and the 'trinitarians' is only verbal and trite. What the Vāiśeṣika philosophy calls ultimate atoms the Sāmkhya terms Prakṛti. The former speak of innumerable ultimate atoms or electrons, whereas the latter take them all as an ggregate and name that aggregate Prakṛti. In this Prakṛti are included time and space as well. Hence the Supreme Being, the individual souls and the Primordial Matter or Prakṛti are the *Three Eternals.*

Man, I say, does not dominate the universe. He does not even understand it. He is groping his way in it and finding out things about it. (*Sir Oliver Lodge, "Science and Religion by Seven Men of Science" p. 17 ll. 15-17.*)

१ २ ३ १ २ ३ १ २ ३ १ २
ॐ ॥ अरं त इन्द्र श्रवसे गमेम शूर त्वावतः ।
१२ ३ १२
अरं शक्र परेमणि ॥ सामवेदे ॥ १ । २०९ ॥

Oh Strong and Omnipotent God! vouchsafe, we beseech Thee, the grace to approach Thee always and everywhere in Thy Glory—Thee, Who hast no equal,—and by all means to take refuge in Thee. (From the Sāmavēda I, 209.)

CHAPTER VI.

SECTION I.

Growth of Human Society.

Atharvavēda VIII, 10, (1)

(१२३) ओ३म् ॥ विराड्वा इदमग्रे आसीत्तस्या जातायाः सर्वमबिभेदियमेवेदं भविष्यतीति ॥१॥

(123) Viraadvaa idamagra aaseet tasyaa jaataayaah sarvam abibhediyamevedam bhavishyateeti ‖ 1.

अग्रे इदम् (जगत) विऽराट् वै आसीत् । तस्याः (विराजः) जाताया इयम् एव इदम् भविष्यति इति सर्वम् अबिभेत् ॥

विराट् =(वि+√राजृ+क्विप=विगतः राट् यस्याः)= state of human socity in which there was no king. **वै** = surely, indeed. **इदम्**=this world, human society. **अग्रे**= in the beginning. **आसीत्** =there was. **तस्याः**=of that (relates to **विराट्**). **जातायाः**=came into being, when it was seen, when it became manifest. **सर्वम्**=the whole world or humanity. **अबिभेत्**=got frightened. **इयम्**=this. **एव**= only. **इदम्**=the world or human society, **भविष्यति**=will become. **इयम्०—इति**=that this state will spread all over the world and become uncontrollable.

In the beginning human society had no king to

unify and rule over it. When men became aware of this they were afraid that this state would spread all over the world and become uncontrollable.

(१२४) सोदक्रामत्सा गार्हपत्ये न्यक्रामत् ॥२॥

(124) Sodakraamat saa gaarhapatye nyakraamat || 2.

सा उत्ऽअक्रामत् (च) सा गार्हऽपत्ये निऽअक्रामत् ॥

उदक्रामत् (उत् + √ क्रम्) = rose up, lifted itself up. **गार्हपत्ये** (गृह + पति + ञ्य) = the consolidation of the family under one head, the government of a family, the position and dignity of a householder. **न्यक्रामत्** = became transformed.

This kingless state however got improved and transformed itself into the consolidation of each human family into a separate unit under a separate head.

(१२५) गृहमेधी गृहपतिर्भवति य एवं वेद ॥३॥

(125) Grahhmedhee grahapatirbhavati ya evam veda || 3.

यः एवम् वेद स गृहऽमेधी (भूत्वा) गृहऽपतिः भवति ॥

गृहमेधी (गृह + √ मेध + णिनि P. III, 2,78) = who manages family affairs. **गृहपतिः** = head of the family.

He who knows this principle, will manage his family affairs well and thus become the head of his family.

(१२६) सोदक्रामत्साहवनीये न्यक्रामत् ॥४॥

(126) Sodakraamat saahavaneeye nyakraamat || 4.

सा उत् ऽअक्रामत् (च) सा आऽहवनीये निऽअक्रामत् ॥

आहवनीये (आ + √ हु दानादनयोरादाने चेत्येके + अनीयर्) = the system of mutual religious, social and other transactions.

It developed still further and transformed itself into a system of mutual religious, social and other transactions amongst human families.

(१२७) यन्त्यस्य दे॒वा दे॒वहूतिं प्रि॒यो दे॒वानां भवति॒ य ए॒वं वेद ॥५॥

(127) Yantyasya devaa devahootim priyo devaanaam bhavati ya evam veda || 5.

अ॒स्य दे॒वऽहूतिम् दे॒वाः यन्ति । यः ए॒वम् वेद (सः) दे॒वानाम् प्रि॒यः भ॒वति॒ ॥

यन्ति=go to, attend. **देवहूतिम् (देव+√ह्वे+क्तिन्)**=an invitation given to the learned. **प्रियः**=beloved, a friend. **देवाः**=the learned.

The learned honour the call of the man who, knowing this secrets of organisation, invites them on special occasions for he befriends the enlightened.

(१२८) सोदक्राम॒त्सा दक्षिणा॒ग्नौ न्यक्रामत् ॥६॥

(128) Sodakraamat saa dakshi*n*aagnau nyakraamat || 6.

सा उत्ऽअ॒क्रा॒म॒त् (च) सा द॒क्षि॒णऽअ॒ग्नौ निऽअ॒क्रा॒म॒त् ॥

दक्षिणाग्नौ (दक्षिण+अग्नि)=still further developed religious and social consolidation.

It rose still higher and became a still further developed religious and social organisation.

(१२९) य॒ज्ञर्तो दक्षि॒णीयो॒ वासतेयो भवति॒ य ए॒वं वेद ॥७॥

(129) Yaj*n*arto dakshi*n*eeyo vaasateyo bhavati ya evam veda || 7.

यः ए॒वम् वेद सः य॒ज्ञऽऋ॒तः द॒क्षि॒णीयः वासतेयः भ॒व॒ति ॥

यज्ञर्तः (यज्ञ+√ऋ+क्त)=devoted to religious observances. **दक्षिणीयः**=deserving of respect. **वासतेयः (वसति+ढञ्)**=giving shelter to others.

The man who knows this truth becomes more devoted to religious observances and therefore is respected by others. He also becomes, so to say, a refuge to the needy and suffering.

(१३०) सोदक्रामत्सा सभायां न्यक्रामत् ॥८॥

(130) Sodakraamat saa sabhaayaam nyacraamat ॥ 8.

सा उत्ऽअक्रामत् (च) सा सभायाम् निऽअक्रामत् ॥

सभायाम्=in the rural (urban or civic) assembly.

It proceeded still further and was changed into the rural (urban or civic) assembly.

(१३१) यन्त्यस्य सभां सभ्यो भवति य एवम् वेद ॥९॥

(131) Yantyasya sabhaam sabhyo bhavati ya evam veda ॥ 9.

यः एवम् वेद सः सभ्यः भवति, अस्य सभाम् (जनाः) यन्ति ॥

सभ्यः (सभा+यः P. IV. 4, 105)=a clever member of the assembly, a clever debater.

He who knows this truth becomes an intelligent member of the assembly, and influenced by him other people also attend its sessions.

(१३२) सोदक्रामत्सा समितौ न्यक्रामत् ॥१०॥

(132) Sodakraamat saa samitau nyakraamat ॥ 10.

सा उत्ऽअक्रामत् (च) सम्ऽइतौ सा निऽअक्रामत् ॥

समितौ (सम्+√इ+क्तिन्)=the king's council, the assembly of the king's counsellors which is one for the whole kingdom.

It went still further and transformed itself into the king's council.

(१३३) यन्त्यस्य समितिं सामित्यो भवति य एवं वेद ॥११॥

(133) Yantyasya samitim saamityo bhavati ya evam veda || 11.

यः एवम् वेद (सः) साम्ऽइत्यः भवति (च) अस्य सम्ऽईतिम् (जनाः) यन्ति ॥

सामित्यः (समिति+ण्यः P. IV, 4, 101)=fit or qualified for the king's council.

He who knows this thing becomes qualified for the king's council and all great men attend it influenced by him.

(१३४) सोदक्रामत्सामन्त्रणे न्यक्रामत् ॥१२॥

(134) Sodakraamat saamantra*n*e nyakraamat || 12.

सा (ततः) उत्ऽअक्रामत् । (उत्क्रम्य च) आऽमन्त्रणे निऽअक्रामत् ॥

आमन्त्रणे (आ+√मन्त्र+ल्युट्)=in the cabinet of ministers.

From there also it proceeded further and became transformed into the king's cabinet of ministers.

(१३५) यन्त्यस्यामन्त्रणमामन्त्रणीयो भवति य एवं वेद ॥१३॥

(135) Yantyasyaamantra*n*am aamantra*n*eeyo bhavati ya evam veda || 13.

यः एवम् वेद (सः) आऽमन्त्रणीयः भवति तस्य (च) आऽमन्त्रणम् (राजा विद्वांसः च) यन्ति ॥

आमन्त्रणीय: (आमन्त्रण+छ)=fit or qualified for the cabinet of ministers. यन्ति=go to, attend (=have a regard for his advice and suggestion).

He who knows this principle becomes fit for the king's cabinet and the king and great men have a regard for his council and suggestions.

॥ ॐ ॥

SECTION II.

Unity.

Ṛgvēda X. 191

Seer:—The Sage Saṃvanana.

Subject:—Verse 1, prayer to God the most Effulgent for Unity; verses 2-4 harmony of hearts.

Metre:—Verse 1, Virāḍanuṣṭup, 2 annṣṭup, 3 triṣṭup and 4 nicṛdanuṣṭup.

Tone:—Verses 1, 2 and 4 gaandhaara and verse 3 dhāivata.

(१३६) ओ३म् ॥ सं समिद्युवसे वृषन्नग्ने विश्वान्यर्य आ। इळस्पदे समिध्यसे स नो वसून्या भर ॥ ऋ० १० । १९१ । १ ॥

(136) Sam samidyuvase vr^{ə}shannagne visvaanyarya aa । I*l*aspade samidhyase sa no vasoonyaa bhara ॥ 1.

पदपाठः—सम् । सम् । इत् । युवसे । वृषन् । अग्ने । विश्वानि । अर्य । आ । इळः ऽपदे । सम् । इध्यसे । सः । नः । वसूनि । आ । भर ।

अन्वयः—(हे) वृषन् अर्य अग्ने ! विश्वानि इत् सम् सम् आ युवसे (च) इळः पदे सम् इध्यसे । सः नः वसूनि आ भर ॥

Word-meaning &c:—**सम् सम्**=the double suffix is here intended to show the intensity and perfection of unity in all God's works. **इत्**=verily. **आ युवसे** (√**यु**)=Thou dost combine perfectly. **वृषन्**=Oh Powerful. **अर्य**=Adorable.

विश्वानि=all things. (The unity of God's design is perceptible in the whole universe.) इळस्पदे=on the earth, in the world, in speech. समिध्यसे=Thou dost fully reveal Thyself. सः=of that description. नः=us. वसूनि=wealth of all kind. आ भर=bestow in every way.

Translation :—Oh Almighty and Adorable God ! in the whole universe Thou dost the work of harmonising and uniting, and most fully reveal Thyself in the world. We therefore, beseech Thee to bestow upon us in every way all the means that will enable us to live in peace and harmony.

Purport:—The devotee should, before asking God for prosperity, observe the world about him and try to understand the Laws working therein. The greatest of God's laws is the law of harmony everywhere and at all times. Creation is the result of the union of atoms and all the natural phenomena are processes of union and harmony. The planets come and go, rise and set in a harmonious succession.

(१३७) सं गच्छध्वं सं वदध्वं सं वो मनांसि जानताम् । देवा भागं यथा पूर्वे सञ्जानाना उपासते ॥२॥

(137) Sa*m* gacchadhvam sa*m* vadadhvam sa*m* vo manaa*m*si jaanataam I Devaa bhaagam yathaa poorve sa*m* jaanaanaa upaasate II 2.

पदपाठः—सम् । गच्छध्वम् । सम् । वदध्वम् । सम् । वः । मनांसि । जानताम् । देवाः । भागम् । यथा । पूर्वे । समऽजानानाः । उपऽआसंते ॥

अन्वयः—सम् गच्छध्वम्, सम् वदध्वम् वः मनांसि सम् जानताम् । यथा पूर्वे देवाः सञ्जानानाः (स्वकर्तव्यस्य) भागम् (अकुर्वन् मां च) उपासते (तथा यूयमपि कुरुत) ॥

Word-meaning &c:—सं गच्छध्वम्=advance forward unitedly. **संवदध्वम्**=hold conferences together in a common language. **संजानताम्**=let them be of one accord to acquire knowledge of the various lores. **देवाः**=the enlightened, **पूर्वे**=before you in all ages. **भागम्**=their task in life. **यथा**=have accomplished together in harmony and co-operation. **संजानानाः**=with their minds in full agreement. **उपासते** = have worshipped or adored Me alone their Omnipotent God.

Translation:—(God says:—)Let all your activities be so directed as to lead you to one common goal (for which) let there be conferences held among you in a common tongue. Let also your minds be all of one accord to acquire knowledge of the various lores. In short do as the enlightened before you in all ages did, performing their tasks in life in cooperation and harmony, with minds in full agreement for the acquisition of knowledge. Like the ancient seers also, worship me alone Who am the only real object of your devotion.

(१३८) समानो मन्त्रः समितिः समानी समानं मनः सह चित्तमेषाम् । समानं मंत्रमभि मंत्रये वः समानेन वो हविषा जुहोमि ॥३॥

(138) Samaano mantrah samitih samaanee samaanam manah saha cittam eshaam | Samaanam mantram abhi mantraye vah samaanena vo havishaa juhomi || 3.

पदपाठः—समानः । मन्त्रः । सम्ऽइतिः । समानी । समानम् । मनः । सह । चित्तम् । एषाम् । समानम् । मन्त्रम् । अभि । मन्त्रये । वः । समानेन । वः । हविषा । जुहोमि ॥

अन्वयः—मन्त्रः समानः समितिः समानी मनः समानम् एषाम् चित्तम् सह । वः समानम् मन्त्रम् अभिमन्त्रये । वः समानेन हविषा जुहोमि ॥

Word-meaning &c:—समानः=common. **मन्त्रः**=counsel; the object of counsel. **समितिः**=the place of assembly.

समानी=common. समानम् मनः=minds at accord. सह चित्तम् =hearts united. समानम् मन्त्रम्=the sacred hymns of the four Vedas which are common to the whole humanity. अभिमन्त्रये=I initiate. समानेन हविषा=common objects of enjoyment. जुहोमि=I give, I provide.

Translation:—Let the object of your counsels be acceptable to all, the place of your assembly common, your minds at accord and your hearts united together. I initiate you in the common inspired hymn and ***provide all of you with common objects of enjoyment.***

(१३९) समानी व आकूतिः समाना हृदयानि वः । समानमस्तु वो मनो यथा वः सुसहासति ॥४॥

(139) Samaanee va aakootih samaanaa hrədayaani vah । Samaanam astu vo mano yathaa vah su sahaasati ॥ 4.

पदपाठः—समानी । वः । आऽकूतिः । समाना । हृदयानि । वः । समानम् । अस्तु । वः । मनः । यथा । वः । सुऽसह । असति ॥

अन्वयः—वः आकूतिः समानी वः हृदयानि समाना वः मनः समानम् अस्तु यथा वः असति सुसह ॥

Word-meaning &c:—आकूतिः=purpose, resolution, object of life. हृदयानि=heart's cravings. मनः = mind. यथा= as. सुसह (शोभनेन=हितेन कल्याणेन, धर्मेण वा सह=सहितं यथा स्यात्तथा)=immensely conducive towards. असति (√अस+अति U. IV, 59) =progress. सुसह असति=so that there may be a great advance in life, so that a high status of life be achieved.

Translation :—Let your object in life be one and the same, your hearts equal (in feeling) and your minds in full agreement so that an excellent common status of life be achieved for all.

Comment :—The first of the four stanzas of this hymn embodies a craving of the devotee for means to live a peaceful and contented life in harmony with all mankind. God 'enlightens' him in the manner mentioned in the next three stanzas the gist of which is :—(1) Men should have common unions. (2) There should be common consultations in which the development of the power of speech should be one of the results aimed at. (3) Minds should be controlled and purged of all unclean and evil impressions by good resolutions taken in union with others. (4) It should become a habit with every one to keep one always in mind of one's duty in life. (5) All should have the same thoughts about the ideal in life, all other thoughts being subservient to this consideration. (6) All should have the same feelings towards one another, in other words, the hearts of all should be in accord. (7) The minds of all should agree on all points and especially with regard to the means and methods of learning with a view to acquire right knowledge. (8) Lives of great men in the past should be studied for guidance. (9) The objects of enjoyment should also be common and approved by all the just in the right direction. (10) All this should be done in commune with God ever remembering that He is Omniscient and Omnipotent, ever ready to help.

Two other and very important points also are suggested which require a special mention. The first is that all mankind in spite of unjust distinctions of caste and creed are equally loved by God. Hence, the advice of harmony and solidarity in this hymn and the others following on the same subject is, that all men should unite for mutual progress as equals. It is clearly hinted in some stanzas that lack of such unity is, in the sight of God, an unpardonable sin. The place where such unity obtains is in His sight holy! The second thing is a very pointed hint about the law of this unity. This is the rule laid down in the Vedas which should be the guide for all who work for social and national harmony and solidarity. Containing laws about human life and principles of right knowledge the Vedas are the Divine Records common to all humanity. As such the study of the Vedas and their right understanding is also a matter to be settled by qualified men meeting together from time to time to discuss questions raised on the subject. The principles laid down in the Vedas for their own interpretation are given in the Introduction to this book.

---

(१४०) ओ३म् ॥ सहृदयं सांमनस्यमविद्वेषं कृणोमि वः । अन्यो अन्यमभि हर्यत वत्सं जातमिवाघ्न्या ॥ अथर्ववेदे ॥ ३ । ३० । १ ॥

(140) Sahr$^{\partial}$dayam saammanasyam avidvesham kr$^{\partial}$nomi vah । Anyo anyam abhi haryata vatsam jaatamivaaghnvaa ॥ Atharveda III, 30, 1.

पदपाठः—सऽहृदयम् । साम्ऽमनस्यम् । अविंऽद्वेषं । कृणोमि । वः । अन्यः । अन्यम् । अभि । हर्यत । वत्सम् । जातम्ऽइव । अघ्न्या ॥

अन्वयः—सहृदयम् सांमनस्यम् अविद्वेषम् वः कृणोमि । अन्यः अन्यम् अभि हर्यत अघ्न्या इव जातम् वत्सम् ॥

Word-meaning &c:—सहृदयम् = concord, agreement. सांमनस्यम् = unanimity. अविद्वेषम् = freedom from enmity. कृणोमि = I ordain. वः = for you. अन्यः अन्यम् = one another. अभिहर्यत = love in every way. वत्सम् = calf. जातम् = new born. अघ्न्या (नञ् + √ हन + यक् + टाप् U. IV, 112 and P. IV, 1, 4) = the cow (literally she who cannot be killed, inviolable Vide Nig. II, 11 and Nir. XI, 43).

Translation :—Oh men ! I ordain for you concord of heart, unanimity of mind and freedom from hatred in dealings with each other. Love one another in every way even as the inviolable cow loves her new-born calf.

Purport :—Men who have any thoughts of social service and uplift of their brethren should cast off all ideas of self and form themselves into a band of workers united by unwavering mutual trust and love. The cow forgets herself at the sight of her new-born calf, licks its body with the tenderest affection, helps it to stand up and gives it suck.

(१४१) अनु॑व्रतः पि॒तुः पु॒त्रो मा॒त्रा भ॑वतु॒ संम॑नाः ।
जा॒या पत्ये॒ मधु॑मतीं वाचं॑ वदतु शन्ति॒वाम् ॥२॥

(141) Anuvratah pituh putro maatraa bbavatu sammanaah I Jaayaa patye madhumateem vaacam vadatu santivaam II 2.

पदपाठः—अनु॑ऽव्रतः । पि॒तुः । पु॒त्रः । मा॒त्रा भ॒वतु॒ । सम्ऽम॑नाः । जा॒या । पत्यै॑ । मधु॑ऽमतीम् । वाचं॑म् । व॒द॒तु । श॒न्ति॒ऽवाम् ॥

अन्वयः—पुत्रः पितुः अनुव्रतः मात्रा संमनाः भवतु । जाया पत्ये मधुमतीम् शन्तिवाम् वाचम् वदतु ॥

Word-meaning &c:—**अनुव्रतः**=obedient, submissive. **पितुः**=to his father. **पुत्रः**=the son. **मात्रा**=with his mother. **भवतु**=let be. **संमनाः**=having agreement of mind. **जाया**=wife. **पत्ये**=to her husband. **मधुमतीम्**=honey-sweet. **शन्तिवाम्**=calm, peaceful. **वाचम्**=words. **वदतु**=let her speak.

Translation :—Let the son be submissive to his father and agreeable to the mind of his mother. Let the wife speak to her husband words calm and sweet as honey.

Purport :—Children should obey their parents and parents should wish well of their children. The wife and husband should impart peace and happiness to each other by the use of sweet and gentle words.

(१४२) मा भ्रा॒ता भ्रात॑रं द्वि॒क्षन्मा स्वसा॑रमु॒त
स्वसा॑ । स॒म्यञ्च॒ः सव्र॑ता भू॒त्वा वाचं॑ वदत भ॒द्रया॑ ॥३॥

(142) Maa bhraataa bhraataram dvikshanmaa svasaaram uta svasaa । Samyaञcah savrataa bhootvaa vaacam vadata bhadrayaa ॥ 3.

पदपाठः—मा । भ्राता । द्विक्षत् । मा । स्वसारम् । उत । स्वसा । सम्यञ्चः । सव्रताः । भूत्वा । वाचम् । वदत । भद्रया ॥

अन्वयः—भ्राता भ्रातरम् मा द्विक्षत् । उत स्वसा स्वसारम् मा (द्विक्षत्) । सम्यञ्चः सव्रताः भूत्वा भद्रया वाचम् वदत ॥

Word-meaning &c:— **मा**=may not. **भ्राता** brother. **भ्रातरम्** =to his brother. **द्विक्षत्**=bear enmity. **स्वसारम्**=to her sister. **स्वसा**=sister. **सम्यञ्चः**=of one mind (literally going together). **सव्रताः (समानं व्रतं येषां ते)**=having the same vows, i. e., ideals. **भूत्वा**=having become. **वाचम्**=speech, words. **वदत**=you should speak. **भद्रया**=gently, courteously.

Translation:—Neither a brother should hate his brother, nor sister be unkind to her sister. You ought to speak with one another most gently being of one mind and keeping the same ideal before you.

Purport :—Courteousness and gentleness towards one another should be the essential feature of the manner of conversation among the members of a family. This is a great and necessary step towards harmony and solidarity.

(१४३) येन देवा न वियन्ति नो च विद्विषते मिथः । तत्कृण्मो ब्रह्म वो गृहे संज्ञानं पुरुषेभ्यः ॥४॥

(143) Yena devaa na viyanti no ca vidvishate mithah । Tat kr^ənmo brahma vo gr^əhe saञjnaanam purushebhyah ॥ 4.

पदपाठः—येन । देवाः । न । विऽयन्ति । नो इति । च । विऽद्विषते । मिथः । तत् । कृण्मः । ब्रह्म । वः । गृहे । सम्ऽज्ञानम् । पुरुषेभ्यः ॥

अन्वयः—येन देवाः न वियन्ति च नो मिथः विद्विषते तत् वः गृहे पुरुषेभ्यः संज्ञानम् कृण्मः ॥

Word-meaning &c:— **येन**=by which. **देवाः**=the wise.

न=not. वियन्ति=go against. नो (न+उ)=nor. च=and. विद्विषते=they bear hatred. मिथः=towards one another. तत्=that. कृण्मः=I ordain (the plural 'we' is used to show authority). ब्रह्म=the Vedic principles or path of life. वः गृहे=home. संज्ञानं=(सम्यक् ज्ञानं) right knowledge, right guiding or leading principle; (समम्=सह ज्ञानम्) understanding or feeling for one another, mutual understanding, sympathy. पुरुषेभ्यः=for all men.

Translation:—We ordain in your home that path of the Vedas from which the enlightened never err, nor do they bear hatred towards one another, so that it may serve as the right guiding principle for all men.

Purport :—Those who aspire after social harmony and solidarity should follow this Vedic path of mutual good feeling and sympathy.

(१४४) ज्यायस्वन्तश्चित्तिनो मा वि यौष्ट संराधयन्तः सधुराश्चरन्तः । अन्यो अन्यस्मै वल्गु वदन्तः एत सध्रीचीनान्वः संमनसस्कृणोमि ॥५॥

(144) Jyaayasvantascittino maa vi yaush*t*a sa*m* raadhayantah sadhuraascarantah I Anyo anyasmai valgu vadanta eta sadhreeceenaan vah sam manasaskr$^{\partial}$*n*omi II 5.

पदपाठः—ज्यायस्वन्तः । चित्तिनः । मा । वि । यौष्ट । सम् । राधयन्तः । सऽधुराः । चरन्तः । अन्यः । अन्यस्मै । वल्गु । वदन्तः । आ । इत । सध्रीचीनान् । वः । सम्ऽमनसः । कृणोमि ॥

अन्वयः—ज्यायस्वन्तः चित्तिनः संराधयन्तः सधुराः चरन्तः मा वि यौष्ट । अन्यः अन्यस्मै वल्गु वदन्तः एत । वः सध्रीचीनान् संमनसः कृणोमि ॥

Word-meaning &c:—ज्यायस्वन्तः (P.V,3,61; VI,4,160; V, 2, 94 and M.B. भूमनिन्दाप्रशंसासु नित्ययोगेऽतिशायने । सम्बन्धेऽस्तिविवक्षायां भवन्ति मतुबादयः ॥) = respectful to the elders. चित्तिनः=possessing noble hearts. मा=do not.

वियौष्ट=be disunited, or separated. **संराधयन्तः**=united in the undertakings of acquiring wealth. **सधुराः**=bearing the same yoke together. **चरन्तः**=walking, going. **अन्यः अन्यस्मै**=to one another. **वल्गु**=sweet, pleasant. **वदन्तः**= speaking. **एत (आ+√इण् गतौ+त)**=come. **सध्रीचीनान् (सह+√अञ्चू गतिपूजनयोः+क्विन्+ख** P. III, 2, 59; VI, 3, 95 and V, 4, 8)=going by the same path (i. e., one-intentioned). **संमनसः**=one-minded. **कृणोमि**=I make.

Translation:—Oh men ! you who are respectful to your elders, possessing noble hearts, friendly in your undertakings of acquiring wealth and walking in the same path bearing the common yoke together, be never disunited one from the other. Come, I make you one intentioned and one-minded. Let each one of you speak sweetly to the other.

Purport:—Followers of the Vedic path of life respect their elders either in age, position or learning, strive for the attainment of good qualities, and work together for the advancement of their society.

(१४५) समानी प्रपा सह वोऽन्नभागः समाने योक्त्रे सह वो युनज्मि । सम्यञ्चोऽग्निं सपर्यतारा नाभिमिवाभितः ॥६॥

(145) Samaanee prapaa saha vo'nnabhaagah samaane yoktre saha vo yunajmi । Samyaंco'gnim saparyataaraa naabhimivaabhitah ॥ 6.

पदपाठः—समानी । प्रऽपा । सह । वः । अन्नऽभागः । समाने । योक्त्रे । सह । वः । युनज्मि । सम्यञ्चः । अग्निम् सपर्यत । अराः । नाभिम्ऽइव । अभितः ॥

अन्वयः—वः प्रपा समानी अन्नभागः सह । समाने योक्त्रे वः सह युनज्मि । सम्यञ्चः अग्निम् सपर्यत इव अराः नाभिम् अभितः ॥

Word-meaning &c:—**समानी**=common. **प्रपा**=place of drinking water. **सह**=together. **वः**=your. **अन्नभागः**=portion of food (partaking of food). **समाने**=to a common. **योक्त्रे**= to a yoke. **युनज्मि**=(√ युज्) I yoke. **सम्यञ्चः** (सम्+√ अञ्चू)= going together, one-intentioned. **अग्निम्**=the Adorable God. **सपर्यत**=serve, adore, worship. **अराः**=spokes. **इव**=like, as. **नाभिम्** =to the nave. **अभि**=all round.

Translation :—Let your place of drinking water be common and let your partaking of food be together as I yoke you to a common yoke. Worship the Adorable God all of you together (attaching yourself to Him) just as the spokes are attached to the nave of the chariot from all round.

Purport:—The Vedic Law, it should be borne in mind, ordains a unity the centre of which is God. Such a unity alone is beneficial to the world at large. A Godless unity is a unity of dacoits.

(१४६) सध्रीचीनान्वः संमनसस्कृणोम्येकश्नुष्टीन्त्संवननेन सर्वान् । देवा इवामृतं रक्षमाणाः सायंप्रातः सौमनसो वो अस्तु ॥७॥

(146) Sadhreeceenaanvah sammanasaskr^{ə}*n*omyeka*s*nushteentsa*m*vananena sarvaan । Devaa ivaamr^{ə}tam rakshamaa*n*aah saayampraatah sammanaso vo astu ॥ 7.

पदपाठः—सध्रीचीनान् । वः । सम्ऽमनसः । कृणोमि । एकंऽश्नुष्टीन् सम्ऽवननेन । सर्वान् । देवाःऽइव । अमृतम् । रक्षमाणाः । सायम्ऽप्रातः । सौमनसः । वः । अस्तु ॥

अन्वयः—संवननेन वः सर्वान् सध्रीचीनान् समनसः एकश्नुष्टीन् कृणोमि । देवाः इव अमृतम् रक्षमाणाः सायं प्रातः सौमनसः वः अस्तु ॥

Word-meaning &c:—**एकश्नुष्टीन्** (एक+√ ष्णस to eat or accept)=having one ideal of life. **संवननेन** (सम्+√ वन)= by mutual help. **सर्वान्**=all. **देवाः**=the wise. **अमृतम्**=liberation of the soul. **रक्षमाणाः**=protecting, having ever before them. **सायंप्रातः**=evening and morning. **सौमनसः**=friendly feelings.

Translation:—I enjoin on all of you to be mutually helping one another, to be united in your mind and to have one goal in life. You should, like the wise of all ages, ever cherish the idea of the liberation of your souls from the trammels of the world and to this end may peace of mind increase among you evening and morning.

Purport—The eternal goal of human life is liberation of the soul. All social harmony and solidarity should have this paramount principle in view. A random ideal of aimlessly and interminably securing wealth or social and political advance is inhuman and no sane man ought to subscribe to such.

---

(१४७) ओ३म् ॥ सं वः पृच्यन्तां तन्वः सं मनांसि समु व्रता । सं वोऽयं ब्रह्मणस्पतिर्भगः सं वो अजीगमत् ॥ अथर्ववेदे ६ । ७४ । १ ॥

(147) Sa*m* vah prəcyantaam tanvah sa*m* manaa*m*si sam u vrataa । Sam vo'yam brahma*n*aspatirbhagah sa*m* vo ajeegamat ॥ Atharvaveda VI, 74,1.

पदपाठः—सम् । वः । पृच्यन्ताम् । तन्वः । सम् । मनांसि । सम् । ऊँ इति । व्रता । सम् । वः । अयम् । ब्रह्मणः । पतिः । भगः । सम् । वः । अजीगमत् ॥

अन्वयः—वः तन्वः सम्, मनांसि सम्, उ व्रता सम्, पृच्यन्ताम् । अयम् ब्रह्मणः पतिः भगः वः वः सम् अजीगमत् ॥

Word-meaning &c:—सम् पृच्यन्ताम्=may unite in harmony. तन्वः=bodies, vast learning or other attainments. ब्रह्मणस्पतिः=Protector of the universe. भगः=the Majestic God. सम् अजीगमत् (√गम्)=has brought you together.

Translation:—Let your bodies (or learning and other attainments) and minds work together in harmony for the achievement of the common ideal. It is for this that the Majestic God, the Protector of the universe, has brought you together in life.

Purport:—It is a principle of the Divine Law that all human beings should unite and work for their general advancement. Otherwise unpleasant clashes and bickerings would be the result.

(१४८) सं ज्ञपनं वो मनसोऽथों संज्ञपनं हृदः ।
अथो भगस्य यच्छ्रान्तं तेन संज्ञपयामि वः ॥२॥

(148) Samjnapanam vo manaso 'tho samjnapanam hr^ədah
Atho bhagasya yacchraantam tena samjnpayaami vah ॥ 2.

पदपाठः—सम्ऽज्ञपनम् । वः । मनसः । अथो इति । सम्ऽज्ञपनम् । हृदः । अथो इति । भगस्य । यत् । श्रान्तम् । तेन । सम्ऽज्ञपयामि । वः ॥

अन्वयः—वः मनसः संज्ञपनम् अथो हृदः संज्ञपनम् अथो भगस्य यत श्रान्तम् तेन वः संज्ञपयामि ॥

Word-meaning &c:—**संज्ञपनम्** (**सम्+√ज्ञा मारणतोषण-निशामनेषु ज्ञापने स्तुतौ च+णिच् +ल्युट्** P. III, 1, 26; 3, 115)= calm and accurate working. **वः**=your. **मनसः**=of the head (mind). **अथो**=in addition to this, also, besides. **संज्ञपनम्**= contented co-operation. **हृदः**=of the heart. **भगस्य**=of the Majestic God, for the right knowledge of the Majestic God. **यत्**=that, what. **श्रान्तम्**=exertion, labour, fatigue. **तेन** =by that, in repayment of. **संज्ञपयामि**=I satisfy your cravings, energize or invigorate you.

Translation:—Let your heads (minds) work in calm and precision and let your hearts join them in contented co-operation. In addition to this for the trouble you have taken to realise the majesty of God, I invigorate you (that you proceed on and reach your goal.)

Purport:—Harmony and solidarity bring peace and peace yields fresh energy to proceed on to the goal of human life—the realisation of God, than which there is nothing more sublime for man to strive for.

(१४९) यथा॑दि॒त्या वसु॑भिः संबभू॒वुर्म॒रुद्भि॑रु॒ग्रा अहृ॑णीयमानाः । ए॒वा त्रि॑णाम॒न्नहृ॑णीयमान इ॒माञ्जना॒न्त्संम॑नसस्कृ॒धीह ॥३॥

(149) Yathaadityaa vasubhih sambabhoovurmarudbhiru-graa ahr^ə*n*eeyamaanaah । Evaa tri*n*aamannahr^ə*n*eeyamaana imaa*u*janaantsammanasaskr^ədheeha ॥ 3.

पदपाठः—यथा॑ । आ॒दि॒त्याः । वसु॑ऽभिः । स॒म्ऽब॒भू॒वुः । म॒रुत्ऽभिः । उ॒ग्राः । अहृ॑णीयमानाः । ए॒व । त्रि॒ऽना॒म॒न् । अहृ॑णीयमानः । इ॒मान् । जना॑न् । सम्ऽम॑नसः कृ॒धि । इ॒ह ॥

Word-meaning &c:—यथा=just as. आदित्याः=enlightened men shining by their mettle. वसुभिः=with wealth, with those that are endowed with good qualities. मरुद्भिः=with brave men who put down their foe. संबभूवुः (√भू)=have lived before you in all past ages. उग्राः=shining valorous, of great mettle. अहृणीयमानः (√हृणीङ्)=unflinching. एव=thus. त्रिणामन् (त्रयाणां लोकानां कालानां वा नामयिता—त्रि+√णम प्रह्वत्वे शब्दे च+मनिन् U. IV, 151)=the Lord God Almighty Who controls the past present and future and the celestial, intermediate and earthly regions. अहृणीयमानः =without being displeased. इमान्=these. जनान्=people. संमनसः कृधि=bind together with common aspirations and common ideals. इह=in this life, in this world, here.

Translation:—Oh Lord God ! Controller of past, present and future and the three worlds, (we beseech Thee) without being displeased (with us for our lack of unity) to bind these people together in common feelings, and ideals, just as, before us, in all the past ages, enlightened men of mettle acting (together) unflinchingly have, with wealth and the co-operation of brave men capable of vanquishing the foe, succeeded in life.

Purport:—Lack of unity is a great sin and cries

to God for justice and brings down His wrath on those that are guilty of it. God is displeased with those who do not polish their angularities and peacefully live and co-operate with their fellow-men.

॥ ॐ ॥

SECTION III.

The Leader

Atharvaveda XV, I, I.

(१५०) ओ३म् ॥ व्रात्यं आसीदीयमान एव स प्रजापतिं समैरयत् ॥ अथर्ववेदे १५ । १ । १ ॥

(150) Vraatya aaseedeeyamaana eva sa prajaapatim samairayat ॥ Atharvveda XV, 1, 1.

व्रात्यः ईयमानः एव आसीत् । सः प्रजाऽपतिम् (जनसंग्रहाय) समऽऐरयत् ॥

व्रात्यः (√ **वृञ् + अतच् + य** Nig. II, 3 and P.V, 1. 5) = benefactor of human society, he who does good to the multitude or a large number of people. **आसीत्**=is. **ईयमानः** (√ **ई+शानच्**)=going, prevailing upon others. **प्रजापतिम्**= the protector of creatures. **समैरयत्** (**सम्+** √ **ईर**)=he successfully prevails upon.

The benefactor of mankind is always moving about preaching people (to be and do good). He succeeds in prevaling upon the Protector of creatures (to bless them with unity.)

---

(१५१) सोऽरज्यत ततो राजन्योऽजायत ॥८।१॥

(151) So'rajyata tato raajanyo'jaayata ॥ Atharvaveda XV, 8, 1.

सः (व्रात्यः) अरज्यत । ततः राजन्यः अजायत ॥

सः=he (the Vrātya, benefactor of human society who is described in the first and succeeding hymns of this book is meant here). **अरज्यत** (√ रञ्ज)=he propitiates, he begins to propitiate or conciliate. (Supply the object **सर्वान्** ='all people,' after this). **ततः**=thereafter. **राजन्यः** (√ राज+**अन्य** U. III, 100)=king, ruler of the people, warrior. **अजायत** (√ जन्)=he becomes.

The benefactor of human society propitiates all and thereafter becomes the ruler of the people.

(१५२) स विशः सबंन्धूनन्नंमन्नाद्यमभ्युदं-तिष्ठत् ॥२॥

(152) Sa visah sabandhoon annam annaadyam abhyudatishthat ॥ 2.

सः सऽबंन्धून् विशः अन्नंम् अन्नऽअद्यम् अभिऽउदंतिष्ठत् ॥

विशः (Nig. II,3)=mankind. **सबन्धून**=along with their kith and kin. **अन्नम्** (√ **अद्**)=food such as cereals. **अन्नाद्यम्**= other edibles. **अभ्युदतिष्ठत्** (**अभि**+**उत**+√ **स्था**)=becomes the manager or controller of.

He then becomes the controller of the subjects with their kith and kin and of all cereals and other edibles.

(१५३) विशां च वै स सबंन्धूनां चान्नंस्य चान्ना-द्यंस्य च प्रियं धामं भवति य एवं वेदं ॥३॥

(153) Visaamca vai sa sabandhoonaam caannasya caannaadyasya ca priyam dhaama bhavati ya evam veda ॥ 3.

यः एवं वेद सः विशां सऽबन्धूनां च अन्नस्य, च अन्नऽअद्यस्य च प्रियं धाम भवति ॥

प्रियम्=loved, beloved. धाम (√धा+मनिन् U.IV,151)= refuge, shelter.

He who knows this truth (and lives up to it) becomes, as it were, the beloved refuge of the subjects with their kith and kin, of cereals and other victuals.

---

(१५४) स विशोऽनुव्यचलत् ॥ ९ । १ ॥

(154) Sa viso 'nuvyacalat || Atharvaveda XV, 9, 1.

सः विशः अनु वि अचलत ॥

अनुव्यचलत् (अनु+वि+√चल)=completely follows the aspirations of.

He (the benefactor of humanity), completely follows the aspirations of his subjects.

(१५५) तं सभा च समितिश्च सेना च सुरा चानुव्यचलन् ॥२॥

(155) Tam sabhaa ca samitisca senaa ca suraa caanu-vyacalan || 2.

सभा च समऽईतिः च सेना च सुरा च तम् अनुऽव्यचलन् ॥

सेना (√सि+नित् U. III, 10)=army. सुरा (√षुर +क +टाप्)=treasury, coffers, riches. अनुव्यचलन्=follow, become amenable to.

The popular assembly, the council, the army, and the treasury of the kingdom, all become amenable to his wishes.

(१५६) सभायाश्च वै स समितेश्च सेनाया सुरा-

याश्च प्रियं धाम भवति य एवम् वेद ॥३॥

(156) Sabhaayasca vai sa samitesca senaayaasca suraayaasca priyam dhaama bhavati ya evam veda || 3.

यः एवम् वेद सः सभायाः च सम् ऽईतेः च सेनायाः च सुरायाः च प्रियम् धाम भवति ॥

He who knows this truth (and lives up to it) becomes, so to say, the beloved refuge of the rural assembly, the council, the army and the treasury.

॥ ओ३म् ॥

SECTION IV.

Prayers for Protection and Prosperity.

SāmavēdaPart I, verses 437-446.

Subject:—Stanzas 437-441 and 444-446 God Almigty; .stanza 442 praise of the righteous and 443 an appreciation of the dawn and prayer to God for the gift of piety.

Metre—Paṃkti.

(१५७) ओ३म् ॥ विश्वतोदावन्विश्वतो न आ भर यं त्वा शविष्ठमीमहे ॥४३७॥

(157) Visvatodaavan visvato na aabhara yam tvaa savishtham eemahe || 437 ||

(हे) विश्वतःऽदावन् विश्वतः नः आ भर यम् त्वा शविष्ठं ईमहे ॥

विश्वतोदावन् (**विश्वतः+√इदाञ्+वनिप्** P. III, 2, 75)= one who confers benefits from all round; God, Who showers benefits from all round. **आभर**=support (us). **शविष्ठम्** (**शवस्+विनि+इष्ठन्** P. V. 2, 121; 3, 55 and 65)= most powerful. **ईमहे**=we entreat Thee.

Oh Lord ! Who conferest benefits on Thy devotees from all round, support us from all directions, we beseech Thee Who art the most Powerful.

(१५८) एष ब्रह्मा य ऋत्विय इन्द्रो नाम श्रुतो गृणे ॥४३८॥

(158) Esha brahmaa ya $r^{ə}$tviya indro naama $sr^{ə}$to $gr^{ə}ne$ ॥ 438.

एषः ब्रह्मा यः ऋत्वियः नाम इन्द्रः श्रुतः (तम् अहम्) गृणे ॥

ब्रह्मा = God Who helps His devotees to advance or progress. **ऋत्वियः** (√ऋ गतिप्रापणयोः + तु + घस् U. I, 72; P. V, 1, 106; & VII, 1, 2) = Who is our benefactor in all seasons. **नाम** = by name **श्रुतः** = known. **गृणे** = I praise Him.

This is the Helper of His devotees in their progress, our Benefactor in all seasons, known as God Omnipotent. I extol Him.

(१५९) ब्रह्माण इन्द्रं महयन्तो अर्कैरवर्धयन्नहये हन्तवा उ ॥४३९॥

(159) Brahmaa*na* indram mahayanto arkairavardhayannahaye hantavaa u ॥ 439.

अहये हन्तवै उ ब्रह्माणः अर्कैः इन्द्रं महयन्तः अवर्धयन् ॥

ब्रह्माणः = the enlightened, learned in the Vedas. **महयन्तः** = adoring Him. **अर्कैः** (= वेदमन्त्रैः) = with Vedic verses. **अवर्धयन्** = propitiate Him. **अहये** = sin, wickedness. **हन्तवै** = for the destruction. **उ** = certainly.

The enlightened who are learned in the Vedic lores adore God Almighty with Vedic verses and propitiate Him that He may certainly dispel all evil,

१ २ ३ २ ३ १ २ ३ २ ३ १ २
(१६०) अनवस्ते रथमश्वाय तक्षुस्त्वष्टा वज्रं
२ ३ १ २
पुरुहूत द्युमन्तम् ॥४४०॥

(160) Anavaste ratham a*s*vaaya takshustvash*t*aa vajram puruhoota dyumantam ॥ 440.

३ ३ १२र १ २र ३ १२र ३ १२र ३ १ २
(हे) पुरुऽहूत अनवः (मोक्षम्) अश्वाय ते रथम् तक्षुः। त्वष्टा द्युमन्तं
१ २र
(त्वां) वज्रं (रचयति कामादिशत्रुसंहननार्थं) ॥

अनवः (√अन् प्राणने+उ U. I, 7 and P. III, 3, 1)= men. ते (त्वाम्)=Thee. रथम् =into a chariot. अश्वाय=for the swift completion of their journey to liberation. तक्षुः= fashion, frame. त्वष्टा=an enlightened person advanced in spiritual knowledge. वज्रम्=a missile (for the killing of foes like, lust, anger etc.) पुरुहूत (पुरुभिर्हूतः P. II, 2, 24)= Who is often invoked by the devotees. द्युमन्तम् (√द्यु अभिगमने+क्विप्+मतुप् or √द्युत दीप्तौ+क्विप्+मतुप् P. III, 2, 178 V, 2, 94 and VI, 3, 109, or √दिवु क्रीडा etc., +क्विच्+मतुप् P. III, 2, 75; VI, 1, 131 and the rest as before)=lustrous.

Oh Lord God, always invoked by the pious! the (righteous) men fashion Thee (by meditation) into a chariot in which they wish to finish quickly the journey to the liberation of their souls, and oh Lustrous One! the enlightened man advanced in spiritual knowledge makes of Thee (by contemplation) a powerful missile with which he desries to kill his foes (in the shape of lust, anger and other passions).

२ ३ २ ३ १ २ ३ २ ३ १ २र ३ १
(१६१) शं पदं मघ ँरयीषिणे न काममव्रतो
२ ३ १ २ ३ २
हिनोति न स्पृशद्रयिम् ॥४४१॥

(161) *S*am padam magha*m* rayeeshi*n*e na Kaamam avrato hinoti na spr^o^*s*adrayim. ॥ 441.

(हे इन्द्र) अऽव्रतः रयिम् न स्पृशत् न कामं हिनोति । रयीषिणे शम् पदं मघं (च भविष्यति) ॥

शम् = happiness, peace. **पदम्** = a high position. **मघम्** = wealth. **रयीषिणे** = to the philanthropic and charitable man. **कामम्** = desire, wish, what is wished for. **अव्रतः (न व्रतम् यस्य)** = an idle man, one who does not attend to his religious and spiritual duties, he who gives no charity. **हिनोति** = obtains, gets, realises. **स्पृशत्** = touches, earns.

Oh Almighty God! it is Thy dispensation that the man who shirks his duties should not touch wealth and that his wishes be not fulfilled, but that the (pious and) philanthropic man should attain a high position and happiness and become rich in worldly possessions.

(१६२) सदा गावः शुचयो विश्वधायसः सदा देवा अरेपसः ॥४४२॥

(162) Sadaa gaavah *s*ucayo vi*s*vadhaayasah sadaa devaa arepasah ॥ 442.

(हे इन्द्र) विश्वऽधायसः देवाः सदा अऽरेपसः शुचयः (भवन्ति यथा गावः सदा (शुचयः भवन्ति) ॥

सदा = always. **गावः*** = the sun's rays, cows, the Vedic lores etc. **शुचयः** (√ ईशुचिर् पूतीभावे+इन् U. IV, 118 and 120) = pure, holy. **विश्वधायसः** (**विश्व** + √ **डुधाञ्** + **युक्** + **असुन्** P. VII, 3, 33, and U. IV, 189) = those who support the world by charity etc. **देवाः** = the righteous. **अरेपसः** (**न विद्यते रेपः यस्य**) = free from the stain of sin.

---

* Vide Nig. I, 1; 4; 5; 11; III, 16; IV, 1 and Nir. 1, 1; 12; II. 5; 6; 14; IV, 24; VIII. 5; XI, 41; 42.

Oh God Almighty! it is Thy will that the righteous men who support the world by charity and good deeds should always be pure and free from the stain of sin just as the sun's rays are always pure (white)

१ २ ३ १२ ३ १ २र ३ १

(१६३) आयाहि वनसा सह गावः सचन्त वर्तनिं

२र

यदूधभिः ॥४४३॥

(163) Aayaahi vanasaa saha gaavah sacanta vartani*m* yadoodhabhih || 443.

२ १२र ३२ २ ३ १ २र

(हे परमात्मन्) यत् (उषः) वनसा सह आऽयाहि (नः) गावः

३ २ १२र ३

वर्तनिं ऊधभिः सचन्त ॥

आयाहि (**आयायात्** 2nd person used for the 3rd)= may come. **वनसा** (√ **वन सम्भक्तौ** + **असुन्**) = with grandeur, glory. **सह** = with. **गावः** = speech. **सचन्त** = may come, join. **वर्तनिम्** (√ **वृतु वर्तने** + **अनि** U. II. 102) = the road. **यत्** (= **यदा**) = when. **ऊधभिः** (√ **वह** + **असुन्** U. IV, 193) = with those that carry i.e., with ejaculations that perfect our praises of Thee, **ऊधस्** generally means the udder. This term is here used for two reasons because:— (1) the name for speech and cow is the same, and (2) because the four types of ejaculations uttered at the time of religions sacrifice viz., **स्वाहा**, **वषट्**, **स्वधा** and **हन्त**, are according to the Śatapatha Br. XIV. 8,9, compared to the four teats of the udder of the cow in the form of speech. **गावः सचन्त वर्तनिम्** = We may be up eulogising Thee, may our joint praises start on their journey towards Thee.

Oh Lord! vouchasafe, we bessech Thee, that when Dawn comes with all her glory, our joint praises may rise

---

* वाचं धेनुमुपासीत। तस्याश्चत्वारः स्तनाः स्वाहाकारो वषट्कारो हन्तकारः स्वधाकारस्तस्यै द्वौस्तनौ देवा उपजीवन्ति स्वाहाकारं च वषट्कारं च। हन्तकारं मनुष्याः स्वधाकारं पितरस्तस्याः प्राण ऋषभो मनो वत्सः ॥ श० १४।८।९॥

up towords Thee with appropriate ejaculations completing our acts of piety.

(१६४) उप प्रक्षे मधुमति क्षियन्तः पुष्येम रयिं धीमहे त इन्द्र ॥४४४॥

(164) Upa prakshe madhumati kshiyantah pushyema rayim dheemahe ta indra ॥ 444.

(हे इन्द्र) मधुमति प्रक्षे उप क्षियन्तः रयिं पुष्येम ते धीमहे ॥

प्रक्षे (प्र+√क्षि निवासगत्योः+ड)=dwelling, abode, state of life. **मधुमति** (मधु+मतुप)=full of spiritual bliss. (**मधु** according to Bṛhad. Up. II, 5, 1* and 16 is the individual and the Supreme Being. **मधु** literally means honey or honey-sweet. Hence that which is the dearest and the most excellent, viz., the soul and God, are here designated **मधु**). **उप क्षियन्तः**=living, residing. **पुष्येम**=may we advance, may we grow. **रयिम्**=wealth. **धीमहे**=meditate, think of.

Oh Omnipotent God! may we, living in a state rich with spiritual bliss, ever meditate on Thee and grow in prosperity.

(१६५) अर्चन्त्यर्कं मरुतः स्वर्का आस्तोभति श्रुतो युवा स इन्द्रः ॥४४५॥

(165) Arcantyarkam marutah svarkaa aastobhati sruto yuvaa sa indrah ॥ 445.

सुऽअर्का मरुतः अर्कं अर्चन्ति स युवा श्रुतः इन्द्रः आ स्तोभति ॥

* इयं पृथिवी सर्वेषां भूतानां मध्वस्यै पृथिव्यै सर्वाणि भूतानि मधु यश्चायमस्यां पृथिव्यां तेजोमयोऽमृतमयो पुरुषो यश्चायमध्यात्मं शारीरस्तेजोमयोऽमृतमयः पुरुषोऽयमेव स योऽयमात्मेदममृतमिदं ब्रह्मेदं सर्वम् ॥ बृ० २।५।१॥

अर्चन्ति=they adore. अर्कम्*=God. मरुतः=sacrificial priests (Nig. III.18.). स्वर्काः (शोभनानि अर्काणि येषाम्)= having good (appropriate for the time) Vedic hymns, provided with good Vedic hymns for the adoration of God. आस्तोभति=is fully praised, extolled in a befitting manner. श्रुतः=renowned in the Vedas, eulogised in the Vedas. युवा (√ यु मिश्रणामिश्रणयोः+कनिन् U. I, 156)=young, strong, powerful. इन्द्रः=God Omnipotent.

Sacrificial priests with hymns appropriate adore God, and the Lord Almighty renowned in the Vedas and the Strongest of all, is (thus) extolled in a befitting manner.

(१६६) प्र व इन्द्राय वृत्रहन्तमाय विप्राय गाथं ।
गायत यं जुजोषते ॥४४६॥

(166) Pra va indraaya vr^ə^trahantamaaya vipraaya gaatham gaayata yam jujoshate ॥ 446.

(हे मनुष्याः) वृत्रऽहन्तमाय विऽप्राय इन्द्राय गाथं प्र गायत वः (यं गाथं सः) जुजोषते ॥

प्रगायत=Sing well. वः=your, the praises sung by you. इन्द्राय=for the Almighty God. वृत्रहन्तमाय (वृत्र+√ हन्+क्विप्+तमप्)=the complete destroyer of all enemies such as lust anger, malice and other passions. विप्राय (√ डुवप बीजसंताने छेदने च+रन् U. II, 28)=for the most wise. गाथम् (√ गै+स्थन् U. II, 4)=praise, a hymn of praise. यम्=which (hymn of praise.) जुजोषते=He accepts, resorts to, appreciates and accepts.

---

* अर्को देवो भवति, यदेनमर्चंति। अर्को मंत्रो भवति, यदनेनार्चन्ति ॥ Nir. V, 5.

† समस्ततेजः परमेश्वर निमित्तेन्द्रपदवाच्यः ॥ *S*abara Svaamin on the Mimaa*m*saasootra.

Oh men! sing well hymns of praise to Almighty God, the Wise, and the Greatest Destroyer of our enemies like lust, anger and other inordinate passions, for He appreciates and accepts such praises offered by you.

---

२ ३ १ २ ३ १ २ ३ १ २ ३ १२ ३ २ ३ २र २र
अग्ने विवस्वदाभरास्मभ्यमूतये महे । देवोह्यसि
३ २
नो दृशे ॥ सामवेदे १ । १ । १ । १० ॥

Oh most Refulgent God! vouchsafe, we beseech Thee, that we may accomplish such religious and philanthropic works as would confer on us perfect safety (in life) for Thou art our Illuminator with Whose light we are able to perceive with our senses (and realise the truth). (Samaveda, I, 1, 1, 10).

यदस्मृति चकृम किंचिदग्न उपारिम चरणे जातवेदः । ततः पाहि त्वं नः प्रचेतः शुभे सखिभ्यो अमृतत्वमस्तु नः ॥ अथर्ववेदे ७ । १०६ । १ ॥

Oh God Most Adorable! whatever we may have done forgetfully—whatever fault we may have committed in our daily life, from that oh Wisest of all! protect Thou us and grant that we, Thy friends, may hereafter be in the right and that the (longing for the) bliss of emancipation may ever be in our hearts. (Atharvaveda VII, 106, 1.)

CHAPTER VII.

Where is God?

The teaching of the Holy Vedic Church with regard to the Supreme Being, the individual soul and matter is quite clear, and very different from what the religious systems of the modern world lay down. These systems, mostly man-made, have all the errors attending upon the half and 'unripe' knowledge of man inseparably mixed with their doctrines, so that it is difficult for an impartial and fair-minded person to distinguish the pure doctrinal part from the spurious, sectarian interpolations. These later accretions have very often the unpleasant odour of imperialism, capitalism, 'nation-worsip' etc., which are as inhuman and absurd as the 'king-worship', instituted by the ancient Roman Caesars. One very horrible muddle which these systems have imparted to modern philosophy is the misunderstanding of the mind and body. Modern, especially Western philosophy, is groping in the dark about the true nature of the mind but yet does not miss any opportunity to call the ancient sages of India 'fools' for their plainly and faultlessly describing mind and body and calling them both material—for, so to say, 'calling a spade a spade.'

The body and mind of man are so closely connected with the noble soul in the composite called a 'human being,' that the slightest mistake on his part in distinguishing them one from the other, is sure to result in the complete blinding of his spiritual vision and leading him into the most horrible pitfalls.

This question is expatiated upon in one of the later Upanishads, viz., The Tējōbindoopaniṣad in stanzas 90-105 in a very simple style. The expanse of the universe, is there said to originate from the identification on the part of the soul, of herself with the body, for otherwise, it is said, she should have long ago attained emancipation. As for the mind, it is through this, says the Upanishad, i. e., through his 'mental' ideas, that, man creates all the horrible trouble of the worldly struggle for himself. His inseparable contact with and dependence upon, the material world is a legerdemain of this mind.* Much in these stanzas smells of sectarianism but yet, the main theme that man should beware his own body and mind, is well worth study.

* देहोऽहमिति संकल्पो महत्संसार उच्यते । देहोऽहमिति संकल्पस्तद्बन्धमिति चोच्यते ॥ देहोऽहमिति संकल्पस्तद्दुःखमिति चोच्यते । देहोऽहमिति यद्भानं तदेव नरकं स्मृतम् ॥ देहोऽहमिति संकल्पो जगत्सर्वमितीर्यते । देहोऽहमिति संकल्पो हृदयग्रन्थिरीरितः ॥ देहोऽहमिति यज्ज्ञानं तदेवाज्ञानमुच्यते । देहोऽहमिति यज्ज्ञानं तदसद्भावमेव च ॥ देहोऽहमिति या बुद्धिः सा चाविद्येति भण्यते । देहोऽहमिति यज्ज्ञानं तदेव द्वैतमुच्यते ॥ देहोऽहमिति संकल्पः सत्यजीवः स एव हि । देहोऽहमिति यज्ज्ञानं परिच्छिन्नमितीरितम् ॥ देहोऽहमिति संकल्पो महापापमिति स्फुटम् । देहोऽहमिति या बुद्धिस्तृष्णा दोषामयः किल ॥ यत्किंचिदपि संकल्पस्तापत्रयमितीरितम् । कामं क्रोधं बन्धनं सर्वदुःखं विश्वं दोषं कालनानास्वरूपम् ॥ यत्किंचेदं सर्वसंकल्पजालं तत्किंचेदं मानसं सोम्य विद्धि ॥ मन एव जगत्सर्वं मन एव महारिपुः । मन एव हि संसारो मन एव जगत्त्रयम् ॥ मन एव महद्दुःखं मन एव जरादिकम् । मन एव हि कालश्च मन एव मलं तथा ॥ मन एव हि संकल्पो मन एव हि जीवकः । मन एव हि चित्तं च मनोऽहंकार एव च ॥ मन एव महद्बन्धं मनोऽन्तःकरणं च तत् । मन एव हि भूमिश्च मन एव हि तोयकम् ॥ मन एव हि तेजश्च मन एव मरुन्महान् । मन एव हि चाकाशं मन एव हि शब्दकम् ॥ स्पर्शं रूपं रसं गन्धं कोशाः पञ्च मनोभवाः । जाग्रत्स्वप्नसुषुप्त्यादि मनोमयमितीरितम् ॥ दिक्पाला वसवो रुद्रा आदित्याश्च मनोमयाः । दृश्यं जडं द्वन्द्वजातमज्ञानम् मानसं स्मृतम् ॥ संकल्पमेव यत्किंचित्तत्तन्नास्तीति निश्चिनु । नास्ति नास्ति जगत्सर्वं गुरुशिष्यादिकं नहि ॥ तेजोबिन्दूपनिषदि ९०-१०५ ॥

With regard to the mind the Atharvaveda (book III hymn 27) gives very plain and sound instruction. It is generally at the time of devotions and meditation that his body and mind began to worry a man most. Lingering pains and itching sensations in some or other part of the body, are signs that the body is not disposed towards one's efforts at sitting quiet at a place. When in spite of this, a man takes to some quiet corner to have a spiritual union with his Creator, the mind sets about heaping all sorts of rubbish on him totally to annihilate his peace. Engaged during daytime in his worldly routine diverted with innumerable knick-knacks man does not always carefully observe the flippancy of his mind. But this becomes very clear and obtrusive at the time of one's spiritual exercises. This hymn provides a wonderful remedy for this malady, which, if utilised is sure to help the devotee get through his devotional exercises successfully.

(१६७) ओ३म् ॥ प्राची दिगग्निरधिपतिरसितो रक्षि-
तादित्या इषवः ॥ तेभ्यो नमोऽधिपतिभ्यो नमो रक्षितृ-
भ्यो नम इषुभ्यो नम एभ्यो अस्तु । यो३स्मान्द्वेष्टि
यं वयं द्विष्मस्तं वो जम्भे दध्मः ॥ अथर्ववेदे ३ । २७ । १ ॥

To his flippant mind and restless body, the devotee, while at his spiritual exercises, thus appeals:—Look here! the Sun is rising (or setting if it is evening time), this is the East (praacee dik), the quarter of the Self-luminous Providence of God (agnih), His Unfettered Omnipotence (asitah), the Protector and Controller of all beings (adhipatih rakshitaa). From It all the beings that are of this vast Earth (aadityaah) are full of desires [for protection and advancement] (ishavah).

Let us look up to these with humility in our eyes (tebhyah namah), let us humbly offer our obeisance to these Protectors and Controllers of all beings [Who protect and lead them in the right path from all directions] (adhipatibhyah namah, rakshitṛbhyah namah, and let us also have good will towards all creatures that are desirous of happiness for protection (ishubhyah namah). In short, let us have a fitting regard for all these (ebhyah namah astu). [Otherwise we shall be failing in our duty towards God Almighty and be regarded as inimical to His Divine Disposal. Though He is pre-eminently merciful, His Omniscient Justice is unfailing and unsparing and its jaws crush all without the slightest distinction of hight or low, just as] we, though finite and erring (vayam), wish to avenge ourselves (jambhe dadhmah) on anyone who bears us ill will (yah asmaan dveshṭi) or to whom we bear ill will (yam vayam dvishmah).

(१६८) दक्षिणा दिगिन्द्रोऽधिपतिस्तिरश्चिराजी रक्षिता पितर इषवः। तेभ्यो नमोऽधिपतिभ्यो नमो रक्षितृभ्यो नम इषुभ्यो नम एभ्योअस्तु । यो३स्मान्द्वेष्टि यं वयं द्विष्मस्तं वो जम्भे दध्मः ॥२॥

Lo here to our right, is the South! (dakshi*n*aa dik). Over this presides His Omnipotent Providence the Controller of all riches and all great virtues and powers whicn He bestows on mankind (indrah adhipatih). As such He protects all beings by means of such useful 'lower' animals [as cows, horses, goats etc., that yield milk and carry burden or can be yoked to conveyances] (tirasciraajee rakshitaa). Of Him all those great men whose duty in life is to protect and guide mankind in the paths of God, are desirous of safety ahd liberality for themselves as well as those in their charge (pitara ishavah).

Let us look up to these with humility in our eyes (tebhyah namah), let us humbly offer our obeisance to these Protectors and Controllers of all beings [who protect and lead them in the right path from all directions] (adhipatibhyah namah rakshitrəbhyah namah) and let us also have good will towards all creatures that are desirous of happiness and protection (ishubhyah namah). In short, let us have a fitting regard for all these (ebhyah namah astu). [Otherwise we shall be failing in our duty towards God Almighty and be regarded as inimical to His Divine Disposal. Though He is pre-eminently merciful, His Omniscient Justice is unfailing and unsparing and its jaws crush all without the slightest distinction of high or low, just as] we, though finite and erring (vayam), wish to avenge ourselves (jambhe dadhmah) on anyone who bears us ill will (yah asmaan dveshti) or to whom we bear ill will (yam vayam dvishmah).

(१६९) प्रतीची दिग्वरुणोऽधिपतिः पृदाकू रक्षितान्नमिषवः । तेभ्यो नमोऽधिपतिभ्यो नमो रक्षितृभ्यो नम इषुभ्यो नम एभ्यो अस्तु । योऽ३स्मान्द्वेष्टि यं वयं द्विष्मस्तं वो जम्भे दध्मः ॥३॥

This is the West now! (prateecee dik) Over this presides His Most Excellent Providence that decides between right and wrong and does full justice to both (varu*n*ah adhipatih). He protects all from ferocious and destructive creatures like the poisonous snake, the lion and the tiger (prədaakoo rakshitaa) but yet long-suffering and patient as He is, all desire their livelihood from Him (annam ishavah).

Let us look up to these with humility in our eyes (tebhyah namah), let us humbly offer our obeisance to these Protectors and Controllers of all beings [who protect and lead them in the right path from all directions] (adhipatibhyah namah rakshitrəbhyah namah) and let us also have good will towards all creatures thar are desirous of happiness and protection (ishubhyah namah).

In short, let us have a fitting regard for all these (ebhyah namah astu). [Otherwise we shall be failing in our duty towards God Almighty and be regarded as inimical to His Divine Disposal. Thou He is pre-eminently merciful, His Omniscient Justice is unfailing and unsparing and its jaws crush all without the slightest distinction of high or low, just as] we, though finite and erring (vayam), wish to avenge ourselves (jambhe dadhmah) on anyone who bears us ill will (yah asmaan dveshti) or to whom we bear ill will (yam vayam dvishmah).

(१७०) उदीची दिक्सोमोऽधिपतिः स्वजो रक्षिता-शनिरिषवः । तेभ्यो नमोऽधिपतिभ्यो नमो रक्षितृभ्यो नम इषुभ्यो नम एभ्यो अस्तु । योऽस्मान्द्वेष्टि यं वयं द्विष्मस्तं वो जम्भे दध्मः ॥४॥

Here to our left is the North (udeecee dik) the Controller of which is His Divine Omnipotence that bestows peace on mankind and all living beings (somo 'dhipatih). Unborn and existing of Himself (svajah), He is our Protector (rakshitaa) from and by means of, such natural phenomena as the lighning (asanih) and we also are full of desires of peace from Him when frightened by such agencies (ishavah).

Let us look up to these with humility in our eyes (tebhyah damah), let us humbly offer our obeisance to these Protectors and Controllers of all beings [who protect and lead them in the right path from all directions] (adhipatibhyah namah rakshitrəbhyah namah) and let us also have good will towards all creatures that are desirous of happiness and protection (ishubhyah namah). In short, let us have a fitting regard for all these (ebhyah namah astu). [Otherwise we shall be failling in our duty towards God Almighty and be regarded as inimical to His Divine Disposal. Though He is pre-eminently merciful, His Omniscient Justice is unfailing and unsparing and its jaws crush all without the slightest distinction of high or low, just as] we, though finite and erring (vayam), wish to avenge ourselves (jambhe dadhmah) on anyone who bears us ill will (yah asmaan dveshti) or to whom we bear ill will (yam vayam dvishmah).

(१७१) ध्रुवा दिग्विष्णुरधिपतिः कल्माषग्रीवो रक्षिता वीरुध इषवः। तेभ्यो नमोऽधिपतिभ्यो नमो रक्षितृभ्यो नम इषुभ्यो नम एभ्यो अस्तु। योऽस्मान्द्वेष्टि यं वयं द्विष्मस्तं वो जम्भे दध्मः ॥५॥

Down below us is the Nether quarter (dhruvaa dik) of which also His Omnipresent Providence is the Controller (vishnuh adhipatih). He is our Protector through dark-hued (and other) trees and plants (kalmaashagreevo rakshitaa) of which we are also the desirers (veerudha ishavah).

Let us look up to these with humility in our eyes (tebhyah namah), let us humbly offer our obeisance to these Protectors and Controllers of all beings [Who protect and lead them in the right path from all directions] (adhipatibhyah namah rakshitrəbhyah namah) and let us also have good will towards all creatures that are desirous of happiness and protection (ishubhyah namah). In short, let us have a fitting regard for all these (ebhyah namah astu). [Otherwise we shall be failing in our duty towards God Almighty and be regarded as inimical to His Divine Disposal. Though He is pre-eminently merciful, His Omniscient Justice is unfailing and unsparing and its jaws crush all without the slightest distinction of high or low, just as] we, though finite and erring (vayam), wish to avenge ourselves (jambhe dadhmah) on anyone who bears us ill will (yah asmaan dveshti) or to whom we bear ill will (yam vayam dvishmah).

(१७२) ऊर्ध्वा दिग्बृहस्पतिरधिपतिः श्वित्रो रक्षिता वर्षमिषवः। तेभ्यो नमोऽधिपतिभ्यो नमो रक्षितृभ्यो नम इषुभ्यो नम एभ्यो अस्तु । योऽस्मान्द्वेष्टि यं वयं द्विष्मस्तं वो जम्भे दध्मः ॥६॥

Overhead is the Upper quarter (oordhvaa dik) presided over by Lord God the Master and Controller of His Eternal Vedic Law and speech (brəhaspatih adhipatih). That most pure (svitrah) God is the Protector of all creatures (rakshitaa) through such natural phenomena as the rain (varsham) of which all creatures are always the most ardent desirers (ishavah).

Let us look up to these with humility in our eyes (tebhyah uamah), let us humbly offer our obeisance to these Protectors and Controllers of all beings [Who protect and lead them in the right path from all directions (adhipatibhyah namah rakshitrəbhyah namah) and let us also have good will towards all creatures that are desirous of happiness and protection (ishubhyah namah). In short, let us have a fitting regard for all these (ebhyah namah astu). [Otherwise we shall be failing in our duty towards God Almighty and be regarded as inimical to His Divine Disposal. Though He is pre-eminetly mercifui, His Omniscient Justice is unfailing and unsparing and its jaws crush all without the slightest distinction of high or low, just as] we, though finite and erring (vayam), wish to avenge ourselves (jambhe dadhmah) on anyone who bears us ill will (yah asmaan dveshti) or to whom we bear ill will (yam vayam dvishmah).

ॐ ॥ तत्सत् ॥ ॐ ॥

शुभं भूयादध्येतुरध्यापकस्य च ॥

BRIEF INDEX.

BIBLIOGRAPHY.

History of Religion, Allan Menzies; John Murray, London 1895.

The Religions of India, A. Barth; Kegan Paul, Trench, Trubner & Co. London 1906.

The Coming Revival of Spiritual Religion, and

The Testimony of science in Favour of Natural Diet; by Sidney H. Beard;

Is Meat eating Sanctioned by Divine Authority? by Sir. W. E. Cooper;

The Cruelties of the Meat Trade, by Josiah Oldfield, all publised by the Order of the Golden Age, London.

Guide to Modern Thought, C. E. M. Joad, Faber & Faber Ltd. London.

Psychology, Prof. William James. (2vols).

Thoughts on Revelation & Life, Brooks Foss Westcott, Macmillan & Co., London, 1891.

A History of Ancient Sanskrit Literature, Max Müller, The Panini Office, Allahabad.

A History of Indian Literature, by M. Winternitz, the Calcutta University 1927. Vol 2 1933.

Psychology Its Facts & Principles, H. L. Hollingworth, D. Appleton & Co., New York & London 1928.

The science of Life, H. G. Wells, J. Huxley & P. G. Wells, Cassell & Co. London.

The New & Revised Outline of History, H. G. Wells, Garden City Publishing Co., New York.

Making of Man by Sir Oliver Lodge, Hodder & Stoughton, London.

History of Sanskrit Literature, A. A. Macdonell, William Heineman 1900.

Mind & Matter, G. F. Stout, Cambridge University, 1931.

The New Dictionary of Thoughts, Tryon Edwards, Classic Pub'ishing Co., London & New York, 1934.

Introduction to the Commentary on the Vedas, Msharshi Dayananda, translated by Ghasi Ram, M.A., L.L.B., 1925.

The Light of Truth, Maharshi Dayananda, Lahore.

Anthology of Vedic Hymns, Bhumananda Sarasvati. Ramlal Kapur & Sons, Anarkali, Lahore, 1935.

The Ashtaadhaayee of Panini with the commentary of Maharshi Dayananda, Vedic Press Ajmer.

The Vedaangaprakaasa of Maharshi Dayananda, Vedic Press, Ajmer.

The Nirukta of Yaaska with the commentary of Durgaa-eaarya, Prof. Rajwade's edition, Anandasrama, Poona.

The Nirukta with the Commentary, by Skanda-Mahesvara, Dr. Lakshman Sarup, Lahore.

A Comparative Grammar of the Dravidian Languages or South Indian Family of Languages by R. Caldwell.

Early History of Assyria to 1000 B. C. Sidney Smith. Chatto & Windus, London, 1928.

Wise Parenthood by Marie. Stopes, G. P. Putnam's Sons, Ltd., London 1923.

Radiant Motherhood do do

Contraception do 1932.

The Golden Bow, Frazer.

Oehler's "Old Testament Theology" T. & T. Clarke, Edinburgh.

Indian Medical Plants by Lt. Col. K. R. Kirtikar, The Panini Office, Allahabad'

The Background of Science by Sir James Jeans.

A Complete Etymological Dictionary of the Vedic Language, first fasciculus, P. Visvabandhu, Lahore.

An Index to all the Brahmanas and Aranyakas do

The Illustrated Weekly of India, July to November 1935:

Life and Letters of Max Müller two vols.

The Vaidika Sampatti by P. Raghunandana Sarma, Soorjee Vallabhdas, Cutch Castle, Chaupati, Bombay.

A History of Vedic Literature by Bhagavaddatta, Lahore 3 vols.

Searul 'Uqool by Asma'iee malek us Sha'araa, the Berut Publishing Co., Berut Palestine.

Hammurabis's Inscriptions by Dr. L. W. King 2 Vols, Luzac & Co., London.

History of Samer and Akkad, L. W. King.

History of Babylon do

Sumerian Reading Book by C. J. Gadd, Oxford University Press.

Semitic Mythology by Dr. S. H. Langdon.

Race Life of the Aryan Peoples by J. P. Widney Funk & Wagnalls Co., New York 1907 Vol II.

N. B. This is only a very brief list.

Printed at the Federal Trade Press, Delhi, India.